The SAGE Encyclopedia of Pharmacology and Society

SAGE was founded in 1965 by Sara Miller McCune to support the dissemination of usable knowledge by publishing innovative and high-quality research and teaching content. Today, we publish more than 850 journals, including those of more than 300 learned societies, more than 800 new books per year, and a growing range of library products including archives, data, case studies, reports, and video. SAGE remains majority-owned by our founder, and after Sara's lifetime will become owned by a charitable trust that secures our continued independence.

Los Angeles | London | New Delhi | Singapore | Washington DC

The SAGE Encyclopedia of Pharmacology and Society

4

Edited by

Sarah E. Boslaugh
Saint Louis University

SAGE reference

Los Angeles | London | New Delhi
Singapore | Washington DC

Los Angeles | London | New Delhi
Singapore | Washington DC

FOR INFORMATION:

SAGE Publications, Inc.
2455 Teller Road
Thousand Oaks, California 91320
E-mail: order@sagepub.com

SAGE Publications Ltd.
1 Oliver's Yard
55 City Road
London, EC1Y 1SP
United Kingdom

SAGE Publications India Pvt. Ltd.
B 1/I 1 Mohan Cooperative Industrial Area
Mathura Road, New Delhi 110 044
India

SAGE Publications Asia-Pacific Pte. Ltd.
3 Church Street
#10-04 Samsung Hub
Singapore 049483

Production Editor: Tracy Buyan
Reference Systems Manager: Leticia Gutierrez
Copy Editors: Suzanne DeRouen, Jim Kelly,
            Rebecca Kuzins, Melinda Masson,
            Terri Lee Paulsen
Typesetter: Hurix Systems (P) Ltd.
Proofreaders: Christina West, Scott Oney,
            Alison Syring
Indexer: J S Editorial
Cover Designer: Candice Harman
Marketing Manager: Teri Williams

DISCLAIMER: All information contained in *The SAGE Encyclopedia of Pharmacology and Society* is intended only for informational and educational purposes. The information is not intended to diagnose medical problems, prescribe remedies for illness, or treat disease. We recommend that you always seek the advice of a health care professional with respect to any medical condition, illness, or disease.

Printed in the United States of America.

Library of Congress Cataloging-in-Publication Data

The SAGE encyclopedia of pharmacology and society / editor, Sarah E. Boslaugh.

p. ; cm.

Encyclopedia of pharmacology and society

Includes bibliographical references and index.

ISBN 978-1-4833-5000-4 (hardcover : alk. paper)

I. Boslaugh, Sarah, editor. II. Title: Encyclopedia of pharmacology and society. [DNLM: 1. Pharmacology—Encyclopedias—English. 2. Drug Industry—Encyclopedias—English. QV 13]

RS51
615.103—dc23   2015036485

15 16 17 18 19 10 9 8 7 6 5 4 3 2 1

Contents

Volume 4

List of Entries   *vii*
Reader's Guide   *xv*

Entries

T   *1345*   W   *1531*
U   *1459*   Y   *1555*
V   *1507*   Z   *1559*

Glossary   *1565*
Resource Guide   *1577*
Appendix: Primary Documents   *1585*
Index   *1705*

List of Entries

Abbott Laboratories
Abuse of Prescription Drugs
Access to Essential Medicines as a Human
   Right: History
Access to Medicines (Developing World)
Access to Medicines (Industrialized World)
Acetaminophen Overdose Risk
Actavis
Addiction to Prescription Drugs
ADHD Drugs
Adherence to Prescription Directions
Adjudicated Claims Data
Adolescents
Adverse Drug Events Reporting Systems
Adverse Drug Reactions (ADR) and Adverse
   Events (AE)
Advertising to Doctors
Advertising to Patients
African Americans
AIDS/HIV Drugs
Alcohol Cessation Drugs
Allergan
Aloe Vera (Herbal Medicine)
American Board of Clinical Pharmacology
American College of Clinical Pharmacy
American Pharmacists Association
American Society of Health-System
   Pharmacists
Amgen
Amphetamines
Anabolic Steroids (Sport)
Anatomical Therapeutic Chemical
   Classification System (WHO)
Animal Testing
Antiaging Medicines

Antianxiety Drugs
Antiasthma Drugs
Antibiotic Revolution, The
Antibiotic/Antimicrobial Resistance
Antibiotics
Anticaries Drugs
Anticholesterol Drugs
Anticoagulants
Anticonvulsant Drugs
Antidepressants
Antidiabetic Medications
Anti-Doping Convention, Council of Europe
Antihistamines
Antihypertensive Drugs
Anti-Inflammatory Drugs
Antimalarials
Antiparasitic Drugs
Antipsychiatry Movement
Antipsychotics
Antipyretic Drugs
Appetite Depressants and Stimulants
Arts: Prescription Drugs and Creativity
Asian Americans
Aspirin
Astellas Pharma
Astemizole (Hismanal) Controversy
AstraZeneca
Athletes
Australia
Austria
Autism and Vaccines
Ayurvedic Medicine

BALCO Scandal
Baseball and Performance-Enhancing Drugs

Bath Salts (Synthetic Cathinones)
Baxter International
Bayer
Behavioral Pharmacology and Substance
    Abuse
Belgium
Belladonna (Traditional Medicine/Poison)
Beta-Blockers (Sport)
Biogen Idec
Biological Passport (Sport)
Blood Doping
Boehringer Ingelheim
Boxing and Performance-Enhancing Drugs
British Pharmacological Society, The

Canada
Canada: Variation in Prescription Drug
    Benefits by Province/Territory
Canadian Provincial Databases
Canadian Society of Pharmacology and
    Therapeutics
Cancer, Drug Treatments for
Canon of Medicine, The (Avicenna)
Cardiovascular Drugs
Cardiovascular Pharmacology
Celgene
Centers for Disease Control and Prevention
Central Nervous System Depressants and
    Stimulants
Cerivastatin (Baycol, Lipobay) Controversy
Chamomile (Herbal Medicine)
Chemical Fertilizers: Human Health Effects
Chemoprevention
Children
Chili (Capsaicin)
China
Classical Pharmacology
Clinical Field Studies
Clinical Pharmacology
Clinical Pharmacology: Developing
    Countries
Clinical Pharmacology: Industrialized
    Countries

Clinical Trials
Clinical Trials, History of
Club Drugs
Cocaine
Cognitive Enhancers
Colombia
Common Rule, The
Comparative Effectiveness Research
Comprehensive Methamphetamine Control
    Act (1996)
Computer-Aided Drug Design
Conscience Clause
Controlled Substances Act
Cosmetic Pharmacology
Costa Rica
Cost-Effectiveness Research
Counterfeit Drugs/Medicines
Cuban Society for Pharmacology
Curandero
Cycling and Performance-Enhancing
    Drugs

Daiichi Sankyo
Dartmouth College
Declaration of Helsinki (1975)
Decongestants
Deinstitutionalization Movement
Denmark
DES (Diethylstilbestrol) Controversy
Developing Countries, Residents of
Diffusion of New Pharmaceutical Drugs
Digitalis
Directly Observed Therapy, Short-Course
Discrimination in Prescribing Practice
Disease Concept of Addiction: History
Disease Management
Diuretics
Diuretics and Masking Agents (Sport)
Dosage Safety Measures
Drug Abuse Control Amendments of
    1965
Drug Allergies
Drug Discovery and Development

Drug Enforcement Administration (U.S.)
Drug Interactions
Drug Labeling: Developing World
Drug Labeling: Industrialized World
Drug Price Competition and Patent Term Restoration Act (1984)
Drug Testing, High School and College Athletes (U.S.)
Drug Testing, Olympic Athletes (Overview)
Drug Testing, Professional Athletes (Overview)
Drug-Resistant Diseases
Drugs as Study Aids

Efalizumab (Raptiva) Controversy
Egbogi (Traditional Yoruba Medicine)
Eisai
Elderly People
Eli Lilly
ENCePP Database (European Network of Centres for Pharmacoepidemiology and Pharmacovigilance)
Endocrine Pharmacology
Ephedra (Herbal Medicine)
EPO (Erythropoietin)
Equity Pricing of Essential Medicines
Ethics of Performance-Enhancing Drugs in Sport
Ethnobotany
EudraCT (European Union Drug Regulating Authorities Clinical Trials)
EudraPharm (European Union Drug Regulating Authorities Pharmaceutical Database)
European Medicines Agency

False Claims Act ("Lincoln Law")
Federal Food, Drug, and Cosmetic Act (1938)
Fen-Phen (Fenfluramine/Phentermine) Controversy
Fertility Control
Fertility Control: History

Fertility Drugs
Fluoridation (Drinking Water)
Food Additives
Food and Drug Administration (U.S.)
Football (American) and Performance-Enhancing Drugs
France

Game of Shadows (Mark Fainaru-Wada and Lance Williams)
Gastric Drugs
Genentech
General Practice Research Database (UK)
Generic Medicines
Geographic Variation in Prescribing Practices
Germany
Gilead Sciences
Ginseng (Herbal Medicine)
Glucocorticosteroids (Sport)
Gray Market Drugs

Hallucinogens
Harm Reduction Policies
Health Care Fraud: United States
Healthcare Cost and Utilization Project (HCUP)
Healthcare Effectiveness Data and Information Set (HEDIS)
Heroin
Heroin-Assisted Treatment
Hispanic Americans
History of Pharmacological Treatments for Mental Health
History of Pharmacology: Ancient China
History of Pharmacology: Ancient Egypt
History of Pharmacology: Europe
History of Pharmacology: Europe, Middle Ages
History of Pharmacology: U.S., Colonial Period to 1865
History of Pharmacology: U.S., 1865 to 1900

History of Pharmacology: U.S., 1900 to
    1945
History of Pharmacology: U.S., 1945 to
    Present
History of Pharmacy as a Profession: Africa
History of Pharmacy as a Profession: Europe
History of Pharmacy as a Profession: Middle
    East
History of Pharmacy as a Profession: United
    States
HMO Research Network (19 Regional
    Health Care Delivery Organizations)
Homeopathy
Hormone Replacement Therapy (HRT)
Hospice Treatment
Hospital Administrative Data
Human Subjects Research: Standards and
    Protections
Human Subjects Research in Developing
    Countries
Hypnotics and Sedatives

Ibogaine
Immigrants and Refugees
India
Indigenous and Ethnic Minorities: Aotearoa
    New Zealand
Inhalants
Intellectual Property Rights
International Opium Convention (1912)
International Pharmaceutical Federation
International Society for Ethnopharmacology
International Society for
    Pharmacoepidemiology
International Society of Regulatory
    Toxicology and Pharmacology

Jamu (Traditional Indonesian Medicine)
Japan
Johnson & Johnson

Kampo (Traditional Japanese Medicine)
Karolinska Institute (Sweden)

Kefauver-Harris Amendments (1962)
Khat
King's College London

Legal Issues in Testing for Performance-
    Enhancing Drugs
Lethal Injection
Levamisole (Ergamisol) Controversy
Lifestyle Drugs
Low-Income People
Low-Literacy and Illiterate People
LSD
Lyme Disease, Treatments for

Mail-Order Pharmacies
Marketed Health Products Directorate
    (Canada)
Mass Drug Administration
Materia Medica
MDMA (Ecstasy)
Me Too Drugs
Medicaid: Prescription Drug Benefits
Medicaid and Medicare Systems
Medical Expenditure Panel Survey
    (MEPS)
Medical Marijuana Legislation
    (Canada)
Medical Marijuana Legislation (Europe)
Medical Marijuana Legislation (Israel)
Medical Marijuana Legislation (U.S.)
Medicare: Prescription Drug Benefits
Medicare Prescription Drug, Improvement,
    and Modernization Act (2003)
Medication Errors
Medication Therapy Management
    (MTM)
Medicinal Plant Species Threatened With
    Extinction
Medicines and Healthcare Products
    Regulatory Agency (UK)
Men
Mental Health Parity
Merck

Methamphetamine
Methaqualone (Quaalude) Controversy
Mexico
Military Pharmaceutical Issues
MRSA (Methicillin-Resistant *Staphylococcus aureus*)
Muti (Traditional Southern African Medicine)
Mylan

Narcotic Antagonists
Narcotics (Prescription)
National Center for Advancing Translational Sciences (NIH)
National Center for Complementary and Alternative Medicine (NIH)
National Childhood Vaccine Injury Act
National Institute for Biological Standards and Control
Native Americans/Alaska Natives
Native Hawai'ians/Pacific Islanders
Naturopathy
Neonatal Abstinence Syndrome
Netherlands
Neuro-Enhancement Through Pharmacy
Neuropharmacology
Nganga (Traditional African Healers)
Nicotine
Nomifensine (Merital, Alival) Controversy
Noonday Demon, The: An Atlas of Depression (Andrew Solomon)
Normal: Definitions and Controversy
Novo Nordisk
Nutritional Supplements: History
Nycomed

Off-Label Use of Pharmaceuticals
Olympics, Summer: Performance-Enhancing Drugs
Olympics, Winter: Performance-Enhancing Drugs
Online Pharmacies
Opiate Replacement Programs

Opioid Prescription Abuse, Misuse, and Overuse
Opium (Herbal Medicine)
Organisation for Economic Co-operation and Development
Orphan Diseases, Drugs for
Over-the-Counter (OTC) Drugs

Pain Control
Pain Disorders
Patient Activism
Patient Protection and Affordable Care Act (Obamacare)
Patient Rights
PCP (Drug of Abuse)
Pediatric Rule (U.S., 1998)
Performance-Enhancing Drugs and Sports: History
Pesticides: Human Health Effects
Pfizer
Pharmaceutical Benefits Within Health Insurance Plans: U.S.
Pharmaceutical Fraud
Pharmaceutical Law
Pharmaceutical Policy: International Cooperation
Pharmaceutical Research and Manufacturers of America
Pharmacists: Training and Certification
Pharmacoeconomics
Pharmacogenomics
Pharmacoinformatics
Pharmacology for Africa Initiative
Pharmacology to Control and Punish
Pharmacovigilance
Pharmacy Benefit Managers
Pharmacy Technicians: Training and Certification
PHARMO Record Linkage System (The Netherlands)
Phenacetin Controversy
Phenformin (Azucaps) Controversy
Philippines

Phytochemicals
Polio Eradication Campaign
Polypharmacy
Prescription Drug Approval Process: Asia
Prescription Drug Approval Process: Australia
Prescription Drug Approval Process: Canada
Prescription Drug Approval Process: Europe
Prescription Drug Approval Process: U.S.
Prescription Drug User Fee Act (1992)
Prescription-Event Monitoring (PEM)
    Database (University of Portsmouth, UK)
Prescriptive Authority
Prison Pharmaceutical Issues
Procter & Gamble
Project Bioshield Act (2004)
Propoxyphene (Darvon, Darvocet)
    Controversy
Pseudoephedrine, Restriction of Access to
Psilocybin
Psychopharmacology
Pure Food and Drug Act (1906)

Quality of Life Research

Race-Based Pharmaceuticals
Racial Minorities: Asia
Racial Minorities: Canada
Racial Minorities: Caribbean
Racial Minorities: Europe
Racial Minorities: Latin America
RAND Health Insurance Experiment
    (1974–1982)
Rational Drug Design
Rational Prescribing
Reimportation of Prescription Drugs
Rimonabant (Acomplia) Controversy
Rofecoxib (Vioxx) Controversy
Russia
RxNorm (National Library of Medicine)

Safety Pharmacology Society
Salvia (Drug of Abuse)
Sanofi-Aventis

Scheduled Drugs (U.S.)
SCHIP (State Children's Health Insurance
    Program): Prescription Drug Benefits
Sex Offenders, Pharmacological
    Interventions for
Sex Reassignment Therapy and Prescription
    Drugs
Sexual Minorities
Shooting Sports and Performance-Enhancing
    Drugs
Siddha Medicine (Dravidian Culture)
Singapore
Sinopharm Group Company Limited
Smallpox Eradication
Smoking Cessation Drugs
Smuggling of Drugs of Abuse
Smuggling of Prescription Drugs
South Africa
State-Sponsored Sports Doping Programs
Stimulants (Sport)
Substance Abuse and Mental Health Services
    Administration (SAMHSA)
Sunscreening Agents
Swimming and Performance-Enhancing
    Drugs
Swiss Society of Pharmacology and
    Toxicology
Switzerland
Synthetic Marijuana

Takeda Pharmaceutical Co.
Technology and Pharmacy Practice
Tennis and Performance-Enhancing
    Drugs
Teva Pharmaceutical Industries
Thalidomide (Contergan) Controversy
Therapeutic Use Exemption (Performance-
    Enhancing Drugs)
Title X Family Planning Program (1970)
*Touched With Fire: Manic-Depressive Illness
    and the Artistic Temperament* (Jamison)
Track and Field and Performance-Enhancing
    Drugs

Traditional and Herbal Medicines,
    Regulation: Africa
Traditional and Herbal Medicines,
    Regulation: Australia and New Zealand
Traditional and Herbal Medicines,
    Regulation: Canada
Traditional and Herbal Medicines,
    Regulation: East Asia
Traditional and Herbal Medicines,
    Regulation: Europe
Traditional and Herbal Medicines,
    Regulation: Latin America
Traditional and Herbal Medicines,
    Regulation: South Asia
Traditional and Herbal Medicines,
    Regulation: United States
Traditional Medicine: Australia (Bush Medicine)
Traditional Medicine: Central America
Traditional Medicine: China
Traditional Medicine: Native American
    Tribes
Traditional Medicine: South Africa
Traditional Medicine: South America
Traditional Medicine: Tibet
Traditional Medicine: Vietnam
Tranquilizers
Translational Pharmacology
TRIPS Agreement (Agreement on Trade-
    Related Aspects of Intellectual Property
    Rights), Doha Declaration, and TRIPS
    Plus
Trovafloxacin (Trovan) Controversy
Tuskegee Experiment
Tylenol Tampering Case

Unani (Muslim Traditional Medicine)
United Kingdom
United States: 1800 to 1850
United States: 1851 to 1900
United States: 1901 to 1950
United States: 1951 to Present
University of California, San Diego
University of California, San Francisco
University of Oxford
University of Toronto
University of Washington
U.S. Anti-Doping Agency
U.S. Pharmacopeial Convention

Vaccination: National and International
    Programs
Vaccines
Valerian (Herbal Medicine)
Venereal Disease Treatment: History
Venereal Diseases, Treatments for
Veterans Administration (U.S.): Prescription
    Drug Benefits
Veterinary Pharmacology

Water Pollution (Prescription Drugs)
WHO Model Lists of Essential Medicines
Women
World Anti-Doping Agency (WADA)
World Health Organization

Yellow Card Scheme

Zero-Tolerance Drug Policies
Zimelidine (Zelmid) Controversy

Reader's Guide

Branches of Pharmacology

Behavioral Pharmacology and Substance Abuse

Cardiovascular Pharmacology

Clinical Pharmacology

Endocrine Pharmacology

Neuropharmacology

Pharmacogenomics

Pharmacoinformatics

Psychopharmacology

Translational Pharmacology

Veterinary Pharmacology

Business of Pharmacology

Diffusion of New Pharmaceutical Drugs

Disease Management

Dosage Safety Measures

Drug Discovery and Development

Equity Pricing of Essential Medicines

Generic Medicines

Gray Market Drugs

Me Too Drugs

Medication Therapy Management (MTM)

Pharmacists: Training and Certification

Pharmacy Benefit Managers

Pharmacy Technicians: Training and Certification

Prescription Drug Approval Process: Asia

Prescription Drug Approval Process: Australia

Prescription Drug Approval Process: Canada

Prescription Drug Approval Process: Europe

Prescription Drug Approval Process: U.S.

Rational Drug Design

Technology and Pharmacy Practice

TRIPS Agreement (Agreement on Trade-Related Aspects of Intellectual Property Rights), Doha Declaration, and TRIPS Plus

Data Sources

Adjudicated Claims Data

Adverse Drug Events Reporting Systems

Canadian Provincial Databases

Centers for Disease Control and Prevention

ENCePP Database (European Network of Centres for Pharmacoepidemiology and Pharmacovigilance)

General Practice Research Database (UK)

Healthcare Cost and Utilization Project (HCUP)

Healthcare Effectiveness Data and Information Set (HEDIS)

HMO Research Network (19 Regional Health Care Delivery Organizations)

Hospital Administrative Data

Medicaid and Medicare Systems

Medical Expenditure Panel Survey (MEPS)

Organisation for Economic Co-operation and Development

PHARMO Record Linkage System (The Netherlands)

Prescription-Event Monitoring (PEM) Database (University of Portsmouth, UK)

Substance Abuse and Mental Health Services
Administration (SAMHSA)
World Health Organization

Ethical Issues in Pharmacology

Abuse of Prescription Drugs
Access to Medicines (Developing
World)
Access to Medicines (Industrialized
World)
Acetaminophen Overdose Risk
Adverse Drug Reactions (ADR) and Adverse
Events (AE)
Antiaging Medicines
Chemoprevention
Cosmetic Pharmacology
Counterfeit Drugs/Medicines
Discrimination in Prescribing Practice
Drug Allergies
Drug Interactions
Fertility Drugs
Homeopathy
Hospice Treatment
Lethal Injection
Lifestyle Drugs
Medicinal Plant Species Threatened With
Extinction
Military Pharmaceutical Issues
Normal: Definitions and Controversy
Orphan Diseases, Drugs for
Pain Control
Pharmaceutical Fraud
Pharmaceutical Policy: International
Cooperation
Pharmacovigilance
Prison Pharmaceutical Issues
Rational Prescribing
Smuggling of Drugs of Abuse
Smuggling of Prescription Drugs
Tuskegee Experiment
WHO Model Lists of Essential
Medicines

Infrastructure of Pharmacology

American Board of Clinical Pharmacology
American College of Clinical Pharmacy
American Pharmacists Association
American Society of Health-System Pharmacists
British Pharmacological Society, The
Canadian Society of Pharmacology and
Therapeutics
Cuban Society for Pharmacology
Drug Enforcement Administration (U.S.)
EudraCT (European Union Drug Regulating
Authorities Clinical Trials)
EudraPharm (European Union Drug
Regulating Authorities Pharmaceutical
Database)
European Medicines Agency
Food and Drug Administration (U.S.)
International Pharmaceutical Federation
International Society for Ethnopharmacology
International Society for
Pharmacoepidemiology
International Society of Regulatory
Toxicology and Pharmacology
Marketed Health Products Directorate
(Canada)
Medicines and Healthcare Products
Regulatory Agency (UK)
National Center for Advancing Translational
Sciences (NIH)
National Center for Complementary and
Alternative Medicine (NIH)
National Institute for Biological Standards
and Control
Pharmaceutical Law
Pharmaceutical Research and Manufacturers
of America
Pharmacology for Africa Initiative
Safety Pharmacology Society
Swiss Society of Pharmacology and
Toxicology
U.S. Pharmacopeial Convention
Yellow Card Scheme

Laws and Regulations

Common Rule, The
Comprehensive Methamphetamine Control
   Act (1996)
Conscience Clause
Controlled Substances Act
Declaration of Helsinki (1975)
Drug Abuse Control Amendments
   of 1965
Drug Price Competition and Patent Term
   Restoration Act (1984)
False Claims Act ("Lincoln Law")
Federal Food, Drug, and Cosmetic Act
   (1938)
Intellectual Property Rights
International Opium Convention (1912)
Kefauver-Harris Amendments (1962)
Medical Marijuana Legislation (Canada)
Medical Marijuana Legislation (Europe)
Medical Marijuana Legislation (Israel)
Medical Marijuana Legislation (U.S.)
Medicare Prescription Drug, Improvement,
   and Modernization Act (2003)
Mental Health Parity
National Childhood Vaccine Injury Act
Off-Label Use of Pharmaceuticals
Patient Protection and Affordable Care Act
   (Obamacare)
Pediatric Rule (U.S., 1998)
Prescription Drug User Fee Act (1992)
Project Bioshield Act (2004)
Pseudoephedrine, Restriction of Access to
Pure Food and Drug Act (1906)
Scheduled Drugs (U.S.)
Title X Family Planning Program (1970)

Pharmaceutical Companies

Abbott Laboratories
Actavis
Allergan
Amgen
Astellas Pharma

AstraZeneca
Baxter International
Bayer
Biogen Idec
Boehringer Ingelheim
Celgene
Daiichi Sankyo
Eisai
Eli Lilly
Genentech
Gilead Sciences
Johnson & Johnson
Merck
Mylan
Novo Nordisk
Nycomed
Pfizer
Procter & Gamble
Sanofi-Aventis
Sinopharm Group Company Limited
Takeda Pharmaceutical Co.
Teva Pharmaceutical Industries

Pharmacological Issues in Society

Advertising to Doctors
Advertising to Patients
Anabolic Steroids (Sport)
Anti-Doping Convention, Council
   of Europe
Arts: Prescription Drugs and Creativity
Astemizole (Hismanal) Controversy
BALCO Scandal
Baseball and Performance-Enhancing Drugs
Beta-Blockers (Sport)
Biological Passport (Sport)
Blood Doping
Boxing and Performance-Enhancing Drugs
Canada: Variation in Prescription Drug
   Benefits by Province/Territory
Cerivastatin (Baycol, Lipobay) Controversy
Clinical Pharmacology: Developing
   Countries

Clinical Pharmacology: Industrialized
    Countries
Cycling and Performance-Enhancing Drugs
DES (Diethylstilbestrol) Controversy
Diuretics and Masking Agents (Sport)
Drug Labeling: Developing World
Drug Labeling: Industrialized World
Drug Testing, High School and College
    Athletes (U.S.)
Drug Testing, Olympic Athletes (Overview)
Drug Testing, Professional Athletes (Overview)
Drugs as Study Aids
Efalizumab (Raptiva) Controversy
EPO (Erythropoietin)
Ethics of Performance-Enhancing Drugs in Sport
Fen-Phen (Fenfluramine/Phentermine)
    Controversy
Fluoridation (Drinking Water)
Football (American) and Performance-
    Enhancing Drugs
Game of Shadows (Mark Fainaru-Wada and
    Lance Williams)
Geographic Variation in Prescribing
    Practices
Glucocorticosteroids (Sport)
Human Subjects Research: Standards and
    Protections
Human Subjects Research in Developing
    Countries
Legal Issues in Testing for Performance-
    Enhancing Drugs
Levamisole (Ergamisol) Controversy
Mail-Order Pharmacies
Medicaid: Prescription Drug Benefits
Medicare: Prescription Drug Benefits
Methaqualone (Quaalude) Controversy
Nomifensine (Merital, Alival) Controversy
Olympics, Summer: Performance-Enhancing
    Drugs
Olympics, Winter: Performance-Enhancing
    Drugs
Online Pharmacies
Over-the-Counter (OTC) Drugs

Performance-Enhancing Drugs and Sports:
    History
Pharmaceutical Benefits Within Health
    Insurance Plans: U.S.
Phenacetin Controversy
Phenformin (Azucaps) Controversy
Polypharmacy
Reimportation of Prescription Drugs
Rimonabant (Acomplia) Controversy
Rofecoxib (Vioxx) Controversy
SCHIP (State Children's Health Insurance
    Program): Prescription Drug Benefits
Sex Offenders, Pharmacological
    Interventions for
Sex Reassignment Therapy and Prescription
    Drugs
Shooting Sports and Performance-Enhancing
    Drugs
State-Sponsored Sports Doping Programs
Stimulants (Sport)
Swimming and Performance-Enhancing
    Drugs
Tennis and Performance-Enhancing Drugs
Thalidomide (Contergan) Controversy
Therapeutic Use Exemption (Performance-
    Enhancing Drugs)
Track and Field and Performance-Enhancing
    Drugs
Trovafloxacin (Trovan) Controversy
U.S. Anti-Doping Agency
Vaccination: National and International
    Programs
Veterans Administration (U.S.): Prescription
    Drug Benefits
Water Pollution (Prescription Drugs)
World Anti-Doping Agency (WADA)
Zero-Tolerance Drug Policies
Zimelidine (Zelmid) Controversy

Pharmacology Around the World

Australia
Austria
Belgium

Canada
China
Colombia
Costa Rica
Denmark
France
Germany
India
Japan
Mexico
Netherlands
Philippines
Russia
Singapore
South Africa
Switzerland
United Kingdom
United States: 1800 to 1850
United States: 1851 to 1900
United States: 1901 to 1950
United States: 1951 to 2012

Public Health Issues

Addiction to Prescription Drugs
Adherence to Prescription Directions
Antibiotic/Antimicrobial Resistance
Autism and Vaccines
Directly Observed Therapy, Short-Course
Drug-Resistant Diseases
Fertility Control
Harm Reduction Policies
Heroin-Assisted Treatment
MRSA (Methicillin-Resistant *Staphylococcus
aureus*)
Neonatal Abstinence Syndrome

Research in Pharmacology

Animal Testing
Classical Pharmacology
Clinical Field Studies
Clinical Trials
Comparative Effectiveness Research
Computer-Aided Drug Design

Cost-Effectiveness Research
Ethnobotany
Pharmacoeconomics
Quality of Life Research
Race-Based Pharmaceuticals
RxNorm (National Library of Medicine)

Social History of Pharmacology

Access to Essential Medicines as a Human
Right: History
Aloe Vera (Herbal Medicine)
Antibiotic Revolution, The
Antipsychiatry Movement
Aspirin
Ayurvedic Medicine
Belladonna (Traditional Medicine/Poison)
Canon of Medicine, The (Avicenna)
Chamomile (Herbal Medicine)
Chili (Capsaicin)
Curandero
Deinstitutionalization Movement
Digitalis
Disease Concept of Addiction: History
Egbogi (Traditional Yoruba Medicine)
Ephedra (Herbal Medicine)
Fertility Control: History
Ginseng (Herbal Medicine)
History of Pharmacological Treatments for
Mental Health
History of Pharmacology: Ancient China
History of Pharmacology: Ancient Egypt
History of Pharmacology: Europe
History of Pharmacology: Europe, Middle
Ages
History of Pharmacology: U.S., Colonial
Period to 1865
History of Pharmacology: U.S., 1865 to
1900
History of Pharmacology: U.S., 1900 to
1945
History of Pharmacology: U.S., 1945 to
Present
History of Pharmacy as a Profession: Africa

History of Pharmacy as a Profession:
    Europe
History of Pharmacy as a Profession: Middle
    East
History of Pharmacy as a Profession: United
    States
Jamu (Traditional Indonesian Medicine)
Kampo (Traditional Japanese Medicine)
Mass Drug Administration
Materia Medica
Muti (Traditional Southern African Medicine)
Naturopathy
Neuro-Enhancement Through Pharmacy
Nganga (Traditional African Healers)
*Noonday Demon, The: An Atlas of
    Depression* (Andrew Solomon)
Nutritional Supplements: History
Opiate Replacement Programs
Opium (Herbal Medicine)
Patient Activism
Patient Rights
Pharmacology to Control and Punish
Polio Eradication Campaign
RAND Health Insurance Experiment
    (1974–1982)
Siddha Medicine (Dravidian Culture)
Smallpox Eradication
*Touched With Fire: Manic-Depressive Illness
    and the Artistic Temperament* (Jamison)
Traditional and Herbal Medicines,
    Regulation: Africa
Traditional and Herbal Medicines,
    Regulation: Australia and New Zealand
Traditional and Herbal Medicines,
    Regulation: Canada
Traditional and Herbal Medicines,
    Regulation: East Asia
Traditional and Herbal Medicines,
    Regulation: Europe
Traditional and Herbal Medicines,
    Regulation: Latin America
Traditional and Herbal Medicines,
    Regulation: South Asia

Traditional and Herbal Medicines,
    Regulation: United States
Traditional Medicine: Australia (Bush
    Medicine)
Traditional Medicine: Central America
Traditional Medicine: China
Traditional Medicine: Native American Tribes
Traditional Medicine: South Africa
Traditional Medicine: South America
Traditional Medicine: Tibet
Traditional Medicine: Vietnam
Tylenol Tampering Case
Unani (Muslim Traditional Medicine)
Valerian (Herbal Medicine)
Venereal Disease Treatment: History

Specific Drugs/Drugs for Specific Conditions

ADHD Drugs
AIDS/HIV Drugs
Alcohol Cessation Drugs
Amphetamines
Anatomical Therapeutic Chemical
    Classification System (WHO)
Antianxiety Drugs
Antiasthma Drugs
Antibiotics
Anticaries Drugs
Anticholesterol Drugs
Anticoagulants
Anticonvulsant Drugs
Antidepressants
Antidiabetic Medications
Antihistamines
Antihypertensive Drugs
Anti-Inflammatory Drugs
Antimalarials
Antiparasitic Drugs
Antipsychotics
Antipyretic Drugs
Appetite Depressants and Stimulants
Bath Salts (Synthetic Cathinones)
Cancer, Drug Treatments for

Cardiovascular Drugs
Central Nervous System Depressants and
    Stimulants
Chemical Fertilizers: Human Health Effects
Club Drugs
Cocaine
Cognitive Enhancers
Decongestants
Diuretics
Food Additives
Gastric Drugs
Hallucinogens
Heroin
Hormone Replacement Therapy (HRT)
Hypnotics and Sedatives
Ibogaine
Inhalants
Khat
LSD
Lyme Disease, Treatments for
MDMA (Ecstasy)
Methamphetamine
Narcotic Antagonists
Narcotics (Prescription)
Nicotine
Pain Disorders
PCP (Drug of Abuse)
Pesticides: Human Health Effects
Phytochemicals
Salvia (Drug of Abuse)
Smoking Cessation Drugs
Sunscreening Agents
Synthetic Marijuana
Tranquilizers
Vaccines
Venereal Diseases, Treatments for

Specific Populations

Adolescents
African Americans
Asian Americans
Athletes
Children
Developing Countries, Residents of
Elderly People
Hispanic Americans
Immigrants and Refugees
Indigenous and Ethnic Minorities: Aotearoa
    New Zealand
Low-Income People
Low-Literacy and Illiterate People
Men
Native Americans/Alaska Natives
Native Hawai'ians/Pacific Islanders
Racial Minorities: Asia
Racial Minorities: Canada
Racial Minorities: Caribbean
Racial Minorities: Europe
Racial Minorities: Latin America
Sexual Minorities
Women

University Research Programs

Dartmouth College
Karolinska Institute (Sweden)
King's College London
University of California, San Diego
University of California,
    San Francisco
University of Oxford
University of Toronto
University of Washington

Takeda Pharmaceutical Co.

Takeda Pharmaceutical Co. is a pharmaceutical corporation headquartered in Osaka, Japan, with more than 30,000 employees. It is as of 2012 the largest Japanese pharmaceutical corporation, and the 14th pharmaceutical corporation in the world in terms of global sales. Takeda's pharmaceutical products are divided among the core therapeutic areas: cardiovascular and metabolic conditions, oncology, the central nervous system, immunology and respiratory conditions, general medicine, and vaccines. Main products in terms of turnover include Actos (marketed as Glustin in Europe) and pioglitazone hydrochloride for the treatment of type 2 diabetes. It was first registered in 1999 and has since been selling in relatively large volumes, including in 2011 when it accounted for approximately 27 percent of the corporation's revenues. However, it lost its exclusivity in August 2012. In fiscal year (FY) 2012, the net sales of Actos/Glustin were ¥122.9 billion, compared to the current Takeda top-seller, Blopress (candesartan cilexetil), which is used for hypertension treatment and sold for ¥169.6 billion. Other large-volume products in terms of sales were Takepron (Prevacid in the United States) for gastric and duodenal ulcers (¥110.2 billion), Leuplin (Enantone in Europe) for prostate and breast cancer and for endometriosis (¥116.5 billion), and Velcade for treating multiple myeloma (¥72.9 billion). The relatively new product Daxan for chronic obstructive pulmonary disease (COPD) had a FY 2012 turnover of ¥3.0 billion.

Corporate Philosophy and Recent Strategic Initiatives

Takeda was established in 1781 as a seller of traditional medicines in Osaka, Japan. After the opening of Japan to the Western world in the late 1860s, Takeda became one of the first companies to start importing Western medicines. The company established itself as a modern pharmaceutical manufacturer in 1895, when it started its own factory in Osaka. It marketed its first multivitamin in Japan in 1952, and started to establish itself in overseas markets from 1962 onward.

In 2013 or thereabouts, Takeda regarded its corporate development as being in the midst of a transformation period. Takeda's overall corporate philosophy, titled Takedaism, lists its core values as ethics (the highest ethical standards); challenge (discover new potential and make the most of one's ingenuity); progress (pursue individual growth and always push oneself further); teamwork (act as a team and develop ties of mutual trust and respect); and steadfastness (seek what matters and embrace a simple, steady approach). After the acquisition of Nycomed in 2011, the corporation implemented a Vision 2020 plan consisting of realizing a New Takeda operating model by 2020 through pursuing concrete measures divided into the core principles.

Globalization, Diversity, and Innovation

Globalization measures concern strengthening the sales of existing brand generics and over-the-counter drugs in countries such as Russia, Brazil, and China, as well as responding to emergent needs in such markets by way of developing new drugs adapted to these markets. At the same time, the corporation aims at maintaining its position in domestic, U.S., and European markets. Diversity concerns fostering a corporate culture, which respects as well as takes advantage of the numerous different personnel and nationalities present within the corporation. The innovation principle concerns are as follows: maintaining a competitive pipeline within key areas, improving R&D productivity, and changing into an efficient operating model while simultaneously fostering global brand marketing efforts.

Takeda is active regarding policies for corporate social responsibility (CSR). It pursues what it calls a holistic approach, consisting of creating as well as sustaining corporate value. Takeda thus strives to maintain cases conducted by Takeda alone, as well as cases with other companies and cases called producer-type activities. Parts of the policy are established with reference to the United Nations (UN) Global Compact principles including human rights, labor practices, and

fair operating practices. General community involvement and development activities are subdivided into externally and internally directed activity areas. As for the former type, Takeda has contributed to support for areas affected by the 2011 Great East Japan Earthquake by way of, for example, conducting long-term and ongoing support programs. There are research grants in a range of fields related to health care, as well as partnerships with NGOs and NPOs. In-company activities include awareness activities established through a dedicated site on the intranet, and a section on the intranet to provide employees with information on volunteering opportunities.

Acquisition History and Collaboration Partners

Takeda has acquired several other companies. Takeda acquired the Cambridge, Massachusetts, corporation Millennium Pharmaceuticals in 2008, and the new subsidiary was subsequently called Millennium: The Takeda Oncology Company. It has approximately 1,200 employees. It was Millennium that had developed the first version of one of Takeda's current core products, Velcade, which was approved by the U.S. Food and Drug Administration (FDA) in 2008, as well as a portfolio of pipeline candidates.

In 2011, Takeda acquired Nycomed. The rationale for this acquisition was multifold. First of all it was conceived of as a strong fit with Takeda's overall growth strategy by way of strengthening the pan-European business platform, leveraging Nycomed's strength in emerging markets to drive further growth. It thus allowed Takeda to maximize the value of its portfolio through enhanced development expertise and commercialization capability in Europe and in emerging markets. An early estimate stated that Takeda's portfolio balance as of 2010 consisted in having approximately 42 percent of its sales in North America, 40 percent in Japan, 15 percent in Europe, and 2 percent in Asia/emerging markets. In 2015 this pattern changed, with approximately 23 percent of sales occurring in North America, 35 percent in Japan, 21 percent in Europe, and 21 percent in Asia/emergent markets. Furthermore, the acquisition would provide a significant growth driver with the COPD drug Roflumilast (the product called Daxas in Europe). Secondly, it constituted according to early estimates a more than 30 percent increase in annual revenue and a more than 40 percent increase in operating income. Thirdly, it constituted an injection of diverse talent that would help to transform Takeda's culture.

Other acquisitions and reorganizations include the 2005 acquisition of the X-ray crystallography company Syrrx, based in San Diego, California. Takeda acquired TAP Pharmaceutical Products, which had been formed in 1977 as a joint venture between Takeda and Abbott Laboratories, in 2008. The split resulted in Abbott acquiring U.S. rights to the drug Lupron. On the other hand, Takeda received rights to the drug Prevacid and TAP's pipeline candidates. The move also increased the number of Takeda employees to 3,000 persons. In 2012, Takeda acquired the Philadelphia-based company URL Pharma in order to obtain the drug Colcrys for gout therapy and subsequently spun out the non-Colcrys generic business to a subsidiary of Sun Pharmaceutical. Also in 2012, Takeda purchased the Brazilian pharmaceutical company Multilab.

Research and Development

Takeda's expenditures for R&D as a percentage in relation to total sales were 20.8 percent in FY 2012, a slight increase from the year before. As of 2015, the corporation has 15 R&D sites worldwide, whereas the Shonan Research Center established in eastern Japan in 2011 is considered to be its global research network hub. It combined the former Tsukuba Research Center and Osaka Research Center. A new organizational framework was announced in May 2013, where the oncology research and development function of Millennium Pharmaceuticals would be integrated into the global R&D organization led by the Chief Medical & Scientific Officer. Takeda considered this move to be in line with their commitment to enhance operational excellence throughout the R&D organization worldwide. Takeda also strives to accelerate innovation in drug discovery, by way of, for example, harnessing the basic technologies acquired through partnerships to diversify identification methods for novel targets.

Recent Controversies

One recent controversy involving Takeda is related to the comparisons used with a rival drug in promotional materials. The materials included a graph that suggested that Biopress was more effective than Novasc (amiodipine), a drug manufactured by Pfizer, at controlling hypertension, as well as language suggesting that Biopress was more effective than Novasc. Takeda was criticized for this promotional material because clinical trial results published in the journal *Hypertension* showed no difference in effectiveness between the two drugs. In March 2014, Takeda CEO Yasuchika Hasegawa publicly apologized for the use of "inappropriate expressions" in the ad, but denied that the company had tampered with data. In 2011, the FDA released a safety announcement warning that using Actos for over a year may be associated with an increased risk of bladder cancer, and the first Actos-related bladder cancer suits were filed the same year.

Terje Grønning
University of Oslo

See Also: Astellas Pharma; Daiichi Sankyo; Eisai; Nycomed.

Further Readings

Astellas Pharma. *Medical Care & the Pharmaceutical Industry 2013*. Tokyo: Astellas Pharma, 2013.

Furukawa, R. and A. Gato. "The Role of Corporate Scientists in Innovation." *Research Policy*, v.35/1 (2006).

Inagaki, K. "Takeda Pharmaceutical Admits to Improper Drug Ads." *The Wall Street Journal*, March 3, 2014.

McColgan, M. *Leading Pharmaceutical Operational Excellence*. Berlin & Heidelberg: Springer, 2013.

Shimura, H., S. Masuda, and H. Kimura. "A Lesson From Japan: Research and Development Efficiency Is a Key Element of Pharmaceutical Industry Consolidation Process." *Drug Discoveries & Therapeutics*, v.8/1 (2014).

Takeda Pharmaceutical Co. *Annual Report 2011*. Osaka: Takeda Pharmaceutical Co., 2011.

Takeda Pharmaceutical Co. *Annual Report 2013*. Osaka: Takeda Pharmaceutical Co., 2013.

TECHNOLOGY AND PHARMACY PRACTICE

Technology implementation in the field of pharmacy involves an increase in health care efficiency, an improvement in medication safety, and an enhancement of the scope of professional pharmacy practice, among other aspects. In fact, if properly implemented, some of the technologies available today could lead to considerable forward progress in pharmacy. The involvement of technology and hence automation in pharmacy began in the 1970s. The role of pharmacists in providing patient care has been both eased and complicated by the use of technology. Subsequently, the increased need for efficiency, safety, and accuracy in the use of medications by consumers, health care professionals, manufacturers, and regulatory authorities has led to significant developments in health information technology (HIT).

Application of Technology

Electronic Prescribing

Electronic prescribing (EP) is a process by which a prescriber (a health care practitioner who is legally entitled to prescribe) can directly send electronic prescriptions to a pharmacy. The automation of supply and prescribing is possible through EP systems. It also reduces the additional burden of medicine administration in the hospital setting, where it can have a huge impact on patient safety by significantly reducing medication-related errors. This reduction in the rate of errors depends in large part on good system design; a poorly designed system can magnify the rate of errors. In the early 1990s, EP was pioneered in the United States and has been implemented in some other countries, including Australia, Denmark, Estonia, Iceland, Sweden, and the United Kingdom. In order to ensure seamless patient care, accurate and timely transmission from the secondary to the primary care setting of a patient's discharge is very important. This can also reduce errors related to miscommunication. Hence, the technology of electronic discharge systems has been adopted by a number of hospitals worldwide.

Identification of Medical Barcode

A medical barcode in the health care setting or hospital is the application of data in an optical, machine-readable format for the identification of medical materials. Completeness of medication history has been improved and medication administration errors have been reduced when, in addition to EP systems, medical barcodes have been applied. However, at the point of administration, the need to scan a medical barcode may constitute an interruption, and hence medical professionals often circumvent barcode scanning by developing "workarounds." In order to inhibit counterfeiting, at the point of dispensing, unique medical identification is called for by the falsified medicines directive of the European Union, to take effect in 2017.

Automated Dispensing

Automated dispensing is the process of computerized drug storage and dispensing at the point of care, while tracking and controlling the distribution of drugs. Robots have been implemented in pharmacy only recently, although they have been in use in distribution and logistics for a number of years. The use of automation was initiated with the *Spoonful of Sugar* report by the Audit Commission in the United Kingdom in 2001, and since then, dispensary robots have been installed at many U.K. hospitals. With the use of pharmacy robots came reductions in dispensing errors, optimized use of pharmacy space, and improvements in the efficiency and speed of dispensing. The implementation of robots in all pharmacy sectors is expected, with the availability of sophisticated, newer, smaller, and more efficient machines.

Telecare

Telecare refers to the provision of remote care to physically challenged and elderly people, offering reassurance and care and allowing them to continue living in their homes. Pharmacy services can be revolutionized and transformed by the use of Internet pharmacy supply services, electronic prescription service, and remote consultations. Its adoption in the field of pharmacy would rely heavily on integration architectures, dependable communications, and the intent of pharmacists to invest in and apply digital technologies in assessing patient demographics.

Monitoring Adherence

Monitoring adherence in the health care setting is the process of evaluation by health care providers of whether patients have adhered strictly to specific treatment plans. Adherence monitoring is now supported by a number of technologies. Smart packaging that consists of tablet blister packs, helpful in monitoring medication adherence, is being designed by some pharmacists. Patients are also asked to record for all their medications any side effects they experience. These data in turn can be transferred to a tablet device or mobile telephone.

Mobile Technology

Mobile technology is widespread in today's society. One common use of mobile technology in pharmacy is the use of text alerts by pharmacists to remind their patients about prescriptions refills. Also under development are sophisticated applications to monitor disease (e.g., blood glucose level, asthma peak flow, medication adherence support). Certainly, once successfully implemented, such applications can considerably influence the practice of pharmacy in the near future.

Current State of Technology-Supported Pharmacy

The use of technology in pharmacy practice involves integration systems and HIT adoption within the electronic health record (EHR) framework. The essential HIT infrastructure represented by the core medication management systems involves pharmacy systems, clinical and computerized provider order entry (CPOE) decision support systems, medication administration systems, and medication reconciliation systems. According to a 2009 report by Surescripts, an American HIT company, EP systems and the adoption of CPOE are far more common in ambulatory care than in hospital settings. It was also reported by Surescripts that nearly 25 percent of office-based physicians use EP, while 70 percent use EP applications within their EHR systems. It was further suggested that compared with the inpatient environment, the adoption of CPOE in ambulatory case showed a steeper growth rate over the previous three years. Today's health care organizations typically lack purely integrated electronic medication reconciliation systems, which are in place in only 10.4 percent of hospitals.

According to a 2007 report by the American Society of Health-System Pharmacists, pharmacy information management systems had been implemented in nearly all the hospitals surveyed; however, only half could operate with core medication-use systems or within the EHR framework, suggesting that the process of pharmacy system integration is still incomplete. In the remaining hospitals, legacy pharmacy systems were in place, which were limited in their ability to integrate or connect with medication reconciliation systems, an essential aspect of generating improvements in medication safety. By 2007, most hospitals had initiated the adoption of storage technologies (83 percent) and medication distribution systems with the automation of repackaging (92 percent). Notwithstanding the tremendous progress made in medication administration systems, including barcodes, electronic medication administration records, and smart pumps, a very low level of integration of these technologies was found:

only 20 percent of hospitals possessed all three systems. Integration between core medication management technologies and medication administration systems, including the EHR, is limited. Depending on the definition of EHR, a level of adoption ranging from 5 percent to 60 percent has been suggested at U.S. hospitals, according to available data on EHR use. According to a study on the use of HIT commissioned by the U.S. Office of the National Coordinator for Health Information Technology, part of the Department of Health and Human Services, it was found that only 8 percent to 12 percent of U.S. hospitals had basic EHR capabilities, while federal meaningful use criteria were met by only 2 percent of hospitals. EHR systems were more likely to be implemented at teaching hospitals, urban hospitals, and large hospitals.

Syed Feroji Ahmed
CSIR-Indian Institute of Chemical Biology

See Also: History of Pharmacy as a Profession: Europe; History of Pharmacy as a Profession: Middle East; History of Pharmacy as a Profession: United States.

Further Readings

American Society of Health-System Pharmacists. "The Consensus of the Pharmacy Practice Model Summit." *American Journal of Health-System Pharmacy*, v.68 (2011).

Hersh, W. "Health Care Information Technology: Progress and Barriers." *JAMA*, v.292/18 (2004).

Howorko, Jason. "Enhancing Pharmacy Practice With Technology: A Utopian Dream?" *Canadian Journal of Hospital Pharmacy*, v.63/6 (2010).

Pedersen, C. A., et al. "ASHP National Survey of Pharmacy Practice in Hospital Settings: Dispensing and Administration." *American Journal of Health-System Pharmacy*, v.69 (2011).

Siska, Mark H. and Dennis A. Tribble. "Opportunities and Challenges Related to Technology in Supporting Optimal Pharmacy Practice Models in Hospitals and Health Systems." *American Journal of Health-System Pharmacy*, v.68/12 (2011).

TENNIS AND PERFORMANCE-ENHANCING DRUGS

Performance-enhancing drugs, known commonly as PEDs and referred to colloquially as "steroids" (because anabolic steroids are some of the most common performance-enhancing drugs, and the ones that first brought about the bans on performance-enhancing drugs in sports), have been around in various sports for years—having been acknowledged internationally as a problem in sports since the 1960s or before and banned by the Olympics since the early 1970s. Despite their ban in most sports, the illegality of many of them, and the health risks they are often associated with, they continue to be a problem in a wide variety of sports. In tennis, the use of performance-enhancing drugs is potentially becoming a serious problem, though it has not gained the level of scandal and attention that it has in other sports, especially baseball.

A Brief History of Performance-Enhancing Drugs

Performance-enhancing drugs, including anabolic steroids and various other banned or illicit drugs, procedures, and methods (ranging from potent stimulants like cocaine and amphetamines to drugs that increase the ability of blood cells to carry oxygen to genetic procedures designed to give athletes unfair advantages), have changed a great deal over time but have plagued sports for decades.

The term *performance-enhancing drug* is an umbrella under which a very wide array of types of drugs and procedures falls, although some are more common than others (with lean body mass builders, such as anabolic steroids and human growth hormone, generally at the forefront of the conversation on PEDs). These drugs and procedures are forbidden because they give players who choose to use them and have access to them unfair advantages over players who do not, and because in the vast majority of cases there are serious health risks, ranging from increased risk of stroke to overdose to addiction, associated with these types of drugs. Many of these drugs are illegal as well as being banned by international sports' governing bodies; however, some may be obtained with a prescription for legitimate medical reasons—that is, a Therapeutic Use Exemption, which is a status granted to particular players at particular times (most usually while experiencing illness or recovering from serious injury) by a major sport's governing body that allows the athlete to use a particular potentially performance-enhancing drug for a short amount of time, as some of them have practical medical uses as well as being used illicitly.

Although they have been regulated by most international, national, and regional sports federations and even by an international body known as the World Anti-Doping Agency (with subsidiaries in various countries, such as the United States Anti-Doping Agency), and often fade from national and international media attention, they are always a problem in various sports, often causing scandals and ruining careers.

Of particular interest to many sports fans is the scandal that rocked the MLB (America's Major League Baseball) for years in the early to mid-2000s (though it has carried on to some degree to this day) after the league's first, very weak antidoping code was enacted following a decade of illicitly enhanced performance that drove the game of baseball to new heights of popularity, but gave unfair advantages to a large number of players while simultaneously endangering their health.

Also disturbing to many fans is the widespread use of recreational drugs, such as marijuana and cocaine, among athletes. Although it is the health effects and illegality of drugs such as these that worry officials more than their performance-enhancing qualities, they can be considered performance enhancers as well, particularly potent stimulants such as cocaine and methamphetamine (which tennis legend Andre Agassi tested positive for and admitted to using in his biography *Open*, leading to some crying out for his titles to be revoked).

However, it is only recently that the effects and widespread use of performance-enhancing drugs are coming to international attention in the world of tennis, though there have been rumors of their use in the ITF (International Tennis Federation, the governing body for tennis and tennis players worldwide) for years, and the World Anti-Doping Agency has long been asking the ITF for more data—in fact, they have been asking since 2006.

Why Tennis Players Dope and the Negative Effects of Their Drug Use

Tennis players "dope"—a formerly colloquial term that has now become acceptable medically and legitimately, referring to the use of forbidden or illicit performance-enhancing drugs—for the same main reasons that athletes in other sports do: for increased physical strength and endurance, primarily, but also to speed up reaction times and provide other unfair advantages.

The issue of greatly increased stamina is the one that is finally drawing attention to tennis in particular, as tennis matches between top players have been getting longer, it seems, every year—with players still playing at the height of their ability. This has led to a surge of accusations against virtually all top tennis players, by fans of the game, former players, and others associated with the industry.

Although all players taking part in International Tennis Federation competitions are required to undergo drug testing, there is widespread concern that the testing procedures allow drug users to pass easily through various methods such as switching urine or using diuretics to rid their systems of evidence of drug use.

Although many fans find these longer, more intense matches at the higher levels of the four Grand Slam tournaments—the U.S. Open, the French Open, the Australian Open, and Wimbledon—to be very exciting, if any of these top players are using performance-enhancing drugs, it is giving them an unfair advantage over their opponents and endangering their health in various ways.

Fans and officials in nations that do not currently have any top-tier players are particularly disturbed by the allegations of performance-enhancing drug use at the highest levels of tennis, as they claim that this may be the factor that is preventing them from breaking into the semifinals and finals of the major tournaments.

That being said, even if these top-tier players are not doping, their careers and legacies are in danger because of the weakness of the ITF's drug enforcement, which is the single greatest factor, besides their performance, that has led to the leveling of so many accusations from officials and fans. Thus, an improvement in the ITF's drug enforcement policies and execution would not only help get rid of cheating players; it would also redeem the reputations of any falsely accused players.

Problems With Tennis's Antidoping Policies

The problems with the ITF's policies and the enforcement thereof related to performance-enhancing drugs has long been apparent to officials within the sports industry, particularly to other antidoping officials (such as those representatives of the World Anti-Doping Agency that have tried to get data on drug use from the International Tennis Federation since 2006), but has only recently been brought to the attention of fans of the sport.

Unfortunately, much of this attention has come about because of accusations leveled at top players and the proliferation of statements by fans, primarily online, about their personal beliefs on players' drug use. While it is possible that this will have a positive outcome in that it will force the ITF to take a hard look at its antidoping procedures, it is also potentially problematic in that the reputation of good players could be unjustly tarnished by such rumors.

It is also troubling to many fans that so much attention is being paid to the issue outside the ITF, but apparently not from within it; this has created a great deal of controversy and has been confusing and difficult both for fans and for ITF officials.

Although the ITF does have drug tests in place and does have official drug policies, there are suggestions from sources as varied as the World Anti-Doping Agency and an anonymous blog created for the sole purpose of leveling accusations of doping at tennis great Rafael Nadal that it would not be difficult for players to get around these tests through various means—one reason the World Anti-Doping Agency has been historically determined to have more of a hand in the International Tennis Federation's doings.

The assumption that it is fairly easy to bypass drug tests even at the highest levels of international sports is exacerbated by the recent scandal involving Lance Armstrong, who took various drug tests and never failed, but was both doping himself and serving as a go-between for other dopers and their suppliers.

Although the exact extent of doping in tennis cannot be established until the International Tennis Federation writes and enforces stricter policies or other international organizations, such as the World Anti-Doping Agency, get involved, many former players have publicly stated that there is a culture of PED use in the ITF, and there is likely at least some effect on the game caused by the use of these illicit drugs.

David Michael Gonzalez
University of Nevada

See Also: Therapeutic Use Exemption (Performance-Enhancing Drugs).

Further Readings

Agassi, Andre. *Open: An Autobiography*. New York: Vintage, 2010.

Kumar, Sanjay. "Tennis Has a Doping Problem." *The Daily Beast*, July 8, 2013.

TEVA PHARMACEUTICAL INDUSTRIES

Teva Pharmaceutical Industries Ltd., established in 1901, is an international pharmaceutical company with its main office in Israel. Teva's motto is "The Passion to Make a Difference—That's Who We Are." One of the goals of Teva, whose name means *nature* in Hebrew, has been to be among the world's largest pharmaceutical companies. Teva is the largest maker of generic drugs globally, and is also in the top 15 pharmaceutical companies worldwide. Two of Teva's plants have been approved by the U.S. Food and Drug Administration (FDA), a key step in the process of pharmaceutical marketing in the United States. Teva began sales to Japan in 2005. Teva holds patents on many drugs: notably, Copaxone (used in the treatment of multiple sclerosis, and a top seller), and Azilect (Agilect), used in the treatment of Parkinson's disease. Teva is also involved in the development, manufacture, and sales of a variety of generic and over-the-counter (OTC) products, specialty medicines, new therapies, and active pharmaceutical ingredients.

Teva Subsidiaries

Teva Pharmaceuticals has many subsidiaries throughout the world, including not only Europe, but also Asia, North America, and South America. Recently efforts are being made to increase Teva's standing in both Brazil, where it is ranked 81st of pharmaceutical firms, and Mexico, where its presence is currently weak. Teva seeks to increase its presence in specific markets such as China, India, Russia, and Brazil, as well as Argentina, Venezuela, Australia, Turkey, South Korea, and Indonesia.

Teva Pharmaceuticals

The range of Teva pharmaceuticals is quite diverse. These products are used in a variety of specialty areas (*vide infra*).

Teva Products and Specialty Areas

A brief outline of Teva's products focuses on several areas: (1) generic pharmaceuticals; (2) central nervous system (CNS) pharmaceuticals; (3) respiratory pharmaceuticals; (4) oncology (cancer) pharmaceuticals; (5) women's health pharmaceuticals; (6) pain pharmaceuticals; and (7) transplant pharmaceuticals.

In the case of generic pharmaceuticals, Teva is the global leader, with high-quality products at competitive prices. Through research and development, these products include not only capsules, creams, liquids, and ointments but also a wide range of different effective dosage forms and delivery systems. Some of the more complex types of generic drugs are also said to be new markets for Teva, including injectable drugs (long term), inhalators and nasal suspensions, and patches and thin films in a quick-dissolving formulation.

In the case of CNS pharmaceuticals, Teva has specialty products such as Azilect for treatment of Parkinson's disease symptoms, Copaxone for treatment of multiple sclerosis (MS), and Nuvigil for treatment of sleep disorders.

In the case of respiratory pharmaceuticals, Teva offers Qvar, not only for prophylactic therapy and maintenance treatment of asthma, but also to reduce or eliminate the need for systemic corticosteroid administration. ProAir HFA is provided for treatment and prevention of bronchospasm in patients either due to reversible obstructive airway disease or exercise-induced bronchospasm. QNASL (beclomethasone dipropionate) is a nasal aerosol for adolescents over 12 and adults having seasonal and perennial allergic rhinitis.

In the case of oncology pharmaceuticals, Teva offers Myocet, cyclophosphamide and doxorubicin in a liposomal formulation for first-line treatment of metastatic breast cancer; Treanda, used in treatment of non-Hodgkin's lymphoma and chronic lymphocytic leukemia; Trisenox, to induce remission in acute promyelocytic leukemia; Tevagrastim, to reduce the duration of neutropenia (low white-blood-cell count) in patients undergoing cytotoxic chemotherapy as well as in patients undergoing bone marrow transplantation, and also used in treatment of patients with advanced human immunodeficiency virus (HIV) infection; Eporatio, used in treatment of anemia in adults, associated with chronic renal failure or in cases of patients receiving chemotherapy for nonmyeloid malignancies; and Synribo (omacetaxine mepesuccinate) for injection, used in treatment of adult patients with chronic or accelerated-phase chronic myeloid leukemia (CML) who are resistant and/or intolerant to two or more tyrosine kinase inhibitors (TKIs). At present, no trials indicate an improvement in disease-related symptoms or increased survival with Synribo.

In the case of women's health pharmaceuticals, Teva offers Quartette, Zoely, Plan B One-step, Enjuvia, Seasonique, and Paragard. Enjuvia is formulated to treat menopause-associated moderate to severe vasomotor symptoms as well as symptoms of vulvar and vaginal atrophy associated with menopause; each of the other products in this category is contraceptive in nature.

Pain pharmaceuticals produced by Teva include Fentora, for management of breakthrough cancer pain; Actiq, for management of breakthrough cancer pain, and Amrix, **for** muscle spasm associated with acute, painful musculoskeletal conditions.

Transplant pharmaceuticals include Tacni (tacrolimus; Austrian brand name is Tacni-transplant and Danish brand name is Tacniteva); Equoral, a ciclosporin gel-based emulsion (German brand name is CiclosporinPro, U.S. brand name is Ciclosporin USP-modified); Ciqorin (ciclosporin, micro-emulsion; U.K., Ireland, Portugal, and Austrian brand name is Vanquoral); and Myfenax (mycophenolate mofetil, mmf; brand name in Croatia, Serbia, Bosnia, Herzegovina, Kosovo, and Macedonia is Trixin).

National Network of Excellence in Neuroscience

Teva has established the National Network of Excellence in Neuroscience (NNE) as a partnership between Teva and Israeli academic and medical institutions. The goals of the NNE are to increase therapeutic developments in neurodegenerative diseases and other key areas of focus. These collaborations address many of the most challenging diseases of our modern society. A combination of increased population and concomitantly increasing longevity has resulted in a significant rise in brain disorders and brain diseases. Israel is a leader in neuroscience research, with a fifth-place global ranking in neuroscience publications per capita. Teva has established the NNE to work with scientists from 10 of the leading universities and teaching hospitals in Israel. Basic research is necessarily a long-term investment as it seeks to understand fundamental origins of complex diseases. However, the NNE collaboration has begun to identify therapeutic approaches that may assist to modify the progression of neurological disorders. Three areas of approach include Alzheimer's disease, multiple sclerosis, and Huntington's disease. For Alzheimer's disease, approaches to memory enhancement are being explored. For multiple sclerosis and Huntington's disease, new approaches aim to halt or slow the disease progression.

The National Network of Excellence in Neuroscience includes the Hebrew University of Jerusalem, the Weizmann Institute of Science, the Technion—Israel Institute of Technology, Ben Gurion University of the Negev, Tel Aviv University, the Tel Aviv Sourasky Medical Center, the Chaim Sheba Medical Center, Rabin Medical Center, Bar-Ilan University, and the University of Haifa.

New Therapeutic Entities Strategy

The New Therapeutic Entities (NTEs) strategy by Teva is an exciting plan for development of new pharmaceuticals. Beginning with an unmet patient need, the program evaluates currently available options and associated problems in order to develop new pharmaceuticals that constitute an advance on present therapies. The flowchart for this process moves from "unmet patient need" to inadequacies of current options and/or problematic issues with current options to the new therapeutic entity with its new options.

Several examples of this approach are particularly interesting.

1. pain (a) unmet patient need—pain control without drug-dependence; (b) current options often result in addiction; (c) new therapeutic entity, abuse-deterrent opiods; (d) benefits—reduction of abuse as well as socioeconomic burdens.

2. schizophrenia (a) unmet patient need—low adherence to oral antipsychotics; (b) current options require daily oral or every 2 weeks intramuscular injection; (c) NTE: long-acting injectable Risperidone (LAI) provides *quarterly* subcutaneous injection; (d) benefits—better adherence with decreased costs.

3. glaucoma (a) unmet patient need—current treatment requires three daily doses with prostaglandin agonist and beta blocker; problems include decreased adherence and systematic side effects; (c) NTE: fixed-dose combination of prostaglandin agonist and beta-blocker once daily; (d) benefits—similar efficacy with lower systemic exposure to beta-blocker; fewer side effects.

4. Crohn's disease (a) unmet patient need—current treatment with 6-MP, an immunosuppressive drug, is associated with systemic side effects such as reduction in white and red blood cell count and greater susceptibility to infection and anemia; (c) NTE: novel formulation for targeted release of 6-MP targets the intestine via delayed release and concomitant rapid release in the intestine; (d) benefits—similar efficacy with reduced adverse events.

Social and Environmental Responsibility

Teva has an Environment Health and Safety (EHS) committee that includes an EHS policy and a commitment to consider both environmental safety and employee health. The program includes "Target Zero," which stands for zero accidents/incidents as well as a healthy and safe workplace. One focus is on energy and emissions, with a goal of minimizing Teva's environmental footprint and to work toward an impact on the environment that is positive. The initial goals of Teva's energy and emissions policy is to decrease greenhouse gas emissions by reduction of energy usage. A second area of environmental concern for Teva is the use of water in its facilities, where it's used predominantly for cooling and/or industrial processes. One example is the biosynthetic plant in Hungary; this facility uses far more water than others. However, this elevated water use is offset by the use of biosynthetic processing instead of processing using organic chemicals, which may themselves be contaminants.

Another arena of positive contribution from Teva is their dedication to helping individuals living with multiple sclerosis. Teva supports a European team that made it to the top of Mount Ventroux, in the recent Climbing Against MS event. This event, sponsored by Teva in 2013, raised 80,000 Euros (US$91,000) for the Netherlands National MS fund.

Laura A. Andersson
Retired Independent Scholar

See Also: Cancer, Drug Treatments for; Generic Medicines; Neuropharmacology; Pain Control.

Further Readings

Gabison, Yoram and Reuters. "For Teva Pharmaceuticals, Stagnation Is the New Growth."

Haaretz News, March 11, 2015. http://www.haaretz
.com/business/1.631780 (Accessed March 10, 2015).
Teva Pharmaceuticals [Web site]. http://www
.tevapharm.com.

THALIDOMIDE (CONTERGAN) CONTROVERSY

Thalidomide, also formerly known under the trade name Contergan, was a sedative at the center of one of the most infamous episodes in pharmaceutical history. During the late 1950s and early 1960s, more than 10,000 children were born with severe malformations of the limbs and organs on account of their mothers' usage of the medication during pregnancy. When news of these births came to light, it provoked an international scandal and drew public attention to the processes of drug testing and regulation. In West Germany, members of the company responsible for producing the medication (Grünenthal) were brought to trial in the late 1960s, although the case was eventually discontinued after the firm agreed to set up a compensation fund for victims. While large numbers of "thalidomide babies," as they were known, were born in countries across the world, only 17 such children were born in the United States since the drug had not received formal approval from the U.S. Food and Drug Administration (FDA). The thalidomide scandal would have a profound effect on the course of pharmaceutical history, as many countries tightened rules for clinical testing and drug regulation in the ensuing years.

In 1954, after thalidomide was first synthesized by chemist Wilhelm Kunz, Grünenthal obtained a patent for it and aimed to sell it as an antihistamine. Although the drug failed in that regard, it demonstrated substantial sedative properties, and Grünenthal would begin to market it under the name Contergan in 1957. Beyond its sedative properties, the drug was also promoted as useful for combating morning sickness in pregnant women. Thalidomide quickly gained in popularity both in West Germany (where it was developed) and abroad, being sold in more than 40 countries under different trade names. The drug seemed to offer substantial promise—unlike many other medications of this type, it acted quickly, produced few immediately apparent side effects, did not result in a sedative "hangover," and only very rarely resulted in overdose—and it quickly rose to become one of the best-selling medications in much of Europe. Available primarily as an over-the-counter (OTC) drug, nearly 700,000 Germans took it on a regular basis and the drug was prescribed for hundreds of thousands of others worldwide.

In late 1959, occasional reports indicated that thalidomide could potentially cause nerve damage in both the hands and feet. These reports did not, however, cause widespread alarm and the drug companies across the world continued to lease the drug and introduce it into new markets. In 1960, the FDA received an application from Merrill to begin marketing the drug under the name Kevadon. The drug's manufacturers had already distributed it to thousands of physicians across the United States to begin trial use, and it was expected to receive a quick approval. The case was assigned to a junior member of staff, Frances Kelsey, a Canadian-born physician and pharmacologist. After examining the data, Kelsey refused Merrill's application, citing that the information presented by the firm did not do enough to demonstrate the safety of the drug. Kelsey and other members of the FDA quickly came under pressure from Merrill representatives, receiving dozens of phone calls and letters urging the drug's approval. When Kelsey raised the issue of reports linking thalidomide to nerve damage, Merrill representatives threatened to sue the FDA for libel. In the meantime, Kelsey continued to delay approval of Kevadon as Merrill continued to put pressure on the agency.

In other parts of the world, by the early 1960s it was becoming apparent that thalidomide had a number of profoundly troubling side effects. In Germany, Widukind Lenz, a pediatrician and professor at the University of Hamburg, first noticed a link between mothers who had taken the drug during pregnancy and children born with phocomelia—a rare syndrome characterized by extreme shortening or absence of bones in the arms or legs. Additionally, many of these children displayed other birth malformations, notably cleft palates and abnormal development of internal organs. While Lenz began gathering data on the abnormalities from colleagues and parents, William McBride, an Australian gynecologist based at the Crown Street Women's Hospital in Sydney, also drew a connection between thalidomide and the troubling births. In December 1961, he published a short letter in *The Lancet* warning that nearly 20 percent of children whose mothers had been exposed to Distaval (the name under which the drug was marketed in Australia) exhibited teratogenic effects.

Shortly after these publications, reports from other parts of the world arrived to confirm these findings. The consequences were considered shocking by the public, medical community, and pharmaceutical industry alike. Over time, it became clear that more than 10,000 thalidomide babies had been born, the largest number of births occurring in Germany. Pictures of children exhibiting phocomelia were resplendent throughout the media, and a

substantial panic ensued given the large numbers of women who had taken the drug. In the United States, people were further outraged when Morton Mintz, a reporter for the *Washington Post*, broke the story regarding Frances Kelsey and Merrill's attempts to put pressure on her to approve the drug despite Kelsey's vocal concerns about insufficient safety testing and potential side effects. Although the drug had not been approved, Merrill had sent samples to more than 1,000 physicians. By mid-1962, thalidomide had been removed from the shelves of most pharmacies worldwide.

Although recalled from pharmacies, thalidomide remained controversial for some time. For her role in keeping thalidomide largely out of the American market, Kelsey was hailed as a hero and given an Award for Distinguished Federal Civilian Service by President Kennedy. She received a promotion within the FDA and would become an important icon in the nascent agency's history. In Germany, meanwhile, federal prosecutors filed a criminal indictment against the manufacturers of Contergan in 1967, arguing that the company had failed to adequately test the drug. The case attracted substantial public attention, lasting nearly 300 days, while the court heard testimony from more than 150 witnesses and scientific experts. Eventually, state prosecutors dropped their case against Grünenthal in exchange for the company agreeing to set up a fund for the children affected by the drug. This agreement freed Grünenthal from any potential further criminal responsibility. Outside of Germany, families affected by thalidomide set up numerous public interest groups and victims' associations to seek out compensation, provide legal and social assistance, and educate the public.

The thalidomide controversy had a profound effect on the ways in which governments, manufacturers, and the medical community thought about drug regulation. Subsequent testing on pregnant animals proved that the drug's teratogenic effect would have been easily spotted had more complete clinical trials been conducted. In the United Kingdom, the government responded by passing the 1968 Medicines Act and setting up the Committee on the Safety of Medicines, an independent body charged with advising the Department of Health on the safety, efficacy, and quality of new drugs. Additionally, formal standards for clinical trials were put into place in hopes of preventing a repeat of the thalidomide tragedy. In West Germany, where regulation before thalidomide had been conducted primarily by medical professionals and pharmacists, the state took a more active role through the passing of two new drug laws in 1964 and 1978. West German drug manufacturers were expected to self-regulate more, however, than their equivalents in the United States where the thalidomide disaster catalyzed Congress to pass new legislation strengthening the FDA. The Kefauver-Harris Drug Amendments required that manufacturers demonstrate that new drugs were both safe and efficacious prior to releasing them to the market. Consequently, new standards for drug testing came into place, establishing the randomized double-blind controlled trial as the de facto gold standard.

Amendments to drug laws prompted by thalidomide also provoked much debate on how much power state regulators should have to restrict new medications. Many of the new regulatory bodies came under attack for "drug lag"—the notion that potentially life-saving medications were being held off the market for fear of a "new thalidomide."

The thalidomide scandal also profoundly shaped public discourse on drugs. The wide extent and visible nature of the side effects served as a potent reminder of the potential dangers of medication, somewhat shattering the public's post-war enthusiasm and optimism for new drugs. Faced with a barrage of criticism, pharmaceutical companies began hiring public relations firms and forming stronger joint organizations to lobby governments and address public concerns. Public skepticism regarding the drug remained high well into the 1990s when researchers began to reconsider the drug as a potential treatment for a host of diseases including Hansen's disease, acquired immunodeficiency syndrome (AIDS) wasting syndrome, and several types of cancer.

Mat Savelli
University of Pittsburgh

See Also: Clinical Trials; Food and Drug Administration (U.S.); Kefauver-Harris Amendments (1962); Prescription Drug Approval Process: U.S.

Further Readings

Carpenter, D. *Reputation and Power: Organizational Image and Pharmaceutical Regulation at the FDA.* Princeton, NJ: Princeton University Press, 2010.

Daemmrich, A. "A Tale of Two Experts: Thalidomide and Political Engagement in the United States and West Germany." *Social History of Medicine*, v.15/1 (2002).

Harris, R. *The Real Voice.* New York: Macmillan, 1964.

THERAPEUTIC USE EXEMPTION (PERFORMANCE-ENHANCING DRUGS)

The Therapeutic Use Exemption, commonly abbreviated as TUE, is an exemption granted by the United States Anti-Doping Agency (USADA), World Anti-Doping Agency (WADA), and other national and international sports federations and regulatory bodies for the legitimate medical use of a substance or method that has been placed on WADA's Prohibited List. This exemption must be granted in accordance with standards for the legitimate use of these substances that have been established by the World Anti-Doping Agency.

Its purpose is to allow athletes access to medications that they need while keeping sporting events in the United States and worldwide fair for all players who are not using performance-enhancing drugs (PEDs). There is a rigorous application process every athlete requesting a Therapeutic Use Exemption must undergo before she or he is allowed to use the drug in question (except in cases of emergency, after which an athlete may apply for an Emergency Therapeutic Use Exemption).

Doping (Use of Performance-Enhancing Drugs) in Sports

The use and subsequent control of performance-enhancing drugs in various sports have a long history. As the name implies, these substances are used by athletes to improve their performance, giving them an unfair competitive advantage over players who do not use PEDs. Their use is called *doping*—hence the names of the national and international organizations created and maintained in order to control the use of these types of drugs in sports, known as antidoping agencies.

Although these drugs are commonly called *steroids* by sportscasters, sports fans, players, coaches, and other people involved with the athletics industry, anabolic steroids are only one category of performance-enhancing drugs, and WADA and its national-level affiliates apply the term to a wide variety of

substances and medical procedures or methods that may enhance athletes' performance unfairly.

However, opinion is varied as to exactly where the line is between what is acceptable in athletic competition and what is not, and what athletes are expected never to use during their careers (including during the off season, between competitions, during recovery from injuries, etc.). Other antidoping organizations and agencies have rules that differ from WADA, and some particular sports competitions have stricter standards; there are also standards within individual sports leagues (such as the National Football League [NFL] and Major League Baseball [MLB]). Some sports officials consider stimulants like caffeine, for example, to be unacceptable during competition, while most (including WADA and the United States Anti-Doping Agency) allow caffeine but forbid more potent stimulants, such as cocaine and amphetamines (including medications like Adderall).

That being said, there are some drugs and supplements that are most definitely performance enhancers but are not forbidden by any agencies because they are legal, harmless in the quantities in which they are supposed to be used, easily accessible, and ubiquitous in sports and medicine. These include vitamins, protein supplements, and OTC (over the counter; i.e., nonprescription) painkillers and anti-inflammatory agents like aspirin and ibuprofen or topical pain relievers (Bengay cream and its generics). Although these drugs and supplements do enhance performance, they are widely considered to do so in a way that is not unfair to other athletes, and to assist in recovery from and coping with normal athletic strain.

The use of performance-enhancing drugs in sports has been considered a problem by many associated with the industry since the

1960s or earlier. However, it was not until 1976 that the use of steroids (again, one of the most common, potent, and potentially harmful PEDs) was banned by the International Olympic Committee (IOC). In 1981, the first player to ever be stripped of a title because of a positive drug test, an American Olympic discus thrower named Ben Plucknett, lost his world record because of his use of anabolic steroids.

However, the antidoping trend did not catch on in the United States until a few years later: In 1987, the NFL began testing players for steroid use, and in 1988 a law was passed making the possession of anabolic steroids (except in situations in which they are prescribed for legitimate medical use) a crime. That being said, steroids and other performance-enhancing drugs were not forbidden by MLB until 2003—and their initial policy was widely criticized for being too lenient. A notable scandal taking place over several of the following years in MLB and in other sporting organizations, including at the college and even high school levels, then brought the conversation about the use of performance-enhancing drugs to the forefront of national attention in America.

More recently, advances in illicit performance-enhancing drug use have been made, as negative offshoots of largely positive research into medicines that manipulate the blood and even the genetics of individuals.

However, despite their risks and the fact that they are widely banned by sporting regulatory bodies and have even been made wholly illegal and classified as controlled substances in some cases, it is important to note that some drugs that are often considered performance enhancers or potential performance enhancers have a legitimate medical use. It is because of these legitimate uses that WADA and the United States Anti-Doping Agency have created the Therapeutic Use Exemption.

How Therapeutic Use Exemptions Work

The process of applying for a Therapeutic Use Exemption is generally a complex and time-consuming one, and time must be allowed for agencies to which athletes apply for TUEs to process the information given and verify the legitimacy of each athlete's claim. TUEs can be granted by various international sports federations and antidoping agencies, and may also be granted in some cases by national sports leagues in various countries. Generally, all sports federations and antidoping regulatory bodies comply with the rules set forth by WADA, but some are stricter, as there are varying ideas as to what exactly enhances performance.

However, all of these bodies grant TUEs to athletes who have a legitimate need for one or more drugs that may be considered performance enhancers. Before the TUE is granted, however, the regulatory body must analyze the claim, verify the legitimate medical need for the drug or drugs, and set forth particular rules about dosing, amount of time the drug may be used, and so on. Generally, retroactive claims for TUEs are not allowed, unless there is some emergency. For example, WADA and the United States Anti-Doping Agency both forbid the use of epinephrine, the active ingredient in fast-acting, lifesaving allergy reducers such as the "Epi-Pen," during athletic competition because it provides an adrenaline rush and is classified as a performance-enhancing stimulant. That being said, the agencies can hardly punish athletes for having life-threatening allergic reactions and will allow an application for a retroactive TUE in this case, which will protect the athlete in the event of a drug test that shows some remnants of the drug in the system. Similarly, retroactive TUEs may be granted for the use of intravenous (IV) drug delivery, which is forbidden by the World Anti-Doping Agency and its subsidiaries, but is often used to quickly deliver lifesaving drugs in the event of various types of emergencies.

When an athlete plans to take part in various competitions that will be drug tested under the authority of the World Anti-Doping Agency and its subsidiaries, she must file separate TUE claims for each competition. In national-level sports leagues and under the umbrella of international sports federations that do their own drug testing and have very frequent athletic competitions, such as FIFA, this stricture does not often apply; instead, the federation granting the TUE will instead allot a specific amount of time during which the potential performance enhancer may be used.

A Therapeutic Use Exemption allows athletes to use these types of drugs for legitimate medical purposes by exempting them from punishments for having specific drugs found in their system during drug tests. That being said, Therapeutic Use Exemptions do not allow for the blanket use of various drugs or exempt athletes from taking required drug tests before or after competitions (or, in many international and national sports federations and leagues, randomly throughout the season). In this way, these exemptions seek to balance the needs of the individual athlete at a particular time with her overall health and with the needs of all others associated with the sport—players, coaches, and fans—the greatest of which is the need for a clean, fair game in which athletes succeed or fail based on their training, focus, and personal skill, not because of their use of drugs that other players choose to abstain from.

David Michael Gonzalez
University of Nevada

See Also: World Anti-Doping Agency (WADA).

Further Readings

CNN Library. "Performance Enhancing Drugs in Sports—Fast Facts." CNN.com, 2014.

FIFA. "FIFA's Approach to Doping in Football." FIFA.com.

United States Anti-Doping Agency. "Therapeutic Use Exemptions (TUEs)." USADA.org.

United States Anti-Doping Agency. "Wallet Card: Examples of Prohibited Substances and Methods." United States Anti-Doping Agency, 2013.

TITLE X FAMILY PLANNING PROGRAM (1970)

The Title X Family Planning Program, commonly known as the Population Research and Voluntary Family Planning Programs, was enacted in 1970 under President Richard Nixon. This legislation on family planning and population emerged from the War on Poverty and was part of the Public Health Service Act. President Nixon's rationale for implementing Title X was to expand research, provide adequate training to family planning and reproductive personnel, and further develop family planning services by increasing population growth information and education. Essentially, Title X's main objective is to increase access to sexual and reproductive health services by fostering methods to enhance affordability for those who are low-income, impoverished, and/or uninsured.

The Title X Program is designed to facilitate access to contraceptive services, supplies, and information to all who want and need them, particularly those living at or below the poverty threshold. Hence, Title X provides funding for a plethora of clinical services associated with reproduction and population growth. These health services include family planning counseling, gynecological examinations, breast and cervical cancer screenings, contraceptive counseling and supplies, screenings for both human immunodeficiency virus/acquired immunodeficiency syndrome (HIV/AIDS) and sexually transmitted diseases (STDs), and pregnancy testing. In addition, it has expanded clinical services to include some general health screenings, such as the testing for diabetes, high blood pressure, and anemia.

As a result of Title X, family clinic staff receive training on a broad range of issues including clinical training, service delivery, management and systems improvement, coordination and strategic initiatives, and quality assurance/improvement and evaluation. Not only do funds cover employee training expenses, but in some cases the staff salary is incorporated into Title X's budget expenses. Also, Title X support has been used to subsidize client expenses such as rent, utilities, and health information technology services. Moreover, other family planning support programs include conducting evaluations for the measurement of quality assurance, research and evaluation to improve delivery methods and communication with the overall reproductive health care field, information dissemination, and community-based education and outreach.

While all clients are eligible to receive financial assistance through Title X funding, the bill specifically prioritizes the needs of low-income individuals, the uninsured, and those who may not qualify to receive government-funded insurance programs such as Medicaid. In order to qualify for Title X's benefits, one must provide proof of income and/or unemployment at the time of the initial visit. After one's income has been verified, patient fees are based on Title X's discounted fee scale: the impact of service fees can range from reduced rates to completely free of charge services. Research indicates that in 2011, 91 percent of those who sought services from Title X–funded establishments had incomes at or below 250 percent of the federal poverty level.

During 2012, clinics funded by the Title X Program served 4.3 million women. Of these reproductive and family planning services clients received, Title X–funded centers provided 1.2 million pap tests, 1.8 million breast exams, nearly 6 million STD tests, and 1.2 million confidential HIV tests. In addition, these public funds have averted an estimated 1 million pregnancies on average per year and subsequently have prevented 760,000 abortions. In 2012, 8.9 percent of the clients were under 18 years old, 51.0 percent were 20 to 29 years old, 20.3 percent were 30 to 39 years old, and 9.2 percent were 40 years and older; 91.9 percent were female; and 20.4 percent were black/African American, 55.9 percent were white, and 28 percent were Hispanic or Latino.

The Title X Program relies on some laws and regulations overseen by the Federal Office of Pharmacy Affairs of the Health Resources and Services Administration in order to provide outpatient drugs at a discounted price. An example is the 340B Drug Pricing Program, which was created through the Veterans Health Care Act. It enables Title X programs to reduce prescription drug prices for patients, increase the scope of services offered, and serve more clients with the same amount of funding. Title X programs are also able to take advantage of 340B's Prime Vendor Program, which utilizes the collective purchasing power of public health authorities to negotiate sub-340B discounts on certain pharmaceuticals.

Funding for Title X programs has been an important issue, because some providers suggest they cannot afford the costs associated with stocking or supplying certain drugs and/or devices. While most Title X programs offer on-site intrauterine devices, far fewer offer on-site contraceptive implants—though larger sites do have these options.

Title X funding works alongside other federal programs to assist groups such as underprivileged women. On March 11, 2009, President Obama signed an executive order creating the White House Council on Women and Girls. The council was created as a means to coordinate federal response to issues that especially affect the lives of women and their families and to ensure that all Cabinet and Cabinet-level agencies across the federal government take into consideration how policies and programs incorporate the needs and concerns of women and girls (including marginalized groups of women such as those of color and those with impairments). Not only have political organizations been established to create more tools for women and families to succeed in the present-day and future economy, but in fiscal 2012, the Title X program received an estimated $296.8 million in federal funding.

When first introduced into law in 1970, Title X received overwhelming bipartisan consensus (in fact, the Senate voted unanimously in favor of the law while there were only 32 dissenting votes in the House). However, over recent years Republican state legislatures have pushed to eliminate Title X funding from the federal budget for a twofold purpose: to decrease federal funding costs and because of the abortion debate. While conservative policy makers believe the defunding of the Title X program will reduce federal expenditures, others argue that eliminating these funds will mean indigent individuals who rely solely on health care services provided by Title X facilities will lose access to both primary and preventive health care.

Research indicates that six in 10 women who access care from a Title X–funded facility consider it to be their main source of health care. Supporters suggest that if the Title X program was abolished, unintended pregnancies would dramatically increase, sexually transmitted infections would go undetected for longer periods of time, and preventive health screenings would be even more difficult to access. They suggest the total costs of cutting such preventive and diagnostic services would be much higher in the long term.

According to Republican leaders, such as Governor Mike Pence and the Republican Party's 2012 presidential nominee, Mitt Romney, clinics that function as providers of both abortion and Title X services should not be eligible to receive federal funding. During 2011, Republican state legislatures passed defunding laws that stripped federal financial assistance from Title X clinics that provided abortions. Among the clinics that were affected by these laws was Planned Parenthood. On average per year, the federal government awards Planned Parenthood with $66 million in Title X family planning grants. However, federal law bans the use of Title X funds to cover abortion procedures.

When Title X was enacted under law, reproductive services were made available to all who may need them—notwithstanding if clients were minors. Thus, grantees of Title X funds provide contraceptive services and reproductive health care to minors. Moreover, services are provided under a confidential basis, meaning parents do not possess the legal right to assent for their minors to receive care, but clinicians do encourage them to involve their guardians in the decision making. Although no state requires parental consent for reproductive services, Texas and Utah forbid minors from receiving contraceptive services without parental consent. In 1998, the House of Representatives passed a parental notification requirement; however, the Senate did not approve it, and therefore the provision was never enacted.

Today, Title X remains the only federal grant program strictly dedicated to providing individuals who are at or below the poverty level with comprehensive family planning and related preventive health services. The U.S. Department of Health and Human Services' Office of Population Affairs (OPA) has been appointed as administrator of Title X. It is estimated that OPA provides funds to over 4,000 family planning centers. This network of providers serves around 5 million clients annually. Nationwide, 10 official offices oversee the Title X program, evaluating and awarding grants to a variety of health care entities. Services are provided through various health care infrastructures such as state, county, and local health departments; community health centers; both hospital-based and school-based facilities; and private nonprofit organizations.

Mark D. Sherry
University of Toledo

Anna Neller
University of Toledo

See Also: Access to Medicines (Industrialized World); Fertility Control; Fertility Control: History.

Further Readings

Beeson, Tishra, et al. "Accessibility of Long-Acting Reversible Contraceptives (LARCs) in Federally Qualified Health Centers (FQHCs)." *Contraception,* v.89/2 (2014).

Wood, Susan, et al. "Scope of Family Planning Services Available in Federally Qualified Health Centers." *Contraception,* v.89/2 (2014).

Touched With Fire: Manic-Depressive Illness and the Artistic Temperament (Jamison)

Touched With Fire: Manic-Depressive Illness and the Artistic Temperament is a 1993 nonfiction book written by Kay Redfield Jamison, an American clinical psychologist and the Dalio Family Professor in Mood Disorders and director of the Mood Disorders Center at the Johns Hopkins University School of Medicine (Baltimore, Maryland, United States). *Touched With Fire* examines the relationship between mood disorders and artistic creativity, and integrates information drawn from artists' and writers' descriptions of their creative process and mood states, biographical and autobiographical information, and scientific information about mental illness.

Jamison's point of departure is the relationship often stated in popular culture, sometimes by creative artists themselves (such as the poet Lord Byron), and in ancient myths and classical literature that creative people are all "touched" or crazy in some way. In fact, sometimes artistic inspiration was described as both a "madness" and a gift of the gods. For instance, Jamison cites a speech attributed to Socrates in Plato's *Phaedrus*, in which Socrates says that "[i]f a man comes to the door of poetry untouched by the madness of the Muses, believing that technique alone will make him a good poet, he and his sane compositions never reach perfection, but are utterly eclipsed by the performances of the inspired madman" (p. 51).

One type of evidence Jamison presents to support her interpretation of the link between artistic creativity and mood disorders is her study of autobiographical, biographical, and medical records for British and Irish poets born in the century between 1705 and 1805. Looking at the available information for 35 major poets, she presents a chart classifying how many suffered from recurrent depression, manic-depressive illness, or psychotic features; were confined to an asylum; or committed suicide, as well as descriptive notes on the evidence available for each poet's mental state. Acknowledging the difficulty of performing a diagnosis from secondary records, each category is coded as definite/probable, possible, or probable. For instance, Jamison codes Samuel Johnson as "definite/probable" for recurrent depression, with notes including "severe recurrent melancholia"; "First severe breakdown at 20, lasting more than 2 years"; and "Felt he had inherited his 'vile melancholy' from his father" (p. 63). She concludes that the poets in her sample were committed to asylums at a rate 20 or more times that of the general population, that two committed suicide, that over half presented evidence of mood disorders, and that over one-third seemed to have suffered from manic-depressive illness.

Similar evidence has been found in a study of contemporary writers. Jamison cites the research of Nancy Andreasen, who studied writers ($n = 30$) participating in the Writers' Workshop at the University of Iowa. Andreasen found lifetime prevalence of 80 percent for affective disorders, 43 percent for bipolar disorders, 37 percent for major depression, and 30 percent for alcoholism among the writers. A control group ($n = 30$; professionals matched for age, education, and sex, but who did not work in the arts) had rates of 30 percent for affective disorders, 10 percent for bipolar disorders, 17 percent for major depression, and 7 percent for alcoholism; the differences between the two groups were statistically significant for affective disorders, bipolar disorders, and alcoholism.

Jamison notes that creative thinking and hypomanic thought share several characteristics, including fluency, rapidity, flexibility, and the ability to combine ideas or categories in order to form new and original connections. She notes that many psychiatrists have remarked on how their manic patients have characteristics also noted in creative people, including a tendency toward divergent rather than convergent thinking and display of a rapid flow of ideas. Research by Nancy Andreasen and Pauline Powers also found similarities between the thought processes of creative writers at the University of Iowa Writers' Workshop and manic patients, but that the thought processes of the writers differed from those of the schizophrenics.

Jamison also addresses an issue that has been raised with regard to those who display both mental illness and creativity: Will treating the mental illness destroy the creativity? She notes that there is not enough research to evaluate the long-term effects of the major drugs used to treat manic-depressive illness. Looking at lithium, one of the most common drugs used for this purpose, the evidence is inconclusive. For instance, a 1971 study by Polatin and Fieve reports that creative individuals treated with lithium felt it inhibited their creativity, and that some preferred to endure their desire rather than be robbed of the "high" they experienced during manic periods. On the other hand, most patients treated with lithium do not report any major side effects, and some studies have found no effect on creativity during lithium treatment. Jamison also notes the negative consequences of not treating manic-depressive illness, including the risk of suicide and of secondary problems such as alcoholism or drug abuse that may indicate an attempt by an individual to self-medicate.

In 2013, Jamison was awarded the Lewis Thomas Prize for Writing About Science in recognition of *Touched With Fire*. This prize is awarded by the board of trustees of Rockefeller University to honor "the rare individual who bridges the worlds of science and the humanities—whose voice and vision can tell us about science's aesthetic and philosophical dimensions, providing not merely new information but cause for reflection, even revelation" ("Lewis Thomas Prize," 2013).

Jamison joined the faculty of the Johns Hopkins University School of Medicine in 1987, following doctoral students at the University of California, Los Angeles (UCLA), and founding and serving as the director of the UCLA Affective Disorders Clinic. Her other books include *An Unquiet Mind* (1995), which discusses her personal experience of bipolar disease; *Night Falls Fast* (1999), a study of suicide; and the medical textbook *Manic-Depressive Illness: Bipolar Disorders and Recurrent Depression* (with Frederick K. Goodwin; 2nd ed., 2007).

Sarah E. Boslaugh
Saint Louis University

See Also: Antipsychiatry Movement; Neuro-Enhancement Through Pharmacy; *Noonday Demon, The: An Atlas of Depression* (Andrew Solomon); Normal: Definitions and Controversy; Psychopharmacology.

Further Readings

Andreasen, Nancy C. "The Relationship Between Creativity and Mood Disorders." *Dialogues in Clinical Neuroscience*, v.10/2 (June 2008). http://www.ncbi .nlm.nih.gov/pmc/articles/PMC3181877/?report=reader (Accessed April 29, 2015).

Bello, Grace. "A Conversation With Kay Redfield Jamison, Professor of Psychiatry." *The Atlantic* (November 11, 2011). http://www.theatlantic.com/ national/archive/2011/11/a-conversation-with-kay-redfield-jamison-professor-of-psychiatry/247995/ (Accessed March 18, 2015).

Goldman, Larry S. *Touched With Fire: Manic-Depressive Illness and the Artistic Temperament* [Book review]. *New England Journal of Medicine*, v.329 (1993). http://www.nejm.org/doi/full/10.1056/ NEJM199310073291520 (Accessed March 31, 2015).

Jamison, Kay Redfield. *Touched With Fire: Manic-Depressive Illness and the Artistic Temperament.* New York: Free Press, 1993.

"Lewis Thomas Prize to Be Awarded to Kay Redfield Jamison." Rockefeller University Newswire (May 7, 2013). http://newswire.rockefeller.edu/2013/05/07/ lewis-thomas-prize-to-be-awarded-to-kay-redfield-jamison/ (Accessed March 18, 2015).

Polatin, Philip and Ronald R. Fieve. "Patient Rejection of Lithium Carbonate Prophylaxis." *Journal of the American Medical Association*, v.218 (November 1971).

Track and Field and Performance-Enhancing Drugs

Performance-enhancing drugs are one of the most well-known scourges of the sports world and affect a wide variety of competitive sports at all levels, ranging from international competition all the way down to, in some cases, middle and high school events. They are commonly called PEDs and also colloquially called steroids, because anabolic steroids and some of their precursors are the most commonly used PEDs in many sports; however, agencies that check for these types of drugs and sports commentators and regulatory bodies in general use the umbrella term *performance-enhancing drugs* to refer to a much wider variety of substances that athletes use to unfairly improve their performance over that of other players.

One sport in which PEDs are used quite often is track and field, a major part of the Summer Olympic Games that attracts millions of spectators live and at home. The sport also has its own world championship, and there are several major national championships that are often associated with the international championship in some way.

Although track and field was not particularly associated with PEDs until relatively recently, since 2002 there has been widespread and virtually constant concern about the drugs' effects on the sport and their growing use among athletes participating in the sport, particularly those at the highest levels (those competing at the Olympic Games and track-and-field national and world championships, who also gain the most attention from the media and are often seen as representatives of or ambassadors for the sport, which does not get as much time in the spotlight, generally speaking, as sports like football and baseball).

PEDs and Their Use in Track and Field and Other Sports: The BALCO Case

Although PEDs have been a problem in sports for a long time, and most major sports leagues and international sports governing and regulatory bodies have had anti-PED rules in their books for years, it was in 2002 that the use of these drugs exploded onto the national and international scene, during an event now known as the BALCO scandal.

PEDs had been an issue in many sports since the late 1960s and early 1970s, and because of their health risks and the unfair playing field their use creates, they were outlawed in many countries and banned by almost all major sports leagues and governing bodies; there were also organizations created for the sole purpose of controlling their use, among these the U.S. Anti-Doping Agency (USADA) and its international counterpart, the World Anti-Doping Agency (*doping* being a previously colloquial, now official, term for the use of PEDs). That being said, Major League Baseball (MLB) in the United States did not have a specific steroid- and drug-regulating and -testing policy until 2003—which it created as a direct result of this scandal.

Because the sports world seemed relatively stable at this time and the tests in place in sports leagues were catching and deterring would-be cheaters, PEDs became mostly invisible in the conversation about sports throughout much of the 1980s and 1990s.

It was in the late 1980s, though, that the company that would grow to create one of the biggest scandals in modern sports began. A man named Victor Conte started a vitamin shop known as Millbrae Holistic with his then wife Aubry Conte. Within a year, he had shut its doors and expanded into the sports nutrition market, founding a company he called BALCO, an abbreviation for Bay Area Laboratory Co-operative. Supposedly, he used advanced equipment and an extensive knowledge of nutrition and the human body to keep track of minerals and minor deficiencies in athletic clients' bodies; either after a lack of success doing this alone or from the very beginning, he also worked with two men named Patrick Arnold (a chemist) and Greg Anderson (a personal trainer) to create and distribute a complex and highly effective cycle of anabolic steroids, human growth hormone (HGH), and other PEDs that could radically change athletes' physiques and go largely undetected even at the highest levels of sport, such as the Olympic Games. The main designer steroid that Conte and the other two men created was nicknamed "The Clear" because it would go undetected on virtually any drug test.

In 1996, Conte signed his first major client, National Football League (NFL) linebacker Bill Romanowski (whose legacy has been tarnished beyond repair by his association with Conte and BALCO, despite the fact that he helped win four Super Bowls). By the time Conte's company was investigated by the U.S. federal government and the USADA in 2002, he had a wide array of high-profile clients across many sports who were found to be using PEDs to increase their strength and endurance unfairly. One of these clients was a track star named Marion Jones, who won five medals (three of the five being gold) at the 2000 Summer Olympics in Sydney.

Jones, who was married to a known PED user, shot-putter and coach C. J. Hunter, at the time and later began a relationship with another, sprinter Tim Montgomery, denied any use of PEDs related to the BALCO scandal until 2007, when she admitted that she lied to federal agents during the course of the investigation. However, she still maintains that she did not mean to use steroids or any other illegal performance enhancer, but that she believed she was taking flaxseed oil. That being said, she returned her medals and retired from the sport the same year.

Other Track-and-Field Drug Scandals

The BALCO scandal and Jones's implication in it cast a shadow over track and field, but the media coverage of and concern over steroids in this sport did not stop there—problems continued with the sport after her confession and retirement, just as many of the problems persisted in other sports as well.

The problem of PEDs has been an international one. In 2013, a major U.S. runner named Tyson Gay and two major Jamaican runners named Asafa Powell and Sherone Simpson tested positive for different types of substances banned by the U.S. and World Anti-Doping Agencies before their participation in the 2013 world championships for track and field. All of them withdrew, with both Jamaican runners claiming absolutely no wrongdoing and Gay being very vague in his admission.

Both countries are concerned that allegations or proof of PED use among their athletes will tarnish their international reputations and throw their athletes' legitimacy into doubt. Jamaican runners, coaches, and commentators are specifically concerned because of their nation's long history of producing star runners.

However, many thinking and writing about the sport believe the problem is much deeper, saying that PEDs have become so deeply rooted in track and field that they are no longer an individual or even a national problem, but a problem for everyone competing in the sport.

Effects of PEDs on Track and Field

These PED-related scandals and others have cast a shadow over the sport, and many in the sports world are hoping for some kind of major change at all levels to prevent this sort of thing from happening. Besides the obvious reasons for wanting to change this aspect of the sport (PEDs' unfairness and ill health effects on users), there are others as well, one example being the fact that it is possible, perhaps even likely, that the ubiquity of PEDs during this era will tarnish the reputations of all the record breakers and other great track-and-field athletes who were active during this time in the future, even if they were clean.

A player many fans and officials are concerned about is sprinter Usain Bolt, commonly known as "The Fastest Man Alive." Many worry that the fact that he legitimately earned his medals through hard work and natural skill will be cast into doubt even though he has never failed a drug test, simply because he is athletic in a time when so many athletes are abusing drugs.

There are a few, though, who believe that PEDs simply make sports more exciting, or that it will be impossible to control their use anyway. Many records that were assumed virtually unbreakable within the sport have been shattered recently, as in other sports, such as baseball. However, because of the unfairness and health concerns of anabolic steroids and other PEDs, there are very few that hold and openly express this view.

David Michael Gonzalez
University of Nevada

See Also: BALCO Scandal.

Further Readings

Davidson, Keay. "Drugs Involved in BALCO Case." *SF Gate* (February 13, 2004).

Fainaru-Wada, Mark and Lance Williams. *Game of Shadows: Barry Bonds, BALCO, and the Steroid Scandal That Rocked Professional Sports.* New York: Gotham, 2006.

Gregory, Sean. "Another Dark Day for Track and Field." *Time* (July 15, 2013).

TRADITIONAL AND HERBAL MEDICINES, REGULATION: AFRICA

Traditional and herbal medicine is an ancient practice that has provided a major source of affordable and accessible health care for the African population. According to the World Health Organization (WHO), traditional and herbal medicine is the major source of primary health care for 80 percent of the African population. Traditional healers and specialists are fundamental to the practice of traditional and herbal medicine. Traditional medicine is defined as the knowledge or practices used in diagnosing, preventing, or eliminating a physical, mental, or social disease that may rely exclusively on past experience or observations handed down from preceding generations verbally or in writing. Traditional medicine also comprises therapeutic practices that have been in existence often for hundreds of years before the development of modern scientific medicine and are still in use today, without any documented evidence of adverse effects. A traditional healer is a person recognized by the community as competent to provide health care by using vegetable, animal, and mineral substances and certain other methods. Traditional specialists are herbalists, bone setters, traditional psychiatrists, traditional pediatricians, traditional birth attendants, herb sellers, and general practitioners.

Progress is being made in the development, regulation, and integration of traditional and herbal medicine in Africa. Progress varies according to country. With the high cost of conventional health care, there is a critical need for a reliable system that is affordable and accessible to African populations, especially those living in rural communities. As an alternative, traditional and herbal medicine provides a health care service that is accessible to and affordable by those in need of primary health care. Countries throughout Africa are developing the profession of traditional and herbal medicine by using a variety of strategies that protect the public, increase the quality of service, and link the practice of traditional and herbal medicine to the scientific method and evidence-based practice.

In resource-poor areas of Africa, those searching for approaches to health conditions such as human immunodeficiency virus (HIV)/ acquired immune deficiency syndrome (AIDS) depend on and choose traditional healers. Traditional healers provide psychosocial counseling and health care services. Given the role in health care of traditional and herbal medicine, the African regional director of the WHO has offered specific input into the development and regulation of processes for traditional and herbal medicine by outlining a framework for African nations to use as a frame of reference.

Developments in Traditional and Herbal Medicine

In Ghana, the government has initiated a directorate for traditional medicine at the Ministry of Health, established policy to guide the integration of traditional and herbal medicine into the health care delivery system, and established initiatives to streamline traditional herbal practice into a professional practice. These three strategic developments have been promoted as a national initiative. A further development in Ghana's development of traditional and herbal medicine is the production of the *Ghana Herbal Pharmacopoeia*, first published in 1993 and most recently in 2007. The development of the *Pharmacopoeia* is intended to provide a scientific base to be adopted by practitioners of traditional and herbal medicine. The content of the *Pharmacopoeia* is based on evidence of the potency of traditional and herbal medicines, and it presents a reliable system of application. Another idea associated with the *Ghana Herbal Pharmacopoeia* is to reduce the risk associated with the practice by treating traditional and herbal medicine as a science. For example, the *Pharmacopoeia* introduces the concepts of dosage forms and chemical composition, and it includes references to other scientific works. The collaboration between the editor of the *Pharmacopoeia*, a well-known traditional and herbal practitioner in Ghana, and the Science and Technology Policy Research Institute represents a model for the integration of traditional and herbal medicine and science.

In Uganda, nongovernmental organizations are participating in the process of developing and regulating traditional and herbal medicine as a profession. The group Traditional and Modern Health Practitioners Together Against AIDS and Other Diseases identified the need to validate and support African traditional medicine. As a result of its efforts, the Eastern & Southern Africa Regional Initiative on Traditional Medicine and AIDS was started. The work of the initiative includes the development of standards for traditional and herbal medicine, which revolve around six themes related to traditional and herbal medicine and HIV/AIDS: the systematic evaluation of traditional remedies; spiritual healing; prevention and care; standardization, processing, and packaging; indigenous knowledge; and intellectual property rights related to traditional health systems. These standards are being incorporated into programs on traditional medicine and HIV/AIDS.

The development of the six standards of practice by the initiative represents the first regional and participatory effort to validate traditional medicine while preserving its integrity. In deeper examination of the six standards, the first standard mirrors the effort in Ghana to align traditional and herbal medicine with scientific evidence. In fact, it calls for observational studies, clinical trials, and the sharing of the results (with the primary beneficiaries of the studies [the scientists], traditional healers, and community stakeholders) through both verbal and written communication methods. The second standard, spiritual healing, is described as something distinctly different from witchcraft. Spiritual healing is a process mediated through spiritual powers not associated with medicine or physical body manipulations. Characteristics of the practice of spiritual healing should be accepted by the community, have no negative social or physical connotations, and be provided free of charge. The community and clients can make voluntary contributions. The third standard is prevention and care. Traditional healers have been reported to be effective HIV/AIDS educators, counselors, and sources of information. This standard recommends training and empowerment of traditional healers in cultural beliefs and practices, basic information on sexually transmitted diseases, HIV/AIDS, tuberculosis, infection control, and other areas related to prevention.

The fourth standard relates to the standardization and packaging of herbal medicines, which will increase their use. The fifth standard, indigenous knowledge, calls for the comprehension of African indigenous knowledge on health and the embrace of all aspects, including rites, practices, and artistic aspects related to the cultures of African peoples. The sixth and final standard is related to intellectual property rights and includes the use of legal documents to protect the processes of traditional healers and providers of services. These standards provide a framework for the development and regulation of the traditional and herbal medicine profession, and the incorporation of the standards into programs related to traditional and herbal medicine provides a basis for continued improvement and further development.

Traditional and herbal medicine is experiencing a renaissance, and this is related to the important role traditional and herbal medicine plays in the HIV/AIDS pandemic. Traditional and herbal medicine is critical in primary health care implementation in Africa and in other developing areas. In Tanzania, legislative actions have been undertaken to address national health needs. The legislation supports the integration and regulation of traditional and herbal knowledge and the development of a resource base for traditional and herbal medicine. In Tanzania, as throughout Africa, the major form of health care is traditional and herbal medicine. Traditional medicine is being recognized for its importance, and it is being integrated into mainstream health care.

Countries in Africa are at different stages in the integration of traditional and herbal medicine into their health care systems, and they are using developmental processes that are complementary to their particular contextual realities. Finding methods and developing health care systems that carefully integrate traditional and herbal medicine with conventional medicine, with minimum perceived and actual threat, is key to the successful integration of traditional and herbal medicine. Recommendations for the institutionalization and integration of traditional and herbal medicine in

health care systems encourage governments to take actions to move their health care agendas forward with traditional and herbal medicine. Some of the actions recommended are the development of supportive policy; the development of legal and regulatory frameworks for the practice of traditional and herbal medicine, within existing national health policies and health legislature frameworks; the promotion of scientific research on medicinal herbs in collaboration with traditional health practitioners, as in Ghana and Tanzania; and the registration of traditional and herbal healers.

In Ghana, traditional and herbal healers are recognized and licensed, through the Ghana Federation of Traditional Medicine Practitioners' Association. The Traditional Medicine Unit was established in 1991 within Ghana's Ministry of Health. In Mali, the Phytotherapy Institute was established in 1968 as the first research establishment for the study of medicinal plants. The institute has since become the Department of Traditional Medicine and is a collaborating center of the WHO. In South Africa, government health services provide only Western medicine, but traditional and herbal medicine is used by most of the population, especially in rural communities. These efforts to increase supportive legislation for and regulation of traditional and herbal medicine in Africa illustrate the importance of traditional and herbal medicine practice and its conservation, especially for the benefit of rural communities.

Traditional and Herbal Medicine as Economic and Cultural Heritage

Traditional and herbal medicine in Africa is viewed by many Africans as a socioeconomic and sociocultural heritage that is practiced and passed on through generations. Some believe that its development has been interrupted by colonial suppression, foreign religions, and lack of political will and that the practice of traditional and herbal medicine, once viewed as primitive, was unfairly challenged by foreign religions and conventional medical practitioners. However, it is now known that traditional and herbal medicine is instrumental in meeting health care goals in Africa and also in other countries throughout the world.

Primary health care is the first level of contact for individuals, families, and communities with the health care system, and one challenge and opportunity in Africa is integrating traditional and herbal medicine into the primary health care system. Such integration may well help achieve the goal of health for all and to overcome the perceived failure of conventional Western medicine, which has failed to provide many Africans with adequate health care services.

P. Qasimah Boston
Florida Department of Children & Families

Ivette A. Lopez
Florida A&M University

See Also: AIDS/HIV Drugs; Medicinal Plant Species Threatened With Extinction; South Africa.

Further Readings

Busia, K. *Ghana Herbal Pharmacopoeia.* Accra, Ghana: Science and Technology Policy Research Institute, 2007.

Elujoba, A. A., O. M. Odeleye, and C. M. Ogunyemi. "Traditional Medicine Development for Medical and Dental Primary Healthcare Delivery System in Africa." *African Journal of Traditional Complementary and Alternative Medicines,* v.2 (2005).

Homsey, J., R. King, J. Tenywa, P. Kyeyune, A. Opio, and D. Balaba. "Defining Minimum Standards of Practice for Incorporating African Traditional Medicine Into HIV/AIDS Prevention, Care and Support: A Regional Initiative in Eastern and Southern Africa." *Journal of Alternative and Complementary Medicine,* v.10/5 (2004).

Stangland, T., S. S. Dhillon, and H. Rekstein. "Recognition and Development of Traditional Medicine in Tanzania." *Journal of Ethnopharmacology,* v.117 (2008).

TRADITIONAL AND HERBAL MEDICINES, REGULATION: AUSTRALIA AND NEW ZEALAND

Both Australia and New Zealand demonstrate high levels of political commitment to traditional medicine (TM) and complementary and alternative medicine (CAM) policy and research. Australia's Therapeutic Goods Act (TGA) of 1989 sets out the legal requirements for the import, export, manufacture, and supply of medicines in Australia. It details the requirements for listing or registering all therapeutic goods in the Australian Register of Therapeutic Goods (ARTG), as well as many other aspects of the law, including advertising, labeling, and product appearance. Australian manufacturers of therapeutic goods must be licensed, and their manufacturing processes must comply with the principles of good manufacturing practice (GMP). All medicines manufactured for supply in Australia must be listed or registered in the ARTG, unless they are specifically exempt or excluded. Listed medicines are considered to be of lower risk than registered medicines. Most complementary medicines (e.g., herbal, vitamin, and mineral products) are examples of listed products. Medicines assessed as having higher levels of risk must be registered. Registered medicines include nonprescription (low-risk, over-the-counter) medicines and prescription (high-risk) medicines. Complementary medicines (also known as "traditional" or "alternative" medicines) include vitamin, mineral, herbal, aromatherapy, and homeopathic products.

Complementary medicines may be either listed or registered, depending on their ingredients and the claims made. Most complementary medicines are listed in the ARTG, and some are registered. In New Zealand, supplements in the marketplace are manufactured largely in the United States. Regulations are not restrictive; there are no limits on ingredients or potencies, and "structure/function" claims are allowed.

Australia

In Australia, indigenous medicines, traditional Chinese medicines, Ayurvedic medicines, homoeopathic medicines, and other medicinal products containing herbs, vitamins, and minerals have been defined and are regulated as complementary medicines. In Australia, the national policy on TM and CAM was issued in 1999. Regulations on TM and CAM in the form of the TGA were issued in 1989. All therapeutic goods that are imported into, supplied in, or exported from Australia must be included on the ARTG prior to supply. The aim is to ensure the quality, safety, and efficacy of therapeutic goods. A two-tiered regulatory system is based on risk assessment. The national office on TM and CAM, known as the Office of Complementary Medicines, was established in 1999; the office is administered by the Ministry of Health. In 1997, the expert Complementary Medicines Evaluation Committee was established. No national research institutes have yet been established for TM, CAM, or herbal medicines. In 1989, Australia began regulating herbal medicines by means of the TGA, which contains partly the same regulations as those issued for conventional medicines. Herbal medicines are regulated as over-the-counter medicines for self-medication; the specific categories are registered goods and listed goods and form part of the ARTG. Medical, health, nutrient content, and structure/function claims may be made for herbal medicines by law.

In place of a national pharmacopoeia, the British pharmacopoeia is used, and it is considered legally binding in cases in which an herbal medicine is listed in the pharmacopoeia. A number of monographs are used in place of national ones; however, they are not considered legally binding. Regulatory requirements for herbal medicines include adherence to information in the pharmacopoeia and monographs and the same GMP rules as those used for conventional pharmaceuticals. Implementation of these requirements is ensured through GMP licensing for finished goods manufacturers. Safety requirements for herbal medicines include the same requirements as for conventional pharmaceuticals, as well as special requirements of traditional use without demonstrated harmful effects and reference to documented scientific research on similar products. Compliance with these requirements is ensured through compositional guidelines for approved complementary medicine substances that describe the identity tests and limits for contaminants and residues, although these are not legally binding on manufacturers. Other control mechanisms include postmarketing reviews, evaluation of toxicological data on new proposed herbal substances, and history-of-use data. There are 1,500 herbal medicines registered in Australia; none is included on the national essential drug list. The postmarketing surveillance system has included adverse effect monitoring since 1970. In Australia, herbal medicines are sold in pharmacies as over-the-counter drugs, in special outlets, by licensed practitioners without restriction.

Warnings About Indifferent Product Claims

Research on complementary medicines used for weight loss showed that some sponsors self-entered indications and/or claims on the ARTG that could not be substantiated. These were then used in promotional materials. Other sponsors made conservative claims on the ARTG but then made very different claims in promotional campaigns. In addition, product names such as Fat Magnet, Weight Loss Accelerate, and Slim-Me could be considered equally misleading and deceptive. The problem of unsubstantiated claims is not limited to weight-loss products. Some recent examples submitted to the Complaint Resolution Panel (CRP) include "All adults should take vitamins to prevent chronic disease," "Homeopathic immunization is a safe and effective way to protect you and your family against childhood and other epidemic diseases," and "There are no reports in the literature of an interaction between glucosamine and warfarin." None of these statements is in accord with the scientific literature, and the last one also contradicts warnings by the Australian Adverse Drug Reaction Advisory Committee.

Currently, the only way to correct such inaccuracies is by submitting complaints. However, the CRP is underresourced and overloaded, and it lacks effective sanctions. It even lacks the resources to follow up its own determinations, which make them easily ignored. It can take multiple complaints before noncompliance with a CRP determination is passed on to the TGA. That organization, citing "commercial-in-confidence" considerations, currently tells complainants nothing and publicizes nothing. However, in response to publicity about this lack of transparency, a government spokesperson has indicated that this policy will change. In 2007, the TGA was asked to review the efficacy of all ingredients used in weight-loss products in the hope that upstream evaluation would reduce the need for downstream complaints. Ultimately, the "Draft Guideline for Levels and Kinds of Evidence for Listed Medicines With Indications and Claims for Weight Loss" was produced, but because of industry opposition it was never finalized. More recently, in response to ongoing concern and a number of government inquiries, the TGA has produced a new consultation document on the levels and kinds of evidence to support indications and claims for listed medicines. It remains to be seen whether this draft will be finalized and, if so, whether effective sanctions will be introduced for sponsors who ignore it. Research by the Australian National Prescribing System (NPS) showed a major disconnection between consumers' perceptions of complementary medicines as natural and risk free and the reality that they contain pharmacologically active substances capable of producing drug-drug interactions and adverse effects. The analysis of advertisements for complementary medicines suggests that this perception is created and/or maintained by extensive promotion that emphasizes the word *natural* and the use of associated imagery and colors.

Warnings about serious drug side effects and drug-drug interactions are currently communicated to health professionals by *Australian Prescriber*, a free, independent drug bulletin published by the NPS. In addition, the TGA may require sponsors to add key warnings to medication labels for consumers (e.g., "Warning: In very rare cases, Black cohosh has been associated with liver failure"). However, there are now numerous Australian Internet sites at which consumers can purchase complementary medicines without having the opportunity to read product labels; there is no requirement that important safety information be communicated on these Web sites, and there is variable implementation of such warnings. Similarly, the perception that complementary medicines are part of a holistic approach to maintaining good health ignores the reality that many of these products are devised and marketed in isolation to take advantage of consumers' anxieties and concerns.

Harm

Although complementary medicines are regarded as "relatively low-risk" products, they are not without adverse effects and interactions with conventional drugs. For example, Echinacea can cause allergic reactions, black cohosh has been associated with rare cases of liver failure requiring liver transplantation, and St. John's wort interacts with a wide range of conventional drugs, including oral contraceptives. In addition, when a number of relatively low-risk ingredients are combined, unexpected adverse effects may result. Recognition of such problems can be difficult because many patients do not tell their doctors that they are taking complementary medicines, and doctors often do not ask. As a result, adverse effects of complementary medicines are almost certainly underrecognized.

New Zealand

In New Zealand, although there is no national policy on TM and CAM currently, such a policy is under consideration. No exclusive laws or regulations on TM and CAM have yet been established, but several are in development. There is no national program, nor are there currently plans to issue one. There is no national office for TM and CAM, but plans for an office of complementary medicine are being discussed. The Ministerial Advisory Committee on Complementary and Alternative Health was established in 2001. No national research institutes on TM and CAM or herbal medicines have been established.

Herbal medicines are regulated under the Medicines Act of 1981, which also regulates conventional pharmaceuticals. Many herbal medicines are regulated under the Dietary Supplements Act of 1985. Herbal medicines are regulated as over-the-counter medicines, as dietary supplements, and as a separate regulatory category. Herbal medicines classified as extemporaneously prepared herbal medicines are exempt from regulation. Medical and health claims may be made only about those herbal medicines approved under the Medicines Act. There is neither a national pharmacopoeia nor national herbal monographs, and none is being prepared. The same regulatory requirements apply to the manufacture of herbal medicines as apply to conventional pharmaceuticals. Special GMP rules apply to the manufacture of dietary supplements, but they are strictly voluntary. Implementation of these requirements is ensured, when mandatory, by auditing and licensing by the regulatory agency Medsafe. Safety requirements apply only to those herbal medicines not classified as dietary supplements; they are the same that apply to conventional pharmaceuticals. For herbal medicines that are supplied commercially, the implementation of safety requirements is ensured by a premarketing evaluation and approval process. There is a registration system in New Zealand, which is used only for products sold commercially and not regulated as dietary supplements; the total number of registered herbal medicines is not available. No herbal medicines are included on the national essential drug list. As part of the postmarketing surveillance system, there is adverse effect monitoring for both conventional pharmaceuticals and herbal medicines. Herbal medicines in New Zealand are sold in pharmacies as prescription and over-the-counter medicines, in special outlets and without restriction.

Conclusion

The Australian regulatory system for complementary medicines is regarded as world best practice. New Zealand also has a successful network to look after the regulation of traditional medicines and their practices. In addition, most health professionals and consumers accept that evidence-based complementary medicines have a place in health care. Despite this, dubious products with unethical claims have proliferated, and it is difficult for individual consumers or health practitioners to distinguish efficacious products from those of uncertain quality and efficacy. There is also no agreed standard for educating health professionals about complementary medicines. Pressure is being brought to bear by health professionals and consumer organizations to improve the regulatory and educational systems, but not surprisingly, others wish to preserve the status quo. However, such problems are not unique to Australia and New Zealand.

Syed Feroji Ahmed
CSIR-Indian Institute of Chemical Biology

See Also: Traditional Medicine: Vietnam.

Further Readings

Australian Government, Department of Health, Therapeutic Goods Administration. "An Overview of the Regulation of Complementary Medicines in Australia." http://www.tga.gov.au/industry/cm-basics-regulation-overview.htm#.VD1VJc7jbF8 (Accessed June 8, 2015).

Braun, L. and M. Cohen. *Herbs and Natural Supplements: An Evidence-Based Guide*, 2nd ed. New York: Elsevier, 2007.

Harvey, Ken J. "Commercialism, Choice and Consumer Protection: Regulation of Complementary Medicines in Australia." *Medical Journal of Australia*, v.188/1 (2008).

Parliamentary Council Office. "Natural Health and Supplementary Products." http://www.legislation.govt.nz/bill/government/2011/0324/latest/whole.html (Accessed June 8, 2015).

Schnauer, David. "Therapeutics Bill Must Pass." *The New Zealand Herald* (2007).

Traditional and Herbal Medicines, Regulation: Canada

Traditional and herbal medicines in Canada are regulated by the Natural and Nonprescription Health Products Directorate (NNHPD), formerly the Natural Health Products Directorate. The mandate of the NNHPD includes the oversight of natural health products, nonprescription drugs, and disinfectant drugs; the latter category includes chemical products meant to clean environmental surfaces and that claim antimicrobial activity. The key legislation governing natural health products is the 2004 Natural Health Products Regulations, which define natural health products (NHPs) as including vitamins and minerals, herbal remedies, homeopathic medicines, traditional medicines, probiotics, and other products such as amino acids and essential fatty acids. NHPs are further defined as over-the-counter (OTC) products that can be sold without presentation of a prescription.

The purpose of the Natural Health Products Regulations is to ensure that Canadians have access to natural health products that are of high quality, safe, and effective, while also honoring cultural and philosophical diversity and freedom of choice. As of 2015, more than 43,000 NHPs were authorized for sale in Canada, and NHPs were used by almost three-quarters (73 percent) of Canadians in 2010, according to a survey by Ipsos Reid, with 32 percent using natural health products on a daily basis. The most common reasons reported for use include health maintenance (85 percent), illness prevention (79 percent), and general health concerns (76 percent). The most common natural health products used include vitamins and minerals (53 percent), Omega 3/essential fatty acids (19 percent), herbal teas (11 percent), and algal and fungal products (10 percent).

Regulations and Licensing

All natural health products sold in Canada must have a product license, and site licenses are required for companies that import, manufacture, package, or label natural health products in Canada. However, retail stores selling NHPs do not require licensing, nor do health care practitioners who compound NHPs for individual patients. The process of obtaining a product license begins with the applicant providing information about the product to Health Canada, including the medicinal ingredients it contains, the source of those ingredients, the dose and potency of the product, nonmedicinal ingredients included, and recommended uses for the product. If Health Canada determines that the product is safe, effective, and of high quality, it issues a product license and a Natural Product Number (an eight-digit number in the form NPN XXXXXXXX) or Homeopathic Medicine Number (a number in the form DIN-HM-XXXXXXXX). The Natural Product Number or Homeopathic Medicine Number indicates that the product has been approved for sale in Canada, and must appear on the product label.

Part of the licensing process for NHPs is the evaluation of scientific evidence regarding the product's safety and effectiveness, such as published studies or reports from clinical trials. The amount and type of evidence required for approval are somewhat different for NHPs making modern health claims, as compared to those used as traditional medicines. For NHPs making modern health claims, the evaluation process involves evidence similar to that used in evaluating pharmaceuticals, including clinical studies, peer-reviewed articles, regulatory authority reports, textbooks, pharmacopoeias, and animal and in vitro studies. NHPs making claims based on traditional health care may draw more on history and tradition than scientific results, and may be "based on the sum total of knowledge, skills, and practices based on theory, beliefs, and experiences indigenous to a specific culture, used in the maintenance of health, as well as prevention, diagnosis, improvement, or treatment of physical and mental illness" (Health Canada, "Pathway").

Passage of the Natural Health Products Regulations in 2004 created an immediate and substantial backlog of NHPs already on the market but that had not gone through the approval process. In order to allow consumers to continue to use the products familiar to them, while also moving forward in the process of evaluating and licensing products for sale, some products were allowed to be sold with an Exemption Number indicating that they have not yet been through the full approval process. These products carry an Exemption Number on their label, with the form EX-XXXXXX. The Exemption Number indicates that the product has passed an initial evaluation concerning efficacy, quality, and safety, but that the review process has not yet been fully evaluated.

Two databases are maintained by Health Canada listing the NHPs that have been licensed or granted an exemption number: The Licensed Natural Health Products Database (www.hc-sc.gc.ca/dhp-mps/prodnatur/applications/licen-prod/lnhpd-bdpsnh-eng.php) and the Exempted Products Database (http://webprod3.hc-sc.gc.ca/product-produit/search-rechercheReq.do?lang=eng). A third database, the Natural Health Products Ingredients Database (http://webprod.hc-sc.gc.ca/nhpid-bdipsn/search-rechercheReq.do), contains information about medicinal and nonmedicinal products used in NHPs, controlled vocabulary (standard terminology) used in the NHP Online Solution, labeling standards, and other relevant information such as single-ingredient and product monographs. Health Canada also collects reports of adverse reactions (unwanted side effects) for NHPs and maintains an online listing of advisories, warnings, and recalls related to NHPs.

Product labels for NHPs must include the name and license number of the product, the quantity of the product, a complete list of all medicinal and nonmedicinal ingredients, recommended use (including dosage, method of administration, and health claims), cautionary statements if applicable (e.g., contraindications for use, potential adverse reactions), and special storage conditions if applicable.

Site licenses are required for all companies that import, manufacture, package, or label NHPs. Site licenses require that the company demonstrate that it meets good manufacturing practice requirements, a series of regulations intended to ensure that products are safe and of high quality and that cover matters such as sanitation, quality assurance, record keeping, product specifications, operations, and recall reporting. Companies must also demonstrate that they maintain appropriate distribution records; have appropriate procedures for the handling, storage, and delivery of their products; and have proper product recall procedures in place.

Sarah E. Boslaugh
Saint Louis University

See Also: Aloe Vera (Herbal Medicine); Chamomile (Herbal Medicine); Ephedra (Herbal Medicine); Ginseng (Herbal Medicine); National Center for Complementary and Alternative Medicine (NIH); Opium (Herbal Medicine); Traditional and Herbal Medicines, Regulation: Europe; Traditional and Herbal Medicines, Regulation: United States.

Further Readings

Health Canada. "Natural Health Products." http://www.hc-sc.gc.ca/dhp-mps/prodnatur/index-eng.php (Accessed March19, 2015).

Health Canada. "Pathway for Licensing Natural Health Products Making Modern Health Claims." http://www.hc-sc.gc.ca/dhp-mps/prodnatur/legislation/docs/modern-eng.php (Accessed March 20, 2015).

Ipsos Reid. "Natural Health Product Tracking Survey—2010 Final Report" (January 13, 2011). http://epe.lac-bac.gc.ca/100/200/301/pwgsc-tpsgc/por-ef/health/2011/135-09/report.pdf (Accessed March 20, 2015).

TRADITIONAL AND HERBAL MEDICINES, REGULATION: EAST ASIA

Conventional views about herbal medicine, as compared with biomedicine, include the following notions: that herbs are more natural than synthetic biomedical pharmaceuticals; that, as an essential part of therapeutic tradition, herbs have a long history of use and thus are safe; that herbal medicine leads to fewer adverse effects and has a gentle therapeutic power; and that herbal medicine has been used for huge populations. So, from a public health perspective, it should be less expensive than biomedicine, which has become burdensome in developed countries.

These views, although not without merit, fall short in their understanding of the transformation of herbal medicine in response to biomedicine, which has existed in East Asia for over 400 years now and has become a permanent component of health services. Also overlooked is the role regulations play in shaping East Asian medical traditions as they undergo modernization and internationalization.

Historical Regulation of Medicinal Herbs

The regulation of medicinal herbs in East Asia can be traced back to 11th-century China, when the court established the first-ever bureau for medical affairs and set up governmental manufacturers and pharmacies. It also revised the official pharmacopoeia, *Bencao Tujing*, and laid down regulations regarding the source, quality, and use of herbs. This included assimilation of common formulas, sales franchises and their accountability, the banning of inferior medicine, and quality and safety control of medicinal herbs. It was during the same period in China that the concept of *didao* (i.e., "genuinely local") gradually developed for selected medical plants such as Sichuan aconite (*Aconitum carmichaelii* Debx) or Hangzhou's garden peony (*Paeonia lactiflora*). The following centuries saw the rise of gigantic markets for medicinal plants in Anguo and Zhangshu and the setting up of trading companies such as Tongrentang, which was founded in 1669.

Under the influence of Chinese culture, Korea and Japan imported medical plants from China and incorporated the formulas into their therapeutic traditions. Although there were no clear national regulations regarding herbs, in big herb distribution centers such as Osaka, Japan, and Daegu and Seoul, South Korea, there were regulations among traders regarding the source and quality of imported plants. Ginseng (mainly *Panax ginseng*), for example, has a long history of medicinal use and is praised as the "king of herbs." Historical records of the ginseng trade in Asian states start as early as the 3rd century C.E., and there were specialist distribution centers in China, in Korea, and later in Japan. Regulations were also in place to govern the harvesting and quality of ginseng.

The history of herb regulation in East Asia is also linked to the development and differentiation of medical traditions in this region. Following the teaching of two Chinese masters, Zhang Zhongjing and Sun Simiao, Japan developed its own interpretations of medical classics in the 16th century, its own diagnostic system based on abdominal examination, and

its own *materia medica*, *Yamato Honzo*. Inspired by Li Shijen's *Bencao Gangmu* ("Compendium of Materia Medica"), this encyclopedia includes herbs that had not been incorporated in any text from China. On the basis of this book, Japanese physicians developed their own formulas such as Taki Motoyasu's *Honchokeikenho* ("Experienced and Tested Remedies in Our Court").

The first recognizable work in Korea's medical tradition is *Dongui Bogam* ("Treasured Mirror of Eastern Medicine"). Compiled mainly by court physician Heo Jun and published in 1613, this 25-volume book includes remedies detailing the collection of herbs and medicinal plants. In contrast with *Hyangyak Jipseongbang* ("Compilation of Native Korean Prescriptions"), an earlier collection of native formulas from Korea, *Dongui Bogam* provides a theoretical framework to classify herbs according to their sources and the diseases it was claimed they could treat. The comprehensiveness of this book led to its later being brought to China and Japan.

Regulating Pharmaceuticals and Medicinal Herbs

The use of herbal medicines has a long history in Western societies. However, these medicines' different approach to body and disease means they have been considered "alternative" and "complementary" to the biomedicine that has dominated the field since the 19th century. When missionaries introduced biomedicine to East Asia in the late 16th century, it was credited as being superior to traditional medicines in the areas of anatomy and surgery. In the 19th century, moreover, East Asian states welcomed biomedicine as a part of Western thinking, and local medical traditions started to lose their predominance when these states pushed for modernization.

Kampo medicine is a case in point. Literally meaning "methods from China" (as distinct from those introduced by the Dutch), *Kampo* became a term that summarized all systematic medicine in traditional Japan. When, in 1876, the Japanese government carried out medical reform by establishing licensing procedures for medical practice, these did not cover *Kampo*. The first *Japanese Pharmacopoeia*, published in 1886, did not include herbs used in *Kampo*. Despite several debates between *Kampo* advocates and modernists, both in Parliament and outside, the government refused to recognize *Kampo* as medicine, and its legal status has remained unchanged ever since.

The effects of the policy of not recognizing *Kampo* as medicine went further than the status of herbal medicines that were no longer considered legal pharmaceuticals in Japan; it also extended to Taiwan, the first Japanese colony, where people used traditional Chinese medicine (TCM). Although during the 50 years of colonial rule (1895–1945) the governor-general of Taiwan did not issue new licenses to TCM practitioners, the consumption of herbal medicine increased with the island's increasing population. Without proper regulation of herbs as drugs, pharmacies freely made medicinal pills, plasters, and boluses and sold them without prescriptions.

Before becoming a part of Japan in 1910, Korea had debated the status of its traditional Oriental medicine, and some initiatives were taken toward modernization. Even so, Oriental medicine soon lost governmental sanction when Japan's rule began. Although practitioners of Oriental medicine were essential for rural health (like TCM practitioners in Taiwan), they, like their Japanese counterparts, had to study biomedicine in order to practice anything called medicine. In 1931, the colonial government set up an investigation committee to try to incorporate local herbs into its public health plan; however, by insisting on using biomedical categories, the committee both recognized the possible therapeutic value of the herbs and denied them any basis in traditional Oriental medical theory.

Still an empire in the 20th century, China met with controversy when it tried to incorporate TCM upon becoming a republic in 1911. Following Japan's policy, progressive intellectuals openly refused to give TCM any part in medical and pharmaceutical education. TCM study groups and pharmacy unions, on the other hand, lobbied the government with nationalist slogans. In the end, although a research institute was founded in 1930 and an ordinance on TCM was passed in 1936, the legal status of TCM remained ambiguous. TCM herbs were not listed in the *Chinese Pharmacopoeia*, first published in 1930, and no regulations governing pharmaceutical affairs include TCM.

Transformation of Herbal Medicines Through Regulation

Without state sanction, herbal medicine practitioners in East Asia had to try to build up therapeutic credibility. At the same time, traditional medicines continued to gain support from the people who considered them an essential part of national identity. In such a context, medicinal herbs developed into healing commodities, and regulations and standards were gradually elaborated to make these herbal medicines competitive with biomedical drugs.

Unlike botanical drugs in Europe and the United States, herbal medicines in East Asia work as formulas that feature multiple medicinal plants, animal parts, and minerals. Thus, one of the first breakthroughs for herbal medicine was mass manufacture. Major Japanese pharmaceutical makers, such as Takeda, Shionogi, and Yamanouchi, produced synthetic drugs, herbal medicines, and home remedies, and they introduced modern manufacturing processes for all products as early as the 1920s. Although these powder, pill, or bolus products were often labeled "scientific," most of them were not *Kampo* but folk medicine. Even so, these herbal medicines quickly became popular and were made available in other East and Southeast Asian states.

Most *Kampo* formulas are decoctions of mixed herbs. The second herbal medicine breakthrough took place in the late 1940s, when an extraction method was developed that could turn decoctions into dried granules. Takeda pharmaceuticals, the developer of this technology, used it for its stomach powder, but it was Kotaro pharmaceuticals that first applied it to *Kampo*. Before the advent of extraction, the preparation of decoctions varied from one pharmacy to another; now, there is a standard method for making modern *Kampo*. As it is much easier to take herbal medicines in packs, *Kampo* extracts gradually replaced traditional decoctions in Japan, and the method was introduced to Taiwan in 1963 to produce "scientific" TCM formulas.

This technology also changed herbal medicines in Japan and Taiwan, where herbal formulas are regulated like biomedical drugs. From 1972 to 1974, Japan's Ministry of Health and Welfare recognized 210 *Kampo* formulas as prescriptive medicines, and they were gradually allowed onto the health insurance formulary. *Kampo* formulas started being listed in the 15th edition of the *Japanese Pharmacopoeia*, published in 2006, and their numbers are increasing. TCM extracts are widely used in Taiwan. Two hundred common formulas are listed in the *Taiwan Herbal Pharmacopoeia*, and for each formula there is a standardized list of the ingredients and their quantities. For both these states, current good manufacturing practice is essential for the makers of herbal medicine to win customers.

In China and Korea, where traditional medicines regained state sanction after World War II, herbal medicines developed in two divergent ways. As an integral part of therapeutics, traditional ways of preparing herbal medicines—in pieces or tinctures—are still popular in Korea. Pharmacies and clinics offer decoction services on request. Meanwhile, the development of Korea's pharmaceutical industry has also benefited from herbal medicine. In addition to the ginseng industry, in 1969 South Korea's Ministry of Health and Welfare allowed the production of Oriental medical formulas from 11 classic medical texts without clinical trials. Since then, major pharmaceutical companies such as Dong-A and Dong Hwa have added herbal medicines to their product lists.

As soon as the Chinese communist government took power, it immediately established regulatory institutions for herbal resources at every administrative level. In universities, hospitals, clinics, and academic associations, China also created an independent TCM system running parallel to biomedicine. The aim of integrating herbal medicine with biomedicine in China has meant that the former's movement toward modernization has sometimes been provocative. TCM research and development are not limited to finding effective herbal substances, but also involve the search to create new formulas, new forms, and new routes of drug delivery. In such a context, TCM cannot be free from adverse effects. Unlike other Asian states, China optimizes the curative power of herbal medicines and risks the side effects that may come with their use.

Regulation as a Way Toward Standardization and Internationalization

With the increasing popularity of traditional medicine outside of East Asia since the 1970s, pharmaceutical regulators have been faced with the problem of whether herbal medicines should be regulated as medicines (and thus subject to the same standards as biomedicine) or regulated separately. In addition, contamination of medicinal herbs through pollution and environmental damage appears to be a serious concern.

As the world's biggest population of TCM users, China currently has an independent regulatory institute that reviews TCM products, but its reviewing process has often come under criticism. Other Asian states, where the regulation of prescription pharmaceuticals has been substantially modified since the 1980s, only approve herbal medicines that are listed in classic medical texts. With the 2004 U.S. Food and Drug Administration (FDA) industry guidelines on botanical drug products, these states hope to develop traditional wisdom into globally marketable pharmaceuticals. Nonetheless, since herbal medicines must be governed by the same regulations as biomedicine, only a handful of products have been approved to date.

Creating an integrated market of consumers who appreciate the value of this kind of drugs seems more feasible than negotiating for FDA approval of herbal medicines. However, again, regulation is the key to this task. Since the 1980s, the World Health Organization (WHO) has led projects on the standardization of traditional medicine and published books on medicinal plants in East Asia. But, even so, no regulatory platform has yet been agreed on. Although a great deal of knowledge on the identification and analysis of herbs has been amassed and included in the various national pharmacopoeias, the attempt to unify the various medical traditions on which herbal medicines are based has been met with problems.

The regulation of herbal sources is another problem. Over 90 percent of medical herbs used in East Asia come from China, but quality is uneven, and herbs often do not meet the rigorous standards of pharmaceuticals. Herbal-medicine-related drug tragedies have been reported in Taiwan, Japan, and Korea. Owing to public health concerns, the European Commission directed that by 2011 traditional herbal medical products had to be licensed before they could be marketed in the European Union, the largest market for herbal medicine outside of East Asia. All these problems create regulatory challenges to the worldwide use of herbal medicines.

In conclusion, regulation ensures the quality of herbal medicines but also decreases accessibility for consumers. This is especially so in East Asian states, where medical traditions have to compete with biomedicine. The task of making herbal medicine reliable but still accessible through appropriate regulation will continue to be a challenge not only for pharmaceutical producers but also for public health advocates and all those who use and believe in herbal medicines.

Wen-Hua Kuo
National Yang-Ming University

See Also: Food and Drug Administration (U.S.); *Kampo* (Traditional Japanese Medicine); Prescription Drug Approval Process: Asia.

Further Readings

Cochran, Sherman. *Chinese Medicine Men: Consumer Culture in China and Southeast Asia*. Cambridge, MA: Harvard University Press, 2006.

European Commission. "Herbal Medicinal Products." http://ec.europa.eu/health/human-use/herbal-medicines/index_en.htm (Accessed April 2014).

U.S. Food and Drug Administration. "Guidance for Industry: Botanical Drug Products." http://www.fda .gov/downloads/Drugs/GuidanceCompliance RegulatoryInformation/Guidances/ucm070491.pdf (Accessed April 2014).

WHO Regional Office for the Western Pacific. "Regional Strategy for Traditional Medicine in the Western Pacific (2011–2020)." http://www.wpro .who.int/publications/PUB_9789290615590/en/ (Accessed April 2014).

Yakuji Nippo Ltd. *The Japanese Pharmacopoeia*, 15th ed. Wickford, Essex, UK: Worldwide Book Service, 2006.

TRADITIONAL AND HERBAL MEDICINES, REGULATION: EUROPE

Herbal medical products require effective regulation to ensure that safe products are available to consumers. There is a wide variety of regulations across Europe. Some countries do not have specific regulations for herbs and alternative medicine but incorporate these into existing laws. This is true of laws that concern manufacturers, importers, and wholesale dealers of herbal medicines.

The assortment of herbal medicine regulations can be shown in the different countries of Europe. Armenia, Austria, the Republic of Belarus, Bulgaria, the Czech Republic, Ireland, Lithuania, the Netherlands, Portugal, the Republic of Moldova, the Russian Federation, Serbia and Montenegro, Slovakia, Slovenia, Spain, Sweden, Switzerland, and the former Yugoslav Republic of Macedonia do not have laws regulating the manufacturing and sale of herbal medicines. For many of these countries, such policies are already included in their laws. Some of these countries, such as the Republic of Belarus, are in the process of developing laws regarding the manufacturing and sale of herbal medicines. Other countries, such as Belgium, have established regulations on traditional medicine (TM) and complementary alternative medicine (CAM), and the countries regulate these in the same way as prescription medicines, over-the-counter (OTC) medicines, and dietary supplements.

A case study of herbal regulation is the United Kingdom. Herbal medicines, for example, in the United Kingdom are regulated under the Medicines Act of 1968. This act established a body called the Medicines Commission to carry out the functions assigned to the commission by the act. This commission oversees the regulation of the practice of medicine other than veterinary medicine, the practice of veterinary medicine, pharmacy practices, and chemistry other than pharmaceutical chemistry, as well as the pharmaceutical industry. There are between 300 and 500 licensed herbal medicines in the United Kingdom for the commission to regulate. However, none of these herbal medicines is on the essential drug list. Essential drug lists include those drugs that meet the priority health care needs of the population such as ibuprofen, antibiotics, or anesthesia. These drugs are selected with regard to relevance to the population that is being served, the evidence of the drug efficacy, and safety with regard to effectiveness of costs. These drugs should be available in a functioning health system and be available in adequate amounts and in appropriate dosage forms. The World Health Organization (WHO) sets separate model lists for adults and for children, but countries are not bound to follow these lists and can set their own criteria for what are essential medications. Herbal medication in the United Kingdom does not meet the essential medicine criteria of being relevant to the population that is being served, or having drug efficacy and safety coupled with a regard to effectiveness of costs.

Many of the countries, to provide coherence to the patchwork of laws concerning herbal medication, have joined under the auspices of the European Union. The European Union, or EU, is an organization of currently 28 sovereign states that have agreed to create legislation that will facilitate trade and defense between the member countries. The European Union was created after World War II as a way to create economic cooperation and to foster interdependent relations between countries. The precursor to the European Union was the European Economic Community created in 1958. Belgium, Germany, France, Italy, the Netherlands, and Luxembourg were the first countries of the emerging union, but this expanded to the current 28 countries. The European Union is founded on voluntary treaties agreed to by all the member countries, which retain their individual sovereign laws.

One of the treaties that the member nations have agreed to is the European Traditional Herbal Medicinal Products Directive (THMPD). This directive was established by the European Parliament and Council on March 31, 2004, to provide a regulatory approval process for traditional herbal medicines in the countries that have joined the European Union. There was not, prior to this legislation, a formal authorization procedure to regulate traditional medicines, and each EU member state regulated these products piecemeal according to its own laws. With the THMPD, EU member nations are able to have a unified standard for manufacturing and selling traditional herbal medicines and facilitate trade of these medicines between member countries.

The THMPD specifications of the legislation set out the manufacturing and sale of traditional herbal medicines. The directive's goal is to protect public health but also allow the manufacturing of herbal medicinal products within the European Union. Currently, herbal medicinal products are licensed nationally by individual EU members, but the THMPD is moving closer to standardizing these licenses across the European Union. For example, articles 21(3) and 21(4) of the transparency and public assessment reports (article 1[19] of Directive 2004/27/EC) state that a new provision in the directive requires competent authorities to make summaries of product

characteristics. They also create assessment reports, including the evidence supporting the judgment of an herb's efficacy and safety available to the public. The deletion of confidential subject matter that might reveal proprietary information is allowed. The information about herbal products will be one standardized set of information on each herbal preparation when brought to market. This information will include the therapeutic uses and recommended safe conditions for use. There will also be a subcategory of "traditional herbal medicinal product" where safety needs to be shown but efficacy does not need to be proved beyond plausible conditions for the traditional indications for the herbal medicine.

The Committee on Herbal Medicinal Products (HMPC) is the decisive organization at the European Medicines Agency (EMA), the medical body in the European Union responsible for preparing opinions on medicines, for herbal medicines. This committee was established in September 2004 and replaced the Committee for Proprietary Medicinal Products (CPMP) Working Party on Herbal Medicinal Products in terms of authorization of herbal medicines. The HMPC is complementary to the Committee for Medicinal Products for Human Use (CHMP) or Committee for Medicinal Products for Veterinary Use (CVMP). Its task, like that of the European Union, is to create standards for herbal medicinal products and to create a regulatory framework for manufacturing and selling herbal medicinal products. The HMPC is composed of scientific experts in the area of herbal medicine whose role is to consult with other experts in the herbal medicine field and to aid dissemination of this information to EU member states and European institutions, both governmental and nongovernmental, through herbal monographs. The committee has one member and one alternate member nominated by each of the European Union member states and by each of the European Economic Area and European Free Trade Association (EEA and EFTA) states of Iceland and Norway. Up to five additional expert committee members may be allowed to provide specialized expertise such as clinical pharmacology. The chair of the HMPC is elected by the committee members.

The committee members of the HMPC have laid out regulations for how herbal substances and preparations can reach the markets of the EU member states. Furthermore, the EMA publishes guidelines to manufacturers and prescribers of herbal medicinal products as to how they can most readily and safely educate their customers and consumers on the use of the herbal products. The herbal medicinal products must fall within three categories to be ready for markets. Under the THMPD, there are specific definitions for what constitutes an herbal product.

An herbal medicinal product is any medicinal product containing the active ingredients of one or more herbal substances or one or more herbal preparations, or several herbal substances in combination with other herbal preparations. Herbal substances are whole, fragmented, or cut plants—parts of plants, algae, fungi, and lichen in a variety of forms that include unprocessed, dried, and fresh. Exudates, the secretions of plants that have not been subjected to other treatments, are also herbal substances. The types of plants and plant parts that are used, as well as the botanical names according to the binomial system of genus, species, variety, and author, are taken into consideration for classification for possible authorization for EU marketing. This extends to herbal preparations from distillation, extraction, expression, fractionation, or separating the herbs into a number of smaller quantities according to a gradient, purification, concentration of herbs, or fermentation. These include

herbs that are powdered, tinctures in alcohol, extracts, essential oils, juices, and secretions. For example, peppermint can be in either an expressed oil form or a tea form and still represent the plant's active ingredient as an herbal medicinal product under EU regulations.

The first way that an herbal medicinal product can be brought to market is under classification of traditional medicinal use provisions ("traditional use") if the product meets sufficient safety data and plausible efficacy. An EU member state grants a traditional use registration through a simplified registration procedure.

The second way that an herbal medicinal product can be brought to market is under the classification of well-established medicinal use provisions or "well-established use." This classification is demonstrated with the scientific literature that establishes the active substances of the herbs in question have been used in the European Union for at least 30 years with a minimum of 15 years in the European Union with safety and efficacy. The product is then given a marketing authorization from a member state or from the EMA.

An herbal medicinal product can also be authorized after evaluation of a marketing authorization application that consists of only safety and efficacy data from a company's own research and development called a "stand-alone" or with a combination of the company's own studies and bibliographic data called a "mixed application." This product can be granted a marketing authorization by a member state or by the EMA through a centralized procedure if all requirements for safety and efficacy are met.

A simplified way of looking at the licensing process is the division between the traditional herbal medicines registration scheme and the licensed herbal medicines scheme. All manufactured herbal medicines that come into the European market must have either a traditional herbal registration (THR) or a product license (PL). The EU legislation classifies traditional herbal medicinal products as those that have been used for at least 30 years within the European Union and are used without the supervision of a medical practitioner and not administered by injection. Some examples of a THR include *Calendula officinalis* L, or common marigold; *Eleutherococcus senticosus* (Rupr. et Maxim.) Maxim, or Siberian ginseng; *Mentha x piperita* L, or peppermint; and *Pimpinella anisum* L, or anise.

Some herbal medicinal products sold in the European Union can have a PL similar to those of pharmaceutical medicines. The products must demonstrate safety and efficacy and have information on safe usage of the product such as interaction with other herbs or drugs and contraindications such as pregnancy and lactation or use in the elderly or very young. Consumers in the European Union can readily see if the product has a PL by looking for the nine-digit PL number on the packaging.

Safety and efficacy must always, irrespective of the means of getting the herbal medicinal product to market, be proven before it is permitted for sale into the EU market. The herbal monographs prepared by the HMPC are relevant for all these types of registration. Whether the herbal medicinal product has a THR or a PL, as of May 1, 2014, all unlicensed herbal medicinal products without a THR or a PL cannot be sold to consumers in the European Union and must be removed from all EU markets.

It is important to remember when considering European laws regarding herbal medicinal products that legislation regarding the manufacturing, distribution, sale, and marketing is an ongoing process, and it is necessary to keep apprised of current developments regarding both laws and scientific knowledge. Current laws only scratch the surface of a complex and evolving environment for the manufacturing, sale, and use of herbal medicinal products in the European Union and its member states.

Anne Cagle
Independent Scholar

See Also: France; Germany; United Kingdom; WHO Model Lists of Essential Medicines; World Health Organization.

Further Readings

British Herbal Medicine Association. "Legislation" (2014). http://bhma.info/index.php/legislation-on-herbal-medicines/ (Accessed May 23, 2015).

European Commission. "Herbal Medicinal Products." http://ec.europa.eu/health/human-use/herbal-medicines/index_en.htm (Accessed May 23, 2015).

European Medicines Agency. "Herbal Medicinal Products." http://www.ema.europa.eu/ema/index.jsp?curl=pages/regulation/general/general_content_000208.jsp (Accessed May 23, 2015).

European Medicines Agency. "HMPC: Overview." http://www.ema.europa.eu/ema/index.jsp?curl=pages/about_us/general/general_content_000122.jsp (Accessed May 23, 2015).

European Union. "How the EU Works." http://europa.eu/about-eu/index_en.htm (Accessed May 23, 2015).

Global Regulatory Services. "Herbal Medicines (Europe)." http://www.globalregulatoryservices.com/industry-sectors/herbal-medicines-europe (Accessed May 23, 2015).

"Medicines Act 1968." http://www.legislation.gov.uk/ukpga/1968/67 (Accessed May 24, 2015).

Medicines and Healthcare Products Regulatory Agency. "How to Register Your Product Under the Traditional Herbal Medicines Registration Scheme: Registration and Fees" (December 31, 2014). https://www.gov.uk/apply-for-a-traditional-herbal-registration-thr

Weerasuriya, Krisantha. "The WHO Essential Drug Concept." http://www.prn.usm.my/old_website/isdb/kris.html (Accessed May 24, 2015).

World Health Organization. "Essential Medicines." http://www.who.int/medicines/services/essmedicines_def/en/ (Accessed May 24, 2015).

World Health Organization. "Essential Medicines and Health Products Information Portal." http://apps.who.int/medicinedocs/en/ (Accessed May 24, 2015).

World Health Organization. "WHO Model Lists of Essential Medicines." http://www.who.int/medicines/publications/essentialmedicines/en/ (Accessed May 24, 2015).

TRADITIONAL AND HERBAL MEDICINES, REGULATION: LATIN AMERICA

Traditional medicines are those medicines used by indigenous people in the prevention, treatment, and overall maintenance of their health. These medicines include herbal preparations as well as animal and mineral components, but plants occupy the bulk of indigenous peoples' treatment modalities. Medicines are selected by native healers after considering the existing relationship of the patient with the cosmos and his or her environment, and not in isolation. In Western society, this would likely be referred to as a "holistic approach." Therefore, although traditional and herbal medicines have been used since ancient times, legislation to specifically address regulations on their manufacture, commercialization, and distribution has been slow to come. Legislation in Latin American countries, nevertheless, has seen significant advances in recent years.

Commercial products based on animal, plant, and mineral components for medicinal purposes have proliferated worldwide in the past decade, bringing concerns of safety and efficacy. The World Health Organization (WHO) called on its member nations in 2009 to respect, preserve, and disseminate knowledge on traditional medicines while formulating policies to regulate their safe and effective use. Nineteen Latin American countries have some type of regulation, either incorporated into legislation covering conventional pharmaceuticals or as resolutions and decrees applying specifically to natural products.

All Latin American national regulations recognize products containing plant, animal, and/or mineral components as medicines, and as with conventional medicines, obtaining sanitary registration with a country's ministry of health is required. One exemption is found in Peruvian legislation, which states that medicinal plants or other natural resources of traditional use do not require sanitary registration, as long as no reference is made to preventive, diagnostic, or therapeutic properties. Argentina, Bolivia, Brazil, Colombia, Cuba, the Dominican Republic, and Ecuador have specific standards and decrees regulating the requirements for registration, preparation, and commercialization of herbal medicines. Five other countries (Costa Rica, Guatemala, El Salvador, Honduras, and Nicaragua) have recently adopted a common regulation on registration requirements for natural medicine products. Only Puerto Rico's legislation lacks specific reference to traditional or herbal medicines, and although the term *natural products* is used in a recent amendment to the legislation, no definition of the term is provided.

There is a lack of standardization in the terminology used in Latin American legislation to refer to traditional and herbal medicines, with some countries incorporating two or more terms. Multiple wording is used, and definitions may also differ considerably from country to country. Some countries use the term *phytomedicines* (*medicamentos fitoterápicos*) or *phytodrugs* (*medicamentos fitofármacos*), which are commonly defined as pharmaceutical products whose active ingredients come from plants or other plant materials (e.g., extracts, tinctures, oils). Phytomedicines are classified as pharmaceutical products because, like conventional drugs, they are used to cure, attenuate, treat, prevent, or diagnose illnesses. Chile's legislation adds that a *phytodrug* also requires standardization of its active ingredients. In Brazil, phytodrugs may be registered as phytomedicines or traditional phytoproducts (*produtos tradicionais fitoterápicos*), depending on whether their safety and efficacy are supported by clinical studies (phytomedicines) or they have been in continuous use for 30 years or more (phytoproducts). As with Brazil, Colombia's term *traditional phytoproducts* refers to plant-based products, the safety and efficacy of which rest on their prolonged use (undefined). In addition, the term *traditional phytoproduct* is reserved for products containing medicinal plants grown locally and manufactured in Colombia. For products not produced in the country, the term *imported traditional phytoproducts* applies.

Terms such as *herbal medicines* (*medicamentos herbarios, medicamentos herbolarios*) and *herbal remedies* (*remedios herbolarios*) are found in the regulations of Argentina, Chile, Peru, and Mexico. Mexico's definition of herbal medicines (*medicamentos herbolarios*) and Peru's definition of herbal medicines of medicinal use (*medicamentos herbarios de uso medicinal*) correspond to that of phytomedicines. Argentina's definition of herbal medicines fits that of phytomedicines as well, except that herbal medicines may also include components from algae and the fungi kingdom. Chile's legislation reserves the term *traditional herbal medicines* (*medicamentos herbarios tradicionales*) for those preparations containing plants as a whole, as parts, ground, fresh, or dried, which are then manually packed and labeled with the name traditionally used by the culture. Traditional herbal medicines must be included in an official list approved by the Ministry of Health, and they may be automatically registered as pharmaceutical products once the place of storage, preparation, and packing has been approved by the appropriate government's office.

Cuba has adopted only one term for natural products: *medicines of natural origin* (*medicamentos de origen natural*). A difference from other legislations is that the active ingredients of medicines of natural origin may be derived not only from animals, plants, and minerals but also from microbial organisms. In addition, justification for their use must be found in traditional medicine records or in scientific studies.

There are two terms related to natural products in the ruling document signed by Guatemala, El Salvador, Nicaragua, Honduras, and Costa Rica, namely, *medicinal natural product* (*produto natural medicinal*), and *traditional medicinal natural product* (*produto natural medicinal tradicional*). Both may include ingredients from the plant, animal, or mineral kingdoms, but a traditional medicinal natural product must have documentation attesting to its medical use for a period of not less than 30 years.

Bolivia and the Dominican Republic use the term *traditional and natural medicines* (*medicamentos naturales y tradicionales*) for those products whose active ingredients come from plants, animals, or minerals and whose use is justified by the practice of traditional medicine or scientific studies. Bolivia's regulations define traditional medicine as that based on ancient practices.

Ecuadorian legislation classifies natural products as processed natural products for traditional medicinal purposes (*productos naturales procesados de uso medicinal tradicional*) and processed natural products for official or demonstrated medicinal use (*productos naturales procesados de uso medicinal oficial o demostrado*). As with some other Latin American countries, Ecuador's ruling defines processed natural products for traditional medicinal purposes as those pharmaceutical products coming from natural resources of traditional medicinal use but requires bibliographic references supporting their safety and efficacy. As for the processed natural products for official or demonstrated medicinal use, Ecuadorian legislation includes pharmaceuticals made from standardized natural resources of medicinal use supported by toxicological, preclinical, and clinical studies. Some other Latin American countries, such as Haiti, Panama, Paraguay, Uruguay, and Venezuela, do not have legislation, have very limited legislation, or are having discussions on upcoming new legislation on traditional and herbal medicines.

Sanitary registration of traditional and herbal medicines requires proof of safety and efficacy in all Latin American countries with enacted legislation on this matter. Proof of the safety and efficacy of nontraditional natural medicines often requires presentation of toxicological, pharmacological, preclinical, and clinical studies. These, however, may be condoned if appropriate information on the subject is found from internationally recognized health organizations, such as the WHO, the U.S. Food and Drug Administration, the European Medicines Agency, and similar agencies. Cuba's legislation is more stringent in this regard, as it requires genotoxicity and reproductive studies as well. Toxicological and pharmacological studies are not necessary, however, for medicines of natural origin with very well established use.

Proof of safety and efficacy for traditional medicines, on the other hand, may be different. Most Latin American countries would accept bibliographic evidence, ethnomedicine reports, technical documentation, and/or documents of interviews of indigenous people attesting to the use, safety, and efficacy of traditional medicines. Moreover, some countries have developed a national list and/or reference book of national medicinal plants considered

safe to use by the ministry of health. Data on botanical characteristics, harvesting and storage, side effects, efficacy, and other attributes may be found here as well. Applicants seeking registration of traditional medicine products containing single active ingredients found in the national medicinal plant lists most often do not need further documentation on safety and efficacy to be compliant with this part of the registration process.

Latin American countries have adopted the WHO's definition of traditional use of herbal medicines in their legislation. Thus, definitions of traditional medicines allude to the long historical use of these products, not necessarily to the applications given by indigenous people. Most countries do not establish minimal times deemed appropriate for traditional products to be considered of long and historical use; others, like Brazil, Colombia, Costa Rica, Cuba, the Dominican Republic, Guatemala, El Salvador, Nicaragua, and Honduras, have added a time frame to this concept.

There are several other similarities found in the language of the legislation of the different countries. First, all regulations available recognize that traditional and herbal medicines are not characterized by defined and well-established chemical compositions. Adding well-defined chemically active ingredients such as allopathic drugs and those isolated from herbs is, therefore, not allowed by any country, except Argentina. Argentina accepts the addition of active ingredients isolated from plants in well-justified cases. Similarly, purified medicinal products obtained after processing raw plant materials cannot be classified as phytomedicines, according to Latin American legislation. Second, all countries but Ecuador exclude narcotics and psychotropic drugs from traditional and herbal medicines. Third, of the countries indicating the routes of administration considered acceptable for traditional and herbal medicines, most include oral and topical as the only appropriate routes, explicitly excluding ophthalmic and parenteral or those routes requiring sterilization. The definition of what constitutes a topical route, however, may vary. A few countries, such as Bolivia and Brazil, include rectal, vaginal, and transdermal administration as topical routes. Brazil also allows nasal, otic, and inhalant administration but prohibits the urethral route. Additional variations include Mexico, which lists only the injectable route as unacceptable, and Ecuador, which does not limit the administration of traditional and herbal medicines to any route; even injectable preparations seem to be acceptable.

The number of active ingredients allowed in traditional and herbal medicines varies somewhat in Latin American legislation. Thus, although no guidance on this aspect is found in some countries' regulations, others, such as Brazil and Mexico, place no restrictions on the number of herbal drugs, preparations of herbal drugs, or natural medicinal products that can be combined. The rulings of Bolivia and the Dominican Republic allow traditional and herbal medicines to be associated, when the association leads to a therapeutic effect (which can be demonstrated, per Bolivian legislation). Traditional herbal medicines, however, cannot be combined per Chilean legislation, which requires that each traditional herbal medicine be packed and commercialized as a separate, well-defined entity.

Standards to ensure the quality of traditional and herbal medicines are found in most countries' legislation, some with detailed steps to be followed to ensure the quality of the medicinal product. Stipulations of good manufacturing practices, qualitative and quantitative composition, determination of heavy metals, pesticides, and other contaminants, and microbiological testing are just a few examples of the requisites.

Prescription requirements for traditional and herbal medicines stated in the laws also vary in the different countries. Except for Mexico and for Chile, where herbal medicines and traditional herbal medicines, respectively, are sold over the counter, obtaining traditional and herbal medicines in most other countries may or may not require a prescription. The decision on this requirement rests with the appropriate office of the ministry of health providing sanitary registration to that particular pharmaceutical entity. Processed natural products of medicinal use containing narcotic or psychotropic drugs, however, do need presentation of a special prescription in Ecuador, the only country where narcotic or psychotropic drugs may be incorporated into traditional and herbal medicines.

Carlota O. Andrews
California Health Sciences University

Mirtha Parada
Instituto de Salud Pública de Chile

See Also: Colombia; Costa Rica; Hispanic Americans; Medicinal Plant Species Threatened With Extinction; Mexico; Racial Minorities: Latin America; Traditional Medicine: Central America; Traditional Medicine: South America.

Further Readings

"Bolivia: Ley de Medicina Tradicional Ancestral Boliviana, 19 de Diciembre de 2013. Ley N° 459." http://www.lexivox.org/norms/BO-L-N459.xhtml (Accessed June 9, 2015).

Robinson, M. M. and X. Zhang. "The World Medicines Situation 2011: Traditional Medicines: Global Situation, Issues and Challenges." http://digicollection.org/hss/documents/s18063en/s18063en.pdf (Accessed June 9, 2015).

World Health Organization. "National Policy on Traditional Medicine and Regulation of Herbal Medicines: Report of a WHO Global Survey." http://apps.who.int/medicinedocs/pdf/s7916e/s7916e.pdf (Accessed June 9, 2015).

TRADITIONAL AND HERBAL MEDICINES, REGULATION: SOUTH ASIA

The southern part of Asia, including Bangladesh, India, Nepal, Pakistan, Nepal, Sri Lanka, and other states, constitutes the World Health Organization's (WHO's) South-East Asia Region (SEAR). In this global region, traditional and herbal medicines are a normal part of health care, particularly in rural areas. The centuries-long, rich, and well-documented heritage of traditional medicine includes a vast reservoir of medicinal plants and huge repositories of knowledge. As of 2003, nearly 2,900 hospitals in India provided Ayurvedic medicines, and both conventional and traditional medicine treatments are offered at the National Health Centre of Bhutan. Five of the 11 SEAR member states have national research institutes for the study of traditional medicine. Many of the SEAR governments have recognized the use of traditional medicine and have established national policies and regulations. As well, medical doctors have been encouraged to work with traditional practitioners at the hospital level, and there has been support for research on traditional medicine.

Traditional Medicine

Specific cultural practices such as the knowledge, practices, and skills used in the sustenance of health, including diagnosis, improvement, prevention, and/or treatment of illnesses, are called traditional medicine. This definition encompasses a diversity of methods and therapies that differ within local regions and countries. Traditional medicine includes the use of animal products, minerals, and herbal preparations. Often, traditional medicines may have been used for significant periods of time without documentation other than oral tradition. The tradition of health practitioners in the local community is an important aspect of health care. A resurgence in the use of traditional medicine has occurred in recent years, with herbal medicines becoming a large and popular market. Of particular interest, the United Nations Committee on Economic, Social and Cultural Rights, in discussing the right to the highest attainable standard of health, indicated that states had an obligation to respect and refrain from hindering or blocking traditional medicines or methods of healing and preventive care.

A global survey of national policies and regulations for herbal medicines and traditional medicines by the WHO reported three areas of concern: evaluation of safety and efficacy of traditional medicine, information sharing, and safety monitoring for herbal medicines. In 2003, a workshop on the regulation of herbal medicines was organized by the WHO South-East Asia Regional Office. As a result, a guideline document was produced that focused on areas of efficacy, quality control, and safety of traditional medicine. This workshop focused on herbal medicines for simplicity.

Classification of Herbal Medicines

A classification system was established for herbal medicines, with four categories. Category 1 includes indigenous herbal medicines, historically used and well known through long use by the local population in terms of composition, treatment, and dosage. Indigenous herbal medicines can be used freely by the local community or region without safety data being required. However, if such local medicines move out of the community, they must meet any national regulations for safety and efficacy, including a review by the established national drug control agency. Action then depends on whether the traditional medicine fits into safety category A, B, or C (below).

Category 2 includes herbal medicines in systems that have a long history of use and are documented along with any concepts or special theories. Examples include the practices and medications of Ayurveda, Unani, and Siddha. Although generally, these traditional medicines have extensive use and documentation, safety review is nonetheless required. Should an herbal medicine fit into safety category C, "herbal medicines of uncertain safety," more documentation and study is needed.

Category 3, modified herbal medicines, are those from categories 1 and 2 that have been altered in some manner, such as alternative medical use, change in dose, form of use, administration mode, and/or different preparation ingredients. Category 3 traditional medicines must meet national regulatory requirements of safety and efficacy. Because traditional medicines in this category include modifications of those in categories 1 and 2, they must meet either safety categories A and/or B or else be deemed "herbal medicines of uncertain safety," requiring further characterization.

Category 4 includes herbal medicines that are imported, including both products and raw materials. These products should be marketed and registered in the exporting countries; as well, safety and efficacy data should be submitted to the importing country. Safety data must meet the requirements for the safety of herbal medicines or for the safety of "herbal medicines of uncertain safety," depending on the requirements of the importing country.

Safety and Identification of Traditional Medicines

A safe herbal medication is defined as one known to cause no potential or known harm to users. Three safety categories for herbal medicines were defined by the WHO-SEAR workshop: category A, safety established by use over a long period of time; category B, safe under specific conditions of use, for example, herbal medicines with strong and well-established documentation; and category C, herbal medicines of uncertain safety. The latter are to be treated as "new" drugs. In the case of new drugs, data will be required on the following: acute toxicity, long-term toxicity, organ-targeted toxicity, immunotoxicity, embryo/fetal and prenatal toxicity, mutagenicity and/or genotoxicity, and carcinogenicity.

Literature Review of Herbal Medicines

The 2003 WHO workshop document outlined a proposal for information sharing. It was suggested that SEAR states share reliable information, beginning with an assessment of bibliographic data. The workshop stated that assessment of traditional medicines requires a clear-cut and unambiguous identification of an herbal medicine, including a well-defined characterization of its constituents. Methods for such identification were outlined to include a detailed and exhaustive literature search, including therapy handbooks; modern textbooks on plant therapy, plant chemistry, and the pharmacology of herbal remedies; scientific journal review; and all relevant data on herbal medicines. It was also suggested that literature reviews focus not only on specific medicinal preparations but also on related plant species and any known data concerning safety and toxicology. In particular, it was suggested that data on herbal medicines be evaluated for comparative characteristics and types of herbal preparations described in the literature and period of experimental use and known safety and toxicity data. For any herbal medicines considered "new drugs," more extensive information should be required, in addition to any documented experience. In particular, a focus on toxicology was suggested, especially for those effects that are less obvious or are difficult to detect, such as genotoxicity. Furthermore, assessments of herbal medicines should consider safe use in vulnerable populations, including pregnant or lactating women and children. Data on herbal medicine abuse (e.g., to induce abortion) should be assessed as well.

Manufacturing

The Association of Southeast Asian Nations met in April 2014 to discuss a rising global demand for alternative and holistic (herbal or traditional) medicines. Guidelines for good manufacturing practice (GMP) were discussed, to ensure consistency of products, quality management control, and risk minimization, particularly with respect to unintended contamination of products. A key goal is to ensure that "health products remain safe for consumers to use." Regulations for herbal medicines vary according to country. In the United States, health supplements and dietary supplements are a category of food under the Dietary Supplement Health and Education Act of 1994. Herbal and traditional medicines are not regulated. Of particular importance, recent data indicate that the U.S. health supplement market is currently valued at about $35 billion and growing. The SEAR nations are in an excellent position to market to the United States, particularly as they address issues of safety and efficacy, along with appropriate regulation.

Bangladesh

In 1995, the People's Republic of Bangladesh issued a national policy on traditional medicines. Herbal medicines began to be regulated in 1992, and the laws applying to conventional pharmaceuticals are applied to herbal medicines. Bangladesh has established national formularies on Unani and Ayurvedic medicine that are legally binding. Present regulations for herbal medicines include GMP and adherence to detailed information from herbal and traditional medicine pharmacopoeias and monographs. A tradition of use of an herbal medicine, without demonstrated harmful effects, is important in terms of safety. Bangladesh requires that herbal medicines be registered. They may be sold by licensed practitioners, over the counter, or by prescription.

India

The Health Ministry of India has a separate Department of Ayurveda, Yoga & Naturopathy, Unani, Siddha and Homoeopathy (AYUSH). The intent is to provide holistic and integrated health care for the benefit of the populace. Each different medical system may be more appropriate for different regions of the country. The AYUSH facilities were first set up in the 1960s in India, in the dispensaries of the Central Government Health Scheme. As well, India has a National Rural Health Mission, which incorporates both traditional medicines and homeopathy into the primary health network.

Regulation of herbal medicine began in India in 1940; regulations for herbal medicines are at least partially the same as those for pharmaceuticals. Herbal medicines may be sold either by prescription or over the counter. The multivolume national pharmacopoeias, the Ayurvedic pharmacopoeia of India and the Unani pharmacopoeia of India, are considered legally binding. As well, there is a national database of medicinal plants used in Ayurvedic medicine. Manufacture of herbal medications must follow the GMP rules required for modern pharmaceuticals, as well as adhering to formulas and data in the pharmacopoeias. Safety requirements for traditional medicines are similar to those for conventional medicines, as well as requirements of traditional medicines with known histories of safety and efficacy. The long history of herbal medicines in the Ayurveda, Unani, and Siddha systems is considered a sufficient basis to verify their safety. In 1999 and 2000, sales of herbal medicines were estimated at 6,705 million Indian rupees ($149 million).

Nepal

Nepal has an ancient tradition of herbal medicine, but a need for management of indigenous plants is arising, as many are on the verge of extinction. Medicinal plants are used for a variety of health issues: for eye problems, *Berberis asiatica* is commonly used; for dandruff, *Sapindus mukorossi* is favored; and for toothache, *Zanthoxylum armatum* was often chosen. Because of the increasing global demand for traditional and herbal medications, it is important not only that local and regional herbs be studied and researched for safety and efficacy but also that management of ethnobotanicals be considered.

Sri Lanka

The health care system in Sri Lanka includes traditional and natural medicine, with about 60 percent to 70 percent of the rural population using Ayurvedic medicine. In 1961, Sri Lanka established a Department of Ayurveda, defined as "all medical systems indigenous to Asia, including Siddha and Unani." In 1970, homeopathy was recognized as a system of medicine; in 1994, the Cabinet Ministry for Indigenous Medicine was established. Traditional medicines also are subject to regulated codes of conduct and ethics. As well, government regulations have been established for Ayurvedic medications, both for internal use and for export.

Regulation of traditional and herbal medicines in South Asia is an ongoing process that encompasses both the strong base of knowledge of medicines used for centuries and more recent empirical studies of safety and efficacy. This regulation strives to permit and maintain the use of herbal medicines of proven efficacy and safety, with an expansion into new studies on less well known herbal preparations. With a growing global interest in herbal and traditional medicines, products from this region are potentially likely to be on our own family shelves soon.

Laura A. Andersson
Retired Independent Scholar

See Also: Ayurvedic Medicine; Ethnobotany; Phytochemicals; Traditional and Herbal Medicines, Regulation: East Asia.

Further Readings

"ASEAN Association of South East Asian Nations: Harmonising Regulation of Traditional Medicines and Health Supplements Ahead of ASEAN Integration." http://www.4-traders.com/news/ASEAN-Association-of-South-East-Asian-Nations-Harmonising-Regulation-of-Traditional-Medicines-and-18266032/ (Accessed October 2014).

"Guidelines for the Regulation of Herbal Medicines in the South-East Asia Region" (WHO Reference Number: SEA-Trad.Med.-82). http://www.searo.who.int/entity/medicines/documents/sea-trad.med-82/en/ (Accessed June 9, 2015).

Kunwar, R. M., L. Mahat, R. P. Acharya, and R. W. Bussmann. "Medicinal Plants, Traditional Medicine, Markets and Management in Far-West Nepal." *Journal of Ethnobiology and Ethnomedicine,* v.9 (2013).

"Legal Status of Traditional Medicine and Complementary/Alternative Medicine: A Worldwide Review." Essential Medicines and Health Products

Information Portal: A World Health Organization Resource. http://apps.who.int/medicinedocs/pdf/h2943e/h2943e.pdf (Accessed June 9, 2015).

Zhang, X. "Regulatory Situation of Herbal Medicines—A Worldwide Review." http://apps.who.int/medicinedocs/pdf/whozip57e/whozip57e.pdf (Accessed June 9, 2015).

TRADITIONAL AND HERBAL MEDICINES, REGULATION: UNITED STATES

Herbal medicines, also referred to as botanicals and phytotherapy, include use of whole plants or plant parts in raw or extract form for therapeutic purposes. Herbal combinations are also used, although this practice is less conventional in Western branches of the field than in others. Common examples of the range of herbs used for medicinal purposes include ginkgo for cognitive functioning, ginseng for energy, echinacea for the common cold, chamomile as a sedative, and flaxseed for cancer and heart disease. Traditional medicines, also referred to as indigenous or folk medicines, are medicinal systems used in a wide range of societies for many generations before introduction of modern medicine. These include health approaches and practices including but not limited to acupuncture, spiritual therapies, homeopathic treatments, traditional Chinese and African medicine, Ayurveda from India, and the traditional Arabic and Islamic medicine systems. Regulation of herbal and traditional medicinal substances in the United States has a rich history linked not only to the country's complex federal system of government, but also to varied challenges posed by changing scientific knowledge, trends in use across the country related to the nation's multicultural society, and ongoing developments in related fields of pharmaceutical use and regulation.

Herbal Medicine Regulation

In the United States, evidence for long-standing popularity of herbal uses for medicinal purposes can be seen since publication of the first edition of the *United States Pharmacopeia* (USP) in 1820 that contained mostly botanicals. In the 1950s and 1960s, U.S. government funding for plant-based pharmaceutical research was high with intensive efforts to screen plants supported by the National Cancer Institute (NCI), resulting in development of a range of medicinal products such as Taxol, extracted from bark found in the Pacific yew. Alkaloids are another product derived from *Rauvolfia serpentina* (Indian snakeroot) with a long history of use to treat hypertension. Interest in this route to new drug development waned by the 1980s. Between 1990 and 2001, use of herbs for medicinal purposes climbed nationally from 4 percent to over one-fifth of the population with spending on herbal and botanical remedies nearing $4.2 billion annually by 2002. Sales for herbal products once limited to health food stores expanded to mainstream retail shops and pharmacies. While information on medicinal uses of herbal substances is widely available on Web sites, recent analysis found these often have few references to scientific literature, adverse effects, drug interactions, or safety information.

Increased popularity influenced national regulation resulting in establishment of the National Institutes of Health (NIH) Office of Alternative Medicine in 1992 and NIH Office of Dietary Supplements two years later to coordinate research on herbs and supplements. By 1998, the Office of Alternative Medicine became the National Center for Complementary and Alternative Medicine (NCCAM).

NCCAM classifies herbal uses for medicine as a complementary approach that encourages utilization of these methods for enhancing health in combination with conventional practices. The agency categorizes herbs as part of natural products versus mind and body practices for health. The center has released three strategic plans, with the last covering through 2015. They report nearly 40 percent of the nation spending just over $33 billion on various complementary and alternative medicines (CAMs) in 2007 in data from the National Center for Health Statistics (NCHS). NCCAM works with a national advisory council to identify knowledge gaps and points to emerging evidence from basic research and clinical trials beginning to reduce the paucity of scientific knowledge on these practices.

In 1990, herbs and similar nutritional substances were integrated into the term *dietary supplement* in the Nutritional Labeling and Education Act (NLEA) of 1990. New rules governing herbal medicine were also embodied in the Dietary Supplement Health and Education Act (DSHEA) enacted in 1994, as an amendment to the Federal Food, Drug, and Cosmetic (FD&C) Act that formally classified herbs and other botanicals as one of six types of dietary supplements. The legislation, originally sponsored by Senators Orrin Hatch (R-UT) and Bill Richardson (D-NM), indicated that dietary supplements must be labeled as such and not be represented as a conventional food. This classification impacted definitions and enforcement and did not set strict legislative standards for safety and effectiveness, distinguishing these products from more rigorous pharmaceutical regulations. Producers are prohibited from making claims that the product can cure, mitigate, or treat a disease and only claims that the product addresses deficiencies in nutrients, supports health, or is linked to bodily function are permitted.

Manufacturers must be able to substantiate that statements about nutritional support are truthful and nonmisleading and to specify that these statements have not been evaluated by the U.S. Food and Drug Administration (FDA). Manufacturers are not required to conduct clinical studies to verify product safety with the burden of proof for safety resting with the government, primarily through postmarket surveillance. The law calls for the FDA to take action quickly against unsafe or adulterated supplements, defined as those that have an unreasonable risk of illness or injury. In addition, the legislation outlines a range of other specific labeling requirements.

Some indicate a need for additional regulation and enforcement, citing studies reporting contaminants of herbal products with heavy metals, over-the-counter drugs, or other undisclosed prescriptions with potential for adverse interactions with other drugs. Use of St. John's wort for depression declined in the five years following 2002 after media reported research showing herb-drug interactions with antiretrovirals, birth control pills, and antidepressants. This resulted in calls for more rigorous adverse effect reporting, disclosure, and manufacturer monitoring. The FDA defines botanical drugs as products classified as drugs made from vegetable or plant materials, algae, or fungi, and some advocate that this categorization poses opportunities to enhance regulation and reduce consumer concern over herbal medicines. New guidelines for herbal mixtures were issued by the FDA in 2004 allowing approval if they can be shown to be safe and effective, and Veregen, a green tea extract produced by Medigene, was the first botanical drug approved under these rules. In spring 2013, the U.S. Pharmacopeial Convention, the independent nonprofit publishing the *United States Pharmacopeia*, published standards for substances in herbal medicines in an Herbal Medicines Compendium (HMC), allowing free public access to monographs designed to form voluntary guidelines for use by both regulators and herbal product manufacturers. These contain information including definitions of ingredients, attributes and analytical procedures, tests, and acceptance criteria.

Regulations governing herbal medicines sometimes vary according to substance and state. The popular plant aloe, for example, which is used in gels, creams, and juice for burns or as a laxative, was subject to increased restriction in 2002 when the FDA called for reformulation or removal of aloe latex as a juice from U.S. markets because of absence of safety data. American ginseng, another popular substance still being researched but often used as an aphrodisiac and for diabetes and energy, is regulated for export under the Convention on International Trade in Endangered Species of Wild Fauna and Flora in addition to being subject to a complex array of state laws governing harvesting, plant age, seasons, and planting on state lands.

Marijuana is another herbal product with a long history of official listing as a medicinal product commonly prescribed by doctors well into the 19th century. Medical uses include relief during chemotherapy, and for symptoms of acquired immunodeficiency syndrome (AIDS), epilepsy, and glaucoma. State prohibitions against use became popular during the 20-year period following 1919, following the initial lead of California. These developments led to action at the national level, with the Marihuana Tax Act (Pub. L. No. 75-238, ch. 553, 50 Stat. 551 [1937]) finally passed in 1937, prohibiting marijuana for medicinal use. In this period, the American Medical Association (AMA) indicated that marijuana had medical potential and should not be blocked by legislation. By 1970, however, the product became classified under the Controlled Substances Act as a Schedule I drug, which includes substances designated as extremely harmful to public health with no medicinal value.

California led the way again in 1996 as the first state to pass legislation allowing medical use of marijuana with Proposition 215, the Compassionate Use Act, allowing primary caregivers and patients with prescriptions to possess and cultivate marijuana. By 2014, 23 states across the country passed medical marijuana laws removing penalties for use with a doctor's permission, although a few of these still ban smoking. With state-level regulation changing rapidly, some unsuccessful efforts thus far have been made to push for federal legislation to remove marijuana from the Controlled Substances Act, and establish a process of federal permits and regulation by the FDA and the Bureau of Alcohol, Tobacco, Firearms and Explosives (ATF).

Traditional Medicine Regulation

These treatments also fall under the broad umbrella of substances under the purview of the U.S. National Center for Complementary and Integrative Health based in the NIH. This office serves as the primary agency to support research and advance the information and decision making based on these practices to enhance health and well-being.

In recent years, Native Americans and Asians are among the most frequent users of CAMs in the United States. Native Americans have a range of traditional medicinal practices including use of herbs and teas, ceremonies, ritual and blood purification, cupping and suction, prayers, chanting, and consultations with traditional healers. Native American healing practices are based on a holistic philosophy of illness linked to disharmony and interconnectedness with nature. The American Indian Policy Review Commission in 1976 explored issues surrounding traditional medicinal use in

Native American populations and challenges concerning integration with the Indian Health Service (IHS), the federal agency that serves as the health advocate for Native Americans. Training programs for traditional healers were established in the 1960s with federal funding including the Navajo School for Medicine Men funded by the National Institute of Mental Health (NIMH). Traditional medicine use by Native Americans was legalized in the American Indian Religious Freedom Act in 1978. In 1979, a Senate Select Committee on Indian Affairs hearing noted requests from Indian tribes asking that traditional medicine be recognized by the IHS as equal to Western medicine and for additional research on the issues. A 1992 policy statement from the agency recognized the value of traditional beliefs, ceremonies, and practices in healing body, mind, and spirit and indicated that the agency encourages a climate of respect and acceptance and policy to protect the rights of American Indian and Alaska Native people to their beliefs and health practices as defined by the tribe's or village's traditional culture.

With respect to Asian populations, while exact data on use of traditional Chinese medicine (TCM) in the United States are not available, the 2007 National Health Interview Survey found that 3.1 million used acupuncture at the time of the survey, up from 2.1 million users in 2001. TCM includes not only Chinese herbal medicine, but also *tai chi* and *qi gong*, acupuncture, *tui na*, Chinese therapeutic massage, and moxibustion (herbal burning applied to acupuncture points). TCM is a system viewing health as a balanced flow of life force energy *qi*, related to balance of opposing *yin* and *yang* (active and passive) forces. TCM remedies often involve complex mixtures of a variety of herbs. TCM substances under study used in cancer treatment and relief include turmeric, ginseng, astragalus,

TJ-41, PHY906, *huachansu*, and *kanglaite*. American ginseng, a substance associated with TCM, was actually originally a native product of the United States introduced into China in the Qing Dynasty. Ayurveda, another long-standing traditional medicinal system used in the United States with ancient roots in India, relies on a variety of herbs, minerals, and metals.

There have been varied approaches with respect to some of these long-standing traditional medicinal practices when it comes to FDA approval. In some cases, the agency has been supportive such as in the case of *Aristolochia*, which is a medicinal vine-like plant used in traditional Chinese and other medicinal systems going as far back as the Egyptians. In 2004, the FDA approved use of leeches as a medical device helpful with blood circulation and blocked veins. In other cases, concerns have been raised. An FDA advisory issued in 2001 cited concerns about cases of kidney damage and urothelial carcinoma from aristolochic acid.

Ephedra is another example of an herb used in TCM for thousands of years that was banned for sale in the United States by the FDA in 2004 after the substance gained national notoriety following linkages to numerous deaths of users including those of pitchers Darryl Kile and Steven Bechler. A substance containing ephedrine alkaloids was used throughout the 1980s and 1990s for weight loss and to enhance athletic performance. Public Citizen eventually filed a petition asking for the ban in 2001 following incidents of adverse health effects from the substance. In 2005, the FDA ban on supplements containing ephedra was struck down by a judge in Utah, who ruled that the burden lay on the FDA to establish the danger in using a supplement, rather than on the manufacturer to demonstrate that it was safe. In the summer of 2006, the Third Circuit Court of Appeals overturned this ruling and upheld the FDA ban, noting the preponderance of evidence used by the FDA in its analysis of risks and benefits.

Interest in acupuncture, another TCM practice, has grown in the United States since the 1970s, and this interest has been reflected in the scientific community. Although scientific studies are still limited, the numbers have increased, particularly after a 1997 NIH consensus conference on acupuncture and increase in federal funding. The practice of acupuncture is regulated at the state level with half of the licenses in the country issued in the state of California alone in 2010. There were just over 13,000 licenses issued by the state in 2009, which was over double the number of licensed practitioners available in 2000. Almost 20 percent of these licenses were in the San Francisco Bay Area. In the 1970s, the state dropped requirements for biomedical physician supervision and referral for acupuncturists. The National Certification Commission for Acupuncture and Oriental Medicine (NCCAOM) is a nonprofit organization created in 1982 that validates competency in the practice of acupuncture and Oriental medicine (AOM) through professional certification. NCCAOM certification or a passing score on the NCCAOM certification exam is required for licensure in 43 states and the District of Columbia. States also have varied eligibility requirements and procedures. Recent debates in the field have included discussions such as the appropriate role of Chinese-language knowledge for students and practitioners of acupuncture.

With respect to the Indian traditional system of Ayurveda, while no states currently license these practitioners, the National Ayurvedic Medical Association is the professional body for these practitioners in the United States that is currently working on building a credentialing and exam system. Over 30 programs across the United States were training practitioners in 2012. In 2007 and 2008, the FDA issued an import alert and notification to use caution with respect to some of these products, noting several studies indicating that a fifth of products made in the United States and India bought on the Internet and in samples from groceries in Boston contained mercury, lead, or arsenic.

A variety of herbs, roots, oils, and other substances have also been part of traditional or folk medicinal practices in other subgroups. For example, in African American communities, turpentine, soot, or cobwebs for cuts; pine for colds or rashes; Betsy bugs for earaches; cranberry for urinary tract infection; and ginger for nausea are some substances among many linked to traditional medicinal practices now more common among older versus younger subgroups. Others link use to distrust or lack of access to conventional pharmacists, doctors, and hospitals. The NCCAM is funding research to further the current nondefinitive evidence that cranberries may be useful in prevention, but not treatment, of infections in urinary tract disease. The FDA has approved camphor, another substance cited in African American tradition, for skin use when dealing with pain. Other policy initiatives recognizing traditional practices include those incorporated in the Native Hawaiian Health Care Improvement Act (NHHCIA), first enacted in 1988, that focused federal policy on efforts to improve the health of Native Hawai'ians. The legislation was recently reauthorized for 10 years under the Patient Protection and Affordable Care Act of 2010 (Pub. L. No. 111-148). This law originated from a report to the secretary of health and human services documenting serious problems with the health status of many Native Hawai'ian populations and noted that this was partially stemming from the lack of recognition of traditional concepts and practices of healing among Native Hawai'ian people. The law, as originally enacted, supported planning and development for a comprehensive health care system building on traditional healing practices including the development of Native Hawai'ian healing centers and working with traditional healers to improve health outcomes for Native Hawai'ian populations.

Pamela Ransom
Metropolitan College of New York

See Also: Aloe Vera (Herbal Medicine); Chamomile (Herbal Medicine); Ephedra (Herbal Medicine); Ginseng (Herbal Medicine); Medical Marijuana Legislation (U.S.); Native Americans/Alaska Natives; Native Hawai'ians/Pacific Islanders; Polypharmacy; Traditional Medicine: Native American Tribes.

Further Readings

Bent, Stephen. "Herbal Medicine in the United States: Review of Efficacy, Safety and Regulation." *Journal of General Internal Medicine*, v.23/6 (2007).

Jesson, Lucinda and Stacey Tovino. *Complementary and Alternative Medicine and the Law.* Durham, NC: Carolina Academic Press, 2010.

McKenzie, Brennen. "CAM and the Law Part 4: Regulation of Supplements and Homeopathic Remedies." *Science Based Medicine* (2010). http://www.sciencebasedmedicine.org/cam-and-the-law-part-4-regulation-of-supplements-and-homeopathic-remedies/ (Accessed May 23, 2015).

Mitchen, Stephanie. *African American Folk Healing.* New York: New York University Press, 2007.

National Center for Complementary and Alternative Medicine. "Traditional Chinese Medicine: An Introduction" (NCCAM Pub No. D428, 2013). http://nccam.nih.gov/health/whatiscam/chinesemed.htm (Accessed July 2013).

National Center for Complementary and Integrative Health. *Exploring the Science of Complementary and Alternative Medicine: NCCAM Third Strategic Plan 2011–2015.* Washington, DC: U.S. Department of Health and Human Services, National Institutes of Health, February 4, 2011.

Paroske, Marcus. "Overcoming Burden of Proof in Science Regulation: Ephedra and the FDA." *Rhetoric and Public Affairs*, v.15/3 (2012).

"S. 784 (103rd): Dietary Supplement Health and Education Act of 1994" (April 7, 1993). http://www.govtrack.us/congress/bills/103/s784 (Accessed May 23, 2015).

U.S. Food and Drug Administration. "Use Caution With Ayurvedic Products" (October 16, 2008). http://www.fda.gov/ForConsumers/ConsumerUpdates/ucm050798.htm (Accessed May 23, 2015).

U.S. Pharmacopeial Convention. "Herbal Medicines Compendium." http://hmc.usp.org (Accessed June 19, 2015).

U.S. Pharmacopeial Convention. "USP-NF." http://www.usp.org/usp-nf (Accessed June 19, 2015).

Van Ornum, Michael and Cheryl Weber. "Dietary Supplements: Applying the Knowledge (Pharmacology Update)." *Journal of Neuroscience Nursing*, v.34/3 (2002).

TRADITIONAL MEDICINE: AUSTRALIA (BUSH MEDICINE)

The traditional medicine of Australia is commonly referred to as bush medicine and is a unique form of traditional medicine that formed without influence from the other regions of the world, largely because of the geographical isolation of the land. Throughout history, the native people of Australia, Aboriginal people, encountered different health threats than their European, African, Asian, and American counterparts and developed medicinal beliefs and techniques to accommodate these needs. Isolated geographically, they were not exposed to the same infectious diseases that affected more densely populated areas. Instead, they were threatened by the natures of the land, snake bites, burns, and stingray stings. As a result, the majority of their medication used plants topically, applied directly to their wounds. When chronic diseases did appear, the

Aboriginal people believed it was because of supernatural causes and tried to remedy their ways and called in spiritual healers to help.

The culture of Aboriginal people did not embrace written communication, preferring instead to pass on information through song, dance, and artwork. The discontinuation of these practices, with the integration of Western culture, has led to many of the health beliefs and medicinal cures becoming a mystery today. In addition to this, Australian bush medicine was not uniform across the vast country but was as diverse as the landscape and communities that inhabited the large land. Nonetheless, it is possible to glean some information from the sources we have available today, some of which are cited in the Further Readings section of this article. Tea tree and eucalyptus oil are both native to Australia and have proved their worth to be included in modern medicine for their properties. Also widely used in Australian bush medicine was the Kakadu plum, emu bush leaves, witchetty grubs, snake vine, kangaroo apple, sandpaper fig, stinking passion flower, and goat's foot plant.

Traditional Australian Health Beliefs and Practices

In order to grasp the logic behind traditional Australian bush medicine, it is essential to establish an understanding of the health beliefs held by those who utilized the methods. These beliefs differed notably from those of the Western world, particularly by placing a larger emphasis on supernatural causes of ill health. This concept enabled them to answer questions about why particular people were affected by diseases at certain times in their lives, questions that remain unanswered in the Western concept of health and medicine.

The typical lifestyle of the Aboriginal people would be considered very healthy by modern standards. Their diet was composed primarily of fruits, vegetables, lean meat, nuts, and seeds with no refined sugar or alcohol. Coupled with regular exercise from their hunter-gatherer lifestyle and geographical isolation from many deadly infectious diseases, this left them with relatively fewer health problems than other populations. It was the harsh land of Australia occupied by natural dangers that posed the greatest threat to the health of the Aboriginal people. The bites and stings of animals such as snakes, spiders, and sea creatures required their attention, and burns from fires in the communities were also common.

The bush medicine remedies were widely known throughout the Aboriginal population, and everyone in the communities knew how to treat common ailments with the plants that grew in the land they inhabited. It was common knowledge, passed down from generation to generation to all people, not only those who were doctors or healers.

It was believed that supernatural forces were the cause of disease and sudden death that appeared in strong people, people not considered young or elderly. There were certain actions and objects that were considered to be positive or negative to evade supernatural ill health, and if struck with chronic disease, the people blamed this and tried to remedy the cause. It is likely that many of these practices to evade supernatural forces did in fact help to avoid diseases as they promoted what is now recognized as a healthier lifestyle. When supernatural ill health did occur, the Aboriginal people sought the help of healers. The healers were usually people external to the affected community and used various methods to banish the evil spirits within the affected person, such as massage, breathing, and singing. This varied among different communities in Australia, but the core idea was to provide a safe environment for the affected person to heal.

Another point of difference in traditional Australian health beliefs is the concept that optimal health is cold, rather than the "not-too-hot and not-too-cold" concept that was widely used in other areas of the world. A simple example of this concept is thirst, which is regarded as hot and, therefore, not a healthy condition. This can be improved by drinking water, which has cooling properties and leads to improving and healing the condition.

When the European population began to settle in Australia late in the 18th century, dramatic changes in the health and remedies of Australian bush medicine began to surface. The greatest impact was seen in the diseases that the European population brought with them for which the Aboriginal population had no immunity, as they had not previously been exposed to such infections. This had a devastating effect on the Aboriginal communities who struggled to understand what supernatural forces were causing this ill health that they had no medicinal cures for. Their healers were called in but had an insignificant effect on the infectious diseases coming from Europe, and a great proportion of the population suffered with their lives.

Another effect of the European settlement in Australia was the relative modernization of traditional Australian bush medicine. As an example, the Aboriginal communities did not previously have access to metal or glass pots and heated the water needed for medicinal concoctions in pits in the ground with hot stones. The European settlers introduced the billycan, a simple metal pot, to the Aboriginal population, and it revolutionized the preparation of medicines, allowing the communities to heat the water and make teas and other concoctions with greater precision, ease, and hygiene.

The introduction of Western medicine also appeared with the integration of Western culture as the Europeans settled in Australia. While traditional bush medicine is still used by some Aboriginal communities in central Australia, the majority of the population has transitioned to the use of Western medication. Interestingly, this is not because of a lack of faith in the bush medicine or a belief that Western medication is superior, but rather because the ease of Western medication in availability and use is preferred. It is largely this phenomenon that continues to cause a significant part of the pharmacological information, which was traditionally passed down from generation to generation, to become lost.

Australian Bush Medicine

Although the central beliefs and practices of traditional Australian bush medicine do not align well with the modern concept of medicine, where science rather than supernatural forces forms the basis of practice, there are several aspects where the traditional practices offer benefits to the health of the current worldwide population. Given the diversity of the countryside that is home to many native Australian plants, there are some useful medicinal compounds that grow exclusively in Australia.

An example of this is eucalyptus oil, coming from a tree that can only be found in Australia. The leaves of the tree were traditionally brewed in water to make a tea that eased pain and fever. Eucalyptus oil has also proved useful to modern society and is commonly used to ease symptoms of respiratory tract infections and is included in several mouthwashes, lozenges, and cough suppressants used in the current day.

Tea tree oil (*Melaleuca alternifolia*) was used on the east coast of Australia for a wide range of ailments. The oil, taken from the crushed bark of the tree, has antiseptic properties that help to disinfect wounds, and it was also brewed to make a tea to treat sore throat and respiratory infections. When the Western world discovered tea tree oil in the early 20th century, it proved to be stronger than the alternative antiseptics available, and it began to be used for a wide range of indications including fungal infections and acne.

Northwestern Australia is home to the Kakadu plum (*Terminalia ferdinandiana*), currently known to be the richest natural source of vitamin C in the world. It formed a major source of nutrients for the tribes living in that area, and it can be predicted that those communities suffered from fewer colds and recovered more quickly when affected because of their high intake of vitamin C.

Emu bush leaves (*Eremophila neglecta*) were traditionally crushed and used by some northern Aboriginal tribes to wash sores and cuts topically. The research on this method has been scarce up until recently, when some studies, such as those cited by Rebecca Thyer, showed efficacy similar to antibiotics; however, there is also some concern of toxicity to mammalian cells. There is a need for further research into the safety and efficacy of emu bush leaves before we can trust them to work for common ailments in modern medicine.

In central Australia, the Aboriginal people often crushed witchetty grubs (*Endoxyla leucomochla*) to make a paste that was used to soothe burns and promote healing. They also treated inflammation such as rheumatoid arthritis, headaches, and open wounds with snake vine (*Tinospora smilacina*). Unfortunately, the efficacy of these practices in comparison to Western alternatives has not been studied in sufficient well-designed trials to recommend or discourage their use at the current point in time.

Kangaroo apple (*Solanum laciniatum* and *Solanum aviculare*) was traditionally used to reduce inflammation on swollen joints. The fruit is found on native Australian shrubs and contains the solasodine steroid that has been shown to have an effect on the production of cortisone. This supports the idea that using kangaroo apple helps to reduce inflammation, and the bush has now been imported to other parts of the world to cultivate its properties on a wider scale.

Along the northern coasts of Australia, the communities inhabiting the land were known to use sandpaper fig (*Ficus opposita*) and stinking passion flower (*Passiflora foetida*) to relieve itching from conditions such as scabies and tinea. The fig leaves were crushed and soaked in water, then rubbed onto the itch, followed by applying the pulp of the passion fruit to the area. The efficacy of this practice, like many of the traditional Australian bush medicines, has not been established.

Australian communities, unlike many other populations of the world, needed to find remedies for stingray and stonefish stings, which were a relatively common occurrence for those that lived near the sea. For this, they crushed and heated the leaves of goat's foot (*Ipomoea pes-caprae*), a plant that grows in the north and along the east coast of Australia, and applied it to the area. It is noted for its antihistamine properties, which explains its efficacy in treating stings and skin infections.

It is evident that many of the traditional bush medicines of Australia have been lost with the integration of Western culture into the Aboriginal communities. The information we currently have available is only a minute fraction of the knowledge that was once held by the common population of the inhabitants of Australia. Importantly, the Aboriginal population lived a healthy lifestyle to promote good health, used bush medicine from the available plants that grew in their area to heal ailments, and resorted to supernatural remedies for unknown causes of disease.

Yolanda Smith
University of South Australia
MedicineHow Founder

See Also: Australia; Prescription Drug Approval Process: Australia; Traditional and Herbal Medicines, Regulation: Australia and New Zealand.

Further Readings

Anakok, F., C. Ndi, M. Barton, H. Griesser, and S. Semple. "Antibacterial Spectrum and Cytotoxic Activities of Serrulatane Compounds From the Australian Medicinal Plant *Eremophila neglecta.*" *Journal of Applied Microbiology,* v.112 (2012).

Clarke, Phillip. "Aboriginal Healing Practices and Australian Bush Medicine." *Journal of the Anthropological Society of South Australia,* v.33 (2008).

Maher, Patrick. "A Review of 'Traditional' Aboriginal Health Beliefs." *Australian Journal of Rural Health,* v.7/4 (1999).

O'Dea, Kerin, P. A. Jewel, A. Whiten, A. Altmann, Simon Strickland, and Olav Oftedal. "Traditional Diet and Food Preferences of Australia Aboriginal Hunter-Gatherers and Discussion." *Philosophical Transactions B,* v.334 (1991).

Stack, Ella. "Aboriginal Pharmacopeia." *Northern Territory Library Service.* Darwin, 1989.

Thyer, Rebecca. "Bush Medicine for a Germ-Killing, Heart-Saving Gargle." *Venture Magazine* (October 2009). http://www.swinburne.edu.au/magazine/7/133/bush-medicine-for-a-germ-killing-heart-saving-gargle/ (Accessed June 19, 2015).

TRADITIONAL MEDICINE: CENTRAL AMERICA

Traditional medicine includes a wide range of health and medicinal practices commonly used prior to the rise of modern Western medication. These methods vary considerably from those used in current times, as did the beliefs of those who practiced them. An appreciation of the health needs of the particular population, as well as their ideals and the available resources, is essential in understanding the traditional medicine of an area. For the purposes of this entry, Central America consists of Belize, Costa Rica, El Salvador, Guatemala, Honduras, Nicaragua, and Panama. Although this area is relatively confined, the populations that inhabited this land area were diverse and lived in small communities with unique traditions. As a result, the health beliefs and treatment of diseases were not always equal, and many differences between tribes were evident.

The indigenous population of Central America placed a strong emphasis on the spiritual world and believed that spiritual imbalances could affect the health of individuals and their communities. This resulted in specific traditional treatments involving shamans, experts of the spiritual realm, in banishing the evil spirits and resetting the balance. In addition to this, plant compounds were also used to heal some ailments, particularly those of a physical nature. The unique landscape in Central America, with rich coastal areas and tropical climate, provided the indigenous people with unique health threats and remedies. Some of the most common medicinal compounds used in traditional medicine were *Ilex vomitoria*, cayenne pepper, papaya, St. John's wort, *Ficis insipida*, and *Biza orellana*, all of which will be discussed in further detail.

Traditional Central American Health Beliefs

Like many traditional health beliefs around the world, the indigenous people of Central America placed a strong emphasis on the spiritual realm in regard to their health. It was believed that for optimal health, their body and soul should exist in harmony, and certain actions and experiences could upset this harmony and cause ill health. An example of this is a shock or a fright that affected someone greatly, which could have resulted in imbalance and ill health. Additionally, venturing to dangerous lands without the proper knowledge and protection was seen as an activity that could upset the harmony between body and soul. It should be noted that many of these beliefs were based on common lifestyle choices that promoted good health and hence were probably effective in reducing the incidence of ill health and disease.

The spiritual health of an individual was not considered to be an isolated case, but was instead expected to affect the health of those surrounding the individual including the individual's family and community. As a result, treatments for sick individuals also often included those close to them, and the shamans used broad medicinal techniques for everyone involved in the illness. Once again, this was in fact likely beneficial to the health of the tribe on the whole, given the nature of many infectious diseases. As an example, a respiratory tract infection in an individual could easily be passed on to the people surrounding them, as the infection is known to be contagious. It was hence good practice for the shamans to include the community in the treatment and likely benefited their health as a whole entity.

When considering the health and beliefs of the indigenous population of Central America, it is essential to also mention their geographical location and how this may have affected their health and requirements from the traditional medicine. Notably, the location has a tropical climate, which led to an increased incidence of infections and parasites. In addition to this, there is a high proportion of coastal areas and tropical jungle, which offer unique threats to the health of the inhabitants of the area. These same land formations also provided the native people with the rich plant sources needed to help heal common ailments and became an essential part of the traditional medicine.

With respect to the healing powers of plants, the native Central American people believed some plants had "hot" properties, while other plants were seen as "cold." These types of plants were then used to reset the right balance in people from conditions that were regarded as hot and cold. To illustrate this point, a hot illness such as inflammation was treated with plants known to have cold properties and the opposite was true for cold diseases. The balance and harmony between the body, soul, and environment had significant importance in the traditional health beliefs of Central America and can clearly be seen when examining their treatment methods and ideology.

When the European population came to inhabit Central America, the effect on the indigenous population was devastating. Many of the coastal populations in particular dropped in number dramatically as the Europeans arrived by way of sea, bringing with them foreign diseases and infections for which the natives had not developed natural antibody protection. The traditional medicine they had available was insufficient to treat these and the practitioners were inexperienced with treating infections of that nature. With time, the two communities began to integrate together and cities inhabited with both populations grew. This led to a decrease in the use of traditional medicine because of the ease and well-researched efficacy of Western medicine, although some areas of Central America still rely primarily on traditional medicinal techniques even today. However, it is undeniable that much of the traditional medicine information has been lost and the information we have today on the subject is only a fraction of what was once well known and used by the indigenous population of Central America.

Pharmacology of Traditional Central American Medicine

A type of tea brewed from the roasted leaves and stems of ilex vomitoria, commonly known as Yaupon Holly, is known today as Black Drink and was common in the traditional medicine of Central America. Research supports the pharmacological use of Black Drink and it has been shown to have emetic properties, which are useful when an individual has need to induce vomiting to expel ingested poisons. Additionally, Black Drink has a therapeutically relevant concentration of iron at 2.5 percent, suggesting the efficacy of its use in the treatment of iron deficiency. The indigenous populations of Panama were known to use Black Drink as a medicinal remedy for these indications and its use continues today by some populations. The emetic properties of Black Drink pose the greatest adverse effect of the compound when used in the treatment of iron deficiency.

Cayenne pepper (*Capsicum frutescens*) is native to Central America and has long been used in the traditional medicine of the region to treat a wide range of ailments. It was used to help with blood circulation, sore throat, colic, and gastrointestinal problems such as excessive wind. For each of these it was ingested as a ground powder, although cayenne pepper was also applied topically in some populations to relieve the pain associated with arthritis. This has since been studied by Western medical research and seems to be pharmacologically effective due to the effect the pepper has on the peripheral nerves, as they carry messages of irritation from the pepper rather than the arthritic pain. It has also gained some

support for use in cardiovascular disease and poses a possibility for treatment also in Western medication.

Papaya is a fruit that grows commonly throughout Central America and was widely used by the indigenous populations that inhabited the land. The fermented fruit was applied directly to external wounds and the seeds were used to eradicate parasitic infections. In addition, there have been claims of papaya being used to treat pain from arthritis, gastrointestinal problems including stomach ulcers, and as an anti-inflammatory for bites and stings. The current evidence to support the use of papaya in modern medicine is lacking; however, fermented papaya for wound healing is widely used in the society of today.

St. John's wort (*Hypericum perforatum*) is not unique to Central America and has been used in traditional medicine throughout many regions of the world, but it was of great importance for the Central American indigenous population. Its pharmacological action is due to the chemical substances hyperforin and hypericin found in the plant, which act on receptors of the central nervous system and have a marked effect on an individual's mood and behavior. It was traditionally used for a wide range of indications including depression, viral infections, and menopause, in addition to aiding wound healing when applied topically to the affected area. Modern Western medication has researched the effects of St. John's wort, and it has become a popular medication worldwide to treat mental health issues, particularly depression. As it is available without a prescription, many people opt to try St. John's wort before resorting to prescription antidepressants; however, this can lead to some complications because of certain drug interactions. As it is extensively metabolized by CYP P450 enzymes, it can have a dramatic effect on the metabolism of the many other drugs metabolized by the same enzymes, including many common prescription antibiotics.

Ficus insipida is a tropical fig tree found throughout the Central America, and the sap from the plant provides the indigenous population of the region a powerful medicinal compound for its body-cleansing properties. In traditional medicine, shamans often used the sap of *ficus insipida* to cleanse the bodies of people suffering from infections and parasites. The highly concentrated sap can be dangerous if it comes into direct contact with skin, so it must be diluted several times before being used to treat and cleanse individuals. Some tribes also used *ficus insipida* to enhance memory and mental alertness. The pharmacological activity and efficacy of the plant has not been studied extensively by modern medical research methods and as a result, the use of the plant in modern society is not widespread.

Achiote (*Bixa orellana*) is a small shrub native to the tropical regions of Central America that yields a strong colored flower that was used to create body paint by the natives in addition to use in the traditional medicine of the area for a selected range of health benefits. These include the treatment of tonsillitis, headaches, leprosy, and common bacterial and fungal infections with varying efficacy. The compound that is responsible for the pharmacological effect of *Bixa orellana* is the carotenoids, which have displayed a moderate antifungal effect. Modern medical researchers have explored the efficacy of *Bixa orellana* in fighting infection and have found that the funus *C. albicans* and *T. mentagrophites*, as well as the bacteria *E. coli*, *S. aureus*, and *P. aeruginosa*, are sensitive to the properties of the plant. This leads to support the use of the compound in infections such as pharyngitis, gingivitis, bronchitis, and infected open wounds and cuts.

The herbal remedies used in Central American traditional medicine are certainly not limited to those listed and discussed here, as the range used was too diverse and lacks modern research to support their use. However, a brief overview has been provided, and then health needs and beliefs that led to the use of these remedies have been discussed.

Yolanda Smith
University of South Australia
MedicineHow Founder

See Also: Traditional Medicine: South America.

Further Readings

Chang, Joseph. "Medicinal Herbs: Drugs or Dietary Supplements?" *Journal of Biochemical Pharmacology*, v.59 (2000).

Dooley, Cassandra. "The Ethnomedical Use of Black Drink to Treat Iron Deficiency Anemia in Bastimentos, Panama." MS Thesis, University of Georgia (2001).

Hansson, Anders. "Reevaluation of Risks With the Use of Ficus Insipida Latex as a Traditional Anthelmintic Remedy in the Amazon." *Journal of Ethnopharmacology*, v.98/3 (2005).

Montenegro, Raul and Carolyn Stephens. "Indigenous Health in Latin America and the Caribbean." *The Lancet*, v.367 (2006).

Raga, Dennis. "A Bioactive Sesquiterpene From Bixa Orellana." *Journal of Natural Medicines*, v.65/1 (2010).

Sandhu, Davinder and Michael Heinrich. "The Use of Health Foods, Spices and Other Botanicals in the Sikh Community in London." *Phytotherapy Research*, v.19 (2005).

World Health Organization. "WHO Traditional Medicine Strategy 2002–2005." Geneva: World Health Organization, 2002.

TRADITIONAL MEDICINE: CHINA

Traditional Chinese medicine (TCM) is a unique and complex medical practice that is deeply based in Chinese philosophy. Dating back at least 23 centuries, TCM is based on philosophies that predate modern orthodox medicine. According to Chinese philosophy, a person is healthy when there is balance between his or her yin and yang and becomes ill when this balance is disturbed; thus the aim of TCM is to maintain and restore balance. This can be achieved through a variety of practices such as Chinese herbal medicine, acupuncture, tai chi, moxibustion, and acupressure. The effectiveness and safety of TCM practices are being scrutinized more heavily because of the rising popularity of TCM in the West; however, as summarized by the National Center for Complementary and Integrative Health, very few reliable scholarly studies have been conducted to help address this issue.

It is important to understand the underlying concepts of TCM as they do not necessarily follow the same theories found in orthodox medicine. Yin and yang, while opposite forces in nature (such as night and day, hot and cold), work together to create balance in the universe but also in all living things within it; therefore, disease results from an imbalance of these two forces. Qi (pronounced "chi") is the life force that flows through all living things. According to TCM, this energy flows through 12 defined paths in our bodies called meridians. When the flow of qi energy is disturbed, this unbalance affects specific organs within our bodies and thus disrupts the balance between yin and yang. In acupuncture, needles are placed into specific parts of the body based on these meridians. This stimulates and adjusts the flow of qi throughout the body with the ultimate goal to rebalance the body's yin and yang. Acupressure functions in the same manner; however, massaging is used in lieu of needles. Moxibustion involves burning incense at acupuncture points, either directly on the skin or combined with acupuncture. These meridians are also tied to *Zang-fu* or the Five Elements (wood, fire, earth, metal, and water). This theory relates these elements to everyday living things and was developed long before anybody mapped out the anatomy of the human body, so they are tied more to the body's function than to its actual parts. The heart, for example, is tied to fire while the kidney and bladder are tied to water. This ancient Chinese philosophy is used to explain a wide array of natural phenomena in addition to interaction between internal organs.

Chinese herbal medicine, or Chinese herbal therapy, makes medicine from herbal formulas to strengthen the body's function and restore balance. *Herbal* can be a misleading term because animals and minerals are used in addition to plant material (although it does make up the majority). The Chinese *Materia Medica*, a famous reference book for TCM practitioners, describes these substances. These medicines are rather complicated and have a mixture that contains anywhere from 3 to 30 ingredients, and are often consumed orally (as a solution made from boiling the ingredients) or used externally, for instance as a cream or lotion. Every herb has distinct properties, and it is the TCM practitioner's responsibility to use the herbs to their fullest healing potential by combining them to readjust the body's energy. Thus there is a high importance to the relationship of the herbs and their function in the body.

Understanding herbal medicine can be difficult as it is very complicated and detailed. All herbs have specific tastes, thermal properties, channel affiliations, and therapeutic effects that determine their healing ability (such as which specific organ they help). Herbs can taste acrid, sweet, sour, bitter, salty, bland, and astringent. Herbs can have more than one taste as well, and if they lack a taste, they are considered bland. Each taste has a specific property that causes a reaction in the body. For example, pungent herbs are considered to have moving, dispersing properties that can dispel excess heat from the lungs and stomach; however, much like our bodies have a hot/cool balance to them, so do herbs. The thermal property includes cold, cool, neutral, warm, and hot herbs that are used to reestablish your body's balance (cool herbs are used to treat warm conditions, hot used to treat cold, etc.). The directional property is closely associated with taste and temperature, but it ultimately breaks down into upward (i.e., coughing), downward (dysentery), inward (pneumonia), and outward (night sweats). Warm, pungent herbs tend to move upward and outward while cold, bitter herbs tend to move downward, for example. Flowers that tend to be light carry upward-moving qi energy while roots move downward. The channels the qi flows through are referred to as meridians, which the medicine can affect in a direct, indirect, or specific way.

TCM is fully integrated into the health care system of China and is regulated by the Chinese government. It is used in parallel with current orthodox medicine, and estimates put TCM use at about 30 to 50 percent of China's medication consumption. Hospitals in China have a TCM department within them, and they have access to both types of care. Some people are diagnosed using Western medicine but then opt for TCM treatment while others prefer TCM for chronic conditions and Western medicine for acute. There have been studies that reflect the latter example in Western practice where patients use orthodox medicine to treat advanced cancer and use TCM to improve their quality of life (nausea from treatment). However, as TCM becomes more popular outside of China, many people are now starting to question the safety of these practices.

Safety

Many people express concerns about the safety of Chinese herbal medicine. The sources of toxicity in Chinese herbs are varied. Some herbs are directly toxic; however, herbs are never used in complete isolation but rather are used in an aqueous solution with up to 30 other materials. So while an herb by itself may be toxic, steps are taken to reduce the level of toxicity. Basic processing usually includes washing the herb and removing unnecessary plant material that may be the source of the toxicity. They are also fried, boiled, or steamed to modify their therapeutic effects (including to detoxify). The chemical makeup of herbs can also vary based on the geographical location, genotype, growth conditions, harvest time, use of herbicides/pesticides, and storage conditions, and other factors such as dosage, extended use, herbal combinations, and mistaking one herb for another can also lead to unexpected side effects. One of the most discussed cases in the literature involves use of the plant *Aristolochia* as a slimming aid: In Belgium, over 100 patients suffered kidney damage after taking this drug. *Aristolochia* and aristolochic acid are known to be potent carcinogens. Herbs with toxic properties are acknowledged in TCM texts. Traditionally, they are ranged as superior, average, and inferior herbs; superior herbs rank as least toxic, and inferior herbs have great toxic potential. Some toxic herbs can be made safe for consumption if processed, formulated, and dosed correctly. In China, most toxicity reports stem from misuse or incorrect use, and herbal medicine is assumed to be relatively safe. It is important to note that reports of adverse effects from TCM also stem from over-the-counter (OTC) medications and dietary supplements. The U.S. Food and Drug Administration (FDA) does not regulate dietary supplements as rigorously as OTC drugs.

The naming of Chinese herbs can further reflect the intricacy of TCM, as there are many aspects of the plant that influence its name, including shape, color, parts of the plant (such as root, branches, or fruit), the geographic region where it grew, and the age of the plant.

When administered by a professional, TCM is safe to practice; however, there is a gap in knowledge between the East and the West. Most of the discrepancy can be traced back to using adulterated or fake ingredients. This is especially evident when looking at OTC herbal supplements. Other factors are unfavorable storage, chemical treatment, and incorporation of Western orthodox medicine. The culture surrounding orthodox medicine is much different from that of TCM, which can make them difficult to compare and understand fully.

The language barrier also can limit the selection of scholarly literature on TCM that is available; however, studies on TCM have often proved to be inadequate, which is a current major obstacle in understanding the safety and effectiveness of TCM. The U.S. National Center for Complementary and Integrative Health (NCCIH), part of the National Institutes of Health, published a summary on its Web page concluding that most systematic reviews of TCM were focused on acupuncture and herbal medicine, and that most were unable to reach conclusions concerning the effectiveness of TCM treatment due to the lack of high-quality studies addressing this issue. Common problems found in Chinese studies include the lack of details concerning how the sample size was determined, the involvement of funders and their influence, and not registering their randomized clinical trials to ensure proper protocol in the study as set forth by the World Health Organization (WHO). Tai chi is generally regarded by the NCCIH as a safe practice. While the effectiveness of acupuncture is not fully understood, it is generally considered safe within the FDA guidelines if performed by a professional. Complications from moxibustion include allergic reactions, burns, and infections, but according to the NCCIH it is not clear how frequently these problems occur.

Some safety studies also look at the herbs in isolation, either in vitro (test tube) or in vivo (living subject) studies, which may not translate perfectly to the herb's effectiveness in practice. Herbal extracts are considered biomedicine in China and are not part of Chinese herbal medicine. TCM requires highly individualized treatment based on the diagnosis of the individual patient, causing there to be many different types of treatment. There have been steps toward establishing more reliable evidence-based medicine practices in China to help bridge this gap in knowledge. Most studies focus on Chinese herbal medicine and acupuncture.

Daniel Lewandowski
D'Youville College

See Also: Ayurvedic Medicine; Clinical Trials; History of Pharmacology: Ancient China; *Kampo* (Traditional Japanese Medicine); *Materia Medica*; Traditional and Herbal Medicines, Regulation: South Asia; Traditional and Herbal Medicines, Regulation: United States.

Further Readings

Chen, John K., Tina T. Chen, and Laraine Crampton. *Chinese Medical Herbology and Pharmacology* (Vol. 369). City of Industry, CA: Art of Medicine Press, 2004.

National Center for Complementary and Integrative Health. "Traditional Chinese Medicine: An Introduction." https://nccih.nih.gov/health/whatiscam/chinesemed.htm (Accessed June 19, 2015).

Shaw, Debbie. "Toxicological Risks of Chinese Herbs." *Planta Medica*, v.76/17 (2010).

Xu, Jonathan S. S. and Daniel Y. T. Yang. "Traditional Chinese Medicine in the Chinese Health Care System." *Health Policy*, v.90/2 (2009).

TRADITIONAL MEDICINE: NATIVE AMERICAN TRIBES

Traditional medicine (TM) is a term used by the World Health Organization (WHO) and others to cover the work of healers accessing a cultural repertoire of beliefs and practices about illness. In many locations, including the United States, curers are members of indigenous groups, although most developed nations also have sizable immigrant populations, many of whom follow customary health precepts to varying degrees.

While American Indians and Alaska Natives have different cultures, languages, and histories, there are some commonalities in health practices. Typically, traditional healers focus on the emotional, social, and spiritual well-being of individuals, as well as physical symptoms, which differs from Western medicine, in which doctors deal primarily with physical health and psychiatrists or psychologists cover mental illness. Given curers' holistic conceptualizations of health to include more than physiology, Native American healers focus on relationships among people, and to the environment, and may include the entire extended family or social group in treatment sessions, in contrast to more mainstream American medical practice, which focuses on the individual and typically isolates people from others for treatment. In a similar manner to Western medicine, TM may support the use of products to improve health, such as herb-infused beverages, or actions to treat illness, such as smudging people with smoke, or chanting. While Western medicine may be provided to people relatively quickly in terms of contact hours, in contrast, TM is time intensive, often requiring lengthy sessions with a curer, which may be challenging to schedule and fund, depending on the desired compensation for services.

In the past, the term *TM* was often used disparagingly in North America and other developed nations to indicate a lower level of treatment efficacy than that provided by Western medically trained doctors in first world hospitals. However, the expansion of the field of complementary or alternative medicine

(CAM), recognized by the WHO and also by American and Canadian medical experts, has encouraged broader recognition of the value of TM for Native Americans. Complementary medicine involves individuals receiving treatment from aboriginal health providers in concert with Western medically trained doctors, while alternative medicine suggests that only traditional healers are providing treatment. In order to understand contemporary Native American TM, it is important to revisit some key historic events, which continue to resonate today for members of Native American tribes. While the past may not be important for understanding Western medicine, it is a part of the practice for indigenous medicine men and women.

History of Native Americans and Traditional Medicine

Native Americans practiced TM for centuries prior to European arrival in the New World. Little is known about the health beliefs of this time period, since the archaeological records are difficult to decipher, and oral histories lack the necessary time depth. In some cases, skeletal evidence shows head binding, trephination, tooth removal, and other practices resulting in bone alteration, but their cultural significance is challenging to uncover. Certainly, skeletal analyses have potential to provide more information, although contemporary American Indians and Alaska Natives may be loath to have researchers examining deceased ancestors, and they have the right under the Native American Graves Protection and Repatriation Act (NAGPRA), enacted in 1990, to decide on reburial of unearthed ancestral remains and associated burial goods, rather than scientific study. In contrast to the limited information from prehistoric times, more understanding of TM can be found in contact-period and later records, now valued by tribal groups seeking to reconstruct early practices. For example, early historic documents speak about Aleut skills in wound care, including cleaning and suturing of deep gashes with sinew thread and bone needles. This instance of medical expertise was appreciated by outsiders, but much traditional knowledge was devalued, and the contact period took an immense toll on Native Americans and their cultures.

With the arrival of Christopher Columbus in Central America in 1502, the first European diseases began their destructive paths across the Americas. Aboriginal peoples had no immunity to measles, smallpox, influenza, and other foreign ailments. As a result, the European exploration and settlement of the future United States was accompanied by tremendous Native American suffering and population decline, decimating vulnerable elders and their stores of cultural knowledge, including healing practices.

American Indians and Alaska Natives then suffered considerable disruption and loss of traditional homelands as the newly arrived colonists gained control of territory and other resources. In 1787, Article I of the U.S. Constitution (Section 8) gave Congress extensive powers over aboriginal people living in the nation. This self-proclaimed authority allowed the United States to negotiate with American Indians and Alaska Natives, although many decisions affecting Native Americans were concluded without aboriginal input or choice. Over the years, this constitutional power, combined with various legal codes and rulings, moved many indigenous peoples to reservations, typically resource-poor locations rejected by Euro-American settlers and, in many cases, not situated in traditional homelands, meaning that people were separated from important sacred sites and medically important flora or fauna.

In addition to the disruptions caused by forced resettlement, disease, and other depredations, American government policy lacked consistency, meaning that aboriginal communities were in a constant state of flux, and it was difficult for people to adapt to constantly changing conditions. Government actions wavered between paternalistic strategies often focused on assimilation, and plans supporting limited self-determination by aboriginal communities. There was little consistency, except a general trend toward loss of rights by Native Americans, interspersed with tremendous abuses and infamous events, such as the 1890 Wounded Knee Massacre, the Indian residential school scandals, and the 1973 Wounded Knee protests, naming just a few of the plentiful examples.

Typically, Native Americans found it difficult to challenge repressive government policies since the Bureau of Indian Affairs (BIA), founded in 1824, had few indigenous employees and was mainly overseen by non–Native Americans. The employment ratios are gradually improving, and appropriately so, given that the BIA is empowered to determine which tribes are federally recognized, controlling access to federal benefits, including health services. Medical decisions were taken over by the new Indian Health Service (IHS) in 1955, which has been chronically underfunded by Congress, creating difficulties in terms of access to basic Western medicine, let alone specialized TM.

Before turning to contemporary treatment and access, the matter of Native American religion and its links to TM should be covered. This is important since for many aboriginal people health practices fit with spiritual beliefs, and healing rites may meld with religious ceremonies. Several Native American religious practices conflicted with American laws, including the ritual use of eagle feathers and the ceremonial consumption of peyote cactus (*Lophophora williamsii*), which contains the hallucinogenic mescaline. The peyote sacrament is an essential part of Native American church rituals. This is a pan-Indian religion, currently practiced in the United States and Canada, primarily in the prairies. Peyote consumption is a thousand-years-old practice that can be archaeologically documented in the southwestern United States and Mexico. Despite the longevity of peyote-based traditions, practitioners found themselves in conflict with American drug laws, while Native American use of eagle feathers contravened eagle protection acts. After years of conflict, finally Congress approved the American Indian Religious Freedom Act (AIRFA) in 1978, which removes some of the legal barriers preventing aboriginal peoples from practicing religious ceremonies, a part of TM. Later agreements sorted out some of the practical barriers in accessing cactus and feathers.

Contemporary Native Americans and Traditional Medicine

As of 2014, according to the National Congress of American Indians, there were 566 federally recognized tribes in the United States, with approximately 1.9 million people listed in the tribal rolls. The tribes range in size from relatively small groups, such as the Louisiana Chitimacha, with an enrollment of approximately 1,300 people, to the sizable Navajo Nation, with more than 250,000 people inhabiting 27,000 square miles, straddling Utah, Arizona, and New Mexico.

While many Native Americans live on reservations, others are urban-based and may lack tribal connections, or federal recognition. There are many American Indians and Alaska Natives who for various reasons are not federally recognized. For example, the Tuscarora Nation of New York is state recognized, but not federally recognized, although other Tuscarora living in Ontario have Indian Status in Canada, the equivalent of federal recognition, and reside in the Six Nations of the Grand River First Nation. The process to achieve federal recognition in the United States is confusing and expensive, and requires lots of documentation, which is just not possible for all Native American groups to achieve.

For those who have achieved federal status, American Indian and Alaska Native reservations are often depressed economically, with substandard housing, located in regions with limited natural resources. Reservations may have schools on the reservation or nearby, but once young people wish to achieve higher education or find jobs, in most cases, they need to leave the reservation and deal with mainstream American society, typified by high levels of stereotyping and discrimination. This may explain why Native Americans typically are paid less for similar types of work than non–Native Americans. Approximately 50 percent of the Native American population under age 65 is considered low income, compared to 25 percent of White Americans in the same age-group.

Native American poverty may be an insurmountable barrier for American Indians and Alaska Natives wanting to get health insurance, and may mean that they only have access to IHS facilities, which may not provide the desired services in a timely manner, given their funding restrictions. A decade ago, per capita funding of IHS patients was approximately half that of Medicaid and a third that of Medicare, and this situation continued to deteriorate until 2010, with the passage of the Patient Protection and Affordable Care Act (ACA, or Obamacare). A major provision of this act for Native American health care was the permanent reauthorization of the IHS system, although it is still too early to really understand the full impacts of the legislation.

Difficulties in accessing medical services are hugely problematic for Native Americans, who suffer from higher rates of mortality and morbidity than the non–Native American population from numerous diseases, including diabetes, alcohol-induced events, pneumonia/influenza, and suicide. There have been attempts to incorporate TM in intervention programs directed toward these major debilitating illnesses, and also substance addiction, gambling, and family violence. In addition, in recent years, greater attention has been paid to documenting the active compounds of TM plants. For example, in the case of the James Bay Cree of Canada, a number of flora are effective in fighting diabetes, but this may only be effectively demonstrated in an evidence-based medical study with the help of university and government scientists.

One way in which Native American TM will be more fully incorporated in urban clinics and hospitals and other off-reservation locations is when more American Indians and Alaska Natives become trained as medical doctors, psychiatrists, and nurses. It is easier to promote change from within the system, and as of 2007, less than 1 percent of graduating medical doctors in the United States were Native American, less than their number in the general population. CAM is most effective when a practitioner is familiar with both health traditions, and is able to utilize knowledge in a truly bicultural manner. Practitioners trained in both traditions may also help alleviate some concerns about the future directions of TM, including ownership of ceremonies, intellectual property rights, cultural appropriation by non–Native Americans often for commercial purposes, altering rituals by shortening or simplifying them, and financial compensation for healers, among many other issues.

Susan J. Wurtzburg
University of Hawai'i at Manoa

See Also: Centers for Disease Control and Prevention; Controlled Substances Act; Drug Enforcement Administration (U.S.); Hallucinogens; Native Americans/Alaska Natives; Traditional and Herbal Medicines, Regulation: United States.

Further Readings

Jesson, Lucinda E. and Stacey A. Tovino. *Complementary and Alternative Medicine and the Law.* Durham, NC: Carolina Academic Press, 2010.

Moghaddam, Jacquelene F. and Sandra L. Momper. "Integrating Spiritual and Western Treatment Modalities in a Native American Substance User Center: Provider Perspectives." *Substance Use & Misuse*, v.46 (2011).

National Congress of American Indians. "Tribal Nations and the United States: An Introduction." http://www.ncai.org/tribalnations/introduction/Tribal_Nations_and_the_United_States_An_Introduction-web-.pdf (Accessed June 19, 2015).

Nebelkopf, Ethan and Mary Phillips, eds. *Healing and Mental Health for Native Americans: Speaking in Red.* Walnut Creek, CA: AltaMira Press, 2004.

Perez, Miguel A. and Raffy R. Luquis, eds. *Cultural Competence in Health Education and Health Promotion,* 2nd ed. San Francisco: Jossey-Bass, 2014.

Spector, Rachel E. *Cultural Diversity in Health and Illness,* 8th ed. Boston: Pearson, 2013.

Traditional Medicine: South Africa

The term *traditional medicine* in South Africa is commonly used to refer to a set of concepts, actions, and relationships that draw on precolonial medicinal ideas and practices to provide interpretations and responses in relation to experiences of illness in contemporary society. Traditional medicine takes a holistic approach to body and mind seen as indivisible from social and spiritual context; illness is subsumed under wider explanatory frameworks of other kinds of misfortune. Traditional medicine is based on the ontological premise that the ancestor spirits remain active in the lives of their descendants and are the ultimate sources of health and prosperity, as well as illness and misfortune. Ancestors are also held to be sources of inspiration for diagnosis and remedial treatment. Traditional medicine is furthermore intimately connected to notions of witchcraft—the alleged ability of persons to use substances and familiars to cause harm to others. While there is a wide social consensus on the ultimate sources of health and illness, only specialists are held to have access to knowledge of how the invisible powers, spirits, and witches interact in particular instances. With regard to ideas of disease causation, roles of healers, and treatment repertoires, there exist broad similarities across cultural groups in South Africa.

According to the World Health Organization (WHO) in a 2002 report, 80 percent of Africans have sought traditional medicine to meet their health care needs. In South Africa, the readiness to consult traditional medicine cuts across gender, age, educational background, and occupation. Traditional medicine includes home herbal remedies that are used to treat minor ailments such as digestive discomforts and fevers by laypeople, and can be bought on the market. But in cases when these conditions persevere, or in the instance of a difficult and chronic illness, specialists of traditional medicine are consulted. Traditional healers are known by the Bantu term *nganga,* or *isangoma* in Nguni languages (*sangoma* in wider parlance). It is the role of the healer to inquire into the symptoms of ill health indivisibly from the social circumstances surrounding the patient, and find their causes in the invisible realm. Healers claim to act as mediums of higher spiritual powers, most frequently their own ancestors or more

generalized ancestral powers that have chosen them for the healing profession.

Traditional medicine frequently involves divination. The need for divination derives from the perception that a particular ailment or misfortune is connected to witchcraft and ancestral agency, and healers are capable of conferring with spiritual entities, their own and their patients' ancestors, to determine the causes of ill being. Individuals, as well as kin groups, may become the subject of divination. Although nuanced in relation to gender, age, and socioeconomic status of the patient(s), the divination process is fairly standardized. It usually involves a type of divinatory apparatus, such as tablets thrown on the floor, through which the healer is expected to reveal not only the present condition of the patient, but also the past and future course. Divinations are highly performative occasions during which the healer demonstrates capability to commune with the spirits, indicating, at first vaguely, the nature of the patient's problems— physical, mental, social, and spiritual—as part of a single narrative. Patients' role is to show approval or disagreement with the healer's pronouncements, and an oracular verdict thus forms the result of dialogues at multiple levels between spirits and humans.

When affliction is identified as resulting from the maleficent activities of a witch, it is the most intimate relations among family members, lovers, coworkers, and friends, rarely those of complete strangers, that are scrutinized for locating the witch's identity. However, the destructive plots of a witch are held to be successful only because the individual or group has lost the ultimate sources of protection grounded in ancestors' benevolence. The state of spiritual vulnerability is ascribed to ancestors' dissatisfaction that they have been neglected by the living kin and is seen to be justified given that one can never do enough to appease the ancestors once and for all. Conversions to a variety of Christian churches that proscribe ancestral sacrifices are often identified by healers as causes of ancestors' anger. Since ancestors are open to human persuasion, during divination, the specific identity of the afflicting ancestors is determined in order that they may be explicitly addressed in further ritual action.

The ancestors are also held to cause misfortune directly in which case they insist that the afflicted individual undergo a ritual *ngoma* (after the Bantu root for "drum") during which the spirits are allowed to take possession of the body of the living descendant, turning the disposition of the person from illness and misfortune to health and well-being. *Ngoma* uses drumming, singing, and playing of rattles as a means of communication between humans and their ancestors, and may be a one-off undertaking, or a periodic participation in *ngoma* may be required by the ancestors. In the latter case, it is understood that the ancestors have given the individual a call to become a healer as a lifelong profession: *Ngoma* is the basis for recruitment of healers. The diviner specifies the appropriate diagnosis and course of action. Members of the ritual group include the afflicted, his or her family and friends, the initiating healer and his or her assistants, and members of the local community. If satisfied with the efforts of the living, the ancestors descend into the bodies of some of those present with the main attention being focused on the afflicted. Often, male spirits possess female mediums and vice versa. *Ngoma* is concluded with animal sacrifice with all the participants sharing the meat with the spirits. If successful, *ngoma* should ensure further health and well-being to the afflicted and his or her family, although in practice this is not always the case, and the need for more remedial action arises. If the afflicted is an adept whom the ancestors

called to become a healer, *ngoma* functions also as a graduation ceremony.

Remedial action following divination typically includes a regimen of medicines, *muti*, as well as a series of rituals to appease the ancestors. The administration of *muti* forms an integral part of traditional medicine in South Africa. The term *muti*, derived from the Bantu root –*ti* signifying "tree," is a semantically broad category including substances that have the power to transform persons, things, or situations in a restorative as well as in a harmful way. In healing, *muti* is used for the purposes of cleansing, protecting, and fortifying; in witchcraft, *muti* is deployed for the destructive ends of depletion and disempowerment. Even healing, however, may seek the aim of annihilation when ridding an afflicted person of the evil influence of witchcraft. Curative and destructive *muti* are not necessarily different substances, and what distinguishes each category is the intention and moral conditions of its use.

Muti is not restricted to indigenous herbal *materia medica* dominating the popular imagination of traditional medicine and includes animal parts, minerals, metallic salts, other substances such as salt or ocean water, and even pharmaceuticals and poisons. Magical and biochemically potent items are not usually distinguished in the deployment of *muti*. *Muti* is effective in treating a variety of disorders such as high blood pressure, diabetes, skin diseases, and sexual diseases; there are also *muti* that are claimed to ensure the attention of a lover, a work promotion, the passing of exams, and the protection of weapons, cars, and businesses from accidents. Also the colors of *muti* carry significance—black substances are associated with evil and as such are used for cleansing and fighting witchcraft; red items increase "hotness" and hasten recovery; whitish shades are seen to "bring light" and are valued for their healing properties.

Muti is administered in many different ways. Curative medicines are mixed with specified kinds of food or drink, rubbed into skin incisions, taken as enemas or baths, and inhaled under a blanket. If a person is suffering from a witchcraft attack on the household, specific *muti* is mixed with urine of the house owner and applied on walls of the homestead. To get rid of witchcraft, *muti* can be blown away from a person to rid him or her of evil influence or can be held in the hand and associated with incantations to return witchcraft to whoever sent it. All these uses of *muti* are secretive, done by the afflicted person(s) according to the instructions of the healer. Healers adjust the kind and dosage of *muti* to individual constitution. "Cleaning the blood" is seen as the primary treatment goal on which further remedies depend for their effectiveness. Healers are a competitive group who constantly innovate their repertoires, using new substances as *muti*, devising new rituals in which these may be used, and deploying established *muti* for new purposes. Witches, likewise, are alleged to be innovative agents: A new form of witchcraft is held to travel through voice on the mobile phone while the witch uses a special kind of *muti*.

However, the ultimate source of efficacy of *muti* in cure is seen to inhere in the establishment of proper relations of the person to his or her ancestor spirits who are divined as the cause of the particular condition. This relationship can be restored through the offering of snuff by the afflicted individual, and/or in more serious instances of affliction or when more members of kin are stricken by misfortune, it is necessary to organize a blood sacrifice (goat, cattle) during which people eat together the flesh of the slaughtered animals while the ancestors are invited to partake in the feast. These rituals are carried out openly, in a socially visible way. The power to transform a person's disposition from health to illness through *muti* is seen as indivisible from transforming his or her relationships with living and dead kin. The ritual of *ngoma,* described earlier, is a special type of ancestor atonement.

In South Africa, traditional healers have been outlawed for over a century under the Witchcraft Suppression Act (passed in 1895, last amended in 1970) although the legislation is currently under review. Traditional medicine still has an ambivalent legal status despite the contemporary South African government's support of traditional medical practices as part of its commitment to "African traditions." Traditional healers have been legally recognized in South Africa as "traditional health practitioners" under the Traditional Health Practitioners Act of 2007 (Act 22 of 2007). Many issues, however, continue to be unresolved such as the very definition of "traditional" healer given the fact that practitioners of traditional medicine, though drawing on centuries of transmitted knowledge, have also been highly innovative agents. It is also unclear how a body of traditional healers may be organized and governed given the fact that their appointment and status is related to communication with the ancestor spirits rather than to principles of bureaucratic authority of the modern state.

Furthermore, the South African Medicines and Medical Devices Regulatory Authority Act (Act 132 of 1998) has required regulation and registration of all medicines including "traditional medicines," which should be sold with disclosure of ingredients. This act has been largely ignored by healers and *muti* vendors who are reluctant to reveal the secrets allegedly passed to them by the ancestors. *Muti*, moreover, has become the subject of rigorous scientific testing. This approach is based on stressing the material and biochemical efficacy of *muti*, ignoring, or even degrading, its spiritual and moral aspects. There have also been attempts by the government to channel cooperation between traditional medicine and biomedicine although its success remains to be seen.

Vendula Rezacova
Charles University

See Also: *Egbogi* (Traditional Yoruba Medicine); Ethnobotany; *Muti* (Traditional Southern African Medicine); *Nganga* (Traditional African Healers); South Africa; Traditional and Herbal Medicines, Regulation: Africa.

Further Readings

Ashforth, Adam. *Witchcraft, Violence and Democracy in South Africa.* Chicago: University of Chicago Press, 2005.

Ngubane, Harriet. *Body and Mind in Zulu Medicine: An Ethnography of Health and Disease in Nyuswa-Zulu Thought and Practice (Studies in Anthropology).* London: Academic Press, 1977.

Van Dijk, Rijk, Ria Reis, and Marja Spierenburg, eds. *The Quest for Fruition Through Ngoma: The Political Aspects of Healing in Southern Africa.* Athens: Ohio University Press, 2000.

World Health Organization. *WHO Traditional Medicine Strategy 2002–2005.* Geneva: World Health Organization, 2002. http://whqlibdoc.who.int/hq/2002/WHO_EDM_TRM_2002.1.pdf

TRADITIONAL MEDICINE: SOUTH AMERICA

The term *traditional medicine* refers to medicinal practices prior to the advance of modern Western medication and includes a wide range of health practices. Various beliefs and approaches to health were prevalent around the world, and therapies from plant, animal, and mineral based sources were commonly used, in addition to spiritual therapies and physical techniques such as massage. The majority of these treatments and techniques have not been studied efficiently in order to compare their efficacy sufficiently with modern Western medication treatment equivalents. In many cases, their worth to modern society is unknown despite their widespread use in past years and previously believed efficacy.

South America is a vast area, and the landscape, flora, and fauna change dramatically between different localities. For the purposes of this article, South America includes the countries of Argentina, Bolivia, Chile, Colombia, Ecuador, French Guiana, Guyana, Paraguay, Peru, Suriname, Uruguay, and Venezuela. Naturally, the traditional medicine used among these South American countries varied wildly, as did the lifestyle and health beliefs. In addition, traditional medicinal plants are strongly tied to the land the people inhabited, and as the flora varies throughout these regions, the plants used to heal the ailments that the people faced also varied considerably.

The indigenous people of South America believed that the right balance was required to maintain optimal health, and they included both spiritual and physical healing methods to reset this balance. Shamans were called in to expel evil spirits and help an individual return from ill health, in addition to the use of several plant-based remedies. These remedies included cat's claw, coca, hot lips, papaya, St. John's wort, lemongrass, dragon's blood, and the San Pedro cactus, all of which will be discussed in further detail.

Traditional South American Health Beliefs

Although the specific health beliefs within South America varied widely, there are some parallels that were prominent throughout vast areas of the region. It was a common belief that ill health and sickness were caused by a lack of harmony between the body and the soul, particularly in relation to the surrounding community and environment. Certain behaviors and choices were associated with falling ill, such as having a fright or going on dangerous terrain, and the population was encouraged to avoid these activities. In addition to this, there was perceived to be a strong connection between the health of an individual and that of the household and community in which they resided. There was likely a large degree of truth to this belief, due to the infectious nature of many diseases that affect the entire community and not only the individual. As a result, when one fell ill it was common to call in a shaman, one who had inherited valuable knowledge of spirits and natural elemental energies, and they would help to reset the harmony imbalance and restore health to the individual and their community. Shamans used a wide range of techniques involving the use of some plants, such as the San Pedro cactus, as well as traditional spiritual practices.

The traditional medicine of South America was not, however, limited to spiritual treatments but also utilized the plant sources available in the locality. The use of these plants was also believed to bring about balance in the ill person once again. Some plants were known as "cold" and others as "hot," and these were used to treat conditions to reset the balance. For example, inflammation was regarded as a hot illness and was hence treated with cold plants, whereas malaria was seen as a cold disease and was treated with plants considered to be hot. Optimal health was seen as having balance and harmony between the body and soul, and the treatments used by the people that inhabited South America reflected this.

It should be noted that traditional health and medicine in South America transformed considerably upon the settlement of Europeans. The indigenous population suffered greatly after the introduction of many bacterial and viral diseases brought with the settlers from Europe, as they had not previously been exposed to these strains and had not developed antibodies to offer them protection. Another consequence was the gradual but general shift toward the use of modern Western medication and the loss of knowledge relating to the traditional medicine. Many indigenous people have since moved to the larger developed cities and have begun to rely entirely on Western medication; thus, the once important health beliefs and treatments are becoming lost. The extinction of some whole indigenous population groups has led to a complete loss of information on the health practices used by the people in that region, including medicinal plants and techniques. Despite this, the efficacy of the health practices once commonly used is not necessarily inferior to current techniques. Further study should be undertaken to assess the full benefits that traditional medicine can offer.

Pharmacology of Traditional South American Medicine

Although many aspects of the traditional medicine of South America relied on spiritual beliefs and resetting the balance back to ill individuals and their communities, the populations also made use of the local flora that grew in the area they inhabited. Due to the diverse nature of the vast land, each community used what was available in the near vicinity, not necessarily the general overview of remedies mentioned in this summary of the most common and effective traditional medicines.

Also known as cat's claw, *uncaria tomentosa* is a plant found commonly throughout Peru and was traditionally taken most commonly as a tea made by boiling the bark in water. It was used for various indications, including inflammation from arthritis, viral infections, depression, and gastrointestinal problems. It works to stimulate the immune system, which has a positive effect on the body's defense against infections. It has been noted that in high doses it can cause damage to the optic nerves and should hence be used in the known recommended doses. Western medical researchers have taken an interest in this plant for its possible anticancer properties, although the safety and efficacy of this has yet to be determined.

The coca plant (*erythoxylum coca*) is native to Bolivia and Peru and is a well-recognized stimulant with extensive research to support its claims of an effect on the central nervous system. In the current society, it is the key ingredient used to make cocaine and has gained a certain reputation as a result. However, the indigenous people of South America traditionally used the coca leaves to make tea and to cure common ailments such as stomachache, sore throat, and fatigue. It was also used by physical labor workers for a boost of energy when needed throughout the workday. The use of the coca plant in current Western society is limited, given its strong reputation as a recreational drug.

Hot lips (*cephaelis elata*), found in many parts throughout South America in the Amazon, has a variety of uses in traditional medicine. It has helped to manage chronic pain in osteoarthritis, in addition to treating both male and female infertility. To date, *cephaelis elata* has not been studied extensively by Western methods and is not commonly used in modern medicine.

In the northern regions of South America, the seeds of papaya were used to eradicate parasites, which commonly affected the native people of those regions. The fruit was also used in the healing of external wounds, a use which continues today also in modern Western medicine. Other medical uses of papaya include the treatment of gastrointestinal problems, arthritis, ulcers, and as an anti-inflammatory.

St. John's wort is a plant that many populations throughout the world discovered and used for its medicinal benefits. The indigenous people of South America were among those that used the plant as an aid for people suffering from mental health problems, particularly depression. It was also used to treat anxiety, ulcers, and physical injuries. St. John's wort is extensively metabolized by cytochrome P450 enzymes and as a result can have a marked effect on other medications used due to drug interactions. It is well recognized in modern Western medication for its antidepressive effects; however, it is essential that all users of the medication are aware of possible drug interactions and are aware of safe doses.

Lemongrass grows commonly in Peru and was used in traditional medicine to help with insomnia, administered as a tea. In addition to this, lemongrass was used on occasion for cardiovascular and gastrointestinal problems, as well as to reduce labor pains for women giving birth due to its soothing effects. Lemongrass is used for its soothing effects in tea and lozenges in modern medicine.

Dragon's blood is the name of the red sap that comes from the croton lechleri tree, commonly found in Peru. In traditional medicine, the sap was used for a wide range of indications, particularly as an antiviral against stomach and respiratory viruses, in addition to treatment of ulcers and hemorrhages. Currently, Western medical scientists are interested in dragon's blood due to the possibility of cancer treatment it presents. The sap of the *ficus insipida* tree was also very useful, particularly in the northern regions of South America. It was used to purify the body from toxins, including drugs, alcohol, and parasites in the intestines. It is essential to dilute the sap in order to use it safely, as it can pose serious adverse effects if used directly and can cause severe burning to the skin. *Ficus insipida* is not used commonly in modern Western medicine, perhaps due to the deterrent of the burning adverse effect.

The San Pedro cactus (*trichocereus pachanoi*), native to Peru, was believed to have a powerful spirit and was traditionally used to help calm nerves and to treat cardiovascular and joint problems, and was also seen to have a detoxifying effect. It was commonly used by the shaman to put sick individuals into a trance during the process of expelling the ill spirits believed to be residing in them. The properties of this plant have since been studied by Western medical researchers, and it has been found to contain mescaline, a hallucinogen that is likely behind the relaxant effects of the San Pedro cactus.

It is clear that the landscape of South America offered the indigenous people residing there rich sources of flora with useful medicinal properties, and they in turn established the experience and knowledge needed of the plants to make use of them. While many of the common medicinal practices and knowledge have been lost with the rise of Western medication, it is evident that some of these still have a place in practice today, which is shown in their continued use and research in the area.

Yolanda Smith
University of South Australia
MedicineHow Founder

See Also: Colombia; Traditional Medicine: Central America.

Further Readings

Borja, Ashley. "Medical Pluralism in Peru—Traditional Medicine in Peruvian Society." Master's Thesis, Brandeis University (2010).

Gonzales, G. and L. Varelio. "Medicinal Plants From Peru: A Review of Plants as Potential Agents Against Cancer." *Anticancer Agents Medical Chemistry*, v.6/5 (2006).

Halpern, John and Harrison Pope. "Hallucinogens on the Internet: A Vast New Source of Underground Drug Information." *American Journal of Psychiatry*, v.158 (2001).

Heras, B. "Antiinflammatory and Antioxidant Activity of Plants Used in Traditional Medicine in Ecuador." *Journal of Ethnopharmacology*, v.61/2 (1998).

Montenegro, Raul and Carolyn Stephens. "Indigenous Health in Latin America and the Caribbean." *The Lancet*, v.367 (2006).

Morales, Glauco. "Antimicrobial Activity of Three Baccharis Species Used in the Traditional Medicine of Northern Chile." *Molecules*, v.13 (2008).

Villegas, León. "Evaluation of the Wound-Healing Activity of Selected Traditional Medicinal Plants From Peru." *Journal of Ethnopharmacology*, v.55/3 (1997).

World Health Organization. "WHO Traditional Medicine Strategy 2002–2005." Geneva: World Health Organization (2002).

TRADITIONAL MEDICINE: TIBET

Traditional Tibetan medicine has advanced and progressed alongside Tibetan culture for the last 2,500 years and is one of the world's oldest medical practices. It is considered a natural and holistic medical science, as it addresses not only the physical needs of the body but its mental and spiritual needs as well. In the development of its practices, the Tibetan people integrated and synthesized knowledge from both Indian and Chinese medical systems, with a particularly dominant Buddhist influence. The majority of its practices are based upon Indian Buddhist literature and Ayurveda, which embraces the belief that the balance of particular bodily functions equals health, while imbalance equals disease.

For diagnosis, practitioners of traditional Tibetan medicine use a multifaceted approach, incorporating philosophy, mental health, and visual analysis. Tibetan medicine considers behavior, nutrition, and lifestyle as essential elements to successful treatment, and utilizes treatment methods like massage, meditation, acupuncture, yoga, and herbal and mineral medicines. The Tibetan herbal pharmacopoeia is complex and involves a large number of medicinal substances, pulling from an array of natural herbs, plants, wildflowers, and mineral substances. Many of these items can be found all over Asia; however, about a third of them are high-altitude plants, found only on the Tibetan high plateau, or in the Himalayas.

Since the Chinese occupation of Tibet in 1950, Tibetans have attempted to reconstruct their cultural heritage and medical tradition in exile. Traditional Tibetan medicine has extended to India and, from there, to many countries of the world under the guidance of a small number of refugee physicians. It continues to be practiced throughout Tibet, China, Mongolia, Siberia, and India, as well as the Himalayan kingdoms of Bhutan, Nepal, and Ladakh.

To understand traditional Tibetan medicine as it is known today, we must explore its history, its relationship with other influential medical systems, and its evolving place in Tibetan refugee health care and the world.

History of Traditional Tibetan Medicine

Though the present Tibetan medical system is considered an offshoot of Indian and Chinese Buddhist medicine, its origins date back to 300 B.C.E. (which predates the 7th-century advent of Buddhism). This period, dating from the beginning of Tibetan civilization until the arrival of Buddhism, is known as the Bon era. At this time, Tibetans had a notable degree of medical knowledge, and their practices followed local folk and shamanistic traditions, which were considered a part of their native religious faith. These shamanistic traditions used practices like divination, astrology, and healing rituals, as well as herbal medicines. These origins were formally recorded by Xiepu Chixi, a physician to the Tibetan King, Niechi Zanpu, in 126 B.C.E.

Aspects of both the traditional Chinese and Indian Ayurvedic medical systems were integrated later. In the beginning of the 4th century, many new ideas about medicine began to enter the country, but the greatest influence happened when Buddhism was adopted in Tibet as the state religion, sometime in the 7th century. During this time, Indian Buddhism and Ayurveda were flourishing in the northern countries, Persian empires were enjoying prosperity, the Chinese Tang Empire developed the Silk Road, and Tibet was unified under King Songzan Ganbu.

This was also a time of prosperity for the Tibetan people, as Songzan Ganbu attempted to make his country a center of cultural, artistic, and spiritual development. He and the Tibetan government promoted an international medical conference in Tibet's Samye Monastery, inviting physicians and scholars from India, China, Persia, and Greece to debate their ideas about health and illness, and to translate their medical texts into Tibetan. These medical systems were allowed to be practiced and diffused along with Tibet's native Bon medical traditions. This collaboration of medical knowledge resulted in the development of the Four Tantras, a single medical doctrine from four perspectives, which soon became the basis for all traditional medical practices. Through these exchanges and the codification of the Four Tantras, Tibetan medicine expanded and shaped its own characteristics, and is now considered one of the oldest complete medical systems in the world.

Medical Principles and the Science of Healing

The Four Tantras, also known as "the science of healing," is a Tibetan text incorporating Indian, Chinese, and Greco-Arab medical systems. Each tantra is a separate book, or chapter, explaining specific aspects of Tibetan medical principles, diagnosis, and treatment. The chapters are as follows: Root (First) Tantra, Exegetical (Explanatory) Tantra, Instructional (Oral Transmissions) Tantra, and Subsequent (Last) Tantra.

The Root Tantra outlines the basic Tibetan medical principles of health and disease and discusses the humors in the body, their potential imbalances, and their link to illness. The Exegetical Tantra discusses, in greater detail, the theory behind the Four Tantras and its beliefs on subjects such as anatomy, physiology, embryology, and treatment. The Instructional Tantra is the longest of the four, and concerns the practical application of treatment. It details the specific cause and treatment of each major category of disease. The Subsequent Tantra focuses on the details of diagnosis, therapies, and the preparation of Tibetan medicines, as well as cleansing techniques.

The basis of these tantras is held firm in the Buddhist belief that the mind is inextricably linked to all phenomena, including illness and wellness. The central aspect of Tibetan medicine is that the five elements of earth, water, fire, air, and space exist in various combinations as different bodily occurrences. The elements are also seen to exist as the principles of function for the body and mind. These corporeal combinations of the elements are known as humors—wind (*rlung*), bile (*mkrhis pa*), and phlegm (*bad kan*). Each of these three humors is considered to constitute the basic energy system in the body, and all are interrelated with vital organs, physiological systems, constituents, and mental processes.

Wind (*rlung*) is considered the source of the body's ability to circulate blood, control the nervous system, and do activities connected with the mind, such as thoughts. Bile (*mkrhis pa*) is characterized by heat in the body and is the source of thermoregulation, digestion, vitality, and critical intellect. Phlegm (*bad kan*) is characterized by fluid in the body and aids in the functioning of bodily stability, joint health, the lymphatic system, and mental stability.

According to Tibetan medical theory, to have good health, it is necessary to maintain balance in the body's three humors. When these principal functions are in balance, health is maintained, and when the equilibrium is lost, one becomes sick. Each of these humors has a corresponding mental "poison," from which Tibetan medicine believes all illnesses arise. According to Tibetan Buddhism, the primary cause that generates imbalance in the humors is ignorance, and the fundamental state of ignorance gives rise to the three mental poisons of attachment, aversion, and indifference.

Since everything in Tibetan medicine is interrelated, imbalance in one organ or one of the humors will affect the rest of the organism. There are three diagnostic methods to explore these imbalances: visual observation, inquiry, and palpating (feeling). The most common method of palpation used by practitioners is pulse and tongue diagnosis, which appears to be derived from the Chinese system, though the method of feeling the pulse and the interpretations differ. Inspection of the tongue and other parts of the body is also an important visual component of diagnosis. One observational method unique to Tibetan medicine is urine analysis, or urinalysis as it is now called. Using the first urine expelled in the morning, the doctor inspects the color, amount of vapor, sediment, and smell. Inquiries into a patient's daily habits, as well as consideration of seasonal influences, all contribute to the analysis. With the various methods of interrogation, visual examination, and tactile examination, a traditional Tibetan doctor will form a diagnosis, and will then use diet and lifestyle guidelines, herbal and mineral medicines, and external therapies (such as massage and acupuncture) to rebalance body, emotions, and mind.

Treatments and Medicinal Materials

Tibetan medicine concentrates on treating the whole person through diet, lifestyle, external therapies, and medicine. Diet can be adjusted for different types of imbalances, depending upon the state of the three humors and whether one's illness is hot or cold in nature. Lifestyle treatments often involve activities such as meditation, breathing exercises, and yoga. These are designed to reduce physical and mental stress, which, according to Tibetan medicine, are the underlying causes for illness.

Physical/external therapies such as *Ku Nye* (massage), acupuncture, and moxibustion are also used, usually in combination with other types of treatment. In Tibetan massage, the word *Ku* means to apply oil, and *Nye* means to apply pressure with a variety of movements. In a *Ku Nye* treatment, the practitioner uses therapeutic herbal oils, while focusing on specific acupressure points and meridians on the body that correspond to different constitutions. Tibetan medicine has held that *Ku Nye* aids in longevity by clearing and sharpening the sensory organs while supporting the function of the internal organs. Acupuncture is used to regulate the flow of vital energy and to help bring about balance. The practitioner will manipulate the body's vital pathways with fine needles, heat, cold, and pressure in order to

affect specific organs and/or systems of the body. Moxibustion is a heating therapy using dried mugwort. Practitioners use *moxa* (mugwort) to warm regions with the intention of stimulating circulation and inducing a smoother flow of blood. There are 20 different types of moxibustion, each using different materials, making the practice of Tibetan moxibustion unique in its diversity.

Herbal medicines are also used, as Tibetan pharmacology is extremely rich in both depth and variety. It makes use of herbal plants, gems, minerals, metals, soils, and saps; complex formulas typically contain 3 to 70 ingredients and include large amounts of unique Himalayan high-altitude plants. At present, there are around 300 different types of medicine that are manufactured. One of these preparations is a commercially available medicine called Padma 28, and is the only Tibetan medicine manufactured outside Asia. Clinical trials have proven it to be effective for vascular diseases, and suggest clinical efficacy in auto-immune and inflammatory conditions, while also possessing antibacterial properties that are beneficial.

Many of the medicinal treatments that are still in use today were established many centuries ago in the Four Tantras. About one-third of the medicinal materials used in Tibetan formulas are unique to the Tibetan region of the Himalayas and bordering countries, while the other two-thirds of the materials can be found all over Asia.

Traditional Tibetan Medicine Today

The Chinese occupation of Tibet led to the exile of over 100,000 Tibetans, and the 1966 Cultural Revolution resulted in their medical traditions being attacked as well as their political, social, and economic structures being dismantled. Thousands of refugees and their government-in-exile resettled in Dharamsala, India, where the new circumstances continued to threaten the disappearance of traditional Tibetan practices.

However, in the late 1970s, the World Health Organization (WHO) developed a policy seeking to incorporate specific indigenous medical practitioners into health care programs. The Tibetan Medical Center of Men-Tsee-Khang (now known as the Tibetan Medical and Astrological Institute) was established in Dharamsala, and institutional support for traditional Tibetan medicine began. The medical college in Dharamsala has research programs as well as a seven-year training course for Tibetan medical students. A second medical college was established in Darjeeling in 1992, boasting a training course along with a pharmacy and two clinics.

So, although some aspects of the traditional Tibetan system of medicine have changed with the population's diaspora and interaction with modern biomedicine, the majority of its concepts have been preserved. The preservation and expansion of Tibetan medical facilities is mainly a result of refugees' dedication to preserve their cultural heritage, which seems unlikely to disappear as these practices are being developed and taught in the wider cultural world. Tibetan herbal medicines are currently prescribed and manufactured by thousands of trained doctors in India and China, as well as the neighboring kingdoms of Bhutan, Nepal, Ladakh, and Sikkim.

Colleen M. Ferguson
*California Polytechnic State University,
San Luis Obispo*

See Also: Siddha Medicine (Dravidian Culture); Traditional and Herbal Medicines, Regulation: South Asia; Traditional Medicine: Vietnam.

Further Readings

Barak, Vivian, Inna Kalickman, Tal Halperin, Shiomo Birkenfeld, and Isaac Ginsburg. "PADMA-28, a Tibetan Herbal Preparation Is an Inhibitor of Inflammatory Cytokine Production." *European Cytokine Network*, v.15/3 (2004).

Cantwell, Cathy. "The Tibetan Medical Tradition and Tibetan Approaches to Healing in the Contemporary World." https://www.repository.cam.ac.uk/bitstream/id/522325/kailash_17_0304_04.pdf (Accessed October 2014).

Dharmananda, Subhuti. "Tibetan Herbal Medicine: With Examples of Treating Lung Diseases Using Rhodiola and Hippophae." http://www.itmonline.org/arts/tibherbs.htm (Accessed October 2014).

Dhonden, Yeshi. *Healing From the Source: The Science and Lore of Tibetan Medicine*. Ithaca, NY: Snow Lion, 2000.

Finckh, Elisabeth. *Foundations of Tibetan Medicine*, Fredericka M. Houser, trans. Dulverton, Somerset, UK: Watkins, 1978.

Tokar, Eliot. "Legal and Regulatory Issues Affecting the Practice of Tibetan Medicine in the United States." http://www.tibetanmedicine.com/html/article4.html (Accessed October 2014).

Tokar, Eliot. "Preservation and Progress: Defining a Role for Tibetan Medicine in the Context of Modern Healthcare." *Asian Medicine Tradition and Modernity*, v.2/2 (2007).

Wen, Fu. "Push to Bring Tibetan Medicine to the World." http://www.globaltimes.cn/content/593924.shtml (Accessed October 2014).

TRADITIONAL MEDICINE: VIETNAM

In the Vietnamese health care system, traditional medicines play an important role. Theories of healing and oriental philosophy underpin Vietnamese traditional medicine. Chinese traditional medicine influences Vietnamese traditional medicine to a large extent, differing in certain aspects. From the clinical point of view, Vietnamese traditional medicine is not evidence based in most cases, but data on subclinical research suggest otherwise, supporting various Vietnamese herbal drugs in traditional use. Knowledge about herb-drug interactions and the occurrence of adverse reactions is necessary so as to safely apply the traditional medicines.

Historical Perspective

Vietnamese traditional medicine, over several thousand years, has undergone evolution, influenced by Chinese traditional medicine, rule, and culture. Therefore, it is a very difficult task to differentiate Thuoc Bac (northern medicine) and traditional Chinese medicine from Thuoc Nam (southern medicine), or Vietnamese traditional medicine, because of their intertwined developments. The classical Vietnamese culture that started in the northern part of Vietnam is actually Thuoc Nam. Even before the 4th or 5th century B.C.E, this part of Vietnam was very much connected with Chinese culture. During that time period, southern China up to northern Vietnam was a large ecological region. Many people living in this part of China were actually not considered by the northern Chinese to be ethnic Chinese people. They even included the Yue, the Chinese term for Viet. By the 4th century B.C.E., southern China and northern Vietnam had come under Chinese rule. The Vietnamese had already developed a medical system, prior to Chinese conquest. Also, from the 4th century B.C.E., Chinese medical texts referred to Yue prescriptions, thereby further confirming the existence of Thuoc Nam. Until the next millennium, the evolution of Chinese and Vietnamese traditional medicine took place very closely together. The Chinese as part of their conquest took, among other valuables, medicinal drugs as tax and tribute. Thus, Chinese traditional medicine incorporated into itself northern Vietnamese folk medicine. Similarly, during the course of 1,000 years of Chinese occupation, Chinese culture and traditional medicine were introduced to Vietnam. Rather than theoretical explanations, a more practical approach would usually be taken by

Vietnamese traditional medicine practitioners. By the 17th century, Chinese traditional practitioners, Vietnamese traditional practitioners, and other ethnic groups of traditional medicine practitioners started identifying Dong Y, or Eastern medicine (also called Oriental medicine), as their class of medicine. This was done to differentiate their class of medicine from Tay Y (Western medicine).

Theories of Traditional Dong Y

There is a difference in practice between Vietnamese and Chinese traditional medicine, but their theoretical foundation is the same. The observational qi (energy) effects are the basis behind the Dong Y theories. Qi has many different forms (mental state, immune, digestive, etc.), but they are all related to food qi, the original source or essence. We inherit essence from our parents, while qi is extracted from food. Hence, both kinetic energy and stored or potential energy are represented by qi, which can be considered to be both energy and matter. Blood is the counterpart of qi. Blood is actually responsible for carrying qi to every body part, itself being a nourishing substance. But to be precise, qi and blood can be considered a single entity. A summary of the functions of qi is as follows: (1) inhibiting pathogens to defend the body, (2) providing movement, and (3) promoting growth and development. Blood functions to provide moistening and nourishment. Qi moves blood, while blood nourishes qi. The concept of qi is thought to be universal: there can be transfer between the universe and our energy. One's qi can be depleted by poor lifestyle, diet, and strenuous work. Energy can also be harvested from the universe through exercises such as tai chi and qigong and through the maintenance of proper health. The major theories surrounding Dong Y are yin and yang and the five elements. A health condition may be described by the combination of these theories.

Yin and Yang

Perhaps the most significant and oldest Dong Y theory is that of the yin and yang. The importance of and existence between the balance of opposing states (action and inaction, hot and cold, etc.) is explained vividly by this theory. It is further subdivided into three major classes: (1) hot and cold, (2) excess and deficiency, and (3) exterior versus interior. The typical manifestations of yin types of diseases are internal symptoms, cold, and malnutrition and other states of deficiency. Typical manifestations of yang types of illnesses are heat, excess, and external symptoms.

Five Elements

The five elements represent another major Dong Y theory. According to this theory, the major body organs are grouped into water, fire, wood, earth, and metal. The same principles are followed by the energy flow within our bodies as in nature: wood brings fire, water nourishes wood, fire forms earth (ashes), and metal is formed by the solidification of earth. According to this theory, balance between these five entities can determine the state of health, with each dependent on the others. Dong Y practitioners, through their observations of these key natural elements, apply the same concept to health. This concept is expanded to include human spiritual, mental, and physical health. A weakness in one element can lead to an excess of another element in a person. For example, water deficiency can cause deficiency in wood and hence excess fire elements. Such a person can be thought to be physically thin and to have a yin health profile. The concepts of the five elements form the basis of teaching in some of the Chinese traditional medicine schools.

Thus, Dong Y practice is guided by the proper conceptualization of its theories, namely, yin and yang, qi, blood, and the five elements, wherein Dong Y practitioners observe the symptoms of their patients and identify and correct disharmonies.

Traditional Vietnamese Medicine

The national medical system of Vietnam has comprehensively and closely integrated Vietnamese traditional medicine. The scope of integration has been subdivided into the following types.

Traditional Medical Management System

This occurs at the central, provincial, and district levels. At the central level, the health ministry oversees a department of traditional pharmacomedicine that looks after the nationwide management of traditional pharmacomedicine. In the provincial medical department, specialists in pharmacomedicine oversee the practice of traditional pharmacomedicine. At the district level, a medical division staffed by part-time or full-time medical officers manages the various aspects of traditional medicine. Nearly 80 percent of the provinces or cities have established management committees to look into matters of traditional pharmacomedicine.

National System of Regulation of Traditional Medicine Treatments

At the central level, the number of traditional medical hospitals is five, with specialist traditional medicine departments present at some other general hospitals. The Pharmacognosis Institute, devoted to the study of herbal plants, has five different specialist centers. Nearly 93 percent of Vietnam's provinces have hospitals with departments for traditional medicine, including 52 traditional medical hospitals. Under the district general hospital, traditional medicine units are present at 93.8 percent of the general hospitals.

Private System

In addition to the traditional medical treatments and examinations at the national level, private-sector systems also have facilities for traditional medicine practice. At present, three provincial traditional medical hospitals exist in Vietnam.

National Policies on Traditional Medicine

The development of traditional pharmacy has always been encouraged by the policies of the Vietnamese government. For example, in 1946, an Oriental medical board was established; in 1957, the Oriental Association and Institute of Research for Traditional Medicine was founded; and in 2005, the Academy of Vietnamese Traditional Pharmacy Medicine was established. All show the intent of the government to foster the development of traditional medicine.

Integration of Modern and Traditional Medicine

Guidelines have been issued by the Vietnamese government for a combinatorial approach involving traditional medicine and modern medicine in order to keep pace with the modern medical world. The combination can be seen as follows:

1. Combining traditional medicine and modern medicine within the national health care system: the whole medical system of Vietnam shows close integration with traditional medicine.

2. Combination in treatment and examination of health, facilitating the use of modern medical tools for treatment and diagnosis by traditional medicine; the latter is used for diagnosis, while both modern and traditional medicine are used for treatment. During the evaluation and observation process, the methods of both traditional and modern medicine are applied rather than traditional medicine alone to make the treatment process far more effective.

3. Combination of modern and traditional medicine depending on treatment period: The treatment rules of traditional medicine are based on four states of disease: chronic, acute, caution, and symptom; both modern and traditional medicine have their own characteristics that define these periods. In some acute periods, it is preferable to use traditional medicine, as in cases of fever and infectious diseases, for which traditional medicine shows better results, with fewer side effects and complications. But in the case of complicated diseases for which surgery becomes inevitable, modern medicine should be used.

Challenges for Vietnamese Traditional Medicine

A number of challenges are faced by Vietnamese traditional medicine that interfere with its successful implementation. Some of the problems are as follows:

- Lack of standardized medical materials
- Lack of indigenous medical materials
- Limited presence of traditional medical industry (e.g., very few factories produce traditional pharmacy products using good manufacturing principles)
- Low level of investment in scientific studies related to traditional medicine
- Officials entrusted with the management of traditional medicine show poor knowledge about their work

- Facilities provided especially for experimental studies are not adequate
- The need for community health care is not satisfied by the community traditional medical system
- Low level of human resources available to handle the growing interest in traditional medicine (only 7.2 percent of the country's medical professionals are engaged in traditional medical systems)
- Within the Association of Southeast Asian Nations (ASEAN) countries, international cooperation is still ineffective

Conclusion

Vietnam has a good opportunity to develop its medical system, incorporating both traditional and general medical techniques. In order to strengthen collaboration among the ASEAN countries for traditional medical practices, Vietnam has participated in traditional medical forums, seminars, and workshops with other ASEAN countries and the rest of the world. The promotion of cooperative activities between the ASEAN countries, particularly with regard to traditional medicine, is an important objective for Vietnam at major international events. Through the organization of different workshops, the health ministry in Vietnam tries to focus on specific areas to promote cooperation for traditional medicine development, particularly in the ASEAN region. Technical and financial support is also sought through such events by the ministry of health in Vietnam from individuals or organizations to promote traditional medicine practice.

Syed Feroji Ahmed
CSIR-Indian Institute of Chemical Biology

See Also: Traditional and Herbal Medicines, Regulation: Australia and New Zealand.

Further Readings

Chu, Quoc Truong. "The Model of Integration of Traditional Medicine With Modern Medicine in Hospitals of Traditional Medicine in Vietnam: Present Status and Prospective Plan." *Chinese Journal of Integrated Medicine*, v.14/3 (2008).

Kalmykova, O. L. "[Traditional Medicine of Vietnam: History and Current Trends]." *Sovetskoe Zdravookhranenie*, v.7 (1990).

Ladinsky, J. L., et al. "The Influence of Traditional Medicine in Shaping Medical Care Practices in Vietnam Today." *Social Science and Medicine*, v.25/10 (1987).

Marr, David. *Vietnamese Tradition on Trial*. Berkeley: University of California Press, 1981.

Wahlberg, A. "Bio-Politics and the Promotion of Traditional Herbal Medicine in Vietnam." *Health (London)*, v.10/2 (2006).

Woerdenbag, Herman J., et al. "Vietnamese Traditional Medicine From a Pharmacist's Perspective." *Expert Review of Clinical Pharmacology*, v.5/4 (2012).

TRANQUILIZERS

The years following World War II have been labeled the Age of Anxiety. This is because of the fear of the atomic bomb, the Cold War, the decline of the nuclear family, and the general climate of social change that swept the nation late in the 1950s and throughout the following decade. It seemed clear that sedatives that had heretofore been adequate to calm neurotics and anxious individuals were not up to the task. Opioids, which were undeniably effective for both pain and sedation, were viewed as dangerous and addictive and were too tightly controlled to be of use in this respect. Likewise, barbiturates were perceived by medical professionals as too risky and dependency producing to meet the growing need of the profession for an anxiolytic—that is, a drug that reduces anxiety without producing excessive sedation. The discovery of various "minor tranquilizers," first meprobamate, then generally the benzodiazepine class, proved a seeming miracle to sufferers of anxiety, to the medical profession, and to large pharmaceutical firms as well. These drugs, initially marketed as safe and non–habit forming, were extremely effective at calming an anxious nation. However, as time passed, it became evident that some users became dependent on the drugs. Another concern was that this class of drugs was criticized, somewhat unfairly, as being used to differentially sedate and control women. Politicians reacting to the perceived excesses of the 1960s began to focus on pharmaceuticals, and doctors by the end of the century became much more reluctant to prescribe this class of drugs so freely. Still, these drugs remain effective and are excellent treatment for anxiety, panic attacks, and muscle spasms and, in some cases, as hypnotics. When the term *tranquilizer* is used, it invariably refers to minor tranquilizers, usually benzodiazepines.

So-called major tranquilizers, more currently known as antipsychotics, are used to calm psychotic and schizophrenic patients and are important in that they allow seriously mentally ill patients to be treated outside institutional settings. However, these drugs have many undesirable and unattractive side effects, and many patients, once released, voluntarily stop using these drugs and have come to constitute a large part of the homeless population. Thus, deinstitutionalization, which once promised to liberate large numbers of the tragically ill and confined population, has been a principal foundation of the seemingly insoluble social problem of homelessness.

The "Miltown Moment"

The development of meprobamate, popularly known as Miltown, is critical in understanding the proliferation of the tranquilizer in American life. Invented in 1950 and first marketed in 1955, meprobamate was a revolutionary product in American culture. It represented a popular recognition that one could self-medicate for the problems of everyday life that had theretofore seemed an insoluble aspect of the human condition. This led to the use of such disparate products as Prozac, Viagra, and Adderall, products to treat depression, sexual dysfunction, and attention deficit/hyperactivity disorder (ADHD). That notwithstanding, the brief Miltown moment gets scant treatment in texts dealing with drugs and drug abuse.

The introduction of the drug was promising, and by the following year, professional and popular interest in the drug was unprecedented. Advertised as a "safe sedative" that would not cause dependency, lead to overdoses, or potentiate with alcohol, the drug was almost an overnight phenomenon. Pharmacy companies began to aggressively market the drug (sold as Miltown or Equanil) through the medium of the medical press and through detail men, or traveling pharmacology company representatives. Doctors were enthusiastically writing prescriptions, sometimes at the behest of eager patients. Pharmacies were literally unable to keep the product in stock and put signs on the doors or sidewalk advertising when new shipments arrived. Patients were queuing up before pharmacies opened in order to ensure being able to fill prescriptions. Newspapers, magazines, and television were full of positive stories about the new "wonder drug." The drug was especially popular in the pressure-filled entertainment industry where comedians used the new "happy pill" as grist for the comedic mill and sitcoms contained sly references to pill-altered amusing comic twists. Even artist Salvador Dali celebrated the drug in an art installation and in paintings. By then, the public had gotten the message: Businessmen and housewives used the drug to cool down after a hard day at the office or in the home. Anxious and stressed college students used the drug to help accustom themselves to being away from home and dealing with college life. Thus, pharmaceutically altering one's mental state for the better and banishing stress, hence the term *happy pills*, became normalized and even fashionable in popular consciousness. By the mid-1960s, other drug companies, noting problems that some patients had with meprobamate, including dependency and overdose, actively began to develop and market yet another "safer tranquilizer" class of drugs, the benzodiazepines, or "benzos."

Librium and Valium: The "Tranquil Trap"

The first drug of the benzodiazepine class to be developed in the Hoffmann-La Roche laboratories was chlordiazepoxide, or Librium, in 1958. Like meprobamate, the drug was an instant success, and by the end of 1960, the drug had captured 20 percent of the tranquilizer market. The same chemist who discovered Librium, Leo Sternbach, in 1959 brought a new more powerful drug to the attention of Hoffmann-La Roche executives—diazepam, or Valium. Valium, like Librium, was marketed as safe, non–habit forming, and versatile. As such, it was to have a dramatic impact on the public. It was the most prescribed drug of the 1970s, and had a place in purses, pockets, and medicine cabinets throughout the nation and the world. At a time when "recreational drugs" such as lysergic acid diethylamide (LSD) and cannabis were being embraced by the counterculture and being stigmatized and increasingly marginalized by politicians, the media, and middle America, Valium was immortalized by The Rolling Stones in "Mother's Little Helper," a cautionary tale about middle-class normalized use and abuse of pharmaceuticals.

The hypocrisy of the normality of self-medication of the middle class was not lost on the young. Moreover, problems with the early benzodiazepines were turning up in doctors' offices and federal regulatory agencies. Some people, usually those who had taken Valium regularly over time, were experiencing alarming symptoms when they stopped using the drug. Reports of nausea, confusion, and anxiety when ceasing use of the drug prompted some physicians and mental health professionals to increase dosages all the while reassuring the patient that the drug was safe. It was discovered that stopping the drug abruptly was ill advised, and patients were subsequently cautioned to gradually reduce the dosage over a period of weeks or even months and to do so under medical supervision. Other criticisms of the drug, and indeed of all benzodiazepines and meprobamate-type drugs, were leveled by a few feminists who saw their use as evidence of victimization of women who were being sedated into becoming passive "Stepford wives" by a male-dominated medical profession. Indeed, congressional hearings into the matter in 1979 were disrupted by antipharmaceutical feminists in the gallery.

This critique has little salience in that men were actually targeted in advertisements and corporate market strategies. A more likely explanation for women being perceived as taking the drug more than men was that women were 3 times more likely to see a doctor than were men, and as such were simply more likely to have the most prescribed drug prescribed. Also, women were more likely than men to complain of stress-related issues and were therefore more likely to have them addressed. The sad fact is, many patients, both men and women, were comorbid with anxiety and depression, and Valium, as a depressant with a long half-life, was not an optimal treatment. It would seem that newer benzodiazepines like alprazolam (Xanax) and lorazepam (Ativan), which both exited the body sooner, would be better to deal with short-term anxiety and panic-type symptoms as they appeared singly or attendant to depression. Thus, Valium and Librium, very important and valuable anxiolytics, continued to fall from favor.

Pharmacological Calvinism, Feminism, and Other Reactions

That notwithstanding, it was clear that meprobamate and benzodiazepines had been somewhat oversold and definitely overprescribed during the 1960s and 1970s. This unsurprisingly led to a situation where a popular and medical overreaction occurred. Prescriptions for both benzodiazepines and meprobamate (still popular even in the face of competition from the benzodiazepines) fell during the 1980s and 1990s to the point where those who really needed the drug for short-term alleviation of symptoms of stress and muscle spasm were hard-pressed to obtain it. Doctors, particularly younger doctors, became much less likely to prescribe tranquilizers because of both responsible medical concerns and media-engendered horror stories and cautionary books and films such as *I'm Dancing as Fast as I Can*.

Patients, having been privy to the same stories and alarmist media reports, were reluctant to ask for the drugs due to a popular stigma, which had gradually inhered to their use. Whereas both comedians and the public had openly joked and given enthusiastic public testimony about the use of Miltown in the 1950s, the therapeutic use of Valium began to be seen as a shameful and secretive practice. Patients were advised to exercise, get other sorts of therapy, take yoga—do anything but take these drugs as a way to deal with stress. This "pharmacological Calvinism," the notion that medicating anxiety demonstrated a lack of character or resolve on the part of both patient and doctor, was a reaction to the perceived abuse of recreational drugs by the counterculture of the 1960s and the notion that the use of benzodiazepines in the 1970s represented a gross example of overprescription and overmedicalization of everyday problems.

Sadly, those with chronic anxiety or temporary muscle spasm disorders suffered and continue to suffer needlessly as these perhaps underprescribed drugs offer significant relief for those issues. Another factor leading to the falling off of tranquilizer prescriptions relates to corporate realities. As these drugs lost their patents, proprietary pharmaceutical companies lost interest in them in favor of publicizing and marketing of other drugs, such as antidepressants, over which they still held market control. However, some have challenged the idea that benzodiazepines pose a serious addiction threat, arguing that if benzodiazepines were so problematic and dependency producing as claimed, there should be huge demand for treatment facilities and a large illegal market to service benzodiazepine addicts should have developed. Neither of these circumstances occurred though there were some highly publicized rehab efforts including that of First Lady Betty Ford. And while there remains some illicit demand for diverted benzodiazepines, this is scarcely a priority issue among drug enforcement agencies. Thus some historians of drug issues, pharmacologists, and physicians suggested that the antibenzodiazepine reaction of the 1980s and 1990s was a hysterical response to some problematic issues with benzodiazepines but was primarily a reaction to the drug abuse of the counterculture and that the drugs of this class had become unfairly stigmatized and had since become underutilized.

Postvalium Tranquilizers: Xanax, Ativan, and Others

The long half-life of diazepam was seen as a major pharmacological issue with the drug. That is, those who were drug dependent and wanted to stop using the drug went through a long withdrawal as the drug took so long to clear their system. Also, a normal short-term therapeutic user might have to cope with a hangover effect due to the aforementioned half-life. It was thought that shorter-acting drugs would be the answer to this problem. Alprazolam and lorazepam were developed with this in mind. However, as is often the case, this solution actually proved to be more problematic than the original problem. Alprazolam clears the system so quickly that patients experiencing panic disorders or illicit users trying to get and maintain a euphoric state find themselves needing to take more, and on a regular basis, than they would if they were taking a longer-acting benzodiazepine. This leads to taking the drug more and thus receiving more positive reinforcement at regular intervals—a situation that only exacerbates the problem. Also, users aver that Xanax provides a more dramatic "high" than other benzodiazepines. Furthermore, it is in demand for polydrug users to potentiate opioid highs, and to cushion anxiety and panic attendant to the use of methamphetamines and cocaine. Some opioid users also use it to cushion withdrawal. Ativan, though having very similar characteristics and seemingly possessing the same potential for abuse, has not been subject to the same pattern of misuse as has Xanax though the reasons for this remain obscure.

Rogue Tranquilizers and Sedatives

Several tranquilizers have been given widespread publicity and enjoyed currency but proved to be so problematic that they were either prohibited by law or banned entirely from American medical practice. The drugs thalidomide, methaqualone, and Rohypnol are the most notorious. Thalidomide was a tranquilizer widely used in West Germany in the late 1950s. An alert U.S. Food and Drug Administration (FDA) reviewer, Frances Kelsey (who withstood intense corporate and political

pressure and persevered), prevented it from being marketed in the United States in 1960 when it was revealed to have severe teratogenic effects. Kelsey received the Distinguished Federal Civilian Service medal for her outstanding effort. The drug was subsequently withdrawn from the European market in 1961. Methaqualone garnered attention as a powerful "club drug" in the late 1960s and into the 1970s. It is very effective as a barbiturate-like antispasmodic and antitussive, and even has local anesthetic qualities. When taken in large doses, it produces an effect akin to drunkenness—loss of coordination, euphoria—and acquired a reputation as an aphrodisiac. Tolerance of the drug developed quickly, and some users became seriously dysfunctional and dependent. As the drug was frequently taken in clubs and discos with alcohol, "drug in combination" overdoses were common. The drug was viewed as so problematic and stigmatized that all legal production of it ceased in the United States. It still appears from time to time in street formulations, however. Rohypnol, or flunitrazepam, commonly known as "roofies," while not legally marketed in the United States, is a powerful Hoffmann-La Roche–developed tranquilizer used primarily as a hypnotic. It is most infamous as a "date rape" drug used to sedate and render individuals helpless, amnesiac, and victims of subsequent sexual assault—which in some cases they cannot recall. It is still legitimately used as a sleep aid in Europe.

Responsible Use of Tranquilizers

In general, tranquilizers, when used for anxiolytic purposes, should not be taken for more than two weeks or a month at most. The smallest effective dose should be calculated by the patient and physician and adhered to with some rigidity. Patients should contact the doctor if the dosage seems insufficient and they want to raise their dose. If patients have been taking the drug daily for more than a few weeks and are ready to quit, they should gradually lower their dosage by taking smaller increments over a period of weeks until the drug is no longer in their system. Drugs of this class should never be stopped abruptly, or serious withdrawal reactions can occur. For long-term users especially, medical supervision of withdrawal is strongly suggested.

That being said, the drugs in question are extremely useful, relatively safe, and important therapeutic agents. "Pharmacological Calvinism" should not deter someone in a serious chronic anxiety state or panic situation from using these drugs under proper medical supervision. Useful drugs for anxiety used today include diazepam, oxazepam, clonazepam, lorazepam, and alprazolam. The last is especially useful in preventing and treating panic attacks. Some benzodiazepines and benzodiazepine-like drugs are primarily used as hypnotics (i.e., for sleep) and are not properly tranquilizers. They include flurazepam (Dalmane), triazolam (Halcion), and temazepam (Restoril). Benzodiazepine-like drugs used as hypnotics include zolpidem (Ambien). Both zolpidem and triazolam have been linked to such bizarre side effects as "sleep eating," "sleep walking," and "sleep driving." That is, a small number of patients report having eaten while "asleep," or having gone for a drive while in a hypnotic state. New research indicates that women should take lower dosages of Ambien than men as they would otherwise receive too much of the drug were they to take the same amount. Triazolam has been linked to temporary amnesia and is now used for preoperative and operative sedation in dental procedures. That notwithstanding, these reactions are few, and the drugs are generally safe when used as directed.

Francis Hawley
Western Carolina University

See Also: Hypnotics and Sedatives.

Further Readings

Carroll, Marilyn and Gary Gallo. "Quaaludes: The Quest for Oblivion." In *The Encyclopedia of Psychoactive Drugs*. New York: Chelsea House, 1985.

Falkowski, Carol. *Dangerous Drugs: An Easy to Use Reference for Parents and Professionals*. Center City, MN: Hazelden Foundation, 2003.

Goode, Erich. *Drugs in American Society*. New York: McGraw-Hill, 2012.

Hart, Carl and Charles Ksir. *Drugs, Society and Human Behavior*. New York: McGraw-Hill, 2013.

Henningfield, Jack E. and Nancy A. Ator. "Barbiturates: Sleeping Pill or Intoxicant?" In *The Encyclopedia of Psychoactive Drugs*. New York: Chelsea House, 1986.

Herzburg, David. *Happy Pills in America: From Miltown to Prozac*. Baltimore, MD: Johns Hopkins University Press, 2009.

Hogshire, Jim. *Pills-A-Go-Go: A Fiendish Investigation Into Pill Marketing, Art, History, and Consumption*. Venice, CA: Feral House, 1999.

Liska, Ken. *Drugs and the Human Body With Implications for Society*. Upper Saddle River, NJ: Prentice Hall, 1997.

Lyman, Michael D. *Drugs in Society: Causes, Concepts and Control*. Waltham, MA: Routledge, 2014.

MacCoun, Robert J. and Peter Reuter. *Drug War Heresies: Learning From Other Vices, Times and Places*. New York: Cambridge University Press, 2001.

Task Force on Benzodiazepine Dependency. *Benzodiazepine Dependence, Toxicity and Abuse*. Washington, DC: American Psychiatric Association, 1990.

Tone, Andrea. *The Age of Anxiety: A History of America's Turbulent Affair With Tranquilizers*. New York: Basic Books, 2009.

Winger, Gail. "Valium: The Tranquil Trap." In *The Encyclopedia of Psychoactive Drugs*. New York: Chelsea House, 1986.

TRANSLATIONAL PHARMACOLOGY

Translational pharmacology is an exciting area tied directly to the concept of personalized medicine. It developed out of the Human

Genome Project, which fully sequenced the human genome in 2002, revealing an estimated 20,000 to 25,000 human protein-encoding genes. Since then, basic science discoveries have proceeded on a genomic level at a rapid pace, hand-in-hand with technological advances in DNA sequencing capabilities and molecular innovations. As disease processes and drug response mechanisms become better understood, new drug therapies are being developed along with associated biomarkers (tests that reveal a disease state) and molecular diagnostics (tests that reveal an individual's genetic capacity to respond to drugs). Translational pharmacology seeks to transform the genomic-level discoveries of basic science into drug treatments that physicians can use to tailor to individual patients for maximum effectiveness. The goal is to bring these new drug therapies to market in a timely manner (within the limits of multiple regulatory agencies), by using an interdisciplinary approach (tapping multiple fields of expertise in a coordinated effort). With each new drug (new molecular entity) under development, it is essential that associated biomarkers be identified so that these new drug treatments have a better chance of successfully passing through clinical trials. After the U.S. Food and Drug Administration's (FDA's) approval, corresponding molecular diagnostics need to be added to genotyping panels and protocols need to be established in order to help physicians prescribe the appropriate dose according to individualized predicted response patterns (taking the long-held concept of "personalized medicine" to a new level).

The outcome of translational pharmacology is the development of a drug that can be prescribed for a specific disease state at a dosage especially suited to an individual's unique genotype/phenotype for maximum effectiveness, and with minimal side effects.

This is based on new understandings of individual genetic variations that can be detected with genotyping panels. These panels detect the presence of genetic variants for specific genes that have been linked to the mechanism of action of a particular drug (gene/drug pairs). The genetic variants detected will indicate whether that individual is predisposed to be a poor, intermediate, or ultrarapid metabolizer of the associated drug, or at what point they may be on the range of drug response, from being a nonresponder to being an adverse responder to a specific drug. This process is closely aligned with the growing field of pharmacogenomics (how individuals react to drugs based on their differences in genetic profile and gene expression), since both have the common goals of maximizing effective drug therapies, minimizing adverse reactions, and using the genomic data of individuals to add to health care providers' current decision-making armamentarium of medical education, continuing education, clinical experience, published research, available population data, and point-of-service electronic resources.

Bringing safe and effective therapies to market quickly is a daunting task due to the strict protocols of regulatory agencies and the enormous expense of clinical trials. But the potential health benefits to society make this an extremely important area that deserves a lot of attention. The U.S. government has stepped up to this challenge by creating agencies and programs, and offering grants dedicated to interdisciplinary approaches in powering a bench-to-bedside (research-to-clinical utility) push. This is more comprehensively referred to as translational biomedicine, which includes the elucidation of disease mechanisms, leading to the development of genetic biomarkers, resulting in diagnostic applications that include sensitive tests, in addition to new treatments utilizing the improved understanding of pharmacologic activity on a genomic scale.

Organizations That Accelerate and Promote Translational Pharmacology

In late 2011, a new center of the U.S. National Institutes of Health (NIH) was created for the express purpose of making changes to the organizational processes that impose scientific and operational roadblocks to an efficient translational process, with the aim to move fundamental discoveries into safe and effective treatments. The new National Center for Advancing Translational Sciences (NCATS) varies from other NIH institutes and centers, in that it focuses on the translational process rather than particular organ systems or diseases.

Three major organizations have been established to provide guidance to clinicians on the appropriate use of genomic tests in conjunction with individualized drug therapy (connecting evidence to practice). The CDC Office of Public Health Genomics established the Evaluation of Genomic Applications in Practice and Prevention (EGAPP) Working Group in 2004. The Royal Dutch Pharmacists Association established the Dutch Pharmacogenetics Working Group (DPWG) in 2005. In 2009, the Clinical Pharmacogenetics Implementation Consortium (CPIC) was formed as a joint effort by Pharmacogenomics Knowledgebase (PharmGKB) and Pharmacogenomics Research Network (PGRN). These three initiatives were created to assess emerging genomic-based tests for clinical utility and validity, and develop peer-reviewed guidelines to help clinicians optimize therapy in connection with the associated drug/gene pairs. An additional resource for genetic-guided drug dosing recommendations is the FDA's Table of Pharmacogenomic Biomarkers in Drug Labeling, which has grown to over 150 drug/gene pairs, some of which include specific genetic evidence-based recommendations.

Translational Pharmacology and Global Data Sharing

The enormous supply of data generated by the Human Genome Project and the subsequent use of those findings by researchers around the world has created the need for its organizational effectiveness and accessibility, thus calling on the field of informatics to come to the rescue with the utilization of electronic medical records (EMRs) and data repositories. In addition to the data sets being generated by research, valuable data is also being derived from clinical practice and captured in ambulatory care and hospital EMRs. This is not to say that all nonprofit and for-profit clinics and hospitals, educational and research institutions, government departments, and regulatory agencies will initially be able or willing to provide de-identified patient data to share and build upon. But the potential exists to develop regional, national, and worldwide grids of databanks that can serve as open access points to promote data sharing and move the cause of translational pharmacology forward with the speed it deserves, considering its potential far-ranging meaningful outcomes.

EMR-derived data has already provided the means for retrospective analysis and data mining to discover new gene/disease and gene/drug associations, as well as the quantification of disease phenotypes, specifically the onset and rate of progression of disease. Accountability becomes a byproduct of this process as treatment outcomes of efficacy and toxicity are tied to measurable genomic factors. Another consequence is that individualized medicine will turn more toward treating the genome when variants show risk of associated disease (taking proactive measures) as opposed to waiting on the development of disease (reactive response). Just as EMRs with DNA biobanks can play a major role in the detection of patterns and relationships of disease states and drug response to genetic variations, they will enable the translation of these pharmacogenomic discoveries into clinical practice on a global scale.

Social Justice Related to Translational Pharmacology

As the mechanisms of disease become understood on a deeper level and drugs are designed with increased efficacy and prescribed with greater accuracy for individuals (resulting in reduced toxicity), the potential for cost savings is substantial through cost-effective health care delivery. Reduced cost will allow a larger segment of society to purchase medications, and thus decrease the gap in health disparities across poor members of all cultures who take part in the movement of translational pharmacology. Since the foundation of translational pharmacology is both broadly protective (by virtue of multidisciplinary participation, data-expansive evidence base, regulatory oversight, and major guidance-focused initiatives) and deeply probing (down to the level of DNA, with rapidly evolving supportive technology driving new insights), the potential is great for this process to lead to improved health outcomes on a large scale and increased patient satisfaction.

The advent of personalized medicine through translational pharmacology's introduction of molecular biomarkers and diagnostics offers physicians methods of optimizing therapy with effective drugs at dosages that maximize efficacy and minimize toxic side effects. This opens up new medicolegal areas that include defensive medicine and personalized justice. This latter concept includes the factor of accountability in relation to the components of adverse drug reactions (behavioral changes, impaired performance, sensitivity, and toxicity). The impact of translational pharmacology will lead to the inclusion of molecular imaging and diagnostic biomarkers that incorporate genomic, proteomic, metabolic, and epigenetic analyses into the justice system. Legal interpretations will be challenging because of the complex nature of pharmacogenomics.

Potential Impact on Primary Care

In spite of all the growing evidence of genetic links to drug response variations and concomitant increases in genetic-testing services, physician education has not kept up with these advances, nor has general public awareness. A number of organizations are supporting efforts to educate medical practitioners and improve the public's understanding of genetic and pharmacogenomic testing services.

The Golden Helix Institute (GHI) is an international nonprofit organization located in Athens, Greece, that performs interdisciplinary research in pharmacogenomics (PGx) and personalized medicine. GHI also supports efforts to improve the implementation of PGx into routine medical practice, with educational activities in Europe, Asia, and Latin America. In the United States, the Mayo Clinic Center for Individualized Medicine has collaborated with the Pharmacogenomics Research Network (PGRN) and the Electronic Medical Records and Genomics (eMERGE) Network to design the Right Drug, Right Dose, Right Time—Using Genomic Data to Individualize Treatment protocol (RIGHT protocol). This translational project goes beyond promoting awareness of the proven clinical utility of genome-guided therapy in that it effectively jump-starts the implementation process by proactively integrating clinically actionable PGx variants into the electronic medical record (EMR). The RIGHT protocol thus gives the EMR the means to drive medical decision-making at the point of care, by connecting the data with the best practices for the utilization of genomic medicine.

Future Directions

Multiple barriers exist to thoroughly implement the many discoveries (biomarkers, molecular diagnostics, new molecular entities, dosage protocols, etc.) translational pharmacology has achieved. In order to fully realize the benefits, an extensive infrastructure needs to be developed.

- Clinical Trials: There is a need for genotype-focused randomized clinical trials to validate the recommended treatment algorithms.
- Electronic Medical Record (EMR): A standardized format of test results is needed to allow entry into an EMR system. Also needed are physician decision-making tools with PGx guidelines to be provided in a translational bioinformatics framework in order to be effectively incorporated into the EMR.
- Laboratory Test Ordering: It is necessary to coordinate genotyping between the ordering physician and a Clinical Laboratory Improvement Amendments (CLIA) approved laboratory, to ensure the accuracy of test results and a rapid turnaround time.
- Insurance Coverage: The value of PGx testing needs to be accepted by insurance companies, and appropriate reimbursement schedules must be developed.
- Clinician Education: It is essential to educate physicians on how to interpret genotyping reports and gain the understanding required to recommend appropriate treatment based on the results.

- Professional Support: Professional medical associations need to be encouraged to provide supportive recommendations and guidelines.

Progress is being made in many of the areas noted above. Collaborations between companies (such as Claritas Genomics and Cerner), research centers (PGRN's Translational Pharmacogenomics Program's six implementation sites), and multidisciplinary efforts within institutions (such as University of California's BRAID, Biomedical Research Acceleration, Integration & Development, initiative) are driving forces of translational pharmacology. A primary goal is the translation of pharmacogenomic data into objective definitions of response (in terms of efficacy and adverse events), according to various clinical phenotypes. This information will be used to produce clinical decision-making tools that will use molecular diagnostic data via electronic medical record platforms to usher in a new era of genomic medicine.

Judith J. Kammerer
Saint Agnes Medical Center

See Also: Adverse Drug Reactions (ADR) and Adverse Events (AE); National Center for Advancing Translational Sciences (NIH); Pharmacogenomics.

Further Readings

Bartlett, G., J. Antoun, and N. K. Zgheib. "Theranostics in Primary Care: Pharmacogenomics Tests and Beyond." *Expert Review of Molecular Diagnostics*, v.12/8 (2012).

Bielinski, S. J., J. E. Olson, and J. Pathak. "Preemptive Genotyping for Personalized Medicine: Design of the Right Drug, Right Dose, Right Time—Using Genomic Data to Individualize Treatment Protocol." *Mayo Clinic Proceedings*, v.89/1 (2014).

Crews, K. R., J. K. Hicks, and C. H. Pui. "Pharmacogenomics and Individualized Medicine: Translating Science Into Practice." *Clinical Pharmacology and Therapeutics*, v.92/4 (2012).

Savonarola, A., R. Palmirotta, F. Guadagni, and F. Silvestris. "Pharmacogenetics and Pharmacogenomics: Role of Mutational Analysis in Anti-Cancer Targeted Therapy." *The Pharmacogenomics Journal*, v.12/4 (2012).

TRIPS Agreement (Agreement on Trade-Related Aspects of Intellectual Property Rights), Doha Declaration, and TRIPS Plus

The Trade-Related Aspects of Intellectual Property Rights (TRIPS) Agreement was negotiated at the end of the Uruguay Round of the General Agreement on Tariffs and Trade (GATT) in 1994. The World Trade Organization (WTO) later replaced GATT as the legal entity for regulating global trade and commerce in 1995. Because of the access to global markets that it provides for its members, countries seeking membership in the WTO are legally bound by the WTO's 18 multilateral trade agreements, which include the TRIPS Agreement. Among these multilateral trade agreements, the TRIPS Agreement has the greatest impact on the pharmaceutical sector, particularly on drug patents and access to medicines. The TRIPS Agreement is of global significance because it introduced global minimum standards for protecting and enforcing almost all forms of intellectual property rights (IPRs), including those for drug patents. Under the TRIPS Agreement, all products and processes in all fields of technology, including pharmaceuticals, enjoy a minimum IPR protection of 20 years provided they meet the patentability criteria of being new, involve an inventive step, and are capable of industrial application. The importance of TRIPS to society lies in its potential for restricting access to medicines for those who need them most and has therefore become a contentious global health and human rights issue, especially in the context of access to life-saving medicines for the HIV/AIDS pandemic. HIV/AIDS has claimed over 39 million lives as of July 2014, the majority of whom are from the developing world, particularly sub-Saharan Africa, which carries the greatest burden of the disease.

Before the TRIPS Agreement came into force in 1995, many countries were operating under the Paris Convention for the Protection of Industrial Property. Countries therefore had more freedom to determine the technological areas for which to grant patent protections in their national laws, and to choose whether to protect only the products or the processes for their production, or both, as well as the length of such protections in their countries. Hence many developing countries and some developed ones previously excluded pharmaceutical products from patent protection. Other countries chose to grant only process patents with respect to the technology and the method or process of production. This allowed alternative technology, or the methods or processes to be used to produce generic copies of patented drug products for use in their local markets and beyond. Brazil and India, for example, excluded pharmaceutical products and processes from patent protection in 1969 and 1970, respectively. This explains the development of the strong local pharmaceutical industry in India, which now supplies over 80 percent of the generic antiretroviral medications (ARVs) used in the developing world.

The TRIPS Agreement covers copyrights, trademarks, patents, industrial designs, and undisclosed information, including trade secrets and test data, among others. Test data includes the data on drug safety, efficacy, and quality that pharmaceutical manufacturers are required to submit to drug regulatory authorities when applying for market authorization for their drug products. In its simplest terms, the TRIPS Agreement protects IPRs, including drug patents, for a minimum of 20 years, and also protects the test data from "unfair commercial use." It is important to note that prior to the TRIPS Agreement, drug regulatory authorities routinely used the innovator brand producers' test data to approve subsequent applications of generic drug equivalents. Generic drug manufacturers simply needed to prove the chemical identity and the bioequivalence (i.e., having similar rate and extent of absorption) of their drug products with the innovator brand product. This procedure was beneficial because it ensured an accelerated entry of generic drug products into the market, with the benefit of price reductions through market competition.

Inasmuch as the TRIPS Agreement sought to stimulate innovation by providing adequate protections for IPRs, the Agreement also included some provisions, known as TRIPS flexibilities or safeguards, under which member states could use inventions such as patented drugs to promote and protect the interest and well-being of their respective peoples. Notable among these TRIPS safeguards are Parallel Importation and Compulsory Licensing. Parallel Importation allows member states of the WTO to import patented drugs from any country, irrespective of the source of original manufacture, by taking advantage of the differential pricing of such drugs in different global markets that come about as the result of generic competition. Compulsory licensing, on the other hand, allows member states to locally produce generic bioequivalent drugs for the use of their populations or, where local manufacturing facilities are not available, to issue such licenses to external sources to produce for them without the approval of the patent holder. This licensing applies to situations when the patent holder refuses to grant voluntary licenses for their products.

All member states of the WTO are required to implement the provisions of the TRIPS Agreement by bringing the needed changes in their national patent laws to make them TRIPS-compliant. However, taking into consideration the different developmental stages of WTO members around the world, two sets of transitional periods were allowed for the developing and the least developed country members of the organization. While the former were expected to become TRIPS compliant by 2005, the latter were given an extended deadline of 2013, which was later extended to January 1, 2016, with the possibility of further extension.

The Doha Declaration

The Doha Declaration on the TRIPS Agreement and Public Health was one of the main achievements of the fourth WTO Ministerial Conference in Doha, Qatar, on November 9 through 14 in 2001. In this Declaration, the WTO confirmed the right of its member states to make effective use of existing TRIPS flexibilities to promote and protect public health. This was a significant achievement for developing countries, especially for the African Group within the WTO, which, faced with the greatest burden of the global HIV/AIDS pandemic and aggravated by multinational pharmaceutical companies' insistence on their patent protections under the TRIPS Agreement, sought the WTO's intervention to address their peculiar concerns regarding access to the life-saving medicines for their peoples. The African Group, supported by others like Brazil, wanted the WTO to clarify the grounds under which member states could effectively use the TRIPS flexibilities to protect the health of their peoples, especially with respect to promoting access to medicines.

The Doha Declaration affirmed that the TRIPS Agreement can and should be interpreted and implemented in such a way that would support member states' right to protect public health in general and to promote access to medicines for all in particular. The Declaration confirmed that each member state has the right to grant compulsory licenses and the freedom to determine the grounds upon which to do so. Furthermore, each member state was allowed to determine what factors constitute a national emergency or other circumstances of extreme urgency, as these would authorize the States to use the TRIPS Flexibilities without challenge from patent holders. With respect to Parallel Importation, the Declaration left each member state "to establish its own regime for such exhaustion (IPRs) without challenge." This means that countries that choose international exhaustion of IPRs can access patented drug products from any country through Parallel Importation. On the other hand, it will be expected that countries with drug patent holders will choose national exhaustion of IPRs, thus preventing any such importation into their countries in order to protect their inventions in their local markets.

Although the goal of the Doha Declaration was to assist WTO member states, especially the developing and the least developed country members, to promote access to essential medicines for their peoples, studies have shown that very few have yet to make the necessary changes in their national patent laws to take full advantage of this Declaration to promote their population's access to these medicines. Notable exceptions here include India. Other countries such as Brazil, China, Indonesia, the Philippines, and Thailand have taken concrete steps to become TRIPS-compliant, enabling them to make use of various flexibilities under TRIPS. However, the majority of the developing world have been held back by the lack of the required technical expertise to address their patent laws accordingly. Alternately, their hands have been tied from using the TRIPS flexibilities due to Free Trade Agreements (FTAs) and other bilateral agreements they have signed with countries such as the United States and those in Europe, which push for TRIPS-Plus obligations on these countries in exchange for trade concessions.

TRIPS Plus

TRIPS-Plus obligations refer to the enforcement of patent protections far beyond those provided for by the TRIPS Agreement. These strategies are employed by patent holders' governments to gain more stringent protections for their drug products than ordinarily required under TRIPS. TRIPS-plus obligations are important to society because they further restrict access to life-saving medicines, ironically, for the populations of those countries who need them most as they carry the greatest global burden of communicable diseases, including HIV/AIDS, tuberculosis, and malaria. TRIPS-plus obligations include the following:

1. Extension of patents beyond the 20-year protection under TRIPS to compensate for delays in patent application examinations or in obtaining market approval for their drug products.

2. Preventing regulatory authorities of the target country from granting marketing approval for generic drug products in that country when patents exist for that drug. This requirement essentially turns these regulatory authorities into enforcers of patent protections, a responsibility outside of their official roles.

3. Requirements for granting patent protections for second indications of known drug products. The TRIPS Agreement requires that patent protections cover new and innovative drugs, among other criteria.

4. Prescribing periods of test data exclusivity or protection during which the country being imposed upon cannot use the innovator drug's test data for granting market authorization for generic bioequivalent drug products.

5. Provisions for enhanced patent enforcement, which include empowering customs officials to seize goods suspected of patent infringement, for example, with respect to drug imports, exports, and in transit. India, for example, made a complaint to the WTO in 2010 regarding the repeated detention of Indian-produced generic drug products while in transit through the European Union (EU) region.

6. Imposing more stringent restrictions on the issuing of Compulsory Licenses for patented drug products.

Unfortunately, the provisions under many U.S. and EU FTAs include a variety of TRIPS-plus obligations on the countries engaged in these trade agreements. India, however, has stood its ground and is determined never to accept TRIPS-plus agreements with the United States, which will jeopardize its own local generic drug manufacturing industry.

Joyce Addo-Atuah
Touro College of Pharmacy

See Also: Access to Essential Medicines as a Human Right: History; Access to Medicines (Developing World); Access to Medicines (Industrialized World); Drug Price Competition and Patent Term Restoration Act (1984); Equity Pricing of Essential Medicines; Generic Medicines; Intellectual Property Rights; WHO Model Lists of Essential Medicines.

Further Readings

Correa, Carlos and Duncan Matthews. "The Doha Declaration Ten Years on and Its Impact on Access to Medicines and the Right to Health—Discussion Paper." http://www.undp.org/content/dam/undp/library/hivaids/Discussion_Paper_Doha_Declaration_Public_Health.pdf (Accessed March 2014).

Johnson, Toni. "The Debate Over Generic-Drug Trade." http://www.cfr.org/drug-trafficking-andcontrol/debate-over-generic-drug-trade/p18055 (Accessed March 2014).

Nicol, Dianne and Owoeye Olasupo. "Using TRIPS Flexibilities to Facilitate Access to Medicines." http://dx.doi.org/10.2471/BLT.12.115865 (Accessed March 2014).

World Health Organization. "WTO and the TRIPS Agreement." http://www.who.int/medicines/areas/policy/wto_trips/en (Accessed March 2014).

World Trade Organization. "Understanding WTO: The Agreements. Intellectual Property: Protection and Enforcement." http://www.wto.org/english/thewto_e/whatis_e/tif_e/agrm7_e.htm (Accessed March 2014).

Trovafloxacin (Trovan) Controversy

Trovafloxacin was a highly touted, broad-spectrum oral antibiotic introduced by Pfizer Inc. into the U.S. marketplace in 1998 as Trovan (the prodrug alatrofloxacin is the intravenous formulation of Trovan). Total sales for Trovan peaked at $300 million in 1999—approximately 300,000 prescriptions per patient per month—but increasing reports of liver toxicity and related patient death greatly reduced the use of the antibiotic. Pfizer stopped promoting the drug in late 1999, and the European Union's Committee for Proprietary Medicinal Products suspended all sales that same year. Because of its broad spectrum of activity, trovafloxacin remained available for use in nursing home patients and/or those experiencing life-threatening infections, but the antibiotic was officially withdrawn from the U.S. marketplace in 2001.

The controversial history of trovafloxacin has proved to be an important case study concerning two overlapping issues in the blockbuster era of drug development: (1) The fraudulent actions of multinational drug companies and, in particular, the ethical shortcomings of global clinical trials networks; and (2) the closely related problem of relying on the *efficacy* of experimental compounds, demonstrated via randomized controlled trials (RCTs) to secure regulatory approval, versus the *effectiveness* of a U.S. Food and Drug Administration (FDA)–approved drug once it is heavily prescribed in the medical marketplace.

A forth-generation member of the fluoroquinolone class of antibiotics, trovafloxacin is bactericidal. The molecule blocks the uncoiling of supercoiled DNA in bacteria by inhibiting DNA gyrase (gram negative bacteria) and topoisomerase IV (gram-positive bacteria). This mechanism of action allows the drug to target and destroy a wide range of microbials, including aerobic and anaerobic bacteria. Fluoroquinolones as a class can cause liver toxicity (1–3 percent). However, only temafloxacin (brand name Omniflox, which was pulled from the U.S. market by Abbott Labs in 1992) and trovafloxacin were designed with a unique difluorinated side chain, which is not found in other quinolones, which makes both drugs highly lipophilic (i.e., potentially hepatotoxic; from acute hepatitis to liver failure).

Pfizer preadvertised Trovan to both Wall Street investors and its field force of drug reps as an extremely safe blockbuster in the making—potentially the first antibiotic to achieve $1 billion annually in sales (Zithromax [azithromycin], another Pfizer antibiotic, would eventually be the first blockbuster anti-infective). In particular, Pfizer advertised the amount of data submitted to the FDA to achieve regulatory approval, claiming at the time that the application was the largest New Drug Application (NDA) in history. Pfizer press releases in early 1998 outlined Trovan's rapid acceptance by the medical community and lauded the company's own ability to secure an unprecedented 14 indications from the FDA for both oral and intravenous formulations. Nevertheless, trovafloxacin was already causing hepatotoxicity in patients in the United States, and litigation was in motion behind the scenes due to the aggressive tactics used by Pfizer to complete RCTs prior to FDA approval.

The legal controversy surrounding trovafloxacin stemmed from a Phase III clinical trial conducted outside the United States in 1996. Pfizer had begun to use new tracking tools to find clean populations to treat with experimental compounds—what medical anthropologist Adriana Petryna has described as "treatment naïve" populations (i.e., test subjects without preexisting conditions and/or not on medication[s]).

Company personnel used the Internet to locate a pediatric outbreak of bacterial meningitis in the city of Kano, Nigeria, and clinicians were dispatched to Africa, where they traveled to a local hospital to recruit patients for the trial. *Médecins Sans Frontières* (Doctors Without Borders) was already providing a cheaper antibiotic in one part of the hospital that is the standard of care for meningitis (i.e., intravenous chloramphenicol in generic form). Pfizer personnel designed their study to be a randomized controlled trial of 200 children, 100 receiving oral trovafloxacin (or intravenous alatrofloxacin if they could not swallow the pill) and 100 receiving 1 gram of intravenous ceftriaxone (Roche's branded Rocephin). Like other multinational drug firms at the time, Pfizer had also begun to outsource clinical trial work through for-profit contract research organizations (CROs). In turn, a Europe-based CRO was hired to analyze spinal fluid samples from infected Nigerian children.

Pfizer dispatched news of the Nigerian study results within the company to managers and pharmaceutical sales representatives as well as publicly to both the press and the FDA. Oral trovafloxacin was shown to be equal to ceftriaxone with a 94 percent survival rate in the Trovan arm of the study. It is not entirely clear if this particular clinical trial was ever published in a peer-reviewed journal, nor is it clear if the data were incorporated into the global Trovan Meningitis Study Group. Nevertheless, drug reps were able to tell this story locally, to their potential prescribers in the United States, by discussing how an oral pill was equal to an intravenous gold standard for a serious, life-threatening infection. This kind of convincing sales narrative can build confidence in doctors to prescribe an antibiotic for more mundane infections, such as sinusitis and cellulitis, which are much larger markets.

Pfizer also promoted the clinical trial as part of its humanitarian (and corporate) mission to help relieve the burden of infectious diseases in developing countries (the epidemic killed approximately 12,000 Nigerians with cholera and measles present as well). Pfizer donated millions of dollars to Kano in medicines and materials. However, almost immediately, reports from government and medical officials in Nigeria, as well as complaints from the parents of patients, began to emerge that questioned the ethics of Pfizer personnel during the study and the side effects of Trovan. Both arms of the study did have high success rates, but 5 children in the Trovan arm and 6 in the Rocephin arm died, and several children were left blind and paralyzed, which parents attribute to the drugs. Over the next 13 years, Pfizer and the plaintiffs engaged in a series of lawsuits, court actions, and appeals concerning compensation for victims enrolled in the clinical trial. Three core issues/questions emerged: (1) Did Pfizer actually have consent

from the Nigerian government to conduct the trial, and/or did parents receive informed consent from Pfizer and subsequently give consent for their children to be part of the clinical trial? (2) Did Pfizer purposefully use a lower dose of ceftriaxone to show better results in the Trovan arm of the study causing unnecessary harm? (3) Did Pfizer and/or the CRO act neglectfully in terms of medical follow-up with subjects/patients in the study?

In 2009, Pfizer settled with the 200 plaintiffs enrolled in the study for $75 million. The outcome of litigation showed that Pfizer did indeed take advantage of an unstable, often corrupt government in order to fast-track a clinical trial to accumulate data for a pending pediatric indication for Trovan in the United States (the FDA eventually rejected the Trovan application for pediatric meningitis). Proper parent/patient consent was never received, and/or the consent forms were backdated/forged, which is a violation of the Nuremberg Code, the Declaration of Helsinki, and the Law of Nations (Pfizer claimed the government did not require consent). And Pfizer personnel and/or the CRO never followed up appropriately with patients. After the two-week clinical trial, researchers never returned to Nigeria to examine patients and review their blood work. Finally, Pfizer argued that the lower-dosed serum levels of ceftriaxone remained bactericidal and limited injection site pain. The usefulness of ceftriaxone to treat meningitis was confirmed in a 2003 clinical trial conducted by Doctors Without Borders in Niger, and reported by Nathan and colleagues, which found that a single shot of ceftriaxone, as compared to the standard treatment with oily chloramphenicol, was a valid treatment alternative, particularly during a mass epidemic.

Hepatotoxicity was also reported in children treated with Trovan in the Nigerian study, and by 1999, similar reports were emerging in the United States. Initially, Pfizer took steps to report adverse drug events in the United States through drug reps, instructing doctors to fill out adverse event reports and forward them to the FDA, while also stressing to clinicians that the types of patients receiving the drug were often compromised (i.e., having preexisting liver dysfunction and/or complicated medical conditions). However, after 100 reported cases of severe liver toxicity in otherwise healthy patients with normal liver function, including patient deaths, the FDA in early 2000 instructed Pfizer to cease all promotion of the drug in the United States.

In retrospect, the trovafloxacin controversy remains an important and multilayered example for understanding the ethical complexities and regulatory shortcomings of fast-tracking experimental compounds to the medical marketplace. William Steere, then CEO of Pfizer, tried to redirect the narrative of Trovan through an efficacy-versus-effectiveness argument. He asked the public and shareholders to think about how experimental drugs in an ideal setting (i.e., RCTs) present one set of facts concerning efficacy and safety versus the real world of patient care, where the effectiveness of a drug in the general population can be unpredictable and produce different outcomes. He was quoted by the *New York Times*: "You put the drug in the general population, and then everyone is taking it . . . We just hold our breath and wait to see if there is something unique with the drug."

Nevertheless, in retrospect, the uniqueness of Trovan, in terms of hepatotoxicity, was clearly known before market introduction. The consumer watchdog group Public Citizen wrote numerous letters to the FDA, citing the agency's own pharmacology reports, indicating that Trovan could be a dangerous drug. Studies submitted by Pfizer and reviewed by FDA medical officers showed abnormal liver functioning and/or hepatotoxicity could occur in both humans and animals. Public Citizen argued the drug should never have been approved because of side effects and the fact that eight other quinolones were available in the United States and, despite Trovan's numerous indications for prescription use, the antibiotic was not novel.

The late 1990s became a key moment in drug history when many experimental compounds that were fast-tracked by the FDA proved to be highly toxic and later were withdrawn from markets. Historians and journalists have revealed that the FDA was under tremendous congressional pressure, stemming from pharmaceutical industry lobbying, to expedite the approval of non-novel drugs with questionable safety profiles. Some of the withdrawn drugs from that era include Rezulin (troglitazone), Posicor (mibefradil), Duract (bromfenac), and Meridia (sibutramine), as well as Trovan. The controversy surrounding trovafloxacin in particular demonstrated what can happen when investor pressure to produce a blockbuster drug for the developed world intersects with a public health crisis in an unstable, developing nation-state. The end result can be life altering and even deadly for extremely marginalized populations (e.g., poor children as clinical trial subjects), as well as dangerous for everyday medical consumers in countries like the United States, who are expected to trust the corporate science, medical practitioners, and regulatory systems that bring new drugs to the health care marketplace.

Michael Oldani
University of Wisconsin–Whitewater

See Also: Pfizer; Pharmaceutical Research and Manufacturers of America.

Further Readings

Abdullahi v. Pfizer, Inc. 2002 U.S. Dist. LEXIS 17436 at *1 (S.D.N.Y. September 17, 2002).

Gartlehner, Gerald, Richard A. Hansen, Daniel Nissman, Kathleen N. Lohr, and Timothy S. Carey. "Criteria for Distinguishing Effectiveness From Efficacy Trials in Systematic Reviews." *Technical Reviews*, No. 12 (Prepared by the RTI-International-University of North Carolina Evidence-Based Practice Center Under Contract No. 290-02-0016). AHRQ Publication No. 06-0046. Rockville, MD: Agency for Healthcare Research and Quality, April 2006.

Hilts, Philip. "Old Fashion Politics." In *Protecting America's Health: The FDA, Business, and One Hundred Years of Regulation*. Chapel Hill: UNC Press, 2003.

Nathan, N., T. Borel, A. Dilbo, D. Eans, S. Djibo, J. F. Corty, M. Guillerm, K. P. Alberti, L. Pinoges, P. J. Guerin, and D. Legros. "Ceftriaxone as Effective as Long-Acting Chloramphenicol in Short-Court Treatment of Meningococcal Meningitis During Epidemics: A Randomized Non-Inferiority Study." *Lancet*, v.366/9482 (July 2005).

National Institutes of Health. "Overview: Fluoroquinolones." http://livertox.hih.gov/Fluoroquinolones.html (Accessed July 2014).

Oldani, Michael. *Filling Scripts: A Multisited Ethnography of Pharmaceutical Sales Practices, Psychiatric Prescribing and Phamily Life in North America* (Chapters 6 and 7). Doctoral dissertation, Department of Anthropology, Princeton University, 2006.

Onyinyechi, U. Daniel. *Concepts of Autonomy and Informed Consent in Developing World Research: The Nigerian Perspective*. Master's thesis, Medical Humanities and Bioethics Program, Feinberg School of Medicine, Northwestern University, 2012.

Perlroth, Nicole. "Pfizer's Nigerian Nightmare." *Forbes*. http://www.forbes.com/forbes/2008/1208/066.html (Accessed July 2014).

Petersen, Melody. "Unforeseen Side Effects Ruined One Blockbuster." *New York Times* (August 27, 2000). http://www.nytimes.com/2000/08/27/business/unforeseen-side-effects-ruined-one-blockbuster.html (Accessed July 2014).

Petryna, Adriana. *When Experiments Travel: Clinical Trials and the Global Search for Human Subjects*. Princeton, NJ: Princeton University Press, 2009.

Public Citizen. "Letter to the Food and Drug Administration to Immediately Ban the Antibiotic Trovafloxacin (Trovan)." http://www.citizen.org/documents/1485.pdf (Accessed July 2014).

Sáez-Llorens, Xavier, Cynthia McCoig, Jesús M. Feris, Sergio L. Vargas, Keith P. Klugman, and Gregory D. Hussey (The Trovan Meningitis Study Group). "Quinolone Treatment for Pediatric Bacterial Meningitis: A Comparative Study of Trovafloxacin and Ceftriaxone With or Without Vancomycin." *Pediatric Infectious Disease Journal*, v.21/1 (January 2002).

Willim, David. "New FDA: How a New Policy Led to Seven Deadly Drugs." *Los Angeles Times* (December 20, 2000). http://www.pulitzer.org/archives/6473 (Accessed July 2014).

TUSKEGEE EXPERIMENT

The Tuskegee experiment, or the "Tuskegee study of untreated syphilis in the Negro male," was a study funded by the federal government about the progression of syphilis among poor African American male residents in Alabama. The U.S. Public Health Service (USPHS) controlled the research, based at the Tuskegee Institute, an African American educational facility founded by Booker T. Washington (1856–1915), a respected African American community leader. The study began in 1932 and continued for four decades.

In contemporary times, this experiment appears typically in research ethics textbooks as an exemplar of how not to proceed in scientific studies of people. Tuskegee is infamous because of the ethical abuse of the participants, which culminated in mortality, impaired health, and other significantly negative outcomes for the men and their families. As a result of Tuskegee and other flawed studies, institutional review boards (IRBs) have been established at research institutions, and contemporary investigators are required to follow strict ethical standards. For all of these reasons, it is important to remember the Tuskegee experiment, which provides a cautionary tale for pharmacologists and others about how a clinical study investigating the symptoms of syphilis developed into an abusive protocol that denied treatment to patients. To understand this progression fully, some information about syphilis is helpful.

History of Syphilis

Syphilis is a sexually transmitted infection (STI). The geographic source of the disease is still debated by specialists, although it was documented in Europe in the late 1400s and may have originated earlier in the Americas. It is difficult to define the origin definitively because most studies have relied on archaeological skeletal evidence, and syphilis is challenging to identify in human bones. Many diseases result in similar types of damage. More convincing substantiation of the geographical source will likely be found in genetic studies, which is a contemporary research mode.

Syphilitic infections may result in sores, rashes, swelling, and major discomfort and disability, often lasting for years and leading to death. Symptoms are diverse, occur in three active phases, and affect vital body organs. Periods of lessened virulence make diagnosis challenging, which is why Canadian physician Sir William Osler (1849–1919) termed syphilis the great imitator.

Despite early identification of the transmission mechanism, it was not until 1905 that the microbe *Spirochaeta pallida* was identified as the cause of syphilis. Within another two years, the Wassermann test was developed, which allowed doctors to identify syphilis definitively in most patients, even during dormant periods. The first effective treatment for syphilis, arsphenamine (Salversan, also known as "compound 606"), was discovered in 1907 by a research team led by Paul Ehrlich, and was an improvement over previous mercury-based treatments, but had serious side effects.

Syphilis and other sexually transmitted diseases were especially prevalent during periods of conflict and population movement such as during World War I when soldiers mingled with prostitutes and infection spread rapidly among the military and civilian populace. In fact, as reported by Frith, sexually transmitted diseases were the second most common reason for disability and absence from duty in the American army during World War I. Approximately 10,000 men left the service because of these illnesses, and about 7 million person days were lost. This was a public health crisis, and postwar fear of syphilis was strong in the United States until better treatment became available.

Despite centuries of attempts to cure syphilis effectively, it was not until 1939, when British scientists purified penicillin, that successful speedy treatment became possible. U.S. penicillin production began in 1941, and the first syphilitic patients were treated in 1943. Two years later, penicillin was dispensed to the liberating forces in Europe, and syphilis changed from being a deadly debilitating disease to a dangerous but treatable infection. By the 1950s, the penicillin cure was available in the civilian world, and its efficacy was well documented by the USPHS.

Alabama Public Health

The deficits of the Tuskegee syphilis investigation resulted from several factors, which coalesced uniquely in Alabama. Previous attention has been paid to the U.S. climate of fear regarding syphilis and the shame connected to its diagnosis. In addition, there was an inaccurate belief in the late 19th and early 20th centuries that White males and Black males experienced syphilis differently, and some descriptions of syphilis in African Americans, as reported by Alan M. Brandt, associated the disease with purported promiscuity or lack of morality. Thus, the disease became ethnically linked with a disadvantaged segment of the population, supporting the attestation that racial stereotypes played a role in the 1932 decision to study syphilis among African Americans.

Contentions of population differences in the syphilitic experience were based on 19th-century ideas that African Americans were mentally and physically inferior to people of European origin, and these notions were common among doctors in slave-holding states such as Alabama, especially prior to and during the Civil War (1861–1865). For this reason, it is reasonable to assume that it is no coincidence that the syphilis study occurred in the southern United States and lasted for so many years without adequate oversight in this locale.

In addition to the influence of southern history in the Tuskegee debacle, the federal government also exerted influence, mainly through public health initiatives affecting the approximately 2.1 million citizens of Alabama. In 1912, Congress provided the fledgling USPHS with its current name and expanded its focus to cover diseases and sanitation amid increasing realization that poverty played a major role in overall U.S. health. Many health officials wanted public funds to improve living standards, including access to water, sanitation, and medical care, and they argued that all American citizens would suffer if the poorer segments of the community lacked health services.

By 1918, the USPHS had created a Division of Venereal Diseases, provided with a mandate to improve treatment and prevention of STIs across the nation. This encouraged state action. In Alabama, the Board of Health opened urban clinics, but the rural poor, mainly African Americans, lacked access to these services, and the cost of syphilis treatment from private doctors was prohibitively expensive and lengthy for impoverished sharecroppers. This meant that syphilis rates continued to grow in these communities, and public health officials became increasingly concerned about the situation.

None of these events occurred in a social vacuum. A public health crisis was colored by the fact that Alabama was segregated, and many in state governments still possessed Civil War–era beliefs. Indeed, the cultural and political climate of Alabama was such that in 1920, less than a decade before the Tuskegee study was launched, seven African American men were lynched. Desegregation of buses did not occur until 1956. Alabama was a racially divided state in 1932, when the experiment began. In addition, African American medical doctors only received Alabama certification to work late in the 19th century, meaning that few members of this community occupied powerful state medical positions. The first African American female medical doctor to work in Alabama was Halle Tanner Dillon, who practiced from 1891 to 1894 at the Tuskegee Institute's John A. Andrew Memorial Hospital. This hospital, a center for African American health and medical practice, featured prominently in the study.

The research was based at Andrew Hospital, and the investigators' focus was the surrounding Macon County, which was predominantly African American, with the population numbering only 27,000 people in 1930. Most adults were illiterate, living in collapsing shacks and scattered across the rural landscape, with unsafe water and sanitation and high levels of malnutrition and poor health. Families barely managed to survive with little cash and no extra funds for medical care. Macon County was extremely poor, exacerbated by the Depression, which lowered the standard of living across the nation. In such circumstances, syphilis treatment was too expensive for adults, meaning that infected mothers passed the disease to their infants, who developed congenital syphilis, and the STI reached epidemic levels in the county.

This was one of many local and national factors encouraging the location of the syphilis study in Macon County, Alabama. These same factors also meant that an investigation of STIs among the African American population in that area ran the risk of valuing the desire of the scientists to conduct research over the ethical rights of the participants. The balance of power was unequal in many ways during segregation.

Another event external to the United States also played a role in supporting the inaccurate notion that a study of syphilis and its symptoms might be medically useful. There was a European precedent for this type of investigation, although it lacked racial overtones and was a retrospective review of Norwegian patients' medical records rather than an ongoing study dealing with sick men over many years; this study is discussed by L. W. Harrison. An important additional difference between the Oslo data and the Macon County patients was that the Norwegian information dated from 1891 to 1910, prior to the invention of the penicillin cure, while the U.S. study denied treatment to ailing participants after penicillin was introduced. These are important distinctions that members of the USPHS tried to gloss over in their use of the Norwegian case to justify the Tuskegee study both before and after it was attacked for ethical violations. However, in the early years of the study, there was little public attention focused on these Alabama men, and for decades the study progressed in an ethical vacuum after its founding in 1932.

The Tuskegee Project Begins in 1932

Many events set the stage for the Tuskegee experiment, including the characteristics of the volunteering men and those of the scientists and medical personnel connected to the project. Health staff had high status at the time and typically made decisions for their patients rather than consulting with clients about options and working together toward medical solutions. Doctors had almost godlike powers in the 1930s and were self-regulating, lacking external boards with supervisory oversight over research other than state and national medical boards, which focused on medical accreditation and were not predisposed to sanction established practitioners.

Given this background, when collaborative meetings were set up between doctors of the USPHS and Alabama state medical personnel to establish the frame of reference for the Tuskegee experiment, it was not surprising that research requirements overpowered patient treatment needs, given the limitations of available time and funding. When the study began in 1932, it focused on studying syphilitic men's health and providing the arsenic cure for a minimal period of time rather than the full course of treatment that was the standard of care for the time. This decision meant sick men would continue to suffer from their illness during and after the short-term research, which was originally envisaged to last less than a year. This research protocol also violated Alabama state laws dating from 1919, 1923, and 1927, encouraging any individual with an STI to visit a physician, receive treatment, and maintain curative practices until the doctor declared the patient to be disease free. However, the law was technically only a principle in

Alabama, since there were no dedicated public funds to support this regulation in 1932.

The research was based at the John A. Andrew Memorial Hospital at the Tuskegee Institute, now called Tuskegee University, an Alabama National Historic Site. The hospital was founded in 1913 and celebrated its 100th anniversary in 2013.

The study location was essential to the success of the research since the local community knew that the hospital and educational institute focused on the well-being of African Americans, and both were staffed predominantly by African Americans. This was the case in 1932 when Eugene H. Dibble (1893–1968) served as medical director of the Andrew Hospital, and Robert Moton (1867–1940) was the Tuskegee Institute president, with an appointment dating from the death of Booker T. Washington in 1915.

The motivations of key African Americans such as Dibble and Moton in facilitating this harmful study are difficult to understand. Perhaps they felt that any treatment of infection was better than no treatment, or perhaps they hoped that focusing medical attention on the region would generate more funding and result in better treatment goals; but whatever their reasoning, they approved it.

In some ways, the involvement of the four powerful White doctors is easier to comprehend, given the prevailing racial norms. Taliaferro Clark and Oliver Wenger both worked for the USPHS and established the Tuskegee research in tandem. Once the project was approved, they hired Raymond H. Vonderlehr to direct the project, and he eventually moved into Clark's position at USPHS, allowing him to continue the study until 1943. At that time, with his retirement, John R. Heller was hired at USPHS; he maintained control of the study until it was concluded in 1972.

Not only did medical authorities involved in the study condone its methods, but many doctors inside and outside of Alabama also ignored their Hippocratic Oath to do no harm and paid little heed to the project's goals. As reported by Brandt, articles and conference presentations provided some documentation of the treatment protocols and the harmful, often deadly results for the men. Journal editors, reviewers, and general readers did not intervene, which broadens the indictment to many members of the medical profession.

In addition to the doctors' supervision of the research, various hospital nurses and administrators were involved. One nurse, Eunice Rivers (1899–1986), played a pivotal role in the study since she was African American and a long-term project employee, presumably garnering her increasing degrees of trust from the research participants. She, along with the other medical staff, argued that she did no harm, and she did receive lesser sanctions than the physicians, in recognition of the fact that given the medical and racial hierarchies of the day, as a nurse and an African American woman, she had limited or no ability to change treatment protocols, especially at the start of the project.

Treatment protocols were applied to 600 African American men, and 399 of these individuals were diagnosed with syphilis. Study recruitment inducements included free medical attention for nonsyphilitic complaints, including transportation to the hospital, meals, and promises of future burial funds. The men were tested and observed but only received minimal treatment for syphilis, and the project's focus was on recording their health decline rather than on improving their well-being. None of these men was given penicillin when this became the standard treatment for syphilis. Instead, the men received painful, risky, unneeded tests such as lumbar punctures or spinal taps to demonstrate the increasing ravages of syphilis on their bodies. Close to 400 men were never informed of their positive syphilis status other than being told that their blood was bad, which was a meaningless phrase. When sick men came to the attention of local doctors or U.S. Army draft facilities, scientists actively prevented them from receiving syphilis treatment. As a final point of outrage, each of these men was autopsied when he died, and his data were recorded by study scientists. In addition to these breaches of trust, other ethical standards were violated.

Ethical Issues

Several national and international ethical codes govern the behavior of contemporary researchers with human study participants. The Nuremberg Code of 1947 arose out of horror at Nazi doctors' torture and abuse, which was disclosed at the Nuremberg Trials at the end of World War II. Because the Nuremberg trials and the development of the Nuremberg Code were widely covered in both the general and medical press, the Tuskegee researchers would presumably have been aware of both the trials and the code. However, all 10 principles of this code were violated by the Tuskegee researchers.

In 1964, the World Medical Association (WMA) adopted the Declaration of Helsinki, which provided additional ethical guidance to medical researchers. The Tuskegee study also breached most of the standards present in this document, which was also widely distributed to U.S. medical doctors.

In addition, the American Medical Association (AMA) developed several ethical codes over the years, which are available from the AMA Web site. The 1903 version was created prior to the start of the Tuskegee project, and a 1957 version would have been operative during the final 15 years of the study. The first principle of the 1957 AMA iteration

encourages medical professionals to respect people's dignity, which did not happen at any stage of the Tuskegee project.

Basically, all extant medical codes of ethics were breeched by the Tuskegee project, and it is important to document the full extent of these ethical violations. The easiest way to describe the problems is to use the format presented by the Belmont Report of 1979, created by the National Commission for the Protection of Human Subjects of Biomedical and Behavioral Research, since this commission and its report arose out of the Tuskegee scandal.

The Belmont Report exhorts researchers to respect people, act with beneficence, and support justice. Respect entails several commitments by researchers, both to allow people to make their own decisions and to provide the tools to help people understand research so they can make informed choices about participation. It is clear that the Tuskegee researchers did not explain the goals of the study to the men, nor were they asked for their consent to take part in the project, which offered neither disclosure of diagnosis nor real treatment options for syphilis. In addition, the provision of free transportation, food, and some medical care served to divert participants' attention from what they were providing to the study in order to receive these benefits. Plus, the researchers were educated, wealthy men for the most part, and the participants were poor, uneducated, mostly illiterate, minority community members. Social and political mores of the time meant that African Americans were unlikely to question the actions of White doctors.

Beneficence builds upon the Hippocratic principle to do no harm, but it extends this basic medical standard further and means that researchers should strive to improve the well-being of their participants. The events that transpired in Macon County resulted in death, disability, pain, and betrayal, and individuals who lived long enough to understand the project's outcomes experienced loss of trust in medical authority. Enduring reduction of confidence by the African American community also resulted in long-term diminished access to medical expertise and care at the time and for the future.

The third Belmont principle of justice attempts to impose some balance on the amount of risk imposed on a community by the research when compared with the accrual of benefits. Research costs should not be borne solely by one population group, with profits flowing to a different set of people. In fact, the Belmont Report cites the case of Tuskegee as an example of how injustice may result from the selection of a disenfranchised community as the locus of research.

Given the broad range of documented ethical violations in the Tuskegee experiment, it is a massive indictment of the USPHS that the study continued until 1972, by which time only 74 men were still living. The research might have continued longer had reports of it not appeared in the national press, as described by Brandt.

Ending the Research and Aftershocks

Jean Heller, who worked for the Associated Press (AP) in Washington, D.C., broke the news about the syphilis project to the U.S. public. Her article appeared in AP-subscribing papers such as the *Washington Star* and the *New York Times* on July 25, 1972. The resulting media frenzy meant that the federal Department of Health, Education, and Welfare was forced to act, finally closing the study four months after the news spread. The project was shut down, with many disavowals of causing harm by all concerned. A government investigation

ensued, and eventually medical assistance and court-mandated financial compensation were provided to the survivors.

In terms of medical harm, a figure that is often cited is that 28 men died of syphilis and possibly 4 times that many from disease complications, but the veracity of these data is arguable. The records also show that several dozen women were infected by their husbands during their study participation, resulting in the birth of 19 children with congenital syphilis.

Eventually, a lawsuit garnered a $9 million settlement for the Tuskegee research participants and their families. To some, this may seem quite generous until the allocation of funds per affected individual is examined. Financial benefits were allotted differently depending on the presence of research survivors and their status. Men still living with syphilis or its effects received $37,500, which is less than $1,000 per year of the 40-year study. Those who had died were considered to have left their recompense to documented family members, who received $15,000. Study participants who had not been diagnosed with syphilis were granted $16,000. If they had died, their heirs received $5,000.

However, some of the men and their families were never compensated, given the court allocation of four years and six months to the plaintiff's lawyer, Fred Gray, for victim location. At the end of this time period, 17 participants had still not been found, meaning that these men and their families never received anything for their suffering. In addition to a financial payout, the settlement included the provision of medical benefits for life to the men, and in 1975, associated women and children were added to the policy, which 20 years later also included wellness benefits.

The lawsuit findings documented the impropriety of the study, but no apologies from the research institutions or medical personnel occurred at the time. Indeed, it was a long wait before any member of the federal government stepped forward to offer an apology. This finally occurred on May 16, 1997, when U.S. President William J. Clinton apologized on behalf of the federal government to the remaining Tuskegee survivors. By this time, only eight men were still alive.

Federal action occurred just in time for the participants, because the last of the men, Ernest L. Hendon, died at the age of 97 in 2004. Five years later, the longest-living widow died. Several children of the original participants are still alive, bearing their story of events, all corroborated in the books and hundreds of articles that have been written about the Tuskegee experiment.

In conclusion, the repercussions of the syphilis study were felt at the level of the individual, the community, medical institutions, and the U.S. government. Participants and their families experienced death, illness, and painful side effects of the disease. Men were not informed about the nature of their illness, nor were they offered cures once effective treatments were available. This ongoing deception, accompanied by many other ethical violations, once exposed by the media, resulted in distrust of researchers, the medical profession, and the U.S. government for good reason. Congress and U.S. health authorities formulated comprehensive ethical codes and established ethical overview of researchers after the Tuskegee experiment was closed down. However, some argue that the negative effects of Tuskegee lived on for many years, not only in the bodies of those directly involved, but also in the broader African American community, where it has contributed to a climate of mistrust between African Americans and the medical establishment.

Susan J. Wurtzburg
University of Hawai'i at Manoa

Sarah J. Simmons
University of Hawai'i at Manoa

Elizabeth A. Souza
University of Hawai'i at Manoa

See Also: Access to Essential Medicines as a Human Right: History; African Americans; Declaration of Helsinki (1975); Human Subjects Research: Standards and Protections; Patient Rights; Venereal Disease Treatment: History.

Further Readings

American Medical Association. "History of AMA Ethics." http://www.ama-assn.org/ama/pub/about-ama/our-history/history-ama-ethics.page (Accessed June 10, 2015).

Brandt, Allan M. "Racism and Research: The Case of the Tuskegee Syphilis Study." *Hastings Center Magazine* (December 1978). Reprinted with permission at http://www.med.navy.mil/bumed/Documents/Healthcare%20Ethics/Racism-And-Research.pdf (Accessed June 10, 2015).

Carmack, Heather J., Benjamin R. Bates, and Lynn M. Harter. "Narrative Constructions of Health Care Issues and Policies: The Case of President Clinton's Apology-by-Proxy for the Tuskegee Syphilis Experiment." *Journal of Medical Humanities*, v.29 (2008).

Frith, John. "Syphilis: Its Early History and Treatment Until Penicillin and the Debate on Its Origins." *Journal of Military and Veterans' Health*, v.20/4 (November 2012). http://jmvh.org/article/syphilis-its-early-history-and-treatment-until-penicillin-and-the-debate-on-its-origins/ (Accessed June 10, 2015).

Gray, Fred D. *The Tuskegee Syphilis Story: The Real Story and Beyond*. Montgomery, AL: NewSouth Books, 1998.

Hagen, Kimberley S. "Bad Blood: The Tuskegee Syphilis Study and Legacy Recruitment for Experimental AIDS Vaccines." *New Directions for Adult and Continuing Education*, v.105 (2005).

Harrison, L. W. "The Oslo Study of Untreated Syphilis Review and Commentary." *British Journal of Venereal Diseases*, v.32/2 (June 1956).

Jones, James H. *Bad Blood: The Tuskegee Syphilis Experiment*. New York: Free Press, 1993.

Lederer, Susan. "Experimentation on Human Beings." *Organization of American Historians Magazine of History*, v.19 (2005).

National Commission for the Protection of Human Subjects of Biomedical and Behavioral Research. "The Belmont Report" (April 18, 1979). http://www.hhs.gov/ohrp/humansubjects/guidance/belmont.html (Accessed June 10, 2015).

Pressel, David M. "Nuremberg and Tuskegee: Lessons for Contemporary American Medicine." *Journal of the National Medical Association*, v.95/12 (December 2003).

Quetel, Claude. *History of Syphilis*. Baltimore, MD: Johns Hopkins University Press, 1990.

Reverby, Susan. *Examining Tuskegee: The Infamous Syphilis Study and Its Legacy*. Chapel Hill: University of North Carolina Press, 2009.

World Medical Association. "Declaration of Helsinki: Ethical Principles for Medical Research Involving Human Subjects." http://www.wma.net/en/30publications/10policies/b3/17c.pdf (Accessed June 10, 2015).

TYLENOL TAMPERING CASE

In 1982, seven people died after taking over-the-counter (OTC) Tylenol Extra Strength capsules containing sodium cyanide. Because the capsules were manufactured and purchased at different locations, police believed someone tampered with the medications as they sat on store shelves. Still unsolved, the investigation reopened in 2009 and remains focused on James W. Lewis, who was convicted of attempting to extort $1 million from Johnson & Johnson, parent of McNeil Consumer Healthcare, manufacturer of Tylenol, to "stop the killings." The Tylenol tampering case altered consumer perceptions of OTC product safety and revolutionized packaging for numerous consumer products, but had the most effect on pharmaceuticals, food, and cosmetics, which are considered higher targets for tampering. The tragedy also set the standard for corporate response to a crisis since Johnson & Johnson dealt quickly and with highest concern for public safety while dealing with the ethical and legal matters surrounding the tragedy.

The case began on September 29, 1982, when a 12-year-old girl from Elk Grove Village, Illinois, died after taking an OTC Tylenol Extra Strength capsule laced with potassium cyanide. Over the next three days, other Chicago-area victims followed, including two brothers in their 20s and the 19-year-old wife of one of the brothers who took capsules from the same bottle, a 35-year-old flight attendant, a 31-year-old mother of two, and a 27-year-old mother of four. Investigators found that the poisonous medications were manufactured in different plants by McNeil Consumer Healthcare, a subsidiary of Johnson & Johnson, and were sold in various drug and grocery stores in the Chicago area, which led to the belief that the tampering occurred after the medications reached store shelves. During the investigation, James W. Lewis, a 49-year-old unemployed accountant who moved from Chicago to New York in September 1982, sent a letter to Johnson & Johnson demanding $1 million to "stop the killings." After a two-month manhunt, Lewis was arrested and admitted sending the letter but said that he never meant to collect the money. Instead, he intended to have the money sent to the bank account of his wife's former employer in retaliation for alleged misdeeds committed against him. During questioning, Lewis maintained that he was innocent of murders, but gave investigators a detailed description of how the killer may have committed the crime. Although investigators suspected Lewis was responsible for the Tylenol murders, he was never charged. Instead, he was convicted of extortion for sending the letter to Johnson & Johnson. In 1995, he was released after serving 10 years of a 20-year sentence for extortion and 2 years for an unrelated tax-fraud charge. In 2009, the case was reopened with new forensic techniques and new tips given to law enforcement because of publicity surrounding the 25th anniversary of the murders. Investigators searched Lewis's Cambridge, Massachusetts, home and a nearby storage locker, taking several bags of evidence, and in 2010, Lewis and his wife, LeAnn, surrendered their fingerprints and DNA samples under court order. Today, the killings remain unsolved, and the $100,000 reward offered by Johnson & Johnson is still unclaimed, with some maintaining that Lewis was just an opportunist who was trying to take advantage of the situation.

The Tylenol tampering incident set off a nationwide alarm, exposing the need for greater consumer protections for OTC products. In the United States, consumers rushed to emergency rooms and called poison hotlines as police drove through streets issuing warnings about the danger over loudspeakers. Sales of Tylenol, which was approximately 35 percent of the OTC analgesic market in the United States, plummeted while merchants rushed to clear Tylenol from their shelves. As public concern rose, society developed a belief that more drugs should be under pharmacists' control. There was also a demand for safer packaging and packaging specialists, which increased the market value of companies producing tamper-resistant packaging. Local and state regulators in Illinois and Massachusetts moved to set new packaging rules as the drug industry encouraged the U.S. Food and Drug Administration (FDA) to set national packaging guidelines, fearing a hodgepodge of local regulations. In November 1982, the FDA issued the first of its rulings describing guidelines for tamper-resistant packaging, and in 1983, the Federal Anti-Tampering Act made it a crime to tamper with any consumer product, including food, drugs, devices, and cosmetics. The FDA describes tamper-resistant packaging as having at least one protection (two protections for two-piece capsules) that would visibly indicate altering has occurred after leaving the manufacturer. Examples of packaging protections include individual push-out compartments, heat-shrunk plastic wrap around the cap, and inner seals laminated to the lip of the container. Although final costs are difficult to measure, one source predicted tamper-resistant packaging would increase OTC product prices by 1 to 2 percent. However, consumers did not seem to mind, preferring safeguards to cost. FDA regulations make products tamper-resistant but never tamper-proof, which might be impossible, regardless of the amount of money spent.

Numerous copycat cases sprouted up across the United States following the Tylenol killings. Notable cases of actual tampering of OTC medications include sulfuric acid in eye drops, instances of mercuric chloride or cyanide in Excedrin Extra Strength capsules, cyanide-laced Sudafed, and strychnine-contaminated Tylenol Extra Strength. However, the 1982 Tylenol tragedy seemed to affect societal attitudes unlike other cases. Public reaction may be linked to the unprecedented media coverage, including 100,000 newspaper stories and hours of radio and television reporting, making about 90 percent of the U.S. public aware of the killings.

To protect consumers and save the Tylenol brand, which was approximately 19 percent of profits, Johnson & Johnson acted quickly, referring back to the corporate philosophy, *Our Credo*, written by Robert Wood Johnson in the 1940s. Considered the highest standard for corporate crisis management, important points include making public safety the company's first concern, while offering an honest appraisal of the situation as did James E. Burke, Johnson & Johnson chairperson, who took decisive command, sharing all details of the case with the media to distribute information to the public quickly. The company stopped all product advertising, set up an 800 number, and issued a worldwide recall of Tylenol Extra Strength offering to exchange Tylenol capsules for Tylenol tablets while spending a half-million dollars to warn physicians, hospitals, and distributors of the situation. Johnson & Johnson also kept its sales force well informed, issuing timely updates and alternative drugs to share with medical personnel. During the recall, Johnson & Johnson examined and destroyed 31 million bottles of Tylenol at a cost of $100 million. Altogether, 44 cyanide-laced capsules were discovered in the five bottles leading to the deaths and in three additional bottles. Therefore, through sound corporate and social responsibility and expert communication strategies, Johnson & Johnson demonstrated that it acted ethically regardless of making a profit, which transformed the company into a champion of the consumer. Ultimately, the public did not seem to blame Johnson & Johnson for the deaths, which were widely thought to be random acts of terrorism. Although consumers said they felt more anxious about taking OTC medications, their anxiety did not result in a change in behavior as shown by the bounce-back in Tylenol sales, which approached pretampering levels within five months of the murders.

The Tylenol tampering case triggered several lawsuits and questions regarding corporate responsibility for intentional criminal actions that might occur after manufacturing. When it came to liability, corporations often argued that they did not cause the actual harm and, thus, were not responsible. Through the early 1980s, U.S. courts generally disagreed with this argument and tended to expand, not limit, corporate responsibility for the unlawful acts of others. However, near the end of the decade, the courts seemed to lessen corporate responsibility for others' actions as was demonstrated by a 1986 incident, in which Diane Elsroth, age 23, died in Yonkers, New York, after taking Tylenol Extra Strength capsules laced with cyanide. In this case, evidence indicated that the triple-sealed medication, which far exceeded FDA regulations for tamper-resistant packaging, was contaminated with cyanide and resealed after manufacturing and shipping to the A&P grocery chain where it was purchased. In 1988, the liability case against McNeil, Johnson & Johnson, and the Great Atlantic & Pacific Tea Company (A&P) was thrown out by the New York court since there was no defect in packaging. This dismissal set a new precedent, making it more difficult for consumers to recover damages from manufacturers whose packaging meets FDA standards and tampering occurs after leaving the manufacturer's control. Even so, in 1991, McNeil and Johnson & Johnson agreed to an undisclosed out-of-court settlement regarding the 1982 Tylenol murders, while maintaining that the tampering victimized both the companies and the seven victims.

Debra L. Frame
University of Cincinnati

See Also: Food and Drug Administration (U.S.); Over-the-Counter (OTC) Drugs; United States: 1951 to Present.

Further Readings

Dershewitz, Robert A. and Gerald S. Levin. "The Effect of the Tylenol Scare on Parent's Use of Over-the-Counter Drugs." *Clinical Pediatrics*, v.23/8 (1983).

Johnson, Robert Wood. *Our Credo*. New Brunswick, NJ: Johnson & Johnson, 1943. http://www.jnj.com/about-jnj/jnj-credo (Accessed June 3, 2015).

Murray, Eileen and Saundra Shohen. "Lessons From the Tylenol Tragedy on Surviving a Corporate Crisis." *Medical Marketing and Media*, v.27/2 (1992).

Tifft, Susan and Lee Griggs. "Poison Madness in the Midwest." *Time*, v.120/15 (1982).

Unani (Muslim Traditional Medicine)

Unani (also spelled Yunani) is a traditional Middle East and Asian subcontinent medicine of Graeco-Arabic origin. *Unani* is an Arabic word that means "Greek." Throughout the world, this traditional medicine continues to assist millions of people and in many cases is their exclusive or main form of health care. Yunani traditional medicine is based upon a set of holistic principles related to a person's "life force" and "humors" (Akhlat). These two principles allow the practitioner (called a *hakim*, or physician) to use a wide assortment of methods to turn a diagnosis into a treatment or therapeutic program. For example, a person's disease is based on his life force or the humors in that he has either too little or too much. A person's emotions primarily affect his life force (age can also). Life force conditions are less common than diseases resulting from disequilibrium of the four humors. A person's humors can be unbalanced by either too little of the humor or if the humor has been degraded by a toxin. These are partly the result of the environment in which one lives, partly by her life force or commonly by food and liquids she has consumed.

History of *Unani* System of Medicine

The origin of this traditional medicine dates back to the "father of medicine," Hippocrates (460–370 B.C.E.) (called *Boharath*), during the age of Pericles (562–430 B.C.E.). At the time, Hippocrates argued for reasoned explanations of infections and diseases. Prior to Hippocrates, infections and diseases were thought to be the product of superstitions, sorcery, or evil spirits that had to be expelled from the person. Hippocrates's teachings maintained that the body needed to be treated as a whole system (holistic) rather than in parts. The fundamentals of his teaching were based on the Humoral Theory, or Humorism. Even though Hippocrates's teaching is the basis of various medicines, the *Unani* traditional medicine is the only one that still follows the principles he set out.

Hippocrates's fundamentals of Graeco-Arabic medicine were built upon by other Greeks such as Galen (131–210 B.C.E.), known as "Jalinoos" in Arabic. Jalinoos's work focused on summarizing the known medical knowledge of the time, confirmed some of Hippocrates's theories, and covered multiple topics such as general medicine and anatomy and physiology. He used cupping therapy as a treatment for the first time. Galen's knowledge of anatomy and physiology was gained largely from dissecting animals rather than humans. It was forbidden during Roman times to dissect human cadavers. He did perform surgeries on humans, and his knowledge of anatomy and physiology was introduced to Arabs.

One of the first scholars to significantly advance *Unani* medicine was Persian Muhammad ibn Zakariyā Rāzī (called Rhazes) (854–925). Rhazes was a medical pioneer who accomplished many things such as using humoralism to differentiate infectious diseases; he published one of the first books on measles and smallpox and is considered the "father of pediatrics." Another *Unani* scholar was Arab Abu al-Qasim Khalaf ibn al-Abbas Al-Zahrawi (936–1013) (called Albucasis), who was considered the preeminent surgeon during medieval times and the "father of modern surgery." He wrote the 30-volume encyclopedia on medical practices around the year 1000, titled *Kitab al-Tasrif*, (The Method of Medicine). Persian Muslim scholar Abu Ali al-Husain ibn Abdullah ibn Sina (936–1037) (called simply Ibn Sina or Avicenna) is one of the most famous *Unani* hakims. He wrote the five-volume encyclopedia that summarized medical knowledge of the time in 1025, titled *al-Qānūn fī al-Ṭibb* (Canon of Medicine). Another Arab hakim, Ala-al-din abu Al-Hassan Ali ibn Abi-Hazm al-Qarshi al-Dimashqi (called Ibn al-Nafis), is best known as being the first to describe the cardiovascular system (pulmonary circulation). Collectively, these Arab and Persian hakims as well as many other medical scholars were responsible for establishing the *Unani* system of medicine as Arab medicine. The *Unani* system of medicine made it to India as a result of the Mongols' raids of Persian and central Asia, and the hakims sought refuge in India.

Fundamentals of the Humoral Theory

The fundamental concept of humoralism is that the body has four humors (e.g., black bile [sauda],

yellow bile [safra], phlegm [balgham], and blood [dam]), which a person could have either an excess or deficiency of. *Unani* philosophy maintains that a person's health and illness are dependent on maintaining an equilibrium or balance of these humors. Each of the humors is related to a temperament (Mizaj). For example, black bile temperament is "cold and dry," yellow bile is "hot and dry," phlegm is "cold and moist," and blood is "hot and moist." A disease is believed to manifest itself if all the four humors are distressed or in a state of disequilibrium. Returning the humors to equilibrium is thus critical for the patient's health. Each person has a unique temperament, which is based on all the humors that are allocated in different proportions that vary from person to person. A person's temperament is typically dominated by one humor and results in four personality archetypes, such as sanguine (blood humor with the person being pleasure-seeking and sociable), choleric (choleric [yellow bile] humor with the person being ambitious and leader-like), melancholic (black bile humor with the person being analytical and literal), and phlegmatic (phlegmatic humor with the person being relaxed and thoughtful).

Unani Medicine Diagnoses and Treatment of Health Problems

In order to diagnose a condition, a hakim takes a full case history of the patient as well as a careful visual inspection (e.g., tongue, eyes, hands, skin, fingernails, posture, tone of voice, etc.). The patient's pulse is commonly taken, and the hakim looks for overt or subtle irregularities in the pulse as a clue to her health. The various body reflexes may be investigated as well as the collection and analysis of urine and stool samples to diagnose health conditions. Thus, a hakim's diagnosis is based on clinical features of the patient.

Treatment is focused on returning the patient's body to a balanced and harmonious state.

The focus of treatment or management of the condition depends on the diagnosis and is based on whether the goal is to eliminate the cause (Izalae Sabab), normalize the humor (Tadeele Akhlat), or normalize the organ (Tadeele Aza). *Unani* traditional medicine utilizes four broad treatments that include Ilaj-Bil-Tadbeer (Regimenal Therapy), Ilaj-Bil-Ghiza (Dietotherapy), Ilaj-bil-Dawa (Pharmacotherapy), and Ilaj-bil-Yad (Surgery). The hakim's treatment will adopt different methods to bring balance to the seven basic principles, which are Arkan (elements), Mizaj (temperament), Akhlat (humors), A'za (organs), Arwah (vital spirit), Quwa (powers), and Af'aal (functions). Therapy options include changes to diet, various herbal medicines, massage (targeted at body reflexes), cupping (cold or hot), musculoskeletal manipulation, and in some cases venesection (bloodletting). The motto of *Unani* is "health is a harmony of the humors."

Unani is still taught and practiced throughout the Middle East and the Asian subcontinent. In India alone, there are at least 40 *Unani* medical colleges offering bachelor's, master's, and Ph.D. degrees in *Unani* medicine. Other countries with colleges, institutes, or programs in *Unani* medicine include Pakistan, Bangladesh, Sri Lanka, and Germany. North America does not recognize *Unani* medicine or license-trained *Unani* health professionals. *Unani* medicine is a unique traditional medicine because it is the basis for modern medicine as well as ancient traditional medicine that has been preserved from Graeco-Arabic times.

Andrew Hund
United Arab Emirates University (previous)

See Also: Access to Medicines (Developing World); History of Pharmacy as a Profession: Middle East.

Further Readings

Bendick, Jeanne. *Galen and the Gateway to Medicine*. Bathgate, ND: Bethlehem Books, 2002.

Lewis, Bernard. *The Arabs in History*. Oxford: Oxford University Press, 2002.

Pormann, Peter E. *Medieval Islamic Medicine*. Georgetown: Georgetown University Press: 2007.

Rahman, Hakim Syed Zillur. *Ḥayāt-i Karam Ḥusain*. 'Alīgaṟh: Ibn Sina Academy of Medieval Medicine and Sciences, 2008.

Rahman, Hakim Syed Zillur. *Tazkirah-yi khāndān-i 'Azīzī*, 2nd ed. 'Alīgaṟh: Academy of Medieval Medicine and Sciences, 2009.

UNITED KINGDOM

The United Kingdom is an island country in northern Europe, with an area of 243,610 square kilometers (94,058 square miles) (80th in the world) and a population of 63.7 million (23rd largest in the world). Almost four-fifths (79.6 percent as of 2011) of the population lives in urban areas, with an annual rate of urbanization of 0.8 percent. Major cities include the capital of London (9.0 million), Birmingham (2.3 million), and Manchester (2.2 million). The population is primarily White (87.2 percent), with substantial minorities of persons with heritage from Africa (3 percent) or the Indian subcontinent (4.2 percent).

The United Kingdom is a prosperous industrialized country with a high standard of living and a modern health care system and a strong system of primary, secondary, and tertiary education, including several notable research universities. In 2013, gross domestic product (GDP) per capita was £24,136.47 (U.S. $37,300) (34th in the world), with an unemployment rate of 7.2 percent and 16.2 percent of the population living below the poverty line. Life expectancy at birth is 80.4 years (29th highest in the world). Health care expenditures comprised 9.3 percent of GDP in 2011. The contraceptive prevalence rate is 84 percent, and the fertility rate of 1.9 children per woman is below replacement levels. Essentially the entire population has access to improved sources of drinking water and sanitation facilities, and literacy is almost universal at 99 percent for both men and women. The United Kingdom rates very well on measures of health care quality, and both the maternal mortality rate (12 deaths per 100,000 live births) and the infant mortality rate (4.4 deaths per 1,000 live births) are low by international comparisons.

National Health Service

The history of the National Health Service (NHS) dates back to 1948, when it was founded under the principle of providing health care services to all, financed by taxation. Today, the United Kingdom provides health care services through four national health services: NHS England, NHS Northern Ireland, NHS Scotland, and NHS Wales. In addition, the Isle of Man and the Channel Islands (Guernsey and Jersey) have independent health service structures. NHS England is the largest system and serves the largest population. NHS England employs 1.3 million people, NHS Scotland 159,748, NHS Wales 84,417, and NHS Northern Ireland 62,603. However, the systems have much in common, and often the four NHS services are treated as a single system. In this entry, NHS refers to all four systems together, but if one of the specific national services is meant, it will be specified (for instance, if statistical or other information pertains to only one system).

NHS coverage is universal for all those "ordinarily resident" in the United Kingdom, with limited coverage for visitors and illegal immigrants (e.g., emergency care, treatment for infectious diseases). NHS services are funded by taxation and provide medical and social care, including coverage for prescription drugs; while many services are free at the point

of service, some, including filling prescriptions and receiving dental treatment, may require payment of a fee. A private medical care sector also exists in the United Kingdom, with about 12 percent of residents having private insurance either provided by their employer or that they pay for directly. Advantages of private insurance include more rapid treatment for elective procedures, and coverage for items not included in NHS coverage. The NHS is generally agreed to provide a high standard of care: For instance, a 2014 study by the Commonwealth Fund rated U.K. health services best overall among 11 peer countries (Australia, Canada, France, Germany, the Netherlands, New Zealand, Norway, Sweden, Switzerland, and the United States, in addition to the United Kingdom). The United Kingdom also ranked first in 7 of the 10 specific categories evaluated: quality care, effective care, safe care, coordinated care, patient-centered care, cost-related problems, and efficiency.

NHS Structure

NHS England, after reorganization in 2013, consists of five main parts. The Department of Health is responsible for leadership and funding for health care and social care in England. It is headed by the secretary of state for health and is supported by 23 agencies and public bodies. NHS England is an independent body whose primary responsibility is to improve health outcomes by providing national leadership to improve quality of care, overseeing the operation of clinical commissioning groups (CCGs) and allocating resources to them, and commissioning primary care and specialist services. CCGs plan and commission health care services for specific local areas and provide most secondary care services, including community health services, planned hospital care, rehabilitative care, urgent and emergency care, and mental health and learning disability services. Health and well-being boards act as a forum for local commissioners and encourage strong working relationships between health care and social care. Public Health England provides national leadership on public health and aids local government and the NHS with emergency response needs.

Licensing of Medicines

Medicines in the United Kingdom are classified into three types, as specified in the Medicines Act 1968. Two of the classifications refer to types of over-the-counter drugs: those on the general sales list, which can be supplied by someone other than a pharmacist, and those that can only be supplied through a pharmacy or by a health care professional. The third type of drug is a prescription-only medication or POM. All medicines sold in the United Kingdom must be licensed and must conform with European Union legislation. Manufactured herbal medicines either must meet the requirements of the traditional herbal registration scheme or must be licensed, but herbal medicines made up for an individual patient following a consultation do not require registration or licensing. Homeopathic medicines are authorized through "product licenses of right" and are assessed for safety and quality only (not effectiveness). Homeopathic medicines may not claim that they are therapeutic for serious conditions, but may make claims regarding the treatment or relief of minor symptoms or conditions that would not ordinarily require a physician's care.

Medicines for human use in the United Kingdom must be licensed by one of two organizations: the Medicines and Healthcare Products Regulatory Agency (MHRA), which grants licenses for use within the United Kingdom, and the European Medicines Agency (EMA), which grants licenses for use within the European Union. The review process before a license is granted includes research on safety and effectiveness using tissue culture, computer analysis, and animal testing, followed by clinical trials in humans (if the medicine passes the initial stages of testing). Medicines are licensed for use only after they have passed all phases of the clinical trial process. Major questions to be answered through the licensing process are whether the medicine is safe and effective for the intended purpose, and whether its benefits outweigh its risks.

The license for a given medicine includes information such as the health conditions for which it is intended, dosage, length of treatment, form of the medicine (e.g., liquid or tablet), restrictions on use (e.g., whether it should only be used for people above a certain age), safety warning, storage instructions, and expiration information. Drugs are provided to health care professionals with a summary of product characteristics (SPC), including this information, and a patient information leaflet (PIL) intended to provide information about the medicine directly to the patient.

In Scotland, details about medicines that have passed the licensing process for the United Kingdom must also be submitted to the Scottish Medicines Consortium (SMC), which will decide if they should be available in Scotland. The New Drugs Committee of the SMC, made up of professionals from the medical, pharmaceutical, statistics, and economics fields, examines information about newly licensed drugs to decide issues such as whether the medicine is effective, whether currently available treatments are superior, and whether the new medicine gives good value for money compared to currently existing treatments.

The SMC gives one of three decisions on a drug: accepted for use, accepted for restricted use (for instance, for a specific patient group), or not recommended for use. Medicines classified as not recommended for use do not need to be made routinely available by the NHS, but they may be available to individual patients under special circumstances. The most common reasons for a not recommended decision are that the manufacturer does not submit the drug to the SMC, that the supporting information is based on an inappropriate comparator (for instance, if the drug was tested against a drug not currently used in Scotland), that the drug is judged no more effective than a less expensive current medicine, and that the cost of the new medicine is not justified in terms of its benefits. The latter reason is common, and may be illustrated by an extreme example: If a drug could lengthen patient life by one day, but cost a million pounds, it could be said to be better (because it does lengthen patient life), but the cost of the drug (1 million pounds) would not be justified by such a minor improvement.

Adverse Event Reporting

The U.K. system for reporting adverse events relating to medicines and health care products is known as the Yellow Card Scheme (YCS). Adverse event reports can be filed by patients, as well as health care professionals, by telephone, over the Internet, or by using a form supplied in pharmacies. The YCS collects information about adverse drug reactions (ADRs), adverse incidents related to medical devices, defective medicines, and fake or counterfeit medicines and medical devices. ADRs can be reported for vaccines, blood factors and immunoglobulin products, and herbal or complementary medicines as well as prescription medicines. Reports of ADRs, also known as side effects, are evaluated by a team of medicine safety experts and evaluated in terms of already-reported side effects for the particular medicine and the side effects known for other medicines used to treat the same condition. New medicines and vaccines, which are

marked by an inverted black triangle in documents such as the *British National Formulary* and in product summary leaflets, are subject to additional monitoring, and health care professionals and patients are urged to report all side effects for products carrying the black triangle symbol.

Examples of adverse events related to medical devices include a thermometer providing an incorrect reading and a wheelchair with faulty brakes. All adverse events with medical devices should be reported, and reported events will be investigated by the MHRA. The category of defective medicines includes products of unacceptable quality as well as problems with packaging or with the information provided (e.g., the patient information leaflet). The Defective Medicines Reporting Centre (DMRC) receives all reports of defective medicines, and may issue drug alerts and recall notices for issues relevant to public health. Reports of fake or counterfeit medicines are investigated by the MHRA, which has the power to seize products from businesses or private property if they are suspected of violating the human medicines regulations of the United Kingdom, and to prosecute offenders.

NHS Medicines Coverage

Prescription drugs were one of the first items supplied by the NHS that required a payment by the user, and the system has moved several times between charging fees for prescriptions and providing them for free. The first prescription fees, of one shilling, were imposed in 1952, and prescription fees remained in place until they were abolished in 1965. However, prescription fees were reintroduced in 1968. As of 2011, NHS Wales and NHS Northern Ireland did not impose prescription fees, and Scotland was scheduled to phase out prescription fees also, while NHS England continued to charge prescription fees.

As of April 2014, the charge for prescription medication under NHS England was £8.05 (U.S. $12.25). Several different prescription prepayment certificates (PPCs) are available to lower costs for people who need to fill many prescriptions, as a PPC provides unlimited prescriptions for £2 (U.S. $3.04) per week during a specified time period in return for payment of a flat fee. A 3-month PPC costs £29.10 (U.S. $44.30) and a 12-month PPC costs £104.00 (U.S. $158.32). Over-the-counter medicines are not covered by the NHS and must be paid for by the individual, although there is an informal practice to assist patients by issuing a prescription for a drug that can also be obtained over the counter.

Some individuals are eligible for free NHS England prescriptions. These include people under age 16 or over age 59, those ages 16 to 18 participating in full-time education, women who are pregnant or have given birth within the past year, those with continuing physical disability, NHS inpatients, and those with war disabilities. Persons with low income, and their partners and dependent children, are eligible for free NHS prescriptions if they are entitled to an NHS tax credit exemption certificate or HC2 certificate or if they receive Income Support, Income-Based Jobseeker's Allowance, Income-related Employment and Support Allowance, Pension Credit, Guarantee Credit, or Universal Credit. In addition, low-income individuals not eligible for free prescriptions may qualify for an HC3 certificate, which entitles them to partial assistance in paying prescription fees.

The Pharmaceutical Industry

Pharmaceutical manufacturing is a significant industry in the United Kingdom. As of 2007, the pharmaceutical industry employed about 67,000 people and produced exports valued at £14.6 billion (more than U.S. $22 billion). The United Kingdom ranked fourth in the world in 2007 on the basis of value of exports, behind Germany, Switzerland, and the United States. The same year, pharmaceutical imports were valued at £10.3 billion (more than U.S. $15.5 billion). In March 2009, there were 10,475 community pharmacies, 38 percent of which were independent, with the remainder part of a chain. Almost all of the population (99 percent) can reach a pharmacy within 20 minutes by car, and 96 percent can reach a pharmacy by walking or using public transportation. In 2005, about 26,000 pharmacists were practicing in the United Kingdom, of which 70 percent worked in community pharmacies, 22 percent in hospitals, and most of the remainder in academia, industry, or primary care.

In 2008, pharmaceutical expenditures for the NHS came to a total of £10.8 billion (more than U.S. $16 billion), with total expenditures on pharmaceuticals including private expenditures of £12.2 billion (more than U.S. $18.5 billion). In 2009, 886 million NHS prescription items were dispensed through NHS England, for an average of 16.4 pharmaceutical items per capita (a 63 percent increase from the average of 10.5 in 1998). Over 40 percent of medicines sold in the United Kingdom are generics.

Sarah E. Boslaugh
Saint Louis University

See Also: Access to Medicines (Industrialized World); Adverse Drug Events Reporting Systems; Adverse Drug Reactions (ADR) and Adverse Events (AE); Advertising to Patients; British Pharmacological Society, The; University of Oxford.

Further Readings

Boyle, Sean. *Health Systems in Transition: United Kingdom (England): Health System Review 2011.* Copenhagen: WHO Regional Office for Denmark,

2011. http://www.euro.who.int/__data/assets/pdf_file/0004/135148/e94836.pdf (Accessed March 19, 2015).

Davis, Karen, Kristof Stremkis, David Squires, and Cathy Schoen. *Mirror, Mirror on the Wall, 2014 Update: How the U.S. Health Care System Compares Internationally.* New York: The Commonwealth Fund, June 2014. http://www.commonwealthfund.org/publications/fund-reports/2014/jun/mirror-mirror (Accessed March 18, 2014).

Fahrni, Mathumalar L., Bryony D. Franklin, Salman Rawaf, and Azeem Majeed. "Improving Medication Safety in UK Care Homes: Challenges and Current Perspective." *JRSM Open*, v.5/2 (February 2014). http://www.ncbi.nlm.nih.gov/pmc/articles/PMC4012648/ (Accessed March 19, 2015).

Medicines and Healthcare Products Regulatory Agency. "Yellow Card." https://yellowcard.mhra.gov.uk (Accessed March 19, 2015).

NHS Inform. "Medicines Information: Licensing of Medicines." http://www.nhsinform.co.uk/health-library/articles/m/medicinesinfo/licensing/ (Accessed March 19, 2015).

Organisation for Economic Co-operation and Development. "Pharmaceutical Price Policies in a Global Market." OECD Health Policy Studies. Paris: Organisation for Economic Co-operation and Development, 2008. http://apps.who.int/medicinedocs/documents/s19834en/s19834en.pdf (Accessed March 19, 2015).

Pharmaceutical Health Information System. "PHIS Pharma Profile: United Kingdom 2010." http://whocc.goeg.at/Literaturliste/Dokumente/CountryInformationReports/PHIS%20Pharma%20Profile%20UK%20Feb2011.pdf (Accessed March 19, 2015).

Smith, Ian. *Building a World-Class NHS.* New York: Palgrave Macmillan, 2007.

United States: 1800 to 1850

The treatment of mental and physical illness from 1800 to 1850 in the United States reveals the promise and potential of the time's conceptualizations, but the folly and ineffectiveness of its practices. Postcolonial but largely premodern, this era began to understand mental illness as a worldly disease, though it could not alleviate mental illness with effective treatments. Homespun wisdom and lifestyle were the mainstays of treating moderate mental illness, while institutionalization became the mainstay of treating severe mental illness. Many scholars date the origins of scientific pharmacology to the mid-19th century, when the first university program in the subject was established at the University of Dorpat in Estonia. The United States lagged behind Europe in establishing pharmacology on a scientific basis, so the practice of pharmacists and apothecaries remained based on supplying a variety of remedies, some based on traditional herbal formulas. In the treatment of mental illness in particular, psychopharmacology from 1800 to 1850 played an adjunctive role, and when used, it either benignly sedated or unintentionally harmed.

Understanding Mental Illness

The late 18th century lit the way for the early 19th century. Within the larger context of Enlightenment progress and scientific advance, mental illness was separated from theology, just as church was separated from state. Even regimens with religious elements, such as the moral treatment, advanced by pious Quakers, were progressively humane in intention as well as largely secular in orientation. Early 19th-century Americans then were able to understand mental illness as an affliction, not entirely different from a bodily affliction. Unlike many in early modern Europe or some in colonial New England, early Americans increasingly understood that mental illness was not a signature of divine wrath or demonic subterfuge. Though they had largely freed themselves of moral and religious explanations, the inhabitants of the early 19th-century United States lacked a compendium of mental illness, but were increasingly acquiring the knowledge necessary to make fine discriminations among different disorders. Still, there was not yet a framework for differential diagnosis or a standardized vocabulary to assist classification and foster discussion. For instance, 19th-century Americans spoke of ennui and doldrums rather than of depression and dysthymia. More importantly, without operational definitions, words such as *melancholia* and *dementia praecox* varied considerably in usage. However, problems of identification, classification, and operationalization were not as crippling as the relative absence of effective treatments.

Treatments of Mental Illness

Correspondence and social communication, riding and walking, work and routine—these were among the remedies employed to stave off mental illness. Rest, diet, baths, waters, diversion, seclusion, and activities were among the common frontline treatments for mental illness. For the severely mentally ill, there were institutions; Philadelphia's Pennsylvania Hospital, opening in 1752 under Quaker direction, as per the National Institute of Mental Health, was one of the earliest examples. Virginia later opened a hospital to care for the mentally ill, but colonial facilities remained uncommon. These vanishingly rare early prototypes set the precedent for the opening of many more mental hospitals in the early 1800s: New York's Bloomingdale Insane Asylum and Utica Psychiatric Center, and Kentucky's Eastern Lunatic Asylum, for instance. Nevertheless, mental hospitals remained rare; this age was not the great age of institutionalization, though it presaged that era. It was during the late 1840s that Dorothea Dix would lobby for the mentally ill,

preparing the legal framework and impassioned atmosphere that would precipitate the construction of countless mental hospitals in the latter part of the 19th century. This expansion was, however, not particular to mental illness, but more generally symptomatic of governmental expansion. As historian Roy Porter notes, the early 19th-century asylum represents a secular, paternalistic reaction of the rational state subsuming responsibilities heretofore relegated to family and parish.

Pharmaceutical treatments were limited. As segregation of the mentally ill was just then becoming commonplace, so was the sedation of the mentally ill. Truly, most early-era 19th-century drugs did sedate more than alleviate. Alcohol was of course used as a method of self-medication, but it was also sometimes suggested as a treatment by physicians. Naturally occurring compounds such as lithium, though discovered and isolated in this age, were not yet applied to the treatment of mental illness in the United States. One emerging medicine was chloral hydrate, variously used as a sedative and stabilizer to treat paresis, mania, depression, and epilepsy. There was also laudanum, a tincture of opium appreciated for its analgesic properties and used to treat anything from dysentery and yellow fever to meningitis and heart disease. Though less frequently, laudanum was also used as a sedative for the agitated and mentally ill. However, as David Healy, author of *The Creation of Psychopharmacology*, asserts, many in the early 1800s had little hope of finding an herb, tincture, tonic, or pill that might bring relief, happiness, hope, or sanity. With the use of hyoscine, bromide, and barbiturates still decades away, and the use of tricyclics, selective serotonin reuptake inhibitors (SSRIs), and antipsychotics much further in the future, there was much reason for pessimism.

The Lincolns as Exemplars

The exceptional life of Abraham Lincoln subsumes many aspects of mental illness within its 56 years: much grief and loss in childhood, multiple bouts of depression in early adulthood, pathology encountered in marriage, and stress and grief imposed by war. Though his life is in many ways exceptional, these particular aspects of his life are less so. Along with frustrated ambitions compounded by financial impositions came the loss of Anne Rutledge. Shortly after losing this first love, a young Lincoln became severely depressed as he pondered the cold rain soaking her buried corpse. Though as a boy he protected turtles from torture and as a man he would not hunt for food, at this time in his life Lincoln took long walks through the woods with a gun. As Joshua Shenk notes, an 1838 edition of the *Sangamo Journal* printed "The Suicide's Soliloquy," an unsigned poem often attributed to Lincoln, which ended thus:

Yes! I've resolved the deed to do; and this the place to do it: This heart I'll rush a dagger through, though I in hell shall rue it!

Using his droll eloquence, Lincoln himself wrote in a letter in 1841 that "I am now the most miserable man living. If what I feel were equally distributed to the whole human family there would not be one cheerful face on the earth." At this time in his relative youth, beset with loss and setbacks, a neighbor thought him crazy as a loon, and a doctor said he came within an inch of being a perfect lunatic for life. One colorful acquaintance said that he had two cat fits and a duck fit. Eventually he was confined to his bed under the care of his doctor who was careful to remove sharp objects and keep constant vigil. For treatment of such a period of hypochondriasis, which seems equivalent to a major depressive episode, Lincoln

was personally prescribed unknown tonics, ether, opium, and morphine, in addition to the standard remedies of inducing vomiting and letting blood. Most famously, Lincoln also, then and later, took the blue mass or the blue pill, which modern researchers have demonstrated to cause neurobehavioral problems. The blue mass contains mercury, a known neurotoxin, which is now strictly regulated by the U.S. Environmental Protection Agency (EPA).

While Abraham Lincoln's most severe bouts of mental illness came early in life, Mary Lincoln's most severe bouts of mental illness came late in life. After her husband's death in 1865, Mary became delusional, imagining the grave illness of her son Robert and believing firmly that poverty stared her in the face despite ample pensioning, investments, and liquid assets. As neatly consolidated by historian Jason Emerson, the postwar years witnessed the height of her mental illness; times when she slandered her son, made a suicide attempt, and was forcibly institutionalized. Yet, as a variety of primary and secondary historical documents show, her mental illness was more mildly manifest throughout her life with Lincoln. For years, Mary showed fascination with the occult, visiting mystics and participating in séances where she could commune with the dead. She also expressed extreme mood lability, leading some to believe that she displayed character pathology, while also expressing protracted mood states, leading some to believe that she displayed bipolar disorder. In response to Mary's mental instability, acquisitiveness, impulsivity, and haughtiness, Lincoln's secretary John Nicolay dubbed her the hellcat, Lincoln's law partner William Herndon called her the tigress and the female wildcat of the age, and the Whitehouse physician Robert Stone called her a perfect devil. Moreover, when a boy who saw Abraham Lincoln dressing for his wedding asked him where he was going, he replied, "To hell I suppose." Not surprisingly, Mary was variously treated with chloral hydrate, laudanum, and placebos.

Benjamin Rush

As the Lincolns serve as exemplars of the 19th-century mental patient, Benjamin Rush serves as an exemplar of the 19th-century psychiatric physician. Rush graduated from the University of Edinburgh and began practicing medicine in Philadelphia in 1769. Gracing the back of the *Diagnostic and Statistical Manual of Mental Disorders*, Rush is widely recognized as the father of American psychiatry, in addition to being a man of letters, founding father, and signer of the Declaration of Independence. Rush is the author of *Medical Inquiries and Observations Upon the Diseases of the Mind*, an 1812 publication representing the culmination of an impassioned career battling psychopathology on rational foundations. The classic text considered causal factors as various as climate, socioeconomic status, loss, mental stimulation, revolution, and injustice. Rush's treatise is scientific in orientation because of its heavy reliance on clinical anecdotes and results of autopsy, as well as its references to large inpatient samples. Especially informative is the inclusion of letters from patients detailing symptoms. Though not formally derived data from controlled studies, his compilation of anecdotes is, nonetheless, used inductively as a foundation for deductions. In other words, the general principles propounded by Rush are based in collections of empirical observations. *Medical Inquiries and Observations Upon the Diseases of the Mind* is properly understood as a product of the Enlightenment, the cosmopolitan intellectual movement that witnessed the mapping of the mathematics of nature in Newtonian law, the isolation of oxygen by Joseph Priestley, and the electrical experiments of Benjamin Franklin. It is an archetypal Enlightenment treatise because of its rationalistic, secular, scientific,

and empirical approach. It is also characteristic of Enlightened thought in the optimism that it radiates—optimism that is embodied in the following passage:

> After the history that has been given of the distress, despair, and voluntary death, which are induced by that partial derangement which has been described, I should lay down my pen, and bedew my paper with tears, did I not know that the science of medicine has furnished a remedy for it, and that hundreds are now alive, and happy, who were once afflicted with it! Blessed Science! which thus extends its friendly empire, not only over the evils of the body, but over those of the minds, of the children of men! (p. 95)

Medical Inquiries and Observations Upon the Diseases of the Mind comes closest to being an authoritative and representative disciplinary statement. Not only did it have the weight of its author's name, but it was influential by virtue of its scope, addressing in a single volume derangement, mania, manicula (a chronic low-level mania, possibly analogous to present descriptions of cyclothymia), manalgia (general insanity accompanied by torpor), *démence* (literally "dementia" in French, this seemed to be used by Rush and also by Philippe Pinel to denote the symptom of dissociation in the context of general madness), hypochondriasis (mood dysregulation; chiefly depression and morbidity), tristimania (nearly synonymous with unipolar depression), fatuity (an absence of memory and reason), disorders of belief (delusions), disorders of sleep, illusions (visual and auditory hallucinations), pathological reverie (attention and concentration problems, which were seen as stemming either from depression or from anxiety), hypersexuality, moral insanity (akin to antisocial behavior), torpor, and dissociation. Though always admirably secular and materialist in orientation, Rush propounded a rather simplistic causal framework, emphasizing circulatory irregularities above cerebral irregularities in his explanation of mental illness. In this way, for all its modernism, Rush shows the continuing influence of Hippocrates and Galen and their theory of humoral imbalance. Noting anecdotes of melancholy persons with low heart rates and agitated persons with high heart rates, Rush looked partially to pulse regulation as a means of imparting mental stability. Following this theory, he advocated the use of digitalis, a compound extracted from certain species of foxglove plants acting as a depressant by activating the parasympathetic branch of the autonomic nervous system. A more properly pharmaceutical version of digitalis, digoxin, is still in use, though it regulates cardiac function with no purported direct effects on mental illness.

Medical Inquiries and Observations Upon the Diseases of the Mind is also notable for its respect of organic and psychosocial origins of madness. Because he had a nuanced appreciation of mental illness, Rush offered many interventions acting, as he put it, "on the body indirectly through the medium of the mind" (p. 96). First, he thought alleviation came partially from compassion and adopting a grave posture by which the physician instilled confidence in patients, and faith in the efficacy of the medicines being prescribed. He also sometimes offered financial relief or marital advice, while sometimes recommending religious counseling, kindness, amusements, music, or travel. Still, direct bodily interventions seemed to be primary, though many of these were not specific to mental illness and some were not pharmaceutical. Rush counseled the use of direct and drastic interference to patients' bodies in an effort to stimulate their constitutions. Drastic interference included bloodletting at rates of 12 pints in four months, rates that exceeded those used for bodily disorders. For various mental maladies,

he also favored cupping and blistering around the temples, administration of diarrhea-inducing drugs, leeches, fasting, mustard rubs, cold and warm baths, exercise on horseback, purges, emetics, restricted diet, friction to the trunk of the body, exercise, and pain stimulation.

Rush also reviewed those treatments that were more consonant with a modern understanding of psychopharmacology. Rush and other physicians of his age advocated the use of errhines, a class of medicines producing nasal mucus. He also suggested the clinical efficacy of Madeira wine, arsenic, and strychnine, as well as niter, which is one of a group of potassium nitrates that comprise saltpeter.

Rush used Peruvian bark, also known as Jesuit's bark, which derives from the *Cinchona* genus of South American trees, and can be refined in the production of quinine, the substance that proved integral in the treatment of malaria. Opium seemed to be his sedative mainstay. Camphor, produced from the camphor laurel tree, valued for its aromatic properties, and presently used in vapor rubs, was then used as an adjunctive treatment for various nervous disorders. Finally, hellebore, which comes from a European perennial of the same name, was sometimes chosen to induce vomiting because of its toxicity.

Physical Illness

In the time after 1850, there came an overwrought dichotomy between mind and body, only now palliated by findings from subdisciplines like psychoneuroimmunology, which demonstrates physical effects of mental stress. However, between 1800 and 1850, the mind–body distinction erred in being insufficiently distinct. In a time when the germ theory of disease was just being articulated, physicians, as was noted in the case of Benjamin Rush, clung to the antiquated theory of humoral imbalance and other tenets suggesting a specious integration of mental and physical maladies, and therefore a credulous blending of mental and physical treatments. In this vein, it will be recalled that laudanum sedated the mentally ill while also treating yellow fever, bloodletting corrected the humoral imbalances common to depression and fever, and the aforementioned blue mass cheered the melancholic and cured the syphilitic.

One can read outsized wisdom into the historical record by suggesting, for instance, that the use of the central nervous system depressant digitalis is representative of some inchoate understanding of the James-Lange theory of emotion (developed in the 19th century by William James and Carl Lange, working independently) and akin to using beta-blockers to inhibit the physiological catalysts of situational anxiety. While there is perhaps some truth in such a reading of events, there is the greater likelihood of anachronistically ascribing modern knowledge to those who were still swayed by the humoral system, and consequently still conflating fundamentals of physical and mental illness.

Dispensing Pharmaceuticals

Prior to the 19th century in America, most medicines were dispensed by physicians, but after 1800 it became more common for drugs to be available in apothecary shops. The apothecary or druggist often sold drugs to both the general public and to physicians and was expect to be able to compound drugs and make common pharmaceutical preparations in the shop. Drugs, mostly patent medicines and herbal preparations, were also sold in general stores, but the owners of these establishments generally sold only prepackaged items. Some drug preparation was also handled by wholesale druggists, who had sufficient knowledge of chemistry and pharmacology to manufacture drugs on a large scale.

The contemporary state of knowledge in terms of pharmaceutical compounding is preserved in the 1820 *Phamacopoeia of the United States*, created by Samuel Latham Mitchill and Lyman Spalding, who had training in both medicine and chemistry. This work gave instructions and recipes for creating drugs such as calomel (mercurous chloride) and silver nitrate from chemicals and other substances. Instructions for creating drugs from chemicals and *materia medica* are also recorded in other publications, such as the *Journal of the Philadelphia College of Pharmacy* founded in 1825.

The quality of the chemicals and other materials used to make drugs became an issue in the 1840s. There was little to no regulation at the time, and as European countries became more strict about the quality of drugs sold, more inferior and adulterated materials began turning up in the United States. The poor quality of available drugs was blamed for the deaths of a number of soldiers during the Mexican-American War (1846–1848), and Congress responded by passing the Drug Importation Act of 1848. Implementing this act, which called for drug materials to be inspected at ports before being allowed to enter the United States, proved difficult because few standards were available to judge the quality of botanical materials. In contrast, manuals already existed providing methods to test the content and quality of chemical materials.

Steven Charles Hertler
College of New Rochelle

See Also: Central Nervous System Depressants and Stimulants; Psychopharmacology; United States: 1851 to 1900.

Further Readings

American Psychiatric Association. *Diagnostic and Statistical Manual of Mental Disorders*, 5th ed. Washington, DC: Author, 2013.

Bynum, William F. *Science and the Practice of Medicine in the Nineteenth Century.* Cambridge, UK: Cambridge University Press, 1994.

Deutsch, Albert. *The Mentally Ill in America: A History of Their Care and Treatment From Colonial Times.* New York: Columbia University Press, 1945.

Emerson, Jason. *The Madness of Mary Lincoln.* Carbondale, IL: Southern Illinois University Press, 2007.

Healy, David. *The Creation of Psychopharmacology.* Cambridge, MA: Harvard University Press, 2004.

Higby, Gregory J. "Chemistry and the 19th-Century American Pharmacist." *Bulletin of the History of Chemistry,* v.28/1 (2003).

Lincoln, Abraham. "Letter to John T. Stuart" (January 23, 1841). http://quod.lib.umich.edu/l/lincoln/lincoln 1/1:248?rgn=div1;view=fulltext (Accessed June 4, 2015).

Porter, Roy. *Madness: A Brief History.* New York: Oxford University Press, 2002.

Rush, Benjamin. *Medical Inquiries and Observations Upon the Diseases of the Mind.* Philadelphia, PA: Kimber & Richardson, 1812.

Scheindlin, Stanley. "A Brief History of Pharmacology." *Modern Drug Discovery,* v.4/5 (May 2001). http://pubs.acs.org/subscribe/archive/mdd/v04/i05/html/05timeline.html (Accessed March 14, 2015).

Shenk, Joshua Wolf. *Lincoln's Melancholy: How Depression Challenged a President and Fueled His Greatness.* New York: Houghton Mifflin, 2005.

Wallace, Edwin and John Gach. *History of Psychiatry and Medical Psychology: With an Epilogue on Psychiatry and the Mind-Body Relation.* New York: Springer, 2010.

UNITED STATES: 1851 TO 1900

Derived from the Greek φάρμακον (*phármakon* meaning "drug"), the term *pharmacy* constitutes both the professional practice that links health sciences with the chemical sciences, and the physical establishment utilized for the purposes of collecting, compounding, preparing, preserving, dispensing, and standardizing drugs and medications. The history of pharmacy practice reveals a distinct relationship between this emerging allied health profession and the evolution of therapeutics and various phases and manifestations of treatment modalities that continues today. For centuries, the only way an individual could enter a health care profession was through apprenticeship. Under this system, an aspiring pharmacist, referred to at the time as an *apothecary* (Latin for "pharmacist"), would learn by observing and performing medication-related activities, often side-by-side under the tutelage of the master craftsman. One such example was Benedict Arnold (1741–1801), who served as an apothecary apprentice for 5 years before operating a successful pharmacy for 12 years. Regrettably, history reveals that Arnold gained infamy when, as a general for the American Continental Army during the Revolutionary War, he became one of the nation's most notorious traitors when he defected to the British Army.

Until pharmacy was established as an independent science, there is a historical evolution that demonstrates the course of this science has a connection to medicine as far back as the 6th century B.C.E. with the *Sushruta Samhita,* an Ayurvedic (Hindu medicine) text that contained a collection of medicinal preparations and surgical procedures for the treatment of various ailments of the time. Consequently, pharmacy practice in the United States also appears to have emerged from the field of medicine, and for much of the 18th century, there was no clear distinction between the two professions. While apothecary shops—mercantile establishments where medicine and other articles are sold—were in existence since the northern American colonies were originally founded, the classic American drugstore did not actually come to exist until the early 1800s. It was not all that uncommon to enter the local drugstore and see shiny soda fountain fixtures, mahogany furnishings, and old "doc," the friendly neighborhood apothecary, standing behind the counter ready to dispense medicines to treat a vast array of minor ailments common at the time. Prior to this period, physicians and their apprentices were responsible for compounding and dispensing medications directly to their patients.

By 1850, American drugstores consisted of a "front end" pharmacy work area and a back area that consisted of a general emporium that contained a small factory to manufacture ingredients and preparations that would eventually be combined into medications for physician prescriptions. Here, the apothecary would supervise the shop and oversee the work of clerks (employed pharmacists) and apprentices who, at the time, not only waited on customers but also were responsible for much of the hard labor associated with sorting, grinding, and filtering the crude ingredients for the drug compounding process. In June 1885, Charles "Doc" Alderton, a pharmacist at Morrison's Old Corner Drug Store in Waco, Texas, applied his pharmaceutical knowledge to blend assorted fruit flavors and conducted various experiments to concoct a soda fountain drink he called the "Waco." In December of the same year, the U.S. Patent Office officially recognized the popular soft drink that Alderton invented as Dr. Pepper. W. B. Morrison, the drugstore owner where Alderton worked and the first person to sample the drink, is largely credited with naming Dr. Pepper after a physician—Dr. Charles T. Pepper—for whom he previously worked in his home state of Virginia.

The mid-18th century also saw a shift from patients being administered strong postoperative medications, including cathartics, emetics, and diaphoretics, to a milder regimen that emphasized a more holistic approach, including clean air, diet, and rest. In the 1840s, the United States made its first great contribution to the field of medicine with the discovery of inhaled anesthesia, including ether, chloroform, and nitrous oxide, which allowed surgeons to delve into lengthy, more complex surgical procedures in the 1850s and 1860s. In 1866, William Warner executed large-scale manufacturing of sugarcoated pills, which, in turn, transformed the pharmaceutical industry by introducing new techniques of mass production. During the 1870s, his noteworthy contribution paved the way for Joseph Lister's (1827–1912) revolutionary approach to antiseptic surgery when he operated in a mist of carbolic acid in an attempt to eliminate microorganisms from the surgical field. Such an unorthodox approach led to the general adoption of aseptic surgery in the 1890s, which, consequently, resulted in hospitals becoming the heart of medical care in the United States. In 1879, to address the issues associated with the varied active alkaloidal and glucosidal content contained in plant remedies (which resulted in two preparations of vegetable drugs seldom having the same strength), Parke, Davis & Company introduced "Liquor Ergotae Purificatus," a controversial medicine for childbirth that, unfortunately, caused severe circulatory and nervous system impairments. Based on the work of Albert Brown Lyons, the company's chief chemist, methods of alkaloidal assay were further developed, which led to Parke and Davis announcing a list of 20 standardized "normal liquids" in 1883. However, perhaps the single most influential advancement in everyday pharmacy practice was the introduction of mass-produced compressed tablets in the 1890s. This revolutionary innovation allowed one person to run multiple machines at once, which, in turn, had the capacity to punch out 1 million headache tablets in a single day.

The 18th century saw pharmacy practice begin to remove itself from medicine to eventually become its own profession. America's first pharmacist, Jonathan Roberts, was hired by Pennsylvania Hospital—the first American hospital, founded in 1752 by Benjamin Franklin (1706–1790) and Thomas Bond

(1712–1784)—soon after opening its doors to arrange medication and other supplies. Roberts, like many early American hospital apothecaries, was an apprentice physician who was expected not only to manage his "shop"—referring to the hospital's pharmacy at that time—but to round on patients, oversee the medical library, and perform minor surgery. As previously mentioned, physicians—not pharmacists—compounded their own prescriptions. Consequently, Roberts was assigned to such general duties at Pennsylvania Hospital. Another pharmacy pioneer was Charles Rice (1841–1901) who, after being discharged as a patient at Bellevue Hospital in New York City in 1865, went to work for the same hospital washing bottles for the hospital's drug department, which, at the time, was the largest in the United States. Because of his intensity, familiarity with contemporary pharmacy and chemistry, and proficiency to both read and speak several foreign languages, Rice gained the respect and admiration of John Frey, head of the drug department. As a result, Rice became Frey's assistant and ultimately succeeded him to become the department head where he not only oversaw the testing of milk consumed in all New York City hospitals, but was responsible for the purchase of all medications and surgical supplies for these hospitals. Martin I. Wilbert (1865–1916) was another prominent early pharmacist who, after graduating from the prestigious Philadelphia College of Pharmacy (founded in 1821 as the first institution of higher education in the United States devoted to pharmacy) in 1890, was hired at the German Hospital in Philadelphia where he redesigned the pharmacy and installed drug assaying and manufacturing equipment before being appointed as the first director of the hospital's roentgenology department. Susan Hayhurst (1829–unknown) was a physician who, after graduating from the Woman's Medical College of Philadelphia in

1857, ran its pharmaceutical department for several years. In 1883, at the age of 63, she was the first woman to graduate from the Philadelphia College of Pharmacy, subsequently becoming the first practicing female pharmacist in the United States. Until this time, when compared to male pharmacists, women were viewed as not physically strong enough to pound the ingredients with sufficient force necessary to properly crush them for use in compounding. Over the next 33 years of her life, Hayhurst served as a preceptor for women pharmacists.

A gathering of 20 pharmacists in Philadelphia led to the founding of the American Pharmacists Association (APhA) in 1852. Under the leadership of its first president, Daniel B. Smith (1792–1883), and first secretary, William Procter Jr. (1817–1874), the association opened its membership to "all pharmaceutists and druggists" of good character who supported its constitution and code of ethics. The objectives of the APhA included not only increasing the professionalism of pharmacy practice, but encouraging its members to represent the organization on governmental matters, particularly those specific to the establishment of standards for drugs and chemicals. Regrettably, even after the APhA was founded, the professional identity of the pharmacy practice developed gradually and erratically in the United States. That same year (1852), pharmacists began to place their compounding areas near the front of their shops in order to not only take advantage of the natural light coming through their windows, but also showcase their professional abilities as pharmacy practitioners. During this period, many pharmacists made their vocation to sell medicines for the sole purpose of making money. It was not until the 1854 APhA meeting that Procter, who in 1846 was elected by association trustees to the newly created professorship of pharmacy at the Philadelphia College of Pharmacy, brought his disapproval for such capitalistic ideals to the forefront by emphasizing that it was the making of medicines, not the selling of them, that was at the heart of pharmacy. Furthermore, Procter and his allies within the organization were against the purchasing of "readymade" pharmaceutical preparations from large manufacturers. While many like-minded professionals rallied behind Procter's cause throughout the remainder of the century, they were unsuccessful in making sweeping changes to the practice as a whole.

In 1857, the second pharmacy journal to be published in the United States, *American Druggists' Circular and Chemical Gazette* (the first being the *Journal of the Philadelphia College of Pharmacy* in 1825, later renamed the *American Journal of Pharmacy* in 1835), provided an independent outlet of communication regarding the daily needs experienced by the average pharmacy practitioner. Sadly, it never attained the notoriety or character of the *American Journal of Pharmacy*. Meanwhile, the profession itself was at a crossroads between those who demonstrated careful manufacturing and compounding of drugs and the increasing threat of quack remedies promising quick relief and unrealistic cures, many of which were a danger to public health. In response to the growing professional and public concern, a number of state laws to regulate pharmacy were enacted in the 1870s and 1880s that improved the quality of pharmacy practice throughout the United States. In addition, the APhA published the first *National Formulary of Unofficial Preparations (NF)* in 1888 that included a collection of prescription recipes for medicinal use that could be easily compounded utilizing standardized ingredients listed in the *United States Pharmacopeia (USP)*, which was a reference publication first released in 1820 during the U.S. Pharmacopeial Convention (USPC) in Washington, D.C.

Although the Civil War split the nation into separate yet distinct alliances in the early to mid-1860s, the emerging pharmaceutical industry flourished with manufacturing entrepreneurs such as E. R. Squibb, a former Navy surgeon and founder of E. R. Squibb & Company, and rival businesses increasing drug preparations for the war effort. In addition, hospital directors, such as those employed at the U.S. Army General Hospital in Philadelphia, actively sought out trained pharmacists, in large part, as not only buyers of medical goods, but experts in the extemporaneous manufacturing of drug preparations. Early attempts at formalized pharmacy education were met with varying degrees of success. During this period, most pharmacy schools operated privately from student fees or the occasional generous contribution from interested pharmacists, some of whom established small member associations and, in turn, presided over a school. The passage of the Morrill Act in 1862 established "land grant" colleges, in which each state was provided 30,000 acres of public land for each U.S. senator and representative under the 1860 census. The act stipulated that the land was to be sold to create an endowment to support formation of a university for the teaching of practical courses. Aside from the Philadelphia College of Pharmacy, six associations of pharmacy were founded in the United States between 1821 and the end of the Civil War, including the Massachusetts College of Pharmacy (1823), Maryland College of Pharmacy (1841), College of Pharmacy of the City (and County) of New York (1847), Cincinnati College of Pharmacy (1850), Chicago College of Pharmacy (1859), and St. Louis College of Pharmacy (1864). By the time the Civil War ended in 1865, all colleges except Cincinnati and Massachusetts offered regular courses of instruction in pharmacy.

Regrettably, by the end of the Civil War, much was forgotten with regard to prescription protocols, medication accountability, and having competent pharmacists on staff. Fortunately, such practices were not forgotten long. Massive immigration from Europe resulted in the near doubling in the number of hospitals in American cities. Increased uniformity with regard to galenical preparations because of the upgrading of the *USP* and new and more effective drugs, including such synthetics as acetanilide, antipyrine, chloral hydrate, and phenacetin, were introduced to the market in the late 1800s. Prior to the Civil War, only five states had laws enacted to regulate pharmacists and medicines, although in most cases, government officials failed to enforce these laws. Between 1869 and 1900, pharmaceutical practice laws were passed in 47 state and territorial legislatures, which regulated the sale of poisons and made the adulteration of medicines illegal. Furthermore, the level of practice within the pharmacy profession was elevated significantly with an increase in the number of state-affiliated pharmacy schools throughout the 1880s and 1890s. Education for the American pharmacist at state universities spanned the gamut from a full-day course of four three-month terms introduced by Albert B. Prescott at the University of Michigan in 1868—where critical attention was aroused because not only was prior pharmaceutical experience not required for admission, but he abandoned the traditional requirement of pre-graduation apprenticeship—to a voluntary four-year course introduced by Edward Kremers at the University of Wisconsin in 1892.

Between 1850 and 1900, pharmacists shifted their practice from small drug manufacturers to skilled master compounders who were skilled in "tailor-made" preparations from prescriptions written by physicians. During this period, pharmacists also began to evolve to become professional drug dispensers, a practice in which a remedy would typically call for a combination of one or more active ingredients in a corked bottle with a label that contained the drugstore's name, the patient's name, and directions for use. While advancements in pharmacy education led to the legitimization of the profession when schools began offering pharmacy diplomas and registration certificates, many ambitious pharmacists chose to practice in hospitals, industry, and academia when retail practice became more commercialized and less scientific. Over the next 50 years, however, those who remained in retail pharmacy faced an uphill battle to be viewed by the public as more than just sellers of chocolate sodas to a credible medical profession while, at the same time, establishing their place in the United States' ever-changing health care environment.

Robert Clegg
California Health Sciences University

See Also: American Pharmacists Association; History of Pharmacy as a Profession: United States; Pharmacists: Training and Certification.

Further Readings

American Pharmacists Association. "History of APhA." http://www.pharmacist.com/history-apha (Accessed June 2014).

Bang, Haakon. "The Practice of Pharmacy in the United States." *Royal Society of Health Journal*, v.84 (1964).

Barker, Kenneth N. and Thomas R. Brown. "Overview of the History of Hospital Pharmacy in the United States." In *Handbook of Institutional Pharmacy Practice*, 4th ed., William A. Zellmer, ed. Bethesda, MD: American Society of Health System Pharmacists, 2005.

Bender, George A. *Great Moments in Pharmacy*. Detroit, MI: Northwood Institute Press, 1967.

Bender, George A. *Parke-Davis's Pictorial Annals of Medicine and Pharmacy*. Morris Plains, NJ: Warner-Lambert, 1999.

Bio-Link. "Pharmaceutical Regulation in the United States: History and a Case Study." http://www.bio-link.org/GMP/KELPOST.html (Accessed June 2014).

Brodie, Donald C. and Roger A. Benson. "The Evolution of the Clinical Pharmacy Concept." *Drug Intelligence and Clinical Pharmacy*, v.10 (1976).

Council on Credentialing in Pharmacy. "Scope of Contemporary Pharmacy Practice: Roles, Responsibilities, and Functions of Pharmacists and Pharmacy Technicians." *Journal of the American Pharmacists Association*, v.50/2 (2010).

Cowen, David L. "The Foundations of Pharmacy in the United States." *Journal of the American Medical Association*, v.236/1 (1976).

Eiler, Lee E. "Pharmacy, by Pharmacists, in Pharmacies." *South Dakota Journal of Medicine and Pharmacy*, v.16 (1963).

Flannery, Michael A. "Building a Retrospective Collection in Pharmacy: A Brief History of the Literature With Some Considerations for U.S. Health Sciences Library Professionals." *Bulletin of the Medical Library Association*, v.89/2 (2001).

Griffenhagen, George B. "*Great Moments in Pharmacy*: Development of the Robert Thom Series Depicting Pharmacy's History." *Journal of the American Pharmacists Association*, v.42/2 (2002).

Hambrick, Judd. "Pharmacist Renames Popular Soft Drink From Waco to Dr. Pepper." http://southernmemoriesandupdates.com/stories/pharmacist-renames-popular-soft-drink-from-waco-to-dr-pepper/ (Accessed July 2014).

Hepler, Charles D. "The Third Wave in Pharmaceutical Education: The Clinical Movement." *American Journal of Pharmaceutical Education*, v.51/4 (1987).

Higby, Gregory J. *One Hundred Years of the National Formulary: A Symposium*. Madison, WI: American Institute of the History of Pharmacy, 1989.

Higby, Gregory J. "American Hospital Pharmacy From the Colonial Period to the 1930s." *American Journal of Hospital Pharmacy*, v.51/22 (1994).

Higby, Gregory J. "American Pharmacy in the Twentieth Century." *American Journal of Health-System Pharmacy*, v.54/16 (1997).

Higby, Gregory J. "American Pharmacy's First Great Transformation: Practice, 1852–1902." *Journal of the American Pharmacists Association*, v.40/1 (2000).

King, Nydia M. *A Selection of Primary Sources for the History of Pharmacy in the United States: Books and Trade Catalogs From the Colonial Period to 1940*. Madison, WI: American Institute of the History of Pharmacy, 1987.

Mrtek, Robert G. "Pharmaceutical Education in These United States: An Interpretive Historical Essay of the Twentieth Century." *American Journal of Pharmaceutical Education*, v.40/4 (1976).

National Association of Boards of Pharmacy. "About." http://www.nabp.net/about (Accessed June 2014).

"Pharmacy." *The Columbia Encyclopedia*, 6th ed. (2014). http://www.encyclopedia.com/topic/pharmacy.aspx (Accessed June 2014).

Reference.com. "Pharmacy." http://www.reference.com/browse/Pharmacy (Accessed June 2014).

Sonnedecker, Glenn. "The American Practice of Pharmacy, 1902–1952." *Journal of the American Pharmacists Association*, v.41/1 (2001).

Starr, Paul. *The Social Transformation of American Medicine: The Rise of a Sovereign Profession and the Making of a Vast Industry*. New York: Basic Books, 1982.

Student Doctor Network. "Pharmacy: A Brief History of the Profession." http://www.studentdoctor.net/2012/01/pharmacy-a-brief-history-of-the-profession/ (Accessed June 2014).

Williams, William H. "Pharmacists at America's First Hospital, 1752–1841." *American Journal of Hospital Pharmacy*, v.33 (1976).

UNITED STATES: 1901 TO 1950

Between 1900 and 1948, although pharmacy practice still had not been completely separated from medicine, the number of active pharmacists increased from approximately 57,000 to nearly 90,000. Moreover, almost 50 percent of all practicing pharmacists managed or owned the establishment in which they were employed, often assuming three roles including proprietor, practicing pharmacist, and salesperson. In fact, the transition from "corner druggist" with soda fountain delights to commercialized chain store retail pharmacy with its contemporary self-service and mass-merchandising strategies became evident when Charles R. Walgreen purchased 116 drugstores between 1901 and 1927, while Louis K. Liggett, founder of Rexall, acquired 672 drugstores between 1907 and 1930. Unfortunately, even after the founding of the American Pharmacists Association (APhA) in 1852, the identity of pharmacy as a profession was still unclear, developing slowly and unevenly across the United States. As the APhA began to assert itself as a credible professional organization, the scientific and technical field of pharmaco-therapeutics was becoming increasingly specialized and complex. Federal and state statutory regulations for drugs and those responsible for compounding and dispensing them were implemented, and the practice of pharmacy began a steady transition of moving the profession out of an apothecary shop, and transitioning a physician's office to one that focused on mass manufacturing and prepackaging dose-specific medications.

As the pharmacy profession changed, so did educational requirements to practice. During this period, it was apparent that a new age of pharmacy education—the scientific era—was on the horizon. Research degrees and graduate programs were flourishing. In 1902, the first Ph.D. in pharmaceutical sciences was awarded at the University of Wisconsin under the direction of Edward Kremers, who first introduced a voluntary four-year course at this institution in 1892. In 1905, New York State led the way by requiring graduation from at least a two-year course in pharmacy. From there, other states followed suit, and by the 1950s, most newly licensed practicing pharmacists had earned a four-year degree. By 1927, at least nine colleges offered a standard academic master's degree program for research-based advanced studies, while an additional four schools offered a Ph.D. for credible graduate programs that incorporated original investigative research into their curriculum. In 1928, the American Association of Colleges of Pharmacy (AACP) approved a four-year bachelor's degree as the national education requirement.

The Great Depression (1929–mid-1940s) resulted when drought struck the South and a severe economic slump ensued when 12.9 million shares of stock were sold in one day, which, consequently, resulted in prices plummeting 23 percent over a four-day period. While the country was reeling in an economic recession, hospital pharmacy was making major strides on several fronts. Edward Spease (1877–1915), dean and professor at Western Reserve University School of Pharmacy in Cleveland, focused much of his efforts on hospital pharmacy where he introduced pharmacy internships into a number of hospitals in Cleveland during the 1930s. Furthermore, he participated in an APhA campaign to upgrade hospital pharmacy, which eventually led him to coauthor the first set of minimum standards for hospital pharmacy.

Unfortunately, the practice requirements were often unclear and erratic throughout the nation. For instance, the introduction of the "assistant pharmacist"—often viewed as a second-class practitioner—required only one to four years of drugstore experience to meet the qualifications for full licensure. Here, an assistant pharmacist could fulfill the duties of a registered pharmacist either under supervision or in the "temporary absence" of that pharmacist. By 1926, there were roughly 20,000 assistant pharmacists employed behind drugstore counters in the United States. To many registered pharmacists who earned a four-year degree to practice, this undermined the credibility of the profession as a whole. Because of this concern and indications of substandard services behind the counter, state legislatures began revoking authorization to license assistant pharmacists in the 1930s. By the 1950s, there were only 1,336 assistant pharmacists who remained before the profession eventually drew to a close.

Biopharmaceuticals, or simply biological drugs, consist of any medicinal product made of or extracted from biological sources, including vaccines, blood and blood products, tissue, somatic cells, allergenics, gene therapies, and extracts of living cells. In 1901, tetanus outbreaks and contaminated smallpox vaccines and diphtheria antitoxins resulting in the death of several children led to the passage of the Biologics Control Act of 1902. This act required that premarket governmental approval be granted not only for every biological drug, but also for the manufacturing process and the facility that produced these drugs. Since such premarket control had never before existed in the United States, this legislation paved the way for more stringent federal regulatory control in the years to follow. As a result of these and other notable substandard practices, the National Association of Boards of Pharmacy (NABP) was founded in 1904 with the goal of protecting the public's health and safety through its pharmacist competency program.

With the passage of another key piece of Progressive Era legislation, the Pure Food and Drug Act of 1906 (also known as the Wiley Act, named after Harvey Washington Wiley, chief chemist of the Bureau of Chemistry in the Department of Agriculture, who was the driving force behind the law and headed its enforcement in the early years of its enactment), pharmacopoeia finally received a national legal standing. The act was originated, in part, because of the release of Upton Sinclair's novel, *The Jungle*, in 1905, which, although fiction, drew attention to the lives of immigrant workers and unsanitary practices in the Chicago meatpacking industry, and because of a number of articles published by Samuel Collins Adams in *Collier's* magazine, which revealed blatant medication and advertising fraud. Included in the law was market oversight over human and animal drugs, medical devices, foods and preservatives, biologics, and vaccines. It also prohibited interstate commerce of contaminated and "misbranded" food and drugs.

The third notable piece of pharmaceutical legislation enacted in the United States was the Harrison Narcotics Tax Act of 1914. The act not only taxed the manufacturing, sale, and use of opium, but it required physician prescriptions for products that exceeded the allowable limit of narcotics. It also required increased record keeping among physicians and pharmacists who were licensed to dispense narcotics. Although the law was originally passed to maintain the systematic marketing of narcotics, it was later clarified to prohibit the supply of narcotics, even to addicts who possessed a physician's prescription. As a result, thousands of physicians throughout the United States were subsequently incarcerated for prescribing narcotics to their patients.

Although its history can be traced back to 1848 when Lewis Caleb Beck was appointed to the U.S. Patent Office to perform chemical analyses of agricultural products, the U.S. Food and Drug Administration (FDA)—originally referred to as the Food, Drug, and Insecticide Administration in 1927 before changing its name in 1930—was empowered by the U.S. Congress to enforce the 1906 Pure Food and Drug Act. Unfortunately, the meagerness of federal control would be apparent in the years to come until another law—the Federal Food, Drug and Cosmetic Act (FD&C Act)—would be enacted nearly a decade later.

First introduced in the 1930s, the antibiotic sulfanilamide was viewed by many in the industry as "the silver bullet" in the treatment of infectious diseases. Since sulfanilamide was relatively insoluble and only available in a pill form, it was difficult to administer to small children. In 1938, the FD&C Act was passed following 358 poisonings and 107 deaths, most of whom were children, the previous year from a sulfanilamide "elixir" in which diethylene glycol (DEG)—an industrial solvent that, upon metabolic conversion, becomes oxalic acid and is toxic to the kidney—was used by a chemist at the S. E. Massengill Company to dissolve the drug into a liquid form. Consequently, the law not only popularized drug reform for the first time in the United States; it also highlighted a shift in the drug industry from a compendium based, in large part, on the extent of drug use to more emphasis placed on dispensing and efficacy. Furthermore, the law required that manufacturers file a New Drug Application (NDA) with the FDA verifying the safety of new drugs following animal and clinical trials.

History reveals that the practice of hospital pharmacy did not develop into a noteworthy movement until the 1920s. One reason behind the push to hire more qualified hospital pharmacists was Prohibition. Led by rural Protestants and social Progressives in the Democratic and Republican parties and coordinated by the Anti-Saloon League, Prohibition was mandated under the Eighteenth Amendment to the U.S. Constitution as a nationwide ban on the sale, production, importation, and transportation of alcoholic beverages between 1920 and 1933. During this period, alcohol was regularly prescribed by physicians for a vast array of ailments, and a pharmacist was needed not only to control its inventory, but to manufacture alcohol-containing preparations that were often commercially expensive.

In 1922, hospital pharmacists established their own committee within the APhA Section of Practical Pharmacy as a means to share knowledge and experience. However, the turning point for hospital pharmacy in the United States occurred in 1925 when the first formal organization of hospital pharmacists—the Hospital Pharmacy Association of Southern California—was founded with 22 members from 12 hospitals. Nationally, organizational efforts in the pharmacy profession were still being funneled through the APhA. At this time, Harvey A. K. Whitney (1894–1957) also joined University Hospital at the University of Michigan where, in 1927, he became the chief pharmacist and, two years later, he instituted the first hospital pharmacy internship program in the United States.

In 1935, a new periodical—*American Professional Pharmacist*—was published and was instrumental in arousing eagerness to establish a national group of hospital pharmacists. Despite the bombing of Pearl Harbor by sea and air forces from the empire of Japan and the consequent entry of the United States into World War II, during the 1942 APhA meeting in Denver, Colorado, the American Society of Hospital Pharmacists (ASHP) was founded as a distinct association within APhA. Unfortunately, because of changes brought on by the war, including wartime rationing of gasoline, the Office of Defense Transportation (ODT) requested a cancellation of all nonessential meetings throughout the United States. This led to a number of hospital pharmacists being discouraged from organizing local professional groups, a notion that many ASHP officers considered to be an essential factor necessary to build a formidable national organization. As such, the ASHP created a constitution that outlined the following objectives, the last three of which were added during its 1943 meeting:

- Establish minimum standards of pharmaceutical service in hospitals
- Ensure an adequate supply of qualified hospital pharmacists by providing standardized hospital training for four-year graduates
- Arrange for interchange of information among pharmacists
- Aid the medical profession in the economic and rational use of medicines
- Establish a one-year hospital pharmacy internship for qualified graduates of an accredited school of pharmacy
- Use for internships American Chemical Society (ACS)– and American Medical Association (AMA)–approved hospitals that meet the minimum standards for a hospital pharmacy, adopted by the ACS

- Persuade all pharmacy boards of examiners to accept such hospital pharmacy internships as experience prerequisite for licensure

With a firm foundation in place, ASHP membership more than tripled in a two-year period from 153 members in 1943 to 460 by 1945. By 1947, there were in excess of 1,100 pharmacists who were members of the ASHP. The following year, membership grew to 1,186 registered pharmacists, 38 percent of whom were women.

During the 1940s, the "Minimum Standard for a Hospital Pharmacy," which elaborated on the original standards drawn up in 1936 by Spease and his colleague, Robert M. Porter, called not only for the hospital's pharmacy and therapeutics (P&T) committee to provide a current hospital formulary to the ASHP, but also for those products requested by a visiting physician that are not carried by the hospital pharmacy to be procured from an outside pharmacy and subsequently charged to the patient. The new version, drafted by Donald Francke, a member of the ASHP's Committee on Minimum Standards, and chaired by W. Arthur Purdum, consisted of six principles including the need for (1) a well-organized pharmacy directed by a legally qualified pharmacist that meets ASHP and division training standards; (2) cooperatively drawn rules and regulations; (3) adequate facilities for compounding, record keeping, library consultation, working, and drug storage; (4) specified pharmaceutical responsibilities, such as preparation and sterilization of hospital-manufactured injectables and drug dispensing; and (5) defined functions of the P&T committee. In 1950, the revised minimum standard was approved by the ASHP's Executive Committee, the APhA's Division of Hospital Pharmacy, and the American Hospital Association (AHA) Council of Professional Practice. The following year, in 1951, the

ASHP Committee on Minimum Standards and the Executive Committee approved the Minimum Standard for Pharmacy Internship in Hospitals, although these standards were not immediately implemented, as a survey published in 1954 showed that 15 U.S. hospitals that offered internships were not linked to academic curriculum while 14 hospitals combined internship opportunities with a graduate program. As a result, Francke, who at this time was the director of the Division of Hospital Pharmacy, emphasized the need for more internship programs in the United States.

With World War II raging throughout Europe and the Pacific Ocean, scientific and technical progress resulted in substantial growth in health care, including the advent of new drug discoveries and the bolstering of pharmacy education. Diethylstilbestrol (DES) was first synthesized in 1938 as a synthetic nonsteroidal estrogen to prevent miscarriage, premature labor, and related complications of pregnancy. The drug was first prescribed to pregnant women in 1940, but its use declined in the 1950s after studies indicated that it was not effective in preventing these problems. In late 1941, the American Foundation for Pharmaceutical Education was formed by representatives of the National Drug Trade Conference (NDTC) to advance and support pharmaceutical education in the United States. Moreover, the Pharmacy Corps Bill was passed in 1943 in which the U.S. Congress recognized that a special need existed for quality pharmaceutical services throughout the nation. Without question, these two events were viewed by many as highlights for pharmacy education during the turbulent war years. Beginning in 1944, the number of new drugs to treat specific disorders multiplied, including the aminoglycoside antibiotic, streptomycin, and a variety of other antimicrobial and chemotherapeutic agents. Following a ruling by the War Emergency Advisory Committee and the results of public opinion surveys that indicated a relatively low regard for pharmacists across the nation, the pharmacy profession responded by launching the Pharmaceutical Survey in 1946. Here, nearly every aspect of the profession was scrutinized, including inconsistencies and the lack of standardization for education, student recruitment, professional organizations, regulatory and legal control, prescription content, licensure, and state boards. In 1948, after hearing testimony from the director of the Committee on the Pharmaceutical Survey and its own Committee on Curriculum, the AACP approved, in principle, an optional six-year pharmacy program and authorized member schools and colleges to, once again, use the Pharm.D. degree once a candidate completed the six-year degree program. That same year, the U.S. Supreme Court ruled that the FDA had the authority to enforce its designation of prescription-only status for certain medications. Such enforcement was viewed by many community pharmacists as persecution, which led to increased antigovernment sentiment within the profession.

Between 1900 and 1950, pharmacy practice saw education and scientific research flourish, hospital pharmacists gain credibility within the industry, the passage of key legislation that focused on patient safety and regulatory control, the Great Depression, World War II, revitalization of chain drugstores, and capitalization of corporate pharmacy on suburban markets. The post–World War II era would soon see the baby boom generation; new drugs and products on the market, including anticoagulants, antipsychotics, corticosteroids, antihypertensives, and antidepressants; and pharmacy begin to emerge as a clinical profession.

Robert Clegg
California Health Sciences University

See Also: American Pharmacists Association; History of Pharmacy as a Profession: United States; Pharmacists: Training and Certification.

Further Readings

American Pharmacists Association. "History of APhA." http://www.pharmacist.com/history-apha (Accessed June 2014).

Bang, Haakon. "The Practice of Pharmacy in the United States." *Royal Society of Health Journal*, v.84 (1964).

Barker, Kenneth N. and Thomas R. Brown. "Overview of the History of Hospital Pharmacy in the United States." In *Handbook of Institutional Pharmacy Practice*, 4th ed., William A. Zellmer, ed. Bethesda, MD: American Society of Health System Pharmacists, 2005.

Bender, George A. *Great Moments in Pharmacy*. Detroit: Northwood Institute Press, 1967.

Bender, George A. *Parke-Davis's Pictorial Annals of Medicine and Pharmacy*. Morris Plains, NJ: Warner-Lambert, 1999.

Bio-Link. "Pharmaceutical Regulation in the United States: History and a Case Study." http://www.bio-link.org/GMP/KELPOST.html (Accessed June 2014).

Brodie, Donald C. and Roger A. Benson. "The Evolution of the Clinical Pharmacy Concept." *Drug Intelligence & Clinical Pharmacy*, v.10 (1976).

Council on Credentialing in Pharmacy. "Scope of Contemporary Pharmacy Practice: Roles, Responsibilities, and Functions of Pharmacists and Pharmacy Technicians." *Journal of the American Pharmacists Association*, v.50/2 (2010).

Cowen, David L. "The Foundations of Pharmacy in the United States." *Journal of the American Medical Association*, v.236/1 (1976).

Eiler, Lee E. "Pharmacy, by Pharmacists, in Pharmacies." *South Dakota Journal of Medicine and Pharmacy*, v.16 (1963).

Flannery, Michael A. "Building a Retrospective Collection in Pharmacy: A Brief History of the Literature With Some Considerations for U.S. Health Sciences Library Professionals." *Bulletin of the Medical Library Association*, v.89/2 (2001).

Griffenhagen, George B. "*Great Moments in Pharmacy*: Development of the Robert Thom Series Depicting Pharmacy's History." *Journal of the American Pharmacists Association*, v.42/2 (2002).

Harris, Ruth R. and Warren E. McConnell. "The American Society of Hospital Pharmacists: A History." *American Journal of Hospital Pharmacy*, v.50/suppl. 2 (1993).

Hepler, Charles D. "The Third Wave in Pharmaceutical Education: The Clinical Movement." *American Journal of Pharmaceutical Education*, v.51/4 (1987).

Higby, Gregory J. "American Hospital Pharmacy From the Colonial Period to the 1930s." *American Journal of Hospital Pharmacy*, v.51/22 (1994).

Higby, Gregory J. "American Pharmacy in the Twentieth Century." *American Journal of Health-System Pharmacy*, v.54/16 (1997).

Higby, Gregory J. "American Pharmacy's First Great Transformation: Practice, 1852–1902." *Journal of the American Pharmacists Association*, v.40/1 (2000).

Higby, Gregory J. *One Hundred Years of the National Formulary: A Symposium*. Madison, WI: American Institute of the History of Pharmacy, 1989.

King, Nydia M. *A Selection of Primary Sources for the History of Pharmacy in the United States: Books and Trade Catalogs From the Colonial Period to 1940*. Madison, WI: American Institute of the History of Pharmacy, 1987.

Mrtek, Robert G. "Pharmaceutical Education in These United States: An Interpretive Historical Essay of the Twentieth Century." *American Journal of Pharmaceutical Education*, v.40/4 (1976).

National Association of Boards of Pharmacy. "About." http://www.nabp.net/about (Accessed June 2014).

"Pharmacy." In *The Columbia Encyclopedia*, 6th ed. (2014). http://www.encyclopedia.com/topic/pharmacy.aspx (Accessed June 2014).

Reference.com. "Pharmacy." http://www.reference.com/browse/Pharmacy (Accessed June 2014).

Sonnedecker, Glenn. "The American Practice of Pharmacy, 1902–1952." *Journal of the American Pharmacists Association*, v.41/1 (2001).

Starr, Paul. *The Social Transformation of American Medicine: The Rise of a Sovereign Profession and the Making of a Vast Industry*. New York: Basic Books, 1982.

Student Doctor Network. "Pharmacy: A Brief History of the Profession." http://www.studentdoctor.net/2012/01/pharmacy-a-brief-history-of-the-profession/ (Accessed June 2014).

U.S. Food and Drug Administration. "About FDA." http://www.fda.gov/AboutFDA/WhatWeDo/History/default.htm (Accessed July 2014).

Williams, William H. "Pharmacists at America's First Hospital, 1752–1841." *American Journal of Hospital Pharmacy*, v.33 (1976).

UNITED STATES: 1951 TO PRESENT

The United States is the third-largest country in the world in terms of area, and the fourth-largest in terms of population, with an estimated July 2014 population of 318,892,103. It is a technologically advanced country with a modern economy, and is classified by the World Bank as a high-income country, with a per capita gross domestic product (GDP) in 2014 of $54,800 (19th-highest in the world). Health expenditures in the United States in 2013 constituted 17.1 percent of GDP, the highest percentage in the world. The United States is both a major producer of pharmaceutical products and a major consumer of them, and is also a site of much medical research, including research and development devoted to discovering and bringing to market new pharmaceutical products.

Health System

Unlike most other countries at its level of economic development, the United States does not have a national system of health care or health insurance, and not all citizens or residents have health coverage. Many individuals have private health insurance, which is often provided as a benefit of employment. Government health insurance is also available to some people through programs including Medicare (a federal program primarily for those over 65 or who are disabled) and Medicaid (a joint federal-state program primarily for low-income people). Both Medicaid and Medicare provide some coverage for prescription drugs, with the specific coverage provided under Medicaid differing by state, and differing by the insurance policy selected through the Medicare Part D program in the case of Medicare.

In 2010, President Barack Obama signed into law the Patient Protection and Affordable Care Act (ACA, also known as "Obamacare"), which provided several different means for uninsured and underinsured individuals (the latter meaning those whose insurance coverage was considered inadequate) to obtain insurance. The ACA used several routes to this goal, including changing laws regarding insurance (for instance, not allowing individuals to be dropped from insurance programs due to preexisting conditions) and providing subsidies to help individuals and families purchase insurance. Different aspects of the ACA took effect over the next several years, and the start of the program was hampered by problems with computers and misunderstanding of how the program worked. However, the percentage of uninsured Americans dropped from 16.4 percent in 2013 to 11.3 percent in 2014, the first year health insurance was available through the exchanges. The groups who benefited most from the ACA included people between the ages of 18 and 34, those with low incomes, those who live in rural areas, and Black and Hispanic people.

Pharmaceutical Industry

According to Pharmaceutical Research and Manufacturers of America, an organization whose members are pharmaceutical manufacturers, U.S. firms lead the world in both research and development in pharmaceutical products, have the most compounds in the research process (about 3,400), and hold the most intellectual property rights for new medicines. Over 810,000 people worked in the U.S. biopharmaceutical industry as of 2012, and the industry is particularly invested in research and development, spending over 10 times as

much per employee on research and development as do manufacturing companies across all industries. In 2015, according to *Forbes* magazine, 5 of the 10 largest pharmaceutical companies in the world were based in the United States: Pfizer, Merck & Co., Eli Lilly & Co., McKesson, and Abbott Laboratories. Pfizer, headquartered in New York City and Groton, Connecticut, was ranked by *Forbes* as the largest pharmaceutical company in the world, with a market value of $211.7 billion, assets of $169.3 billion, sales of $49.6 billion, and profits of $9.1 billion.

The pharmaceutical industry in the United States can be divided into four subsectors: innovative, biopharmaceutical, biologics, and generics. The innovative pharmaceutical industry researches, tests, and produces new drugs derived from chemicals, which are subject to an extensive testing and approval process before being brought to market. Often the research and development is a multinational process and/or is conducted in partnership with researchers in universities or government labs. Drugs produced by the innovative pharmaceutical industry are granted patent protection for 20 years in the United States, a rule intended to help the manufacturer recoup the cost of the drug.

The biopharmaceutical industry produces drugs from biologics, including proteins and nucleic acids. One method to produce drugs from biologics is through transgenic organisms, including plants and animals that have been genetically engineered to produce the drug. Much research in biopharmaceuticals is conducted at universities or small companies, and independent financing or the support of a larger company may be required to bring a promising product to market. Biologics include products such as vaccines and blood components, and are differentiated from biopharmaceuticals by being extracted directly from a nonengineered source. The biologics market includes biosimilars, products that have similar properties to biologics.

The generic pharmaceutical industry produces versions of drugs for which patent protection has expired. Under U.S. law, once a patent on a brand-name pharmaceutical has expired, other manufacturers are allowed to produce drugs identical to those previously produced only as brand-name products. Generic pharmaceuticals are usually sold for a lower price than brand-name drugs, which are still covered by patent protection, and have become increasingly popular as a means to control health care costs.

Pharmaceutical Market

The United States is also the largest market in the world for pharmaceutical products. As the population is aging, and because for the most part pharmaceutical prices are not controlled by the government, the size of the U.S. market for pharmaceuticals is expected to increase in the future.

From 2008 through 2012, almost half (48.7 percent) of Americans reported taking at least one prescription drug in the previous 30 days, with 21.8 percent reporting using three or more prescription drugs during that period, and 10.7 percent reporting using five or more prescription drugs during that period. All figures represent increases over previous years: For instance, from 1988 to 1994, only 39.1 percent of individuals reported using at least one prescription drug in the past 30 days, 11.8 percent three or more prescription drugs, and 4.0 percent five or more prescription drugs. From 2009 to 2012, increasing age was associated with increased use of prescription drugs: For instance, 89.8 percent of people age 65 or older reported taking at least one prescription drug in the past 30 days, as compared to 23.5 percent of those under 18 years. The discrepancy is even greater among those taking five or more prescription drugs in the past 30 days, which was reported by 39.1 percent of those age 65 or older as compared to 0.8 percent of those under 18 years.

The most commonly used class of drugs in the United States from 2009 to 2012 was antihyperlipidemic agents (used to prevent or control high cholesterol), as 13.1 percent of the population reported taking at least one drug from this class in the last 30 days. The second most common type of drug reported was antidepressants (9.0 percent of the population reported taking at least one drug from this class in the last 30 days), followed by analgesics (drugs taken for pain relief), reported by 8.8 percent of the population, and proton pump inhibitors and H2 antagonists (taken to treat ulcers or gastric reflux disease), taken by 8.2 percent of the population. The most commonly used drugs varied considerably by age, with bronchodilators (taken for asthma or to improve breathing) most common among those under 18 years, analgesics most common for those age 18 to 44 years, and antihyperlipidemic agents most common for both the 45 to 64 and 65-plus age categories.

Sarah E. Boslaugh
Saint Louis University

See Also: Access to Medicines (Industrialized World); Centers for Disease Control and Prevention; History of Pharmacy as a Profession: United States; Medicaid and Medicare Systems; Medicare: Prescription Drug Benefits; Medicare Prescription Drug, Improvement, and Modernization Act (2003); Traditional and Herbal Medicines, Regulation: United States.

Further Readings

Centers for Disease Control and Prevention. "Therapeutic Drug Use." http://www.cdc.gov/nchs/fastats/drug-use-therapeutic.htm (Accessed June 9, 2015).

Forbes. "The World's Biggest Companies." http://www.forbes.com/global2000/list/#industry:Pharmaceuticals (Accessed June 9, 2015).

Quealy, Kevin and Margot Sanger-Katz. "Obama's Health Law: Who Was Helped Most." *New York Times* (October 29, 2014). http://www.nytimes.com/interactive/2014/10/29/upshot/obamacare-who-was-helped-most.html?_r=0&abt=0002&abg=1 (Accessed June 9, 2015).

U.S. Department of Commerce. "The Pharmaceutical and Biotech Industries in the United States." http://selectusa.commerce.gov/industry-snapshots/pharmaceutical-and-biotech-industries-united-states (Accessed June 9, 2015).

University of California, San Diego

The University of California at San Diego (UCSD) is a public research university. Established in 1960 and located in La Jolla, near San Diego, this university is recognized for being a student-centered, research-focused, and service-oriented institution. The research program at UCSD is conducted in a multifaceted and multidisciplinary approach. The faculty have received global honors for their work in their respective fields, including the Pulitzer Prize, Guggenheim fellowships, and the Nobel Prize for their achievements. In addition, UCSD's entrepreneurial spirit is displayed by students and researchers who are responsible for more than 300 San Diego–based start-ups.

The campus includes six colleges, three graduate schools, and two professional medical schools. In addition, it is home to Scripps Institution of Oceanography, which focuses on scientific research and education about the ocean, earth, and atmosphere. The UCSD Health System is responsible for providing patient care and medical research and educating future health care professionals. The health system encompasses the UC San Diego Medical Center, UC San Diego Thornton Hospital, Moores Cancer Center, Shiley Eye Center, and Sulpizio Cardiovascular Center.

Department of Pharmacology

The Department of Pharmacology includes 21 full-time and 15 adjunct faculty members, 10 research scientists, 50 postdoctoral investigators, 49 support staff, and 65 Ph.D. students. The Department specializes in research in four areas: signal transduction, computational biology and drug design, integrated system and animal models, and pharmacogenomics. In addition, the Superfund Research Center at UCSD, supported by a grant from the National Institute of Health Sciences, conducts research related to toxicology and Superfund sites. A particular strength of the department is the study of basic cellular and molecular mechanisms of signal transduction, with research often leading to drug discovery or other direct impact on human health. Among the diseases studied by the department are hypertension, cancer, neurological and inflammatory diseases, and cardiovascular regulation.

The department has the highest number of research grant awards among U.S. pharmacology departments. Grant-funded studies have been performed in the areas of hypertension, cardiovascular regulation, cancer, and neurological and inflammatory diseases. UCSD has partnered with other institutions to complete this research. Affiliations with San Diego Supercomputer Center facilitate the research in computational and molecular science, drug design, and bioinformatics. As of 2015, 7 members of the National Academy of Science and 3 Howard Hughes Medical Institute Investigators are affiliated with the UCSD Pharmacology Department. Other honors recently won by members of the department include France's Legion of Honour Award, granted to Palmer Taylor in July 2013, and the Biochemical Society 2014 Centenary Award, granted to Susan Taylor in March 2013.

Grant-funded projects in the fields of environmental health sciences and pharmacogenomics are performed by the School of Pharmacy and Pharmaceutical Sciences (SPPS) at UCSD. This department collaborates closely with adjunct faculty at the Salk Institute, the Scripps Research Institute, the Burnham Institute, and adjunct faculty and affiliates from the local biotechnology and pharmaceutical industries. This multidisciplinary approach allows for open communication between the science efforts of each partnering institution, while moving forward in the research and study of technology and drug discovery.

Shivaun Williams
Writer

See Also: Neuropharmacology; University of California, San Francisco.

Further Readings

Boarder, Michael, David Newby, and Phyllis Navti. *Pharmacology for Pharmacy and the Health Sciences: A Patient-Centered Approach.* Oxford, UK: Oxford University Press, 2010.

Brunton, Laurence, John Lazo, and Keith Parker. *Goodman & Gilman's The Pharmacological Basis of Therapeutics.* New York: McGraw-Hill Professional, 2005.

University of California, San Diego. Department of Pharmacology. http://pharmacology.ucsd.edu/ (Accessed May 10, 2015).

UNIVERSITY OF CALIFORNIA, SAN FRANCISCO

The University of California, San Francisco (UCSF) is the branch of the University of California system that focuses exclusively on health care. In existence for more than 150 years, UCSF includes schools of pharmacy, medicine, dentistry, and nursing and is the second largest employer in the city of San Francisco. The faculty of UCSF include many distinguished scholars who have made instrumental contributions in the study of health-related issues such as cancer, neurodegenerative diseases, and stem cell research.

School of Pharmacy

UCSF is a member of the American Association of Colleges of Pharmacy (AACP). Studies and research are centered on drug-related sciences and specialized pharmacy patient care. The School of Pharmacy is comprised of three academic departments; Bioengineering and Therapeutic Sciences, Clinical Pharmacy, and Pharmaceutical Chemistry. The Doctor of Pharmacy (Pharm.D.) professional degree includes the following courses of study: Pharmaceutical Care, Health Services & Policy Research, and Pharmaceutical Sciences. The missions of the UCSF School of Pharmacy Departments of Bioengineering and Therapeutic Sciences, Clinical Pharmacy, and Pharmaceutical Chemistry are in line with the mission of the University of California system.

The Medical Center at UCSF is devoted to developing new treatment approaches in cancer, heart disease, neurological disorders, immunological disorders, HIV/AIDS, and organ transplantation, as well as specialty services for women and children. The Medical Center is a treatment destination for patients from all over the United States in search of life-saving health care. People from all parts of the United States—and from across the world—come to UCSF to receive life-saving health care services. The Medical Center at UCSF is ranked among the best U.S. hospitals. The center has two locations; one at Parnassus campus and the other at Mount Zion campus.

UCSF is also committed to serving vulnerable populations within its own community. In collaboration with San Francisco General Hospital and Trauma Center and the San Francisco Veteran Affairs Medical Center as well as several health care facilities, including St. Anthony Free Clinic, Buchanan Dental Center and Glide Health Services, they are committed to serving the community and patients' needs.

Research

In 2010, UCSF was the top-ranked pharmacy school in the United States in terms of grants and contracts received from the National Institutes of Health (NIH), with over $30 million in awards. The UCSF pharmacy school also placed first in the 2012 ranking of pharmacy schools by *U.S. News and World Report*, a status based on surveys of faculty and administrators at accredited pharmacy schools.

Shivaun Williams
Writer

See Also: Pharmacists: Training and Certification; University of California, San Diego.

Further Readings

Boarder, Michael, David Newby, and Phyllis Navti. *Pharmacology for Pharmacy and the Health Sciences: A Patient-Centered Approach*. Oxford, UK: Oxford University Press, 2010.
University of California, San Francisco. School of Pharmacy. https://pharmacy.ucsf.edu (Accessed September 4, 2015).

University of Oxford

The University of Oxford, located in Oxford, England, is the oldest institution of higher learning in the English-speaking world. While the exact date of its establishment remains unknown, it is documented that some classes were being taught there as early as 1096. The official founding date has been estimated to be 1167. By the late 12th century, Oxford had begun to attract scholars from other countries. The first of the 38 colleges that comprise the university system was established during the medieval period. Long recognized as a force in humanistic studies, Oxford began adding a new emphasis on natural and applied science in the 20th century. In 1912, the Department of Pharmacology was established in a room at the university's museum. In the early 21st century, the department was one of only two pharmaceutical departments in the United Kingdom to receive a five-star ranking. Oxford's Pharmacology Department is divided into five major areas: Cardiovascular/Autonomic; In Vivo/Systems Neuroscience; Drug Discovery/Medicinal Chemistry; Cell Signaling, Molecular Neuroscience, and Disease; and Cellular Neuroscience.

The Department of Pharmacology is part of the Medical Sciences Division. Operating with a budget of approximately £4M (US$6,422,608), the department employs 180 researchers. The focus of their research is on studying the interactions between chemical and biological systems and advancing knowledge of gene functions in living organisms. Oxford pharmacologists have established international reputations in calcium imaging, which is used in developing treatments for human conditions that range from cardiovascular diseases to reproductive issues. Oxford also specializes in neuropharmacology, which has major implications for conditions of the nervous system, and pharmacogenomics, which deals with the impact of genetics on the responses of patients to particular drugs.

While keeping its major focus on the interaction between chemical and biological systems, Oxford's Department of Pharmacology promotes collaboration among pharmacologists and other researchers involved in physiological sciences and clinical medicine, as well as with those involved in other disciplines, including the humanities. Departmental researchers are engaged in studying the fundamental mechanisms of chemical physiology and pathology and understanding all aspects of drug actions and interactions. Areas of study include molecular pharmacology, cardiovascular pharmacology, cell signaling, and pharmacogenetics. Oxford's Department of Pharmacology has established partnerships with a large number of global pharmaceutical and biotech companies with the intent of benefiting global society.

Continued innovation is a major priority, and the department is working on developing minimally invasive microendoscope-based imaging methods of collecting images of cells from deep within the brains of living human beings. Plans are under way to establish the Oxford Medical Chemistry Institute as a joint endeavor of the Department of Pharmacology, Medical Sciences Division, and the Chemistry Department. The institution is expected to provide an environment conducive to drug discovery and tools for probing biological systems.

Researchers

Major researchers within the Cardiovascular/ Autonomic group include Dr. Derek Terrar, Dr. Chris Garland, Dr. Kim Dora, Dr. Rebecca Sitsapesan, and Dr. Ming Lei. Dr. Terrar is a professor of cardiac electrophysiology who specializes in the influence of drugs on cardiac muscle contraction. He pays close attention to drugs and mechanisms that either positively or negatively influence the functions of the heart. Dr. Garland is a professor of vascular pharmacology and a fellow of Magdalen College. His research deals with the mechanisms that

regulate the tone of vascular smooth muscle cells. In 2009, he was honored by the British Pharmacological Society for his outstanding contributions to cardiovascular pharmacology. Dr. Dora, a member of the Vascular Pharmacology Research Group, concentrates on cell-to-cell communication in resistance arteries and arterioles. Her work has led to increased understanding of the impact of current and Ca^{2+} signals on controlling arterial diameter. Dr. Sitsapesan's work, which is funded by the British Heart Foundation, studies the role of Ca^{2+} release from intracellular stores in initiating and regulating particular cell functions. Dr. Ming Lei is the head of the Cardiac Signaling Group. He is particularly interested in cardiac arrhythmias, hypertrophy, and heart failure. He is also engaged in developing new therapies for cardiovascular conditions and is working on creating novel optogenetic model systems for use in treating heart disease.

The two professors that form the core of the In Vivo/Systems Neuroscience research team are Dr. Trevor Sharp and Dr. Daniel Anthony. Dr. Sharp is a professor of neuropharmacology, a Radcliffe Medical Fellow in neuroscience at Oxford's University College, and a lecturer on pharmacology at Oxford's Corpus Christi College. His research involves studying the physiology and pharmacology of midbrain monoamine systems, the neuropharmacology of antidepressants, and the neural mechanisms of mood and anxiety. Dr. Anthony is head of the Experimental Neuropathology Laboratory. His research focuses on the relations between brain injury and disease and other organs of the body. His work has significant implications for patients with diseases such as multiple sclerosis.

Faculty members involved in Drug Discovery and Medicinal Chemistry include Dr. Grant Churchill and Dr. Angela Russell. Dr. Churchill studies the various aspects of cyclic ADP-ribose and NAADP levels and the development of caged and cell-permeant messengers. Dr. Russell is engaged in research on medical chemistry, and she is involved in multidisciplinary research collaborations designed to develop new treatments for tuberculosis and cancer.

Faculty members engaged in cell signaling, molecular neuroscience, and disease include Dr. Antony Galione, Dr. John Parrington, Dr. Fran Platt, and Dr. Paolo Tammaro. Dr. Galione serves as the chair of the Department of Pharmacology. His research focuses on molecular pharmacology, with particular focus on calcium signaling and stimulus-secretion coupling in exocrine and endocrine pancreas excitation-contraction coupling in both striated and smooth muscle. Dr. Parrington's research is concerned with the molecular aspects of egg activation and calcium signaling and in vivo gene transfer into the testis and sperm. He also studies calcium signaling in sea urchin gametes. As a biochemist and a pharmacologist, Dr. Platt studies glycosphingolipids in health and heart disease. Dr. Tammaro is concerned with the molecular basis of hypertension, and his research is directed toward identifying the molecular mechanisms that influence vascular ion channels and developing new drugs capable of modulating blood vessels.

The team involved in research in cellular neuroscience consists of Dr. Nigel Emptage, Dr. Colin Akerman, Dr. Karri Lämsä, and Dr. Liliana Minichiello. Dr. Emptage focuses his research on basic synaptic transmission and synaptic plasticity. His studies of the central nervous system of mammals have significant potential for improved treatment for conditions such as Alzheimer's and schizophrenia. Dr. Akerman is involved in studying synaptic circuit development and plasticity and is particularly focused on studying the role of intercellular signaling events in regulating neural circuit formation and plasticity.

Dr. Lämsä is engaged in the study of inhibitory circuit dynamics in health and disease, focusing on synaptic plasticity in inhibitory circuits in hippocampal formation, neuromodulation of inhibition, the neuropathy of schizophrenia, and the pathology of epilepsy. Dr. Minichiello is involved in the study of molecular and cellular mechanisms in synaptic plasticity, learning, and memory; the molecular basis of age-related cognitive decline; the role of neuronal subtypes and networks in animal behavior and neurological conditions; and discovering ways to repair damage caused by neuronal dysfunction and degeneration.

Elizabeth Rholetter Purdy
Independent Scholar

See Also: Cancer, Drug Treatments for; Cardiovascular Pharmacology; Neuropharmacology; Pharmacogenomics; United Kingdom.

Further Readings

Cordes, Eugene H. *Hallelujah Moments: Tales of Drug Discovery.* Cambridge, NY: Oxford University Press, 2014.

Hochman, Michael E. *50 Studies Every Doctor Should Know: The Key Studies That Form the Foundation of Evidence Based Medicine.* Oxford, UK: Oxford University Press, 2013.

University of Oxford. "Department of Pharmacology." http://www.pharm.ox.ac.uk/ (Accessed October 2014).

UNIVERSITY OF TORONTO

The University of Toronto was initially established as King's College in 1827. In its current form, the university has one campus in Mississauga and another in Scarborough in addition to the original Toronto campus. The university is affiliated with 10 hospitals in metropolitan Toronto, and its research library is the largest in Canada. The student body has grown to include 67,128 undergraduates and 15,885 graduates, and the faculty is made up of 12,589 scholars in a range of disciplines.

The Department of Pharmacology was established at the University of Toronto in 1887 along with the Departments of Physiology and Biochemistry. In 1907, Professor Velyien Henderson (1877–1945) took over as head of the Department of Pharmacy. He is considered one of the founders of North American experimental pharmacology, which concentrates on studying drugs and their impacts. In 2007, it was determined that the name of the department should be changed to the Department of Pharmacology and Toxicology to reflect the training being carried out for both graduates and undergraduates. The Department of Pharmacology and Toxicology also offers interdepartmental programs in biomedical toxicology, addiction studies, cardiovascular sciences, neuroscience, women's health, and resuscitation sciences. Pharmaceutical research is carried out in 12 major areas that include biochemical and molecular pharmacy; cardiovascular pharmacy; clinical pharmacology; drug addiction; drug metabolism, distribution, and pharmaceuticals; endocrine pharmacology; immunopharmacology; neuropharmacology/psychopharmacology; pharmacogenetics; receptor pharmacology; second messengers and signal transduction; and toxicology.

Research Areas

The field of biochemical pharmacology builds on methods used in biochemistry, biophysics, molecular biology, structural biology, cell biology, and cell physiology to determine the mechanisms by which drugs act and understand how they affect various organisms. The end goal of such studies at the University of Toronto is to use research on biosynthetic and cell signaling pathways and their kinetics to develop effective treatments for various diseases and disorders. Researchers involved with molecular pharmacology seek to identify the molecular basis behind drug actions and interactions using the techniques of mathematics, physics, chemistry, molecular biology, biochemistry, and cell biology.

The Heart and Stroke Foundation estimates that 70,000 heart attacks occur in Canada each year, and close to 16,000 Canadians die each year after suffering a heart attack. Because heart disease is so prevalent in Canada and other developed countries, the research of cardiovascular pharmacologists has taken on new urgency. Researchers at the University of Toronto study the impact of particular drugs on cardiac mechanical function, electrophysiological function, arterial pressure, vascular bed blood flow, the release of physiological mediators, and neural activity that derives from the structures of the central nervous system.

Clinical pharmacology at the university serves as the link between basic pharmacology and the different branches of clinical medicine. Researchers are involved in discovering drugs and getting them into the hands of the people who need them. Aspects of clinical pharmacology within the department include research on pharmacogenetics, genomics, drug metabolizing enzymes, drug transporters, pharmacoepidemiology, pharmacoeconomics, and toxicoepidemiology.

Departmental researchers studying drug addiction look at the mechanisms and risk factors that affect the behaviors of addicts. In addition to studying cellular models, researchers examine human drug abusers, self-administration of drugs in animals, genetically modified or bred animals, and genetic variation in receptors, transporters, and enzymes. Researchers engaged in the study of drug metabolism, distribution, and pharmacokinetics are concerned with identifying the correct concentrations of drugs that determine their ability to safely and effectively treat disease. This requires researchers to understand the ways in which drugs affect all parts of the body.

At the University of Toronto, endocrine pharmacology deals with hormones and hormone derivatives and drugs that affect the synthesis or action of hormones that are normally secreted. The field of immunopharmacology is concerned with identifying, delivering, and monitoring drugs that either suppress or enhance the immune system. This research is particularly important in treating diseases such as HIV/AIDS and cancer and in preventing rejections in transplant patients.

The field of neuropharmacology is concerned with the impact of drugs on the nervous system and has particular application to patients suffering from brain and spinal cord injury. The field of psychopharmacology is closely related because it deals with the ways that drugs affect behavior and cognitive functions. Subjects for study among department researchers include Alzheimer's disease, Parkinson's disease, epilepsy, depression, and schizophrenia. Pharmacogenetics allows researchers to focus on the impact of gene structure on responses to drugs and foreign chemicals in the human body.

Receptor pharmacologists use both molecular and biochemical methods to study the compounds with which drugs are able to bind, producing particular effects. Researchers study common receptors found within the human body, including those that bind endogenous hormones, neurotransmitters, and cytokines and enzymes. Signal transduction systems in cells and organs may be affected by a variety of therapeutic agents. Researchers in the field of toxicology are concerned with studying the negative impact of chemical agents and finding ways to offset these effects, which can cause disease, death, disruption of bodily systems, or interference with normal growth patterns.

Selected Faculty Research Areas

Susan George focuses on studying G protein-coupled receptors (GPCR), signal transduction, drug addiction, and neuropsychiatric disorders, paying particular attention to the molecular pharmacology of neurotransmitters in the brain and their role in drug addiction and psychiatric disorders. Denis Grant concentrates on the study of drug metabolism, pharmacogenetics, and carcinogenesis. As the head of the Division of Clinical Pharmacology and Toxicology and a member of the staff of the Hospital for Sick Children, Shinya Ito focuses on cellular drug transport and pediatric pharmacology. Rebecca Laposa is involved in research on toxicology, neuropharmacy, and biochemical and molecular pharmacology, particularly focusing on DNA damage and repair in neurodegeneration and on neural stem cells. Ruth Ross serves as the chair of the Department of Pharmacology and Toxicology. Her focus is on cannabinoid pharmacology, GPCR, cannabis, and orphan GPCR.

Michelle Arnot is concerned with identifying potential targets for drugs based on her study of the role of ion channels in brain and cardiac cells. Paul Dorian is engaged in the study of the impact of antiarrhythmic drugs on cardiac refractoriness, arterial and ventricular fibrillation, and defibrillation. Benjamin Goldstein's focus is on bipolar disorder, and he is attempting to identify biomarkers to treat adolescent bipolar disorder and to enhance understanding of the association between bipolar disorder and cardiovascular disease.

Gideon Koren is a pediatric pharmacologist whose research focuses on the impact of drugs on developing organs. He is particularly interested in very-low-weight infants and pediatric cancer chemotherapy. Jack Uetrecht specializes in idiosyncratic drug reactions that occur in particular individuals but have not been identified as a side effect when the drug was tested. Cindy Woodland is engaged in research on drug-induced toxicity, focusing particularly on drug metabolizing enzymes and drug transporters.

Bernard Le Foll is focused on tobacco and alcohol addiction, and he serves as head of the Translational Addiction Research Laboratory and head of the Alcohol Research and Treatment Clinic at the Centre for Addiction and Mental Health. Art Petronis studies the epigenetics of non-Mendelian diseases such as schizophrenia, diabetes, and Crohn's disease. Bruce Pollock specializes in geriatric clinical psychopharmacology.

Elizabeth Rholetter Purdy
Independent Scholar

See Also: Canada; Cancer, Drug Treatments for; Cardiovascular Pharmacology; Neuropharmacology; Pharmacoeconomics; Pharmacogenomics.

Further Readings

Department of Pharmacology and Toxicology, University of Toronto. http://www.pharmtox .utoronto.ca/home.htm (Accessed October 2014).

Frankel, Grace, Christopher Louizos, and Austin Zubin. "Canadian Educational Approaches for the Advancement of Pharmacy Practice." *American Journal of Pharmaceutical Education,* v.78/7 (2014).

Koren, Gideon. "Training Clinicians in Pediatric Pharmacology-Toxicology." *Pediatric Drugs,* v.11/1 (2009).

University of Washington

The University of Washington was founded in Seattle, Washington, in 1861, and additional branches have since been established in Tacoma and Bothell. The Department of Pharmacology is located within the School of Medicine. Within the Department of Pharmacology, research is focused on advancing knowledge of the ways in which molecules affect the development and behavior of cells and organisms. Researchers also seek to understand the role that pharmacology plays in combating disease and the human aging process, as well as the impact of drugs on human health and behavior.

Pharmacological research at the University of Washington is divided into six areas: cellular signaling, neurophysiology, drug addiction, stem cell, gene regulation, and protein structure and function. In addition to the six core areas of research, pharmacologists at the University of Washington are involved in advancing knowledge concerning the role of biology in diseases and disorders that affect human society, focusing on muscular dystrophy, Alzheimer's disease, Parkinson's disease, Huntington's disease, cancer, heart disease, and obesity.

In the area of inter- and intracellular signaling, researchers examine the relationship between molecules and peptides and their receptors and the ways in which those receptors impact intracellular signaling. Researchers are also concerned with influences such as kinases and phosphatases on signaling and the impact of signaling on changes in gene expression.

Studies in neurophysiology focus on the relationship between neuron physiology and human behavior and memory. Certain labs examine the role of generation and regulation in nerve impulses, the transmission of signaling molecules between neurons, the impact of small molecules on neuronal chemistry and physiology, the interactions between receptors and channels, and the ways in which experience can impact neuroplasticity.

Drug and alcohol addiction are major problems in modern society, and pharmacologists at the University of Washington are involved in understanding the molecular basis of drug and alcohol addictive behaviors and in discovering new ways for treating those addictions. Lab work focuses on studying mice with genetic lesions in order to identify specific genes that play a role in addictive behaviors associated with alcohol, opioid, cannabinoid, and psychostimulant drugs.

Stem cell biology is involved in studying the role of stem cells in allowing the human body to renew itself. Pharmacological research focuses on examining signaling pathways that affect the differentiation of cells that are used in self-renewal. These studies are particularly important in developing pharmaceuticals that can be used to treat degenerative diseases such as Alzheimer's disease and Parkinson's disease.

Within the Department of Pharmacology, the study of gene regulation is concerned with examining cellular responses to external signaling cues. Certain studies look at the initiation, maintenance, and termination of gene transcription, the regulation of gene silencing, the repair of DNA, and the role of chromatin higher structure in gene function.

The study of protein structure and function focuses on identifying the ways in which proteins adopt defined structures and the role of those structures in determining the functions of particular proteins. Studies in this area seek to answer questions about the assembly of protein complexes, the interaction between small molecules and proteins in altering structure and function, and the role of residues in producing catalytic activity and binding capacity.

Faculty Research Areas

At the time of this writing, the following faculty was on staff. Dr. William Catteral serves as the chair of the Pharmacology Department. His research focuses on the molecular basis of electrical excitability, the regulation of excitability of nerve and muscle cells, the impact of drugs and toxins on electrical excitability, and the molecular biology of ion channels. Dr. Sandra Bajjalieh is involved in studying the molecular basis of neurotransmission. She pays particular attention to the role of Synaptic Vesicle Protein 2 in controlling neurotransmitter release and the impact of lipid modifying enzymes on the functioning of neurons. Dr. Joseph Beavo studies the mechanism of action of cyclic nucleotides. He addresses problems associated with isozymes of cyclic nucleotide-phosphodieterases in regulating cyclic nucleotide action and metabolism and looks at enzyme fractionation, monoclonal antibodies, selective inhibitors, and molecular genetic techniques. Dr. Charles Chavkin is the Allan Phyllis Treuer Professor of Pain Research. His research deals with the study of neurophysiology of opioid peptides and opioid receptor function, opioid receptor diversity, and the regulation of receptor function.

The research of Dr. Richard Gardner concentrates on studying ubiquitin-mediated regulation in the nucleus, focusing particularly on nuclear protein quality control and its ability to protect humans from contracting protein aggregation diseases. He also studies the regulation of chromatin structures in telomere silencing, gene activation, and gene repair. Dr. Chris Hague is involved in studying pharmacological and molecular characterization of G-protein coupled receptor expression and signaling. He also studies molecular impacts on muscular dystrophy and diseases of the heart and nervous systems. Dr. G. Stanley McKnight's work focuses on signaling transduction pathways. He uses molecular genetic techniques to examine the role of cAMP-dependent protein kinases in the hormonal regulation of gene expression differentiation and uses mice models to study the expression of wild-type and mutant kinase genes.

In addition to serving in the Department of Pharmacology, Dr. Randall Moon is investigator for the Howard Hughes Medical Institute and the director for the Institute for Stem Cell and Regenerative Medicine at the University of Washington. His research uses Xenopus frogs and zebrafish to study embryonic development, seeking to learn more about signaling of wnt proto-oncogenes. Dr. Neil Nathanson examines the cell and molecular biology of neural signal transduction proteins. He looks at the regulation, function, and neuroplasticity of muscarinic acetylcholine receptors, G proteins, and receptors for neuronal differentiation factors. Dr. John Neumaier, Dr. Paul Phillips, and Dr. Nephi Stella are all also on the staff of Psychiatry and Behavioral Sciences. Neumaier specializes in studying the regulation of serotonin receptor expression in the brain, and Phillips focuses on the role of phasic dopamine release in mental illness, decision-making, and motivated behavior. Stella concentrates on studying the immune cells of the central nervous system (CNS) and looks at how they interact with degenerating neurons as a means of identifying plant-based therapies such as marijuana and echinacea. Dr. John Scott is the Edwin G. Krebs–Hilma Speights Professor of Pharmacology and an investigator with the Howard Hughes Medical Institute. His work is concerned with the impact of anchoring proteins on spatial and temporal specificity of signal transduction events.

Dr. Daniel Storm's work is involved with studying the molecular basis of neruoplasticity, and he is particularly interested in studying the central nervous system, neuron growth, and calmodulin- and calcium-regulated systems. Dr. Bruce Tempel, who is also on the faculty of the Otolaryngology Department and the Virginia Merrill Bloedel Hearing Research Center, concentrates on the molecular and genetic basis of membrane excitability. He uses mice models and electrophysiological, biochemical, and molecular techniques to study normal and mutant potassium channel genes. Dr. Edith Wang focuses on the regulation of gene expression, concentrating on cell proliferation and muscle differentiation. Also an investigator with the Howard Hughes Medical Institute, Dr. Ning Zheng is concerned with the structural biology of protein ubiquitination and degradation, focusing on cell progression, signal transduction, transcription, and DNA repair and the impact of ubiquitin ligases on cancer and viral infections. Dr. Larry Zweifel is involved in studying the genetic dissection of neural circuit function and behavior. He focuses on examining the impact of phasic dopamine on human behaviors such as reward and punishment and fear and anxiety.

Elizabeth Rholetter Purdy
Independent Scholar

See Also: Antiaging Medicines; Cancer, Drug Treatments for; Central Nervous System Depressants and Stimulants; Opium (Herbal Medicine).

Further Readings

Mitra, Ashim K., Chil H. Lee, and Kun Cheng. *Advanced Drug Delivery*. Hoboken, NJ: Wiley, 2014.

Stella, Nephi and Paul Schweitzer. "A Second Endogenous Cannabinoid That Modulates Long-Term Potentiation." *Nature*, v.388/6644 (1997).

University of Washington. "Department of Pharmacology." http://depts.washington.edu/phcol/ (Accessed October 2014).

U.S. Anti-Doping Agency

Doping, the use of drugs to enhance performance in sports, has existed since ancient times. Only relatively recently, however, have organizations been created to regulate the use of drugs in sport; such organizations include the World Anti-Doping Agency (WADA) and the U.S. Anti-Doping Agency (USADA). USADA is a not-for-profit nongovernmental organization and the national antidoping organization of the

United States. It aims to preserve fair play and protect the safety of athletes.

According to some sources, the word *dop* was used by Zulu warriors to denote an alcoholic beverage taken as a stimulant during religious ceremonies, and this word may be the root of the present-day term *doping*. Doping in sports took place at least as early as the time of the ancient Greeks, whose Olympic athletes reportedly used special diets and "magical" potions believed to improve performance; they had an incentive to use these means because of the rewards given to successful Olympic competitors.

Given the potential for doping to compromise the safety and health of athletes, and because of its prevalence, an international framework was created to monitor fairness in sports. In the early 1990s, doping resulted in injuries and even deaths among participants in football matches. Likewise, numerous doping scandals occurred in the late 1990s, most notably in road cycling. Later, the international sports community discussed the evolving challenges of doping in sports at the First World Conference on Doping in Sport, held in Lausanne, Switzerland, in 1999. WADA was then created, with the aim of overseeing antidoping policies that would be enforced at the international level, most importantly at the Olympic Games. WADA provides a set of regulations for all national and international sports organizations, which must be adhered to for participation in the Olympic Games. Table 1 provides a history of some notable doping events in modern athletic competition.

Table 1   History of Some Notable Doping Events in Modern Athletic Competition

Year	Event
1865	An unnamed performance-enhancing drug was used by swimmers during an event in Amsterdam
1867	During a popular six-day cycling race, French athletes used mixtures based on caffeine, Belgians used sugar mixed with ether, and others used alcoholic beverages or nitroglycerin
1896	English cyclist Arthur Linton suffered the first reported death caused by doping (ephedrine) during a race from Paris to Bordeaux
1904	At the St. Louis marathon, racers consumed strychnine and cognac before the race
1910	The first reported case involving accusations of doping in athletes takes place
1920	Amphetamine use becomes common in sports
1952	During an ice-skating event in Oslo, ampules and syringes are found in athletes' locker rooms
1960	During the Olympic Games in Rome, the Danish cyclist Knud Jensen died after abusing amphetamines
1967	The British cyclist Tom Simpson (amphetamines) and the runner Dick Howard (heroin overdose) die
1976	In the Olympic Games in Montreal, the Polish athlete Zbiegniew Kaczmarek and the Bulgarian athlete Valentin Hristov (both weight lifters) are forced to return their gold medals after being proved to have engaged in doping
1988	The use of a banned anabolic steroid (stanozolol) is detected at the Olympic Games in Seoul

Once WADA was established, many countries created their own antidoping agencies to monitor their athletes' adherence to WADA's regulations. USADA was established on the U.S. Olympic Committee's recommendation to endorse fair play and to ensure that athletes would be eligible for international competition. On October 1, 2000, USADA was created and given full authority to establish a comprehensive national antidoping program, including testing, education, research, policy formation, and procedures to ensure fairness in all U.S.-sanctioned events that could qualify an athlete for the Olympic Games.

World Anti-Doping Code

USADA is a signatory to WADA and fully complies with the World Anti-Doping Code's international standards. The World Anti-Doping Code is a document whose aim is to harmonize antidoping regulations in all sports and countries. It embodies an annual list of prohibited substances and methods athletes are not allowed to take or use. The code works in conjunction with five international standards for uniform testing programs across the globe and is widely considered the basis for the strongest and strictest antidoping programs in sports. The code works in conjunction with the following international standards:

- The WADA Prohibited List (outlining the substances and methods prohibited in sport)
- The International Standard for Testing and Investigations (test planning and sample collection process)
- International Standard for Laboratories (standard for the caliber of laboratories that can process athletes' samples)
- International Standard for Therapeutic Use Exemptions (TUEs) (the approval process for allowing athletes to obtain exemptions for prohibited substances when a legitimate medical reason exists)

- International Standard for the Protection of Privacy and Personal Information (privacy protections when collecting and using athletes' personal information)

Programs of USADA

USADA organizes a number of programs to make athletes aware of the programs and protect their rights to ensure fair play.

Education

USADA provides extensive antidoping education to thousands of athletes each year, helping athletes understand their rights and responsibilities with regard to the drug-testing process. The topics of discussion during the education sessions include the following:

- Prohibited substance details
- Required information for the out-of-competition testing program
- Details on the sample collection process and expectations during a urine or blood test
- Awareness about dietary supplements
- Medication information and how to apply for a TUE
- Results management information
- General rules and guidelines for competing clean

USADA provides its antidoping education and athlete resources in a number of ways, including in-person education training and presentations; webinars for general and select audiences; online, interactive tutorials; and brochures and online education resources.

Drug Reference

USADA provides a number of drug reference resources for athletes to assist with questions on prohibited medications, TUEs, and dietary supplement safety.

Global Drug Reference Online

The Global Drug Reference Online (Global DRO) describes the "prohibited" or "not prohibited" status of medications with specific and generic brand names as well as individual medical ingredients and assists athletes, parents, coaches, support personnel, and others. It is specific to those substances prohibited only in certain sports. It was created through a partnership between the Canadian Centre for Ethics in Sport, UK Anti-Doping, and USADA. The Japan Anti-Doping Agency also became an official Global DRO licensee in 2013.

Drug Reference Phone Line

USADA's athlete express service allows athletes and support personnel to speak with experts regarding a host of topics related to medications and prohibited substances.

Supplement 411

Supplement 411 is one of the most comprehensive educational tutorials for athletes, their support personnel, and general consumers regarding the safety of over-the-counter dietary supplement products. The use of dietary supplements can pose both a health risk and an antidoping risk, as there have been positive test results linked to the use of dietary supplement products around the world.

Therapeutic Use Exemptions

USADA provides a TUE application process for athletes who have a legitimate medical need to use prohibited substances or methods. USADA's TUE application process is compliant with both the World Anti-Doping Code and WADA's International Standard for TUE.

A therapeutic use exemption can be requested for an athlete which permits him or her to use a prohibited medication for a legitimate medical purpose. This can be requested when (1) an alternative nonbanned medication is not available, (2) the medication would significantly impair the athlete if not taken, (3) the substance has no additional performance-enhancing ability aside from returning the athlete to a more normal state of health, and (4) there is appropriate physician documentation.

Sample Collection

A safe and secure sample collection process is one of the most important pieces of an effective antidoping program. USADA's sample collection processes are fully compliant with the World Anti-Doping Code and the International Standard for Testing and Investigations. USADA employs highly trained doping control officers (DCOs) and support staff members to maintain an effective sample collection process.

USADA's regulations require that a chaperone or DCO be present throughout the collection process to validate the sample. If necessary, the DCO or chaperone may allow the athlete to hydrate, although rehydration is avoided, because a urine sample must have an appropriate specific gravity. Specific regulations for urine- and blood-sampling procedures are provided in Annexes D and E of the International Standard for Testing and Investigations (January 2012), respectively.

For urine drug testing, an athlete is required provide at least 90 mL of urine with specific gravity greater than 1.005. The pH of the urine must be in the range of 4.5 to 7.5.

According to WADA, the amount of blood drawn from an athlete depends on the required testing. For further immediate processing of a blood sample (e.g., centrifugation), the athlete remains at the site until the final sealing in a tamper-evident kit. The athlete must secure the seal prior to its transportation to the testing site.

Testing Notification

The test distribution plan of USADA determines the number of in- and out-of-competition drug-testing events. Athletes are notified prior to a test unless the drug test is a "no advance notice" test. Before an athlete undergoes testing, he or she may eat or drink at his or her own risk.

Athletes are also required to sign a notification form certifying that they have been informed of the drug-testing requirement. WADA and USADA notify athletes of missed tests. If an athlete misses or fails a test, a probation period of 18 months is ordered. Athletes are penalized if they have a combination of three missed tests or whereabouts-filing failures the same as if they had positive drug test results.

Sample Analysis

Blood or urine samples of athletes are analyzed at WADA-accredited laboratories. The samples are accurately and promptly shipped to the labs, and the integrity of each sample is maintained.

There are currently 32 laboratories accredited to conduct human doping control sample analyses around the world. The UCLA Olympic Analytical Laboratory in Los Angeles and the Sports Medicine Research and Testing Laboratory in Salt Lake City, Utah, are WADA-accredited laboratories in the United States.

Implications of a Failed Test

An athlete can fail a drug test for a number of reasons, mostly because of the presence of a banned substance. The list of violations causing a failed drug test is as follows:

- A prohibited substance or its metabolites or makers
- A prohibited method
- Reusing or failing to submit to the sample collection without justification

- Violating requirements of availability for out-of-competition testing
- Tampering or attempting to tamper with the doping control process
- Possessing prohibited substances or using prohibited methods
- Trafficking or attempting to traffic prohibited substances or prohibited methods
- Administration or attempted administration of a prohibited substance to any athlete in competition

Athletes who violate WADA's antidoping regulations can be sanctioned with lifetime bans, on the basis of the extent of the violation.

Results Management

USADA is also involved in the results management and judgment process for U.S. athletes. This eliminates the inherent conflict of interest associated with sport organizations that try to both grow and promote their sports.

TrueSport

The main objective of USADA's TrueSport movement is to ensure a positive youth sport experience through parents, coaches, athletes, educators, camps, ambassadors, and more. TrueSport emphasizes clean competition, sportsmanship, and peak performance.

Innovative Technologies Developed by USADA

USADA Paperless Sample Collection System

USADA has developed a state-of-the-art electronic sample collection system that allows DCOs to seamlessly collect and transmit completed test data to their test management databases. It provides real-time data transfer, improving efficiency and ensuring the accuracy of data entry into an antidoping management system. In addition, it permits a significant reduction in collection paperwork, printing, and shipping fees.

Simon

USADA's Simon database serves as an operational tool that integrates with the Paperless Sample Collection System. It has a user-friendly interface and is currently being used by national antidoping agencies in other countries, such as Canada, Ireland, Switzerland, and New Zealand. Simon's integration with the Paperless Sample Collection System allows antidoping organizations to communicate sensitive data to relevant parties.

Chronos

The USADA has developed Chronos, an interactive application for tracking, reviewing, plotting, and analyzing samples for authenticated users. Chronos can provide detailed information about sample collection, including athlete timelines and athlete monitoring lists. The tracking of relevant internal information and ongoing commentary to benefit future test planning and results case management can also be obtained.

Contract Testing

USADA also provides services to assist any organization in promoting clean competition.

The WADA Prohibited List

The WADA Prohibited List is the comprehensive document that serves as the international standard for identifying substances and methods prohibited in sport. It is one of the most important parts of harmonization globally across the antidoping movement. The Prohibited List is updated annually.

WADA bans substances on the basis of the following criteria:

- The potential to enhance performance
- An actual or potential health risk
- Whether they violate the spirit of sport

When a substance is banned, its entire class is usually banned as well, regardless of whether the specific substance is named. Avoiding consumption of a banned substance is an athlete's personal responsibility.

The International Olympic Committee listed approximately 40 to 50 compounds, including only stimulants, narcotics, and analgesics, in its prohibited list in 1967. After WADA was launched in 1999, the list was updated. Table 2 lists the banned drugs according to category.

Prohibited Substances

Nonapproved substances (S0): This category was included in 2011 in the WADA Prohibited List. The category includes substances that are not approved by any authority for therapeutic use (drugs under development, etc.). These drugs are prohibited at all times in sports.

Anabolic agents (S1): These agents were banned in 1975. They are used to treat various ailments therapeutically. However, athletes may use them for building muscle mass. Examples include testosterone, nandrolone, and so on.

Peptide hormone, growth factors (S2): Erythropoietin (EPO) is used to increase the number of red blood cells (RBCs) in anemic patients. However, athletes may use EPO to improve their endurance, due to increased oxygen capacity as a result of increased RBCs.

Beta-2 antagonists (S3): For USADA, all β_2 agonists are prohibited, including optical

Table 2 WADA's List of Prohibited Substances

Category	Group/Methods	Prohibited Drugs
Prohibited substances in sports		
S0	Clinically nonapproved substances	Drugs under preclinical or clinical development or discontinued, designer drugs, or veterinary drugs
S1	Anabolic agents	Testosterone, DHEA, etc.
S2	Peptide hormones, growth hormones	Erythropoietin, human chorionic gonadotropin, insulin-like growth factors, etc.
S3	β_2 antagonists	All taken orally, except inhaled formoterol, salbutamol, and salmeterol
S4	Hormone and metabolic modulators	Aromatase inhibitors, selective estrogen receptor modulators
S5	Diuretics and other masking agents	Agents that increases plasma volume
S6	Stimulants and optical isomers	Except imidazole derivatives for topical use and those for the 2014 monitoring program
S7	Narcotics	Buprenorphine, dextromoramide, diamorphine (heroin), opium, etc.
S8	Cannabinoids	Natural or synthetic THC and THC-like cannabinoids (e.g., hashish, marijuana, Spice, JWH018, HU-210)
S9	Glucocorticoids	Systemic use of glucocorticosteroids is prohibited in competition, including oral intake (e.g., Medrol Dosepak), a systemic IV or IM injection, or by rectal routes
Prohibited methods		
M1	Manipulation of blood and blood components	RBCs or artificial oxygen by physical or chemical means
M2	Chemical and physical manipulation	Tampering or attempting to tamper with a collected sample to affect its validity
M3	Gene doping	The transfer of polymers of nucleic acids or nucleic acid analogues or the use of normal or genetically modified cells
Substances prohibited in specific sports		
P1	Alcohol	Banned in specific games such as archery, shooting,
P2	β-blockers	billiards, karate, etc.

Source: Athlete Guide to the 2015 Prohibited List (includes substances prohibited at all times, both in and out of competition).
Note: DHEA = dehydroepiandrosterone; IM = intramuscular; IV = intravenous; RBC = red blood cell; THC = tetrahydrocannabinol.

isomers, except for formoterol, salbutamol, and salmeterol when used by inhalation. According to USADA, concentrations greater than 1,600 µg per 24 hours require a TUE of a drug taken by inhalation.

Hormone and metabolic modulators (S4): WADA and USADA prohibit the use of aromatase inhibitors, antiestrogenic chemicals, selective estrogen receptor modulators, and agents that modify myostatin function. Insulin can be used with a TUE.

Diuretics and other masking agents (S5): Diuretics, which increase plasma volume, have been banned since 1988.

Stimulants (S6): Stimulants were the first drugs to be banned in sports, in 1967. Stimulants that are used for therapeutic purposes, such as cough and cold, can be taken up to a threshold limit. Using more than the threshold limit results in sanctions.

Narcotics (S7): Narcotics are generally used as painkillers in postsurgical treatments, but athletes may use them to mask their pain to sustain performance for longer periods.

Prohibited Methods

M1: The administration of blood products or artificial delivery of oxygen to provide extra endurance is prohibited.

M2: Tampering with the integrity and validity of samples (e.g., adulteration of urine) is prohibited.

M3: Transfer of normal or genetically modified genes for enhancing performance is also prohibited.

Substances Prohibited in Specific Sport Events

Categories P1 and P2 include alcohol and β-blockers, which are prohibited in specific sports category such as archery, shooting, golf, and so on.

Nutritional Supplements in Sports

An athlete must use certified nutritional supplements, because supplements may contain substances with different names instead of the active compounds (in the case of herbal products), substances that are precursors of endogenous steroids (e.g., norandrostenedione as a precursor of nandrolone), or contaminations of other products.

Conclusion

USADA is responsible for banning substances and for upholding drug-testing requirements to ensure fair play and maintain the safety of athletic competitions. The number of substances on the WADA Prohibited List grows annually. Antidoping agencies update their lists of banned substances and methods on a yearly basis on their Web sites and offer resources to athletes and regulatory bodies.

Manoj Poonia
*Narsee Monjee Institute
of Management Studies*

See Also: Drug Testing, Olympic Athletes (Overview); Ethics of Performance-Enhancing Drugs in Sport; Olympics, Summer: Performance-Enhancing Drugs; Olympics, Winter: Performance-Enhancing Drugs.

Further Readings

Conti, A. A. "Doping in Sports in Ancient and Recent Times." *Medicine Nei Secoli,* v.22/1–3 (2012).
Global Drug Reference Online. http://www.globaldro .org (Accessed June 10, 2015).
U.S. Anti-Doping Agency. "Athlete Guide to the 2015 Prohibited List." http://www.usada.org/substances/ prohibited-list/athlete-guide/ (Accessed June 10, 2015).
U.S. Anti-Doping Agency. "Therapeutic Use Exemptions (TUEs)." http://www.usada.org/ substances/tue/ (Accessed June 10, 2015).

U.S. Anti-Doping Agency. "USADA's Anti-Doping Programs." http://www.usada.org/about/programs/ (Accessed June 10, 2015).

U.S. PHARMACOPEIAL CONVENTION

The U.S. Pharmacopeial Convention (USP) is a scientific nonprofit organization that sets standards for the identity, strength, quality, and purity of medicines, food ingredients, and dietary supplements that are manufactured, distributed, and consumed worldwide. The USP publishes the *U.S. Pharmacopeia*. The standards set by the USP are observed in over 140 countries, and within the United States are enforced by the U.S. Food and Drug Administration (FDA). The USP is headquartered in the U.S. city of Rockville, Maryland.

History

The USP was founded in 1820 with the assistance of 11 physicians. The first version of its pharmacopeia, released the same year, contained 217 products. In 1848, the pharmacopeia was officially recognized by the U.S. federal government. In 1975, the USP (organization) acquired the National Formulary and Drug Standards Laboratory.

Structure

The three bodies composed of volunteers from around the world govern the USP. These are as follows:

- USP Convention Membership: The USP Convention constitutes more than 400 member organizations and includes academic institutions, health practitioner and scientific associations, consumer organizations, manufacturer and trade associations, government bodies and associations, and nongovernmental standards-setting and conformity assessment bodies.
- Board of Trustees: The USP Board of Trustees is elected every five years by the Convention membership. The board makes decisions that guide the USP's policies, finances, and strategic direction.
- Council of Experts and its Expert Committees: The Council of Experts is the body that makes the USP's scientific and standards-setting decisions. Members of the Council are elected by the USP Convention membership.

The activities of the USP are conducted according to a Code of Ethics. The USP Code of Ethics requires that USP employees and volunteers operate in accordance with ethical standards.

U.S. Pharmacopeia

The *U.S. Pharmacopeia* is the official pharmacopeia of the United States, published dually with the National Formulary as the *USP-NF*. The pharmacopeia contains directions for the identification of compound medicines. The pharmacopeia is, like the Convention, also commonly abbreviated to *USP*.

Prescription and over-the-counter medicines and other health care products, as well as dietary supplements that are sold in the United States, are required to follow the standards in the *USP-NF*. This is a requirement of U.S. federal law. The inclusion of dietary supplements is the most recent addition to the *USP*. The 1994 Dietary Supplement Health and Education Act (DSHEA), an amendment to the Federal Food, Drug, and Cosmetic Act (FDCA), provided a regulatory framework to allow marketing of vitamins, minerals, herbs or other botanicals, amino acids, and substances such as enzymes, organ tissues, glandulars, and metabolites. For this, standardization and definition in the *USP* was required.

The USP's standards are presented in a monograph (documentary standard), with references to general chapters and allied reference materials that are required to demonstrate conformance to the documentary standard. The makeup of the pharmacopeia is as follows:

- Monographs: Each monograph includes the name of the ingredient or preparation; the definition; packaging, storage, and labeling requirements; and the specification. The specification consists of a series of tests, procedures for the tests, and acceptance criteria. Monographs are numbered 999 and below in the text. Where compliance needs to be shown, the monographs are mandatory.
- General Chapters: Tests and procedures referred to in multiple monographs are described in detail in the *USP-NF* general chapters. General chapters are numbered 1000 and above. They are nonmandatory and offer practical guidance.
- General Notices: The General Notices provide definitions for terms used in the monographs, as well as information that is necessary to interpret the monograph requirements.

The aim of public standards is to allow first parties (manufacturers), second parties (purchasers), and third parties (governmental bodies and others independent of sellers and buyers) to test the quality of food and medicines. USP standards are developed and revised by more than 900 volunteer experts, including international participants, who work with the USP under strict conflict-of-interest rules. Thus the standards can be used by regulatory agencies and manufacturers to help ensure that pharmaceutical products are of the appropriate identity, as well as strength, quality, purity, and consistency.

The pharmacopeia has, since the 2000s, embarked on a process, where agreement can be reached, of international harmonization with other global pharmacopeias. Here the USP works with the European Pharmacopoeia and the Japanese Pharmacopoeia (with the World Health Organization as an observer) in the Pharmacopoeial Discussion Group (PDG). When agreement is reached, the USP signs a Memorandum of Understanding (MOU), and a harmonized standard is published across the three pharmacopeias. Standards in development are available for public comment through the Pharmacopeial Forum publication.

Other Compendia

In addition to the pharmacopeia, the Convention also publishes the following:

- Food Chemicals Codex (FCC): A compendium of internationally recognized standards for the purity and identity of food ingredients. The guideline includes monographs relating to food-grade chemicals, processing aids, foods (such as vegetable oils, fructose, whey, and amino acids), flavoring agents, vitamins, and functional food ingredients (such as lycopene, olestra, and short chain fructooligosaccharides).
- Dietary Supplements Compendium (DSC): The guidance provides documentary specifications of identity, strength, quality, and purity for dietary supplements, dietary ingredients, and other components of dietary supplements.
- USP on Compounding: A compilation of standards designed to help compounding practitioners adhere to widely acknowledged, scientifically sound procedures and practices, and facilitate the delivery of consistent and good-quality prepared medicines to patients.
- Medicines Compendium (MC): A compendium of public standards (monographs with reference materials) relating to approved medicines.

Safety of Medicines

The Convention has, since the 1960s, examined and collated information to support creation of safe medication use and quality of care standards. Many of these standards are incorporated into the pharmacopeia. The Convention also issues reports to guide practitioners to promote safe medication use. On occasion, the USP's product standards call for the adjustment of labels and labeling to reduce the likelihood of error.

New Medicines

The USP has a legal role in the naming of both pharmaceutical ingredients and products. This is through the USP's membership of the U.S. Adopted Names Council. The Council is made up from the American Medical Association (AMA), the American Pharmacists Association (APA), and the USP. The USAN Program sets out to select simple, informative, and unique nonproprietary names (also called generic names) for drugs by establishing logical nomenclature classifications based on pharmacological and/or chemical relationships.

Promoting the Quality of Medicines

The Promoting the Quality of Medicines (PQM) Program is operated by the USP in tandem with the U.S. Agency for International Development. The aim of the program is to improve drug quality and the appropriate use of drugs in countries in Asia, Africa, and Latin America. The main focus is on medicines intended to treat malaria, HIV/AIDS, and tuberculosis. One of the core activities of the PQM is to reduce the presence of substandard and counterfeit medicines.

In relation to its PQM activities, the USP operates the Technical Assistance Program (TAP). This initiative is designed to provide developing countries with tools and training to increase their capacity to test the quality of medicines provided for their citizens.

Reference Materials

The USP manufactures and sells a number of reference standards. USP reference materials are highly characterized physical specimens used in connection with USP's documentary standards to help ensure the quality and benefit of food and drugs. These are made available to laboratories to purchase.

Tim Sandle
*Pharmaceutical Microbiology
Interest Group (Pharmig)*

See Also: Food and Drug Administration (U.S.); History of Pharmacology: U.S., 1945 to Present; United States: 1951 to Present.

Further Readings

Russo K. A., S. de Mars, and W. F. Koch. "USP Response to Stimuli Article European Pharmacopoeia–US Pharmacopeia Prospective Harmonization: API Pilot Project—Industry Perspective." *Pharmacopeial Forum*, v.36/6 (2010).

Wiggins, J. M., P. M. Travis, A. Park, and R. A. Fitzgerald. "Ph Eur/USP Prospective Harmonization—API Pilot Project: Industry Perspective." *Pharmacopeial Forum*, v.6 (2010).

VACCINATION: NATIONAL AND INTERNATIONAL PROGRAMS

As arguably the most cost-effective strategy for modern disease prevention, vaccination use has become more common throughout the 20th century. Of course, this is only effective if large segments of the population have been protected; the World Health Organization (WHO) estimates that "herd immunity," or the protection from disease that occurs when a large segment of the population is vaccinated, exists when 95 percent of the population is compliant. While there are policies and programs that strongly encourage vaccination in the United States, including mandatory vaccination for schoolchildren and individuals in the military, nonmilitary individuals are able to exempt themselves or their children in order to keep these programs constitutional. The situation is similar in developed nations around the world.

United States Vaccination Policies and Programs

The National Vaccine Program Office is the primary federal overseer of vaccine programs in the United States. This office ensures collaboration between all federal agencies involved in immunization activities. It is this office that advises the U.S. National Vaccine Plan under the Department of Health and Human Services. The current national vaccine plan includes strategizing with scientists to make safer, more efficient vaccines and increasing awareness to raise the number of people receiving vaccination. Beyond this, there is not a comprehensive mandatory vaccination system. While these debates seem like a modern phenomenon, the American government has been grappling with their implications for over two centuries.

The first federal legislation in the United States regarding vaccination policy was the Vaccine Act of 1813. This act established the United States Vaccine Agency, which attempted to provide large-scale smallpox vaccination and sought to protect consumers against fraudulent quacks. The most comprehensive portion of this act was the requirement for the post office to carry, for free, smallpox vaccine material in an attempt to educate the masses. This was controversial, and Congress repealed the act in 1822 after unsafe material was sent through the mail. It was not until 1855 that a compulsory vaccination law appeared in the United States, when Massachusetts required smallpox vaccination for schoolchildren.

There was enough antivaccine sentiment during the 19th century to seriously question these laws, encouraging revision throughout the 20th century. In 1905, a United States Supreme Court case, *Jacobson v. Massachusetts*, ruled that compulsory vaccination was legal when it was performed for the common good. The ruling was determined by using the Tenth Amendment of the United States Constitution, which states that the police powers of public health are constitutional if the power exercised over a person and property is reasonable. It was determined that providing exemptions for schoolchildren would ensure this reasonable control. Although controversies surrounding school vaccination still exist, these programs continue to be protected by this Supreme Court case.

As part of the Centers for Disease Control and Prevention (CDC), the Advisory Committee on Immunization Practices provides scientific evidence and advisory counsel for the routine administration of vaccines for adults and the vaccine schedule for schoolchildren. Today, it is required that children receive vaccinations for a variety of infectious diseases, including diphtheria, pertussis, tetanus, measles, mumps, rubella, and hepatitis B, before their entry into public schools. Most states offer exemptions for religious or philosophical reasons, in addition to allowing for medical exemptions.

Arguably, the largest vaccination program targeted toward children in the United States was for protection against polio in the 1950s. Polio crippled approximately 35,000 people a year throughout the 1940s. Scientists were vying to be the first to create a reliable and efficient vaccine to protect against one of the most feared diseases of the 20th century. In 1954, Jonas Salk's polio vaccine began large-scale clinical trials on schoolchildren. This was not without incident—260 incidents and 10 deaths from polio directly related to the Salk vaccine resulted in Sabin's oral "sugar cube" being the preferred method for children. The large-scale administration to schoolchildren, funded by the organization now known as the March of Dimes, is largely responsible for jump-starting the worldwide eradication of polio. WHO dates polio eradication to 1994.

Besides compulsory vaccination schedules for schoolchildren, the U.S. government requires all military personnel and those applying for immigration to have their vaccines. Whereas the parents of schoolchildren are able to exercise exemptions, these are not as readily available for those in the military. Military vaccine programs have been instrumental in the development and implementation of many effective vaccination programs going back further than we may realize; during the Revolutionary War, Gen. George Washington required inoculation against smallpox for all American soldiers. For the British army, this was voluntary. More soldiers died from smallpox than they did combat, and thus some historians have argued that Washington's order, which was the first of its kind, was a weapon in itself. Similar programs have existed for diseases like yellow fever and adenovirus.

In 1997, the Clinton administration required that all military personnel become vaccinated with BioThrax, a vaccine against anthrax. This would be in addition to its normal vaccine routines, including tetanus, pneumococcal, Japanese encephalitis, and after 2001, smallpox. To refuse these vaccines, including the controversial BioThrax, is grounds for dishonorable discharge.

In some cases, military vaccination policy affects civilian vaccination policy. In 1976, when an Army private at Fort Dix died from a strain of swine flu appearing similar to the 1918 influenza strain, public health officials suggested to President Gerald Ford that mass vaccination would prevent another deadly pandemic. Costing $135 million, the response was unprecedented; from October to December 1976, over 40 million Americans, or roughly one-quarter of the population, were vaccinated against swine flu. While later studies have revealed that this vaccination program likely resulted in greater immunity during the 2009 outbreak of swine flu, there were several adverse reactions to the 1976 vaccine. While only one person, the initial Army private, died from swine flu, 25 Americans died from vaccine-related illnesses. Another 500 vaccine recipients reported cases of Guillain-Barré syndrome. This crisis lessened confidence in the CDC, the United States Public Health Service, and vaccination more generally.

In order to mitigate the damage to vaccines' reputations, and to account for the injuries that vaccines cause, a national program was established. In 1986, the U.S. Congress passed the National Childhood Vaccine Injury Act. In addition to improving informed consent and better reporting of vaccine-adverse effects, this act also allowed the Department of Health and Human Services to establish a tax of $0.75 per vaccine from vaccine manufacturers. This fund requires those injured from a childhood vaccine to file a claim with the United States Court of Federal Claims before suing the vaccine manufacturer. Based on a formula, a claimant may be reimbursed for injuries sustained.

United States' Global Vaccine Involvement

The United States is involved in the administration of vaccines in countries of the Global South. The CDC Global Immunization Division estimates that its work is responsible for saving the lives of up to 3 million individuals annually. By protecting people from vaccine-preventable diseases abroad, the CDC argues that it is, in fact, protecting Americans as global pandemics do not obey geographic or political borders. The CDC Global Immunization Division's goals and strategies align with WHO's Global Vaccine Action Plan, ensuring a long and cooperative partnership. Nearly every country on earth has endorsed the "Decade of Vaccines" initiative, which pledges to make the delivery of vaccination more equitable by 2020. It was this collaboration that was able to advise the World Health Organization's Global Vaccine Action Plan.

The work of these organizations globally would be much more difficult without philanthropic assistance. Specifically, the Bill & Melinda Gates Foundation and the GAVI Alliance spend billions of dollars partnering with WHO and UNICEF to make vaccine development and delivery more efficient.

International Vaccine Programs

Developed nations around the world have national vaccine programs similar to those in the United States. Australia, Malaysia, the Republic of Ireland, and the United Kingdom require vaccination before receiving social welfare services, including a public education, although there are exemption eligibilities. Slovenia has one of the strictest vaccination policies of any country; vaccination for nine diseases is mandatory during childhood. While medical exemptions exist, there are no exemptions for religious or philosophical reasons. Failure to receive these vaccines results in a fine for Slovenians, ensuring a compliance rate of over 95 percent.

Jessica Nickrand
University of Minnesota

See Also: Centers for Disease Control and Prevention; Military Pharmaceutical Issues; National Childhood

Vaccine Injury Act; Polio Eradication Campaign; Smallpox Eradication; Vaccines; World Health Organization.

Further Readings

Centers for Disease Control and Prevention. "Global Vaccines and Immunization." http://www.cdc.gov/globalhealth/immunization/ (Accessed March 2014).

College Physicians of Philadelpha. "History of Vaccines." http://www.historyofvaccines.org (Accessed March 2014).

Heller, Jacob. *The Vaccine Narrative*. Nashville, TN: Vanderbilt University Press, 2008.

Largent, Mark. *Vaccine: The Debate in Modern America*. Baltimore, MD: Johns Hopkins University Press, 2012.

Newton, David E. *Vaccine Controversies*. New York: ABC-CLIO, 2013.

VACCINES

Vaccines are biological preparations administered to prevent disease or lessen disease severity, and the process of administering a vaccine to an individual is called vaccination. There are several types of vaccines, but all operate on the principle of introducing an antigen (for instance, the virus that causes measles) in a weakened or inactivated state into an individual's body for the purpose of stimulating the individual's immune system to produce antibodies against that antigen. In this way, vaccines make recipients immune or less susceptible to the disease caused by that antigen (in this case, measles), thus protecting them from the health consequences of becoming infected with that disease. Vaccination is an important public health measure and has led to widespread reduction in the occurrence of many formerly common diseases and played a key role in the campaign to eradicate smallpox. New types of vaccines are currently in development, including vaccines to promote immune responses against different types of cancer.

History

The root of the word *vaccine* comes from the Latin word *vacca* meaning *cow*. The modern history of vaccines dates from the work of the British physician Edward Jenner, who demonstrated in 1796 that infection with cowpox provided immunity against smallpox, hence the reference to "cow" in the term *vaccination*; today, the terms *vaccination* and *immunization* are often used interchangeably. Unlike Jenner's vaccinations, modern vaccines are generally based on a form of the antigen causing the disease they are intended to protect against.

The history of vaccination and related procedures intended to protect individuals against disease is much older than Jenner, however: for instance, attempts to protect individuals against smallpox by introducing matter from an infected individual to a healthy individual (inoculation) took place in China around 1000 C.E., and smallpox inoculation was also practiced in Europe and Colonial America in the 18th century. Inoculation against smallpox was based on the fact that individuals who had the disease and survived could not become infected with it again, so the hope was that inoculation would produce a mild case of smallpox that the individual would survive and thus be immune to the disease.

Some countries passed laws requiring smallpox vaccination in the 19th century, but these requirements were controversial, particularly when the prevalence of smallpox declined (ironically, in part due to the effectiveness of vaccination), so that people were less familiar with the consequences of contracting the disease. In addition, some saw compulsory vaccination as an infringement of their personal rights, and/or a requirement imposed by the upper classes on people of the working class, rather than as a public health measure intended to safeguard the health of everyone.

The 20th century saw the discovery of the development of many types of vaccines, addressing both dreaded diseases like polio and smallpox, and common childhood diseases such as measles and chicken pox. Two types of vaccine were introduced in the mid-20th century. The first, discovered by Jonas Salk, used an inactivated form of several strains of polio virus and was administered by injection. Large-scale human testing of the Salk vaccine began in 1954, and following the successful results of these trials, campaigns promoting the widespread use of the Salk vaccine began in 1955. Another type of polio vaccine, using a live but weakened form of the virus, and which could be administered orally, was developed in 1961 by Albert Sabin. The Sabin vaccine became more used in the global campaign to eradicate polio (as of 2015, polio is endemic in only Afghanistan, Nigeria, and Pakistan), but the Salk vaccine is also used today.

The campaign to eradicate smallpox relied heavily on mass vaccination. Smallpox was chosen as a good candidate for eradiation because an effective vaccine existed, and because the disease only infects humans (i.e., it has no animal reservoirs). In 1959, the World Health Organization (WHO) declared the goal of eradicating smallpox, and in 1966 intensified efforts toward this goal. Mass vaccinations were effective because of herd immunity—when most of the population is immune to a disease, a new case of infection will not spread through the population. The last known "wild" case of smallpox (i.e., a case not caused by infection with smallpox used for lab research) was recorded in 1977, and the disease was declared eradicated in 1980.

Vaccination against smallpox used to be routine in the United States, but following eradication of the disease in 1972, routine vaccination against smallpox ceased. Recent awareness of the bioterrorism potential of smallpox has renewed interest in the smallpox vaccine (although the disease does not exist in the wild, the antigen that causes it still exists in laboratories), and as of 2004, the Centers for Disease Control and Prevention (CDC) reported that it had stockpiled enough smallpox vaccine to immunize every person in the United States. However, routine vaccination has not resumed, and instead the CDC is maintaining a supply of the vaccine to be used in case a smallpox emergency occurs.

Vaccination Schedules

Many diseases that used to be common in childhood are now preventable by vaccines, and the percentage of children receiving these vaccines is considered an important measure of the level of medical care and public health available in a country. Besides preventing children from experiencing the illness caused by a particular disease, one reason vaccination is considered important is because some children contracting a disease may have severe complications or die as a result. For instance, while many children who contract the measles recover without serious or long-lasting effects, some percentage of those infected may become deaf or blind, or die, as a result of the disease.

WHO publishes recommendations for vaccinations for persons in different age-groups. For children in all countries, the following vaccinations are recommended (detailed vaccination schedules and other information, including exceptions to the recommendations, are available from the WHO Web site):

- BCG (Bacillus Calmette-Guerin)
- Hepatitis B
- Polio
- DPT (diphtheria, pertussis, tetanus)

- Hib (*Haemophilus influenzae* type b)
- Pneumonia
- Rotavirus
- Measles
- Rubella

For children living in certain regions where these diseases are prevalent, vaccination is also recommended against Japanese encephalitis, yellow fever, and tick-born encephalitis. For certain high-risk populations, vaccinations are also recommended against typhoid, cholera, meningitis, hepatitis A, and rabies. In some cases, vaccinations are also recommended against mumps, varicella (chicken pox), and seasonal influenza.

For adolescents, recommended vaccinations include a booster for tetanus and diphtheria, vaccination for high-risk groups not previously vaccinated against hepatitis B, vaccination against rubella for females of child-bearing age if not previously vaccinated, and HPV (human papillomavirus) vaccination for girls. Vaccination recommendations for adults include a booster for tetanus and diphtheria in early adulthood or pregnancy, vaccination against hepatitis B if not previously vaccinated, and vaccination against rubella for women of child-bearing age if not previously vaccinated. For high-risk populations of adolescents and adults, vaccination is recommended against typhoid, cholera, meningitis, hepatitis A, and rabies, and for some countries, vaccination is also recommended against seasonal influenza and varicella.

Individual countries sometimes issue recommendations that differ from those of the World Health Organization, based in part on the resources available in that country and the risk posed by different diseases. For instance, the United States recommends the Zoster (shingles) vaccine for persons aged 60 and older, and a one-time Tdap (tetanus, diphtheria, pertussis) for adults, followed by a Td (tetanus, diphtheria) booster every 10 years.

Sarah E. Boslaugh
Saint Louis University

See Also: Access to Medicines (Developing World); Access to Medicines (Industrialized World); Autism and Vaccines; National Childhood Vaccine Injury Act; Smallpox Eradication; Vaccination: National and International Programs; WHO Model Lists of Essential Medicines; World Health Organization.

Further Readings

Butterfield, Lisa H. "Cancer Vaccines." *BMJ* (April 22, 2015).

Centers for Disease Control and Prevention. "Vaccines & Immunizations." http://www.cdc.gov/vaccines/ (Accessed June 11, 2015).

Stern, Alexandra Minna and Howard Markel. "The History of Vaccines and Immunization: Familiar Patterns, New Challenges." *Health Affairs*, v.24/3 (May 2005). http://content.healthaffairs.org/content/24/3/611.full (Accessed June 11, 2015).

World Health Organization. "Immunization, Vaccines, and Biologicals: Fact Sheets." http://www.who.int/immunization/newsroom/factsheets/en/ (Accessed June 11, 2015).

World Health Organization. "Summary of WHO Position Papers: Recommendations for Routine Immunization" (updated February 27, 2015). http://www.who.int/immunization/policy/Immunization_routine_table1.pdf?ua=1 (Accessed June 11, 2015).

VALERIAN (HERBAL MEDICINE)

Valerian is a flowering herb that was originally cultivated in regions of Asia and Europe. It was eventually brought to the Americas. While extracts made from the petals of valerian were used as perfume, the root of valerian is typically what is used in pharmaceutical and herbal medicine. Valerian has many healing properties attributed to it. While valerian is more commonly known as an herbal treatment for sleep disorders, it is also used to alleviate physical discomfort and to treat a variety of mental disorders. These disorders include anxiety disorders, attention deficit hyperactivity disorder (ADHD), and depression.

Although valerian has been used for thousands of years, the precise physiological mechanism that aids in its healing capability has not been solidly determined. However, based on valerian's traditional use as a sleeping aid and pain reliever, it has been linked to increasing the amount of gamma aminobutyric acid (more commonly known as GABA) that is present in the brain. GABA is a neurotransmitter that regulates the frequency of neuron excitability in the central nervous system. Drugs that increase the amount of GABA in the brain tend to have calming and anticonvulsive effects on the body.

Valerian and Physical Ailments

Valerian can be used to alleviate both muscle and joint discomfort. It is also often used to ease the pain related to menstrual cramps along with the hot flashes that can accompany menopause. Since valerian is linked to having a calming effect on the body, it can be used as an alternative to pharmaceutical medications when it comes to treating physical ailments. However, since the mechanism of valerian hasn't been comprehensively examined, the full range of side effects is yet to be determined. This makes valerian an herbal remedy that should only be used under close supervision due to the impact it may have on the central nervous system.

The popularity of valerian as a pain reliever may stem from the negative connotation that is connected to the use of prescription pain medications. Due to the increasing prevalence of the abuse of prescription pain relievers,

individuals who are legitimately suffering from chronic pain may be wary of depending on prescribed medication. This can be due to a fear of becoming addicted to such medication. It may also be due to the social stigmas that are linked to needing such medication, especially for illnesses that don't manifest themselves outwardly.

Using a natural remedy takes away the necessity of explaining an illness to health professionals. Since so many health professionals have encountered individuals who have lied about illnesses to gain access to prescriptions, some may be suspicious due to these encounters. Studies have shown that it is becoming increasingly difficult for patients with chronic pain to find physicians who are willing to prescribe the medication that these legitimate patients need. Without suitable treatment, these patients find themselves unable to function through their debilitating pain. By taking herbal alternatives such as valerian, many patients hope to elude the extensive search for a physician who will assist them and avoid having to justify their pain to someone who may not believe them. In doing so, they can avoid what they might perceive to be an uncomfortable encounter. However, due to the lack of concrete knowledge regarding valerian's efficacy, these patients may be adversely affected by side effects or may not receive the pain relief that they need.

Valerian and Mental Health

Valerian was first used thousands of years ago by the ancient Greeks, Indians, Chinese, and Romans. While the ancient Greek physician Hippocrates and his counterparts used valerian for a wide range of ailments, its use as an antihysteric persisted well into the 20th century. Hysteria was classified as an illness that primarily afflicted women and that produced symptoms such as faintness, severe fluctuations in sexual desire, shortness of breath, nervousness, and anxiety. Valerian was one of the treatments administered to treat mild cases of hysteria, but depending on the severity of the symptoms present, other treatments were also administered. Since hysteria had so many symptoms, it was often the umbrella under which illnesses that could not be identified fell. However, as medicine made advances and the general public became more informed, the diagnoses of hysteria sharply declined. Today, female hysteria is no longer classified as an illness.

Valerian's sedative ability makes it a popular herbal option for those who suffer from insomnia. Valerian is said to produce relatively few side effects when compared to its prescribed equivalents. Typically, those who have taken prescribed sleep medication have experienced withdrawal symptoms when they fail to continue taking their medication. Some of these individuals have also experienced a "sleep hangover," which generally involves feeling extremely tired and groggy after awakening. Valerian, on the other hand, is touted as an herbal remedy for insomnia that assists in inducing sleep without producing tiredness upon awaking or withdrawal symptoms.

Unlike many prescription medications that begin working almost immediately, it has been found that valerian needs to be taken for several weeks in order to reach an effective level. Another issue with valerian stems from the lack of proper regulation and studies performed on it. Due to this issue, it can be difficult for a person to determine a proper dosing amount and schedule for maximum effectiveness. Additionally, contrary to the claims that valerian is without side effects, studies have shown that taking valerian for long periods of time can indeed produce withdrawal effects similar to those found when taking prescription sleep aids.

These symptoms can include heart palpitations, headaches, nausea, and, in rare instances, liver damage.

Potential issues may arise with valerian since it interacts with alcohol and prescribed medications such as Xanax, benzodiazepines, CNS depressants, and medications containing cytochrome P450 3A4 substrates. One of the problems with over-the-counter medication is that patients often forget to tell their doctors about adding valerian to their medicine regimen. Additionally, since the medication isn't prescribed, pharmacists are not able to act as the last line of defense since they would likely be equally uninformed. If those who intend to use valerian fail to tell their physicians prior to using it, medication may be prescribed that can cause unwanted interactions, resulting in excessive sleepiness or exaggerated medicine potency and side effects.

Karen Knaus
University of Colorado Denver

Halimah Hamidu
University of Colorado Denver

See Also: Aloe Vera (Herbal Medicine); Chamomile (Herbal Medicine); Ginseng (Herbal Medicine).

Further Readings

American Cancer Society. "Valerian" (November 28, 2008). http://www.cancer.org/treatment/treatmentsandsideeffects/complementaryand alternativemedicine/herbsvitaminsandminerals/valerian.

Barrish, C. "Crackdown on Painkiller Epidemic Hurts Legitimate Patients." *USA Today*, February 27, 2012. http://usatoday30.usatoday.com/news/health/story/health/story/2012-02-26/Crackdown-on-painkiller-epidemic-hurts-legitimate-patients/53255904/1.

Bhatia, J. "Herbal Remedies for Natural Pain Relief." *Everyday Health*, August 3, 2012. http://www.everydayhealth.com/pain-management/herbal-remedies-for-pain.aspx.

Briggs, L. "The Race of Hysteria: 'Overcivilization' and the 'Savage' Woman in Late Nineteenth-Century Obstetrics and Gynecology." *American Quarterly*, v.52/2 (2000). doi:10.1353/aq.2000.0013

Ehrlich, S. "Valerian." University of Maryland Medical Center, May 4, 2011. http://umm.edu/health/medical/altmed/herb/valerian.

Hobbs, C. "Valerian and Other Anti-Hysterics in European and American Medicine (1733–1936)" (1998). http://www.christopherhobbs.com/website/library/articles/article_files/valerian_antihysterics.html.

Meltzer, E. C. "Stigmatization of Substance Use Disorders Among Internal Medicine Residents." *Substance Abuse*, v.34/4 (2013). doi:10.1080/08897077.2013.815143.

Morgenthaler, T. "Valerian: A Safe and Effective Sleep Aid?" Mayo Clinic (April 3, 2012). http://www.mayoclinic.org/diseases-conditions/insomnia/expert-answers/valerian/faq-20057875.

Watanabe, M. "GABA and GABA Receptors in the Central Nervous System and Other Organs." *International Review of Cytology*, v.213 (2002). doi:10.1016/S0074-7696(02)13011-7.

Watson, S. "The Stigma of Chronic Migraine." *Harvard Health Blog* (January 23, 2013). http://www.health.harvard.edu/blog/the-stigma-of-chronic-migraine-201301235828.

VENEREAL DISEASE TREATMENT: HISTORY

Venereal diseases are sexually contagious illnesses. Major types of venereal diseases include chlamydia, gonorrhea, genital herpes, human immunodeficiency virus/acquired immune deficiency syndrome, human papillomavirus, syphilis, bacterial vaginosis, trichomoniasis, and viral hepatitis.

The history of venereal disease is an important topic because it demonstrates the connections between sex, disease, fear of contagion, prejudice, and medicine. For centuries, sexually transmitted diseases (STDs) have been connected to larger cultural norms about virtue, sin, intimacy, and gender norms. They have also been cloaked in secrecy, stigma, and discrimination. Historically, people with STDs often faced a great deal of stigma and were considered morally degenerate. Such was the shame associated with STDs that many doctors would write false causes of death on death notices in order to protect the reputation of a family.

Attitudes about sexual and social practices often influence medical treatment (and vice versa). The shame of catching a disease that is transmitted sexually has greatly influenced the ways in which such diseases are understood and disclosed, but it has also historically affected the ways in which people who contracted the diseases were diagnosed and treated.

Venereal disease was initially named after the Greek goddess of love, Venus. Some of the initial attempts to medically explain how STDs are contracted date back as early as the 1500s. In 1530, poet and physician Girolamo Fracastoro wrote a poem about a young boy named Syphylis. The boy had offended the sun god, Apollo, and subsequently was infected with the disease now recognized as the STD syphilis.

Penis coverings (which subsequently became known as condoms) were believed to prevent venereal disease as early as the Renaissance. Condoms have been made from various materials across the ages, including intestine and bladder, leather, linen, and small pieces of cloth. However, they were often incredibly expensive, were not pleasurable for many men, and were considered immoral by some religious leaders.

The ways in which gender and STDs intersect can often be seen in the treatment of female prostitutes. In England, the Contagious

Diseases Acts of 1864 and 1866 mandated the registration and police supervision of prostitutes. These women could be subjected to detention and regular hospitalization as a way of policing their behaviors, as well as monitoring STDs. STDs were considered so dangerous that the Poor Laws of 1909 recommended detention orders for patients with venereal disease, and the Divorce Law of 1912 indicated that transmission of venereal disease was an act of cruelty second to none and was unmistakably grounds for divorce.

The fear of STDs, and the need to control them, was so profound that in 1913, the Royal Commission on Venereal Disease was created, which led to the establishment of treatment centers. These centers were influenced by feminists, physicians, and the social hygiene movement and usually emphasized the importance of morality when it came to sexual behavior, a strategy known as "moral prophylaxis." One symptom of advanced venereal disease could be the loss of the nose. Medical treatment of this symptom in some cases involved the use of a prosthetic nose. This problem was so common that "no-nose clubs" arose in some parts of England, and clandestine parties were held for people without noses.

In the mid-19th century, some doctors suggested that STDs were caused by excessive sexual intercourse and recommended marriage as an appropriate treatment. Often women were blamed; the sexism of the day identified "unclean women" as the source of the disease. However, research by Charles-Paul Diday and Alfred Fournier on the transmission of venereal disease to newborn babies (and, more broadly, within pregnancy) challenged the status quo of medical thinking. They identified the key role of men in the transmission of the disease: while the mother had transferred the disease in utero to the child, she had usually contracted it from her husband.

People in colonized countries were also blamed for contagious diseases, including venereal disease. Countries such as Britain had specific laws about venereal disease in every colony, though they often differed from colony to colony. Ideas about nation, race, sex, and gender were deeply important to the whole ideology of colonialism. Moral judgments about sex, the family, gender, and even prostitution were all a part of the colonial project. Colonialists blamed the "new world" (colonized countries) for the introduction of such diseases, even suggesting that some of these cultures had histories of sex with animals.

The treatment of venereal disease was important in the development of progressive medicine, because it enabled physicians to examine the links between social practices and pathologies, in particular the ways in which sex and contagious diseases intersected. By the 1870s, medicine recognized that venereal disease could spread throughout the body, leading to problems such as partial paralysis. The development of germ theory suggested that the infection could be transferred through the blood to the internal organs.

One of the historical treatments for venereal disease (in particular syphilis) involved the use of mercury, which was thought to remove the humors that caused syphilis. However, the amounts of mercury that were administered to patients have subsequently been found to be so toxic that they may have been responsible for many of the symptoms that were identified and for many deaths. For instance, some of the effects of these large doses of mercury included the loss of teeth, hemorrhaging of the bowel, and tongue fissures. These treatments were incredibly painful for patients.

In 1909, Paul Ehrlich, a German physician and scientist, designed the arsenic-based drug Salvarsan to treat "sleeping sickness," a nonvenereal disease caused by a microbe. Although

Ehrlich did not fulfill his initial intention of curing the sleeping sickness, he discovered other treatment uses for the drug, such as the treatment of syphilis. In 1910, after reportedly achieving complete cures within three weeks and with no dead animals, Salvarsan was introduced into the clinical setting as an effective drug to cure patients with syphilis. Although Salvarsan was a better alternative in antisyphilitic medications, especially in comparison with previously used mercury-based remedies, it did possess drawbacks. For example, the medication required specific, complicated administration. Also, the drug had significant side effects, including rashes, liver damage, possible limb loss, and fatality. The potential of experiencing these severe side effects was increased by mishandling and improper administration of the drug.

Another treatment, which was used in World War I, involved urethral irrigation with antiseptic solutions such as potassium permanganate through syringes and later from bottles placed 9 feet above the pelvis. This caused complications such as epididymitis in almost every patient. Eventually, the strength of potassium permanganate was reduced in order to limit these complications, and the bottles were lowered to 3 feet above the patient. Shortly after World War I, some physicians used a thin surgical instrument heated by an electric current and inserted into the urethra.

Other treatments involved the administration of boiling water into the bodies of patients. This method was introduced by Colonel L. W. Harrison, who is historically known as the father of British venereology. At the start of the 20th century, Colonel Harrison was assigned to establish standards in the diagnosis of venereal diseases at the Millbank Military Hospital in London. At the time, physicians and medical personnel at this base were frustrated because they were unable to effectively manage the symptoms and the further spread of gonorrhea within this particular military population. Harrison devised a new treatment regimen: heated, electric currents applied within the urethra. Physicians in other Western countries also adopted this treatment. For example, the Kettering Institute in Dayton, Ohio, constructed a specialized heating chamber that was designed to heat the body to 105.8°F. The means of heating the body to rid it of venereal disease became known as the Kettering hypertherm method. This procedure was commonplace until the 1930s.

At the beginning of the 20th century, medical professionals such as Dr. Albert E. Carrier began to discuss the need for collecting anonymous data on reported cases of venereal diseases. Along with health care professionals, in 1905, the Michigan State Medical Society began to question the benefits of reporting cases of venereal diseases to state health boards. However, after much debating of the necessity of state reporting, it was not until 1913 that the U.S. Public Health Service adopted the Model State Law for Morbidity Reports. The primary intent of the model was to control preventable diseases such as gonorrhea and syphilis.

In 1930, the Rosenwald Memorial Fund undertook a study of the prevalence of syphilis among African Americans and found that a lack of social and economic resources was more important than race in terms of the incidence of syphilis. The poorest county they studied had an infection rate of approximately 40 percent. Treatment was not a priority in this study—it simply aimed to establish how widespread the disease was—but when treatment was given, it involved eight or nine injections of arsenic.

The Public Health Service and the Tuskegee Institute launched the Tuskegee Study of

Untreated Syphilis in the Negro Male in 1932. The study involved a total of 600 African American men, 399 of whom had syphilis and the remainder of whom were diagnosed with medical issues such as anemia and/or fatigue. Although the study was projected to last only 6 to 8 months, it persisted from 1932 to 1972. In return for volunteering, subjects received free meals, free medical services, and free burial insurance. The Tuskegee experiment was unethical for several reasons. First, professionals involved in the study failed to ask for medical consent from any of their research volunteers. Furthermore, they deceived the participants about the true nature of the study. Although the men were told that they were receiving treatment for their conditions, none of them ever actually received appropriate treatment for syphilis. Additionally, in 1945, when penicillin was medically determined to be the frontline defense for combating syphilis, it was not incorporated in the treatment regimens of the men. In October 1972, an ad hoc advisory panel appointed by the assistant secretary for health and scientific affairs ruled that the Tuskegee experiment posed many risks to participants and was therefore unethical. Thus, in 1972, the experiment ended. In 1997, President Bill Clinton made a formal apology to the Tuskegee victims.

However, other victims of deliberate and unethical infection have not received the same attention as those involved in the Tuskegee experiment. For instance, between 1944 and 1946, prostitutes in Guatemala were deliberately infected with venereal disease, with the hope of spreading it to prisoners. These prostitutes were infected with *Treponema pallidum*. When the rates of transmission of the disease from these prostitutes were not as high as authorities had hoped, they moved to applying *T. pallidum* directly to the foreskins of prisoners, people in mental institutions, and soldiers. Participants in this study were not told the nature of the experiment and were simply offered items such as cigarettes to participate. Most patients were treated with penicillin, but there were complications, including one death in a patient with epilepsy and other deaths associated with underlying conditions.

Efforts to implement effective treatments for venereal disease also involved the development of registries of patients. However, a national survey in the late 1960s found that the vast majority of doctors who treated patients with either syphilis or gonorrhea did not report them. In fact, almost 90 percent of physicians who treated patients with these diseases indicated that they would not report such cases to relevant authorities. Additionally, people who think they may have a venereal disease may not report it because of the fear of shame and stigma. Unfortunately, however, a failure to report can increase the spread of the disease, because the individuals who have contracted the disease are not being treated. This underreporting also makes estimating the true number of people with venereal disease more difficult.

By the 1960s, treatment of patients with venereal disease involved the administration of penicillin. A 1969 survey suggested that approximately 6.5 percent of patients reported sensitivity to penicillin, but less than 1 percent of those treated with such medications had penicillin reaction. The most frequent allergic reaction was urticaria, and there was a very small number of anaphylactic reactions. From 1947 to 1957, there was a dramatic decrease in reported cases of syphilis, and there was a shift in treatment from public facilities to private physicians. Easily accessible penicillin therapy was a remarkably effective public health intervention in this period. However, other medications were also tried, including the administration of terramycin hydrochloride.

The history of treatment for venereal disease is an example of the ways in which limited scientific knowledge, medical experimentation, and social stigmas can result in poor treatment of patients with particular diseases. Knowledge about venereal disease has changed remarkably over time; modern medicine has been able to identify more than 20 different types of venereal disease. Additionally, medical knowledge about these types of disease (and the therapies used to treat them) has also undergone significant improvements. However, the history of deliberate infection of vulnerable populations is an important reminder of the importance of ethics, honesty, disclosure, and informed consent when it comes to patient diagnosis and treatment.

Mark D. Sherry
University of Toledo

Anna Neller
University of Toledo

See Also: History of Pharmacology: U.S., 1865 to 1900; History of Pharmacology: U.S., 1900 to 1945; History of Pharmacology: U.S., 1945 to Present; Tuskegee Experiment.

Further Readings

Adler, M. W. "The Terrible Peril: A Historical Perspective on the Venereal Diseases." *BMJ*, v.281/6234 (1980).

Brandt, Allan M. *No Magic Bullet: A Social History of Venereal Disease in the United States Since 1880.* Oxford, UK: Oxford University Press, 1987.

Hüntelmann, Axel C. "A Different Mode of Marketing? The Importance of Scientific Articles in the Marketing Process of Salvarsan." *History and Technology,* v.29/2 (2013).

Levine, Philippa. *Prostitution, Race, and Politics: Policing Venereal Disease in the British Empire.* London: Routledge, 2003.

Sherman, Irwin W. *Twelve Diseases That Changed Our World.* Washington, DC: ASM Press, 2007.

VENEREAL DISEASES, TREATMENTS FOR

Venereal diseases (VDs) are contracted or transmitted through sexual contact. Commonly known as sexually transmitted diseases (STDs), VDs have various forms, including human papillomavirus (HPV), chlamydia, gonorrhea, herpes, human immunodeficiency virus (HIV), syphilis, and trichomoniasis. Because many STDs do not cause symptoms, sexually active individuals should undergo regular checkups and testing. If an individual has an STD, obtaining prompt treatment is crucial to managing the disease and preventing transmission.

Some VDs are curable with medications, while others are incurable. For example, STDs caused by bacteria, including gonorrhea, chlamydia, and syphilis, are cured typically with the administration of antibiotics. STDs caused by viruses, including HIV, herpes, and HPV, are not curable but can be treated to control symptoms.

The terms *sexually transmitted disease* and *sexually transmitted infection* (STI) are sometimes used interchangeably. In the medical sector, the term *STI* is often used instead of *STD*, because an infection does not always manifest symptoms or cause a disease. Therefore, the term *STD* is sometimes used when the infection has actually transformed into a disease.

The U.S. Centers for Disease Control and Prevention (CDC) publishes periodic treatment guidelines for STDs. For example, the CDC recommends oral azithromycin 1 g or oral doxycycline 100 mg twice daily at a frequency of seven days for adults and adolescents with uncomplicated chlamydial infections. Pregnant women with uncomplicated chlamydial infections may receive oral azithromycin 1 g or oral amoxicillin 500 mg thrice daily. Alternative medications, such as erythromycin, ofloxacin, and levofloxacin, may be used if the recommended regimens for chlamydia are not suitable for the patient. CDC recommendations are presented only as clinical guidelines and should not be used as clinical standards. Health care providers should consider and treat each patient on a case-by-case basis.

Continuing research on STDs has resulted in a marked improvement in the fight against these diseases. For example, advances in biopharmaceutical research have largely contributed to HIV infection's becoming a severe, manageable condition rather than a death sentence.

Infections, Diseases, and Treatments

A number of antiviral medications are used to treat (though not cure) VDs caused by viral infections. Acyclovir (marketed as Zovirax) is one of the most frequently used antivirals for infection caused by the herpes simplex virus–2, which causes genital herpes. The drug works by slowing the growth and expansion of the virus in the body. Although the medication does not cure the virus, it can reduce symptoms of the infection. Acyclovir can be taken three to five times daily and is available in oral (pill and liquid), injectable, and topical forms. Acyclovir is given intravenously when the infection is more serious, such as in immune-compromised individuals or infants. Patients with kidney problems should be given lower doses.

Because acyclovir is regarded as a pregnancy category B drug, it is typically safe to take during pregnancy. The medication can be given during childbirth, because if the mother has an active lesion, the herpes virus can be transmitted to the newborn child during delivery. Although studies have shown that acyclovir is generally safe to use, it has been noted that it can cause potential harm to an infant if expelled into the breast milk of a lactating mother.

Like the herpes virus, acquired immune deficiency syndrome (AIDS) currently has no cure. However, there are many pharmaceuticals, known as antiretroviral drugs, that are used to suppress the reproduction of HIV, the virus that causes AIDS. People with HIV infection can be treated with a combination of at least three drugs; this process is typically referred to as "highly active antiretroviral therapy." These medications are used to lower the chance of the virus becoming resistant.

Nucleoside reverse transcriptase inhibitors (NRTIs) became available in 1987 and were the first available drugs to treat HIV infection. To have the ability to infect healthy cells and replicate itself in the body, HIV requires an enzyme called "reverse transcriptase." NRTIs inhibit reverse transcriptase and stop HIV from infecting cells and reproducing itself. Nonnucleoside reverse transcriptase inhibitors (NNRTIs) were approved for the treatment of HIV infection in 1997. They serve the same purpose as NRTIs, except that they join in a different way to stop the duplication and spread of the virus in the body. First approved in 1995, protease inhibitors prevent protease, which is one of the digestive enzymes HIV uses to replicate itself. Protease inhibitors prevent the infection of new cells and slow the reproduction of the virus. Whereas NRTIs and NNRTIs affect only newly infected cells, protease inhibitors are also effective in cells that have been infected for a considerable amount of time. Fusion or entry inhibitors (such as enfuvirtide, marketed as Fuzeon) are the fourth and most recently approved group of antiretroviral drugs. Fuzeon works by blocking one of the proteins HIV carries, as well as slowing the duplication of the virus. Unlike the other three types of antiretroviral drugs that can be taken orally, Fuzeon is a protein, which can be digested in the stomach; therefore, it must be injected.

HPV, which is the most common VD in the United States, has no treatment. The virus can cause genital warts, which, if left untreated, may go away on their own, remain the same, or grow in size. Genital warts can be treated (by the patient) with podofilox solution or gel, imiquimod cream, or sinecatechins ointment. Provider-administered treatments include cryotherapy, podophyllin, and trichloroacetic or bichloroacetic acid.

Trichomoniasis, which is regarded as the most commonly curable STD in the United States, is caused by the protozoan parasite *Trichomonas vaginalis*. The infection can be cured with a single dose of metronidazole or tinidazole antibiotic pills.

Bacterial infections, such as gonorrhea, syphilis, and chlamydia, are generally curable and can be easily treated with the right antibiotic. Penicillin, the first type of antibiotic, was discovered in 1928 by Alexander Fleming. Since then, the number of antibiotics has grown to more than 100 in the United States. Gonorrhea, which is caused by the bacterium *Neisseria gonorrhoeae*, can be treated with one dose of ceftriaxone (marketed as Rocephin), which is typically administered as an injection in the arm. Depending on the patient, other options for treating gonorrhea may include azithromycin and doxycycline.

Syphilis, which is caused by the bacteria *Treponema pallidum*, is treatable with penicillin G benzathine (marketed as Bicillin). Depending on the severity of the disease, a single dose, double dose, or triple dose of the drug may be required. Individuals with neurosyphilis, a life-threatening disease that can develop if syphilis goes untreated, may be treated with aqueous crystalline penicillin or, alternatively, procaine penicillin and the gout treatment probenecid, which makes the penicillin more effective.

Penicillin allergies, such as skin rash, hives, and difficulty breathing, are the most frequently reported drug allergies. In such cases, an STD patient may need to avoid penicillin and a class of medications called cephalosporins, which are similar in structure to penicillin, is used instead. Depending on whether a patient is anaphylactic (has serious allergic reactions), he or she may need to be treated with unrelated antibiotics.

Developing Studies on VD Treatments

A new drug has been developed to lower the rate of viral shedding in patients with genital herpes simplex virus–2. Viral shedding happens when a virus makes its way from the nerves up to the surface of the skin; during this process, the virus can be transmitted to others via skin-to-skin contact. The new herpes simplex virus drug, pritelivir, is designed to obstruct replication and lower the risk for transmission.

To improve HIV/AIDS treatment regimens, biopharmaceutical companies are concentrating on preventive vaccines and useful therapies that are currently in clinical trials or awaiting government approval. In the development stages are 44 vaccines and medications, including 25 antivirals, 16 vaccines, and 3 gene therapies. For example, potential therapies include "attachment inhibitors," a new class of HIV drugs designed to safeguard cells from infection, and "gene modification," which modifies the specific receptor that makes it easy for HIV to infect cells.

With more than 100 million new gonococcal infections around the world yearly, gonorrhea has made its way onto the CDC's list of urgent threats. A study conducted in the United States revealed that a new gonorrhea treatment (based on an anticancer therapy) has successfully eliminated gonococcal infection from female mice and stopped reinfection. On the basis of the results of the animal-based study, researchers received the go-ahead to develop the technology needed to treat the disease and suppress reinfection.

Grace Ferguson
Independent Scholar

See Also: AIDS/HIV Drugs; Antibiotic Revolution, The; Antibiotic/Antimicrobial Resistance; Antibiotics; Centers for Disease Control and Prevention; Disease Management; Food and Drug Administration (U.S.).

Further Readings

Bernstein, D. I., L. R. Stanberry, and S. L. Rosenthal. *Sexually Transmitted Diseases: Vaccines, Prevention and Control.* San Diego, CA: Academic Press, 2013.

Centers for Disease Control and Prevention. "Antibiotic-Resistant Gonorrhea." http://www.cdc.gov/Std/gonorrhea/arg/default.htm (Accessed October 2014).

Centers for Disease Control and Prevention. "Sexually Transmitted Diseases (STDs)." http://www.cdc.gov/std/ (Accessed October 2014).

Faro, S. *Sexually Transmitted Diseases in Women.* Philadelphia: Lippincott Williams & Wilkins, 2003.

Pharmaceutical Research and Manufacturers of America. "44 Medicines and Vaccines Being Developed for Those Living With HIV/AIDS." http://www.phrma.org/research/new-medicines-development-hivaids (Accessed October 2014).

VETERANS ADMINISTRATION (U.S.): PRESCRIPTION DRUG BENEFITS

The Veterans Administration is a shortened name for the Veterans Health Administration, also known as the VHA, which is the largest arm of the United States Department of Veterans Affairs, often known simply as the VA. The VHA, which is a totally distinct organization from the Department of Defense Military Health System, provides medical care for all veterans who have met certain requirements (serving for a certain amount of time). Originally, pensions and free medical care served as incentives to convince young people to enlist in the United States military, but over time the services that the VA provides have come to be seen as a civic duty and a way of repaying those who have served the United States.

The Veterans Health Administration provides various benefits for enrollees, including hospital care and doctor visits, and can also provide pharmaceuticals at a greatly reduced rate when prescribed by a VHA doctor, because it has the right to negotiate drug prices with pharmaceutical companies and can use taxpayer funding in order to repay those that have served the United States through free medication or medication at a reduced cost.

The History of VA Prescription Drug Benefits

The Department of Veterans Affairs has been a long time in the making, with influences as old as the 1636 declaration among the colonists at Plymouth Rock that those who fought in the wars the colony was waging against Native Americans at that time would be cared for by the colony after fulfilling their duty.

Since the American Revolution, lifelong benefits for veterans have been promised by recruiting organizations (then state militias), but over time the view of veterans' benefits as an incentive to join the military has changed to a view of them as the civic duty of the rest of society, in that society must repay veterans for what they have done to maintain peace and order, often under very difficult circumstances.

Although the Department of Veterans Affairs did not achieve the cabinet-level status that it enjoys today until 1989, it was formed in its most modern iteration in 1930, when various other government agencies that were caring for veterans medically, financially, and otherwise were consolidated into one entity to make them more effective and easier to manage.

Although the Department of Veterans Affairs even then dealt with helping veterans in a wide variety of ways, not just with their physical and mental well-being, medical care was always an important part of what the Department of Veterans Affairs did for its members. The depth and breadth of care being offered has been continually expanded since the organization's inception in 1930; for example, it has grown from encompassing only 54 VA hospitals to being made up of over 150 hospitals, as well as more than 800 outpatient clinics and over 100 nursing homes or similar facilities.

As the focus has shifted from only providing surgeries and other higher levels of medical care to improving all aspects of veterans' lives and allowing them the freedom and dignity of outpatient proceedings and self-managed treatment, prescription medications have simply come over time to be included in the system. The development of more effective and affordable prescription medications has also had a great deal to do with this, as medicine has certainly advanced a good distance since the 1930s. As it has become more effective, it has also become more necessary and ubiquitous—meaning that the VHA's need to procure it for patients has also increased.

The system by which the Veterans Health Administration negotiates prices with pharmaceutical companies also came about over time and has undergone a few changes throughout the years, though it essentially has remained the same. The VHA uses its status within the federal government as its main negotiating point, because negotiating fairly with the VHA will allow drug companies to access other markets that are run by the federal government, such as the huge Medicaid program.

While many believe that this is the most effective method of both saving taxpayers' money and taking care of veterans, it has been criticized for various reasons by various individuals. Some veterans and veterans' advocates claim that it results in too small a selection of drugs for veterans undergoing treatment with the Veterans Health Administration to choose from. On the other hand, drug companies and their lobbyists and advocates claim that the low prices prevent them from doing research that will result in the development of new drugs.

The Veterans Health Administration's negotiation rights and techniques were brought to the forefront of the national conversation in 2008, when a bill was proposed in the U.S. Congress that would allow Medicare, which subsidizes the payments the elderly must make for their drugs with its "Part D" program, to negotiate with drug companies in the same way that the Veterans Health Administration does. Advocates of the bill said that this would continue to save program members money while also reducing government spending on overpriced drugs, while groups across the aisle came out strongly against such a law, saying that it would do far more damage to drug companies' research and development funding than the federal government is already doing.

Although the bill did not become a law, the issue is still debated among many advocacy groups and lobbying groups on both sides today, and it may become a legal issue again in the future.

That being said, the practices the VA uses to negotiate with drug companies are here to stay, at least for the time being, and form an integral part of the entire VHA system, in that they are at the center of the program's effort to bring prescription drugs to veterans at prices that reflect their needs and their invaluable service to their country.

How VA Prescription Drug Benefits Work

Because the VHA is able to negotiate bulk prices for prescription drugs with drug manufacturers, it can procure prescription drugs for its patients at a greatly reduced cost. Most veterans are then eligible to receive those drugs prescribed to them by VHA physicians at a highly discounted rate, while some, usually those with service-related health problems or disabilities, those with lower incomes, or those who underwent particularly trying circumstances during their service (such as being prisoners of war, or POWs), can actually get their medication for free. Benefits to veterans and prioritizing their treatment are based on their economic need, the seriousness of the conditions requiring treatment, and their experiences during service (meaning whether or not the injuries or strain they received during service has had a direct or indirect impact on their later health).

That being said, these drugs must be prescribed by VHA physicians, and never by outside physicians alone. Every veteran who has served a particular amount of time is allowed to sign up for Veterans Affairs benefits, and upon signing up will receive a primary care physician or primary care team, which will then be assigned to him or her as long as he or she is part of the program. While this model is fair in theory, a great deal of controversy has arisen from its execution, with some saying that it is too difficult to sign up for the program and that the amount of time required to sign up and then wait to meet with a VHA physician is unfair. Still others complain that the list of drugs the VHA allows its patients to purchase, a list called a *formulary*, generated by its dealings with various drug companies during the negotiation process for particular prices for veterans, is too small and does not offer veterans enough choice when it comes to what medications they want to take for their conditions.

There is also a great deal of tension with regard to the amount of time it takes a veteran to see a VHA physician in that VHA physicians often do not or cannot easily share medical records with non-VHA physicians, and are not obligated to fill or sign off on prescriptions for drugs or procedures recommended by non-VHA physicians.

With the recent VHA scandal still looming over the climate surrounding the VHA, there is greater concern than ever about the fairness of VHA policies and the extent to which veteran patients have access to a wide variety of drugs and procedures when they need them. There is also a wide-ranging movement to update the treatments and drugs available to take into account new information on mental illness, the rising number of women in the military, and several other important trends that are changing the way today's medicine and today's military are defined.

Change is likely in the future for the VHA, but certain things about it, such as its core values and general negotiation method for keeping costs manageable for taxpayers *and* patients, will likely remain the same.

David Michael Gonzalez
University of Nevada

See Also: Access to Medicines (Industrialized World); Military Pharmaceutical Issues; United States: 1951 to Present.

Further Readings

New York Times [Editorial]. "Negotiating Lower Drug Prices." *New York Times*, January 12, 2007.

U.S. Department of Veterans Affairs [Web site]. "History—VA History." http://www.va.gov/about_va/vahistory.asp.

VETERINARY PHARMACOLOGY

Veterinary pharmacology encompasses a vast category of varying methods for medicating and therapeutic techniques due to the large array of patients that are being treated. Every form of medication varies because of factors like dosage, microbial resistance, environmental implications, and host conditions. Similar to Western medicine, different ailments require different forms of medications. Each varies with what category it belongs to and the method of delivery to the patient. The basic principles studied are absorption, distribution, metabolism, and elimination, which determine the methods of administering the medication.

History of Pharmacology

The beginning developments of veterinary pharmacology are deeply rooted and paralleled to human pharmacology. For many years, it was hard to distinguish differences between human and veterinary pharmacology. Recent archaeological evidence indicates that a hospital was erected in India, specifically for military elephants and horses, around 5000 B.C.E., which was the first recorded method of veterinary medicine. The formal coursework that is taught now stems from the 1760s in veterinary hospitals and universities in France, Austria, Germany, and the Netherlands because of epidemics spreading through animals across western Europe. In 1791, the Royal Veterinary College Veterinary Surgeons in London was established, while the earliest veterinary universities in North American were not formed until the late 1800s. At this time, the pharmacology taught in these schools was equivalent to the pharmacology taught in the medical schools. The field of pharmacology shifted to focusing on the actual science of veterinary pharmacology in 1954 because of a publication by Professor L. Meyer Jones in the first edition of *Veterinary Pharmacology and Therapeutics*. Organizations, such as the American Academy of Veterinary Pharmacology and Therapeutics founded in 1977, began to appear in the late 1970s. The U.S. Food and Drug Administration (FDA) Center for Veterinary Medicine now oversees the production and safety of animal drugs that are produced. Veterinary pharmacology is now a course required by veterinary colleges for students that are planning to become veterinarians. Not much change or shifting within the field has occurred in recent years.

Delivery Methods

Oral medications can be administered in the form of liquids, semi-solids, and solids. Liquids are produced as solutions, suspensions, and emulsions. Solutions are a mixture of multiple ingredients that become homogeneous at a molecular level and are easily absorbed in the animal. These are most commonly used to medicate infantile and adolescent animals. Suspensions are an aqueous agent combined with an insoluble medicine. They are typically used for poorly soluble or insoluble medications and treatments that target specific material in the gastrointestinal system. Emulsions contain two liquids that are not miscible and are typically used for oil medications. Semi-solids only come in the form of paste, which is a powder-like medication in an aqueous or fatty acid type of base. It is mostly used to administer treatments to horses and cats. Solids come in more common forms like tablets, capsules, powders, and granules. There is also a premix, which contains a specific active ingredient and an excipient for ruminants, pigs, and poultry. The specific active ingredient is determined by the medical condition that is being treated. A final solid form that is only used for ruminants, pigs, and poultry are medication blocks. The blocks contain a compressed feed block, typically corn, along with surfactant to prevent bloating, and a nutritional supplement that is determined based on the needs of the patient.

Parenteral dosages are administered via injections, intramammary infusions, intravaginal delivery systems, and implants. Injections contain solutions, suspensions, and emulsions that are completely similar to oral methods. The only difference is that one is injected, while one is ingested. A dry powder injection can also be used by immediately introducing it into a solution right before injection. Intramammary infusions are used to treat inflamed breast tissue for lactating and nonlactating cows by infusing the medication so that it attaches to udder tissues at a fast and equal rate. Intravaginal delivery systems are used only in sheep, cows, and goats for estrus synchronization, similarly to birth control. The methods include time-released drugs, progesterone-releasing devices, and vaginal sponges. Implants in veterinary medicine are tablets and matrix systems that allow the drug to be released in a uniform manner and are typically only used for reproduction and breeding behaviors.

Topical dosages are used to transport the medicine onto the ectoderm and into the bloodstream. The most common forms of topical dosages are solids, semi-solids, and liquids. The only solid is in the form of a dusting powder, which is an insoluble powder that contains talc, zinc, or starch. Dusting powders are preferred because they absorb moisture and prevent bacterial growth, while also serving as a lubricant for the skin. Semi-solids consist of creams, ointments, and pastes. Creams are emulsions that are used for the skin or mucous membranes and are most commonly oil and water combinations. Ointments are a greasy semi-solid that contains a dissolved medication, mostly for chronic lesions on the skin. Paste contains the powders that are present in dusting powders and are used for ulcerated lesions. Liquid topical forms are solution, suspension concentrate, and suspo-emulsions and emulsifiable concentrates. The solutions category is used for eyes, ears, and as a lotion. Eye drops can contain antibiotics, anesthetics, anti-inflammatory properties, and drugs that focus on the autonomic nervous system. Ear drops contain antibiotics, insecticides, and anti-inflammatory properties. Lotions are used to evaporate solvents and cool off the skin, typically in hair-covered areas. Suspension concentrates are only for topical use and contain a mixture of insoluble active ingredients in a water or oil base. Suspo-emulsion combines both emulsions and suspensions that allow multiple active ingredients to be combined into a medicinal use. Emulsifiable concentrate involves two immiscible liquids that are used for topical conditions. Transdermal delivery gel contains some form of a "vehicle," typically a pluronic lecithin organogel that provides medication into the bloodstream via transdermal transmission. A transdermal delivery patch is similar to the gel, except that it uses an adhesive patch that secures to the skin and is used on cats, dogs, and horses.

The final form of medication is inhalation and only contains two forms of medication. The first form is inhalational anesthetics, which is the method of delivery for anesthesia for surgeries in animals. The second form, inhalation therapy, delivers high concentrations of drugs to the lungs without having extreme side effects. The most common form of this therapy is nebulizers that are used on animals with upper respiratory infections.

Prescribing Veterinary Medications

Prescribing medications for animals is similar to human pharmacology, but varies in many different ways. For a nonfood animal, such as a dog, cat, or guinea pig, to receive medication, a veterinarian-patient relationship must exist. Extra-label medications are medications that do not follow the original label for the prescription, such as giving a different dosage or different time interval, and are prescribed for food animals. These medications require a veterinary-patient relationship, similar to household pets. Extra-label medications were legalized in 1994 by the Animal Medicinal Drug Use Clarification Act (AMDUCA) to aid the food animal industry in their quest to treat ill and injured animals. The medications must also be FDA approved, therapeutic only, and are not allowed to increase the production of goods, such as eggs or milk, from the animal. In 2005, the FDA banned certain medications from being prescribed for food animals because they violated the rules that regulate medications for these animals. The drugs banned are chloramphenicol, diethylstilbestrol, dimetridazole, ipronidazole, other nitroimadazoles, furazolidone, nitrofurazone, sulfonamide drugs in cattle that are lactating, clenbuterol, fluoroquinolones, and glycopeptides, phenylbutazone in cattle that are used for dairy production and are over 20 months, and amandatine or neuraminidase inhibitor class drugs. Amandatine and neuraminidase are used to treat influenza A in poultry animals. For prescribed medications, generic forms can be used. Recently, a new animal drug rule has been created to have more strict rules for prescribing human medications for animals and vice versa. According to the rule, the medication prescribed for the animal must be intended to only be used for animals, it must be recognized as safe and effective for the conditions treated, and it must have suggested labeling on the prescription. This movement was to prevent the inaccurate prescription of medications for the incorrect animal.

Drug Categories

There are a variety of different categories of medications. The categories are vaccinations and immunotherapy, antiseptics and disinfectants, anti-inflammatory agents, antineoplastic agents, anthelmintics, antibiotics, growth promotants, ectoparasiticides, antiviral agents, and antifungal agents. Vaccinations and immunotherapy produce protective antibodies to respond to a microbial invasion by attacking the invading microbial and producing a long-term resistance to the microbial. This method enters the body via an injection. Antiseptics and disinfectants are anti-infective agents that are applied topically; the usage for antiseptics ranges from sanitization to sterilization within the area that it is applied to. They are extremely crucial for surgeries, like spay and neuters, to sterilize the equipment used and at the surgical site on the animal. The mechanism that provides sterilization of the surfaces is to denature the protein, alter the cell membrane, or inhibit enzymes. Antiseptics in veterinary pharmacology are the same as antiseptics in human pharmacology. Anti-inflammatory agents are used specifically to help with inflamed, or vascularized, muscles within the patient. Anti-inflammatory medications are the drug of choice for many injured muscles because it can be incredibly dangerous to put an animal under anesthesia. Many veterinarians avoid anesthetizing animals because they are susceptible to not surviving the operation, so they choose to turn to anti-inflammatories to aid with the healing process instead. Anti-inflammatory agents in veterinary medicine are the same as anti-inflammatories used with human pharmacology.

Antineoplastic agents are equivalent to chemotherapeutic treatments to treat various cancers of the body. Antineoplastics are produced specifically for small-animal practices and treating tumors in cows and horses. The decision to use this form of medication is determined by the size of the tumor, the stage that the cancer is in, the condition of the health of the animal, and financial stability of the individual paying for the patient. The drug specifically targets the cancerous cells and eliminates them, while allowing the healthy cells to continue growing. Unlike normal medications, dosages are determined by body surface area instead of body mass due to the specific properties in the drug for larger animals; however, dosage for cats and dogs is determined by body mass. The differences in determining the dosages all relate to the success and research associated with previous trials. Based on the research, it is concluded that larger animals versus smaller animals have different needs in regard to dosage and treatment. There is no specific method of administering this medication, as it varies for every animal based on the conditions of their health, treatment plan, and physical response to the medication. Anthelmintics are another form of chemotherapy for animals, but this method is less likely to be used because it requires optimum conditions for usage. It must be used accurately and correctly, have a favorable clinical response and a beneficial reaction between the host body and the cell, and minimize cell death of the healthy cells.

It is very possible to underdose or overdose on this treatment, and both can lead to many problems. Typically, anthelmintics are chosen less frequently than the latter treatment.

Antibiotics in veterinary pharmacology differ slightly from their human counterparts. This category contains penicillin, monobactam, carbapanem, cephalosporin, and cephamycins. They work to interrupt bacterial infections by attacking the development that occurs within the cell membranes of the bacteria. Similarly to other antibiotics, veterinary antibiotics are subject to resistance. About 50 to 60 percent of *Staphylococcus spp* strains and 40 to 70 percent of strains of *E. coli* are resistant to penicillin, while 15 to 40 percent of *E. coli* strains in household and farm animals are resistant to ampicillin. Antibiotics are also overused for food animals because they are injected into the animal as a means of prevention of illness. Many times this translates to increased levels of antibiotics in the animal, which are then taken in by the consumer later down the line. Growth promotants are used to convert the feed ingested by the animal into muscles, fat, and bone. This is only used on livestock that are being raised for human consumption, such as meat and milk. The two forms are hormonal treatments and antimicrobial feed additives. Hormonal treatments contain anabolic steroids, growth hormones, and insulin-like growth factor, whereas antimicrobial feeds add antibiotics to the food to decrease bacteria that hosts itself in the intestinal system, as mentioned above. This form of medication is extremely controversial at this time because of the implications that it has had on the consumer and quality of the products being produced. Ectoparasiticides are topical or parenteral products that are used to remove ectoparasites from livestock and fleas and ticks from household pets. The treatments for livestock are typically more aggressive than those used on household pets, but both are toxic if ingested by the animal. They are specifically formulated to kill the parasites that attach to the animal's body by poisoning them. The methods of poison used are insect growth regulators, chloronicotinyls, formamidines, macrocyclic lactones, pyrethins, organophosphates, carbamates, and organochlorides. Since ectoparasites only live for brief times and are a seasonal problem, the medication only needs to be administered as needed until the animal is rid of the parasite. It can also be used as a preventive measure before to make sure that the animal does not contract a parasite. Ectoparasiticides are over-the-counter medications that can be bought at any pet store or veterinarian's office, but they do not require a prescription.

Antiviral medications are used when vaccinations are not an option for prevention and the illness is caused by a virus, not bacteria. The overall task of the medication is to eradicate the virus without causing extreme damage to the host body's cells. Due to the nature of the genetic variations in viruses, it is incredibly difficult to produce a specific antiviral medication that treats every type of virus. Very few antiviral medications have been proven to be safe and effective in treating different types of viruses, in which most have only been tested on humans for human immunodeficiency virus (HIV). Very few have been tested on animals with limited success for treating feline immunodeficiency virus (FIV) in cats. FIV is the equivalent of HIV in humans, but it is only found in cats. These medications work specifically to interfere with the nucleic acids in the virus by disrupting their synthesis and regulation. Others work specifically to enhance the immune system of the animal. Either way, they are not completely effective for their purpose. Antifungal agents are used specifically to attack pathogenic fungi, such as molds and yeasts, on animals. The success rate of the medications is determined based on different factors for the fungi, varying from host response to response of the drug to the chitin present in the fungi. Antifungals are applied topically to the ectoderm, cornea, mucus membranes, or auditory canal. These medications are used to treat a wide variety of different fungal agents around the world and have significantly decreased mortality rates of animals with fungal diseases.

Karen Knaus
University of Colorado Denver

Alexandra Kjelstrom
University of Colorado Denver

See Also: Antibiotic/Antimicrobial Resistance; Antibiotics; Food and Drug Administration (U.S.).

Further Readings

Cunningham, F., J. Elliott, and P. Lees. "Principles of Pharmacodynamics and Their Applications in Veterinary Pharmacology." *Journal of Veterinary Pharmacology and Therapeutics*, v.27/6 (2004).

Moses, M. "Pharmacology." *Merck Veterinary Manual* (2004). http://www.merckmanuals.com/vet/pharmacology.html (Accessed October 10, 2014).

Papich, M. "Veterinary Pharmacology and Therapeutics." *The Canadian Veterinary Journal*, v.31/1 (1990).

Riviere, Jim E. and Mark G. Papich, eds. "Principles of Pharmacology." In *Veterinary Pharmacology and Therapeutics*, 9th ed. Ames, IA: Wiley-Blackwell, 2009.

WATER POLLUTION (PRESCRIPTION DRUGS)

Pharmaceuticals, prescriptions, and over-the-counter medications have been found in surface water, ground water, and drinking water across the globe. Contaminated water samples have been documented for several decades. Interest has intensified in the past 10 years, with increased studies on water contamination, sources, environmental impact, and solutions. Practitioners' prescribing habits and available over-the-counter medications are reflected in the contamination seen in local bodies of water. The most common source of contamination is human waste after medication consumption; additional sources of contamination have been identified as medication disposal and agricultural medication use. Studies documenting changes seen in animals and bacteria have triggered environmental concerns over pharmaceutical contamination. Health care concerns have stemmed from the unknown effect of lifelong low-dose medication exposure in humans. Solutions for decreasing pharmaceuticals in water vary from changes in chemical processing in waste water treatment plants (WWTP) to changes in prescribing habits to the design of more ecofriendly medications.

Environmental Observations

Scientists are concerned about changes in the ecosystems from pharmaceutical contamination. High levels of estrogen, notably from birth control consumption, have been observed in some rivers and have been associated with the gender changes of fish from male to female. An increase in the number of female fish has led to population increases and changes in the surrounding ecosystem. Other studies of fish farms using antibiotics to improve fish survival tested the bacteria in the sediment for antibiotic resistance. All of the bacteria samples were found to be 100 percent resistant to the antibiotic used by that particular farm. The results from these studies have intensified the amount of research conducted in pharmaceutical water pollution.

Sources of Contamination

Human consumption and elimination is the most common source of prescription drug pollution of the water supply. Many medications are eliminated without being metabolized by the body and leave as the active parent molecule. Other medications can be metabolized by the body to a different active molecule, also known as an active metabolite, and then can be eliminated from the body into the water system. Active molecules tend to be more persistent in the environment due to their decreased ability to be degraded. The types of medications contaminating the water from human consumption can vary by the site of discharge. Hospitals and long-term care facilities discharge acute care medications such as analgesics and antibiotics. Private residencies discharge some of the same medications but also more chronic disease state medications such as antidepressants and antihypertensive.

Medication disposal by flushing down the toilet is another source of contamination. Topical medications such as ointments, creams, and lotions can enter the water through the drain when the skin is washed. These routes lead to medications entering WWTP, septic systems, or directly into the waterway. Surveys of the general population show patients are uncertain how to dispose of expired and unwanted medications. Studies have shown some health systems also flush expired or unwanted medications, further leading to contamination of the water system. Flushing of medications is fast and easy, therefore making it an attractive option. Advice from the U.S. Food and Drug Administration (FDA) regarding medication disposal may also be confusing to some people. The FDA recommends disposing of most drugs by wrapping them in plastic and disposing of them as trash, with only those which carry a high potential for abuse or serious consequences due to accidental exposure being flushed. This further creates confusion surrounding proper medication disposal. Over the last decade, health-system education, governmental policies, and protocols have helped to decrease flushing and increase the use of medication processing plants, most of which use incineration for medication disposal.

The contamination seen from disposal has led to research on buying and prescribing practices that contribute to the abundance of medications. Large package sizes of over-the-counter medications can lead to the expiration of medication prior to container completion. Another source is the prescribing practices of "just in case," when a practitioner gives a prescription so that the patient or family does not need to come back to the office. For example, a practitioner writes a prescription for two siblings for antibiotics when only one child shows signs of infection, and the second prescription is given just in case the second child becomes infected. This can lead to excessive medications being purchased without an actual medical need.

Human are also not the only consumers of medications; animals also consume similar medication classes. The increasing use of antibiotics and hormones to promote growth and survival of animals in aquatic and livestock agriculture has contributed to pharmaceutical water contamination. Runoff and excrement from agricultural farms does not go through a WWTP and therefore enters waterways directly. Household pets and veterinarian clinics also have the same sources of pharmaceutical water contamination as do humans: disposal, consumption, large package sizes, and prescribing practices.

Common Contaminating Medications

Analgesic and nonsteroidal anti-inflammatories
Acetaminophen, naproxen, ibuprofen, diclofenac, morphine, ketamine, fentanyl

Antidepressants
Fluoxetine, paroxetine

Antacids
Ranitidine, famotidine

Beta-blockers
Atenolol, propranolol, sotalol

Lipid-lowering agents
Gemfibrozil, benzafibrate

Antiepileptics
Carbamazepine

Antibiotics
Ampicillin, azithromycin, cephalexin, cefazolin, cefotaxime, ciprofloxacin, clarithromycin, erythromycin, lincomycin, metronidazole, oxytetracycline, sulfamethozazole, sulfathiazole, tetracycline, trimethoprim

Hormones
Estriol, estradiol, progesterone, testosterone

Medication Design

Referring to the list of commonly occurring medications above, it is important to note the different classes, chemical structures, and chemical properties. The medications that are persistent in the environment tend to have a few similar chemical properties: more than one ionizable group and lipophilic with moderate water solubility. These properties allow the medications to stay in the water system for a longer period of time before degradation, leading to extended environmental exposure.

Solutions and Current Research

Scientists are looking at ways to decrease contamination and eliminate medications in water. One step is to further educate patients on proper disposal of medications. Patients should be instructed to place unwanted or expired medications into a sealable bag, add water if it is a solid dosage form, and add a deterrent such as kitty litter, sawdust, or coffee grounds. After all this is done, seal the bag and discard into the household trash. If the trash is then taken to a landfill, the medication degrades via hydrolysis and anaerobic bacteria breakdown. If the trash

is incinerated, the chemicals are degraded through that process.

Another solution is to decrease the number of unneeded or expired medications. By decreasing the number of unnecessary prescriptions, this also decreases the number of medications that are disposed. Decreasing the package size of over-the-counter medications may help decrease the number of expired medications and therefore medication disposal. Increasing patient adherence could also lead to a decrease in expired and unwanted medications. Even with a decrease in medications to dispose of, there would still be human consumption and agriculture sources, leading to research in these areas of contamination.

Currently, WWTPs are not required to look for pharmaceutical products in the water, so the overall extent of the environmental contamination is unknown. Conventionally, water treatment with chlorine is used to disinfect drinking water; it has also been shown to help degrade certain pharmaceutical products such as acetaminophen. Biological reactors, another conventional treatment, have also been shown to remove some pharmaceutical products such as anti-inflammatory agents. Since conventional treatments do not remove all known pharmaceutical contaminants, current research in other areas include activated carbon from varying sources, ultraviolet radiation, gamma radiation, and electro-oxidation (alone or in combination with one another). These treatments only look at water that enters a water treatment facility; there are many areas across the planet were water does not enter a treatment facility.

Environmental groups are asking for purposeful development of ecofriendly medications, along with the development of improved education to prescribing practitioners on ecofriendly medications. This may lead to changes in prescribing habits and a decrease in the medications that persist in the environment. Scientists are beginning to understand the types of medications that persist in water and some of their properties. Changes in drug development and prescribing habits could lead to benefits in ecosystems across the planet.

Jennifer Towle
MCPHS University

See Also: Chemical Fertilizers: Human Health Effects; Pesticides: Human Health Effects.

Further Readings

Mostofa, Khan M. G. "Sources, Factors, Mechanisms, and Possible Solutions to Pollutants in Marine Ecosystems." *Environmental Pollution,* v.182 (2013).

Rivera-Utrilla, Jose. "Pharmaceuticals as Emerging Contaminants and Their Removal for Water. A Review." *Chemosphere,* v.93 (2013).

Samuelsen, Ole Bent. "Long-Range Changes in Oxytetracycline Concentrations and Bacterial Resistance Towards Oxytetracycline in a Fish Farm Sediment After Medication." *The Science of the Total Environment,* v.114 (1992).

U.S. Environmental Protection Agency. "Pharmaceuticals and Personal Care Products (PPCPs)." http://www.epa.gov/ppcp (Accessed July 2014).

WHO Model Lists of Essential Medicines

The term *model list of essential drugs* in its widest sense signifies social, economic, and human rights efforts to secure basic medicines for developing countries. More narrowly, the term denotes the legislation that recognizes and establishes these rights. International appreciation of these rights initially came in 1977, when the World Health Organization (WHO) compiled its first Model List of Essential Drugs, followed in 1978 by the Declaration of Alma-Ata and culminating in the United Nations Millennium Development Goals of 2015. The terms *Model List of Essential Drugs* and *Model List of Essential Medicines* are interchangeable since both are commonly used to describe blueprints for selecting safe, effective, and affordable medicines to meet urgent health needs. WHO compiles both an adult and a pediatric version of the model list, both of which are updated every two years.

Since 1977, the number of countries with their own essential medicines lists has increased worldwide, from 12 countries in 1977 to at least 134 in 2007, and the number of people with regular access to essential medicines rose from 2.1 billion in 1977 to over 4 billion in 2003. The United Nations Children Fund (UNICEF), the United Nations High Commissioner for Refugees (UNHCR), and many international nongovernmental organizations routinely consult the WHO Model Lists of Essential Medicines to procure medicines for vulnerable groups, including children, women, and the elderly.

The goal of universal access to essential drugs has not been achieved: basic drugs especially elude the poor and vulnerable populations across the globe. Challenges to closing the access gap remain in developing countries where essential drugs are often unavailable due to low investment in health and the high cost of medicines, and poor supply and distribution systems. Although initially aimed at developing countries, the concept of essential medicines has become more relevant for industrialized countries due to increasing demand and rising medicine costs. This topic is of great importance because it addresses questions of ethics and equitable access to health care by vulnerable groups.

Essential Medicines: WHO Model List (2013)

The current adult WHO Model List of Essential Medicines, which is the 18th edition published since 1977, has over 350 medicines. Included in the current list are medications needed to treat infectious diseases such as malaria, human immunodeficiency virus/ acquired immunodeficiency syndrome (HIV/ AIDS), and tuberculosis as well as chronic diseases, such as cancer and diabetes, and for reproductive health. The WHO Model List of Essential Medicines guides countries to develop their own national lists of essential medicines. Since health needs vary across the world, countries determine independently which drugs they want to select from the WHO model. Countries typically purchase lower-cost generic drugs, if they are shown safe and effective, compared to more costly brand names. Since essential medicines are almost entirely generic, the WHO list of essential medicines can help countries control their costs, thereby reducing the overall burden on the health system.

Specific types of essential drugs include antibacterial medicines: a type of medicine typically used for the treatment and prevention of acute respiratory infections, tuberculosis, malaria, and sexually transmitted diseases; anesthetics: frequently used to treat severe pain and other debilitating symptoms common among patients with cancer, HIV, and other life-threatening diseases, particularly during the later stages; antianemia medicines: used to reduce anemia (a deficiency in red blood cells) in pregnant women and infants; antiviral medicines: medicines frequently given for the treatment and prevention of HIV and hepatitis C; cardiovascular medicines: used to treat hypertension (high blood pressure) and heart attacks, strokes, and heart failure; gastrointestinal medicines: medicines

often prescribed to treat diarrhea in children; and vaccines: typically used to prevent common infectious diseases such as tuberculosis, polio, diphtheria, tetanus, pertussis, and measles.

WHO Lists and Barriers to Access

Numerous researchers have stated emphatically that one-third of the world's population does not have regular access to essential medicines and now urge that countries adopt essential medicine programs to improve access to the most basic drugs. In 2013, WHO warned that 10 million people could die annually (mostly in developing countries) because they do not have access to existing medicines and vaccines. Studies conducted across the world indicate that many essential drugs are often not available at public health care facilities, which constitute a major part of the health systems in most developing countries and which are especially important for poor families seeking affordable services. In fact, survey results from Africa, the Americas, and Europe show that in low-income countries the average chance of finding essential medicines in the public sector is as low as 38 percent.

One possible reason for the unavailability of essential drugs in the public sector is insufficient public spending on essential drugs. Since drugs can consume as much as 66 percent of the health budgets in developing countries, many countries are unable to purchase a sufficient supply. Due to the scarcity of essential drugs in the public sector, patients are often forced to buy these medicines in the private sector where they are more readily available though at an exorbitant price.

The high cost of medicines is another likely cause for the poor access to essential drugs. Medicines are typically the largest out-of-pocket household health expenditure in developing countries. Out-of-pocket payments consume 61 percent of household health expenditures in Azerbaijan, 73 percent in Bangladesh, 80 percent in Mali, and 85 percent in Burkina Faso, for example. Researchers have pointed out that prohibitive drug prices are often the result of strong intellectual property protection that allows a pharmaceutical company to sell its product exclusively in order to recoup money spent during drug research and development (after spending an average of US$500 million on R&D) and to generate a profit. In fact, in 2003 the antimalarial drug lumefantrine, taken in combination with artemether, is 25 times more expensive than chloroquine, the first-line treatment for malaria. Many innovative and new medications for cancer, HIV/AIDS, and other chronic conditions are prohibitively expensive and unaffordable to many millions of people. In addition, intellectual property protection sometimes makes it more difficult for poor countries to produce cheaper generic drugs, including antiretrovirals that are used to treat patients with HIV. In 2000, the United Nations Millennium Development Goals (MDG) acknowledged the need to improve the availability of affordable medicines for the world's poor. It encouraged pharmaceutical companies to reduce the costs of essential medicines for developing countries where cheaper generic drugs are often not available, to increase funding for drugs relevant to developing countries and their health needs, and to promote the production of generic medicines there. In 2001, the World Trade Organization (WTO) recognized the potential effects that patent protection can have on drug prices. On August 30, 2003, the WTO implemented *Paragraph 6 of the Doha Declaration on the Trade-Related Aspects of Intellectual Property Rights (TRIPS) Agreement and Public Health*, which allows WTO members to circumvent patent rights to bring

affordable, life-saving medicines to countries that need them desperately.

A third likely explanation for the lack of access to essential drugs is a poor medicine supply and distribution system. Studies conducted in Ethiopia, Malawi, and Rwanda indicated that essential drugs for the treatment of pneumonia, diarrhea, and malaria, which are the three most deadly diseases in children, are often unavailable in local clinics because of a breakdown in the drug delivery system. Since drugs are rarely delivered to local clinics, community health workers typically have to collect medicines from supply centers by traveling an hour or longer, usually on foot or by bicycle depending on the country, the terrain, and the season. In addition, since community health workers are typically volunteers and not compensated for their travel time or costs, the motivation to pick up medicines is often low. In 2013, researchers recommended that countries address problems associated with local transportation systems and develop affordable and sustainable solutions to ensure that essential drugs are more readily available at the community level.

In addition, researchers have stressed that the WHO Model Lists of Essential Medicines could result in more equitable access to health care in industrialized countries where the costs of medicines have skyrocketed due to an aging population. Research conducted in the United States indicates that the pharmaceutical expenditure, which includes spending on prescription medicines and over-the-counter products, rose by 18 percent in 1999, 16 percent in 2000, and 17 percent in 2001. In Canada, costs for prescription drugs increased by an average of 93 percent between 1987 and 1993. Researchers recommend a systematic approach to controlling the cost of drugs in developed countries that could include price reductions or rebates on pharmaceuticals or a general cap on pharmaceutical companies' profits.

Angela Matysiak
Policy Studies Organization (PSO)

See Also: Access to Essential Medicines as a Human Right: History; Access to Medicines (Developing World); Access to Medicines (Industrialized World); Generic Medicines; TRIPS Agreement (Agreement on Trade-Related Aspects of Intellectual Property Rights), Doha Declaration, and TRIPS Plus; World Health Organization.

Further Readings

Bazargani, Yaser T., Margaret Ewen, Anthonius de Boer, Hubert G. M. Leufkens, and Aukje K. Mantel-Teeuwisse. "Essential Medicines Are More Available Than Other Medicines Around the Globe." *PLOS ONE*, v.9/2 (2014).

Hogerzeil, Hans V. "The Concept of Essential Medicines: Lessons for Rich Countries." *British Medical Journal*, v.329/7475 (2004).

Quick, Jonathan D. "Essential Medicines Twenty-Five Years On: Closing the Access Gap." *Health Policy and Planning*, v.18/1 (2003).

Yasmin Chandani, Megan Noel, Amanda Pomeroy, Sarah Andersson, Michelle K. Pahl, and Timothy Williams. "Factors Affecting Availability of Essential Medicines Among Community Health Workers in Ethiopia, Malawi, and Rwanda: Solving the Last Mile Puzzle." *American Journal of Tropical Medicine and Hygiene*, v.87/5 (2012).

WOMEN

The anatomy and physiology of male and female bodies differ considerably and, as a result, the pharmacology of medicine throughout the body is also different. This is important for the use of drugs in society, as an awareness of how gender can affect the function of medicine is essential for the safe and effective use of medications. The changes are not due to one sole factor but rather a combination of many that contribute to the effect of the medication in men and women. A sound understanding of the anatomy, physiology, and pharmacokinetics of the body and the pharmacodynamics of drugs is essential to grasp this concept.

Some conditions are exclusive to women's health, particularly those related to female reproduction organs, contraception, pregnancy, and menopause. These conditions will be discussed and the use of medications in these circumstances will be considered. In addition to this, while evident in both genders, there are some health conditions that are markedly more prominent in females. This can be a result of various reasons, such as the diet and lifestyle common within a particular gender, as well as physiological susceptibilities. Health conditions that are more prevalent in females include urinary tract infections, bowel disorders, osteoporosis, and depression, each of which will be discussed in more details in due course.

A well-documented difference of gender in health is that women in society are more likely than men to experience adverse drug reactions, an observation that is closely related to the composition of the female body. The size, proportion of muscle to fat, and efficacy of the liver and kidney all play a role, as they tend to increase the blood concentration of the drug, which leads to a higher risk of toxic effects on the body. It is essential to consider the particulars of the drug used and how doses should differ for use in different genders and body composition in order to obtain the best results.

Women's health is a complicated matter involving the medications for use in the management of conditions and the pharmacology of these drugs specifically in relation to women. A general overview of the expansive topic will be given, along with some specific examples and ideas for how medications can best be used in the current society of women.

Gender Differences in Physiology and Pharmacology

The composition of a woman's body has a significant effect on the way in which medications are absorbed into the body, distributed throughout the body, metabolized within the body, and excreted from the body. Each of these can change the concentration and, therefore, the effect of the drug on the body dramatically and should hence be considered closely.

For the vast majority of orally administered medications, the active component must be absorbed into the bloodstream from the gastrointestinal tract in order for it to reach its target receptors and exert its effect on the body. This process is dependent on several factors such as the transit time in the gut, the acidity of the gastrointestinal tract, and the lipid solubility, ionization, and molecular weight of the drug. The transit time for food to pass through the gastrointestinal tract is considerably longer for females than males, which has a notable effect on the amount of active components absorbed into the blood stream. In practical terms, the increase in transit time provides the drug greater opportunity to be absorbed and results in a higher drug concentration in the blood. This can then lead to greater efficacy of the medication but also increased risk of adverse reactions, particularly if the drug has a narrow therapeutic index. Women also tend to have more acidic gastric fluids than men, which results in increased absorption of weak bases and decreased absorption of weak acids.

There are notable differences in the bile acid composition between genders, with men exhibiting higher concentrations of cholic acid in comparison to women who have higher concentrations of chenodeoxycholic acid. This changes the environment in the gastrointestinal tract, which then affects the solubility of different drugs and the extent to which they are absorbed into the bloodstream from the gastrointestinal tract. Contrary to the transit time in the gut, this does not necessarily indicate higher or lower concentrations of the drug but rather the drugs will absorb differently in women in comparison to their male counterparts and the particular drug determines how it will differ. In some cases, this may result in increased absorption for females, whereas for other drugs the absorption rate will be less than for men.

When using alternative methods of drug administration, there are other factors that play a major role. Women have a higher body fat content than males, and it has been hypothesized that the increase in subcutaneous lipid content improves the bioavailability of lipid soluble drugs administered transdermally, although there is currently limited evidence supporting this claim. In addition to this, some data has found that women ingest a lower volume of inhaled aerosol drugs as a result of their lower tidal volume and greater respiratory minute ventilation in respect to males. These changes may call for a difference in dosing between genders; however, guidelines on the matter have yet to be created.

The way in which the drug distributes throughout the body is also greatly affected by the composition of the body. Volume of distribution is a value assigned to a drug based on the extent to which it is distributed throughout the body. As women generally have lesser total body weight, body water, and blood volume, the volume of distribution for most drugs is usually lower, which leads to an increase in drug concentration. The fat content of the body also plays a role and is an evident difference between males and females. Women are known to have a higher percentage of body fat, which increases the volume of distribution of lipid soluble drugs in females as the drug has a greater propensity to distribute to the fatty tissues. On the contrary, for water-soluble drugs the volume of distribution is significantly lower, resulting in higher concentrations in the blood and an increased risk of adverse reactions. An example of this is alcohol, which is a water-soluble compound and should be taken in lower quantities by females, as the maximum concentration of the drug in the blood is higher due to their smaller body mass and high body fat content. Another important factor to consider about the distribution of drugs throughout the body is the extent to which the drug binds to plasma proteins and the fraction of the drug that is available to exert its effect. Whilst the concentration of albumin has not been shown to vary significantly between men and women, estrogens increase the levels of serum-binding globulins and can have an effect on the proportion of drugs bound to proteins and active drug.

The metabolism of the drug in the liver is also vital in the explanation of how drugs work differently for men and women. As particular enzymes are essential in the metabolism of specific drugs, a variance in the levels of these enzymes between the genders can have a significant effect on the metabolism of certain drugs. The cytochrome P450 (CYP) enzymes are of particular note, as they play a major role in the metabolism of drugs in the body. Whilst some of the CYP enzymes are equally present regardless of sex, some enzymes in the group (CYP1A, CYP2D6, and CYP3A) are notably different in presence and as a result have an altered ability to work an effect in the metabolism of drugs in the liver. These differences are summarized in Table 1, along with the specific drugs that are usually metabolized by these enzymes and are hence affected by gender.

Table 1   Sex Difference in Cytochrome P450 Metabolism and Hepatic Clearance

Metabolic Route	Drugs Metabolized by Route	Sex Difference
CYP1A	Clomipramine, clozapine, olanzapine, paracetamol, tacrine, theophylline	Men > Women
CYP2D6	Codeine, encainide, flecainide, fluoxetine, hydrocodone, metoprolol, paroxetine, mexilitine, phenformin, propranolol, sertraline, timolol, haloperidol, clomipramine, desipramine, imipramine, propafenone, testosterone	Men < Women
CYP3A	Alprazolam, alfentanil, astemizole, atorvastatin, carbamazepine, cisapride, clarithromycin, cyclophosphamide, cyclosporin, diazepam, diltiazem, erythromycin, estradiol, fentanyl, indinavir, itraconazole, ketoconazole, lovastatin, nimodipine, nisoldipine, quinidine, ritonavir, simvastatin, tacrolimus, tamoxifen, tirilazad, troglitazone, verapamil, vinblastine, vincristine	Men < Women

Source: Adapted from Soldin, Offie, et al. "Sex Differences in Drug Disposition." *Journal of Biomedicine and Biotechnology* (2011).

The excretion of the drug via urine depends greatly on the function and effectiveness of the kidneys, which is not equal for men and women. The renal excretion depends on the blood flow to the kidneys, the glomerular filtration, and the tubular secretion and reabsorption, all of which are higher in males than females when standardized for body size. The practical difference as a result of this is that men are more efficient at eliminating drugs via the renal system. Women, on the other hand, take longer to clear the drug and experience higher concentrations of drugs in the bloodstream that extends for longer periods of time after ingesting the same dose as men.

There are also other, less prominent methods of drug clearance such as the elimination of drug via the pulmonary route. Once again, as women have lower tidal volume and greater respiratory minute ventilation than men, they are less efficient at eliminating the drug via this mechanism. However, due to the minimal quantities of drugs usually excreted via the pulmonary tract, this is unlikely to make a notable difference in the concentration of most medications, and dosage changes are unlikely to be needed for gender.

Drugs in Pregnancy, Contraception, and Menopause

In the current society, both males and females are responsible for family planning and contraceptive methods and often multiple methods of contraception are used with the involvement of both genders. However, the most common form of contraception used in the United States and many other parts of the world is the oral contraceptive pill, which is taken by the female, and hence it is the woman that experiences the effects of the drug.

The pharmacology of the oral contraceptive pill relies on the woman's natural response to the female sex hormones progesterone and estrogen. Progesterone is the essential component that is given in a sufficient quantity to supersede the natural hormone levels of the woman to provide contraception. The increased levels of the progesterone hormone communicate to the woman's body that she is nearing the end of her menstruation cycle and hence this prevents her from ovulating and becoming pregnant. Both hormones are included in the majority of formulations available, as the combination allows for more convenient daily dosing and a larger window of time to remember to take the medication in the event that a pill was missed, thus decreasing the risk of contraceptive failure. There are, however, several progesterone-only pill brands on the market that provide an equally effective contraceptive method, provided each dose is taken on time.

In today's society, where the majority of the population is taking multiple medications, it is essential to understand the effect other medications have on the oral contraceptive pill and vice versa. Cytochrome P450 enzymes are involved in the metabolism of the oral contraceptive pill, leading to substantial drug interactions with other medications metabolized by the same enzymes. For the majority of these reactions, the main concern is not of drug toxicity of either drug but rather the increased metabolism of the oral contraceptive pill and a subsequent drop in efficacy of the hormonal contraception. Drugs that pose a major concern in this way are antiepileptic drugs such as carbamazepine and phenytoin; antibacterial drugs such as rifabutin and rifampicin; antiretrovirals such nevirapine, nelfinavir, and ritonavir; and other drugs, including some herbal medications such as St. John's wort. Where possible, it is preferable to avoid these combinations, but in some instances it is unavoidable, and we must find a solution to use both medications while not compromising on the efficacy of the oral contraceptive. This is usually done in practice by increasing the dose of the oral contraceptive pill, which counteracts the increase in metabolism and ensures there are sufficient hormone levels in the body to prevent ovulation and unwanted pregnancies.

Taking the oral contraceptive pill can affect the likelihood of other health conditions related to women, which has a marked effect on the health of women today and into the projected future. Several studies have shown a link between taking an oral contraceptive for an extended period of time with an increased risk of breast cancer. Thus, women should be made aware of this, and women at higher risk of breast cancer, such as those with a family history of the disease, should at a minimum consider other contraceptive options. Additionally, there is a higher risk of venous thromboembolism and stroke associated with the use of the oral contraceptive pill and, similar to breast cancer, women at risk of these conditions should reconsider if the oral contraceptive pill is the best option for them.

Pregnancy is a specific circumstance unique to female health and involves the woman's individual health in addition to that of her baby. During this period, the health requirements of a pregnant woman differ considerably from other women and men. Of particular note, she has higher requirements for some nutrients, such as folic acid, iron, and iodine, because of the growing fetus inside her. Additionally, the other medications women take throughout their pregnancy can have a significant effect, both with prescription and freely available medicines. The safe use of many drugs in pregnancy has been studied extensively and each has a different level of caution associated with it. Some should be avoided entirely as they pose serious risks to the mother or baby, while others have been used widely among pregnant women and have not been found to pose significant risks to the mother and baby to prevent their use. Of particular concern are lipophilic drugs, as they are more easily able to cross the blood-brain barrier and, importantly in pregnancy, cross the placental barriers and reach the blood circulation of the unborn baby. Alcohol is an example of such a substance and can produce severe defects to babies that were exposed to high volumes of alcohol in the womb; it is for this reason that it is recommended to avoid the consumption of alcohol whilst pregnant. There are many drugs that can pose health threats to a pregnant woman and her baby.

The growth stage of the baby is a factor that carries an important weight in the use of drugs in pregnancy. The first trimester, for example, is the prime time of formation of the central nervous system of the baby. During this period, it is essential that pregnant women consume sufficient levels of folic acid, which plays a crucial role in this process. With inadequate folic acid in the woman's body to assist in the formation of the central nervous system, the baby can develop neural tube defects as a result. Later in the pregnancy, however, during the second and third trimester, the majority of the central nervous system has already been formed and lower levels of folic acid have a less detrimental effect. It is for this reason that folic acid is recommended to be given early in pregnancy and before conception if it is possible and the baby was planned.

In addition to women who are currently pregnant or intending to become pregnant, all women of childbearing age should be considered carefully before taking medications that can be harmful to the woman or her baby should an unexpected pregnancy occur. There are several drugs that should be avoided in pregnancy and only used when the woman is taking sufficient contraceptive precautions, and the reasons behind these recommendations can usually be explained by the pharmacology of the specific drugs and the possible effects they could have. An example of such a drug is the antiepileptic medication sodium valproate, which greatly increases the risk of congenital malformations. Due to the detrimental effects this medication can have on a pregnant woman and her baby, it is recommended that all women of childbearing age taking valproate use sufficient contraception methods, preferably two methods such as condoms and the oral contraceptive pill, to reduce the risk of an unintended pregnancy.

Menopause plays a big role in women's health, and the changes to her body as a result of the hormone changes can have a significant impact on subsequent health outcomes. This time of life can be very uncomfortable, and many women seek the assistance of medications, both prescription hormone replacement therapy and alternative herbal remedies, to lessen the symptoms that arise because of hormonal changes. In addition to this, women are more susceptible to certain health conditions following menopause, such as cardiovascular disease and osteoporosis, furthering the need for some form of intervention to promote the health of older women.

Hormone replacement therapy is used to substitute the estrogen and progesterone hormones that the woman is no longer producing, and this has been shown to help lessen menopausal symptoms as well as minimize the risk of osteoporosis and cardiovascular disease by maintaining bone density and reducing cardiovascular risk factors respectively. While they are the same hormones taken in the oral contraceptive pill, they are used in lower doses for menopausal women and are insufficient to provide contraceptive cover. However, the risks associated with the use of hormone replacement therapy are closely linked to those associated with the oral contraceptive pills. Notably, there is an increased risk of breast cancer, stroke, and thromboembolism, which echoes the risks posed by long-term use of the oral contraceptive pill.

For women unable to take hormone replacement therapy due to the reasons indicated, there are minimal alternatives currently available. There are some herbal and alternative remedies, such as black cohosh, but the long-term safety and efficacy of these methods has not been established by quality scientific trials. Instead, we look to symptomatic treatments that may help for specific symptoms and risks associated with menopausal women. For associated vaginal dryness, lubricant can ease this system; to decrease the risk of osteoporosis and subsequent bone fractures, calcium and vitamin D supplements are recommended.

Relevant Health Conditions

Health conditions affect males and females to varying degrees, which is the result of both the anatomy and physiology of the female body and the common lifestyle habits of women. Those involving hormonal contraception, pregnancy, and menopause are clearly exclusive to female health and have been discussed extensively in the previous section. Additionally, some conditions affect women to a significantly greater degree than men, which can be explained by various reasons. Both are important to consider in the health of women in society and how the medications can be optimized in their use for better health outcomes.

Vaginal infections such as thrush and bacterial vaginosis are exclusive to female health and are a common occurrence for many women, with increased incidence in women with particular risk factors such as pregnancy and diabetes. While often these infections are self-limiting, the majority of women seek medical aid to lessen the duration due to the uncomfortable nature of the symptoms. Antithrush treatments are commonly used for vaginal infections and are available in several formulations including a cream and pessaries to be applied intravaginally, as well as an oral tablet that can be taken in uncomplicated cases. The primary aim behind this treatment is to reset the natural balance of the vagina and eliminate the infection present.

While it is possible for males to be affected by breast cancer, it is overwhelmingly more prevalent in females. The immediate treatment of breast cancer involves surgery, chemotherapy, radiotherapy, and oral drugs, separately or individually depending on the individual situation. Of particular importance for the pharmacology of the drugs used in breast cancer are the long-term medications used after diagnosis with breast cancer to prevent relapse once remission has been achieved. There is a range of drugs available, including aromatase inhibitors and modulators of estrogen, the choice of which depends on the type of cancer and the history of the disease in the woman. The pharmacology of these drugs is focused on limiting the growth factors that promote the regrowth of cancer. As an example, tamoxifen is a selective estrogen receptor modulator and exerts its effect by down regulating the estrogen receptors, which has a marked effect on reducing the reemergence of hormone-dependent breast cancer. Therefore, the use of this drug is reserved for women recovering from, and occasionally for prevention in women with extremely high risk of hormone-dependent breast cancer. The adverse effects of tamoxifen are once again closely related to the specific pharmacology of the drug and are largely hormonal, producing a similar effect to menopause, although on a more severe scale. These effects include hot flashes, mood swings, vaginal dryness, and weight gain.

Women have a significantly higher risk of experiencing a urinary tract infection in respect to males, which can largely be explained by the anatomical differences of the urinary tract, as the female urethra is shorter in length and offers less protection from external infections. Although women experience a higher incidence of urinary tract infections than males, they are also usually less severe due to the same anatomical reason; it is easier for an infection to enter but also to exit. However, medications are still usually needed in the treatment of urinary tract infections in women, thus it is beneficial to discuss their use and pharmacology. Symptomatic treatments are used to neutralize the acidity, and therefore pain on urination, in addition to antibiotics to treat the cause of the infection. Trimethoprim is the most commonly used antibiotic for urinary tract infections and inhibits the reduction of particular acids essential for bacteria to thrive. The treatment time with antibiotics is notably shorter than for the treatment time used in males, due to the more common nature of female urinary tract infections with less severity in most cases.

Irritable bowel syndrome (IBS) is a functional bowel disorder involving abdominal pain associated with a change in bowel movements, either or both of constipation and diarrhea, and is more prevalent in women worldwide. The projected reasons for this gender susceptibility are differences in the physiology of the body, as well as diet, lifestyle, and stress differences. There is a range of medications used for the treatment of IBS, which are mainly used to relieve specific symptoms. For example, the antidiarrheal drug loperamide is used to address symptoms of diarrhea, whereas if the individual is experiencing constipation, various forms of laxatives are used, including bulk-forming and osmotic laxatives. The unique pathophysiology of IBS leads to contrasting symptoms of the bowels, and an individual may experience both at different periods and require both types of medication. In addition, some other drugs such as antibiotics, probiotics, and serotonin receptor antagonists may be used to reset the gastrointestinal tract to its normal function. IBS can affect individuals on a chronic basis, and many women experience symptoms intermittently for extended periods of time.

It has been observed in several studies that the incidence of mental health conditions, such as depression, is higher in women than men. Although there has been some speculation about diet and lifestyle, a definite reason behind this has not been clearly established. Women also tend to be more emotional and susceptible to mood changes than men, which could account for some of the increased cases of depression. It is, however, undeniable that mental health and antidepressant treatments are becoming an increasingly important aspect of women's health. The treatments available for mental health illness such as depression often present women with several uncomfortable adverse effects that can be difficult to manage, such as weight gain, insomnia or drowsiness, sexual problems, and gastrointestinal problems. In some cases, these adverse effects can make the initial problems worse; taking weight gain as an example, the woman may experience lower self-esteem as a result of societal pressure on women to maintain slender appearance, which could worsen feeling of depression. Mental health is also likely to continue being a major concern for women's health into the future.

Adverse Drug Reactions

Adverse drug reactions are a serious concern in the current society, resulting in up to 5 percent of all hospital admissions. It has been observed that women experience more adverse drug reactions than men and studies have shown an age-standardized odds ratio of 1.6 (95 percent confidence interval 1.5–1.7). From a general perspective, women have a greater tendency to take medications and are therefore subject to the possibility of experiencing an adverse reaction. However, even when standardized for actual drug use, women tend to experience these reactions with much greater frequency and severity than their male counterparts.

The physiology of the female body and the way in which it interacts with drugs pharmacologically is partially the cause of the increased incidence of adverse effects observed in women. The particular differences between the physiology of the male and female body have been described in detail in the previous section about gender differences. The female body is generally more effective at absorbing and less effective at eliminating the majority of drugs, resulting in a higher blood concentration of the drug in the body. Several studies have noted a higher maximum drug concentration in addition to a greater area under the curve in women, which is an indicator of total drug exposure. It is logical that greater drug exposure and higher drug concentrations will be more likely to lead to adverse effects, an observation that is evident in the actual use of drugs by women.

The physical composition of the female body is of particular importance in the consideration of adverse drug reactions, particularly as it differs vastly from the male body, yet both genders are most often given identical doses of medications regardless of their sex. The female body is generally smaller in size than the male body and has a lower muscle content and higher fat content. As discussed previously, all of these factors can result in higher concentrations of drugs in the body for the same doses, and hence adverse drug reactions are more likely to occur. Women also have a longer transit time in the gut, which gives orally administered drugs an extended time to dissolve in the gastric acids and be absorbed into the blood stream. This then leads to an increase in the bioavailability of the drug and increases the risk of toxic doses and adverse reactions. The volume of distribution of the drug is another parameter that has a significant effect on the incidence of adverse drug reactions. As mentioned previously, it describes the level to which the drug disperses throughout the body. As women usually have a lower volume of distribution—although this also depends on the pharmacology of the drug—there is once again a higher concentration in the blood and an increased risk of adverse effects.

It is important to consider the therapeutic index of the drug to understand the level of severity the adverse reaction could pose to women. A drug with a narrow therapeutic index has a smaller window of drug concentrations that are accepted to be in the optimal range, which is sufficient to work effectively but less than required to lead to toxic effects. These are the drugs that pose the biggest concern in relation to adverse effects, as there is only a small difference in concentration between ineffective and over-effective or toxic. For women, who are at higher risk of adverse effects, these drugs should be monitored more closely for toxicity in order to reduce the risk of adverse effects.

In practice, this knowledge of the relationship between women and an increased risk of adverse effects can be used to alter the way we use drugs in women, hence managing and reducing the risk. If we know, for example, that a hydrophilic drug is likely to have a low volume of distribution in women due to their high fat content, we can expect that women would need a lower dose of the drug to achieve the same effects as a man. In most cases, currently males and females are given identical doses of most medications, although this may change in the future as healthcare professionals develop a more pronounced emphasis on the individual. Already some categories of medications, such as antipsychotics, are taking gender into consideration when prescribing doses, as the adverse effect profile has been well documented and changes in practice have begun to take place.

Yolanda Smith
University of South Australia
MedicineHow Founder

See Also: Men.

Further Readings

Anderson, Gail. "Gender Differences in Pharmacological Response." *International Review of Neurobiology*, v.83 (2008).

Blencowe, Hannah. "Folic Acid to Reduce Neonatal Mortality From Neural Tube Disorders." *International Journal of Epidemiology*, v.39 (2010).

Briggs, Gerald. *Drugs in Pregnancy and Lactation: A Reference Guide to Fetal and Neonatal Risk.* New York: Lippincott Williams & Wilkins, 2012.

Canavan, Caroline. "The Epidemiology of Irritable Bowel Syndrome." *Clinical Epidemiology*, v.6 (2014).

Lee, C. Rhoda. "Drug Interactions and Hormonal Contraception." *Trends in Urology, Gynaecology and Sexual Health*, v.14/3 (2009).

Morrow, James. "Malformation Risks of Antiepileptic Drugs in Pregnancy: A Prospective Study From the UK Epilepsy and Pregnancy Register." *Journal of Neurology, Neurosurgery and Psychiatry*, v.77 (2006).

Mosher, William and Jo Jones. "Use of Contraception in the United States: 1982-2008." *National Center for Health Statistics*, v.23/29 (2010).

Quigley, Eamonn. "Irritable Bowel Syndrome: A Global Perspective." *World Gastroenterology Organization Global Outline* (April 20, 2009).

Rademaker, Marius. "Do Women Have More Adverse Drug Reactions?" *American Journal of Clinical Dermatology*, v.2/6 (2001).

Reynolds, F. and C. Knott. "Pharmacokinetics in Pregnancy and Placental Drug Transfer." *Oxford Reviews of Reproductive Biology*, v.11 (1989).

Seeman, Mary. "Gender Differences in the Prescribing of Antipsychotic Drugs." *American Journal of Psychiatry*, v.161/8 (2004).

Soldin, Offie P., Sarah H. Chung, and Donald R. Mattison. "Sex Differences in Drug Disposition." *Journal of Biomedicine and Biotechnology*, v.2011 (2011).

Venturini, Carina. "Gender Differences, Polypharmacy, and Potential Pharmacological Interactions in the Elderly." *Journal of Clinical Science*, v. 66/11 (2011).

World Anti-Doping Agency (WADA)

The World Anti-Doping Agency (WADA) is a private law foundation chartered in Lausanne, Switzerland, with headquarters located in Montreal, Canada. It is focused on promoting, coordinating, and leading a collaborative world-wide effort for doping-free sports. Legally, WADA is a private law foundation as defined under the provisions of the Swiss Civil Code. The entity was formed through initiation of the International Olympic Committee (IOC), governed by a constitutive instrument and Articles 80 et seq. of the Swiss Civil Code. It was established as a foundation under private law with the vision by the European Union that it should eventually evolve into an agency governed under public law. Typical of foundations, the WADA structure includes a 38-member board, executive committee, several standing committees, and an auditing arm, in addition to a director general and staff.

Pharmaceuticals influence the body and its performance in a variety of subtle ways, and the use of these and other substances by athletes involved in high-stakes sport competitions worldwide has led to a large number of complex policy concerns. WADA was launched in 1999 as a result of initial groundwork resulting from the First World Conference on Doping in Sports held in Switzerland, which produced a statement called the Lausanne Declaration on Doping in Sports. It called for establishing an agency to help expand testing outside of competition, prevention, and education, as well as research coordination and creating greater integration among the standards, procedures, and methods of analysis among countries, interested stakeholders, and organizations with respect to the issues of doping in sports. The organization remains at the forefront of policy with respect to these issues.

History and Organizational Structure

Much of the drive for a new agency came from the crises resulting from scandals surrounding use of performance-enhancing drugs (PEDs), culminating in extensive publicity related to these substances at the Tour de France in 1998, resulting in decisions by the International Olympic Committee of the need for an independent body to create greater oversight and coordination of the issues. The Second World Conference on Doping in Sports resulted in ratification of a World Anti-Doping Code, which first went into effect in 2004 and provides the framework for rules and regulation in this sphere.

The agency is governed by a 38-member foundation board and a 12-member policy-making executive committee that is comprised of governments and Olympic Movement representatives, along with several committees dealing with areas including athletes, ethics, education, finance, and health. The organization has a network of other regional offices in Cape Town, South Africa; Tokyo, Japan; Lausanne, Switzerland; and Montevideo, Uruguay, to carry out the work of the organization, which is international in scope. The agency receives funding from both governments and the Olympic Movement. In 2012, for example, Canada was the largest government contributor, allocating $26.4 million toward the agency, with only two other countries, including the United States, giving more than $1 million to the organization.

Organizational Activities

The World Anti-Doping Program defines doping and includes the World Anti-Doping Code, which sets forward rules, regulations, and policies with respect to doping. The program also includes international standards for operational issues related to antidoping programs as well as guidelines and models of best practices for various problematic areas in antidoping. *Doping* is defined within the framework of infractions of rule violations based on specific articles in the code that ban prohibited substances from entering athletes' bodies and make them clearly responsible for the presence of these substances, metabolites, or markers in samples, as well as for activities such as failure to comply with protocols set out for testing and filing of information on athlete whereabouts to facilitate monitoring, among others.

WADA is responsible not only for implementing various procedures and policies related to the World Anti-Doping Code but also for publishing a prohibited list at least yearly, which identifies substances and methods that may not be used by athletes in—and in some cases outside of—sports competitions. The list is wide ranging, from anabolic agents, peptide hormones, diuretics, and other masking agents to illegal drugs such as narcotics, marijuana, and stimulants including some amphetamines, to name a few. However, for a substance or method to reach the stage of being placed on the list there must be strictly determined medical, scientific, or pharmacological evidence that the substance meets two

out of three basic criteria, including that it enhances or has potential to enhance performance in sports, poses a health risk, or otherwise violates the spirit of sports. While some substances are specifically listed, there is also language including substances with similar chemical structures or biological effects.

WADA also monitors code compliance by signatories, helps finance antidoping services, and provides support and advice through entities such as Sportacord, the organization composed of sports federations and associations worldwide. The organization works with stakeholders such as the various international sports federations and organizers of major games and a wide range of national and regional antidoping organizations. WADA publishes model rules and guidelines to provide some guidance for these organizations, although use of these is not mandatory. WADA reviews formulation and enforcement of antidoping regulations to ensure harmony with respect to the code, which works in conjunction with an International Convention Against Doping in Sport that was signed by 148 countries in 2010 and serves as the formal treaty through which governments agree to adopt rules complying with the code.

While national antidoping organizations are responsible for testing athlete use of prohibited substances, all collected samples are sent to laboratories accredited by WADA. Rules for out-of-competition monitoring of athlete whereabouts went into effect in early 2009, with complaints from some top athletes that the system was too invasive. Under this system, national antidoping authorities must have advance notice of where top athletes can be found for certain times of the day. In recent years this system has evolved into using apps and smartphones for those in a testing pool, which help with a range of tasks including reminding them of location tracking obligations and requirements for submitting information. In the 10-year period following the founding of WADA, the number of checks for doping was reported to have nearly doubled, from 120,000 to 200,000. As of 2009, three missed tests in 18 months is considered a violation that is sufficient to open a disciplinary proceeding, with potential sanctions of one to two years depending on the circumstances.

WADA also runs an Independent Observer Program that has sent teams to monitor, gain perspectives from various stakeholders, and issue unbiased reports on various aspects of doping control at over 30 major sports competitions and events. The agency also has responsibility for monitoring and appealing doping cases to a Court of Arbitration for Sport, and intervening to ensure a fair and consistent process for granting exemptions. For example, if an athlete is prescribed a medication that might involve a prohibited substance for a legitimate medical condition, they may apply to be allowed the right to use this medication through an exemption called a Therapeutic Use Exemption to a federation. WADA has a special committee to monitor these exemptions and deal with appeals when the exemption is not granted. The agency is active in terms of cooperating with governments and international policing agencies, such as Interpol, facilitating policy enforcement in a range of activities to stem availability and use of problematic substances in sports.

WADA also promotes an active agenda related to research on doping, including improving detection of prohibited substances, primarily through a grant program of more than $56 million since 2001 that involves proposal review by independent experts. In some cases, controversies have been reported such as media attention to a program involving WADA cooperation with pharmaceutical firms on monitoring of drugs that might attract attention of future offenders.

Another pillar for the agency is wide-ranging efforts for education and training for athletes and the general public about issues related to antidoping through a variety of creative tools such as an Athlete Outreach Center, "Say No to Doping" campaign, Athlete Learning Program About Health and Anti-Doping, as well as through books, videos, and toolkits. The organization also holds two forums on antidoping annually. Model guidelines are also produced to help organizations work through each of the stages of analysis, planning, development, implementation, and evaluation of an education and information strategy related to preventing doping in sports.

Pamela Ransom
Metropolitan College of New York

See Also: Drug Testing, Olympic Athletes; Drug Testing, Professional Athletes; Ethics of Performance-Enhancing Drugs in Sport; Olympics, Summer: Performance-Enhancing Drugs; Olympics, Winter: Performance-Enhancing Drugs; Performance-Enhancing Drugs and Sports: History.

Further Readings

Anderson, Jack. "Doping, Sport and the Law: Time for Repeal of Prohibition?" *International Journal of Law in Context*, v.9/2 (2013).

"Anti-Doping Agency in Sports Defends New Rules." *Swiss Info* (February 25, 2009).

Casini, L. "Global Hybrid Public-Private Bodies: The World Anti-Doping Agency." Draft paper for Global Administrative Law Conference, Practical Legal Problems of International Law, Geneva, March 20–21, 2009. http://www.academia.edu/1378653/Global_Hybrid_Public-Private_Bodies_the_World_Anti-Doping_Agency_WADA_.

"CGI Group: World Anti-Doping Agency Introduces App." *Entertainment Close-Up* (2013). http://www.highbeam.com/doc/1G1-353669057.html (Accessed September 2015).

Commission of the European Communities. "Communication From the Commission to the Council, the European Parliament, the Economic and Social Committee and the Committee of the Regions: Community Support Plan to Combat Doping in Sport" (December 1, 1999). http://aei .pitt.edu/3537/1/3537.pdf.

Cox, Thomas Wyatt. "The International War Against Doping: Limiting the Collateral Damage From Strict Liability." *Vanderbilt Journal of Transnational Law*, v.47/1 (2014).

Kondro, Wayne. "Anti-Doping Allocation." *Canadian Medical Association Journal* (May 15, 2012). http:// go.galegroup.com/ps/i.do?id=GALE%7CA2896208 07&v=2.1&u=nysl_me_mcolny&it=r&p=AONE&s w=w&asid=983015cd8eec6517cab5a8b8d538f8ea (Accessed July 2014).

"Pharmaceutical Firms Cooperate With World Anti-Doping Agency." *Pharma Marketletter* (December 15, 2008). http://go.galegroup.com/ps/i.do?id=GALE %7CA190365077&v=2.1&u=nysl_me_mcolny&it= r&p=ITOF&sw=w&asid=f80d8e5f54c03cd99c4e2f 47547826d8 (Accessed July 2014).

World Anti-Doping Agency. *World Anti-Doping Code*. Montreal: World Anti-Doping Agency, 2015. https:// www.wada-ama.org/en/resources/the-code/world-anti-doping-code (Accessed June 2015).

World Anti-Doping Agency/Council of Europe Cooperation. "Model Guidelines for Core Information/Education Programs to Prevent Doping in Sports," Draft 4.6 (April 26, 2005). https:// wada-main-prod.s3.amazonaws.com/resources/ files/WADA_Guidelines_EducationPrograms_ EN.pdf (Accessed September 2015).

World Health Organization

The World Health Organization, commonly known as WHO, is an agency run by the United Nations (UN) that seeks to improve and maintain health worldwide, focusing on a variety of areas ranging from communicable and noncommunicable diseases such as acquired immunodeficiency syndrome (AIDS), malaria, and cancer to substance abuse and basic hygiene. It has existed since July 22, 1946, when its constitution was signed by 61 countries; it now consists of almost 200. It is considered a part of the United Nations Development Group, which seeks to implement UN practices and ideas at the level of individual nations and has been active since 1997, consolidating the management and regulating and keeping track of the interaction of various UN agencies so that they can work together more effectively to have a more serious impact on the lives of individuals.

Essentially, the goal of WHO is to combat serious health problems around the globe, whether the results of communicable diseases or resulting from unhealthy lifestyle decisions, such as eating poorly or smoking. WHO seeks to use its resources and knowledge to increase both life expectancy and quality of life around the globe, in both developed and underdeveloped countries, by pooling international resources and thoughts and issuing various statements and policies that affect the ways individuals and systems involved in the health care process go about their daily operations.

The History of the World Health Organization

The World Health Organization, when its constitution was written and ratified by the United Nations in 1946, became the first specialized agency of the United Nations that every UN member country agreed to; the constitution was also signed by countries outside of the United Nations at the time.

It combined two previous organizations, the Office International d'Hygiène Publique and the Health Organization that existed as part of the League of Nations. The Office International was a world health group based in Paris that preceded the creation of the League of

Nations, and focused almost exclusively on the containment of communicable diseases, especially with regard to international maritime trade. The Health Organization was created as part of the League of Nations to serve essentially the same purposes that the World Health Organization fulfils today, but it was less effective because the League of Nations as a whole was less effective. When the League of Nations became defunct and was supplanted by the United Nations, the World Health Organization simply took over where the League of Nations Health Organization left off.

Since its inception, WHO has sought to serve as a truly global organization that helps people in all nations and of all socioeconomic and ethnic backgrounds. To this end, it sponsors events such as World Health Day and provides operational support and leadership whenever there are health crises the world over, while also gathering and processing data that is free for all to access. It serves two purposes, as it seeks to scientifically show individuals and health systems how they may assist in promoting better worldwide health and also shows the progress that WHO has made in combating certain worldwide health problems (AIDS and child mortality being two major areas of interest), which in turn allows the organization to set benchmarks and goals for itself in the future.

The organization began work on April 7, 1948—prompting April 7 to now be celebrated as World Health Day in many UN member states with a focus on public health, and is used to draw attention to the organization and particular health issues with which the organization is helping populations cope, as each year has a different theme or particular public health issue focus. On July 24 of the same year, its governing body, the World Health Assembly (also known as the WHA and consisting of a meeting between health ministers and similar officials from all of WHO's member states, consisting today of 194 countries) met, having established a budget with the UN, and elected its first director general, Andrija Stampar.

The WHA continues to meet every year, outlining major issues upon which WHO will focus on for that year, electing a director general (who serves a single five-year term), establishing a budget, and setting public health policies that will be endorsed or enforced by WHO. It is the largest health policy body in the world.

Since its creation, the World Health Organization has proven itself effective in many areas, combating diseases such as polio quite well (reducing cases by 99 percent and hoping to eradicate it entirely in the near future) and eradicating smallpox entirely by 1979. That being said, there is still much progress to be made in the area of world health, and there are some areas in which WHO is still working to reduce the impact of particular diseases. WHO has, since its inception, improved the overall level of world health by greatly reducing incidences and mortality rates of certain diseases, making health information more accessible to the general public, and bringing public health to the forefront of the international conversation on worldwide survival and well-being. On the 50th anniversary of WHO's formation, April 7, 1998, the director general at the time made public statements about the organization's progress and positive impact over the years, but also highlighted areas upon which it would need to focus in the future.

The World Health Organization has also been the subject of a few major controversies over the years, one of the most notable and public being its passionate disagreement with the Catholic Church on the use of condoms to prevent the spread of AIDS—a conflict born out of the fact that the church authorities forbid the use of contraceptives, but the World Health Organization actively promotes the use of condoms during sexual intercourse, as they have been scientifically proven to greatly reduce the spread of AIDS.

The World Health Organization has also had notable and public disagreements with the sugar industry (because WHO released statements that sugar should only make up very small portions of healthy persons' diets) and has even created controversy through its actions regarding another agency that operates under and reports to the United Nations (despite being established separately from and independently of the UN), the International Atomic Energy Agency; there is widespread belief that an agreement formed between WHO and the International Atomic Energy Agency stating that they will share information and report to each other whenever the actions of one body could affect the other actually limits the ability of WHO to observe the ill effects of radiation on public health, including during radiation disasters such as those as Chernobyl and Fukushima.

The Priorities of the World Health Organization

Although the specifics of the priorities of the World Health Organization have changed over time, it has always focused itself on a few key areas and is currently focused on these major areas in particular: communicable diseases, noncommunicable diseases (including mental health problems, cancers, and others), development and aging, reproductive health and safe sex, nutrition and widespread access to healthy food, substance abuse, occupational hazards, and the gathering and dispersing of data related to public health worldwide. It is also highly concerned with the relationship between ill health and poverty, and has recently backed various national initiatives to establish or reinforce universal health care.

Although the World Health Organization is often directly involved with health care—especially in times of great health care crises such as the 2009 flu pandemic, in which its scientists directly interfaced with those working in the pharmaceutical and other health care industries—it primarily seeks to offer support and leadership that will create independently successful health care systems and correct the problems in existing health care programs within member states. As such, it provides various types of support to governments and others involved with the delivery of health care within member nations, particularly by establishing health goals and policies for all member nations to work toward.

Many associate the WHO with developing or underdeveloped nations, but it in fact does a great deal of work in wealthy, industrialized nations as well, increasing access to health care across racial and economic groups, and attempting to mitigate effects from environmental pollution, unhealthy food, and the widespread use of alcohol and tobacco products, as well as illegal and improperly used drugs.

There is also a new focus on multilingualism in WHO policies, which is in keeping with its long-standing idea that health information should be accessible to all. A great deal of work is currently being done on this front, with a particular focus on publishing all materials in the six official languages of the World Health Organization (English, Arabic, Chinese, French, Spanish, and Russian) and allowing external bodies license with which to translate WHO publications into the many other languages individuals the world over use daily. The official languages were established at the 1978 World Health Assembly, when multilingualism first became a focus of the World Health Organization.

The Structure of the World Health Organization

The World Health Organization is currently made up on 194 member nations, with several other "associate members," "observers," and newly invited members; membership of any nation that applies is granted by a simple majority at the World Health Assembly the following year.

The director general is elected by the WHA every five years and spearheads the worldwide efforts of WHO for the next five years. The WHA also appoints 34 members to its executive board, which organizes WHO's efforts and publishes reports to keep the assembly updated on its progress on various fronts. Each member of the executive board serves a three-year term.

These bodies control WHO as a whole, but much of the actual work of WHO is done at the regional level. Between 1949 and 1952, the world was divided into various regions by WHO, each of which has its own regional offices and governing body; the governing bodies for each region determine who will represent each of the member states in their associated regions at each World Health Assembly and also have a great deal of influence over other important WHO considerations, such as budget.

The structure of WHO at the regional level mirrors its structure at its global level, in that regional offices generally have assemblies once a year (usually occurring in autumn) and elect a regional director who serves as the regional equivalent of the director general of the WHO proper.

The regions recognized and maintained by the World Health Organization are as follows: Africa, Europe, Southeast Asia, Eastern Mediterranean, Western Pacific, and the Americas. Each regional office is located in a major city within its region; for example,

the Eastern Mediterranean office is located in Cairo, and the Americas regional office is in Washington, D.C. The African regional office does not serve a great deal of North Africa, which is considered geographically and culturally to be more similar to the Eastern Mediterranean region, which serves all of the Middle East, except for Israel, which is served by the European regional office.

The World Health Organization also has offices in most of its member countries, across all of its regions, and also has offices that serve as liaisons between it and other prominent international organizations, such as the European Union and International Monetary Fund. It also operates a cancer research center in Lyon, France, and the WHO Centre for Health Development in Kobe, Japan.

Worldwide Impact of the World Health Organization

Although it has not yet achieved all of its goals, the World Health Organization has made great strides in increasing life expectancy and quality of life since its creation, and has participated in the eradication or serious reduction of several major diseases, which it labeled as "scourges." Although it has sometimes been the subject of controversy and is, as all national and supranational organizations are, subject to politics, it has also been an internationally unifying body and has measurably improved the world health situation and the ability of member nations to work together. We can all agree, regardless of politics, that disease and premature death are enemies of humanity, and the idea of a common enemy has helped to unify many nations with seemingly irreconcilable political differences.

The World Health Organization has also been at the forefront of a great deal of information gathering and dispersion, and its records and information are available to all, across class and linguistic borders, on paper and via the Internet. It has made great strides since its 1948 beginnings, while sticking to the same ideals and using many of the same motifs, in everything from its policy to its advertising, and is expected to continuing evolving in the future.

The Future of the World Health Organization

The World Health Organization is an adaptive institution, its annual assemblies allowing it to restructure its approaches and the specific applications of its values, techniques, and thoughts to respond to new challenges and combat new health concerns, therefore increasing life expectancy and quality of life across the globe.

In the future, WHO hopes to continue its study of the relationship between health and socioeconomic status, while also adapting to new challenges such as the growing antivaccine movement and the Ebola epidemic.

Over the long term, WHO is expected to maintain the same kinds of relationships with governmental systems, nongovernmental organizations (NGOs), and private sector health care providers as it has in the past, providing leadership and resources while also sometimes directly involving itself in research and directly dealing with massive public health problems such as epidemics and natural disasters (when they may impact public health worldwide).

However, WHO is also changing in its new focus on the patient, with training programs being implemented that encourage Ebola survivors to talk directly to WHO and other Ebola treatment workers to describe the physical experience of having Ebola, the endorsement of universal health care and the pledge to support any nations seeking to create or reform universal health care programs, and a new spin on the study of the relationship between money and health. While much of their past research has sought to prove that people in poorer countries and poorer people in wealthy countries have greater difficulty maintaining good health, they are now providing research that shows that negative health situations and choices can also lead to economic decline and loss of economic opportunity. Much of this research is heavily intertwined with their new programs to advance universal health care, as they are promoting the belief that it is unfair for individuals to suffer economic consequences for being in bad health, which already causes such a great reduction of quality of life.

David Michael Gonzalez
University of Nevada

See Also: Access to Medicines (Developing World); Smallpox Eradication; WHO Model Lists of Essential Medicines.

Further Readings

Mann, Jim. "Sugar Revisited—Again." *Bulletin of the World Health Organization* (2003).

World Health Organization. "About WHO." United Nations, World Health Organization (2014).

World Health Organization. "Liberia: Survivors Help Train Health Workers for Ebola Care." United Nations, World Health Organization (October 2014).

World Health Organization. "Staff Regulations and Staff Rules." United Nations, World Health Organization (2013).

Yellow Card Scheme

The Yellow Card Scheme (YCS) is the United Kingdom's (UK's) system for collecting information on suspected Adverse Drug Reactions (ADRs) to medicines. It is run by the Medicines and Healthcare Products Regulatory Agency (MHRA), the branch of the UK's Department of Health, which is responsible for the safety and efficacy of medicines, and the Commission on Human Medicines (CHM), the government's independent scientific advisory body on medicines' safety. Health care professionals and patients voluntarily report adverse drug reactions that they suspect are caused by a prescription medicine or an over-the-counter product, vaccine, or herbal remedy. By law, pharmaceutical companies holding marketing authorizations from the MHRA must report adverse effects including those they have identified through the literature within 14 days.

The YCS system was originally created in 1964, after the thalidomide disaster. At first, only doctors and dentists participated; coroners were added in 1969 and hospital pharmacists in 1997. In 1999, a pilot project found that community pharmacists submitted a high proportion of reports associated with herbal products and generic inequivalence, where an adverse effect occurs after switching from a brand to generic drug. As a result, all pharmacists were encouraged to submit reports. Nurses and midwives have been submitting reports since 2002. In 2005, a pilot scheme was launched for patients to report ADRs directly to the MHRA. The pilot showed that patient reports added value to the system, and since February 2008, all patients have been able to report ADRs directly to the MHRA.

Although the original color of the document used to report adverse effects was yellow, today health care professionals can report online, by mail, or from various clinical systems, while the public can report online, by mail, or by phone. The forms used by the public and by health care professionals are different.

For established medicines, herbal remedies, and over-the-counter drugs, health care professionals and companies are only supposed to report "serious" suspected adverse reactions, defined to include those that are fatal, life-threatening, disabling or incapacitating, or medically significant, or that result in prolonged hospitalization. Causality does not have to be established for reporting to be encouraged. Medicines or vaccines that have a black triangle after their names are being monitored particularly closely by regulatory authorities in the European Union (EU). In England, the black triangle indicates that the medicine or vaccine is new, is being used for a new indication, or is being given by a new route of administration. All reactions for these are to be reported including those that are not serious. Practitioners are also required to report any adverse reaction that occurs in children or the elderly even if they are not serious. European pharmacovigilance legislation adopted in July 2012 required a number of changes in what must be reported. The adverse drug reactions that must be reported now include ADRs arising from medication error, off-label use, misuse, and abuse. Pharmaceutical companies that hold marketing authorizations must now submit any report they receive from a consumer, even if it is not medically confirmed.

When the MHRA gets a report, it is entered into a database, and a staff made up of expert health professionals along with lay representatives decide whether they should investigate further or if they need to take immediate action. They can update information about the medicine, such as changing the recommended dosage or advising against use by certain groups of patients. They can add warnings to the product information and, in very rare cases, withdraw the product. They base their decisions on case reports in the literature, pre- and post-marketing clinical trials, epidemiological studies, record linkage databases, and data from other drug regulatory agencies.

The MHRA and CSM publish *Drug Safety Updates*, an electronic bulletin that includes up-to-date information on adverse reactions. Anyone can sign up to receive an e-mail when a new issue is released, or they can go directly to the MHRA Web page.

From the beginning of the YCS, underreporting has been a problem. In 2006, the British Medical Association estimated that only 10 percent of serious reactions and 2 to 4 percent of nonserious reactions were reported. From the mid-1980s until 2004, the number of reports filed annually has been fairly consistent at 20,000. The one exception was in 2000 when reporting increased because of a mass meningitis C vaccination campaign. Reasons for underreporting have included lack of time, not having easy access to report forms, misunderstanding what should be reported, lack of certainty that the reaction was caused by the medicine, and fear of liability. Between 2005 and 2007, there were 26,269 reports of side effects—19.8 percent were from patients and 80.2 percent were from health professionals. Compared with patients, health care professionals tended to report more adverse drug reactions that caused hospitalizations, were life threatening, or caused death than patients. They also reported more adverse effects from newly marketed drugs, which is not surprising since they are supposed to report all reactions for black triangle drugs. Patient reports tended to give more detail on the impact of adverse drug reactions on daily life and activities, and patients reported more adverse reactions from drugs used to treat the central nervous system than health care practitioners. Reporting via the Web was introduced in 2002, and in February 2008, the online form was redesigned to be less cumbersome and easier to use. The MHRA collected adverse drug reaction reports from 2008 to 2012 and found reporting had increased. From 2008 to 2012, the number of reports went from 25,012 to 26,037, a 4.1 percent increase. The percentage of reports made electronically went from 25 percent in 2008 to 68 percent in 2012. The group that uses electronic reporting the most is the public. In spite of the decrease in reporting by paper and phone, there are currently no plans to eliminate these modes of reporting. Another group that does not submit many reports is dentists. This is probably because dental prescriptions represented only 0.6 percent of overall prescriptions in England, and dental prescriptions usually come from a well-established list of drugs and not black triangle medications.

Patient reporting peaked in 2009 after the formal launch of patient yellow card reporting. Since then it has decreased, although there was a slight increase from 2011 to 2012.

Natalie Kupferberg
Ohio State University

See Also: European Medicines Agency; Medicines and Healthcare Products Regulatory Agency (UK); Thalidomide (Contergan) Controversy.

Further Readings

BMA Board of Science. *Reporting Adverse Drug Reactions: A Guide for Healthcare Professionals.* London: British Medical Association, 2006. http://bmaopac.hosted.exlibrisgroup.com/exlibris/aleph/a21_1/apache_media/GYVFNJ1RT2PFNDUJ8IUK PUNTFVRF8G.pdf (Accessed September 2015).

Griffith, Richard. "Nurses Must Report Adverse Drug Reactions." *British Journal of Nursing*, v.22/8 (2013).

McLernon, David J. "Adverse Drug Reaction Reporting in the UK: A Retrospective Observational Comparison of Yellow Card Reports Submitted by Patients and Healthcare Professionals." *Drug Safety,* v.33/9 (2010).

Medicines and Healthcare Products Regulatory Agency. "Report a Problem With a Medicine or Medical Device." http://www.mhra.gov.uk/Safetyinformation/ Reportingsafetyproblems/Reportingsuspectedad versedrugreactions/index.htm (Accessed July 2014).

Medicines and Healthcare Products Regulatory Agency. *Trends in UK Spontaneous Adverse Drug Reaction (ADR) Reporting Between 2008-2012.* London: MHRA, 2014.

Rees, Judith, Ian Smith, and Jennie Watson. *Pharmaceutical Practice.* Edinburgh: Churchill Livingstone/Elsevier, 2014.

Taylor, J. and M. N. Pemberton. "Yellow Card Scheme (letter)." *British Dental Journal*, v.215/9 (2013).

ZERO-TOLERANCE DRUG POLICIES

In general, the term *zero tolerance* is referred to as a consistently enforced policy, in response to weapons, drugs, and violence. It has been applied in schools, the workplace, the military, and law enforcement. Over time, zero tolerance has led to mandated, predetermined, harsh consequences for a wide degree of rule violations. The policies were developed to protect the safety of students, citizens, and employees so they can live in a conducive environment.

Some of the first examples of zero-tolerance policies were found in the enforcement tactics related to narcotics during the War on Drugs under President Ronald Reagan, to curb the transfer of drugs at borders in the United States. Strict enforcement of personal use was thought to reduce demand and strike at the cause of the drug problem. The term *zero tolerance* did not actually appear in a report until 1994, though its roots can be traced back to research in 1973 conducted by James Q. Wilson and George L. Kelling. Their theory, titled Broken Windows, was based on the notion that small problems lead to bigger problems. So, if a few broken windows are not repaired in a neighborhood, vandals are more likely to break more

windows. Then, they might enter the building. The less respect for that building with the broken windows, the more likely persons will litter around that property. The cycle could then continue, until there is disrespect for the entire neighborhood.

New York City Mayor Rudy Giuliani utilized the zero-tolerance policy in his law enforcement tactics. Although the decline of crime started before his administration, reports show that crime declined in large part because of his application of this policy. By enforcing the law against the minor crime of turnstile jumping, for example, a robbery on the subway could be prevented.

These polices have also been applied in schools because they allow quick removal of problematic individuals, which sends a clear message to the offenders and the onlookers that certain behaviors are not acceptable. In the workplace, these policies allow for safer working conditions, better performance, fewer workplace accidents and injuries, less absenteeism, less employee theft, and less violence on the job.

When driving a motor vehicle, these policies have been enforced to make the roads safer for all drivers. In fact, there are various types of driving under the influence of drug laws in every state devised to crack down on persons who operate a vehicle under the influence of a controlled substance. This is especially important in certain occupations (such as long-distance truckers and delivery personnel). However, forensic toxicologists have not agreed on specific levels that could be designated as impairment, so it is difficult to prosecute drugged drivers.

About 88 percent of schools have zero-tolerance policies and practices for drugs. In the workplace, employees often receive policies in writing that they need to sign as a condition of being hired. Most companies clearly state that employees who test positive for drugs or alcohol will immediately be terminated.

In the school setting, students are usually prohibited from being under the influence of illegal drugs while in the classroom, on campus, or while participating in school-sanctioned or sponsored activities. Testing can be done randomly throughout school enrollment, with reasonable suspicion, or post-incident (an accident or report of erratic or dangerous behavior). The basis for reasonable suspicion and the steps taken after must be documented. Students must sign policies, which should clearly state that they cannot use drugs, that they can be subject to screening, and that refusal to submit to testing will lead to dismissal. Zero tolerance at the high school level might include expulsion, suspension, and exclusion from extracurricular activities.

Consequences

Although zero-tolerance policies were developed with good intentions, there are some unintentional negative consequences associated with the use of any policy that does not individualize the treatment of offenders. There are nonquantifiable costs that must be weighed (such as the effect of persons being labeled and punished across the board—especially in a school setting). In the military and the workforce, the use of drug screening is likely to reduce the number of qualified individuals who will even apply for positions. If the discovery of use leads to automatic dismissal, the cost of random drug testing itself and the cost of finding new qualified individuals to fill their spots, becomes expensive. Some individuals might not even apply for jobs where there is drug testing, as they may feel it is an invasion of their privacy.

There is even a cost associated with employer-sponsored treatment programs. The positive notion of helping an employee can backfire since success rates are not 100 percent. Then, the company is paying for treatment of a person who cannot be rehabilitated and then cannot be rehired.

Another issue is random testing versus "for cause" testing. Both circumstances need to be clearly stated in a written policy, and those who qualify for "for cause" testing must only be used if there is reasonable suspicion of involvement in drug use in violation of the policy. The terms used in the policy need to be clear and applied fairly. It is acceptable to only test certain employees (those who operate machinery or those in the construction industry) if there are serious safety concerns.

Proper Procedure

Consent forms must be properly worded and results must be reported in a way that does not violate one's confidentiality rights, or there could be a claim or lawsuit arising from testing. An employer cannot physical force an employee to submit to a search, and they need to be very careful when conducting pre-employment drug testing. Understanding that employers must use proper techniques to detect drug use is also important. Most zero-tolerance legislation allows for law enforcement to require a suspect to have bodily fluids screened through urine, blood, or saliva. Urine analysis is the most popular form of drug detection (especially in the workplace setting), but it only detects the presence of inactive drug metabolites, not THC. Drawing blood is the second method, but it is generally viewed as more invasive, so medical personnel must be used to collect this data. Saliva testing only detects the presence of cannabis for a short period (one to two hours following the use of the drug). But, it is noninvasive and therefore ideal.

Regardless of the technique, clarity is essential. It must be very clear (whether in the classroom or workplace setting) what is prohibited under the policy. There is usually a zero-tolerance approach to have a prohibited substance in one's system. In general, the unlawful manufacture, distribution, dispensation, possession, or use of controlled substances would be prohibited at any workplace. Next, a company should not begin any drug testing unless it has a drug testing lab that is reliable and reputable.

To avoid a lawsuit, an employer must have a policy that prohibits positive drug test results, evidence to establish that the employee consented to the drug testing, a document to establish the chain of custody of the sample, and documentation from a drug testing lab to establish conformation of the method, as well documentation of the positive results.

Conclusion

Imposing consistent and firm consequences for behavior is associated with decreasing the likelihood of negative behavior and has been a part of the definition of deterrence theory. However, broad application of the zero-tolerance polices results in suspensions and expulsions for serious infractions as well as mild ones, especially for minorities.

Research has shown that in the long run, zero-tolerance policies are ineffective because they lead to increased rates of school drop-out and discriminatory application of disciplinary practices. Evidence does not suggest that zero tolerance reduces violence or drug abuse by students. Those with behavioral problems tend to be punished repeatedly (but the punishment might not be getting to the root of the problem). Additionally, those who drop out might be exposed to a lack of parental supervision and negative peer associations, crime, and delinquency.

Some studies find that there are more effective alternative strategies, such as systemic schoolwide violence prevention programs, social skills training, and utilizing mental health experts, to research and develop policies that focus on positive behavior. Involving families and community resources, helping students with emotional disorders and deficits in social skills, applying zero-tolerance policies with some flexibility, and early intervention before problems escalate can reduce the need for harsh consequences.

Gina Robertiello
Felician College

See Also: Cost-Effectiveness Research; Drug Testing, High School and College Athletes (U.S.); Harm Reduction Policies.

Further Readings

Caplan, Y. "Technology for Testing Drugs of Abuse in DUID." In *Developing Global Strategies for Identifying, Prosecuting, and Treating Drug-Impaired Drivers: Symposium Report*, J. Michael Walsh, Leo A. Cangianelli, and Nei-Hyn Park, eds. The Walsh Group, June 2004.

Cassuto, Y. and D. Shinar. "Effects of THC on Driving Performance, Physiological State and Subjective Feelings Relative to Alcohol." *Accident, Analysis and Prevention*, v.40/3 (2007).

Goldberg, L., D. L. Elliot, D. MacKinnon, E. Moe, K. Kuehl, L. Nohre, and D. Lockwood. "Drug Testing Athletes to Prevent Substance Abuse." *Journal of Adolescent Health*, v.32 (2003).

Mehay, S. and N. J. Webb. "Workplace Drug Prevention Programs: Does Zero Tolerance Work?" *Applied Economics*, v.39 (2007).

Skiba, R. *Zero Tolerance, Zero Evidence: An Analysis of School Disciplinary Practice*. Indiana Education Policy Center, 2000.

ZIMELIDINE (ZELMID) CONTROVERSY

The controversy surrounding the licensing, marketing, and subsequent speedy withdrawal of the drug Zimelidine in the early 1980s is a case study in both the extraordinary promise of new drug research and the impact of revisionist data that leads ultimately to a field-wide reinvestigation of a drug's apparently promising profile. In this case, the story of Zimelidine offers an instance of the dangers of rushing drugs into use without sufficient study. In addition, the often incendiary controversy surrounding Zimelidine provides a clear picture of how the pharmaceutical industry can react efficiently and effectively, unhampered by concerns for profits or by paranoia over protecting brand identification. But can that reaction itself be too hasty? In the case of Zimelidine, despite being the product of years of methodical and careful research (among its earliest developers was a future Nobelist), its widespread use quickly revealed unsuspected and potentially dangerous side effects. The industry's quick and decisive response to the problems associated with the new drug, and that with the full cooperation of the parent company chiefly responsible for its development, provides an important contemporary template for how to proceed when data is presented that significantly undercuts a new drug's reliability, even in the face of years of testing and despite initially maintaining a highly favorable drug profile.

In retrospect, Zimelidine perhaps appeared too good to be true. Can the brain simply be told not to permit anxiety? Can the brain's neural system of messaging simply be rewired, redirected, essentially rerouted to prevent bad emotional responses from ever registering? Can a patient essentially be made happy? Zimelidine was initially researched (and licensed) as the world's first serotonin reuptake inhibitor antidepressant, a type of drug developed to treat psychiatric disorders, specifically depression. The brain communicates with the body through a highly developed system of cellular transmitters that essentially creates and sustains moods. Inhibitors, it was believed, could be used to counter the effects of depression by simply intercepting the serotonin transmitters within the brain cells themselves. Block the signal, block the depression. By inhibiting these neurotransmitters, by impacting and rerouting their signals, serotonin reuptake inhibitors appeared to reprogram the brain itself, realigning balance to lighten moods and in turn to significantly decrease the anxiety and emotional trauma associated with manic depression. (Zoloft is perhaps the most familiar serotonin reuptake inhibitor antidepressant prescribed today.) Although accepted and even standard in pharmaceutical field today, in the early 1980s research into this process was relatively new, and much less was understood about the possibility of drugs that could intercept and basically reprogram the brain to heighten a patient's receptivity to more positive emotional codes.

As early as 1971, teams of researchers in Sweden first proposed the molecular structure of what would be eventually developed as

Zimelidine. Historically, the first medical journal articles outlining the results of clinical trials with Zimelidine were published in mid-decade—the results appeared promising, indeed extraordinarily so. Research teams reported that carefully controlled clinical trials administering Zimelidine in patients with acute depression revealed such patients would experience a significant and relatively rapid decline in anxiety levels. In turn, this reduction in anxiety levels led to a decrease in general depression and a lessening of impulses given to moodiness or irritability. Without debating the ethics of essentially reprogramming patients, interfering with the brain functions and controlling emotional states, these clinicals offered abundant hope for patients that had long struggled with the effects of acute depression. And because the drug appeared not to encourage the usual side effects of drugs administered to combat depression—extreme fatigue, general listlessness, and often paralyzing catatonic indifference as well as a variety of potentially long-term cardiovascular impacts—Zimelidine was heralded as a real breakthrough, an authentic new direction in antidepression treatment. At last, the brain itself could be reordered, its most distressing message-impulses interdicted. That no less than the Swedish wunderkind Dr. Arvid Carlsson had worked on the research and development of the new drug only added to its prestige—his endorsement meant quite a bit. Carlsson at the time was perhaps the most-respected chemist and medical researcher in Scandinavia (he would later share the 2000 Nobel Prize in Medicine for his work in developing dopamine, a drug used successfully to combat the worst symptoms of Parkinson's disease). It appeared the pharmaceutical field was about to be realigned. In 1982, given the nearly universal endorsement among researchers of its potential benefits and its entirely favorable drug profile, Zimelidine was quickly approved for production and marketing in Sweden and in turn made available to the international market.

The drug proved an immediate success, and its parent company, the Swedish drug conglomerate Astra AB, quickly enjoyed international accolades for its groundbreaking drug. Patients reported immediate results—a lightening of mood, a diminishment in debilitating mood swings, a general stabilizing of emotional reactions. Zimelidine appeared to deliver on its promise. Patients reported not only a lessening of depression anxieties but a general lessening of an assortment of other phobias, including anxieties over closed-in spaces and even heights. Even more potentially important, initial research revealed significant success in elderly patients, a segment of the patient population that had been put at significant risk with other antidepressant regimens given their potential to negatively impact the heart. Although some patients, particularly patients without a significant history of antidepression treatments, reported a general lethargy while taking the drug and episodes of nausea early in the regimen, that appeared to be of minimal concern and not entirely unexpected when dealing for the first time with antidepressants.

But within the year, after more than a quarter of a million patients had already been prescribed Zimelidine (most with moderate to significant success), distressing indications pointed to a potential side effect to the drug. On average one out of every 10,000 patients who received Zimelidine evidenced symptoms consistent with Guillain-Barré syndrome, a relatively rare nervous system disorder in which patients experienced initially flu-like symptoms but that quickly degenerated into extreme paralysis in their extremities and the compromise of significant motor response within the neural system. Normally, that is in the broader field of patients of Guillain-Barré syndrome, the disease impacted only one in 500,000. Thus the difference with patients treated with Zimelidine was considered statistically significant, that is sufficient to warrant reconsideration of the drug's market approval. Guillain-Barré syndrome was seldom lethal, and in fact about 96% of treated patients recovered.

The medical community was alarmed that a drug effective in treating one disorder was creating other symptoms. There were further problems. What was found was that in rare cases—fewer than one out of 100,000 treated with Zimelidine—patients actually reported an excess of anxiety, indeed a significant percentage of those patients reported that under the drug protocol they had actually experienced worst depression manifestations, including genuine suicidal ideation. In short, the drug was enhancing and increasing the very psychological disorder it had been designed to control and contain. On September 17, 1983, less than eight months after the initial reports questioning the efficacy of Zimelidine, Astra AB agreed to withdraw the drug from its international markets.

The reaction was split. Many applauded the drug company's swift and decisive action—too often, they argued, drug companies would bury such damaging evidence and in some cases actually prevent that information from being accessed in the interests of preserving its profit margins, particularly when, as with Zimelidine, the immediate impact had registered so widely. But the response was not entirely favorable. Many found the action questionable at best, accusing Astra AB of kowtowing to a minority panic. Many doctors, particularly in Europe, took great exception to the action, calling it precipitous and unwarranted. The drug, they argued, had had far more positive effects and had, in fact, provided revolutionary treatments for depression. It had helped far, far more than it had hurt. Not surprisingly, even after Astra AB pulled the drug from its global enterprises, the drug was still made available in Sweden—and doctors, convinced of the drug's potential and unswayed by the relatively small percentage of patients with negative side effects, continued to prescribe the drug for depression disorders with the tacit understanding that doctors would be on the lookout for any evidence of extreme side effects and that doctors would caution patients that taking the drug, while it would far more likely help, might in fact cause just such a reaction. Doctors agreed that transparency would be the best approach—much as today with new drugs introduced to the marketplace, drug companies routinely provide cautions over potential negative effects that have been recorded in a relatively minor number of patients tested during clinicals. But the ban remained in place and, after a time, newer SSRIs, such as Fluvoxamine and Fluoxetine, were developed and subsequently endorsed by the U.S. Food and Drug Administration, and Zimelidine faded from prescriptions.

Joseph Dewey
Broward College

See Also: AstraZeneca; Thalidomide (Contergan) Controversy.

Further Readings

DrugBank. "Zimelidine." http://www.drugbank.ca/drugs/db04832.

Fagius, Jan. "Guillain-Barré Syndrome Following Zimeldine [sic] Treatment." *Journal of Neurology, Neurosurgery, and Psychiatry*, v.48 (1985).

Glossary

Abstinence: In the context of substance abuse and treatment, nonuse of alcohol or any illicit drugs, as well as nonabuse of medications normally obtained by prescription or over the counter.

Addiction: Combination of the physical dependence on, behavioral manifestations of the use of, and subjective sense of need and craving for a psychoactive substance, leading to compulsive use of the substance either for its positive effects or to avoid negative effects associated with abstinence from that substance.

ADME: Abbreviation for the four steps in a medicine's journey through the body: absorption, distribution, metabolism, and excretion.

Adverse Drug Reaction (ADR): In the preapproval clinical experience with a new medicinal product or its new usages, particularly as the therapeutic dose(s) may not be established, all noxious and unintended responses to a medicinal product related to any dose should be considered adverse drug reactions. The phrase "responses to a medicinal product" means that a causal relationship between a medicinal product and an adverse event is at least a reasonable possibility, that is, the relationship cannot be ruled out.

Adverse Event (AE): Any untoward or unfavorable medical occurrence in a human subject, including any abnormal sign (for example, abnormal physical exam or laboratory finding), symptom, or disease, temporally associated with the subject's participation in the research, whether or not considered related to the subject's participation in the research.

Agonist: A molecule that triggers a cellular response by interacting with a receptor.

Analgesic: A compound that alleviates pain without causing loss of consciousness. Opioid analgesics are a class of compounds that bind to specific receptors in the central nervous system to block the perception of pain or affect the emotional response to pain. Such compounds include opium and its derivatives, as well as a number of synthetic compounds.

Antibiotic: A substance that can kill or inhibit the growth of certain microorganisms.

Antibody: A protein of the immune system, produced in response to an antigen (a foreign, often disease-causing, substance).

Anti-Inflammatory: A drug's ability to reduce inflammation, which can cause soreness and swelling.

Antipyretic: Fever-reducing; the term comes from the Greek word *pyresis*, which means fire.

Audit: Independent on-site quality assurance of monitoring performed at clinical research sites (including pharmacies and laboratories). Auditors must be fully distinct and independent from entities providing site monitoring services.

Benzodiazepines: Group of medications having a common molecular structure and similar pharmacological activity, including antianxiety, sedative, hypnotic, amnestic, anticonvulsant, and muscle-relaxing effects. Benzodiazepines are among the most widely prescribed medications (e.g., diazepam, chlordiazepoxide, clonazepam, alprazolam, lorazepam).

Best-Treatment Practices: Methods determined, often by a consensus of experts, to be optimal for defined therapeutic situations. Such guidelines usually are based on both an analysis of published research findings and the experience of experts.

Bioavailability: The ability of a drug or other chemical to be taken up by the body and made available in the tissue where it is needed.

Bioinformatics: A field of research that relies on computers to store and analyze large amounts of biological data.

Biological Product: Any virus, therapeutic serum, toxin, antitoxin, or analogous product available to prevent, treat, or cure diseases or injuries in man. The terms *biological product* or *biologic* are deemed to be synonymous within DAIDS policies.

Biotransformation: The conversion of a substance from one form to another by the actions of organisms or enzymes.

Blinding: See *Masking*.

Blood–Brain Barrier: A blockade consisting of cells and small blood vessels that limits the movement of substances from the bloodstream into the brain.

Carcinogen: Any substance that, when exposed to living tissue, may cause cancer.

Case History: A detailed account of relevant information gathered about a subject. This information includes the case report forms and supporting data including, for example, signed and dated consent forms and medical records, including, for example, progress notes of the physician, the individual's hospital chart(s), and the nurses' notes, as required for both IND and IDE clinical trials.

Causality Assessment: An evaluation performed by a medical professional concerning the likelihood that a therapy or product under study caused or contributed to an adverse event.

Clinical Development Plan: A document that describes the collection of clinical studies that are to be performed in sequence, or in parallel, with a particular active substance, device, procedure, or treatment strategy, typically with the intention of submitting them as part of an application for a marketing authorization. The plan should have appropriate decision points and allow modification as knowledge accumulates.

Clinical Investigation: Any experiment that involves a test article and one or more human subjects, and that either must meet the requirements for prior submission to the U.S. Food and Drug Administration (FDA), or the results of which are intended to be later submitted to, or held for inspection by, the FDA as part of an application for a research or marketing permit. FDA has defined clinical investigation to be synonymous with research.

Clinical Investigator: A qualified professional who conducts clinical research activities, including collaboration and information exchange with community representatives, recruitment, enrollment, protocol visit conduct, management of study products, assessment and reporting of critical events, collection and management of clinical research data, communication of data, and creation, maintenance, and storage of research records, including participant files, source documents, regulatory files, subject identification information, clinical reports, and case report forms.

Clinical Research: Research conducted on participants, material, or data of human origin with an identifiable person as the source. Clinical research includes exploratory, behavioral, and observational studies. All clinical trials are a subset of clinical research.

Clinical Research Records: The records that describe or record the methods, conduct, and/or results of a clinical trial, and the actions taken. Examples of these documents may include, but are not limited to, all essential and source documents listed in the DAIDS Policy on Essential Documents Appendix. The records may be in any form, including written, electronic, magnetic, and optical records; and scans, X-rays, and electrocardiograms. Clinical research records include case histories and source documents.

Clinical Significance: Change in a subject's clinical condition regarded as important whether or not due to the test intervention. Some statistically significant changes (in blood tests, for example) have no clinical significance. In research, the criterion or criteria for clinical significance should be stated in the protocol.

Clinical Trial: A prospective study of human subjects designed to answer questions about biomedical or behavioral interventions, for example, drugs, treatments, devices, or new ways of using known treatments to determine whether they are safe and effective.

Closed Formulary: Closed formularies are exclusive lists of specific drugs that often limit prescribers to only some of the commercially available products in each therapeutic class. Drugs that do not appear on the list of approved products (nonformulary drugs) are not covered by the health plan, PBM, or employer, and patients must pay additional out-of-pocket expenses to obtain nonformulary prescriptions (or use a prior approval or nonformulary exceptions process).

Community Advisory Board (CAB): Community Advisory Board (CAB) is an active group representing the local population(s) impacted by human immunodeficiency virus/acquired immunodeficiency syndrome (HIV/AIDS). CAB members work in close communication with clinical treatment unit investigators and staff to include the local perspective in the implementation of a clinical research plan.

Conflict of Interest (COI): A situation when someone has or is perceived to have competing professional obligations or personal or financial interests that would make it difficult to fulfill his duties fairly.

Control: The comparator against which the study treatment is evaluated (e.g., concurrent [placebo, no treatment, dose-response, active], and external [historical, published literature]).

Critical Event: Any unanticipated, study-related incident that causes or increases the risk of harm to participants or others, or has a significant adverse impact on study outcomes or integrity. A single incident that is determined to be a critical event may represent more than one class of critical event.

Cross-Tolerance: Condition in which repeated administration of a drug results in diminished effects, not only for that drug but also for one or more drugs from a similar class to which the individual has not been exposed recently.

Cyclooxygenase: An enzyme, also known as COX, that makes prostaglandins from a molecule called arachidonic acid; the molecular target of nonsteroidal anti-inflammatory drugs.

Data Integrity: A dimension of data contributing to its trustworthiness and pertaining to the systems and processes for data capture, correction, maintenance, transmission, and retention. Key elements of data integrity include security, privacy, access controls, a continuous pedigree from capture to archive, stability (of values, of attribution), protection against loss or destruction, ease of review by users responsible for data quality, proper operation and validation of systems, and training of users.

Declaration of Helsinki: A set of recommendations or basic principles that guide medical doctors in the conduct of biomedical research involving human subjects. It was originally adopted by the 18th World Medical Assembly (Helsinki, Finland, 1964) and recently revised (52nd WMA General Assembly, Edinburgh, Scotland, October 2000).

Dependence: The state of physical adaptation that is manifested by a drug class–specific withdrawal syndrome that can be produced by abrupt cessation, rapid dose reduction, and/or decreasing blood level of a substance and/or administration of an antagonist.

Detoxification: Treatment for addiction to an illicit substance in which the substance is eliminated gradually from a patient's body while various types and levels of reinforcing treatment are provided to alleviate adverse physical or psychological reactions to the withdrawal process.

Drug: An article intended for use in the diagnosis, cure, mitigation, treatment, or prevention of disease in man or other animals.

Drug Testing: The examination of an individual to determine the presence or absence of illicit or nonprescribed drugs or alcohol, or to confirm maintenance levels of treatment medications.

Drug Utilization Review (DUR): Also called drug use evaluation, or medication use evaluation, it is a formal performance improvement program for assessing data on drug use against explicit, prospective standards (criteria) and, as necessary, introducing remedial strategies to achieve some desired end.

Effectiveness: The capacity of a drug or treatment (study intervention) to produce beneficial effects on the course or duration of a disease at the dose tested and against the illness (and patient population) for which it is designed. Effectiveness measures how well a study intervention works under real-life conditions, and takes into account tolerability of a drug, acceptability of a behavioral intervention, ease of use, and so on.

Efficacy: The measure of a study intervention's desired influence on a disease or condition as demonstrated by substantial evidence from adequate and well-controlled investigations. Efficacy measures how well a study intervention works in an ideal, controlled setting.

Elimination Half-Life: The time required after administration of a substance (e.g., methadone) for one-half the dose to leave the body. Elimination half-life affects the duration of action of a substance or medication and can be influenced by patient factors such as absorption rate, variable metabolism and protein binding, changes in urinary pH, concomitant medications, diet, physical condition, age, pregnancy, and even use of vitamins and herbal products.

Enzyme: A molecule (usually a protein) that speeds up, or catalyzes, a chemical reaction without being permanently altered or consumed.

Equivalence Trial: A trial with the primary objective of showing that the response to two or more treatments differs by an amount that is clinically unimportant. This is usually demonstrated by showing that the true treatment difference is likely to lie between a lower and an upper equivalence margin of clinically acceptable differences.

Exclusion Criteria: List of characteristics in a protocol, any one of which may exclude a potential subject from participation in a study.

Fabrication: Making up data or results and recording or reporting them.

Falsification: Manipulating research materials, equipment, or processes, or changing or omitting data or results such that the research is not accurately represented in the research record.

Generalizability: The extent to which the findings of a clinical trial can be reliably extrapolated from the subjects who participated in the trial to a broader patient population and a broader range of clinical settings.

Generic Substitution: The substitution of drug products that contain the same active, chemically identical ingredient(s) and are identical in strength, concentration, dosage form, and route of administration to the drug product prescribed.

Good Clinical Practice (GCP): An international ethical and scientific quality standard for designing, conducting, recording, and reporting trials that involve the participation of human subjects.

Hormone: A messenger molecule that helps coordinate the actions of various tissues; made in one part of the body and transported, via the bloodstream, to tissues and organs elsewhere in the body.

Inclusion Criteria: The criteria in a protocol that prospective subjects must meet to be eligible for participation in a study. Exclusion and inclusion criteria together define the study population.

Independent Safety Monitor: The physician or other appropriate expert who is independent of the study and available to review serious adverse events (SAEs) and other safety data in a timely fashion and recommends appropriate actions to the study team and any governing organizations.

Informed Consent Process: A process by which a participant voluntarily confirms his or her willingness to participate in a particular study after having been informed of all aspects of the trial that are relevant to the participant's decision to participate.

Institutional Review Board/Ethics Committee (IRB/EC): The board, committee, or other group formally designated by an institution to review, to approve the initiation of, and to conduct periodic review of research involving human subjects. The primary purpose of such review is to assure the protection of the rights and welfare of participants in research.

Intention to Treat: A strategy for analyzing data in which all participants are included in the group to which they were assigned, whether or not they completed the intervention given to the group. Intention-to-treat analysis prevents bias caused by the loss of participants, which may disrupt the baseline equivalence established by random assignment and which may reflect nonadherence to the protocol.

International Conference on Harmonisation (ICH) Guidelines: A set of guidelines developed, through a collaboration between the FDA and regulatory agencies in Japan and the European Union, to "harmonize" regulatory requirements to produce marketing applications acceptable to the United States, Japan, and the countries of the European Union.

Investigational Device Exemption (IDE): Analogous to an Investigational New Drug (IND), an Investigational Device Exemption (IDE) allows an unapproved medical device to be used for investigational purposes.

Investigational New Drug (IND): A drug or biological product that is used in a clinical investigation.

Masking: Also known as blinding, a procedure in which one or more parties to the trial are kept unaware of the treatment assignment(s). Single masked usually refers to the subject(s) being unaware, and double masked usually refers to the subject(s), investigator(s), monitor, and, in some cases, data analyst(s) being unaware of the treatment assignment(s).

Medically Supervised Withdrawal: In the context of the treatment of opiate use and treatment, dispensing of a maintenance medication in gradually decreasing doses to alleviate adverse physical or psychological effects incident to withdrawal from the continuous or sustained use of opioid drugs. The purpose of medically supervised withdrawal is to bring a patient maintained on maintenance medication to a medication-free state within a target period.

Metabolite: A chemical intermediate in metabolic reactions; a product of metabolism.

Methadone: The most frequently used opioid agonist medication. Methadone is a synthetic opioid that binds to mu (μ)-opiate receptors and produces a range of μ-agonist effects similar to those of short-acting opioids such as morphine and heroin.

Minimal Risk: The probability and magnitude of harm or discomfort anticipated in the research are not greater in and of themselves than those ordinarily encountered in daily life or during the performance of routine physical or psychological examinations or tests.

Model Organism: A bacterium, animal, or plant used by scientists to study basic research questions; common model organisms include yeast, flies, worms, frogs, and fish.

Monitors: In a clinical trial, individuals qualified by education or experience, whose primary role is to ensure compliance with the applicable regulations, policies, and standard procedures, as well as compliance with the study protocol as approved by the institutional review board or research ethics board.

Monoclonal Antibody: An antibody that recognizes only one type of antigen; sometimes used as immunotherapy to treat diseases such as cancer.

Neurotransmitter: A chemical messenger that allows neurons (nerve cells) to communicate with each other and with other cells.

Nonsteroidal Anti-Inflammatory Drug (NSAID): Any of a class of drugs that reduces pain, fever, or inflammation by interfering with the synthesis of prostaglandins.

Observational Study: A type of study in which individuals are observed or certain outcomes are measured, but no treatments or interventions are assigned by the study.

Open or Unrestricted Formulary: An open formulary is a very comprehensive listing of medications typically offering almost every commercially available product in each therapeutic category. Physicians who prescribe from an open formulary are not restricted and may prescribe virtually any drug. Payers, including employers, health plans, and third-party administrators, provide coverage for all medications since there are no restrictions.

Opiate Receptors: Areas on cell surfaces in the central nervous system that are activated by opioid molecules to produce the effects associated with opioid use, such as euphoria and analgesia. Opiate receptors are activated or blocked by opioid agonist or antagonist medications, respectively, to mediate the effects of opioids on the body. Mu (μ)- and kappa (κ)-opiate receptor groups principally are involved in this activity.

Opioid: Natural derivative of opium or synthetic psychoactive substance that has effects similar to morphine or is capable of conversion into a drug having such effects. One effect of opioid drugs is their addiction-forming or addiction-sustaining liability.

Partially/Selectively Closed Formulary: These are formulary hybrids that limit prescribing choices within certain therapeutic classes and offering unlimited choice within other drug classes. Such formularies direct prescribers to preferred agents within therapeutic classes, which may be included in a treatment protocol or clinical guideline. In some cases, entire categories, such as drugs used solely for cosmetic purposes, may be closed to prevent payment for those drugs that are excluded from coverage.

Participant: In clinical trials, a living individual about whom an investigator conducting research obtains (1) data through intervention or interaction with the individual or (2) identifiable private information.

Patient-Treatment Matching: Process of individualizing therapeutic resources to patient needs and preferences, ideally by a participatory process involving both the treatment provider and patient.

Pharmacodynamics: The study of how drugs act at target sites of action in the body.

Pharmacogenomics: Science that examines inherited variations in genes that dictate drug response and explores the ways such variations can be used to predict whether a person will respond favorably, adversely, or not at all to an investigational product.

Pharmacokinetics: The study of how the body absorbs, distributes, breaks down, and eliminates drugs.

Pharmacology: Science that addresses the origin, nature, chemistry, effects, and uses of medications and drugs.

Pharmacopoeia: A compendium of drug standards for purity and strength.

Pharmacotherapy: Treatment of disease with prescribed medications.

Pharmacovigilance: All scientific and data gathering activities relating to the detection, assessment, and understanding of adverse events.

Prevalence: Number of cases of a disease in a population, either at a point in time (point prevalence) or over a period (period prevalence). Prevalence rate is the fraction of people in a population who have a disease or condition at one time. (The numerator of the rate is the number of existing cases of the condition at a specified time, and the denominator is the total population.)

Principal Investigator (PI): In a research context, the qualified person designated by the applicant institution to direct the funded research program. PIs oversee the scientific and technical aspects of an award and the day-to-day management of the research.

Prostaglandins: Any of a class of hormone-like, fat-soluble, regulatory molecules made from fatty acids such as arachidonic acid; prostaglandins participate in diverse body functions, and their production is blocked by NSAIDs.

Protocol: A document that describes the objective(s), design, methodology, statistical considerations, and organization of a trial. The protocol usually also gives the background and rationale for the trial, but these could be provided in other protocol-referenced documents.

Quality Assurance (QA): A periodic, systematic, objective, and comprehensive examination of the total work effort to determine the level of compliance with accepted Good Clinical Practice (GCP) standards. For example, in a clinical trial, a monthly peer review of source documents compared to case report form pages to determine adherence to protocol requirements.

Quality Control (QC): The real-time, ongoing (day-to-day) observation and documentation of a site's work processes to ensure that accepted procedures are being followed. For example, in a clinical trial, reviewing demographic information for accuracy on each Case Report Form (CRF) page prior to entry into the database.

Quality Management: The overall system that includes all activities involved in quality assurance and quality control during a clinical trial, including the assignment of roles and responsibilities, the reporting of results, and the resolution of issues identified during the review.

Receptor: A specialized molecule that receives information from the environment and conveys it to other parts of the cell; the information is transmitted by a specific chemical that must fit the receptor, like a key in a lock.

Research Hypothesis: The proposition that a study sets out to support (or disprove); for example, "blood pressure will be lowered by [specific endpoint] in subjects who receive the test product." The null hypothesis is the converse to what the researcher expects to happen in reference to the target outcome. Inferential statistical analyses are designed around accepting or rejecting the null hypothesis.

Research Misconduct: Fabrication, falsification, or plagiarism in proposing, performing, or reviewing research, or in reporting research results. Research misconduct does not include honest error or differences of opinion.

Sample Informed Consent (SIC): In a clinical trial, an informed consent developed by the protocol team for a specific protocol that will help guide participating sites in the development of their site-specific informed consent.

Sedative: Medication with central nervous system sedating and tranquilizing properties. An example is any of the benzodiazepines.

Most sedatives also promote sleep. Overdoses of sedatives can lead to dangerous respiratory depression (slowed breathing).

Self-Medication: Medically unsanctioned use of drugs by a person to relieve any of a variety of problems (e.g., pain, depression).

Serious Adverse Drug Experience: Any adverse drug experience occurring at any dose that results in any of the following outcomes: death, a life-threatening adverse drug experience, inpatient hospitalization or prolongation of existing hospitalization, a persistent or significant disability/incapacity, or a congenital anomaly/birth defect. Important medical events that may not result in death, be life threatening, or require hospitalization may be considered a serious adverse drug experience when, based upon appropriate medical judgment, they may jeopardize the patient or subject and may require medical or surgical intervention to prevent one of the outcomes listed in this definition.

Serious Adverse Event (SAE): Any untoward medical occurrence that at any dose results in death, is life threatening, requires inpatient hospitalization or prolongation of existing hospitalization, results in persistent or significant disability/incapacity, or is a congenital anomaly/birth defect. This includes important medical events that may not be immediately life threatening or result in death or hospitalization but may jeopardize the patient or may require intervention to prevent one of the outcomes listed in the definition above.

Serum Half-Life: The time required for the amount of a compound (e.g., an opioid) in blood serum to be halved through metabolism or excretion.

Side Effect: Consequence (especially an adverse result) other than that for which a drug is used—especially the result produced on a tissue or organ system other than that being targeted.

Site of Action: The place in the body where a drug exerts its effects.

Site-Specific Informed Consent: An informed consent developed by a participating site based upon the sample informed consent that is reviewed and approved by the site's designated IRB/IEC and is used to consent subjects at the site for a specific clinical trial.

Source Data: All information in original records and certified copies of original records of clinical findings, observations, or other activities in a study necessary for the reconstruction and evaluation of a clinical trial. Source data are contained in source documents (original records or certified copies).

Source Documents: The original documents, data, and records containing clinical findings, observations, or other activities in a clinical research study that allows the reconstruction and evaluation of the study. Examples of source documents include hospital records, clinical and office charts, laboratory notes, memoranda, subjects' diaries or evaluation checklists, pharmacy dispensing records, recorded data from automated instruments, copies or transcriptions certified after verification as being accurate and complete, microfiches, photographic negatives, microfilm or magnetic media, X-rays, subject files, and records kept at the pharmacy, at the laboratories, and at medico-technical departments involved in the clinical trial.

Sponsor: A person (individual, corporation, or agency) who initiates a clinical investigation, but who does not actually conduct the investigation.

Sponsor-Investigator: An individual who both initiates and actually conducts, alone or with others, a clinical investigation. For example, under whose immediate direction the test article is administered, dispensed to, or used involving a subject and who also submitted the IND.

Standard Operating Procedures (SOPs): Written procedures designed to ensure data and analysis quality by requiring uniform performance of specific functions by the group(s) that fall within their scope. An SOP is designed to provide a high-level overview of tasks or functions performed. An SOP, by definition, must be followed unless a documented exception is approved.

Step Protocol: A treatment protocol that recommends beginning a trial of drug therapy for a medical condition with one drug or class of drugs (often of lower cost or risk) before proceeding to other drugs or drug classes.

Steroid: A type of molecule that has a multiple ring structure, with the rings sharing molecules of carbon.

Structural Biology: A field of study dedicated to determining the three-dimensional structures of biological molecules to better understand the function of these molecules.

Subject: A living individual about whom an investigator conducting research obtains (1) data through intervention or interaction with the individual or (2) identifiable private information. For research conducted under U.S. Food and Drug Administration (FDA) regulations, a subject is an individual who is or becomes a participant in research, either as a recipient of the test article or as a control. A subject may be either a healthy individual or a patient.

Substance Use Disorder: Frequently referred to as substance abuse or dependence, it is a maladaptive pattern of drug or alcohol use manifested by recurrent, significant adverse consequences related to the repeated use of these drugs or alcohol. The substance-related problem must have persisted and occurred repeatedly during a 12-month period. It can occur sporadically and mainly be associated with social or interpersonal problems, or it can occur regularly and be associated with medical and mental problems, often including tolerance and withdrawal.

Suspected Unexpected Serious Adverse Reaction (SUSAR): A suspected unexpected serious adverse reaction (SUSAR) in a clinical trial is an event that is (1) serious, (2) related (i.e., there is a reasonable possibility that the adverse event may be related to the study agent), and (3) unexpected.

Therapeutic Alternates: Drug products differing in composition or in their basic drug entity, but of the same pharmacological and/or therapeutic class, that are considered to have very similar pharmacological and therapeutic activities and adverse reaction profiles when administered to patients in therapeutically equivalent doses.

Therapeutic Drug: A drug used to treat a disease or condition; contrast with drug of abuse.

Therapeutic Equivalence: Similar pharmacological and therapeutic activity of drugs.

Toxicology: The study of how poisonous substances interact with living organisms.

Unanticipated Problems: Unanticipated problems involving risks to subjects or others, any serious or continuing noncompliance with policy requirements or determinations of the internal review board (IRB), and any suspension or termination of IRB approval.

Unanticipated Problems Involving Risk to Subjects or Others: Any adverse event occurring in one or more subjects in a research protocol, the nature, severity, or frequency of which suggests the risk is (1) unexpected given the research procedures that are described in the protocol-related documents, and the characteristics of the subject population being studied; and (2) related or possibly related to a subject's participation in the research, and suggests that the research places subjects or others at a greater risk of harm than was previously known or recognized.

Unexpected Adverse Drug Experience: Any adverse drug experience, the specificity or severity of which is not consistent with the current investigator brochure; or, if an investigator brochure is not required or available, the specificity or severity of which is not consistent with the risk information described in the general investigational plan or elsewhere in the current application, as amended.

Unexpected Adverse Event: Any adverse event occurring in one or more subjects in a research protocol, the nature, severity, or frequency of which is not consistent with either (1) the known or foreseeable risk of adverse events associated with the procedures involved in the research that are described in (a) the protocol-related documents, such as the IRB-approved research protocol, any applicable investigator brochure, and the current IRB-approved informed consent document, and (b) other relevant sources of information, such as product labeling and package inserts; or (2) the expected natural progression of any underlying disease, disorder, or condition of the subject(s) experiencing the adverse event and the subject's predisposing risk factor profile for the adverse event.

U.S. Food and Drug Administration (FDA): A public health agency within the United States Department of Health and Human Services. FDA's mission is to promote and protect public health by helping safe and effective products reach the market in a timely way and monitoring of products for continued safety after they are in use as authorized by the Federal Food, Drug, and Cosmetic Act. The agency regulates all clinical investigations in support of marketing applications.

Vaccine and Prevention Research Program (VPRP): The VPRP is a program within the Division of AIDS of the National Institute of Allergy and Infectious Diseases (DAIDS) in the United States that supports the discovery and development of vaccines and other biomedical and behavioral interventions to prevent acquired immunodeficiency syndrome (AIDS).

Virus: An infectious agent composed of a protein coat around a DNA or RNA core; to reproduce, viruses depend on living cells.

X-Ray Crystallography: A technique used to determine the detailed, three-dimensional structure of molecules based on the scattering of X-rays through a crystal of the molecule.

Source: Adapted from publications of the National Institutes of Health and other sources.

Resource Guide

Books

Abraham, John and Helen Lawton Smith, eds. *Regulation of the Pharmaceutical Industry*. New York: Palgrave Macmillan, 2003.

Al-Achi, Antoine. *An Introduction to Botanical Medicines: History, Science, Uses, and Dangers*. Westport, CT: Praeger Publishers, 2008.

Amyes, Sebastian G. B. *Magic Bullets, Lost Horizons: The Rise and Fall of Antibiotics*. New York: Taylor & Francis, 2001.

Arnold, Ken and Danielle Olsen, eds. *Medicine Man: The Forgotten Museum of Henry Welcome*. London: British Museum Press, 2003.

Arnold, Renee J. G., ed. *Pharmacoeconomics: From Theory to Practice*. Boca Raton, FL: Taylor & Francis, 2010.

Arsdall, Anne and Timothy Graham, eds. *Herbs and Healers From the Ancient Mediterranean Through the Medieval West: Essays in Honor of John M. Riddle*. Burlington, VT: Ashgate, 2012.

Attaran, Amir and Brigitte Granville. *Delivering Essential Medicines*. London: Chatham House, 2004.

Bagchi, Debasis and Harry G. Preuss, eds. *Phytopharmaceuticals in Cancer Chemoprevention*. Boca Raton, FL: CRC Press, 2005.

Barnard, Marina. *Drug Addictions and Families*. Philadelphia, PA: Jessica Kingsley Publishers, 2009.

Beamish, Rob. *Steroids: A New Look at Performance-Enhancing Drugs*. Santa Barbara, CA: Praeger, 2011.

Berry, Ira R. and Robert P. Martin. *The Pharmaceutical Regulatory Process*, 2nd ed. New York: Informa Healthcare, 2008.

Bing, Eric G. and Marc J. Epstein. *Pharmacy on a Bicycle: Innovative Solutions to Global Health and Poverty*. San Francisco: Berrett-Koehler, 2013.

Bolton, Sanford. *Pharmaceutical Statistics: Practical and Clinical Applications*, 5th ed. New York: Informa Healthcare USA, 2010.

Bonamin, Leonia Villano, ed. *Signals and Images: Contributions and Contradiction About High Dilution Research*. New York: Springer, 2008.

Bouchard, Ron A. *Patently Innovative: How Pharmaceutical Firms Use Emerging Patent Law to Extend Monopolies on Blockbuster Drugs*. Oxford: Biohealthcare, 2012.

Brachmachari, Goutam, ed. *Chemistry and Pharmacology of Naturally Occurring Bioactive Compounds*. Boca Raton, FL: CRC Press, Taylor & Francis Group, 2013.

Brody, Howard. *Hooked: Ethics, the Medical Profession, and the Pharmaceutical Industry*. Lanham, MD: Rowman & Littlefield, 2007.

Carpinella, Maria Cecilia and Mahendra Rai, eds. *Novel Therapeutic Agents From Plants*. Enfield, NH: Science Publishers, 2009.

Chase, Kate. *Buying Rx Drugs Online: Avoiding a Prescription for Disaster*. Boston: Thomson, 2005.

Chaudhuri, Sudip. *The WTO and India's Pharmaceuticals Industry: Patent Protection, TRIPS, and Developing Countries.* New Delhi: Oxford University Press, 2005.

Cho, William C. S., ed. *Evidence-Based Anticancer Materia Medica.* New York: Sprinter, 2011.

Chow, Shein-Chung. *Controversial Statistical Issues in Clinical Trials.* Boca Raton, FL: CRC Press, 2011.

Clark, Patricia Ann. *A Cretan Healer's Handbook in the Byzantine Tradition: Text, Translation, and Commentary.* Burlington, VT: Ashgate, 2011.

Cohen, Jillian Clare, Patricia Illingworth, and Udo Schuklenk, eds. *The Power of Pills: Social, Ethical, and Legal Issues in Drug Development, Marketing, and Pricing.* Ann Arbor, MI: Pluto, 2006.

Cragg, Gordon M., David G. I. Kingston, and David J. Newman, eds. *Anticancer Agents from Natural Products.* Boca Raton, FL: Taylor & Francis, 2005.

Craig, David. *Familiar Medicine: Everyday Health Knowledge and Practice in Today's Vietnam.* Honolulu: University of Hawaii Press, 2002.

Daemmrich, Arthur A. *Pharmacopolitics: Drug Regulation in the United States and Germany.* Chapel Hill: University of North Carolina Press, 2004.

Daniel, M. *Medicinal Plants: Chemistry and Properties.* Enfield, NH: Science Publishers, 2006.

Darke, Shane. *The Life of the Heroin User: Typical Beginnings, Trajectories and Outcomes.* New York: Cambridge University Press, 2011.

Dasgupta, Amitava. *Beating Drug Tests and Defending Positive Results: A Toxicologist's Perspective.* New York: Humana Press, 2010.

Dasgupta, Amitava. *Effects of Herbal Supplements in Medicine.* New York: Walter de Gruyter, 2011.

David, Paul. *A Guide to the World Anti-Doping Code: The Fight for the Spirit of Sport.* New York: Cambridge University Press, 2008.

Denning, Patt, Jeannie Little, and Adina Glickman. *Over the Influence: The Harm Reduction Guide for Managing Drugs and Alcohol.* New York: Guilford, 2004.

Dewick, Paul M. *Medicinal Natural Products: A Biosynthetic Approach,* 3rd ed. Chichester, West Sussex: Wiley, 2009.

Dietrich, Alexa S. *The Drug Company Next Door: Pollution, Jobs, and Community Health in Puerto Rico.* New York: NYU Press, 2013.

Dreyfuss, Rochelle C. and Cesar Rodriguez-Garavito, eds. *Balancing Wealth and Health: The Battle Over Intellectual Property and Access to Medicines in Latin America.* Oxford: Oxford University Press, 2014.

Duffin, C. J., ed. *A History of Geology and Medicine.* London: The Geological Society, 2013.

Dukes, M. N. G., John Braithwaite, and J. P. Moloney. *Pharmaceuticals, Corporate Crime and Public Health.* Cheltenham, UK: Edward Elgar Publishing, 2014.

Eban, Katherine. *Dangerous Doses: How Counterfeiters Are Contaminating America's Drug Supply.* Orlando, FL: Harcourt, 2005.

Eliassen, Lars P., ed. *Nonprescription Drugs: Considering a New Class for Behind-the-Counter Drugs.* New York: Nova Science Publishers, 2010.

Etkin, Nina L. *Edible Medicines: An Ethnopharmacology of Food.* Tucson: University of Arizona Press, 2006.

Farooqui, Akhlaq A. and Tahira Faroqui, eds. *Phytochemicals and Human Health: Pharmacological and Molecular Aspects.* New York: Nova Science Publishers, 2011.

Finegold, David L., ed. *Bioindustry Ethics.* Boston: Elsevier Academic Press, 2005.

Flannery, Michael A. *Civil War Pharmacy: A History of Drugs, Drug Supply and*

Provision, and Therapeutics for the Union and Confederacy. New York: Pharmaceutical Products Press, 2004.

Forman, Lisa and Jillian Clare Kohler, eds. *Access to Medicines as a Human Right: Implications for Pharmaceutical Industry Responsibility.* Toronto: University of Toronto Press, 2012.

Freye, Enno. *Pharmacology and Abuse of Cocaine, Amphetamines, Ecstasy and Related Designer Drugs: A Comprehensive Review on Their Mode of Action, Treatment of Abuse and Intoxication.* Dordrecht, Netherlands: Springer, 2009.

Furdell, Elizabeth Lane. *Fatal Thirst: Diabetes in Britain Until Insulin.* Boston: Brill, 2009.

Genillous, Olga and Francisca Vicente, eds. *Drug Discovery from Natural Products.* Cambridge, UK: Royal Society of Chemistry, 2012.

Gerlach, Manfred. *Psychiatric Drugs in Children and Adolescents: Basic Pharmacology and Practical Applications.* Vienna: Springer, 2014.

Goozner, Merrill. *The $800 Million Pill: The Truth Behind the Cost of New Drugs.* Berkeley: University of California Press, 2004.

Gould, Ian M. and Jos. W. M. van der Meer, eds. *Antibiotic Policies: Controlling Hospital Acquired Infection.* New York: Springer, 2011.

Grace, Fergal and Julien S. Baker, eds. *Perspectives on Anabolic Androgenic Steroids (AAS) and Doping in Sport and Health.* New York: Nova Science Publishers, 2012.

Greene, William. *The Emergence of India's Pharmaceutical Industry and Implications for the U.S. Generic Drug Market.* Washington, DC: U.S. International Trade Commission, 2007.

Greenfield, Robert. *Timothy Leary: A Biography.* Orlando, FL: Harcourt, 2006.

Griffith, John, Heleen Weyers, and Maurice Adams. *Euthanasia and Law in Europe.* Oxford: Hart Publishing, 2008.

Habenicht, Ursula F. and R. John Aitken, eds. *Fertility Control.* London: Springer, 2010.

Halperin, John J., ed. *Lyme Disease: An Evidence-Based Approach.* Cambridge, MA: CABI, 2011.

Hehmeyer, Ingrid and Hanne Schonig, eds. *Herbal Medicine in Yemen: Traditional Knowledge and Practice, and Their Value for Today's World.* Boston: Brill, 2012.

Hermann, Andrea M. *One Political Economy, One Competitive Strategy? Comparing Pharmaceutical Firms in Germany, Italy, and the UK.* New York: Oxford University Press, 2008.

Heyman, Gene M. *Addiction: A Disorder of Choice.* Cambridge, MA: Harvard University Press, 2009.

Higgs, John. *I Have America Surrounded: The Life of Timothy Leary.* Fort Lee, NJ: Barricade Books, 2006.

Ho, Cynthia M. *Access to Medicine in the Global Economy: International Agreements on Patents and Related Rights.* New York: Oxford University Press, 2011.

Hollen, Kathryn H. *Encyclopedia of Addictions.* Westport, CT: Greenwood Press, 2009.

Humi, Raymond A. *Pharmaceutical Competitive Intelligence for the Regulatory Affairs Professional.* New York: Springer, 2012.

Institute of Medicine, Committee on HIV Screening and Access to Care. *HIV Screening and Access to Care: Exploring the Impact of Policies on Access and Provision of HIV Care.* Washington, DC: National Academies Press, 2011.

Institute of Medicine, Committee on the Review of the National Immunization Program's Research Procedures and Data Sharing Programs. *Vaccine Safety Research, Data Access, and Public Trust.* Washington, DC: National Academies Press, 2005.

Iwu, Maurice M. *Handbook of African Medicinal Plants,* 2nd ed. Boca Raton, FL: CRC Press, 2014.

Iwu, Maurice M. and Jacqueline C. Wootton, eds. *Ethnomedicines and Drug Discovery.* New York: Elsevier, 2002.

Jackson, Emily and John Keown. *Debating Euthanasia.* Portland, OR: Hart Publishing, 2012.

Karch, Steven B., ed. *Pharmacokinetics and Pharmacodyamics of Abused Drugs.* Boca Raton, FL: CRC Press, 2008.

Kilic, Burcu. *Boosting Pharmaceutical Innovation in the Post-TRIPS Era: Real-Life Lessons for the Developing World.* Cheltenham, UK: Edward Elgar, 2014.

Kirschmann, Anne Taylor. *A Vital Force: Women in American Homeopathy.* New Brunswick, NJ: Rutgers University Press, 2004.

Kitta, Andrea. *Vaccination and Public Concern in History: Legend, Rumor, and Risk Perception.* New York: Routledge, 2012.

Kronenfeld, Jennie J. *Medicare.* Santa Barbara, CA: Greenwood, 2011.

Kuanpoth, Jakkrit. *Patent Rights in Pharmaceuticals in Developing Countries: Major Challenges for the Future.* Northampton, MA: Edward Elgar, 2010.

Kurtz, Lisa A. *Understanding Controversial Therapies for Children With Autism, Attention Deficit Disorder, and Other Learning Disabilities: A Guide to Complementary and Alternative Medicine.* Philadelphia, PA: Jessica Kingsley Publishers, 2008.

LaMattina, John L. *Devalued and Distrusted: Can the Pharmaceutical Industry Restore Its Broken Image?* Hoboken, NJ: John Wiley & Sons, 2013.

Larson, Richard S., ed. *Bioinformatics and Drug Discovery.* New York: Humana Press, 2012.

Lattin, Don. *The Harvard Psychedelic Club: How Timothy Leary, Ram Dass, Huston Smith, and Andrew Weil Killed the Fifties and Ushered in a New Age for America.* New York: HarperOne, 2010.

Lev, Efraim and Zohar Amar. *Practical Materia Medica of the Medieval Eastern Mediterranean According to the Cairo Genizah.* Boston: Brill, 2008.

Lewis, Walter H. and Memory P. F. Elvin-Lewis, 2nd ed. *Medical Botany: Plants Affecting Human Health.* Hoboken, NJ: John Wiley & Sons, 2003.

Li, Jie Jack. *Triumph of the Heart: The Story of Statins.* New York: Oxford University Press, 2009.

Liu, Shao-hua. *Passage to Manhood: Youth Migration, Heroin, and AIDS in Southwest China.* Stanford, CA: Stanford University Press, 2011.

Lu, Hong, Terrance D. Miethe, and Bin Liang. *China's Drug Practice and Policies: Regulating Controlled Substances in a Global Content.* Burlington, VT: Ashgate Publishing, 2009.

Macdonald, Dave. *Drugs in Afghanistan: Opium, Outlaws, and Scorpion Tales.* London: Pluto, 2007.

Mann, John. *Life Saving Drugs: The Elusive Magic Bullets.* Cambridge: Royal Society of Chemistry, 2004.

Mayes, Rick, Catherine Bagwell, and Jennifer Erkulwater. *Medicating Children: ADHD and Pediatric Mental Health.* Cambridge, MA: Harvard University Press, 2009.

Mazumdar, Mainak. *Performance of Pharmaceutical Companies in India: A Critical Analysis of Industrial Structure, Firm Specific Resources, and Emerging Strategies.* New York: Physica-Verlag, 2013.

McPherson, Sandra B., Harold V. Hall, and Errol Yudko. *Methamphetamine Use: Clinical and Forensic Aspects,* 2nd ed. Boca Raton, FL: CRC Press, 2008.

Mehlhorn, Heinz, ed. *Nature Helps: How Plants and Other Organisms Contribute to Solve Health Problems.* New York: Springer, 2011.

Millichap, J. Gordon. *Attention Deficit Hyperactivity Disorder Handbook: A Physician's Guide to ADHD*, 2nd ed. New York: Springer, 2010.

Mold, Alex. *Heroin: The Treatment of Addiction in Twentieth-Century Britain*. DeKalb: Northern Illinois University Press, 2008.

Morrison, Linda Joy. *Talking Back to Psychiatry: The Psychiatric Consumer/Survivor/Ex-Patient Movement*. New York: Routledge, 2005.

Mosher, Clayton J. and Scott Akins. *Drugs and Drug Policy: The Control of Consciousness Alternation*. Thousand Oaks, CA: Sage, 2007.

Mossalos, Elias, Monique Mrazek, and Tom Walley, eds. *Regulating Pharmaceuticals in Europe: Striving for Efficiency, Equity and Quality*. Maidenhead, UK: Open University Press, 2004.

Ng, Chee H., ed. *Ethno-Psychopharmacology: Advances in Current Practice*. New York: Cambridge University Press, 2008.

Osling, Alan W., ed. *Intellectual Property Rights and International Trade*. Hauppauge, NY: Nova Science Publishers, 2010.

Osseo-Asare, Aben Dove. *Bitter Roots: The Search for Healing Plants in Africa*. Chicago: University of Chicago Press, 2014.

Paterson, Craig. *Assisted Suicide and Euthanasia: A Natural Law Ethics Approach*. Burlington, VT: Ashgate, 2008.

Patil, Popat N. *Discoveries in Pharmacological Sciences*. Hackensack, NJ: World Scientific, 2012.

Petryna, Adriana, Andrew Lakoff, and Arthur Kleinman, eds. *Global Pharmaceuticals: Ethics, Markets, Practices*. Durham, NC: Duke University Press, 2006.

Pogge, Thomas, Matthew Rimmer, and Kim Rubenstein, ed. *Incentives for Global Public Health: Patent Law and Access to Essential Medicines*. New York: Cambridge University Press, 2010.

Rai, Mahendra, ed. *Medicinal Plants: Biodiversity and Drugs*. Boca Raton, FL: CRC Press, 2012.

Ramesh, Santhanam, Rajabalaya Rajan, and Ramasamy Santhanam. *Freshwater Phytopharmaceutical Compounds*. Boca Raton, FL: CRC Press, 2014.

Rapaka, Rao S. and Wolfgang Sadee, eds. *Drug Addiction: From Basic Research to Therapy*. New York: Springer, 2008.

Rasmussen, Susan J. *Those Who Touch: Tuareg Medicine Women in Anthropological Perspective*. DeKalb: Northern Illinois University Press, 2006.

Regitz-Zagrosek, Vera, ed. *Sex and Gender Differences in Pharmacology*. New York: Springer, 2012.

Rosen, Daniel M. *Dope: A History of Performance Enhancement in Sports From the Nineteenth Century to Today*. Westport, CT: Praeger, 2008.

Rosenberg, David and Samuel Gershon, eds. *Pharmacotherapy of Child and Adolescent Psychiatric Disorders*, 3rd ed. Chichester, UK: John Wiley & Sons, 2011.

Salek, Sam and Andrew Edgar, eds. *Pharmaceutical Ethics*. Hoboken, NJ: John Wiley & Sons, 2002.

Sashegyi, Andreas, ed. *Benefit-Risk Assessment in Pharmaceutical Research and Development*. Boca Raton, FL: CRC Press, 2014.

Sampath, Padmashree Gehl. *Regulating Bioprospecting: Institutions for Drug Research, Access, and Benefit-Sharing*. New York: United Nations University Press, 2005.

Schaler, Jeffrey A., ed. *Szasz Under Fire: A Psychiatric Abolitionist Faces His Critics*. Chicago: Open Court, 2004.

Schlaes, David M. *Antibiotics: The Perfect Storm*. New York: Springer, 2010.

Schotsmans, Paul and Tom Meulenbergs, eds. *Euthanasia and Palliative Care in the Low Countries*. Dudley, MA: Peeters, 2005.

Shadlen, Kenneth C., ed. *Intellectual Property, Pharmaceuticals, and Public Health: Access to Drugs in Developing Countries.* Cheltenham, UK: Edward Elgar, 2011.

Shaver, Lea. *Access to Knowledge in Brazil: New Research on Intellectual Property, Innovation and Development.* New Haven, CT: Information Society Project, Yale Law School, 2008.

Sosa, Anibl de J., ed. *Antimicrobial Resistance in Developing Countries.* New York: Springer, 2010.

Souto, Eliana, B., ed. *Patenting Nanomedicines: Legal Aspects, Intellectual Property and Grant Opportunities.* New York: Springer, 2012.

Stanford, Clare and Rosemary Tannock, eds. *Behavioral Neuroscience of Attention Deficit Hyperactivity Disorder and Its Treatment.* New York: Springer, 2012.

Storz, Ulrich, Wolfgang Flasche, and Johanna Driehaus. *Intellectual Property Issues: Therapeutics, Vaccines and Molecular Diagnostics.* New York: Springer, 2012.

Strom, Brian L., ed. *Pharmacoepidemiology,* 4th ed. Hoboken, NJ: John Wiley & Sons, 2005.

Sukul, Nirmal C. *High Dilution Effects: Physical and Biochemical Basis.* Boston: Kluwer Academic, 2004.

Szaz, Thomas. *Antipsychiatry: Quackery Squared.* Syracuse, NY: Syracuse University Press, 2009.

Taylor, David, Martin Knapp, and Robert Kerwin, eds. *Pharmacoeconomics in Psychiatry.* London: Martin Dunitz, 2002.

Taylor, Kevin, Sarah Nettelton, and Geoffrey Harding. *Sociology for Pharmacists: An Introduction,* 2nd ed. New York: Taylor & Francis, 2003.

Taylor, Yolanda, ed. *Battling HIV/AIDS: A Decision Maker's Guide to the Procurement of Medicines and Related Supplies.* Washington, DC: World Bank, 2004.

Thieme, Detief and Peter Hemmersbach, eds. *Doping in Sports.* Berlin: Springer, 2010.

Thompson, Frank J. *Medicaid Politics: Federalism, Policy Durability, and Health Reform.* Washington, DC: Georgetown University Press, 2012.

Tone, Andrea. *The Age of Anxiety: A History of America's Turbulent Affair With Tranquilizers.* New York: Basic Books, 2009.

Tone, Andrea and Elizabeth Siegel Watkins, eds. *Medicating Modern America: Prescription Drugs in History.* New York: New York University Press, 2007.

Tringali, Corrado, ed. *Bioactive Compounds From Natural Sources: Natural Products as Lead Compounds in Drug Discovery,* 2nd ed. Boca Raton, FL: CRC Press, 2012.

Tsuang, Ming T. and Mauricio Tohen, ed. *Textbook in Psychiatric Epidemiology,* 2nd ed. New York: Wiley-Liss, 2002.

Tulloch, Gail. *Euthanasia, Choice and Death.* Edinburgh: Edinburgh University Press, 2005.

Tunnell, Kenneth D. *Pissing on Demand: Workplace Drug Testing and the Rise of the Detox Industry.* New York: NYU Press, 2004.

Varela, Alejandro and Jasiah Ibanez, eds. *Medicinal Plants: Classification, Biosynthesis and Pharmacology.* New York: Nova Biomedical Books, 2009.

Verster, Joris C., ed. *Drug Abuse and Addiction in Medical Illness: Causes, Consequences and Treatment.* New York: Springer, 2012.

Walsh, Christopher. *Antibiotics: Actions, Origins, Resistance.* Washington, DC: ASM Press, 2003.

Walsh, David. *From Lance to Landis: Inside the American Doping Controversy at the Tour de France.* New York: Ballantine Books, 2007.

Wang, Feng, ed. *Biomarker Methods in Drug Discovery and Development.* Totowa, NJ: Humana Press, 2008.

Wang, Mei-Ling. *Global Health Partnerships: The Pharmaceutical Industry and BRICA.* New York: Palgrave Macmillan, 2009.

Washington, Harriet A. *Deadly Monopolies: The Shocking Corporate Takeover of Life Itself, and the Consequences for Your Health and Our Medical Future.* New York: Doubleday, 2011.

Weedle, Peter and Leonie Clarke, eds. *Pharmacy and Medicines in Ireland.* Chicago: Pharmaceutical Press, 2011.

Journals

Addiction (Carfax Publishing)

Advances in Pharmacology (Academic Press)

Adverse Drug Reaction Bulletin (Lippincott Williams & Wilkins)

African Journal of Traditional, Complementary, and Alternative Medicines (African Networks on Ethnomedicines)

American Journal of Drug and Alcohol Abuse (Taylor & Francis)

Annual Review of Pharmacology and Toxicology (Annual Reviews Inc.)

Behavioural Pharmacology (Clinical Neuroscience Publishers)

Biotechnology & the Law (Thomson Reuters)

BMC Pharmacology (BioMed Central)

British Journal of Pharmacology and Chemotherapy (British Medical Association)

British Journal of Social Medicine (British Medical Association)

Canadian Adverse Reaction Newsletter (Health Canada)

Canadian Journal of Physiology and Pharmacology (NRC Research Press)

Drug Abuse & Alcoholism Review (Haworth Press)

Economic and Medicinal Plant Research (Academic Press)

Environmental Toxicology and Pharmacology (Elsevier Science)

European Journal of Medicinal Plants (Sciencedomain International)

European Journal of Pharmacology (Elsevier Science)

Experimental and Clinical Psychopharmacology (American Psychological Association)

Expert Opinion on Drug Safety (Ashley Publications)

Health Sociology Review (Australian Sociological Association)

Herbs, Spices, and Medicinal Plants: Recent Advances in Botany, Horticulture, and Pharmacology (Oryx Press)

International Journal of Phytomedicine (Advanced Research Journals)

International Journal of Public Health (Birkhäuser)

Japanese Journal of Pharmacology (Japanese Pharmacological Society)

Journal of Addictive Diseases (Haworth Press)

Journal of Clinical Pharmacy and Therapeutics (Blackwell Science)

Journal of Clinical Psychopharmacology (Lippincott Williams & Wilkins)

Journal of Epidemiology & Community Health (British Medical Association)

Journal of Ethnopharmacology (Elsevier)

Journal of Health & Social Policy (Haworth Press)

Journal of Herbs, Spices & Medicinal Plants (Haworth Press)

Journal of Pharmacology and Experimental Therapeutics (American Society for Pharmacology and Experimental Therapeutics)

Journal of Pharmacy & Pharmaceutical Sciences (Canadian Society for Pharmaceutical Sciences)

Journal of Pharmacy & Pharmacology (Royal Pharmaceutical Society of Great Britain)

Journal of Pharmacy Teaching (Haworth Press)

Journal of Traditional and Complementary Medicine (Wolters Kluwer Health)

Open Pharmacology Journal (Bentham Science Publishers)

Pharmacoepidemiology and Drug Safety (John Wiley & Sons)
Pharmacognosy Magazine (Elsevier)
Pharmacy Education (Informa UK Ltd.)
Phytotherapy Research (Heyden & Son)
Research in Social and Administrative Pharmacy (Elsevier)
Scandinavian Journal of Social Medicine (Almqvist & Wiksell)
Side Effects of Drugs Annual (Elsevier/North Holland)
Social Science & Medicine (Elsevier)
Therapeutic Advances in Drug Safety (SAGE Publications)
Therapeutic Advances in Psychopharmacology (SAGE Publications)
Trends in Pharmacological Sciences (Elsevier)
World Drug Report (Oxford University Press)

Web Sites

American Pharmacists Association
http://www.pharmacist.com/
American Society for Pharmacology and Experimental Therapeutics
http://www.aspet.org/
Antimicrobial Resistance (World Health Organization)
http://www.who.int/mediacentre/factsheets/fs194/en/
British Pharmacological Society
http://www.bps.ac.uk/view/index.html
Canadian Society of Pharmacology and Therapeutics
http://pharmacologycanada.org/

Counterfeit Drugs (World Health Association)
http://www.who.int/medicines/services/counterfeit/overview/en/
Essential Medicines (World Health Organization)
http://www.who.int/topics/essential_medicines/en/
European Drug Monitoring Centre for Drugs and Drug Addiction
http://www.emcdda.europa.eu/
Food and Drug Administration (U.S.)
http://www.fda.gov/
Guttmacher Institute (contraception and reproductive health)
http://www.guttmacher.org/
National Center for Complementary and Integrative Health (U.S.)
http://nccam.nih.gov/
National Institutes of Health: Clinical Trials Database (U.S. and non-U.S.)
http://clinicaltrials.gov/
Pharmaceutical Group of the European Union
http://www.pgeu.eu/
Substance Abuse and Mental Health Services Administration (U.S.): Data, Outcomes, and Quality
http://www.samhsa.gov/data/
Traditional and Complementary Medicine (World Health Organization)
http://www.who.int/medicines/areas/traditional/en/
World Anti-Doping Agency
https://www.wada-ama.org/

Appendix

Primary Documents

Prescription Medication Use

Information in these tables was drawn from *Health, United States, 2013*, the 37th annual overview of the nation's health, compiled by the National Center for Health Statistics (NCHS) of the Centers for Disease Control and Prevention. The full report, including detailed information about data sources, definitions, and methods, is available for free download from the Internet (http://www.cdc.gov/nchs/data/hus/hus13.pdf).

The 2013 edition of *Health, United States* includes a special feature on prescription drug use in the United States, which includes the tables included in this appendix. Topics covered include the number and classes of drugs used by Americans, access problems, the impact of drugs used to treat chronic diseases, antibiotic misuse, opioid misuse, adoption of electronic health records (EHRs), and the growth in spending on prescription drugs.

Data table for Figure 20. Prescription drug use in the past 30 days, by number of drugs taken and age: United States, 1988–1994 through 2007–2010

Excel and PowerPoint: http://www.cdc.gov/nchs/hus/contents2013.htm#fig20

Characteristic	1988–1994		1999–2002		2003–2006		2007–2010	
	Percent	Standard error	Percent	Standard error	Percent	Standard error	Percent	Standard error
Number of prescription drugs in past 30 days								
Total, crude:								
No drugs	62.2	0.5	55.0	1.1	52.7	0.8	51.5	0.9
1–4 drugs.	34.2	0.5	37.6	0.6	37.1	0.5	37.9	0.7
5 or more drugs	3.6	0.2	7.4	0.3	10.1	0.5	10.6	0.5
Total, age-adjusted:[1]								
No drugs	60.9	0.5	54.8	0.9	53.1	0.6	52.5	0.7
1–4 drugs.	35.2	0.5	37.7	0.8	36.9	0.4	37.3	0.6
5 or more drugs	4.0	0.1	7.5	0.3	10.0	0.3	10.1	0.4

2007–2010	Under 18 years		18–44 years		45–64 years		65 years and over	
	Percent	Standard error	Percent	Standard error	Percent	Standard error	Percent	Standard error
No drugs	76.0	0.7	61.3	1.2	33.8	1.2	10.3	0.6
1–4 drugs	23.2	0.7	35.6	1.0	49.4	1.1	50.0	1.1
5 or more drugs	0.8	0.1	3.1	0.5	16.8	0.9	39.7	1.2

[1]Estimates are age-adjusted to the year 2000 standard population using four age groups: under 18 years, 18–44 years, 45–64 years, and 65 years and over.

NOTES: Data are for the civilian noninstitutionalized population. Only prescriptions the respondent themselves took are included. Prescriptions administered in other health care settings, such as physician offices and hospital outpatient departments, are not collected. See Appendix II, Age adjustment; Drug. See related Table 92.

SOURCE: CDC/NCHS, National Health and Nutrition Examination Survey. See Appendix I, National Health and Nutrition Examination Survey (NHANES).

Data table for Figure 21. Prescription drug use in the past 30 days, by age and selected drug class: United States, 1988–1994 and 2007–2010

Excel and PowerPoint: http://www.cdc.gov/nchs/hus/contents2013.htm#fig21

Age and drug class (common indications for use)	1988–1994		2007–2010	
	Percent	Standard error	Percent	Standard error
Under 18 years				
Antiasthmatics (asthma, allergies, breathing)[1]	3.2	0.4	6.8	0.4
Antibiotics (bacterial infections)[2]	10.1	0.6	6.1	0.5
Central nervous system stimulants (attention deficit disorder)[3]	*0.8	0.2	4.2	0.4
Analgesics (pain relief)[4]	1.2	0.2	1.3	0.2
Antidepressants (depression and related disorders)[5]	*	*	1.3	0.2
18–64 years				
Cardiovascular agents (high blood pressure, heart disease, kidney disease)[6]	10.0	0.4	17.7	0.7
Cholesterol-lowering drugs (high cholesterol)[7]	1.6	0.2	10.7	0.5
Anti-acid reflux drugs (gastric reflux, ulcers)[8]	3.0	0.2	9.0	0.7
Antidiabetic agents (diabetes)[9]	2.4	0.2	5.3	0.4
Anticoagulants (blood clot prevention)[10]	0.7	0.1	1.8	0.2
Analgesics (pain relief)[4]	8.6	0.4	10.5	0.7
Antidepressants (depression and related disorders)[5]	2.2	0.2	10.6	0.6
65 years and over				
Cardiovascular agents (high blood pressure, heart disease, kidney disease)[6]	51.5	0.9	70.2	1.2
Cholesterol-lowering drugs (high cholesterol)[7]	5.9	0.5	46.7	1.1
Anti-acid reflux drugs (gastric reflux, ulcers)[8]	7.5	0.7	21.5	1.2
Antidiabetic agents (diabetes)[9]	9.0	0.6	18.4	0.9
Anticoagulants (blood clot prevention)[10]	6.1	0.5	18.1	0.7
Analgesics (pain relief)[4]	13.8	0.7	17.5	1.1
Antidepressants (depression and related disorders)[5]	3.0	0.4	13.7	0.8

* Estimates are considered unreliable. Data preceded by an asterisk have a relative standard error (RSE) of 20%–30%. Estimates not shown have an RSE greater than 30%.

[1]Includes one or more asthma drugs, including bronchodilators, mast cell stabilizers, inhaled corticosteroids, leukotriene modifiers, and antiasthmatic combinations (level 2, class 125, 130, 131, or 243). For a full list of drug classes included, see Technical Notes.

[2]Includes one or more antibiotic drugs, including penicillins, tetracyclines, cephalosporins, and macrolide derivatives (level 2, class 6, 8–18, 240, 315, or 406). For a full list of drug classes included, see Technical Notes.

[3]Includes one or more central nervous system stimulants (level 2, class 71).

[4]Includes one or more analgesic drugs (level 2, class 58).

[5]Includes one or more antidepressant drugs (level 2, class 249).

[6]Includes one or more cardiovascular agents, including drug classes such as ACE inhibitors, beta blockers, calcium channel blockers, and diuretics (level 1, class 40). For a full list of drug classes included, see Technical Notes.

[7]Includes one or more cholesterol-lowering (antihyperlipidemic) drugs (level 2, class 19).

[8]Includes one or more anti-acid reflux (proton pump inhibitors or H2 antagonists) drugs (level 2, class 94 or 272).

[9]Includes one or more antidiabetic drugs (level 2, class 99).

[10]Includes one or more anticoagulants or antiplatelet agents (level 2, class 82 or 83).

NOTES: Data are for the civilian noninstitutionalized population. Only prescriptions the respondent themselves took are included. Prescriptions administered in other health care settings, such as physician offices and hospital outpatient departments, are not collected. Drug classes are from Lexicon Plus (Cerner Multum, Denver, CO), a proprietary comprehensive database of all prescription and some nonprescription drug products available in the U.S. drug market. For more information on the drug classes in each category, see Technical Notes. See Appendix II, Drug; Multum Lexicon Plus therapeutic class. See related Table 93.

SOURCE: CDC/NCHS, National Health and Nutrition Examination Survey. See Appendix I, National Health and Nutrition Examination Survey (NHANES).

Data table for Figure 22. Number of prescription drugs taken in the past 30 days among adults aged 18 and over, by selected characteristics: United States, 2007–2010

Excel and PowerPoint: http://www.cdc.gov/nchs/hus/contents2013.htm#fig22

| | Number of drugs in past 30 days | | | | | | | |
| | Total | | No drugs | | 1–4 drugs | | 5 or more drugs | |
Characteristic	Percent distribution	Standard error	Percent distribution	Standard error	Percent distribution	Standard error	Percent distribution	Standard error
Sex								
Male............................	48.3	0.4	56.3	0.8	42.4	0.7	41.8	1.4
Female..........................	51.7	0.4	43.7	0.8	57.6	0.7	58.2	1.4
Race and Hispanic origin								
White only, not Hispanic..................	68.4	2.5	56.9	3.0	76.8	1.9	78.3	2.3
Black only, not Hispanic..................	11.5	1.0	13.8	1.2	9.4	0.9	10.7	1.4
Mexican origin..........................	8.6	1.3	13.5	1.8	5.2	0.9	*3.9	1.1
Age								
18–44 years	48.9	0.9	69.2	1.0	40.7	1.1	10.8	1.4
45–64 years	34.5	0.7	26.9	1.0	39.8	0.9	41.7	1.1
65 years and over	16.6	0.5	3.9	0.3	19.5	0.7	47.5	1.5
Health status (respondent-assessed)								
Excellent or very good...................	44.4	1.2	49.7	1.2	46.8	1.4	20.9	1.6
Good................................	38.5	0.8	37.8	0.9	38.9	1.2	39.6	1.5
Fair or poor...........................	17.1	0.7	12.5	0.7	14.3	0.9	39.6	1.3

NOTES: Data are for the civilian noninstitutionalized population. In 2007–2010, 43.4% of adults took no drugs in the past 30 days, 42.8% took 1–4 drugs, and 13.9% took 5 or more drugs. Only prescriptions the respondent themselves took are included. Prescriptions administered in other health care settings, such as physician offices and hospital outpatient departments, are not collected. Estimates include all race and Hispanic origin groups not shown separately, except for the race and Hispanic origin-specific estimates. Race and Hispanic origin estimates do not sum to 100% because of respondents in other racial and ethnic groups. See Appendix II, Drug.

SOURCE: CDC/NCHS, National Health and Nutrition Examination Survey. See Appendix I, National Health and Nutrition Examination Survey (NHANES).

Data table for Figure 23. Nonreceipt of needed prescription drugs in the past 12 months due to cost among adults aged 18–64, by insurance status and percent of poverty level: United States, 2002–2012

Excel and PowerPoint: http://www.cdc.gov/nchs/hus/contents2013.htm#fig23

Insurance status and poverty level	2002	2003	2004	2005	2006	2007	2008	2009	2010	2011	2012
Insurance status in the past 12 months						Percent					
Total	7.6	8.1	9.2	9.4	9.3	9.6	10.7	11.2	11.2	10.5	9.4
Insured all 12 months	3.9	3.8	4.9	5.0	4.6	4.8	5.6	6.0	6.2	5.9	5.0
Uninsured all or part of past 12 months	20.9	22.7	23.6	24.1	23.9	25.5	27.3	26.7	25.8	24.1	22.4
						Standard error					
Total	0.2	0.2	0.2	0.2	0.3	0.3	0.3	0.3	0.3	0.3	0.2
Insured all 12 months	0.2	0.2	0.2	0.2	0.2	0.2	0.2	0.2	0.2	0.2	0.2
Uninsured all or part of past 12 months	0.6	0.6	0.7	0.7	0.8	0.8	0.9	0.9	0.7	0.6	0.7

Insurance status in the past 12 months and percent of poverty level, 2011–2012	Percent	Standard error
Insured all 12 months	5.5	0.1
Below 100%	10.8	0.6
100%–199%	11.5	0.5
200%–399%	6.2	0.3
400% or more	2.2	0.1
Uninsured all or part of past 12 months	23.2	0.5
Below 100%	30.7	0.9
100%–199%	23.2	0.8
200%–399%	19.4	0.8
400% or more	14.9	1.3

NOTES: Data are based on household interviews of a sample of the civilian noninstitutionalized population. Based on adults responding to the question, "During the past 12 months was there any time when you needed prescription medicine but did not get it because [person] couldn't afford it?" Persons not covered by private insurance, Medicaid, Children's Health Insurance Program (CHIP), public assistance (through 1996), state-sponsored or other government-sponsored health plans (starting in 1997), Medicare, or military plans are considered to have no health insurance coverage. Persons with only Indian Health Service coverage are considered to have no health insurance coverage. Percent of poverty level is based on family income and family size and composition using U.S. Census Bureau poverty thresholds. Missing family income data were imputed. See Appendix II, Family income; Health insurance coverage; Poverty; Table VI. See related Table 74.

SOURCE: CDC/NCHS, National Health Interview Survey. See Appendix I, National Health Interview Survey (NHIS).

Data table for Figure 25. Use of prescription antidepressants in the past 30 days among adults aged 18 and over, by sex and age: United States, 1988–1994 through 2007–2010

Excel and PowerPoint: http://www.cdc.gov/nchs/hus/contents2013.htm#fig25

Sex and age	1988–1994		1999–2002		2003–2006		2007–2010	
	Percent	Standard error	Percent	Standard error	Percent	Standard error	Percent	Standard error
Total, crude	2.3	0.2	8.0	0.4	10.9	0.4	11.1	0.5
Total, age-adjusted[1]	2.4	0.2	7.9	0.4	10.8	0.4	10.8	0.5
18–44 years	1.6	0.2	6.0	0.5	7.5	0.5	7.9	0.6
45–64 years	3.5	0.5	10.5	0.7	15.8	0.9	14.4	0.8
65 years and over	3.0	0.4	9.3	0.6	12.0	0.8	13.7	0.8
Male, crude	1.5	0.2	5.2	0.4	6.7	0.4	6.7	0.4
Male, age-adjusted[1]	1.6	0.2	5.2	0.4	6.7	0.4	6.6	0.4
18–44 years	*1.0	0.2	3.6	0.5	3.5	0.4	4.4	0.6
45–64 years	*2.3	0.5	7.0	0.7	10.5	1.0	8.9	0.7
65 years and over	*2.3	0.5	7.2	0.8	9.8	1.0	9.4	0.7
Female, crude	3.1	0.3	10.5	0.6	14.8	0.6	15.2	0.8
Female, age-adjusted[1]	3.2	0.3	10.5	0.6	14.6	0.6	14.8	0.8
18–44 years	2.3	0.4	8.5	0.7	11.4	0.8	11.3	0.9
45–64 years	4.6	0.7	13.8	1.2	20.9	1.2	19.6	1.2
65 years and over	3.5	0.4	10.8	0.8	13.7	1.1	17.0	1.2

* Estimates are considered unreliable. Data preceded by an asterisk have a relative standard error (RSE) of 20%–30%. Data not shown have an RSE greater than 30%.

[1]Estimates are age-adjusted to the year 2000 standard population using three age groups: 18–44 years, 45–64 years, and 65 years and over.

NOTES: Data are for the civilian noninstitutionalized population. Antidepressant use includes one or more antidepressant drugs (level 2, class 249). Only prescriptions the respondent themselves took are included. Prescriptions administered in other health care settings, such as physician offices and hospital outpatient departments, are not collected. Drug classes are from Lexicon Plus (Cerner Multum, Denver, CO), a proprietary comprehensive database of all prescription and some nonprescription drug products available in the U.S. drug market. See Appendix II, Age adjustment; Drug; Multum Lexicon Plus therapeutic class. See related Table 93.

SOURCE: CDC/NCHS, National Health and Nutrition Examination Survey. See Appendix I, National Health and Nutrition Examination Survey (NHANES).

Data table for Figure 26. Antibiotics ordered or provided during emergency department, outpatient, and physician visits for cold symptom diagnoses, by age: United States, average annual, 1995–1996 through 2009–2010

Excel and PowerPoint: http://www.cdc.gov/nchs/hus/contents2013.htm#fig26

	All ages		Under 18 years		18 years and over	
Year	Percent of visits for colds	Standard error	Percent of visits for colds	Standard error	Percent of visits for colds	Standard error
1995–1996	44.7	3.0	37.5	4.3	58.5	3.4
1997–1998	36.5	2.6	26.8	2.8	52.0	3.9
1999–2000	27.7	2.8	20.4	2.5	37.8	5.1
2001–2002	36.1	3.0	26.8	2.8	52.9	4.9
2003–2004	30.4	3.6	20.9	3.0	45.1	6.3
2005–2006	27.1	2.9	14.8	2.4	44.1	4.4
2007–2008	32.1	2.3	26.3	2.9	42.5	3.8
2009–2010	27.1	2.8	21.5	2.9	39.5	4.3

NOTES: Visits for cold symptoms are those with the 9th Revision of the *International Classification of Diseases, Clinical Modification* codes 460 [acute nasopharyngitis (common cold)] or 465 (acute upper respiratory infections) and no other diagnoses. Until 2002, up to six prescription and nonprescription medications were recorded on the patient record form (PRF). Starting with 2003 data, up to eight prescription and nonprescription medications are recorded on the PRF. To be consistent over time, only the first six medication fields were considered. Antibiotics were identified based on drug codes. For a list of drug codes included, see Technical Notes. Visits with unknown drug codes (99980 and 99999) were excluded.

SOURCE: CDC/NCHS, National Ambulatory Medical Care Survey, National Hospital Ambulatory Medical Care Survey: Emergency Department and Outpatient Components. See Appendix I, National Ambulatory Medical Care Survey (NAMCS); National Hospital Ambulatory Medical Care Survey (NHAMCS).

Data table for Figure 27. Computerized systems for prescription drugs, by provider and system type: United States, 2010

Excel and PowerPoint: http://www.cdc.gov/nchs/hus/contents2013.htm#fig27

	Provider type							
	Physician offices		Hospital outpatient departments		Hospital emergency departments		Residential care facilities[1]	
System type	Percent of providers	Standard error	Percent of providers	Standard error	Percent of providers	Standard error	Percent of providers	Standard error
Ordering prescriptions	53.7	2.0	50.3	4.5	58.1	4.6	19.7	0.9
Warning of drug interactions and contraindications	46.0	2.0	38.7	4.5	45.9	4.6	17.9	0.9
Submitting prescriptions electronically to pharmacy	44.6	2.0	30.3	4.5	19.7	2.9	8.2	0.6
Including patient's allergies and current medications (in clinical notes system)	51.0	2.0	56.4	5.0	66.0	4.3	28.3	1.1
All four system types..................	33.3	1.8	24.3	4.3	15.7	2.5	3.3	0.4

[1]Includes residential care facilities, assisted living residences, board and care homes, and other licensed shared housing establishments that offer help with personal care or health-related services and other services. Residences licensed to serve exclusively persons with mental illness, mental retardation, or developmental disabilities are excluded.

NOTE: For variables used, see Technical Notes.

SOURCE: CDC/NCHS, National Ambulatory Medical Care Survey, National Hospital Ambulatory Medical Care Survey: Emergency Department and Outpatient Components, and National Survey of Residential Care Facilities. See Appendix I, National Ambulatory Medical Care Survey (NAMCS); National Hospital Ambulatory Medical Care Survey (NHAMCS); and National Survey of Residential Care Facilities (NSRCF).

Data table for Figure 28. Drug poisoning deaths involving opioid analgesics among persons aged 15 and over, by race and Hispanic origin, sex, and age: United States, 1999–2000 through 2009–2010

Excel and PowerPoint: http://www.cdc.gov/nchs/hus/contents2013.htm#fig28

Characteristic	1999–2000	2001–2002	2003–2004	2005–2006	2007–2008	2009–2010
	Deaths per 100,000 population					
Aged 15 and over, age-adjusted[1]	1.9	2.9	4.0	5.2	6.1	6.6
Aged 15 and over, crude	1.9	2.9	4.0	5.2	6.0	6.5
Age						
15–24 years	0.7	1.5	2.4	3.2	3.8	3.7
25–34 years	1.9	2.8	4.1	6.1	7.2	8.1
35–54 years	3.4	4.9	6.6	8.2	9.2	9.9
55–64 years	1.0	1.6	2.4	3.5	4.8	6.0
65 years and over	0.3	0.5	0.6	0.9	1.0	1.2
Sex[1]						
Male	2.6	3.7	5.0	6.6	7.5	8.1
Female	1.3	2.1	3.0	3.9	4.6	5.1
Race and Hispanic origin[1,2]						
White, not Hispanic	2.2	3.5	5.1	6.7	8.0	8.9
Black, not Hispanic	1.1	1.5	1.7	2.8	2.4	2.7
Hispanic or Latino	1.8	1.7	2.0	2.3	2.6	2.4
American Indian or Alaska Native	1.7	2.6	4.2	5.4	6.1	7.1
Asian or Pacific Islander	0.2	0.3	0.3	0.6	0.5	0.7

[1]Rates are age-adjusted using eight age groups. Age-adjusted rates are calculated using the year 2000 standard population with unrounded population numbers. See Appendix II, Age adjustment.

[2]The race groups, Asian or Pacific Islander and American Indian or Alaska Native, include persons of Hispanic and non-Hispanic origin. Persons of Hispanic origin may be of any race. Death rates for the American Indian or Alaska Native, Asian or Pacific Islander, and Hispanic populations are known to be underestimated. Starting with 2003 data, some states allowed the reporting of more than one race on the death certificate. The multiple-race data for these states were bridged to the single-race categories of the 1977 Office of Management and Budget standards, for comparability with other states. See Appendix II, Race.

NOTES: Rates are based on resident population. Drug poisoning deaths with the drug type unspecified (up to 25% of the total) are not included. Drug poisoning deaths involving opioid analgesics among children under 15 is low, 0.1 per 100,000 population in 2010. Therefore this analysis is limited to those aged 15 and over. Opioid analgesics include pharmaceutical opioids such as hydrocodone, codeine, and methadone, and synthetic narcotics such as fentanyl, meperidine, and propoxyphene. Drug poisoning deaths involving opioid analgesics include those with an underlying cause of drug poisoning and with opioid analgesics mentioned in the 10th Revision of the *International Classification of Diseases* (ICD–10) multiple causes of death. See Appendix I, National Vital Statistics System (NVSS), Multiple Cause-of-death File, for information about tabulating cause-of-death data in this table. These deaths include all manners and intents. See Appendix II, Age adjustment; Cause of death; Hispanic origin; Table IV. See related Table 32.

SOURCE: CDC/NCHS, National Vital Statistics System. See Appendix I, National Vital Statistics System (NVSS).

Data table for Figure 29. Retail prescription drug expenditures, annual percent change, and spending by payer: United States, 2001–2011

Excel and PowerPoint: http://www.cdc.gov/nchs/hus/contents2013.htm#fig29

Year	Annual percent change
2001	14.7
2002	14.0
2003	11.3
2004	9.2
2005	6.5
2006	9.5
2007	5.2
2008	2.8
2009	5.0
2010	0.4
2011	2.9

Payer	2001	2011
	Percent	
Out-of-pocket	26.4	17.1
Private health insurance	50.9	46.5
Medicare	1.8	24.2
Medicaid[1]	17.1	7.8
Other health insurance programs[2]	1.8	3.0
Other third-party payers[3]	2.0	1.4

[1]Includes both the state and federal portions. Also includes Children's Health Insurance Program (CHIP) and Medicaid CHIP expansions.

[2]Includes Department of Defense and Department of Veterans Affairs programs.

[3]Includes worksite health care, other private revenues, Indian Health Service, workers' compensation, general assistance, maternal and child health, vocational rehabilitation, other federal programs, Substance Abuse and Mental Health Services Administration, other state and local programs, and school health.

NOTES: See Appendix II, Health expenditures, national. See related Table 115.

SOURCE: Centers for Medicare & Medicaid Services, Office of the Actuary, National Health Statistics Group, National Health Expenditure Accounts. See Appendix I, National Health Expenditure Accounts (NHEA).

Information in these figures was drawn from the National Health and Nutrition Examination Survey (NHANES), a cross-sectional survey conducted by the National Center for Health Statistics (NCHS) of the Centers for Disease Control and Prevention (CDC). The data on trends in opioid use among Americans in these figures are drawn from NHANES data from 1999–2002 through 2011–2012, while the use of opioid analgesics among population subgroups is drawn from NHANES data from the years 2007–2008, 2009–2010, and 2011–2012. More technical information about the data is available from http://www.cdc.gov/nchs/data/dataBriefs/db189.pdf.

Figure 1. Trend in prescription opioid analgesic use in the past 30 days among adults aged 20 and over: United States, 1999–2012

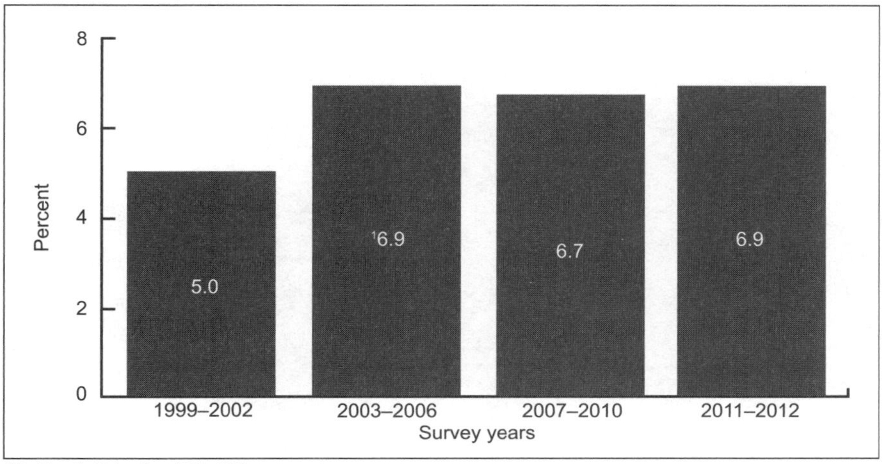

¹Significantly higher than 1999–2002.
NOTE: Access data table for Figure 1 at: http://www.cdc.gov/nchs/data/databriefs/db189_table.pdf#1.
SOURCE: CDC/NCHS, National Health and Nutrition Examination Survey, 1999–2012.

Figure 2. Trends in the use of different strength opioid analgesics among adults aged 20 and over who used opioids in the past 30 days: United States, 1999–2012

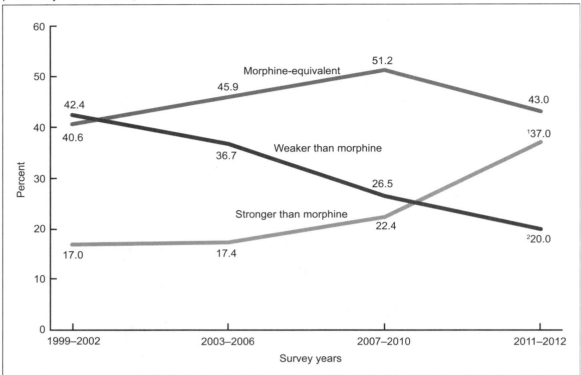

[1]Significant linear trend for use of stronger-than-morphine opioid analgesics.
[2]Significant linear trend for use of weaker-than-morphine opioid analgesics.
NOTES: Respondents who reported using two or more opioid analgesics of different strengths were categorized based on the strongest opioid analgesic reported.
Access data table for Figure 2 at: http://www.cdc.gov/nchs/data/databriefs/db189_table.pdf#2.
SOURCE: CDC/NCHS, National Health and Nutrition Examination Survey, 1999–2012.

Figure 3. Prescription opioid analgesic use in the past 30 days among adults aged 20 and over, by age, sex, and race and Hispanic origin: United States, 2007–2012

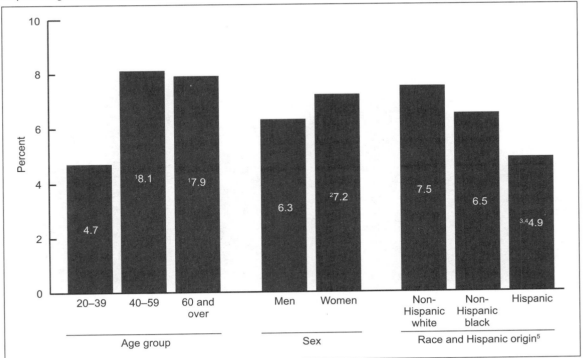

[1]Significantly higher than adults aged 20–39.
[2]Significantly higher than men.
[3]Significantly lower than non-Hispanic white adults.
[4]Significantly lower than non-Hispanic black adults.
[5]Estimates were age-adjusted by the direct method to the 2000 U.S. census population using age groups 20–39, 40–59, and 60 and over.
NOTE: Access data table for Figure 3 at: http://www.cdc.gov/nchs/data/databriefs/db189_table.pdf#3.
SOURCE: CDC/NCHS, National Health and Nutrition Examination Survey, 2007–2012.

Figure 4. Prescription opioid analgesic use in the past 30 days among adults aged 20 and over, by sex and age: United States, 2007–2012

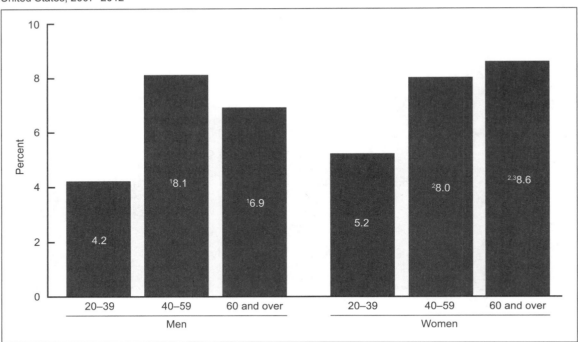

[1]Significantly higher than men aged 20–39.
[2]Significantly higher than women aged 20–39.
[3]Significantly higher than men aged 60 and over.
NOTE: Access data table for Figure 4 at: http://www.cdc.gov/nchs/data/databriefs/db189_table.pdf#4.
SOURCE: CDC/NCHS, National Health and Nutrition Examination Survey, 2007–2012.

Figure 5. Prescription opioid analgesic use in the past 30 days among adults aged 20 and over, by sex and race and Hispanic origin: United States, 2007–2012

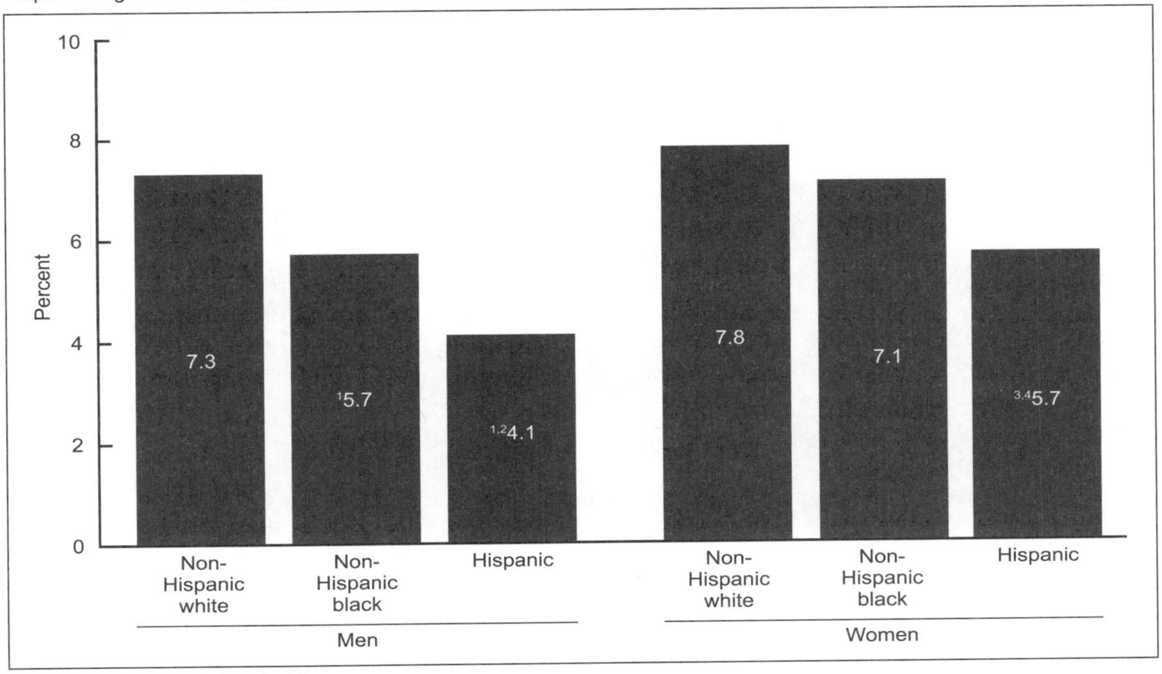

[1]Significantly lower than non-Hispanic white men.
[2]Significantly lower than non-Hispanic black men.
[3]Significantly lower than non-Hispanic white women.
[4]Significantly higher than Hispanic men.
NOTES: Estimates were age-adjusted by the direct method to the 2000 U.S. census population using age groups 20–39, 40–59, and 60 and over. Access data table for Figure 5 at: http://www.cdc.gov/nchs/data/databriefs/db189_table.pdf#5.
SOURCE: CDC/NCHS, National Health and Nutrition Examination Survey, 2007–2012.

Information for this figure was drawn from the National Health Interview Survey (NHIS), a survey conducted by the National Center for Health Statistics (NCHS) of the Centers for Disease Control and Prevention (CDC). More information about the NHIS is available from http://www.cdc.gov/nchs/nhis/about_nhis.htm and more technical information about the data in this figure is available from http://www.cdc.gov/diabetes/statistics/meduse/methods.htm.

CDC - Percentage Using Diabetes Medication by Type of Medication - Treating Diabetes - Data & Trends - Diabetes DDT

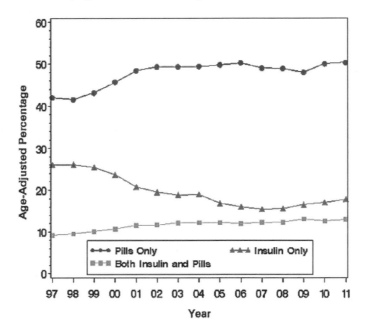

Antibiotic Resistance

Information for this table was drawn from a 2013 report from the Centers for Disease Control and Prevention (CDC). The complete report is available from http://www.cdc.gov/drugresistance/threat-report-2013/pdf/ar-threats-2013-508.pdf, and more information about antibiotic resistance is available from the CDC Web site at http://www.cdc.gov/drugresistance/.

Minimum Estimates of Morbidity and Mortality from Antibiotic-Resistant Infections*

Antibiotic-Resistant Microorganism	Infections Included in Case/Death Estimates	Infections Not Included	Estimated Annual Number of Cases	Estimated Annual Number of Deaths
Carbapenem-resistant Enterobacteriaceae (CRE)	Healthcare-associated Infections (HAIs) caused by *Klebsiella* and *E. coli* with onset in hospitalized patients	Infections occurring outside of acute care hospitals (e.g., nursing homes) Infections acquired in acute care hospitals but not diagnosed until after discharge Infections caused by Enterobacteriaceae other than *Klebsiella* and *E. coli* (e.g., *Enterobacter spp.*)	9,300	610
Drug-resistant *Neisseria gonorrhoeae* (any drug)	All infections	Not applicable	246,000	<5
Multidrug-resistant *Acinetobacter* (three or more drug classes)	HAIs with onset in hospitalized patients	Infections occurring outside of acute care hospitals (e.g., nursing homes) Infections acquired in acute care hospitals but not diagnosed until after discharge	7,300	500
Drug-resistant *Campylobacter* (azithromycin or ciprofloxacin)	All infections	Not applicable	310,000	28
Drug-resistant *Candida* (fluconazole)	HAIs with onset in hospitalized patients	Infections occurring outside of acute care hospitals (e.g., nursing homes) Infections acquired in acute care hospitals but not diagnosed until after discharge	3,400	220
Extended-spectrum β-lactamase producing Enterobacteriaceae (ESBLs)	HAIs caused by *Klebsiella* and *E. coli* with onset in hospitalized patients	Infections occurring outside of acute care hospitals (e.g., nursing homes) Infections acquired in acute care hospitals but not diagnosed until after discharge Infections caused by Enterobacteriaceae other than *Klebsiella* and *E. coli* (e.g., *Enterobacter spp.*)	26,000	1,700

Antibiotic-Resistant Microorganism	Infections Included in Case/Death Estimates	Infections Not Included	Estimated Annual Number of Cases	Estimated Annual Number of Deaths
Vancomycin-resistant *Enterococcus* **(VRE)**	HAIs with onset in hospitalized patients	Infections occurring outside of acute care hospitals (e.g., nursing homes); Infections acquired in acute care hospitals but not diagnosed until after discharge	20,000	1,300
Multidrug-resistant *Pseudomonas aeruginosa* **(three or more drug classes)**	HAIs with onset in hospitalized patients	Infections occurring outside of acute care hospitals (e.g., nursing homes); Infections acquired in acute care hospitals but not diagnosed until after discharge	6,700	440
Drug-resistant non-typhoidal *Salmonella* **(ceftriaxone, ciprofloxacin†, or 5 or more drug classes)**	All infections	Not applicable	100,000	40
Drug-resistant *Salmonella* **Typhi (ciprofloxacin†)**	All infections	Not applicable	3,800	<5
Drug-resistant *Shigella* **(azithromycin or ciprofloxacin)**	All infections	Not applicable	27,000	<5
Methicillin-resistant *Staphylococcus aureus* **(MRSA)**	Invasive infections	Both healthcare and community-associated non-invasive infections such as wound and skin and soft tissue infections	80,000	11,000
Streptococcus pneumoniae **(full resistance to clinically relevant drugs)**	All infections	Not applicable	1,200,000	7,000

1603

Antibiotic-Resistant Microorganism	Infections Included in Case/Death Estimates	Infections Not Included	Estimated Annual Number of Cases	Estimated Annual Number of Deaths
Drug-resistant tuberculosis (any clinically relevant drug)	All infections	Not applicable	1,042	50
Vancomycin-resistant *Staphylococcus aureus* (VRSA)	All infections	Not applicable	<5	<5
Erythromycin-resistant Group A *Streptococcus*	Invasive infections	Non-invasive infections including common upper-respiratory infections like strep throat	1,300	160
Clindamycin-resistant Group B *Streptococcus*	Invasive infections	Non-invasive infections and asymptomatic intrapartum colonization requiring prophylaxis	7,600	440
Summary Totals for Antibiotic-Resistant Infections			2,049,442	23,488
Clostridium difficile Infections	Healthcare-associated infections in acute care hospitals or in patients requiring hospitalization	Infections occurring outside of acute care hospitals (e.g., nursing homes, community) Infections acquired in acute care hospitals but not diagnosed until after discharge	250,000	14,000

†Resistance or partial resistance

Youth Drug Use

Information for these tables was reproduced from the Centers for Disease Control and Prevention's (CDC's) *Morbidity and Mortality Weekly Report* and drawn from the 2013 Youth Risk Behavior Surveillance System (YRBSS), including both the national survey and surveys conducted at the state and local levels. The YRBSS, conducted by the CDC and state and local health agencies, gathers information about six types of health-related behaviors among youth and young adults: those relating to injuries and violence; tobacco use; alcohol and drug use; sexual behavior; diet; and physical inactivity. Further information about the YRBSS is available from http://www.cdc.gov/healthyyouth/data/yrbs/index.htm.

Surveillance Summaries

TABLE 49. Percentage of high school students who ever used marijuana* and who tried marijuana for the first time before age 13 years, by sex, race/ethnicity, and grade — United States, Youth Risk Behavior Survey, 2013

	Ever used marijuana						Tried marijuana before age 13 years					
	Female		Male		Total		Female		Male		Total	
Category	%	CI[†]	%	CI	%	CI	%	CI	%	CI	%	CI
Race/Ethnicity												
White[§]	34.8	(31.6–38.1)	38.6	(34.8–42.6)	**36.7**	**(33.4–40.1)**	4.5	(3.6–5.7)	8.6	(6.7–10.9)	**6.6**	**(5.3–8.1)**
Black[§]	45.4	(41.1–49.7)	48.2	(44.3–52.2)	**46.8**	**(43.6–50.0)**	6.1	(4.4–8.3)	17.0	(14.7–19.6)	**11.5**	**(9.9–13.2)**
Hispanic	47.6	(42.3–52.9)	50.0	(46.3–53.7)	**48.8**	**(44.6–52.9)**	9.8	(7.8–12.2)	13.7	(11.0–16.8)	**11.7**	**(9.8–13.8)**
Grade												
9	29.0	(26.0–32.3)	31.1	(27.6–34.8)	**30.1**	**(27.1–33.2)**	7.7	(6.2–9.6)	11.8	(9.4–14.7)	**9.8**	**(8.0–11.9)**
10	37.4	(32.1–43.2)	40.7	(35.5–46.1)	**39.1**	**(34.3–44.1)**	7.8	(5.3–11.5)	11.4	(9.3–13.9)	**9.6**	**(7.7–11.9)**
11	45.1	(41.4–48.9)	47.8	(44.2–51.4)	**46.4**	**(43.6–49.3)**	5.7	(4.2–7.6)	11.6	(9.1–14.7)	**8.6**	**(7.0–10.5)**
12	46.4	(41.4–51.4)	50.9	(45.9–55.9)	**48.6**	**(44.1–53.2)**	3.0	(2.1–4.1)	9.5	(7.7–11.6)	**6.2**	**(5.1–7.4)**
Total	**39.2**	**(36.1–42.3)**	**42.1**	**(39.3–45.1)**	**40.7**	**(37.9–43.5)**	**6.2**	**(5.0–7.6)**	**11.1**	**(9.5–12.9)**	**8.6**	**(7.4–10.1)**

* One or more times during their life.
[†] 95% confidence interval.
[§] Non-Hispanic.

TABLE 50. Percentage of high school students who ever used marijuana* and who tried marijuana for the first time before age 13 years, by sex — selected U.S. sites, Youth Risk Behavior Survey, 2013

Site	Ever used marijuana						Tried marijuana before age 13 years					
	Female		Male		Total		Female		Male		Total	
	%	CI†	%	CI	%	CI	%	CI	%	CI	%	CI
State surveys												
Alabama	31.5	(26.3–37.3)	37.2	(30.8–44.2)	**34.4**	**(29.1–40.0)**	7.0	(5.0–9.9)	9.0	(6.7–12.0)	8.1	(6.2–10.3)
Alaska	38.1	(32.3–44.3)	39.5	(34.7–44.4)	**39.0**	**(34.7–43.5)**	9.9	(7.0–13.8)	10.5	(8.3–13.3)	10.4	(8.4–12.9)
Arizona	39.6	(33.8–45.8)	47.0	(41.5–52.5)	**43.3**	**(38.3–48.4)**	7.6	(5.3–10.7)	12.0	(9.5–15.1)	9.8	(7.9–12.1)
Arkansas	33.9	(30.1–38.0)	40.1	(35.7–44.7)	**36.9**	**(33.5–40.5)**	5.9	(4.3–8.1)	13.7	(10.3–18.1)	9.8	(7.9–12.2)
Connecticut	38.0	(33.6–42.6)	46.1	(41.4–50.8)	**42.1**	**(38.5–45.8)**	3.8	(2.5–5.6)	10.0	(7.8–12.7)	7.0	(5.4–8.9)
Delaware	39.0	(35.9–42.2)	46.1	(42.4–49.7)	**42.6**	**(40.0–45.2)**	6.1	(4.6–8.0)	12.8	(10.9–15.0)	9.6	(8.2–11.1)
Florida	35.8	(33.6–38.1)	41.5	(39.1–44.1)	**38.7**	**(36.8–40.7)**	5.4	(4.6–6.2)	11.1	(9.9–12.5)	8.3	(7.6–9.0)
Georgia	33.7	(29.8–37.7)	38.0	(32.6–43.7)	**35.9**	**(31.7–40.2)**	5.3	(3.8–7.4)	12.3	(9.6–15.7)	9.0	(7.3–11.0)
Hawaii	—§	—	—	—	—	—	9.2	(7.6–11.3)	11.5	(9.1–14.4)	10.4	(8.5–12.6)
Idaho	29.1	(25.3–33.3)	30.8	(25.6–36.5)	**30.0**	**(26.2–33.9)**	3.8	(2.5–5.6)	5.8	(4.4–7.7)	4.8	(3.8–6.1)
Illinois	36.0	(30.1–42.4)	44.5	(39.3–49.7)	**40.4**	**(35.2–45.8)**	6.2	(4.9–7.7)	11.3	(8.1–15.4)	8.9	(6.9–11.3)
Kansas	27.0	(23.8–30.5)	31.3	(26.9–36.0)	**29.2**	**(26.1–32.6)**	4.3	(3.0–6.1)	7.5	(5.7–9.9)	6.0	(4.9–7.4)
Kentucky	30.6	(24.7–37.1)	36.9	(32.7–41.4)	**34.0**	**(29.9–38.3)**	6.0	(3.7–9.5)	10.6	(8.4–13.2)	8.5	(6.6–10.7)
Louisiana	29.0	(23.7–34.9)	36.4	(29.0–44.5)	**32.9**	**(28.2–37.9)**	7.3	(5.0–10.6)	11.2	(8.6–14.4)	9.5	(7.4–11.9)
Maine	—	—	—	—	—	—	5.2	(4.3–6.3)	8.8	(7.6–10.1)	7.1	(6.2–8.1)
Maryland	34.0	(32.9–35.2)	37.6	(36.6–38.7)	**35.9**	**(35.0–36.8)**	5.8	(5.4–6.3)	11.3	(10.6–12.1)	8.8	(8.3–9.3)
Massachusetts	39.1	(35.8–42.5)	43.2	(39.5–47.1)	**41.3**	**(38.4–44.2)**	4.7	(3.8–5.9)	8.5	(6.9–10.3)	6.6	(5.5–7.9)
Michigan	31.4	(28.6–34.4)	34.4	(31.1–37.8)	**33.0**	**(30.5–35.5)**	4.4	(3.4–5.8)	7.6	(6.2–9.3)	6.1	(5.1–7.3)
Mississippi	29.3	(25.8–33.0)	37.3	(32.3–42.7)	**33.3**	**(29.8–36.9)**	6.1	(4.2–8.8)	13.9	(11.3–17.0)	10.0	(8.2–12.1)
Missouri	—	—	—	—	—	—	—	—	—	—	—	—
Montana	36.9	(33.2–40.9)	38.4	(35.2–41.6)	**37.6**	**(34.5–40.9)**	6.6	(5.0–8.8)	9.0	(7.4–10.9)	7.9	(6.4–9.7)
Nebraska	22.7	(18.6–27.4)	24.6	(19.9–30.0)	**23.6**	**(19.8–27.8)**	3.7	(2.5–5.6)	7.3	(5.4–9.6)	5.5	(4.2–7.3)
Nevada	41.5	(35.4–47.9)	41.3	(35.5–47.5)	**41.5**	**(36.0–47.2)**	7.1	(5.2–9.6)	12.0	(8.2–17.0)	9.6	(7.0–13.0)
New Hampshire	37.7	(32.8–42.9)	42.1	(38.2–46.0)	**39.9**	**(36.3–43.6)**	5.1	(3.6–7.2)	7.8	(5.9–10.2)	6.6	(5.3–8.2)
New Jersey	35.5	(31.8–39.4)	42.3	(37.8–46.9)	**38.9**	**(35.8–42.0)**	3.1	(2.3–4.1)	7.2	(4.5–11.3)	5.1	(3.5–7.4)
New Mexico	—	—	—	—	—	—	13.7	(11.0–16.8)	20.8	(17.7–24.2)	17.3	(14.6–20.4)
New York	—	—	—	—	—	—	4.6	(3.2–6.5)	9.8	(8.1–11.8)	7.3	(6.0–8.7)
North Carolina	36.7	(32.0–41.6)	44.7	(40.1–49.3)	**40.8**	**(36.5–45.2)**	5.2	(3.8–7.0)	12.3	(9.6–15.6)	8.9	(7.0–11.1)
North Dakota	—	—	—	—	—	—	5.5	(3.7–8.1)	5.8	(4.2–7.9)	5.6	(4.1–7.6)
Ohio	33.9	(28.4–40.0)	37.2	(30.1–44.9)	**35.7**	**(29.9–42.0)**	3.4	(2.3–5.0)	7.9	(5.4–11.4)	5.8	(4.2–7.9)
Oklahoma	32.1	(27.9–36.6)	38.4	(33.3–43.7)	**35.3**	**(31.5–39.4)**	4.3	(2.8–6.7)	8.3	(6.1–11.1)	6.4	(4.8–8.3)
Rhode Island	38.0	(33.5–42.6)	40.8	(36.3–45.4)	**39.5**	**(36.0–43.2)**	4.2	(2.8–6.3)	9.1	(6.6–12.5)	6.8	(4.9–9.4)
South Carolina	33.8	(29.1–38.7)	39.1	(33.9–44.6)	**36.6**	**(32.8–40.7)**	5.0	(3.5–7.1)	10.8	(7.8–14.7)	8.0	(6.2–10.3)
South Dakota	27.9	(21.5–35.5)	31.3	(23.7–40.0)	**29.6**	**(23.1–37.1)**	5.8	(3.5–9.5)	8.6	(5.5–13.2)	7.2	(4.6–11.2)
Tennessee	38.3	(33.8–43.1)	43.4	(36.8–50.3)	**41.0**	**(36.1–46.2)**	6.8	(4.8–9.7)	14.0	(10.9–17.9)	10.6	(8.7–12.9)
Texas	35.1	(30.7–39.8)	40.0	(35.5–44.6)	**37.5**	**(33.5–41.7)**	5.9	(4.6–7.4)	10.5	(8.7–12.6)	8.2	(6.9–9.8)
Utah	16.4	(12.0–21.9)	17.2	(13.7–21.3)	**16.8**	**(13.3–20.8)**	3.0	(1.8–5.1)	4.3	(2.7–6.5)	3.7	(2.6–5.4)
Vermont	—	—	—	—	—	—	5.6	(4.3–7.2)	10.9	(9.5–12.6)	8.4	(7.2–9.8)
Virginia	30.5	(27.2–34.0)	33.4	(30.5–36.4)	**32.1**	**(29.4–35.0)**	5.0	(4.1–6.0)	9.6	(8.2–11.2)	7.5	(6.5–8.7)
West Virginia	36.0	(31.2–41.1)	42.0	(37.5–46.6)	**39.0**	**(34.9–43.2)**	7.1	(5.4–9.2)	11.1	(8.1–15.0)	9.1	(7.1–11.6)
Wisconsin	29.9	(25.4–34.9)	32.3	(28.3–36.7)	**31.2**	**(27.5–35.3)**	5.1	(3.7–7.1)	7.4	(5.6–9.8)	6.3	(4.9–8.1)
Wyoming	33.5	(29.9–37.3)	38.8	(35.7–41.9)	**36.3**	**(33.6–39.1)**	6.3	(4.2–9.5)	10.7	(8.8–13.1)	8.7	(6.8–11.0)
Median	*33.9*		*38.8*		*36.6*		*5.5*		*10.5*		*8.1*	
Range	*(16.4–41.5)*		*(17.2–47.0)*		*(16.8–43.3)*		*(3.0–13.7)*		*(4.3–20.8)*		*(3.7–17.3)*	

See table footnotes on the next page.

TABLE 50. (*Continued*) Percentage of high school students who ever used marijuana* and who tried marijuana for the first time before age 13 years, by sex — selected U.S. sites, Youth Risk Behavior Survey, 2013

Site	Ever used marijuana						Tried marijuana before age 13 years					
	Female		Male		Total		Female		Male		Total	
	%	CI†	%	CI	%	CI	%	CI	%	CI	%	CI
Large urban school district surveys												
Baltimore, MD	43.1	(38.5–47.9)	41.8	(35.1–48.8)	**42.9**	**(38.3–47.7)**	10.3	(7.6–13.8)	16.0	(12.3–20.7)	**13.6**	**(10.9–16.8)**
Boston, MA	43.3	(37.4–49.3)	40.3	(35.0–45.8)	**41.9**	**(37.6–46.4)**	6.3	(4.3–9.2)	8.8	(6.8–11.3)	**7.5**	**(6.0–9.3)**
Broward County, FL	35.6	(31.5–39.9)	40.3	(35.4–45.4)	**38.0**	**(34.3–41.9)**	5.4	(3.9–7.4)	9.8	(7.2–13.3)	**7.8**	**(6.1–10.1)**
Charlotte-Mecklenburg, NC	45.9	(41.2–50.7)	52.2	(47.9–56.4)	**49.3**	**(45.7–52.8)**	6.5	(4.5–9.4)	13.6	(10.5–17.4)	**10.1**	**(8.1–12.5)**
Chicago, IL	45.9	(40.7–51.1)	53.9	(48.9–58.9)	**50.0**	**(45.7–54.3)**	9.5	(6.9–12.8)	16.6	(13.1–20.7)	**13.2**	**(10.3–16.7)**
Detroit, MI	34.7	(30.0–39.7)	31.9	(27.3–36.9)	**33.7**	**(30.1–37.5)**	9.4	(6.7–13.0)	12.7	(9.8–16.4)	**11.2**	**(9.3–13.4)**
District of Columbia	—	—	—	—	—	—	12.6	(11.6–13.7)	22.6	(21.2–24.1)	**17.5**	**(16.6–18.5)**
Duval County, FL	40.0	(37.2–42.9)	47.1	(44.0–50.3)	**43.5**	**(41.3–45.6)**	8.2	(6.8–9.8)	15.9	(13.9–18.2)	**12.0**	**(10.7–13.5)**
Houston, TX	43.1	(38.1–48.3)	44.1	(40.2–48.1)	**43.6**	**(40.0–47.2)**	10.0	(7.7–12.9)	15.1	(12.4–18.4)	**12.7**	**(10.7–15.1)**
Los Angeles, CA	40.4	(34.0–47.1)	38.4	(32.8–44.3)	**39.3**	**(34.2–44.7)**	9.0	(6.2–12.8)	9.6	(7.0–12.9)	**9.3**	**(7.0–12.1)**
Memphis, TN	42.1	(37.2–47.2)	52.1	(47.5–56.6)	**47.2**	**(43.7–50.8)**	7.2	(5.1–9.9)	18.6	(14.8–23.2)	**13.2**	**(11.1–15.6)**
Miami-Dade County, FL	34.1	(29.4–39.2)	34.9	(30.6–39.4)	**34.6**	**(30.9–38.6)**	4.7	(3.3–6.5)	8.3	(6.8–10.2)	**6.5**	**(5.3–7.9)**
Milwaukee, WI	53.6	(46.3–60.7)	54.8	(48.8–60.7)	**54.4**	**(48.8–59.8)**	12.9	(10.5–15.9)	22.4	(18.0–27.6)	**17.8**	**(14.7–21.4)**
New York City, NY	—	—	—	—	—	—	4.2	(3.4–5.1)	10.3	(8.6–12.3)	**7.4**	**(6.4–8.5)**
Orange County, FL	31.4	(26.9–36.2)	37.2	(33.0–41.6)	**34.5**	**(30.7–38.6)**	4.7	(3.3–6.8)	9.0	(7.0–11.6)	**7.2**	**(5.9–8.8)**
Palm Beach County, FL	39.7	(35.1–44.4)	48.2	(43.1–53.3)	**44.2**	**(40.2–48.2)**	6.1	(3.8–9.7)	12.4	(9.8–15.5)	**9.5**	**(7.5–12.1)**
Philadelphia, PA	44.5	(38.5–50.7)	44.7	(39.1–50.4)	**44.6**	**(39.8–49.5)**	6.5	(4.7–9.0)	9.6	(7.0–13.1)	**8.0**	**(6.4–10.1)**
San Bernardino, CA	41.0	(36.1–46.0)	46.3	(40.6–52.1)	**43.7**	**(39.2–48.3)**	8.5	(6.5–10.9)	15.3	(12.5–18.6)	**12.0**	**(9.9–14.4)**
San Diego, CA	40.3	(35.1–45.7)	40.3	(35.3–45.6)	**40.5**	**(35.9–45.2)**	6.2	(4.3–8.9)	10.6	(8.1–13.7)	**8.5**	**(6.8–10.6)**
San Francisco, CA	27.8	(23.6–32.4)	28.3	(23.7–33.4)	**28.2**	**(24.7–32.0)**	6.0	(4.2–8.5)	5.3	(3.9–7.1)	**5.9**	**(4.6–7.4)**
Seattle, WA	33.3	(28.9–38.1)	36.5	(31.9–41.3)	**35.2**	**(31.6–39.0)**	7.1	(5.2–9.6)	8.8	(6.6–11.7)	**8.2**	**(6.6–10.1)**
Median	*40.4*		*41.8*		*42.9*		*7.1*		*12.4*		*9.5*	
Range	*(27.8–53.6)*		*(28.3–54.8)*		*(28.2–54.4)*		*(4.2–12.9)*		*(5.3–22.6)*		*(5.9–17.8)*	

* One or more times during their life.
† 95% confidence interval.
§ Not available.

TABLE 51. Percentage of high school students who currently use marijuana,* by sex, race/ethnicity, and grade — United States, Youth Risk Behavior Survey, 2013

Category	Female		Male		Total	
	%	CI†	%	CI	%	CI
Race/Ethnicity						
White§	18.0	(15.0–21.3)	22.8	(20.0–25.9)	**20.4**	**(17.8–23.3)**
Black§	27.1	(23.5–31.0)	30.6	(27.4–34.1)	**28.9**	**(26.3–31.6)**
Hispanic	27.4	(24.0–31.2)	27.7	(24.2–31.5)	**27.6**	**(24.6–30.7)**
Grade						
9	17.6	(15.0–20.6)	17.7	(15.3–20.4)	**17.7**	**(15.5–20.1)**
10	22.7	(18.9–27.1)	24.3	(19.6–29.7)	**23.5**	**(19.9–27.5)**
11	22.8	(19.2–26.8)	28.4	(24.9–32.0)	**25.5**	**(22.9–28.4)**
12	24.6	(21.0–28.6)	30.9	(27.2–35.0)	**27.7**	**(24.7–31.0)**
Total	**21.9**	**(19.4–24.6)**	**25.0**	**(22.8–27.4)**	**23.4**	**(21.3–25.7)**

* One or more times during the 30 days before the survey.
† 95% confidence interval.
§ Non-Hispanic.

Surveillance Summaries

TABLE 52. Percentage of high school students who currently use marijuana,* by sex — selected U.S. sites, Youth Risk Behavior Survey, 2013

Site	Female %	Female CI†	Male %	Male CI	Total %	Total CI
State surveys						
Alabama	16.2	(13.6–19.2)	22.1	(17.1–27.9)	19.2	(16.3–22.4)
Alaska	17.7	(13.8–22.4)	21.2	(18.1–24.8)	19.7	(17.1–22.5)
Arizona	19.3	(15.5–23.7)	27.6	(22.7–33.1)	23.5	(20.1–27.4)
Arkansas	16.5	(13.8–19.6)	21.8	(18.0–26.2)	19.0	(17.1–21.2)
Connecticut	22.6	(18.6–27.1)	29.4	(26.0–33.0)	26.0	(23.2–29.1)
Delaware	22.9	(20.3–25.7)	28.1	(24.9–31.5)	25.6	(23.3–27.9)
Florida	20.1	(18.1–22.2)	23.9	(21.9–26.1)	22.0	(20.4–23.7)
Georgia	19.1	(15.8–22.9)	21.3	(17.5–25.7)	20.3	(17.0–23.9)
Hawaii	18.0	(15.0–21.4)	19.7	(16.4–23.5)	18.9	(16.0–22.1)
Idaho	14.1	(11.7–17.0)	16.5	(13.5–20.1)	15.3	(13.2–17.7)
Illinois	20.9	(16.9–25.6)	26.8	(23.3–30.6)	24.0	(20.7–27.6)
Kansas	12.4	(10.4–14.7)	16.1	(12.7–20.2)	14.3	(12.1–16.9)
Kentucky	15.3	(11.7–19.7)	20.0	(16.6–23.8)	17.7	(14.9–21.0)
Louisiana	14.5	(11.0–18.9)	20.4	(16.1–25.5)	17.5	(14.7–20.6)
Maine	18.8	(16.9–20.9)	23.5	(21.5–25.6)	21.3	(19.5–23.2)
Maryland	17.8	(17.0–18.7)	21.6	(20.8–22.4)	19.8	(19.1–20.5)
Massachusetts	21.8	(19.6–24.2)	27.6	(24.4–31.1)	24.8	(23.0–26.8)
Michigan	16.8	(15.2–18.6)	19.6	(17.6–21.8)	18.2	(16.8–19.8)
Mississippi	14.1	(11.5–17.1)	21.5	(18.3–25.1)	17.7	(15.2–20.6)
Missouri	17.0	(13.0–21.8)	23.7	(19.3–28.7)	20.5	(17.2–24.4)
Montana	19.9	(17.3–22.8)	22.1	(19.7–24.7)	21.0	(18.8–23.5)
Nebraska	9.9	(7.6–12.8)	13.4	(10.5–16.9)	11.7	(9.6–14.0)
Nevada	19.1	(16.1–22.5)	18.3	(14.4–22.9)	18.7	(15.5–22.2)
New Hampshire	22.6	(19.1–26.7)	26.0	(23.0–29.3)	24.4	(21.8–27.2)
New Jersey	18.1	(15.3–21.4)	23.9	(20.3–27.9)	21.0	(18.5–23.6)
New Mexico	25.7	(21.5–30.3)	29.8	(26.6–33.3)	27.8	(24.3–31.5)
New York	19.0	(16.3–22.0)	23.8	(21.4–26.3)	21.4	(19.4–23.5)
North Carolina	19.5	(15.7–24.0)	26.5	(22.5–31.0)	23.2	(19.5–27.3)
North Dakota	15.6	(12.7–19.0)	16.3	(13.6–19.4)	15.9	(13.6–18.6)
Ohio	18.6	(13.8–24.5)	22.5	(17.3–28.8)	20.7	(16.3–25.8)
Oklahoma	14.1	(11.4–17.3)	18.4	(14.0–23.7)	16.3	(13.3–19.8)
Rhode Island	22.3	(18.5–26.6)	25.1	(20.1–30.8)	23.9	(20.0–28.4)
South Carolina	17.3	(14.5–20.4)	21.7	(18.3–25.6)	19.6	(17.2–22.3)
South Dakota	14.2	(9.1–21.5)	18.0	(11.6–26.7)	16.1	(10.7–23.3)
Tennessee	18.0	(14.6–22.0)	24.5	(20.8–28.7)	21.4	(18.1–25.2)
Texas	18.9	(16.2–21.9)	22.0	(19.0–25.3)	20.5	(17.9–23.2)
Utah	6.8	(5.0–9.2)	8.2	(6.0–11.1)	7.6	(6.1–9.3)
Vermont	21.4	(19.3–23.6)	29.7	(26.9–32.7)	25.7	(23.9–27.5)
Virginia	16.4	(14.5–18.6)	19.2	(17.5–21.2)	17.9	(16.3–19.7)
West Virginia	17.4	(14.7–20.4)	20.5	(16.7–24.9)	18.9	(16.1–22.0)
Wisconsin	14.8	(12.1–18.1)	19.6	(16.8–22.7)	17.3	(15.1–19.7)
Wyoming	16.0	(13.9–18.4)	19.4	(17.0–22.1)	17.8	(16.3–19.5)
Median	*17.9*		*21.7*		*19.7*	
Range	*(6.8–25.7)*		*(8.2–29.8)*		*(7.6–27.8)*	

See table footnotes on the next page.

TABLE 52. (*Continued*) Percentage of high school students who currently use marijuana,* by sex — selected U.S. sites, Youth Risk Behavior Survey, 2013

Site	Female %	Female CI†	Male %	Male CI	Total %	Total CI
Large urban school district surveys						
Baltimore, MD	22.0	(18.9–25.4)	26.5	(20.6–33.4)	24.7	(21.5–28.2)
Boston, MA	24.0	(19.8–28.8)	27.2	(22.4–32.5)	25.6	(22.1–29.5)
Broward County, FL	18.8	(16.0–21.9)	27.0	(22.6–31.9)	22.9	(20.1–26.1)
Charlotte-Mecklenburg, NC	26.6	(23.1–30.4)	31.8	(27.8–36.1)	29.2	(26.2–32.4)
Chicago, IL	25.3	(21.7–29.2)	31.7	(28.4–35.3)	28.5	(25.8–31.4)
Detroit, MI	17.4	(14.4–20.9)	16.5	(13.2–20.5)	17.1	(14.6–19.9)
District of Columbia	30.4	(28.9–31.9)	33.9	(32.3–35.5)	32.2	(31.0–33.3)
Duval County, FL	21.6	(19.4–24.1)	27.0	(24.2–30.1)	24.3	(22.4–26.3)
Houston, TX	21.9	(18.0–26.3)	25.0	(21.8–28.5)	23.4	(20.5–26.6)
Los Angeles, CA	20.7	(15.2–27.6)	20.0	(15.8–25.0)	20.3	(16.1–25.3)
Memphis, TN	23.8	(20.1–28.0)	29.8	(25.8–34.1)	26.9	(24.1–29.9)
Miami-Dade County, FL	19.9	(16.3–23.9)	19.7	(16.6–23.2)	19.8	(17.5–22.3)
Milwaukee, WI	29.0	(23.2–35.6)	35.4	(30.2–41.0)	32.2	(28.0–36.8)
New York City, NY	14.8	(12.9–16.8)	17.3	(15.1–19.8)	16.2	(14.5–18.0)
Orange County, FL	15.0	(12.2–18.3)	22.5	(19.2–26.2)	18.9	(16.6–21.6)
Palm Beach County, FL	24.5	(20.7–28.7)	30.9	(27.4–34.8)	27.8	(24.8–31.1)
Philadelphia, PA	24.8	(21.2–28.8)	25.3	(20.1–31.4)	25.1	(21.6–28.9)
San Bernardino, CA	20.5	(16.9–24.6)	25.6	(21.1–30.6)	22.9	(19.6–26.6)
San Diego, CA	21.1	(17.3–25.6)	22.3	(18.4–26.8)	21.9	(18.6–25.7)
San Francisco, CA	15.6	(12.7–18.9)	16.7	(13.2–20.9)	16.3	(13.6–19.3)
Seattle, WA	21.2	(17.8–25.0)	24.4	(21.0–28.3)	22.9	(20.1–25.9)
Median	*21.6*		*25.6*		*23.4*	
Range	*(14.8–30.4)*		*(16.5–35.4)*		*(16.2–32.2)*	

* One or more times during the 30 days before the survey.
† 95% confidence interval.

TABLE 53. Percentage of high school students who ever used cocaine* and who ever used hallucinogenic drugs,† by sex, race/ethnicity, and grade — United States, Youth Risk Behavior Survey, 2013

Category	Ever used cocaine Female %	Female CI§	Male %	Male CI	Total %	Total CI	Ever used hallucinogenic drugs Female %	Female CI	Male %	Male CI	Total %	Total CI
Race/Ethnicity												
White¶	3.7	(2.9–4.8)	5.9	(4.7–7.4)	4.8	(3.9–5.9)	5.4	(4.4–6.7)	9.8	(7.8–12.3)	7.6	(6.3–9.3)
Black¶	1.2	(0.7–1.9)	3.0	(2.1–4.3)	2.1	(1.5–2.8)	1.0	(0.5–2.0)	3.4	(2.3–5.1)	2.2	(1.5–3.2)
Hispanic	8.1	(5.7–11.3)	10.9	(8.5–14.0)	9.5	(7.5–11.9)	8.0	(5.8–11.1)	8.9	(7.0–11.1)	8.4	(6.8–10.5)
Grade												
9	4.2	(3.0–5.8)	4.6	(3.5–6.1)	4.4	(3.4–5.6)	4.1	(3.0–5.7)	5.0	(3.7–6.9)	4.6	(3.7–5.7)
10	3.1	(2.0–4.8)	5.0	(3.5–7.1)	4.0	(3.1–5.3)	5.0	(3.4–7.4)	8.1	(5.9–10.9)	6.6	(4.8–8.9)
11	5.8	(4.3–7.8)	7.9	(6.0–10.2)	6.8	(5.6–8.3)	6.6	(5.0–8.7)	11.0	(8.6–13.8)	8.7	(7.2–10.6)
12	4.7	(3.2–6.7)	9.5	(7.5–11.9)	7.1	(5.7–8.7)	5.9	(4.4–7.9)	11.7	(9.5–14.3)	8.8	(7.2–10.6)
Total	**4.5**	**(3.6–5.6)**	**6.6**	**(5.5–7.9)**	**5.5**	**(4.7–6.6)**	**5.5**	**(4.5–6.7)**	**8.8**	**(7.4–10.5)**	**7.1**	**(6.0–8.4)**

* Used any form of cocaine (e.g., powder, crack, or freebase) one or more times during their life.
† Used hallucinogenic drugs (e.g., LSD, acid, PCP, angel dust, mescaline, or mushrooms) one or more times during their life.
§ 95% confidence interval.
¶ Non-Hispanic.

Surveillance Summaries

TABLE 54. Percentage of high school students who ever used cocaine,* by sex — selected U.S. sites, Youth Risk Behavior Survey, 2013

Site	Female %	CI†	Male %	CI	Total %	CI
State surveys						
Alabama	4.2	(3.0–5.7)	8.3	(6.0–11.4)	6.6	(5.1–8.6)
Alaska	4.9	(3.3–7.3)	6.0	(4.4–8.1)	5.8	(4.4–7.5)
Arizona	8.3	(6.1–11.1)	11.6	(8.9–15.0)	10.1	(8.3–12.3)
Arkansas	5.7	(4.1–8.1)	9.9	(8.0–12.2)	8.1	(6.7–9.9)
Connecticut	2.7	(1.9–3.9)	6.9	(5.4–8.8)	4.9	(3.9–6.0)
Delaware	2.4	(1.7–3.5)	5.4	(4.2–7.0)	4.0	(3.3–4.9)
Florida	3.8	(3.1–4.5)	7.7	(6.7–8.9)	5.8	(5.1–6.6)
Georgia	5.6	(4.2–7.6)	8.0	(5.8–10.9)	7.0	(5.4–9.1)
Hawaii	6.5	(4.7–8.7)	6.5	(4.9–8.7)	6.5	(5.2–8.1)
Idaho	4.8	(3.6–6.4)	6.0	(4.3–8.4)	5.4	(4.2–7.0)
Illinois	5.3	(3.9–7.2)	9.8	(7.7–12.5)	7.8	(6.3–9.5)
Kansas	—§	—	—	—	—	—
Kentucky	2.0	(1.2–3.3)	6.5	(4.5–9.2)	4.5	(3.4–5.9)
Louisiana	5.2	(3.4–7.8)	10.9	(8.2–14.3)	8.3	(6.6–10.5)
Maine	—	—	—	—	—	—
Maryland	4.2	(3.9–4.5)	8.1	(7.6–8.6)	6.5	(6.1–6.9)
Massachusetts	2.9	(2.1–4.0)	4.4	(3.2–6.1)	3.7	(2.9–4.8)
Michigan	2.4	(1.6–3.7)	5.6	(3.8–8.0)	4.0	(2.8–5.7)
Mississippi	2.5	(1.5–4.1)	5.9	(4.2–8.2)	4.2	(3.1–5.5)
Missouri	—	—	—	—	—	—
Montana	4.9	(4.0–6.0)	7.7	(6.6–9.0)	6.4	(5.6–7.3)
Nebraska	2.0	(1.2–3.3)	4.4	(2.9–6.5)	3.2	(2.3–4.4)
Nevada	5.7	(4.1–7.8)	9.6	(7.1–12.7)	7.7	(5.9–10.0)
New Hampshire	3.1	(2.0–4.6)	6.4	(4.7–8.8)	4.9	(3.6–6.5)
New Jersey	2.6	(1.8–3.7)	7.1	(4.6–11.0)	4.8	(3.4–6.8)
New Mexico	8.5	(6.0–11.8)	12.0	(9.8–14.6)	10.3	(8.1–13.0)
New York	3.7	(2.5–5.6)	6.8	(5.2–8.9)	5.3	(4.2–6.7)
North Carolina	2.5	(1.6–3.9)	7.2	(5.8–8.9)	4.9	(3.9–6.3)
North Dakota	—	—	—	—	—	—
Ohio	2.6	(1.3–4.8)	5.1	(3.8–6.7)	3.8	(2.9–5.1)
Oklahoma	2.8	(1.6–4.6)	4.8	(3.3–7.0)	3.8	(3.1–4.7)
Rhode Island	3.2	(2.2–4.6)	5.1	(3.6–7.3)	4.5	(3.4–5.8)
South Carolina	2.6	(1.5–4.7)	7.0	(4.4–10.9)	5.2	(3.7–7.3)
South Dakota	—	—	—	—	—	—
Tennessee	4.2	(2.9–6.1)	7.4	(5.6–9.8)	6.0	(4.6–7.8)
Texas	5.3	(4.2–6.7)	11.2	(8.8–14.2)	8.3	(6.8–10.2)
Utah	2.9	(1.7–5.2)	3.8	(2.5–5.6)	3.5	(2.3–5.2)
Vermont	4.3	(3.7–5.0)	7.9	(6.6–9.5)	6.3	(5.4–7.2)
Virginia	4.2	(3.5–5.1)	6.6	(5.2–8.2)	5.7	(4.8–6.7)
West Virginia	5.0	(3.3–7.5)	5.4	(3.8–7.6)	5.2	(4.1–6.6)
Wisconsin	3.1	(2.1–4.4)	5.5	(3.8–7.7)	4.3	(3.2–5.8)
Wyoming	5.1	(3.8–6.7)	8.7	(7.0–10.7)	7.1	(5.8–8.6)
Median	4.2		6.9		5.4	
Range	(2.0–8.5)		(3.8–12.0)		(3.2–10.3)	

See table footnotes on the next page.

TABLE 54. (*Continued*) Percentage of high school students who ever used cocaine,* by sex — selected U.S. sites, Youth Risk Behavior Survey, 2013

Site	Female %	CI[†]	Male %	CI	Total %	CI
Large urban school district surveys						
Baltimore, MD	5.1	(3.3–7.7)	10.7	(7.8–14.4)	8.4	(6.5–10.9)
Boston, MA	2.3	(1.2–4.3)	4.6	(2.8–7.5)	3.5	(2.3–5.4)
Broward County, FL	2.9	(2.1–4.2)	6.3	(4.6–8.6)	4.9	(3.8–6.4)
Charlotte-Mecklenburg, NC	3.0	(2.0–4.3)	6.9	(5.0–9.6)	5.3	(4.1–6.8)
Chicago, IL	3.8	(2.5–5.7)	10.1	(8.1–12.5)	7.1	(5.6–8.9)
Detroit, MI	2.1	(1.2–3.8)	6.4	(3.9–10.4)	4.4	(2.9–6.6)
District of Columbia	4.4	(3.8–5.1)	7.8	(6.9–8.7)	6.4	(5.9–7.0)
Duval County, FL	4.4	(3.4–5.7)	9.2	(7.5–11.2)	7.1	(5.9–8.5)
Houston, TX	8.7	(6.7–11.3)	12.6	(9.9–15.9)	11.2	(9.3–13.6)
Los Angeles, CA	5.4	(4.0–7.2)	7.5	(6.0–9.3)	6.5	(5.3–7.8)
Memphis, TN	4.6	(3.0–7.0)	7.0	(4.7–10.3)	6.1	(4.4–8.4)
Miami-Dade County, FL	5.9	(4.4–7.9)	4.6	(3.2–6.7)	5.3	(4.2–6.7)
Milwaukee, WI	4.4	(3.0–6.5)	9.1	(6.8–12.1)	7.0	(5.5–9.0)
New York City, NY	2.9	(2.3–3.6)	6.2	(5.0–7.6)	4.7	(3.8–5.6)
Orange County, FL	3.7	(2.4–5.8)	5.3	(3.8–7.3)	4.7	(3.6–6.1)
Palm Beach County, FL	6.8	(4.7–9.6)	8.4	(6.2–11.3)	7.8	(6.1–9.8)
Philadelphia, PA	2.9	(1.6–5.2)	2.9	(1.6–5.2)	3.1	(1.9–4.9)
San Bernardino, CA	5.0	(3.4–7.3)	8.0	(5.5–11.6)	6.5	(4.9–8.5)
San Diego, CA	4.3	(2.9–6.2)	9.1	(6.9–11.9)	6.9	(5.4–8.8)
San Francisco, CA	6.6	(5.1–8.4)	6.0	(4.1–8.7)	6.5	(5.2–8.1)
Seattle, WA	—	—	—	—	—	—
Median	*4.4*		*7.3*		*6.4*	
Range	*(2.1–8.7)*		*(2.9–12.6)*		*(3.1–11.2)*	

* Used any form of cocaine (e.g., powder, crack, or freebase) one or more times during their life.
[†] 95% confidence interval.
[§] Not available.

TABLE 55. Percentage of high school students who ever used inhalants* and who ever used ecstasy,[†] by sex, race/ethnicity, and grade — United States, Youth Risk Behavior Survey, 2013

	Ever used inhalants						Ever used ecstasy					
	Female		Male		Total		Female		Male		Total	
Category	%	CI[§]	%	CI	%	CI	%	CI	%	CI	%	CI
Race/Ethnicity												
White[¶]	9.1	(7.7–10.7)	8.1	(6.4–10.1)	8.6	(7.4–10.0)	4.6	(3.5–6.1)	6.9	(5.5–8.7)	5.8	(4.8–7.0)
Black[¶]	7.9	(6.1–10.3)	5.5	(4.2–7.3)	6.8	(5.6–8.2)	2.1	(1.2–3.4)	7.0	(5.3–9.1)	4.4	(3.4–5.7)
Hispanic	14.3	(11.5–17.6)	8.9	(7.4–10.8)	11.7	(9.9–13.7)	10.1	(7.0–14.4)	8.7	(6.8–11.0)	9.4	(7.1–12.4)
Grade												
9	11.9	(9.7–14.5)	8.2	(6.6–10.3)	10.1	(8.4–12.0)	3.3	(2.4–4.5)	4.7	(3.2–6.8)	4.0	(3.0–5.3)
10	9.4	(7.0–12.4)	6.4	(4.9–8.5)	7.9	(6.2–10.0)	4.2	(3.0–5.8)	6.7	(5.2–8.6)	5.5	(4.4–6.8)
11	11.0	(8.7–13.8)	8.7	(6.8–11.2)	9.9	(8.3–11.7)	7.5	(5.8–9.8)	9.4	(7.2–12.3)	8.5	(7.1–10.0)
12	7.1	(5.6–8.9)	8.1	(6.3–10.4)	7.6	(6.2–9.3)	7.1	(5.1–9.8)	10.1	(8.0–12.7)	8.6	(7.0–10.6)
Total	**10.0**	**(8.7–11.5)**	**7.9**	**(6.8–9.1)**	**8.9**	**(7.9–10.1)**	**5.5**	**(4.6–6.7)**	**7.6**	**(6.4–8.9)**	**6.6**	**(5.6–7.7)**

* Sniffed glue, breathed the contents of aerosol spray cans, or inhaled any paints or sprays to get high one or more times during their life.
[†] Used ecstasy (also called "MDMA") one or more times during their life.
[§] 95% confidence interval.
[¶] Non-Hispanic.

Surveillance Summaries

TABLE 56. Percentage of high school students who ever used inhalants* and who ever used ecstasy,† by sex — selected U.S. sites, Youth Risk Behavior Survey, 2013

Site	Inhalants Female %	Female CI§	Inhalants Male %	Male CI	Inhalants Total %	Total CI	Ecstasy Female %	Female CI	Ecstasy Male %	Male CI	Ecstasy Total %	Total CI
State surveys												
Alabama	12.5	(9.6–16.0)	12.9	(10.2–16.1)	13.1	(10.7–15.9)	5.1	(3.6–7.0)	10.4	(8.5–12.6)	7.9	(6.5–9.7)
Alaska	5.3	(3.5–7.8)	7.2	(5.3–9.8)	6.6	(5.1–8.5)	5.8	(3.7–9.0)	6.3	(4.5–8.8)	6.3	(4.7–8.4)
Arizona	10.0	(7.8–12.8)	11.0	(7.4–15.9)	10.7	(8.0–14.2)	—¶	—	—	—	—	—
Arkansas	11.0	(8.8–13.7)	14.7	(12.1–17.7)	13.1	(11.2–15.3)	4.8	(3.4–6.5)	11.6	(8.9–15.0)	8.3	(6.9–10.0)
Connecticut	7.5	(6.0–9.3)	8.5	(7.0–10.3)	8.1	(6.9–9.5)	4.3	(3.2–5.8)	8.5	(6.9–10.6)	6.5	(5.6–7.6)
Delaware	6.8	(5.5–8.3)	8.2	(6.7–10.0)	7.5	(6.4–8.8)	4.2	(3.0–5.9)	7.0	(5.5–8.7)	5.7	(4.7–6.9)
Florida	—	—	—	—	—	—	—	—	—	—	—	—
Georgia	8.2	(6.7–9.9)	11.2	(8.6–14.5)	9.9	(8.2–12.0)	5.0	(3.8–6.7)	8.7	(6.6–11.4)	7.1	(5.6–8.8)
Hawaii	9.8	(8.2–11.7)	8.2	(6.6–10.2)	9.2	(7.8–11.0)	7.0	(5.6–8.7)	8.9	(6.1–12.7)	8.0	(6.1–10.5)
Idaho	9.5	(7.4–12.1)	7.8	(6.2–9.8)	8.6	(7.0–10.5)	6.1	(4.6–8.2)	7.2	(5.0–10.3)	6.7	(5.1–8.7)
Illinois	11.2	(8.8–14.1)	12.4	(9.7–15.7)	12.0	(10.1–14.3)	6.3	(4.6–8.7)	10.9	(8.6–13.7)	8.8	(6.9–11.1)
Kansas	7.5	(5.9–9.4)	8.0	(6.1–10.3)	7.7	(6.5–9.2)	3.0	(2.1–4.3)	7.2	(5.3–9.8)	5.2	(4.0–6.8)
Kentucky	7.2	(5.6–9.1)	6.7	(4.9–9.2)	7.1	(5.9–8.5)	2.1	(1.2–3.7)	5.8	(4.3–8.0)	4.2	(3.3–5.4)
Louisiana	14.0	(10.3–18.6)	14.1	(10.8–18.3)	14.5	(12.0–17.4)	6.4	(4.5–9.1)	14.0	(11.6–16.8)	10.6	(8.7–12.8)
Maine	8.2	(7.3–9.3)	9.8	(8.6–11.2)	9.1	(8.3–10.1)	—	—	—	—	—	—
Maryland	9.3	(8.7–9.9)	10.7	(10.1–11.3)	10.4	(9.9–10.9)	5.7	(5.3–6.1)	10.3	(9.7–11.0)	8.3	(7.9–8.8)
Massachusetts	—	—	—	—	—	—	3.7	(2.4–5.5)	5.5	(4.1–7.4)	4.7	(3.8–5.8)
Michigan	7.4	(6.2–8.8)	7.3	(5.7–9.4)	7.4	(6.3–8.7)	—	—	—	—	—	—
Mississippi	10.0	(8.2–12.1)	10.0	(7.6–13.0)	10.0	(8.6–11.7)	3.7	(2.4–5.5)	6.9	(4.6–10.0)	5.3	(3.9–7.0)
Missouri	—	—	—	—	—	—	—	—	—	—	—	—
Montana	10.4	(8.6–12.5)	9.4	(8.1–10.9)	9.9	(8.7–11.2)	6.6	(5.5–8.0)	9.4	(8.1–11.0)	8.2	(7.2–9.3)
Nebraska	6.6	(4.8–9.0)	7.4	(5.6–9.6)	7.0	(5.7–8.6)	2.4	(1.4–4.0)	4.1	(2.8–5.9)	3.2	(2.4–4.5)
Nevada	10.9	(7.9–15.0)	9.4	(7.2–12.3)	10.3	(8.3–12.6)	8.9	(7.5–10.6)	13.4	(10.4–17.1)	11.2	(9.5–13.2)
New Hampshire	8.2	(6.5–10.5)	7.4	(5.6–9.6)	8.0	(6.7–9.6)	5.4	(3.9–7.4)	8.8	(6.7–11.4)	7.4	(5.8–9.2)
New Jersey	8.6	(5.9–12.2)	10.8	(8.6–13.5)	9.7	(7.9–11.8)	5.7	(3.9–8.1)	7.8	(5.6–10.7)	6.7	(5.1–8.9)
New Mexico	—	—	—	—	—	—	8.1	(6.3–10.4)	10.1	(8.7–11.7)	9.2	(7.8–10.8)
New York	—	—	—	—	—	—	5.8	(4.1–8.2)	8.2	(6.1–10.8)	7.0	(5.7–8.7)
North Carolina	9.3	(7.2–11.9)	7.4	(5.5–9.9)	8.3	(7.1–9.7)	—	—	—	—	—	—
North Dakota	11.9	(9.6–14.7)	9.2	(7.3–11.5)	10.5	(9.0–12.3)	—	—	—	—	—	—
Ohio	7.6	(5.3–10.9)	10.0	(7.1–13.8)	8.8	(7.1–10.8)	—	—	—	—	—	—
Oklahoma	8.3	(6.5–10.6)	7.8	(6.1–10.0)	8.0	(6.7–9.7)	4.4	(3.0–6.3)	5.6	(3.8–8.1)	5.0	(4.2–5.9)
Rhode Island	—	—	—	—	—	—	—	—	—	—	—	—
South Carolina	10.8	(7.6–15.1)	10.2	(7.6–13.6)	10.7	(8.7–13.2)	4.3	(2.8–6.4)	8.6	(6.3–11.5)	6.8	(5.3–8.6)
South Dakota	10.2	(6.7–15.3)	11.3	(8.8–14.2)	10.7	(8.0–14.1)	—	—	—	—	—	—
Tennessee	11.1	(9.2–13.4)	11.4	(8.9–14.5)	11.4	(9.8–13.3)	5.2	(3.6–7.6)	8.4	(6.3–11.0)	7.0	(5.3–9.3)
Texas	9.5	(7.7–11.6)	9.5	(7.4–12.0)	9.5	(8.1–11.1)	7.4	(5.7–9.7)	10.1	(8.3–12.2)	8.8	(7.2–10.6)
Utah	7.6	(5.9–9.7)	5.5	(4.2–7.1)	6.6	(5.3–8.1)	2.6	(1.6–4.1)	4.5	(3.0–6.6)	3.6	(2.6–5.0)
Vermont	8.3	(7.3–9.3)	8.3	(7.0–9.8)	8.4	(7.4–9.5)	—	—	—	—	—	—
Virginia	8.3	(7.1–9.5)	8.8	(7.4–10.3)	8.8	(7.8–9.9)	5.0	(4.1–6.1)	7.9	(6.7–9.2)	6.6	(5.7–7.5)
West Virginia	7.0	(5.5–8.9)	11.3	(8.9–14.3)	9.2	(7.7–11.0)	4.0	(2.3–6.7)	5.9	(4.6–7.5)	4.9	(4.1–5.9)
Wisconsin	5.1	(3.9–6.6)	6.5	(5.1–8.3)	5.9	(4.9–7.0)	—	—	—	—	—	—
Wyoming	10.5	(8.8–12.4)	11.4	(9.6–13.5)	11.1	(9.6–12.8)	5.9	(4.6–7.6)	10.6	(8.8–12.7)	8.5	(7.1–10.1)
Median	*8.9*		*9.4*		*9.2*		*5.1*		*8.4*		*6.9*	
Range	*(5.1–14.0)*		*(5.5–14.7)*		*(5.9–14.5)*		*(2.1–8.9)*		*(4.1–14.0)*		*(3.2–11.2)*	

See table footnotes on the next page.

TABLE 56. (*Continued*) Percentage of high school students who ever used inhalants* and who ever used ecstasy,† by sex — selected U.S. sites, Youth Risk Behavior Survey, 2013

	Ever used inhalants						Ever used ecstasy					
	Female		Male		Total		Female		Male		Total	
Site	%	CI§	%	CI	%	CI	%	CI	%	CI	%	CI
Large urban school district surveys												
Baltimore, MD	—·	—	—	—	—	—	3.8	(2.6–5.7)	10.7	(7.9–14.3)	**8.0**	**(6.2–10.1)**
Boston, MA	—	—	—	—	—	—	2.7	(1.5–4.6)	6.5	(4.8–8.8)	**4.6**	**(3.4–6.2)**
Broward County, FL	5.8	(4.1–8.2)	6.9	(5.2–9.0)	**6.5**	**(5.2–8.3)**	6.2	(4.8–8.0)	8.6	(6.3–11.8)	**7.7**	**(6.3–9.3)**
Charlotte-Mecklenburg, NC	10.5	(8.0–13.6)	9.6	(7.4–12.3)	**10.4**	**(8.6–12.5)**	—	—	—	—	—	—
Chicago, IL	9.0	(6.8–11.9)	10.2	(7.6–13.5)	**9.9**	**(7.9–12.5)**	4.4	(3.0–6.4)	10.8	(8.8–13.2)	**7.8**	**(6.5–9.3)**
Detroit, MI	11.2	(8.8–14.2)	8.6	(6.0–12.1)	**10.4**	**(8.3–12.9)**	—	—	—	—	—	—
District of Columbia	13.9	(12.9–15.0)	12.1	(11.0–13.2)	**13.4**	**(12.6–14.2)**	5.6	(4.9–6.3)	9.1	(8.1–10.1)	**7.5**	**(6.9–8.2)**
Duval County, FL	8.8	(7.4–10.6)	11.9	(10.2–13.8)	**10.5**	**(9.3–11.9)**	7.2	(5.9–8.8)	11.3	(9.6–13.4)	**9.5**	**(8.3–11.0)**
Houston, TX	10.7	(8.7–13.1)	11.1	(9.2–13.2)	**11.3**	**(10.0–12.9)**	6.7	(5.2–8.5)	11.2	(9.3–13.5)	**9.4**	**(8.1–10.9)**
Los Angeles, CA	12.7	(10.2–15.8)	8.4	(5.9–11.9)	**10.5**	**(8.7–12.7)**	11.5	(8.5–15.4)	10.2	(7.6–13.7)	**10.9**	**(8.5–13.8)**
Memphis, TN	11.0	(8.7–13.8)	9.4	(7.1–12.3)	**10.7**	**(8.7–12.9)**	3.8	(2.5–5.8)	6.7	(4.7–9.3)	**5.6**	**(4.1–7.5)**
Miami-Dade County, FL	7.2	(5.3–9.6)	4.6	(3.5–6.2)	**6.0**	**(4.8–7.4)**	11.4	(9.0–14.3)	9.0	(7.0–11.6)	**10.3**	**(8.5–12.5)**
Milwaukee, WI	7.7	(6.0–10.0)	13.3	(9.4–18.4)	**10.6**	**(8.2–13.6)**	6.4	(4.9–8.4)	11.1	(7.9–15.5)	**9.0**	**(7.2–11.3)**
New York City, NY	—	—	—	—	—	—	3.3	(2.5–4.4)	5.9	(4.8–7.2)	**4.8**	**(4.1–5.5)**
Orange County, FL	8.2	(6.6–10.1)	8.8	(7.1–10.9)	**8.8**	**(7.5–10.3)**	4.2	(3.2–5.6)	8.8	(6.7–11.5)	**6.8**	**(5.4–8.6)**
Palm Beach County, FL	9.0	(6.2–12.9)	10.6	(7.8–14.3)	**10.1**	**(7.9–13.0)**	11.3	(8.5–14.9)	16.8	(13.4–21.0)	**14.5**	**(11.8–17.8)**
Philadelphia, PA	7.4	(5.4–10.0)	5.7	(3.8–8.5)	**6.7**	**(5.3–8.5)**	3.0	(2.0–4.3)	4.9	(2.9–8.2)	**4.1**	**(2.8–6.0)**
San Bernardino, CA	14.7	(11.3–19.0)	11.0	(8.4–14.3)	**13.0**	**(10.7–15.7)**	7.1	(5.0–10.0)	9.8	(7.1–13.4)	**8.4**	**(6.4–10.9)**
San Diego, CA	7.5	(5.8–9.7)	8.4	(6.6–10.6)	**8.0**	**(6.8–9.4)**	10.7	(8.1–14.1)	10.6	(8.5–13.1)	**10.7**	**(8.9–12.9)**
San Francisco, CA	5.3	(3.9–7.1)	6.1	(4.5–8.3)	**5.9**	**(4.8–7.2)**	8.1	(6.3–10.3)	8.6	(6.3–11.6)	**8.5**	**(6.7–10.6)**
Seattle, WA	—	—	—	—	—	—	—	—	—	—	—	—
Median	*9.0*		*9.4*		*10.4*		*6.3*		*9.4*		*8.2*	
Range	*(5.3–14.7)*		*(4.6–13.3)*		*(5.9–13.4)*		*(2.7–11.5)*		*(4.9–16.8)*		*(4.1–14.5)*	

* Sniffed glue, breathed the contents of aerosol spray cans, or inhaled any paints or sprays to get high one or more times during their life.
† Used ecstasy (also called "MDMA") one or more times during their life.
§ 95% confidence interval.
¶ Not available.

TABLE 57. Percentage of high school students who ever used heroin* and who ever used methamphetamines,† by sex, race/ethnicity, and grade — United States, Youth Risk Behavior Survey, 2013

	Ever used heroin						Ever used methamphetamines					
	Female		Male		Total		Female		Male		Total	
Category	%	CI§	%	CI	%	CI	%	CI	%	CI	%	CI
Race/Ethnicity												
White¶	1.1	(0.6–1.9)	2.3	(1.6–3.3)	**1.7**	**(1.2–2.4)**	2.8	(2.1–3.8)	3.2	(2.3–4.4)	**3.0**	**(2.4–3.8)**
Black¶	0.8	(0.4–1.7)	2.4	(1.5–3.7)	**1.6**	**(1.1–2.3)**	0.5	(0.2–1.2)	2.1	(1.3–3.3)	**1.3**	**(0.9–1.9)**
Hispanic	3.0	(2.0–4.5)	3.9	(2.9–5.3)	**3.4**	**(2.6–4.5)**	4.9	(3.4–6.9)	4.2	(3.0–5.9)	**4.5**	**(3.4–6.1)**
Grade												
9	1.6	(1.0–2.8)	2.4	(1.4–4.0)	**2.0**	**(1.3–3.1)**	2.2	(1.4–3.3)	2.7	(1.8–4.1)	**2.4**	**(1.7–3.5)**
10	1.1	(0.6–2.0)	2.8	(1.9–4.3)	**2.0**	**(1.4–2.9)**	3.1	(2.1–4.4)	3.0	(2.0–4.3)	**3.0**	**(2.3–4.0)**
11	2.0	(1.1–3.4)	2.8	(1.8–4.4)	**2.4**	**(1.8–3.3)**	4.3	(3.0–6.0)	3.6	(2.5–5.2)	**3.9**	**(3.1–5.0)**
12	1.2	(0.6–2.3)	3.1	(2.2–4.4)	**2.1**	**(1.6–2.9)**	2.2	(1.1–4.1)	4.4	(3.3–5.7)	**3.3**	**(2.4–4.4)**
Total	**1.6**	**(1.1–2.2)**	**2.8**	**(2.2–3.6)**	**2.2**	**(1.7–2.8)**	**3.0**	**(2.3–3.8)**	**3.4**	**(2.7–4.3)**	**3.2**	**(2.6–4.0)**

* Used heroin (also called "smack," "junk," or "China White") one or more times during their life.
† Used methamphetamines (also called "speed," "crystal," "crank," or "ice") one or more times during their life.
§ 95% confidence interval.
¶ Non-Hispanic.

Surveillance Summaries

TABLE 58. Percentage of high school students who ever used heroin* and who ever used methamphetamines,† by sex — selected U.S. sites, Youth Risk Behavior Survey, 2013

	Ever used heroin						Ever used methamphetamines					
	Female		Male		Total		Female		Male		Total	
Site	%	CI§	%	CI	%	CI	%	CI	%	CI	%	CI
State surveys												
Alabama	3.8	(2.1–6.9)	5.9	(4.2–8.1)	**5.3**	**(3.7–7.5)**	4.8	(3.1–7.4)	7.3	(5.0–10.6)	**6.2**	**(4.4–8.7)**
Alaska	1.2	(0.5–2.7)	2.8	(1.6–4.9)	**2.2**	**(1.4–3.6)**	1.8	(1.0–3.4)	2.8	(1.7–4.5)	**2.6**	**(1.8–3.9)**
Arizona	3.7	(2.4–5.6)	5.6	(3.6–8.6)	**4.7**	**(3.2–6.9)**	3.9	(2.5–6.0)	5.3	(3.3–8.5)	**4.7**	**(3.3–6.7)**
Arkansas	4.0	(2.2–7.0)	8.5	(5.7–12.5)	**6.6**	**(4.6–9.5)**	4.5	(3.2–6.3)	9.2	(6.5–12.8)	**7.2**	**(5.6–9.1)**
Connecticut	1.2	(0.7–2.2)	5.4	(4.2–6.8)	**3.4**	**(2.7–4.3)**	2.0	(1.3–2.9)	6.4	(4.6–8.9)	**4.3**	**(3.3–5.6)**
Delaware	1.3	(0.8–2.3)	4.0	(3.0–5.4)	**2.8**	**(2.1–3.6)**	1.5	(0.9–2.5)	3.8	(2.8–5.1)	**2.7**	**(2.1–3.5)**
Florida	—¶	—	—	—	—	—	—	—	—	—	—	—
Georgia	—	—	—	—	—	—	—	—	—	—	—	—
Hawaii	3.2	(2.2–4.6)	3.3	(2.3–4.8)	**3.4**	**(2.8–4.2)**	4.2	(3.1–5.6)	3.9	(2.6–5.7)	**4.3**	**(3.2–5.6)**
Idaho	1.5	(0.7–3.1)	2.7	(1.7–4.4)	**2.1**	**(1.4–3.2)**	2.9	(1.9–4.4)	2.7	(1.8–4.1)	**2.8**	**(2.1–3.8)**
Illinois	1.9	(1.2–3.1)	5.6	(3.8–8.0)	**3.9**	**(2.8–5.5)**	2.7	(1.8–4.1)	5.9	(4.2–8.4)	**4.5**	**(3.2–6.2)**
Kansas	—	—	—	—	—	—	2.0	(1.2–3.4)	3.9	(2.8–5.3)	**3.1**	**(2.3–4.1)**
Kentucky	—	—	—	—	—	—	2.5	(1.6–4.1)	4.3	(2.9–6.3)	**3.7**	**(2.7–5.0)**
Louisiana	5.0	(2.8–8.8)	9.8	(7.4–12.7)	**7.8**	**(5.9–10.1)**	5.5	(3.3–9.2)	11.7	(8.4–15.9)	**8.9**	**(6.9–11.5)**
Maine	—	—	—	—	—	—	—	—	—	—	—	—
Maryland	2.8	(2.5–3.1)	6.3	(5.8–6.8)	**4.9**	**(4.6–5.3)**	3.0	(2.7–3.3)	6.4	(5.9–6.9)	**5.0**	**(4.7–5.4)**
Massachusetts	—	—	—	—	—	—	1.3	(0.7–2.4)	1.9	(1.2–3.0)	**1.6**	**(1.1–2.5)**
Michigan	1.7	(1.2–2.6)	3.8	(2.6–5.5)	**2.8**	**(2.0–4.0)**	1.6	(1.0–2.3)	3.7	(2.4–5.6)	**2.7**	**(1.9–3.8)**
Mississippi	1.7	(1.0–3.1)	4.7	(2.9–7.5)	**3.2**	**(2.2–4.6)**	2.0	(1.1–3.7)	4.4	(2.8–6.8)	**3.2**	**(2.2–4.5)**
Missouri	—	—	—	—	—	—	—	—	—	—	—	—
Montana	1.7	(1.3–2.4)	3.3	(2.6–4.2)	**2.6**	**(2.1–3.2)**	2.7	(2.0–3.5)	4.4	(3.5–5.4)	**3.6**	**(3.0–4.3)**
Nebraska	0.9	(0.4–2.0)	1.6	(0.9–2.8)	**1.2**	**(0.8–2.0)**	1.4	(0.7–2.6)	2.6	(1.6–4.4)	**2.0**	**(1.4–3.0)**
Nevada	1.6	(1.1–2.3)	4.6	(3.0–7.0)	**3.3**	**(2.2–5.0)**	3.1	(2.1–4.4)	7.0	(4.8–10.3)	**5.2**	**(3.7–7.1)**
New Hampshire	1.8	(1.1–2.9)	3.3	(2.1–5.1)	**2.7**	**(1.9–3.9)**	1.5	(0.9–2.6)	3.6	(2.4–5.2)	**2.9**	**(2.1–3.9)**
New Jersey	1.1	(0.7–1.8)	3.7	(2.4–5.4)	**2.4**	**(1.7–3.3)**	1.2	(0.8–1.7)	4.1	(2.6–6.5)	**2.6**	**(1.8–3.8)**
New Mexico	3.0	(2.0–4.4)	4.8	(4.1–5.8)	**4.0**	**(3.2–5.0)**	4.1	(2.7–6.2)	5.8	(4.6–7.2)	**5.0**	**(3.8–6.5)**
New York	2.7	(1.7–4.1)	4.5	(3.2–6.3)	**3.7**	**(2.7–4.8)**	3.1	(2.0–4.7)	5.8	(4.2–8.0)	**4.5**	**(3.4–6.0)**
North Carolina	—	—	—	—	—	—	—	—	—	—	—	—
North Dakota	—	—	—	—	—	—	3.7	(2.5–5.5)	3.3	(2.2–4.8)	**3.5**	**(2.6–4.7)**
Ohio	0.5	(0.2–1.3)	3.3	(2.1–5.3)	**2.0**	**(1.2–3.1)**	—	—	—	—	—	—
Oklahoma	1.2	(0.5–2.8)	1.1	(0.4–2.6)	**1.1**	**(0.6–2.1)**	3.6	(2.4–5.3)	2.8	(1.6–4.7)	**3.2**	**(2.3–4.4)**
Rhode Island	—	—	—	—	—	—	1.8	(1.2–2.8)	4.2	(2.7–6.5)	**3.3**	**(2.3–4.8)**
South Carolina	—	—	—	—	—	—	2.1	(1.3–3.4)	5.9	(3.9–9.0)	**4.4**	**(3.1–6.2)**
South Dakota	—	—	—	—	—	—	3.1	(2.1–4.6)	5.3	(2.8–9.7)	**4.2**	**(2.6–6.7)**
Tennessee	2.4	(1.5–3.6)	6.0	(4.4–8.3)	**4.4**	**(3.3–5.9)**	2.8	(1.6–4.8)	6.6	(4.9–8.8)	**4.9**	**(3.7–6.6)**
Texas	1.9	(1.0–3.4)	5.5	(3.5–8.6)	**3.8**	**(2.5–5.7)**	3.2	(2.1–5.0)	6.4	(4.5–9.0)	**4.8**	**(3.5–6.6)**
Utah	1.4	(0.8–2.8)	2.4	(1.7–3.4)	**2.0**	**(1.4–3.0)**	2.1	(1.2–3.5)	2.8	(1.9–4.1)	**2.6**	**(1.8–3.6)**
Vermont	1.9	(1.5–2.4)	4.1	(3.2–5.2)	**3.1**	**(2.6–3.7)**	2.4	(1.8–3.2)	4.6	(3.4–6.3)	**3.6**	**(2.9–4.4)**
Virginia	2.5	(1.9–3.3)	4.8	(3.8–6.0)	**3.9**	**(3.3–4.7)**	2.7	(2.2–3.4)	5.0	(3.8–6.6)	**4.1**	**(3.3–5.1)**
West Virginia	1.8	(0.9–3.7)	2.4	(1.6–3.6)	**2.1**	**(1.4–3.1)**	3.5	(2.2–5.3)	3.8	(2.4–5.9)	**3.6**	**(2.7–4.7)**
Wisconsin	—	—	—	—	—	—	—	—	—	—	—	—
Wyoming	2.3	(1.6–3.2)	5.2	(3.9–6.9)	**4.0**	**(3.1–5.0)**	3.0	(2.0–4.5)	5.2	(4.0–6.8)	**4.3**	**(3.3–5.6)**
Median	*1.8*		*4.5*		***3.3***		*2.7*		*4.4*		***3.7***	
Range	*(0.5–5.0)*		*(1.1–9.8)*		***(1.1–7.8)***		*(1.2–5.5)*		*(1.9–11.7)*		***(1.6–8.9)***	

See table footnotes on the next page.

TABLE 58. (*Continued*) Percentage of high school students who ever used heroin* and who ever used methamphetamines,† by sex — selected U.S. sites, Youth Risk Behavior Survey, 2013

| | Ever used heroin | | | | | | Ever used methamphetamines | | | | | |
| | Female | | Male | | Total | | Female | | Male | | Total | |
Site	%	CI§	%	CI	%	CI	%	CI	%	CI	%	CI
Large urban school district surveys												
Baltimore, MD	3.8	(2.3–6.1)	8.2	(5.4–12.1)	7.2	**(5.2–9.9)**	3.5	(2.2–5.6)	9.5	(6.8–13.2)	7.3	**(5.5–9.7)**
Boston, MA	1.2	(0.5–3.1)	4.3	(2.7–6.9)	2.8	**(1.7–4.4)**	—	—	—	—	—	—
Broward County, FL	1.6	(0.6–3.9)	2.4	(1.2–4.6)	2.3	**(1.3–4.3)**	2.1	(1.3–3.3)	3.3	(2.0–5.2)	3.0	**(2.1–4.3)**
Charlotte-Mecklenburg, NC	1.0	(0.5–2.2)	2.9	(1.7–4.8)	2.2	**(1.3–3.5)**	1.6	(0.7–3.3)	4.6	(3.1–6.9)	3.3	**(2.3–4.8)**
Chicago, IL	1.7	(0.8–3.6)	6.1	(3.8–9.6)	4.1	**(2.6–6.5)**	2.5	(1.3–4.7)	4.8	(2.9–7.9)	3.7	**(2.4–5.5)**
Detroit, MI	1.7	(0.7–3.8)	5.8	(3.7–9.0)	3.9	**(2.5–6.1)**	3.0	(1.7–5.3)	5.9	(3.9–8.8)	4.7	**(3.4–6.6)**
District of Columbia	2.8	(2.4–3.4)	5.2	(4.6–6.0)	4.3	**(3.9–4.9)**	3.0	(2.5–3.6)	5.5	(4.7–6.4)	4.6	**(4.1–5.2)**
Duval County, FL	—	—	—	—	—	—	4.1	(2.9–5.8)	6.6	(5.1–8.6)	5.7	**(4.5–7.2)**
Houston, TX	3.6	(2.4–5.3)	7.2	(5.1–10.2)	5.9	**(4.4–7.8)**	4.8	(3.4–6.6)	7.6	(5.4–10.4)	6.6	**(5.2–8.5)**
Los Angeles, CA	1.8	(0.9–3.4)	4.0	(2.4–6.6)	3.0	**(2.1–4.3)**	3.8	(2.7–5.1)	6.4	(4.1–9.8)	5.1	**(3.6–7.3)**
Memphis, TN	2.3	(1.2–4.3)	5.8	(3.8–8.7)	4.3	**(3.0–6.3)**	2.4	(1.3–4.2)	6.6	(4.5–9.6)	4.9	**(3.5–7.0)**
Miami-Dade County, FL	1.1	(0.5–2.3)	2.4	(1.6–3.6)	1.9	**(1.2–2.8)**	2.4	(1.5–3.8)	2.2	(1.4–3.4)	2.4	**(1.7–3.4)**
Milwaukee, WI	4.0	(2.5–6.6)	10.1	(6.8–14.9)	7.4	**(5.0–10.9)**	3.5	(1.9–6.1)	9.1	(6.3–13.0)	6.6	**(4.4–9.6)**
New York City, NY	1.4	(1.0–2.1)	3.9	(2.9–5.2)	2.8	**(2.1–3.6)**	1.8	(1.3–2.5)	4.7	(3.7–5.9)	3.4	**(2.7–4.2)**
Orange County, FL	1.5	(0.8–2.6)	3.5	(2.4–5.0)	2.8	**(2.0–3.9)**	1.6	(0.9–2.8)	3.7	(2.5–5.5)	2.9	**(2.1–3.9)**
Palm Beach County, FL	3.1	(1.8–5.5)	7.4	(5.2–10.6)	5.7	**(3.9–8.2)**	5.7	(3.3–9.6)	8.1	(5.9–11.1)	7.2	**(5.1–10.1)**
Philadelphia, PA	0.7	(0.2–2.1)	2.9	(1.7–4.7)	1.8	**(1.1–2.9)**	2.2	(1.0–4.5)	3.0	(1.5–6.2)	2.8	**(1.5–5.1)**
San Bernardino, CA	1.1	(0.6–2.2)	2.2	(1.2–3.9)	1.6	**(1.0–2.6)**	2.6	(1.6–4.3)	3.6	(2.2–5.9)	3.1	**(2.1–4.5)**
San Diego, CA	—	—	—	—	—	—	1.2	(0.6–2.4)	4.5	(3.2–6.2)	2.9	**(2.2–3.9)**
San Francisco, CA	2.5	(1.5–4.0)	3.3	(2.2–5.0)	3.0	**(2.2–4.1)**	3.4	(2.1–5.3)	4.1	(2.8–5.9)	4.0	**(3.0–5.3)**
Seattle, WA	—	—	—	—	—	—	—	—	—	—	—	—
Median	1.7		4.1		**3.0**		2.6		4.8		**4.0**	
Range		(0.7–4.0)		(2.2–10.1)		**(1.6–7.4)**		(1.2–5.7)		(2.2–9.5)		**(2.4–7.3)**

* Used heroin (also called "smack," "junk," or "China White") one or more times during their life.
† Used methamphetamines (also called "speed," "crystal," "crank," or "ice") one or more times during their life.
§ 95% confidence interval.
¶ Not available.

TABLE 59. Percentage of high school students who ever took steroids* and who ever took prescription drugs,† by sex, race/ethnicity, and grade — United States, Youth Risk Behavior Survey, 2013

| | Ever took steroids without a doctor's prescription | | | | | | Ever took prescription drugs without a doctor's prescription | | | | | |
| | Female | | Male | | Total | | Female | | Male | | Total | |
Category	%	CI§	%	CI	%	CI	%	CI	%	CI	%	CI
Race/Ethnicity												
White¶	1.8	(1.2–2.6)	3.8	(3.0–4.8)	2.8	**(2.3–3.4)**	18.0	(15.3–21.1)	19.4	(16.8–22.3)	18.7	**(16.4–21.3)**
Black¶	1.3	(0.8–2.3)	3.3	(2.2–4.8)	2.3	**(1.7–3.1)**	11.1	(8.3–14.6)	15.7	(12.9–19.0)	13.3	**(11.1–15.9)**
Hispanic	3.6	(2.4–5.2)	5.0	(3.7–6.6)	4.2	**(3.2–5.6)**	19.9	(16.4–23.8)	18.5	(15.7–21.6)	19.2	**(16.5–22.2)**
Grade												
9	2.3	(1.6–3.3)	3.5	(2.4–5.0)	2.9	**(2.2–3.8)**	14.0	(11.4–17.0)	10.9	(9.1–12.9)	12.4	**(10.7–14.4)**
10	2.8	(1.9–4.1)	3.5	(2.5–5.0)	3.2	**(2.5–4.1)**	16.9	(13.2–21.4)	17.6	(13.9–22.0)	17.3	**(13.9–21.3)**
11	2.4	(1.3–4.3)	4.0	(2.7–5.8)	3.1	**(2.3–4.2)**	19.5	(16.8–22.4)	22.3	(19.7–25.2)	20.8	**(18.8–23.1)**
12	1.2	(0.7–2.0)	5.1	(3.8–6.7)	3.1	**(2.4–4.0)**	18.6	(15.6–22.0)	24.0	(21.0–27.4)	21.3	**(18.8–24.0)**
Total	2.2	**(1.8–2.8)**	4.0	**(3.4–4.8)**	3.2	**(2.7–3.6)**	17.2	**(15.0–19.8)**	18.3	**(16.4–20.4)**	17.8	**(15.9–19.9)**

* Took steroid pills or shots without a doctor's prescription one or more times during their life.
† Took prescription drugs (e.g., OxyContin, Percocet, Vicodin, codeine, Adderall, Ritalin, or Xanax) without a doctor's prescription one or more times during their life.
§ 95% confidence interval.
¶ Non-Hispanic.

Surveillance Summaries

TABLE 60. Percentage of high school students who ever took steroids* and who ever took prescription drugs,[†] by sex — selected U.S. sites, Youth Risk Behavior Survey, 2013

	Ever took steroids without a doctor's prescription						Ever took prescription drugs without a doctor's prescription					
	Female		Male		Total		Female		Male		Total	
Site	%	CI[§]	%	CI	%	CI	%	CI	%	CI	%	CI
State surveys												
Alabama	3.7	(2.4–5.6)	8.3	(5.7–11.8)	6.3	(4.4–8.9)	17.9	(13.4–23.5)	21.2	(17.5–25.5)	19.7	(16.5–23.3)
Alaska	—[¶]	—	—	—	—	—	12.5	(9.5–16.3)	14.0	(11.2–17.3)	13.5	(11.4–16.1)
Arizona	4.7	(3.2–6.8)	6.6	(4.0–10.9)	5.9	(3.9–8.8)	—	—	—	—	—	—
Arkansas	5.2	(3.7–7.3)	8.7	(6.4–11.6)	7.1	(5.4–9.3)	20.4	(17.7–23.4)	22.3	(18.9–26.2)	21.5	(19.4–23.9)
Connecticut	—	—	—	—	—	—	—	—	—	—	—	—
Delaware	2.2	(1.5–3.2)	4.0	(3.0–5.3)	3.2	(2.5–4.1)	11.7	(10.6–12.8)	13.7	(12.1–15.6)	12.8	(11.7–14.0)
Florida	2.5	(1.9–3.2)	5.3	(4.4–6.4)	4.0	(3.4–4.6)	15.7	(13.4–18.4)	19.5	(16.7–22.6)	17.7	(16.1–19.5)
Georgia	—	—	—	—	—	—	14.2	(12.0–16.6)	11.5	(9.2–14.4)	12.9	(10.9–15.3)
Hawaii	—	—	—	—	—	—	17.8	(15.2–20.7)	14.8	(12.0–18.2)	16.3	(14.1–18.7)
Idaho	1.8	(1.2–2.8)	3.2	(2.3–4.6)	2.5	(1.9–3.4)	16.1	(12.4–20.5)	20.2	(16.3–24.8)	18.4	(14.8–22.5)
Illinois	2.2	(1.5–3.2)	5.5	(3.9–7.7)	4.0	(2.9–5.5)	13.4	(11.4–15.8)	16.1	(12.9–19.8)	14.9	(13.0–16.9)
Kansas	—	—	—	—	—	—	12.0	(9.4–15.1)	12.6	(9.9–16.0)	12.4	(10.3–14.8)
Kentucky	1.5	(0.9–2.4)	3.8	(2.6–5.5)	2.9	(2.2–3.8)	16.5	(13.4–20.1)	20.0	(15.7–25.0)	18.4	(15.9–21.3)
Louisiana	7.6	(4.7–12.0)	9.3	(6.5–13.3)	8.8	(6.5–11.9)	10.9	(9.8–12.2)	13.5	(12.7–14.4)	12.4	(11.6–13.3)
Maine	—	—	—	—	5.1	(4.8–5.5)	13.6	(13.1–14.3)	16.3	(15.5–17.1)	15.2	(14.7–15.8)
Maryland	3.2	(2.9–3.5)	6.3	(5.8–6.9)	1.5	(1.1–2.0)	—	—	—	—	—	—
Massachusetts	0.7	(0.4–1.5)	2.2	(1.6–3.0)	2.9	(2.1–4.0)	15.9	(13.8–18.2)	16.4	(13.5–20.0)	16.2	(14.0–18.6)
Michigan	2.0	(1.3–3.1)	3.7	(2.7–5.1)	3.7	(2.7–5.1)	15.4	(12.2–19.3)	16.8	(13.1–21.2)	16.2	(13.9–18.7)
Mississippi	2.3	(1.4–3.7)	5.2	(3.4–7.8)	2.6	(2.2–3.2)	15.3	(13.7–17.2)	16.8	(15.0–18.8)	16.2	(14.7–17.7)
Missouri	—	—	—	—	2.3	(1.6–3.3)	9.7	(7.4–12.6)	11.1	(8.8–14.0)	10.4	(8.7–12.4)
Montana	1.4	(1.0–2.0)	3.7	(3.0–4.6)	4.0	(2.7–5.8)	20.9	(17.5–24.8)	18.0	(14.4–22.2)	19.4	(16.2–23.1)
Nebraska	1.2	(0.7–2.2)	3.3	(2.2–5.1)	—	—	17.4	(14.3–21.1)	15.5	(12.5–19.0)	16.5	(14.3–19.0)
Nevada	2.4	(1.6–3.6)	5.5	(3.6–8.5)								
New Hampshire	—	—	—	—	—	—						
New Jersey	0.8	(0.4–1.9)	3.8	(2.2–6.4)	2.3	(1.5–3.7)	10.5	(8.3–13.2)	13.0	(10.9–15.5)	11.8	(9.8–14.0)
New Mexico	—	—	—	—	—	—	16.1	(12.9–20.0)	16.4	(14.8–18.1)	16.3	(14.2–18.6)
New York	—	—	—	—	—	—	—	—	—	—	—	—
North Carolina	2.1	(1.2–3.9)	1.9	(1.1–3.1)	2.1	(1.5–2.9)	16.4	(12.7–20.9)	17.8	(14.6–21.5)	17.2	(14.4–20.3)
North Dakota	—	—	—	—	—	—	17.6	(15.3–20.1)	17.6	(14.8–20.9)	17.6	(15.6–19.9)
Ohio	1.8	(1.0–3.2)	3.6	(2.3–5.6)	2.7	(1.8–4.0)	—	—	—	—	—	—
Oklahoma	3.1	(2.1–4.5)	2.9	(2.0–4.1)	3.0	(2.3–3.8)	18.5	(15.6–21.9)	17.5	(14.5–20.9)	18.0	(15.8–20.4)
Rhode Island	—	—	—	—	—	—	12.4	(8.7–17.3)	13.9	(10.3–18.6)	13.5	(10.3–17.4)
South Carolina	—	—	—	—	—	—	15.5	(12.7–19.0)	19.1	(15.1–23.8)	17.6	(14.8–20.8)
South Dakota	—	—	—	—	—	—	11.0	(9.0–13.4)	14.5	(11.0–18.9)	12.8	(10.5–15.4)
Tennessee	4.7	(3.3–6.8)	7.2	(5.4–9.7)	6.1	(4.9–7.7)	17.9	(15.3–20.8)	19.9	(17.3–22.8)	19.0	(16.7–21.5)
Texas	3.2	(2.4–4.2)	5.9	(3.8–8.9)	4.6	(3.2–6.4)	17.0	(14.1–20.4)	20.8	(17.9–24.1)	19.0	(16.5–21.7)
Utah	2.5	(1.4–4.4)	3.0	(2.1–4.4)	2.9	(1.9–4.2)	8.0	(6.1–10.4)	9.3	(7.6–11.4)	8.7	(7.2–10.5)
Vermont	—	—	—	—	—	—	15.4	(14.0–17.0)	16.3	(14.8–17.9)	15.9	(14.9–17.0)
Virginia	2.4	(1.8–3.1)	4.7	(3.8–5.8)	3.7	(3.0–4.5)	16.9	(13.8–20.6)	16.1	(12.9–20.0)	16.5	(14.5–18.7)
West Virginia	1.5	(0.8–3.0)	5.4	(3.6–8.1)	3.6	(2.4–5.2)	13.8	(11.7–16.2)	15.8	(13.1–18.9)	14.9	(13.0–17.0)
Wisconsin	—	—	—	—	—	—	17.0	(14.4–19.9)	20.8	(17.8–24.2)	19.1	(16.7–21.7)
Wyoming	2.4	(1.7–3.3)	4.5	(3.4–5.9)	3.6	(2.9–4.4)						
Median	*2.3*		*4.6*		*3.6*		*15.6*		*16.3*		*16.2*	
Range	*(0.7–7.6)*		*(1.9–9.3)*		*(1.5–8.8)*		*(8.0–20.9)*		*(9.3–22.3)*		*(8.7–21.5)*	

See table footnotes on the next page.

TABLE 60. (*Continued*) Percentage of high school students who ever took steroids* and who ever took prescription drugs,† by sex — selected U.S. sites, Youth Risk Behavior Survey, 2013

| | Ever took steroids without a doctor's prescription | | | | | | Ever took prescription drugs without a doctor's prescription | | | | | |
| | Female | | Male | | Total | | Female | | Male | | Total | |
Site	%	CI§	%	CI	%	CI	%	CI	%	CI	%	CI
Large urban school district surveys												
Baltimore, MD	—	—	—	—	—	—	11.7	(9.0–15.1)	17.3	(13.0–22.6)	**15.5**	**(12.8–18.6)**
Boston, MA	1.7	(0.8–3.3)	4.5	(2.9–6.7)	3.1	(2.1–4.5)	6.8	(4.6–9.9)	8.8	(6.6–11.8)	**7.8**	**(6.2–9.8)**
Broward County, FL	1.8	(0.9–3.5)	2.9	(1.8–4.7)	2.6	(1.7–4.0)	9.7	(7.5–12.3)	13.9	(11.2–17.2)	**12.2**	**(10.4–14.3)**
Charlotte-Mecklenburg, NC	2.6	(1.5–4.5)	4.5	(2.9–6.9)	3.7	(2.6–5.2)	16.9	(13.8–20.5)	19.2	(15.9–23.0)	**18.1**	**(15.6–20.9)**
Chicago, IL	2.3	(1.3–4.1)	5.4	(3.7–8.0)	4.2	(2.8–6.2)	8.0	(6.4–10.0)	14.2	(10.6–18.6)	**11.3**	**(9.2–13.8)**
Detroit, MI	3.0	(1.9–4.8)	7.0	(4.6–10.4)	5.1	(3.6–7.2)	12.4	(9.6–15.8)	13.4	(10.1–17.5)	**12.9**	**(10.7–15.5)**
District of Columbia	3.0	(2.5–3.6)	5.3	(4.6–6.2)	4.5	(4.0–5.0)	11.6	(10.7–12.5)	14.9	(13.7–16.1)	**13.5**	**(12.8–14.3)**
Duval County, FL	3.2	(2.2–4.4)	7.9	(6.4–9.8)	5.6	(4.6–6.9)	—	—	—	—	—	—
Houston, TX	5.0	(3.4–7.4)	6.5	(4.5–9.2)	6.3	(4.7–8.4)	13.4	(10.9–16.4)	20.6	(17.3–24.3)	**17.4**	**(15.1–20.0)**
Los Angeles, CA	2.5	(1.5–4.2)	3.8	(2.2–6.4)	3.2	(2.1–4.8)	9.4	(6.8–13.0)	11.7	(9.0–15.2)	**10.6**	**(8.1–13.8)**
Memphis, TN	2.4	(1.4–3.9)	6.8	(4.8–9.5)	5.0	(3.5–6.9)	13.2	(10.4–16.5)	19.0	(16.2–22.1)	**16.3**	**(14.2–18.7)**
Miami-Dade County, FL	1.8	(1.2–2.6)	2.7	(1.9–3.8)	2.4	(1.8–3.1)	12.1	(10.1–14.3)	10.5	(8.6–12.9)	**11.3**	**(9.7–13.2)**
Milwaukee, WI	—	—	—	—	—	—	14.5	(11.7–17.9)	19.6	(15.5–24.5)	**17.3**	**(14.4–20.6)**
New York City, NY	—	—	—	—	—	—	—	—	—	—	—	—
Orange County, FL	1.3	(0.7–2.3)	3.3	(2.2–4.9)	2.6	(1.8–3.7)	11.3	(9.1–13.9)	15.7	(13.4–18.4)	**13.8**	**(12.0–15.8)**
Palm Beach County, FL	3.8	(2.0–7.0)	7.7	(5.6–10.5)	6.0	(4.5–8.0)	10.7	(8.3–13.6)	17.9	(14.7–21.8)	**14.6**	**(12.5–17.1)**
Philadelphia, PA	2.8	(1.5–5.3)	4.1	(2.6–6.3)	3.4	(2.2–5.4)	10.4	(8.2–13.1)	12.2	(9.4–15.5)	**11.4**	**(9.4–13.9)**
San Bernardino, CA	2.6	(1.5–4.3)	3.5	(2.1–5.7)	3.0	(2.0–4.4)	13.7	(11.0–16.8)	15.5	(11.3–21.0)	**14.6**	**(11.9–17.7)**
San Diego, CA	1.3	(0.5–2.9)	2.7	(1.7–4.5)	2.0	(1.3–3.2)	10.1	(7.8–12.9)	12.9	(10.7–15.5)	**11.6**	**(9.8–13.7)**
San Francisco, CA	—	—	—	—	—	—	11.1	(9.1–13.6)	10.8	(8.5–13.6)	**11.1**	**(9.3–13.3)**
Seattle, WA	—	—	—	—	—	—	—	—	—	—	—	—
Median	2.5		4.5		*3.5*		11.4		14.5		*13.2*	
Range	(1.3–5.0)		(2.7–7.9)		*(2.0–6.3)*		(6.8–16.9)		(8.8–20.6)		*(7.8–18.1)*	

* Took steroid pills or shots without a doctor's prescription one or more times during their life.
† Took prescription drugs (e.g., OxyContin, Percocet, Vicodin, codeine, Adderall, Ritalin, or Xanax) without a doctor's prescription one or more times during their life.
§ 95% confidence interval.
¶ Not available.

TABLE 61. Percentage of high school students who injected illegal drugs* and who were offered, sold, or given an illegal drug by someone on school property,† by sex, race/ethnicity, and grade — United States, Youth Risk Behavior Survey, 2013

| | Ever injected any illegal drug | | | | | | Offered, sold, or given an illegal drug on school property | | | | | |
| | Female | | Male | | Total | | Female | | Male | | Total | |
Category	%	CI§	%	CI	%	CI	%	CI	%	CI	%	CI
Race/Ethnicity												
White¶	0.9	(0.6–1.5)	2.1	(1.4–3.0)	1.5	(1.0–2.2)	17.5	(15.7–19.5)	23.1	(20.1–26.5)	**20.4**	**(18.2–22.7)**
Black¶	0.8	(0.5–1.5)	1.7	(1.1–2.8)	1.3	(0.9–1.9)	15.6	(13.2–18.3)	21.7	(18.6–25.2)	**18.6**	**(16.4–20.9)**
Hispanic	2.0	(1.1–3.9)	2.4	(1.6–3.5)	2.2	(1.4–3.5)	26.7	(22.8–31.0)	28.1	(25.8–30.6)	**27.4**	**(24.6–30.4)**
Grade												
9	1.4	(0.8–2.6)	1.5	(0.8–2.8)	1.5	(0.9–2.5)	21.9	(19.2–24.7)	22.9	(20.0–26.1)	**22.4**	**(20.2–24.8)**
10	1.2	(0.7–2.0)	2.3	(1.5–3.6)	1.7	(1.2–2.5)	21.7	(18.1–25.9)	24.6	(21.1–28.5)	**23.2**	**(20.3–26.5)**
11	1.0	(0.6–1.8)	2.2	(1.4–3.6)	1.6	(1.0–2.4)	20.2	(16.9–23.9)	26.4	(23.2–29.9)	**23.2**	**(20.7–26.0)**
12	1.1	(0.6–2.2)	2.6	(1.8–3.9)	1.9	(1.3–2.7)	13.7	(11.6–16.2)	24.0	(20.6–27.7)	**18.8**	**(16.6–21.1)**
Total	**1.3**	**(0.8–2.0)**	**2.2**	**(1.7–2.8)**	**1.7**	**(1.3–2.3)**	**19.7**	**(17.9–21.5)**	**24.5**	**(22.1–27.0)**	**22.1**	**(20.2–24.1)**

* Used a needle to inject any illegal drug into their body one or more times during their life.
† During the 12 months before the survey.
§ 95% confidence interval.
¶ Non-Hispanic.

Surveillance Summaries

TABLE 62. Percentage of high school students who injected illegal drugs* and who were offered, sold, or given an illegal drug by someone on school property,† by sex — selected U.S. sites, Youth Risk Behavior Survey, 2013

Site	Ever injected any illegal drug						Offered, sold, or given an illegal drug on school property					
	Female		Male		Total		Female		Male		Total	
	%	CI§	%	CI	%	CI	%	CI	%	CI	%	CI
State surveys												
Alabama	2.6	(1.6–4.2)	5.9	(3.8–9.0)	4.4	(3.0–6.6)	22.4	(18.6–26.7)	28.2	(24.9–31.7)	25.3	(23.0–27.7)
Alaska	1.3	(0.6–2.7)	2.6	(1.4–4.7)	2.0	(1.2–3.2)	—¶	—	—	—	—	—
Arizona	—	—	—	—	—	—	28.3	(24.5–32.4)	34.2	(29.9–38.9)	31.3	(28.3–34.5)
Arkansas	2.3	(1.3–3.8)	6.2	(4.6–8.4)	4.2	(3.2–5.6)	25.0	(21.4–29.0)	29.3	(26.0–32.9)	27.4	(24.8–30.1)
Connecticut	0.9	(0.5–1.6)	3.6	(2.5–5.2)	2.4	(1.8–3.2)	24.9	(23.1–26.8)	29.0	(26.2–32.0)	27.1	(25.3–28.9)
Delaware	1.2	(0.7–2.0)	3.3	(2.4–4.5)	2.3	(1.7–2.9)	14.0	(12.1–16.3)	24.4	(22.1–26.9)	19.1	(17.6–20.8)
Florida	—	—	—	—	—	—	16.6	(15.3–18.0)	23.3	(21.4–25.4)	20.0	(18.7–21.3)
Georgia	—	—	—	—	—	—	22.0	(19.0–25.3)	31.0	(27.3–35.0)	26.5	(23.9–29.4)
Hawaii	2.7	(2.1–3.6)	2.1	(1.6–2.9)	2.6	(2.1–3.1)	28.4	(25.0–32.0)	34.2	(32.1–36.4)	31.2	(29.3–33.2)
Idaho	1.2	(0.7–2.3)	3.0	(2.0–4.5)	2.1	(1.4–3.1)	22.9	(19.9–26.1)	21.4	(18.1–25.2)	22.1	(19.6–24.9)
Illinois	2.1	(1.4–3.2)	4.2	(3.1–5.6)	3.2	(2.4–4.2)	23.5	(21.3–26.0)	30.5	(27.5–33.7)	27.2	(25.1–29.4)
Kansas	—	—	—	—	—	—	18.1	(14.9–21.9)	20.2	(17.6–23.0)	19.4	(17.3–21.6)
Kentucky	—	—	—	—	—	—	15.9	(13.2–19.1)	24.8	(21.4–28.5)	20.6	(18.3–23.0)
Louisiana	—	—	—	—	—	—	—	—	—	—	—	—
Maine	1.5	(1.0–2.0)	3.2	(2.6–3.8)	2.4	(2.0–2.8)	14.8	(13.2–16.7)	21.6	(19.6–23.8)	18.4	(16.7–20.3)
Maryland	2.5	(2.2–2.9)	5.0	(4.6–5.4)	3.9	(3.6–4.2)	25.0	(24.1–25.9)	33.0	(32.2–33.9)	29.1	(28.4–29.9)
Massachusetts	0.6	(0.3–1.2)	1.2	(0.7–2.0)	1.0	(0.6–1.5)	20.5	(17.9–23.3)	25.1	(22.5–28.0)	23.0	(21.2–24.9)
Michigan	1.5	(1.0–2.3)	2.6	(1.7–3.9)	2.1	(1.5–3.0)	20.7	(18.0–23.7)	26.9	(24.5–29.5)	23.8	(21.9–25.8)
Mississippi	1.4	(0.6–2.8)	3.7	(2.1–6.4)	2.5	(1.6–4.0)	9.7	(7.6–12.4)	14.4	(10.6–19.3)	12.1	(10.1–14.4)
Missouri	—	—	—	—	—	—	—	—	—	—	—	—
Montana	1.7	(1.2–2.4)	3.0	(2.4–3.9)	2.4	(1.9–3.0)	20.6	(18.7–22.6)	24.9	(23.0–26.9)	22.8	(21.4–24.2)
Nebraska	0.8	(0.3–1.8)	2.9	(1.9–4.4)	1.9	(1.2–2.8)	16.4	(14.0–19.0)	21.9	(18.9–25.3)	19.2	(17.0–21.6)
Nevada	2.2	(1.3–3.6)	4.5	(2.3–8.6)	3.3	(2.0–5.4)	28.9	(24.6–33.7)	33.5	(28.8–38.6)	31.2	(27.3–35.4)
New Hampshire	—	—	—	—	—	—	18.5	(16.1–21.2)	21.6	(18.3–25.2)	20.1	(18.1–22.3)
New Jersey	0.6	(0.2–1.4)	3.3	(2.3–4.8)	2.0	(1.5–2.7)	27.5	(23.5–32.0)	33.9	(29.5–38.5)	30.7	(27.2–34.4)
New Mexico	2.4	(1.5–3.6)	3.8	(3.0–4.9)	3.1	(2.4–4.1)	30.7	(28.4–33.1)	34.7	(30.8–38.9)	32.8	(30.6–35.0)
New York	2.2	(1.4–3.3)	4.5	(3.1–6.5)	3.4	(2.5–4.4)	—	—	—	—	—	—
North Carolina	—	—	—	—	—	—	20.6	(17.3–24.2)	26.5	(22.4–31.1)	23.6	(20.4–27.2)
North Dakota	—	—	—	—	—	—	12.2	(10.1–14.8)	15.5	(13.3–18.0)	14.1	(12.6–15.7)
Ohio	1.0	(0.5–2.0)	3.3	(2.1–5.2)	2.2	(1.5–3.3)	16.9	(13.5–21.1)	22.6	(19.6–25.9)	19.9	(17.1–23.0)
Oklahoma	0.8	(0.3–2.1)	1.7	(0.9–3.1)	1.3	(0.7–2.1)	11.6	(9.4–14.3)	16.3	(13.6–19.3)	14.0	(12.0–16.4)
Rhode Island	—	—	—	—	—	—	18.2	(16.2–20.4)	26.5	(22.9–30.4)	22.6	(20.1–25.2)
South Carolina	1.5	(0.7–3.2)	3.9	(2.5–6.1)	2.8	(1.8–4.4)	22.2	(18.3–26.6)	26.4	(22.6–30.5)	24.5	(21.6–27.6)
South Dakota	2.4	(1.4–3.9)	3.7	(2.3–6.1)	3.0	(1.9–4.8)	11.9	(9.7–14.6)	18.8	(14.1–24.7)	15.4	(12.2–19.2)
Tennessee	3.4	(2.4–4.8)	5.7	(4.0–8.1)	4.7	(3.5–6.3)	21.5	(17.5–26.2)	27.9	(24.4–31.7)	24.8	(21.7–28.2)
Texas	1.8	(1.0–3.5)	3.9	(2.5–6.0)	2.9	(1.9–4.3)	23.8	(20.7–27.2)	28.8	(25.9–32.0)	26.4	(23.8–29.0)
Utah	1.0	(0.7–1.5)	2.4	(1.4–4.1)	1.7	(1.1–2.7)	18.2	(14.8–22.2)	21.8	(18.3–25.7)	20.0	(17.0–23.4)
Vermont	—	—	—	—	—	—	—	—	—	—	—	—
Virginia	1.9	(1.4–2.7)	4.9	(3.7–6.4)	3.5	(2.7–4.6)	—	—	—	—	—	—
West Virginia	1.9	(1.0–3.4)	2.3	(1.4–3.6)	2.1	(1.4–3.1)	12.6	(10.3–15.3)	21.5	(18.2–25.3)	17.1	(14.8–19.7)
Wisconsin	—	—	—	—	—	—	17.1	(14.7–19.8)	19.4	(16.5–22.7)	18.3	(16.3–20.4)
Wyoming	2.3	(1.5–3.4)	3.8	(2.8–5.2)	3.1	(2.4–4.1)	17.6	(15.7–19.7)	22.6	(20.3–25.1)	20.2	(18.8–21.8)
Median	*1.7*		*3.6*		*2.5*		*20.5*		*25.0*		*22.7*	
Range	*(0.6–3.4)*		*(1.2–6.2)*		*(1.0–4.7)*		*(9.7–30.7)*		*(14.4–34.7)*		*(12.1–32.8)*	

See table footnotes on the next page.

TABLE 62. (*Continued*) Percentage of high school students who injected illegal drugs* and who were offered, sold, or given an illegal drug by someone on school property,† by sex — selected U.S. sites, Youth Risk Behavior Survey, 2013

| | Ever injected any illegal drug | | | | | | Offered, sold, or given an illegal drug on school property | | | | | |
| | Female | | Male | | Total | | Female | | Male | | Total | |
Site	%	CI§	%	CI	%	CI	%	CI	%	CI	%	CI
Large urban school district surveys												
Baltimore, MD	4.5	(2.9–6.9)	9.1	(6.4–12.7)	7.2	(5.4–9.6)	23.3	(19.2–27.8)	29.1	(24.5–34.2)	26.4	(23.1–30.1)
Boston, MA	—	—	—	—	—	—	19.0	(16.1–22.4)	24.4	(20.4–28.8)	21.9	(19.1–24.9)
Broward County, FL	1.8	(0.9–3.3)	2.3	(1.3–4.0)	2.2	(1.3–3.7)	28.9	(25.1–33.0)	36.1	(31.7–40.7)	32.6	(30.0–35.2)
Charlotte-Mecklenburg, NC	—	—	—	—	—	—	28.2	(25.1–31.6)	36.8	(32.7–41.1)	32.5	(29.8–35.4)
Chicago, IL	1.5	(0.7–3.1)	3.4	(2.2–5.2)	2.6	(1.6–4.1)	28.7	(25.1–32.5)	32.9	(28.4–37.8)	30.9	(27.4–34.6)
Detroit, MI	2.6	(1.4–5.0)	4.4	(2.9–6.6)	3.8	(2.6–5.5)	24.1	(20.4–28.2)	36.2	(30.9–41.7)	29.5	(26.2–32.9)
District of Columbia	—	—	—	—	—	—	—	—	—	—	—	—
Duval County, FL	2.2	(1.5–3.3)	5.1	(4.0–6.6)	3.7	(3.0–4.7)	26.4	(23.7–29.3)	36.0	(33.1–39.0)	31.2	(28.8–33.6)
Houston, TX	2.5	(1.6–3.8)	4.9	(3.5–6.8)	3.8	(3.0–4.9)	30.6	(27.6–33.7)	33.3	(29.1–37.8)	32.2	(29.3–35.2)
Los Angeles, CA	0.8	(0.5–1.4)	3.0	(1.9–4.9)	2.1	(1.4–3.2)	27.8	(23.9–32.0)	31.1	(27.6–34.8)	29.5	(26.6–32.6)
Memphis, TN	1.7	(0.8–3.4)	5.1	(3.4–7.5)	3.5	(2.4–5.0)	20.3	(17.6–23.2)	24.8	(21.5–28.4)	22.6	(20.4–24.9)
Miami-Dade County, FL	1.1	(0.5–2.3)	2.0	(1.2–3.3)	1.6	(1.1–2.5)	23.3	(20.2–26.7)	24.0	(21.7–26.5)	23.7	(21.6–25.9)
Milwaukee, WI	—	—	—	—	—	—	23.0	(20.0–26.3)	34.6	(30.4–39.1)	28.7	(25.9–31.7)
New York City, NY	1.6	(1.2–2.2)	3.1	(2.4–4.1)	2.5	(1.9–3.2)	—	—	—	—	—	—
Orange County, FL	1.1	(0.6–2.1)	2.3	(1.5–3.7)	2.0	(1.4–3.0)	21.8	(19.0–24.9)	30.7	(27.5–34.0)	26.4	(24.1–28.9)
Palm Beach County, FL	4.1	(2.7–6.2)	7.7	(5.4–10.7)	6.1	(4.5–8.2)	23.6	(20.5–26.9)	29.2	(25.6–33.2)	26.5	(24.0–29.3)
Philadelphia, PA	2.6	(1.3–5.2)	2.3	(1.4–3.7)	2.6	(1.7–3.9)	21.1	(18.5–24.0)	29.4	(25.5–33.6)	25.1	(22.3–28.1)
San Bernardino, CA	1.2	(0.6–2.7)	2.5	(1.4–4.5)	1.9	(1.1–3.1)	24.5	(21.4–28.0)	33.5	(29.2–38.1)	29.1	(26.0–32.4)
San Diego, CA	1.0	(0.4–2.1)	3.0	(1.5–5.8)	2.1	(1.2–3.4)	29.6	(25.2–34.4)	30.5	(27.4–33.8)	30.1	(27.2–33.2)
San Francisco, CA	—	—	—	—	—	—	24.7	(21.6–28.1)	29.1	(25.4–32.9)	27.0	(24.2–29.9)
Seattle, WA	2.1	(1.1–4.0)	3.1	(1.7–5.4)	2.7	(1.8–4.2)	25.4	(22.4–28.7)	29.4	(25.4–33.6)	27.5	(25.1–30.1)
Median	1.7		3.1		2.6		24.5		30.7		28.7	
Range	(0.8–4.5)		(2.0–9.1)		(1.6–7.2)		(19.0–30.6)		(24.0–36.8)		(21.9–32.6)	

* Used a needle to inject any illegal drug into their body one or more times during their life.
† During the 12 months before the survey.
§ 95% confidence interval.
¶ Not available.

TABLE 67. Percentage of high school students who used a condom during last sexual intercourse* and who used birth control pills before last sexual intercourse,*,† by sex, race/ethnicity, and grade — United States, Youth Risk Behavior Survey, 2013

| | Condom use | | | | | | Birth control pill use | | | | | |
| | Female | | Male | | Total | | Female | | Male | | Total | |
Category	%	CI§	%	CI	%	CI	%	CI	%	CI	%	CI
Race/Ethnicity												
White¶	53.2	(47.9–58.3)	61.8	(57.0–66.4)	57.1	(52.9–61.1)	30.7	(26.9–34.7)	20.1	(16.6–24.0)	25.9	(23.0–29.0)
Black¶	55.3	(49.0–61.3)	73.0	(66.4–78.8)	64.7	(59.9–69.1)	7.3	(4.6–11.5)	9.0	(6.3–12.7)	8.2	(5.8–11.4)
Hispanic	50.7	(45.7–55.7)	66.5	(60.8–71.7)	58.3	(54.5–61.9)	7.3	(4.8–10.8)	10.8	(7.7–15.1)	9.0	(6.7–11.9)
Grade												
9	56.5	(47.5–65.2)	69.5	(62.8–75.4)	62.7	(56.3–68.7)	14.7	(10.0–21.0)	7.7	(4.7–12.3)	11.4	(7.9–16.2)
10	55.5	(47.5–63.2)	69.3	(60.7–76.7)	61.7	(55.7–67.4)	19.2	(14.2–25.3)	13.7	(9.2–19.9)	16.7	(13.4–20.6)
11	54.8	(49.8–59.6)	70.6	(65.0–75.6)	62.3	(58.7–65.7)	23.2	(17.4–30.2)	15.1	(12.3–18.4)	19.3	(16.0–23.2)
12	48.4	(44.7–52.2)	58.0	(52.9–63.1)	53.0	(49.4–56.5)	27.6	(22.2–33.8)	19.3	(15.3–24.2)	23.7	(19.9–28.0)
Total	53.1	(49.5–56.7)	65.8	(62.4–69.1)	59.1	(56.3–61.9)	22.4	(19.2–25.9)	15.1	(12.6–18.0)	19.0	(16.6–21.7)

* Among the 34.0% of students nationwide who were currently sexually active.
† To prevent pregnancy.
§ 95% confidence interval.
¶ Non-Hispanic.

Surveillance Summaries

TABLE 68. Percentage of high school students who used a condom during last sexual intercourse* and who used birth control pills before last sexual intercourse,*,† by sex — selected U.S. sites, Youth Risk Behavior Survey, 2013

| | Condom use | | | | | | Birth control pill use | | | | | |
| | Female | | Male | | Total | | Female | | Male | | Total | |
Site	%	CI§	%	CI	%	CI	%	CI	%	CI	%	CI
State surveys												
Alabama	48.6	(39.0–58.3)	54.2	(44.8–63.2)	**51.3**	**(45.6–57.0)**	19.5	(14.3–25.9)	17.7	(11.9–25.7)	**18.6**	**(14.2–24.0)**
Alaska	59.6	(51.6–67.2)	61.9	(52.7–70.2)	**60.4**	**(54.3–66.1)**	21.3	(14.6–30.0)	25.1	(17.0–35.4)	**23.4**	**(17.4–30.8)**
Arizona	48.5	(41.5–55.6)	62.2	(54.4–69.3)	**55.1**	**(49.8–60.3)**	19.6	(15.0–25.3)	14.3	(9.5–20.9)	**17.5**	**(13.8–22.1)**
Arkansas	45.6	(38.6–52.7)	58.2	(47.1–68.5)	**51.1**	**(45.4–56.8)**	19.0	(14.5–24.5)	21.4	(15.6–28.6)	**20.2**	**(16.8–24.0)**
Connecticut	56.0	(50.0–61.8)	65.7	(59.9–71.0)	**60.7**	**(57.0–64.4)**	32.8	(25.9–40.5)	22.7	(16.4–30.5)	**27.9**	**(23.1–33.2)**
Delaware	55.8	(51.3–60.3)	71.5	(66.3–76.1)	**63.4**	**(60.0–66.7)**	22.1	(18.2–26.5)	13.1	(10.1–16.8)	**17.9**	**(15.4–20.8)**
Florida	57.2	(53.6–60.6)	66.9	(63.3–70.3)	**62.4**	**(59.7–65.0)**	18.6	(15.3–22.5)	12.8	(10.3–15.9)	**15.6**	**(13.3–18.2)**
Georgia	—¶	—	—	—	—	—	—	—	—	—	—	—
Hawaii	41.5	(36.0–47.3)	53.5	(45.9–61.0)	**45.9**	**(41.5–50.4)**	16.4	(11.3–23.2)	12.8	(8.8–18.2)	**14.9**	**(11.4–19.2)**
Idaho	54.5	(47.1–61.7)	63.5	(57.7–69.0)	**58.5**	**(53.5–63.4)**	—	—	—	—	—	—
Illinois	54.4	(48.8–59.8)	61.3	(52.8–69.1)	**57.7**	**(52.1–63.1)**	21.6	(16.9–27.1)	17.0	(11.7–24.2)	**19.4**	**(15.1–24.5)**
Kansas	49.9	(43.1–56.6)	64.3	(57.0–70.9)	**56.2**	**(51.6–60.8)**	25.1	(19.2–32.2)	21.7	(16.6–27.9)	**23.3**	**(19.4–27.8)**
Kentucky	45.1	(37.8–52.6)	62.1	(55.2–68.5)	**53.1**	**(48.0–58.1)**	24.2	(18.7–30.7)	15.3	(11.3–20.3)	**19.9**	**(16.2–24.1)**
Louisiana	—	—	—	—	—	—	—	—	—	—	35.7	(33.4–38.1)
Maine	52.9	(49.8–56.0)	64.4	(61.2–67.5)	**57.8**	**(55.3–60.3)**	40.6	(37.4–43.8)	29.7	(27.1–32.5)	**18.7**	**(17.7–19.8)**
Maryland	56.4	(54.7–58.1)	67.2	(65.7–68.7)	**61.5**	**(60.4–62.7)**	21.9	(20.4–23.4)	15.5	(14.3–16.7)	**27.4**	**(23.7–31.5)**
Massachusetts	50.8	(44.3–57.3)	65.2	(60.1–69.9)	**57.6**	**(52.9–62.2)**	31.6	(26.7–37.0)	23.0	(18.1–28.8)	**21.7**	**(18.7–25.0)**
Michigan	55.6	(52.2–59.0)	66.6	(59.8–72.8)	**61.0**	**(56.7–65.1)**	26.7	(22.4–31.4)	16.7	(12.9–21.4)	**13.6**	**(10.1–18.1)**
Mississippi	51.2	(44.1–58.3)	69.7	(63.2–75.5)	**61.0**	**(54.5–67.1)**	18.2	(14.0–23.2)	9.5	(6.3–14.2)	**16.0**	**(11.6–21.8)**
Missouri	51.8	(44.8–58.8)	64.3	(53.7–73.7)	**58.1**	**(51.9–64.0)**	17.6	(11.4–26.1)	14.5	(8.9–22.8)	**24.9**	**(21.6–28.7)**
Montana	57.2	(53.0–61.4)	65.9	(61.6–69.9)	**61.5**	**(58.1–64.8)**	29.0	(24.9–33.4)	20.7	(17.1–24.7)	**16.4**	**(12.4–21.5)**
Nebraska	56.9	(50.1–63.5)	67.7	(60.1–74.5)	**62.5**	**(57.3–67.4)**	20.4	(15.2–26.7)	12.7	(7.9–20.0)	**20.1**	**(16.8–23.9)**
Nevada	53.9	(49.2–58.6)	63.9	(57.2–70.2)	**59.0**	**(55.2–62.7)**	26.7	(22.0–31.9)	13.5	(9.1–19.6)	**34.4**	**(29.8–39.3)**
New Hampshire	53.1	(46.5–59.6)	58.6	(50.3–66.3)	**55.2**	**(50.2–60.1)**	37.0	(31.3–43.2)	30.9	(24.1–38.7)		
New Jersey	49.6	(41.6–57.7)	68.4	(62.1–74.0)	**58.6**	**(53.8–63.3)**	26.5	(19.4–34.9)	16.0	(11.0–22.8)	**21.5**	**(17.2–26.4)**
New Mexico	53.3	(48.1–58.4)	61.3	(57.5–65.0)	**57.2**	**(54.0–60.3)**	19.6	(14.2–26.3)	11.9	(9.0–15.5)	**15.9**	**(12.0–20.7)**
New York	57.1	(50.2–63.6)	69.5	(64.4–74.2)	**63.3**	**(59.0–67.3)**	26.1	(19.4–34.1)	14.5	(10.2–20.1)	**20.1**	**(15.7–25.4)**
North Carolina	52.6	(43.9–61.1)	69.4	(60.5–77.0)	**60.8**	**(53.9–67.4)**	—	—	—	—	—	—
North Dakota	—	—	—	—	—	—	—	—	—	—	—	—
Ohio	46.3	(40.6–52.2)	56.0	(45.7–65.7)	**50.8**	**(45.3–56.3)**	29.7	(23.1–37.3)	17.6	(12.4–24.2)	**24.1**	**(19.5–29.4)**
Oklahoma	51.0	(44.3–57.7)	65.3	(56.1–73.5)	**58.2**	**(51.7–64.4)**	13.7	(10.1–18.2)	11.1	(6.6–18.0)	**12.3**	**(9.1–16.6)**
Rhode Island	64.8	(57.5–71.5)	71.0	(60.7–79.6)	**67.6**	**(61.3–73.3)**	31.0	(24.7–38.2)	20.0	(13.4–28.7)	**26.0**	**(20.6–32.4)**
South Carolina	51.2	(43.1–59.2)	67.7	(61.5–73.3)	**59.1**	**(54.7–63.4)**	21.0	(15.1–28.4)	12.5	(7.4–20.6)	**17.0**	**(13.3–21.5)**
South Dakota	60.8	(52.3–68.8)	59.3	(51.3–66.7)	**60.0**	**(53.1–66.6)**	23.5	(18.6–29.2)	19.0	(12.2–28.5)	**21.2**	**(16.5–26.8)**
Tennessee	53.8	(46.3–61.0)	64.2	(57.3–70.6)	**58.6**	**(53.0–63.9)**	18.7	(12.8–26.4)	13.5	(9.1–19.7)	**16.1**	**(12.5–20.5)**
Texas	44.0	(37.6–50.5)	61.8	(57.8–65.7)	**52.9**	**(49.4–56.3)**	13.2	(8.6–19.7)	14.2	(9.7–20.5)	**13.7**	**(9.4–19.6)**
Utah	—	—	—	—	—	—	—	—	—	—	—	—
Vermont	—	—	—	—	—	—	—	—	—	—	—	—
Virginia	—	—	—	—	—	—	21.1	(16.7–26.3)			**25.9**	**(22.9–29.2)**
West Virginia	49.6	(43.8–55.4)	56.9	(49.4–64.1)	**53.4**	**(48.7–58.0)**	30.8	(25.9–36.2)	20.7	(15.1–27.8)	**23.7**	**(19.7–28.2)**
Wisconsin	57.8	(52.2–63.2)	68.3	(60.7–75.1)	**62.5**	**(57.9–66.8)**	26.4	(21.0–32.7)	16.9	(13.2–21.4)	**19.2**	**(16.3–22.5)**
Wyoming	52.7	(47.2–58.1)	63.9	(58.9–68.6)	**57.9**	**(54.0–61.8)**	21.6	(18.1–25.7)	16.9			
Median	*53.0*		*64.3*		*58.5*		*22.0*		*16.3*		*20.0*	
Range	*(41.5–64.8)*		*(53.5–71.5)*		*(45.9–67.6)*		*(13.2–40.6)*		*(9.5–30.9)*		*(12.3–35.7)*	

See table footnotes on the next page.

TABLE 68. (*Continued*) Percentage of high school students who used a condom during last sexual intercourse* and who used birth control pills before last sexual intercourse,*,† by sex — selected U.S. sites, Youth Risk Behavior Survey, 2013

| | Condom use | | | | | | Birth control pill use | | | | | |
| | Female | | Male | | Total | | Female | | Male | | Total | |
Site	%	CI§	%	CI	%	CI	%	CI	%	CI	%	CI
Large urban school district surveys												
Baltimore, MD	57.9	(49.6–65.7)	72.5	(63.9–79.7)	**64.8**	**(59.3–69.9)**	12.9	(7.3–21.8)	8.6	(4.5–15.8)	**10.6**	**(7.2–15.4)**
Boston, MA	53.6	(43.4–63.5)	73.6	(64.6–81.0)	**62.6**	**(55.8–68.9)**	14.9	(9.0–23.7)	13.4	(8.1–21.4)	**14.1**	**(9.4–20.6)**
Broward County, FL	59.6	(53.5–65.4)	78.1	(70.2–84.3)	**70.0**	**(64.4–75.1)**	16.0	(10.4–23.9)	10.1	(6.3–15.7)	**13.3**	**(9.9–17.6)**
Charlotte-Mecklenburg, NC	61.6	(53.1–69.5)	73.8	(65.6–80.6)	**67.6**	**(61.8–72.9)**	14.5	(10.6–19.6)	12.7	(8.3–18.9)	**13.6**	**(10.4–17.6)**
Chicago, IL	51.9	(43.4–60.2)	70.3	(63.2–76.6)	**61.3**	**(55.8–66.5)**	11.1	(7.8–15.6)	10.1	(7.0–14.4)	**10.6**	**(8.4–13.1)**
Detroit, MI	56.7	(48.2–64.9)	75.3	(66.6–82.4)	**65.5**	**(59.5–71.0)**	11.9	(6.5–20.9)	8.0	(4.7–13.3)	**10.1**	**(6.7–15.0)**
District of Columbia	62.0	(59.3–64.6)	78.2	(75.7–80.4)	**70.1**	**(68.2–71.8)**	9.2	(7.7–11.0)	6.9	(5.6–8.4)	**8.0**	**(7.0–9.2)**
Duval County, FL	59.3	(53.7–64.6)	68.6	(63.1–73.5)	**64.0**	**(60.1–67.7)**	15.6	(12.1–19.7)	13.3	(9.4–18.5)	**14.4**	**(11.9–17.2)**
Houston, TX	47.1	(39.6–54.8)	64.6	(57.7–70.9)	**55.7**	**(50.9–60.3)**	14.1	(10.4–18.8)	5.9	(3.2–10.6)	**10.0**	**(7.7–13.0)**
Los Angeles, CA	62.4	(51.5–72.1)	64.4	(54.0–73.5)	**63.3**	**(58.8–67.6)**	8.1	(4.0–16.0)	6.8	(3.1–14.1)	**7.4**	**(4.3–12.3)**
Memphis, TN	62.5	(54.8–69.6)	72.8	(64.6–79.7)	**67.5**	**(62.5–72.2)**	13.6	(10.0–18.4)	7.7	(4.9–11.7)	**10.5**	**(8.4–13.1)**
Miami-Dade County, FL	56.5	(49.3–63.5)	76.0	(72.3–79.3)	**66.4**	**(61.0–71.3)**	10.1	(6.2–16.1)	7.2	(4.8–10.5)	**8.7**	**(6.3–12.0)**
Milwaukee, WI	50.8	(40.9–60.6)	73.7	(65.4–80.7)	**61.5**	**(54.3–68.3)**	11.6	(7.4–17.8)	7.2	(3.5–14.1)	**9.4**	**(6.3–14.0)**
New York City, NY	61.3	(56.3–66.1)	73.3	(68.2–77.9)	**67.8**	**(64.2–71.2)**	10.6	(7.7–14.6)	8.7	(6.4–11.7)	**9.6**	**(8.0–11.5)**
Orange County, FL	58.4	(50.5–66.0)	67.4	(59.6–74.3)	**62.6**	**(57.4–67.6)**	13.1	(8.2–20.1)	9.2	(5.6–14.8)	**11.0**	**(7.5–15.9)**
Palm Beach County, FL	61.3	(53.6–68.6)	69.2	(61.1–76.3)	**65.8**	**(59.7–71.3)**	21.8	(15.6–29.8)	11.5	(6.6–19.3)	**16.1**	**(12.0–21.3)**
Philadelphia, PA	51.5	(43.2–59.7)	64.6	(52.5–75.1)	**57.8**	**(50.9–64.5)**	16.4	(13.3–20.1)	13.5	(7.6–22.7)	**14.9**	**(11.4–19.3)**
San Bernardino, CA	48.9	(42.3–55.7)	64.5	(54.0–73.8)	**56.9**	**(49.4–64.2)**	12.7	(7.8–20.0)	4.6	(2.1–9.7)	**9.1**	**(6.0–13.7)**
San Diego, CA	54.7	(45.4–63.7)	57.7	(50.1–64.9)	**56.6**	**(50.4–62.5)**	25.2	(17.8–34.5)	19.8	(14.6–26.3)	**22.4**	**(17.4–28.3)**
San Francisco, CA	—		—		**—**		—		—		**—**	
Seattle, WA	53.0	(44.2–61.6)	68.5	(60.3–75.7)	**61.2**	**(54.9–67.2)**	30.0	(22.3–39.0)	18.3	(12.4–26.2)	**24.2**	**(18.8–30.5)**
Median	*57.3*		*71.4*		***63.6***		*13.3*		*8.9*		*10.6*	
Range	*(47.1–62.5)*		*(57.7–78.2)*		***(55.7–70.1)***		*(8.1–30.0)*		*(4.6–19.8)*		*(7.4–24.2)*	

* Among students who were currently sexually active.
† To prevent pregnancy.
§ 95% confidence interval.
¶ Not available.

TABLE 69. Percentage of high school students who used an IUD* or implant† before last sexual intercourse§,¶ and who used a shot,** patch,†† or birth control ring§§ before last sexual intercourse,§,¶ by sex, race/ethnicity, and grade — United States, Youth Risk Behavior Survey, 2013

| | IUD or implant use | | | | | | Shot, patch, or birth control ring use | | | | | |
| | Female | | Male | | Total | | Female | | Male | | Total | |
Category	%	CI¶¶	%	CI	%	CI	%	CI	%	CI	%	CI
Race/Ethnicity												
White***	2.0	(1.2–3.3)	1.8	(1.0–3.4)	**1.9**	**(1.2–2.9)**	4.8	(3.7–6.2)	4.8	(3.2–7.0)	**4.8**	**(3.8–6.0)**
Black***	1.7	(0.7–4.1)	0.4	(0.1–1.4)	**1.1**	**(0.5–2.1)**	10.1	(5.9–16.8)	1.8	(0.9–3.3)	**5.7**	**(3.6–9.0)**
Hispanic	1.4	(0.7–2.8)	1.1	(0.3–3.4)	**1.3**	**(0.7–2.2)**	5.2	(2.9–9.3)	3.3	(1.4–7.7)	**4.3**	**(2.3–8.1)**
Grade												
9	1.0	(0.3–3.2)	0.0	(0.0–0.2)	**0.5**	**(0.2–1.7)**	2.9	(1.4–6.0)	0.6	(0.1–2.6)	**1.8**	**(0.9–3.5)**
10	1.3	(0.5–3.1)	0.4	(0.1–1.3)	**0.9**	**(0.4–1.8)**	5.5	(3.5–8.6)	3.3	(1.6–6.7)	**4.5**	**(3.1–6.5)**
11	1.7	(0.9–3.1)	1.3	(0.6–2.8)	**1.5**	**(1.0–2.3)**	6.6	(4.3–10.0)	3.3	(2.0–5.4)	**5.0**	**(3.6–6.9)**
12	2.5	(1.4–4.5)	2.4	(1.3–4.5)	**2.5**	**(1.6–3.9)**	6.3	(4.4–9.1)	5.7	(3.6–9.0)	**6.0**	**(4.5–8.0)**
Total	**1.8**	**(1.2–2.7)**	**1.3**	**(0.8–2.2)**	**1.6**	**(1.1–2.2)**	**5.6**	**(4.5–7.0)**	**3.7**	**(2.6–5.2)**	**4.7**	**(3.8–5.8)**

* Such as Mirena or ParaGard.
† Such as Implanon or Nexplanon.
§ Among the 34.0% of students nationwide who were currently sexually active.
¶ To prevent pregnancy.
** Such as Depo-Provera.
†† Such as OrthoEvra.
§§ Such as NuvaRing.
¶¶ 95% confidence interval.
*** Non-Hispanic.

Surveillance Summaries

TABLE 70. Percentage of high school students who used an IUD* or implant† before last sexual intercourse§,¶ and who used a shot,** patch,†† or birth control ring§§ before last sexual intercourse,§,¶ by sex, race/ethnicity, and grade — United States, Youth Risk Behavior Survey, 2013

Site	IUD or implant use — Female %	CI¶¶	Male %	CI	Total %	CI	Shot, patch, or birth control ring use — Female %	CI	Male %	CI	Total %	CI
State surveys												
Alabama	4.7	(2.2–9.7)	1.0	(0.2–5.5)	3.0	(1.6–5.7)	14.0	(10.2–18.9)	4.3	(2.0–8.8)	9.5	(6.7–13.3)
Alaska	5.9	(3.2–10.7)	3.6	(0.9–13.3)	4.9	(2.5–9.4)	9.1	(5.7–14.4)	6.6	(3.0–13.7)	8.0	(5.2–11.9)
Arizona	1.5	(0.5–4.8)	1.1	(0.3–4.3)	1.3	(0.5–3.7)	7.4	(4.1–12.9)	3.2	(1.6–6.0)	5.4	(3.3–8.5)
Arkansas	2.3	(1.4–3.9)	3.2	(1.4–7.2)	2.7	(1.6–4.6)	10.0	(6.2–15.8)	4.0	(2.0–7.7)	7.3	(5.0–10.6)
Connecticut	1.9	(0.8–4.5)	1.9	(0.8–4.3)	1.9	(1.2–3.1)	5.2	(2.4–11.0)	3.1	(1.5–6.2)	4.2	(2.3–7.4)
Delaware	2.3	(1.2–4.2)	0.4	(0.1–1.7)	1.3	(0.8–2.3)	7.4	(5.0–10.8)	1.8	(0.9–3.6)	4.6	(3.3–6.5)
Florida	1.0	(0.4–2.5)	0.6	(0.2–1.4)	0.8	(0.4–1.5)	4.4	(3.0–6.2)	2.6	(1.6–4.4)	3.4	(2.5–4.7)
Georgia	—***	—	—	—	—	—	—	—	—	—	—	—
Hawaii	6.0	(3.3–10.7)	2.0	(0.8–5.0)	4.4	(2.4–8.0)	6.7	(4.7–9.5)	5.0	(3.2–7.7)	6.3	(4.8–8.3)
Idaho	—	—	—	—	—	—	—	—	—	—	—	—
Illinois	2.3	(1.1–5.0)	2.5	(1.2–5.2)	2.4	(1.3–4.4)	8.0	(5.2–12.0)	3.1	(1.6–5.8)	5.7	(3.7–8.7)
Kansas	3.0	(1.2–7.2)	1.5	(0.5–4.6)	2.3	(1.1–4.6)	10.1	(6.3–15.8)	2.4	(0.7–8.3)	6.6	(4.3–10.0)
Kentucky	2.7	(1.1–6.4)	2.5	(1.3–4.8)	2.6	(1.4–4.8)	6.8	(4.3–10.7)	2.9	(1.5–5.5)	4.9	(3.2–7.4)
Louisiana	—	—	—	—	—	—	—	—	—	—	6.2	(4.9–7.8)
Maine	3.1	(2.2–4.4)	2.3	(1.4–3.8)	2.7	(2.0–3.8)	8.3	(6.7–10.3)	3.6	(2.4–5.4)	4.3	(3.9–4.9)
Maryland	1.8	(1.4–2.3)	1.0	(0.7–1.3)	1.5	(1.2–1.8)	5.7	(5.0–6.4)	2.8	(2.3–3.4)	4.5	(2.9–6.9)
Massachusetts	4.4	(2.5–7.6)	1.0	(0.3–3.0)	2.8	(1.6–4.7)	6.0	(3.5–10.1)	2.9	(1.6–5.2)	4.5	(2.9–6.9)
Michigan	1.4	(0.5–3.7)	2.1	(0.9–5.0)	1.8	(0.8–3.8)	7.8	(5.3–11.4)	4.0	(1.9–8.1)	6.0	(4.3–8.3)
Mississippi	4.1	(1.4–11.1)	1.0	(0.3–3.5)	2.5	(1.0–6.1)	7.5	(4.4–12.6)	3.8	(2.2–6.6)	5.6	(3.7–8.4)
Missouri	5.2	(2.6–10.3)	1.8	(0.6–5.0)	3.5	(2.0–6.2)	7.9	(4.4–13.8)	1.7	(0.6–4.5)	4.8	(2.9–7.9)
Montana	2.1	(1.2–3.7)	1.6	(0.9–2.8)	1.9	(1.2–2.8)	8.6	(6.8–11.0)	3.9	(2.6–5.9)	6.3	(5.0–8.0)
Nebraska	3.1	(1.3–7.1)	0.7	(0.1–4.7)	1.8	(0.8–4.1)	6.1	(2.9–12.5)	6.9	(3.3–14.0)	6.5	(3.9–10.7)
Nevada	1.1	(0.5–2.5)	1.7	(0.4–6.3)	1.4	(0.5–3.8)	2.1	(0.7–5.8)	0.6	(0.1–2.6)	1.3	(0.5–3.4)
New Hampshire	4.0	(2.3–6.7)	0.5	(0.1–3.4)	2.4	(1.4–4.1)	8.0	(5.5–11.4)	2.5	(1.0–6.1)	5.4	(3.8–7.8)
New Jersey	0.0	—	0.7	(0.2–2.9)	0.3	(0.1–1.4)	3.4	(1.4–7.8)	1.5	(0.7–3.2)	2.5	(1.2–4.9)
New Mexico	6.8	(3.8–11.9)	3.0	(1.6–5.3)	5.0	(2.9–8.3)	8.6	(6.2–11.8)	4.5	(2.3–8.5)	6.6	(4.8–9.1)
New York	1.5	(0.6–4.1)	1.6	(0.5–4.6)	1.6	(0.8–2.9)	6.8	(3.7–12.2)	1.6	(0.7–3.6)	4.2	(2.2–7.6)
North Carolina	—	—	—	—	—	—	—	—	—	—	—	—
North Dakota	—	—	—	—	—	—	—	—	—	—	—	—
Ohio	2.3	(0.8–6.3)	1.3	(0.2–8.5)	1.8	(0.7–4.5)	11.8	(7.4–18.3)	4.1	(2.3–7.4)	8.3	(5.7–12.0)
Oklahoma	2.9	(1.1–7.6)	2.6	(0.9–7.4)	2.7	(1.2–6.1)	13.3	(8.8–19.7)	1.4	(0.4–4.4)	7.3	(4.7–11.0)
Rhode Island	3.3	(1.3–8.2)	0.0	—	2.0	(0.8–5.1)	4.1	(1.8–9.3)	1.8	(0.4–7.2)	3.1	(1.6–5.9)
South Carolina	4.7	(2.8–7.9)	0.5	(0.1–3.8)	2.7	(1.5–4.7)	10.6	(6.8–16.0)	2.6	(0.7–9.0)	6.7	(4.2–10.4)
South Dakota	3.4	(1.0–10.5)	0.8	(0.2–3.6)	2.1	(0.8–5.4)	6.2	(2.5–14.3)	7.7	(3.3–17.2)	7.0	(3.3–14.1)
Tennessee	3.8	(2.0–7.1)	0.5	(0.1–3.8)	2.4	(1.2–4.6)	10.6	(6.5–16.8)	3.5	(1.8–6.8)	7.2	(4.5–11.2)
Texas	2.6	(1.7–4.1)	1.1	(0.3–3.3)	1.8	(1.2–2.8)	7.7	(5.3–10.9)	1.7	(0.6–4.6)	4.7	(3.2–6.7)
Utah	—	—	—	—	—	—	—	—	—	—	—	—
Vermont	—	—	—	—	—	—	—	—	—	—	—	—
Virginia	—	—	—	—	—	—	7.1	(4.1–12.1)	2.8	(1.0–7.6)	4.9	(3.4–7.0)
West Virginia	1.3	(0.4–4.6)	1.0	(0.2–4.2)	1.1	(0.4–3.0)	10.3	(6.9–15.0)	4.8	(2.6–8.6)	7.8	(5.6–10.9)
Wisconsin	5.3	(2.7–9.9)	1.1	(0.3–4.2)	3.3	(1.7–6.3)	10.3	(6.9–15.0)	4.5	(2.8–7.2)	7.5	(5.8–9.6)
Wyoming	3.7	(2.4–5.8)	1.2	(0.4–3.7)	2.6	(1.7–4.0)	10.4	(8.1–13.3)	4.5	(2.8–7.2)	7.5	(5.8–9.6)
Median	*2.9*		*1.1*		*2.3*		*7.7*		*3.1*		*5.8*	
Range	*(0.0–6.8)*		*(0.0–3.6)*		*(0.3–5.0)*		*(2.1–14.0)*		*(0.6–7.7)*		*(1.3–9.5)*	

See table footnotes on the next page.

TABLE 70. (*Continued*) Percentage of high school students who used an IUD* or implant[†] before last sexual intercourse[§,¶] and who used a shot,** patch,[††] or birth control ring[§§] before last sexual intercourse,[§,¶] by sex, race/ethnicity, and grade — United States, Youth Risk Behavior Survey, 2013

| | IUD or implant use | | | | | | Shot, patch, or birth control ring use | | | | | |
| | Female | | Male | | Total | | Female | | Male | | Total | |
Site	%	CI[¶¶]	%	CI	%	CI	%	CI	%	CI	%	CI
Large urban school district surveys												
Baltimore, MD	2.6	(0.8–7.7)	3.2	(1.2–8.6)	**3.1**	**(1.5–6.3)**	17.6	(12.3–24.4)	3.0	(1.0–8.6)	**11.0**	**(7.5–15.7)**
Boston, MA	4.3	(2.0–9.0)	1.9	(0.5–6.7)	**3.2**	**(1.7–6.0)**	11.1	(6.6–18.2)	2.4	(0.7–8.3)	**7.2**	**(4.0–12.4)**
Broward County, FL	0.0	—	0.7	(0.1–5.2)	**0.4**	**(0.1–2.9)**	1.6	(0.5–5.2)	2.7	(1.2–6.2)	**2.5**	**(1.2–4.8)**
Charlotte-Mecklenburg, NC	4.6	(2.2–9.5)	2.2	(0.9–5.7)	**3.3**	**(1.8–5.8)**	6.3	(3.2–11.8)	2.3	(1.0–5.5)	**4.4**	**(2.6–7.4)**
Chicago, IL	2.0	(0.7–5.3)	2.1	(1.0–4.3)	**2.0**	**(1.2–3.3)**	9.8	(6.4–14.8)	3.7	(1.9–7.1)	**6.7**	**(4.6–9.8)**
Detroit, MI	1.6	(0.5–5.2)	0.9	(0.2–4.0)	**1.3**	**(0.4–3.9)**	5.4	(2.7–10.4)	2.8	(1.1–7.1)	**4.2**	**(2.4–7.3)**
District of Columbia	3.8	(2.8–5.0)	1.0	(0.6–1.7)	**2.4**	**(1.8–3.1)**	9.8	(8.3–11.6)	2.1	(1.5–3.0)	**5.9**	**(5.0–6.8)**
Duval County, FL	2.3	(1.2–4.2)	2.2	(1.0–4.8)	**2.2**	**(1.3–3.6)**	5.3	(3.4–8.2)	3.0	(1.8–5.1)	**4.1**	**(2.9–5.7)**
Houston, TX	2.0	(0.6–6.1)	0.4	(0.1–2.8)	**1.2**	**(0.4–3.3)**	3.5	(1.7–7.1)	1.9	(0.6–5.4)	**2.7**	**(1.5–4.7)**
Los Angeles, CA	0.9	(0.1–7.1)	0.7	(0.1–5.6)	**0.8**	**(0.2–3.5)**	0.6	(0.1–4.5)	3.4	(1.0–11.4)	**2.1**	**(0.7–6.4)**
Memphis, TN	2.7	(1.2–6.3)	0.7	(0.1–5.2)	**1.7**	**(0.8–3.7)**	6.9	(3.9–11.9)	0.6	(0.1–3.3)	**3.7**	**(2.2–6.1)**
Miami-Dade County, FL	0.9	(0.3–3.2)	0.2	(0.1–0.7)	**0.6**	**(0.2–1.6)**	1.0	(0.3–4.1)	2.9	(1.2–6.7)	**2.0**	**(1.2–3.2)**
Milwaukee, WI	5.5	(2.6–11.5)	1.0	(0.2–5.1)	**3.3**	**(1.7–6.4)**	14.9	(10.6–20.6)	6.6	(3.5–12.2)	**11.2**	**(8.4–14.7)**
New York City, NY	2.7	(1.5–4.8)	1.5	(0.7–3.0)	**2.0**	**(1.3–3.1)**	8.3	(5.7–12.1)	2.9	(1.3–6.6)	**5.4**	**(3.7–7.8)**
Orange County, FL	4.0	(1.9–8.4)	0.9	(0.1–6.5)	**2.4**	**(1.2–5.0)**	0.0	—	1.0	(0.3–4.1)	**0.5**	**(0.1–2.0)**
Palm Beach County, FL	1.6	(0.5–5.3)	0.3	(0.1–2.3)	**0.9**	**(0.3–2.5)**	3.6	(1.6–7.7)	3.1	(1.3–7.2)	**3.3**	**(1.8–6.1)**
Philadelphia, PA	0.5	(0.1–3.6)	0.0	—	**0.3**	**(0.0–1.9)**	7.7	(4.0–14.1)	3.3	(1.2–8.8)	**5.6**	**(3.1–9.8)**
San Bernardino, CA	0.9	(0.2–3.7)	2.1	(0.6–7.0)	**1.5**	**(0.6–4.1)**	3.9	(1.3–11.0)	2.3	(0.5–10.0)	**3.0**	**(0.9–9.4)**
San Diego, CA	2.0	(0.7–6.1)	0.0	—	**1.0**	**(0.3–3.2)**	3.6	(1.3–9.6)	1.8	(0.6–5.7)	**2.7**	**(1.1–6.4)**
San Francisco, CA	—	—	—	—	**—**	**—**	—	—	—	—	**—**	**—**
Seattle, WA	10.5	(6.6–16.1)	5.4	(2.1–13.3)	**7.8**	**(5.2–11.6)**	16.0	(10.7–23.2)	2.7	(1.1–6.6)	**9.4**	**(6.3–13.7)**
Median	*2.1*		*0.9*		*1.8*		*5.8*		*2.7*		*4.1*	
Range	*(0.0–10.5)*		*(0.0–5.4)*		*(0.3–7.8)*		*(0.0–17.6)*		*(0.6–6.6)*		*(0.5–11.2)*	

* Such as Mirena or ParaGard.
[†] Such as Implanon or Nexplanon.
[§] Among the 34.0% of students nationwide who were currently sexually active.
[¶] To prevent pregnancy.
** Such as Depo-Provera.
[††] Such as OrthoEvra.
[§§] Such as NuvaRing.
[¶¶] 95% confidence interval.
*** Not available.

Surveillance Summaries

TABLE 71. Percentage of high school students who used birth control pills; an IUD* or implant;[†] or a shot,[§] patch,[¶] or birth control ring** before last sexual intercourse[††,§§] and who used both a condom during last sexual intercourse and birth control pills; an IUD* or implant;[†] or a shot,[§] patch,[¶] or birth control ring** before last sexual intercourse,[††,§§] by sex, race/ethnicity, and grade — United States, Youth Risk Behavior Survey, 2013

| | Birth control pill; IUD or implant; or shot, patch, or birth control ring use | | | | | | Condom use and birth control pill; IUD or implant; or shot, patch, or birth control ring use | | | | | |
| | Female | | Male | | Total | | Female | | Male | | Total | |
Category	%	CI[¶¶]	%	CI	%	CI	%	CI	%	CI	%	CI
Race/Ethnicity												
White***	37.5	(33.8–41.4)	26.6	(23.2–30.4)	32.6	(29.6–35.8)	13.0	(10.9–15.4)	9.2	(7.6–11.1)	11.3	(10.0–12.7)
Black***	19.2	(12.9–27.6)	11.2	(8.1–15.3)	15.0	(11.0–20.1)	7.1	(4.1–12.2)	4.3	(2.6–6.9)	5.6	(3.6–8.7)
Hispanic	13.9	(9.9–19.2)	15.2	(10.3–21.9)	14.5	(10.7–19.4)	3.0	(1.6–5.5)	6.1	(4.1–9.0)	4.5	(3.0–6.6)
Grade												
9	18.6	(12.8–26.2)	8.3	(5.2–12.9)	13.7	(9.6–19.2)	7.0	(4.4–10.9)	2.4	(1.2–4.8)	4.8	(3.1–7.4)
10	26.0	(20.4–32.4)	17.4	(11.6–25.1)	22.1	(18.0–26.7)	9.0	(5.5–14.3)	4.7	(2.8–7.8)	7.0	(4.9–10.1)
11	31.5	(25.5–38.2)	19.7	(17.0–22.8)	25.9	(22.6–29.4)	11.7	(8.0–16.9)	10.5	(8.4–13.2)	11.1	(8.7–14.2)
12	36.5	(30.0–43.5)	27.4	(23.2–32.1)	32.2	(27.3–37.5)	11.1	(8.4–14.5)	7.9	(6.3–10.0)	9.6	(7.6–12.1)
Total	29.8	(26.1–33.8)	20.1	(17.3–23.3)	25.3	(22.4–28.4)	10.2	(8.3–12.4)	7.2	(6.1–8.5)	8.8	(7.5–10.3)

    * Such as Mirena or ParaGard.
    † Such as Implanon or Nexplanon.
    § Such as Depo-Provera.
    ¶ Such as OrthoEvra.
  ** Such as NuvaRing.
  †† Among the 34.0% of students nationwide who were currently sexually active.
  §§ To prevent pregnancy.
  ¶¶ 95% confidence interval.
*** Non-Hispanic.

Surveillance Summaries

TABLE 72. Percentage of high school students who used birth control pills; an IUD* or implant;[†] or a shot,[§] patch,[¶] or birth control ring** before last sexual intercourse[††,§§] and who used both a condom during last sexual intercourse and birth control pills; an IUD* or implant;[†] or a shot,[§] patch,[¶] or birth control ring** before last sexual intercourse,[††,§§] by sex — selected U.S. sites, Youth Risk Behavior Survey, 2013

| | Birth control pill; IUD or implant; or shot, patch, or birth control ring use | | | | | | Condom use and birth control pill; IUD or implant; or shot, patch, or birth control ring use | | | | | |
| | Female | | Male | | Total | | Female | | Male | | Total | |
Site	%	CI[¶¶]	%	CI	%	CI	%	CI	%	CI	%	CI
State surveys												
Alabama	38.2	(31.1–45.8)	23.0	(16.0–32.1)	**31.1**	**(25.4–37.5)**	10.8	(5.9–18.9)	6.7	(4.2–10.7)	**8.9**	**(5.7–13.6)**
Alaska	36.4	(28.8–44.7)	35.3	(25.9–46.0)	**36.3**	**(29.5–43.7)**	17.5	(12.2–24.4)	15.1	(9.7–22.8)	**16.4**	**(12.5–21.3)**
Arizona	28.6	(22.4–35.6)	18.6	(13.8–24.6)	**24.2**	**(19.7–29.4)**	8.5	(5.4–13.2)	5.7	(3.5–9.0)	**7.6**	**(5.3–10.8)**
Arkansas	31.4	(26.0–37.4)	28.6	(22.3–35.7)	**30.2**	**(26.5–34.2)**	8.4	(4.9–13.9)	10.0	(5.7–16.9)	**9.0**	**(6.1–13.3)**
Connecticut	39.9	(33.1–47.2)	27.7	(20.8–35.9)	**34.0**	**(30.1–38.1)**	12.4	(8.8–17.3)	8.5	(5.5–12.9)	**10.5**	**(8.0–13.7)**
Delaware	31.7	(27.0–36.9)	15.4	(12.3–19.1)	**23.9**	**(20.9–27.1)**	10.5	(7.7–14.1)	6.4	(4.4–9.3)	**8.6**	**(6.8–10.9)**
Florida	24.0	(20.3–28.1)	16.1	(13.4–19.2)	**19.8**	**(17.4–22.4)**	8.3	(6.3–10.9)	6.2	(4.5–8.6)	**7.2**	**(5.7–9.1)**
Georgia	—***	—	—	—	—	—	—	—	—	—	—	—
Hawaii	29.1	(23.2–35.7)	19.8	(15.0–25.5)	**25.6**	**(21.3–30.4)**	8.7	(6.5–11.6)	4.8	(2.8–8.2)	**7.2**	**(5.8–8.8)**
Idaho	—	—	—	—	—	—	—	—	—	—	—	—
Illinois	31.9	(27.2–37.0)	22.6	(16.6–30.1)	**27.5**	**(22.8–32.8)**	10.8	(8.7–13.4)	6.6	(3.8–11.2)	**8.8**	**(7.5–10.4)**
Kansas	38.2	(32.2–44.6)	25.6	(19.7–32.5)	**32.2**	**(28.0–36.7)**	12.5	(8.8–17.5)	10.2	(7.0–14.7)	**11.3**	**(9.0–14.1)**
Kentucky	33.7	(28.1–39.8)	20.6	(15.8–26.4)	**27.3**	**(23.1–31.9)**	8.5	(5.6–12.8)	4.6	(2.9–7.3)	**6.6**	**(4.6–9.4)**
Louisiana	—	—	—	—	—	—	—	—	—	—	—	—
Maine	52.0	(48.9–55.0)	35.6	(32.2–39.2)	**44.6**	**(41.7–47.6)**	18.6	(16.4–21.0)	15.2	(13.0–17.5)	**17.0**	**(15.7–18.4)**
Maryland	29.4	(27.7–31.1)	19.3	(17.9–20.7)	**24.5**	**(23.4–25.7)**	10.8	(9.8–11.8)	7.4	(6.6–8.3)	**9.2**	**(8.5–9.9)**
Massachusetts	42.0	(36.8–47.4)	27.0	(21.6–33.1)	**34.8**	**(30.6–39.2)**	13.1	(9.4–17.9)	10.7	(7.8–14.4)	**11.9**	**(9.6–14.6)**
Michigan	35.9	(30.6–41.6)	22.8	(18.9–27.4)	**29.5**	**(26.0–33.2)**	12.7	(9.6–16.6)	8.0	(5.4–11.5)	**10.3**	**(8.1–13.1)**
Mississippi	29.8	(23.8–36.5)	14.3	(10.7–19.0)	**21.7**	**(17.3–26.8)**	12.0	(9.1–15.7)	6.3	(3.4–11.3)	**9.0**	**(6.9–11.7)**
Missouri	30.8	(23.7–38.8)	18.1	(11.8–26.7)	**24.4**	**(19.6–29.9)**	10.0	(6.2–15.8)	9.1	(5.0–15.9)	**9.5**	**(7.0–12.8)**
Montana	39.7	(35.8–43.7)	26.2	(22.1–30.7)	**33.2**	**(29.7–36.8)**	16.2	(13.6–19.1)	9.7	(7.4–12.7)	**13.1**	**(11.2–15.3)**
Nebraska	29.5	(22.2–38.0)	20.3	(13.1–30.1)	**24.8**	**(19.1–31.5)**	13.2	(8.4–20.1)	5.9	(2.8–11.8)	**9.4**	**(6.2–14.1)**
Nevada	29.8	(24.3–36.1)	15.8	(11.8–20.9)	**22.9**	**(19.3–26.9)**	12.3	(9.2–16.2)	5.8	(3.4–9.6)	**9.0**	**(7.1–11.4)**
New Hampshire	49.0	(42.7–55.4)	33.9	(26.5–42.1)	**42.2**	**(37.2–47.4)**	16.4	(12.9–20.6)	14.2	(9.4–20.9)	**15.3**	**(12.7–18.3)**
New Jersey	29.8	(22.0–39.0)	18.3	(12.6–25.7)	**24.3**	**(19.5–29.8)**	8.5	(5.3–13.3)	7.0	(3.3–14.0)	**7.8**	**(5.6–10.6)**
New Mexico	35.0	(27.7–43.1)	19.3	(15.3–24.0)	**27.5**	**(22.1–33.6)**	13.1	(10.2–16.6)	6.6	(4.2–10.3)	**10.0**	**(7.8–12.8)**
New York	34.5	(27.5–42.2)	17.6	(13.8–22.3)	**25.8**	**(22.3–29.8)**	14.3	(11.1–18.3)	7.1	(4.7–10.6)	**10.7**	**(8.5–13.3)**
North Carolina	—	—	—	—	—	—	—	—	—	—	—	—
North Dakota	—	—	—	—	—	—	—	—	—	—	—	—
Ohio	43.8	(37.2–50.6)	23.0	(17.8–29.2)	**34.2**	**(29.7–39.1)**	13.3	(9.3–18.7)	2.5	(1.0–6.1)	**8.4**	**(5.9–11.7)**
Oklahoma	29.9	(24.8–35.5)	15.0	(10.5–21.0)	**22.3**	**(18.8–26.4)**	11.0	(7.6–15.7)	6.2	(3.6–10.3)	**8.6**	**(6.0–12.1)**
Rhode Island	38.5	(31.2–46.3)	21.8	(16.1–28.8)	**31.1**	**(25.6–37.3)**	18.7	(13.0–26.1)	9.8	(5.7–16.3)	**14.9**	**(10.7–20.4)**
South Carolina	36.3	(28.2–45.2)	15.7	(10.0–23.9)	**26.4**	**(21.3–32.2)**	14.5	(9.6–21.3)	6.7	(3.6–12.1)	**10.7**	**(8.0–14.2)**
South Dakota	33.0	(26.0–40.9)	27.6	(17.8–40.2)	**30.3**	**(24.0–37.4)**	14.2	(10.3–19.1)	9.8	(4.9–18.5)	**11.9**	**(8.8–16.1)**
Tennessee	33.0	(26.9–39.7)	17.5	(12.6–23.9)	**25.6**	**(21.9–29.7)**	13.3	(9.9–17.7)	7.3	(5.1–10.5)	**10.4**	**(8.1–13.2)**
Texas	23.5	(17.8–30.3)	17.0	(11.8–23.8)	**20.2**	**(15.4–26.2)**	6.5	(4.2–9.7)	7.5	(4.9–11.2)	**7.0**	**(4.8–9.9)**
Utah	—	—	—	—	—	—	—	—	—	—	—	—
Vermont	—	—	—	—	—	—	—	—	—	—	—	—
Virginia	—	—	—	—	—	—	—	—	—	—	—	—
West Virginia	39.3	(33.4–45.6)	24.8	(19.6–31.0)	**32.0**	**(28.6–35.5)**	13.1	(8.6–19.6)	9.0	(5.9–13.5)	**11.0**	**(8.7–13.9)**
Wisconsin	41.9	(35.4–48.7)	26.6	(20.8–33.3)	**34.9**	**(30.6–39.5)**	16.1	(12.4–20.6)	11.6	(7.3–17.9)	**14.0**	**(11.4–17.1)**
Wyoming	35.8	(31.4–40.4)	22.6	(18.5–27.2)	**29.3**	**(25.8–33.1)**	14.0	(10.7–18.1)	8.3	(6.2–11.1)	**11.2**	**(9.1–13.6)**
Median	*34.1*		*21.2*		***27.5***		*12.6*		*7.3*		***9.8***	
Range	*(23.5–52.0)*		*(14.3–35.6)*		***(19.8–44.6)***		*(6.5–18.7)*		*(2.5–15.2)*		***(6.6–17.0)***	

See table footnotes on the next page.

Surveillance Summaries

TABLE 72. (*Continued*) Percentage of high school students who used birth control pills; an IUD* or implant;[†] or a shot,[§] patch,[¶] or birth control ring** before last sexual intercourse[††,§§] and who used both a condom during last sexual intercourse and birth control pills; an IUD* or implant;[†] or a shot,[§] patch,[¶] or birth control ring** before last sexual intercourse,[††,§§] by sex — selected U.S. sites, Youth Risk Behavior Survey, 2013

| | Birth control pill; IUD or implant; or shot, patch, or birth control ring use | | | | | | Condom use and birth control pill; IUD or implant; or shot, patch, or birth control ring use | | | | | |
| | Female | | Male | | Total | | Female | | Male | | Total | |
Site	%	CI[¶¶]	%	CI	%	CI	%	CI	%	CI	%	CI
Large urban school district surveys												
Baltimore, MD	33.0	(24.2–43.2)	14.8	(9.4–22.5)	24.7	(19.7–30.5)	15.9	(9.7–24.9)	6.3	(3.4–11.2)	11.7	(8.3–16.3)
Boston, MA	30.3	(23.4–38.3)	17.7	(12.0–25.3)	24.5	(19.1–30.9)	10.4	(5.5–18.7)	10.2	(5.7–17.8)	10.3	(6.8–15.2)
Broward County, FL	17.6	(11.8–25.5)	13.5	(9.0–19.7)	16.1	(12.5–20.6)	5.7	(2.9–10.8)	4.5	(2.2–8.7)	5.0	(3.2–7.8)
Charlotte-Mecklenburg, NC	25.4	(19.9–31.8)	17.3	(12.4–23.5)	21.3	(17.6–25.5)	8.2	(5.0–13.3)	6.5	(4.0–10.4)	7.6	(5.4–10.6)
Chicago, IL	22.9	(18.0–28.7)	15.9	(12.6–19.9)	19.3	(16.5–22.4)	8.9	(6.2–12.5)	9.6	(6.8–13.5)	9.2	(7.6–11.1)
Detroit, MI	19.0	(12.5–27.7)	11.7	(7.4–18.1)	15.6	(11.6–20.6)	6.4	(3.8–10.6)	4.5	(2.0–10.0)	5.4	(3.5–8.3)
District of Columbia	22.8	(20.5–25.3)	10.0	(8.3–11.8)	16.3	(14.8–17.9)	8.8	(7.4–10.5)	4.3	(3.3–5.6)	6.5	(5.7–7.5)
Duval County, FL	23.1	(19.0–27.8)	18.5	(14.1–23.8)	20.7	(17.9–23.7)	10.8	(8.0–14.5)	8.2	(5.8–11.4)	9.4	(7.5–11.8)
Houston, TX	19.5	(15.5–24.4)	8.2	(4.6–14.1)	13.9	(11.3–16.9)	4.5	(2.2–9.2)	1.8	(0.4–7.2)	3.2	(1.7–5.9)
Los Angeles, CA	9.6	(4.6–19.2)	10.8	(6.1–18.5)	10.2	(6.4–16.0)	3.3	(1.3–8.2)	1.9	(0.4–8.8)	2.6	(1.0–6.4)
Memphis, TN	23.3	(17.7–29.9)	9.0	(6.1–13.3)	15.9	(13.1–19.2)	12.6	(8.8–17.8)	3.8	(2.1–6.6)	8.1	(6.1–10.6)
Miami-Dade County, FL	12.1	(8.1–17.6)	10.3	(7.2–14.4)	11.2	(8.3–15.1)	3.9	(1.6–9.2)	4.8	(2.6–8.9)	4.5	(2.4–8.3)
Milwaukee, WI	32.1	(26.2–38.6)	14.8	(9.9–21.7)	23.9	(19.7–28.6)	12.4	(7.8–19.3)	5.6	(2.5–11.7)	9.1	(6.1–13.4)
New York City, NY	21.6	(17.8–26.1)	13.1	(10.4–16.3)	17.0	(14.6–19.6)	9.6	(6.5–13.8)	6.2	(4.0–9.3)	7.7	(6.1–9.8)
Orange County, FL	17.1	(11.9–23.8)	11.2	(6.8–17.7)	13.9	(10.2–18.8)	3.2	(1.4–7.2)	1.7	(0.5–5.6)	2.4	(1.1–5.0)
Palm Beach County, FL	27.0	(20.2–35.1)	15.0	(9.4–23.1)	20.3	(15.8–25.7)	13.8	(9.2–20.2)	3.7	(1.6–8.2)	8.3	(6.0–11.4)
Philadelphia, PA	24.6	(20.7–28.9)	16.8	(10.7–25.5)	20.7	(16.8–25.3)	8.3	(5.4–12.4)	5.0	(2.8–8.8)	6.7	(4.9–9.2)
San Bernardino, CA	17.5	(10.6–27.3)	9.0	(4.6–16.8)	13.6	(8.7–20.8)	5.8	(2.7–12.1)	3.9	(1.7–8.5)	4.7	(2.7–7.9)
San Diego, CA	30.9	(22.6–40.6)	21.7	(16.4–28.1)	26.1	(20.8–32.2)	11.0	(6.8–17.4)	3.3	(1.5–7.1)	7.2	(4.7–10.8)
San Francisco, CA	—	—	—	—	—	—	—	—	—	—	—	—
Seattle, WA	56.4	(46.4–65.9)	26.4	(18.5–36.2)	41.4	(34.8–48.4)	21.5	(15.4–29.1)	9.1	(5.8–14.1)	15.7	(12.0–20.4)
Median	*23.0*		*14.1*		*18.1*		*8.8*		*4.6*		*7.4*	
Range	*(9.6–56.4)*		*(8.2–26.4)*		*(10.2–41.4)*		*(3.2–21.5)*		*(1.7–10.2)*		*(2.4–15.7)*	

* Such as Mirena or ParaGard.
[†] Such as Implanon or Nexplanon.
[§] Such as Depo-Provera.
[¶] Such as OrthoEvra.
** Such as NuvaRing.
[††] Among students who were currently sexually active.
[§§] To prevent pregnancy.
[¶¶] 95% confidence interval.
*** Not available.

TABLE 73. Percentage of high school students who did not use any method to prevent pregnancy during last sexual intercourse* and who drank alcohol or used drugs before last sexual intercourse,* by sex, race/ethnicity, and grade — United States, Youth Risk Behavior Survey, 2013

| | Did not use any method to prevent pregnancy | | | | | | Drank alcohol or used drugs before last sexual intercourse | | | | | |
| | Female | | Male | | Total | | Female | | Male | | Total | |
Category	%	CI[†]	%	CI	%	CI	%	CI	%	CI	%	CI
Race/Ethnicity												
White[§]	11.9	(9.7–14.4)	10.1	(8.3–12.2)	11.1	(9.7–12.6)	18.2	(15.4–21.3)	25.1	(21.5–29.1)	21.3	(19.4–23.4)
Black[§]	21.2	(16.2–27.3)	11.2	(7.3–16.8)	15.9	(12.8–19.7)	20.5	(16.4–25.4)	24.9	(20.0–30.5)	22.8	(19.2–26.8)
Hispanic	23.7	(20.0–27.9)	15.4	(11.1–20.8)	19.7	(17.2–22.5)	21.3	(16.6–26.9)	27.0	(22.2–32.5)	24.0	(20.4–28.0)
Grade												
9	18.1	(13.0–24.7)	14.3	(9.6–20.8)	16.3	(13.0–20.3)	16.7	(12.0–22.8)	27.6	(21.1–35.3)	22.0	(17.9–26.8)
10	17.3	(13.7–21.6)	10.2	(6.5–15.6)	14.1	(11.3–17.5)	22.0	(18.0–26.5)	22.6	(17.7–28.5)	22.3	(18.8–26.2)
11	12.9	(9.9–16.8)	11.9	(9.0–15.5)	12.4	(10.4–14.8)	19.0	(15.2–23.4)	27.8	(23.3–32.9)	23.2	(21.1–25.4)
12	15.5	(11.6–20.5)	10.9	(8.0–14.6)	13.3	(10.9–16.2)	18.4	(14.9–22.5)	25.7	(22.4–29.2)	21.9	(19.2–24.8)
Total	**15.7**	(13.5–18.2)	**11.5**	(9.6–13.8)	**13.7**	(12.2–15.4)	**19.3**	(17.4–21.3)	**25.9**	(23.2–28.8)	**22.4**	(20.7–24.3)

* Among the 34.0% of students nationwide who were currently sexually active.
[†] 95% confidence interval.
[§] Non-Hispanic.

TABLE 74. Percentage of high school students who did not use any method to prevent pregnancy during last sexual intercourse* and who drank alcohol or used drugs before last sexual intercourse,* by sex — selected U.S. sites, Youth Risk Behavior Survey, 2013

| | Did not use any method to prevent pregnancy | | | | | | Drank alcohol or used drugs before last sexual intercourse | | | | | |
| | Female | | Male | | Total | | Female | | Male | | Total | |
Site	%	CI†	%	CI	%	CI	%	CI	%	CI	%	CI
State surveys												
Alabama	14.0	(8.6–21.8)	14.5	(10.1–20.3)	14.1	(10.5–18.8)	18.6	(13.3–25.4)	26.7	(20.2–34.3)	22.6	(18.3–27.5)
Alaska	15.6	(9.1–25.4)	11.8	(7.1–19.1)	13.8	(9.0–20.8)	14.3	(9.3–21.4)	16.6	(10.3–25.5)	15.3	(11.5–20.0)
Arizona	19.3	(13.3–27.3)	15.8	(9.9–24.1)	17.5	(12.5–23.9)	15.4	(10.9–21.3)	26.6	(19.1–35.8)	20.6	(16.1–25.9)
Arkansas	23.0	(16.8–30.8)	11.2	(6.5–18.6)	17.8	(14.3–21.9)	13.4	(10.2–17.4)	28.6	(22.9–35.2)	20.1	(16.3–24.5)
Connecticut	8.4	(5.4–13.0)	9.1	(5.9–13.7)	8.8	(6.5–11.8)	16.0	(12.5–20.3)	24.8	(18.8–31.9)	20.3	(16.9–24.1)
Delaware	13.7	(10.0–18.4)	9.3	(6.3–13.4)	11.5	(9.2–14.4)	18.4	(14.7–22.8)	24.8	(20.6–29.6)	21.8	(18.7–25.2)
Florida	14.9	(12.1–18.1)	10.7	(8.7–13.0)	12.6	(11.0–14.5)	18.5	(15.6–21.7)	26.5	(22.9–30.4)	22.8	(20.2–25.7)
Georgia	—§	—	—	—	—	—	—	—	—	—	—	—
Hawaii	17.5	(13.4–22.6)	11.9	(8.4–16.7)	15.6	(12.4–19.4)	21.9	(17.2–27.5)	26.9	(18.6–37.2)	24.0	(19.0–30.0)
Idaho	—	—	—	—	—	—	17.5	(12.5–24.0)	23.3	(18.6–28.7)	20.1	(16.7–24.0)
Illinois	16.3	(12.7–20.6)	13.8	(10.7–17.7)	15.1	(12.2–18.4)	18.1	(13.4–24.0)	27.6	(22.8–33.1)	22.7	(18.5–27.4)
Kansas	12.9	(8.2–19.7)	9.6	(5.9–15.1)	11.5	(8.2–16.0)	16.0	(11.8–21.4)	20.6	(15.1–27.4)	18.0	(14.2–22.6)
Kentucky	18.6	(13.9–24.4)	11.2	(8.2–15.0)	15.1	(12.0–19.0)	13.6	(9.3–19.6)	23.8	(18.7–29.7)	18.7	(14.8–23.3)
Louisiana	—	—	—	—	—	—	—	—	—	—	—	—
Maine	8.5	(6.7–10.8)	9.4	(7.5–11.8)	9.0	(7.5–10.8)	16.9	(14.7–19.4)	19.8	(17.2–22.6)	18.4	(16.4–20.5)
Maryland	15.2	(14.0–16.5)	13.3	(12.0–14.6)	14.3	(13.4–15.2)	20.1	(18.9–21.4)	27.9	(26.3–29.5)	24.0	(22.9–25.1)
Massachusetts	8.8	(6.0–12.7)	12.1	(9.0–16.2)	10.5	(8.6–12.7)	18.2	(13.9–23.4)	29.1	(24.0–34.8)	23.5	(19.9–27.5)
Michigan	9.8	(7.6–12.5)	8.1	(5.6–11.6)	8.9	(7.2–11.0)	20.3	(16.7–24.5)	22.1	(17.4–27.7)	21.3	(18.1–24.8)
Mississippi	16.1	(11.9–21.4)	11.9	(8.2–17.0)	13.9	(11.0–17.6)	19.1	(13.2–26.7)	23.1	(16.4–31.4)	21.2	(15.7–27.9)
Missouri	18.9	(13.1–26.4)	13.5	(7.7–22.7)	16.2	(11.6–22.0)	17.9	(14.4–22.0)	23.5	(17.9–30.3)	20.7	(17.0–25.0)
Montana	8.6	(6.6–11.1)	6.6	(5.0–8.7)	7.6	(6.2–9.4)	20.0	(17.5–22.8)	23.5	(20.1–27.2)	21.7	(19.5–24.0)
Nebraska	15.9	(11.5–21.6)	8.8	(5.1–14.7)	12.2	(8.9–16.6)	16.3	(10.9–23.6)	22.9	(16.1–31.6)	19.7	(15.1–25.3)
Nevada	16.6	(11.3–23.6)	14.7	(9.9–21.4)	16.0	(11.5–21.9)	22.3	(18.2–27.0)	23.1	(17.0–30.6)	23.0	(18.6–28.1)
New Hampshire	6.9	(4.4–10.8)	10.7	(7.0–16.1)	8.6	(6.3–11.5)	18.6	(14.8–23.0)	23.0	(17.3–29.8)	20.7	(17.3–24.6)
New Jersey	15.9	(9.4–25.8)	11.4	(8.4–15.4)	13.8	(9.1–20.3)	16.4	(11.8–22.5)	26.7	(19.9–34.7)	21.4	(17.4–26.1)
New Mexico	16.1	(11.9–21.5)	11.3	(9.2–13.9)	13.8	(11.1–17.0)	14.6	(10.8–19.5)	23.7	(20.4–27.4)	19.1	(15.8–22.9)
New York	13.3	(9.3–18.5)	11.6	(7.8–16.9)	12.6	(9.8–16.2)	25.5	(21.9–29.5)	30.1	(23.9–37.0)	27.7	(24.0–31.9)
North Carolina	—	—	—	—	—	—	18.2	(13.5–24.1)	24.1	(17.7–31.9)	21.2	(16.3–27.0)
North Dakota	—	—	—	—	—	—	—	—	—	—	—	—
Ohio	12.8	(8.8–18.4)	11.0	(5.9–19.5)	12.0	(9.0–15.8)	13.6	(8.3–21.4)	24.0	(16.5–33.6)	18.4	(13.4–24.7)
Oklahoma	17.8	(13.0–24.0)	9.2	(5.8–14.3)	13.5	(10.1–17.9)	14.0	(10.1–19.2)	19.9	(14.6–26.6)	17.0	(13.4–21.2)
Rhode Island	12.2	(8.6–17.0)	6.9	(4.2–11.2)	10.0	(7.2–13.7)	—	—	—	—	—	—
South Carolina	14.9	(9.9–22.0)	13.1	(8.1–20.5)	14.0	(10.7–18.2)	17.1	(12.5–23.0)	23.1	(17.7–29.5)	20.0	(16.0–24.7)
South Dakota	11.4	(6.7–18.7)	13.9	(7.2–25.0)	12.7	(7.4–20.8)	22.8	(17.8–28.9)	25.9	(16.7–38.0)	24.4	(17.7–32.7)
Tennessee	20.6	(15.2–27.4)	16.1	(11.0–23.0)	18.8	(15.0–23.3)	12.3	(8.7–17.0)	22.7	(17.3–29.1)	17.6	(13.6–22.4)
Texas	20.9	(16.4–26.1)	17.1	(12.7–22.5)	19.0	(15.9–22.4)	19.3	(14.7–24.9)	28.4	(23.6–33.8)	23.8	(20.5–27.5)
Utah	—	—	—	—	—	—	—	—	—	—	—	—
Vermont	—	—	—	—	—	—	—	—	—	—	—	—
Virginia	—	—	—	—	—	—	—	—	—	—	—	—
West Virginia	12.7	(9.6–16.5)	13.9	(10.8–17.5)	13.2	(10.7–16.3)	14.2	(10.5–18.9)	22.5	(16.1–30.6)	18.3	(14.5–22.9)
Wisconsin	10.3	(6.7–15.5)	11.1	(7.2–16.8)	10.7	(8.1–14.0)	15.5	(10.1–23.2)	29.5	(23.4–36.4)	21.9	(18.3–26.1)
Wyoming	12.8	(8.7–18.5)	11.4	(8.2–15.7)	12.3	(9.1–16.3)	17.0	(13.9–20.5)	24.6	(20.7–29.1)	20.8	(18.3–23.6)
Median	*14.9*		*11.4*		*13.3*		*17.5*		*24.0*		*20.8*	
Range	*(6.9–23.0)*		*(6.6–17.1)*		*(7.6–19.0)*		*(12.3–25.5)*		*(16.6–30.1)*		*(15.3–27.7)*	

See table footnotes on the next page.

TABLE 74. (Continued) Percentage of high school students who did not use any method to prevent pregnancy during last sexual intercourse* and who drank alcohol or used drugs before last sexual intercourse,* by sex — selected U.S. sites, Youth Risk Behavior Survey, 2013

| | Did not use any method to prevent pregnancy | | | | | | Drank alcohol or used drugs before last sexual intercourse | | | | | |
| | Female | | Male | | Total | | Female | | Male | | Total | |
Site	%	CI†	%	CI	%	CI	%	CI	%	CI	%	CI
Large urban school district surveys												
Baltimore, MD	21.9	(16.6–28.2)	20.5	(12.4–32.0)	**21.2**	**(16.3–27.1)**	12.1	(7.2–19.6)	32.6	(20.8–47.1)	**22.5**	**(15.8–30.9)**
Boston, MA	18.4	(11.7–27.7)	17.7	(11.8–25.9)	**18.3**	**(14.0–23.5)**	24.5	(16.5–34.7)	21.3	(14.8–29.7)	**23.5**	**(17.2–31.2)**
Broward County, FL	15.2	(10.3–21.9)	9.8	(6.4–14.6)	**12.0**	**(9.2–15.6)**	18.6	(12.9–26.1)	25.6	(18.8–33.8)	**22.4**	**(17.1–28.8)**
Charlotte-Mecklenburg, NC	13.5	(9.1–19.6)	10.8	(6.8–16.8)	**12.1**	**(8.6–16.7)**	23.6	(17.3–31.3)	29.2	(22.2–37.2)	**26.7**	**(21.8–32.4)**
Chicago, IL	22.1	(16.8–28.6)	13.3	(8.7–19.6)	**17.6**	**(13.7–22.3)**	13.1	(8.4–19.8)	23.9	(17.9–31.2)	**18.8**	**(14.5–23.9)**
Detroit, MI	18.1	(12.4–25.7)	11.3	(6.8–18.2)	**15.3**	**(11.8–19.5)**	33.6	(22.5–46.8)	30.6	(23.0–39.5)	**32.5**	**(25.3–40.7)**
District of Columbia	20.3	(18.1–22.7)	13.6	(11.7–15.7)	**17.0**	**(15.5–18.5)**	16.0	(14.2–17.9)	24.9	(22.5–27.5)	**20.5**	**(19.0–22.2)**
Duval County, FL	16.7	(13.1–21.1)	13.6	(10.0–18.2)	**15.2**	**(12.4–18.6)**	19.0	(15.2–23.5)	32.6	(27.0–38.8)	**26.1**	**(22.5–30.1)**
Houston, TX	28.4	(22.6–35.1)	19.6	(14.4–26.0)	**24.2**	**(20.5–28.2)**	20.2	(14.8–26.9)	29.0	(22.1–36.9)	**24.8**	**(19.5–30.9)**
Los Angeles, CA	20.2	(14.0–28.2)	20.9	(11.2–35.5)	**21.0**	**(14.4–29.6)**	18.9	(12.2–28.0)	15.6	(7.7–29.0)	**17.1**	**(11.4–24.9)**
Memphis, TN	24.4	(18.8–31.2)	19.1	(13.4–26.5)	**22.0**	**(17.7–26.9)**	17.2	(11.5–25.0)	24.7	(18.9–31.6)	**21.0**	**(16.7–26.0)**
Miami-Dade County, FL	19.2	(13.4–26.7)	10.4	(6.9–15.6)	**14.9**	**(11.8–18.7)**	19.9	(15.9–24.6)	24.2	(19.2–30.0)	**22.1**	**(18.6–26.2)**
Milwaukee, WI	22.4	(15.7–30.9)	10.2	(5.9–16.9)	**16.4**	**(12.2–21.6)**	18.4	(12.3–26.6)	24.6	(17.0–34.3)	**21.3**	**(16.3–27.3)**
New York City, NY	18.3	(14.2–23.2)	17.1	(13.0–22.1)	**17.6**	**(14.4–21.3)**	14.2	(10.7–18.8)	22.1	(18.1–26.7)	**18.5**	**(15.8–21.6)**
Orange County, FL	20.0	(14.3–27.2)	21.2	(15.7–28.1)	**21.3**	**(17.1–26.3)**	16.6	(11.0–24.5)	26.2	(20.4–32.9)	**21.8**	**(17.3–27.1)**
Palm Beach County, FL	12.3	(8.7–17.2)	11.6	(6.9–18.9)	**11.8**	**(8.6–16.0)**	25.7	(19.9–32.4)	28.0	(22.6–34.1)	**27.1**	**(23.3–31.4)**
Philadelphia, PA	21.5	(13.6–32.3)	20.3	(13.7–28.9)	**20.8**	**(14.8–28.4)**	15.3	(11.0–20.9)	28.7	(20.8–38.0)	**21.7**	**(17.1–27.0)**
San Bernardino, CA	25.0	(17.8–34.0)	13.4	(8.6–20.2)	**18.4**	**(14.2–23.5)**	14.5	(9.2–22.1)	26.7	(19.3–35.6)	**21.1**	**(16.3–26.8)**
San Diego, CA	19.1	(13.4–26.5)	14.5	(9.9–20.8)	**16.7**	**(12.6–21.8)**	11.0	(6.7–17.6)	24.4	(18.9–31.0)	**18.4**	**(14.2–23.5)**
San Francisco, CA	—		—		**—**		—		—		**—**	
Seattle, WA	5.9	(3.0–11.2)	8.0	(4.1–15.2)	**7.0**	**(4.2–11.2)**	24.1	(18.5–30.7)	28.4	(20.4–38.1)	**26.2**	**(20.9–32.2)**
Median	19.6		13.6		*17.3*		18.5		25.9		*21.9*	
Range	(5.9–28.4)		(8.0–21.2)		*(7.0–24.2)*		(11.0–33.6)		(15.6–32.6)		*(17.1–32.5)*	

* Among students who were currently sexually active.
† 95% confidence interval.
§ Not available.

TABLE 75. Percentage of high school students who were ever taught in school about acquired immunodeficiency syndrome (AIDS) or human immunodeficiency virus (HIV) infection and who were ever tested for HIV,* by sex, race/ethnicity, and grade — United States, Youth Risk Behavior Survey, 2013

| | Taught in school about AIDS or HIV infection | | | | | | Tested for HIV | | | | | |
| | Female | | Male | | Total | | Female | | Male | | Total | |
Category	%	CI†	%	CI	%	CI	%	CI	%	CI	%	CI
Race/Ethnicity												
White§	86.8	(83.2–89.8)	86.3	(82.0–89.7)	**86.6**	**(82.9–89.6)**	12.7	(10.7–15.0)	8.7	(7.0–10.7)	**10.7**	**(9.1–12.5)**
Black§	83.0	(78.6–86.7)	80.6	(77.2–83.6)	**81.9**	**(79.3–84.2)**	20.9	(16.9–25.6)	18.7	(15.9–21.8)	**19.8**	**(17.2–22.7)**
Hispanic	84.9	(82.2–87.2)	83.9	(80.3–86.9)	**84.4**	**(81.9–86.6)**	13.4	(9.8–18.2)	12.2	(10.1–14.7)	**12.8**	**(10.3–15.8)**
Grade												
9	80.1	(75.4–84.1)	82.4	(78.5–85.7)	**81.3**	**(77.8–84.3)**	7.8	(5.7–10.7)	10.4	(8.2–13.0)	**9.1**	**(7.4–11.2)**
10	86.2	(82.3–89.3)	84.5	(79.4–88.4)	**85.3**	**(81.7–88.3)**	12.6	(10.4–15.2)	8.5	(6.5–11.1)	**10.6**	**(8.8–12.7)**
11	88.2	(85.8–90.3)	86.7	(84.0–88.9)	**87.4**	**(85.4–89.2)**	17.3	(14.9–20.0)	13.2	(10.6–16.2)	**15.3**	**(13.4–17.4)**
12	89.3	(87.0–91.2)	86.6	(83.4–89.3)	**88.0**	**(85.6–90.0)**	21.3	(18.9–24.0)	13.1	(11.3–15.2)	**17.2**	**(15.6–19.0)**
Total	85.8	(83.3–87.9)	85.0	(82.3–87.3)	**85.3**	**(83.0–87.4)**	14.6	(12.8–16.5)	11.2	(9.8–12.9)	**12.9**	**(11.5–14.4)**

* Not including tests done when donating blood.
† 95% confidence interval.
§ Non-Hispanic.

Information in this table was drawn from the National Youth Risk Behavior Survey (YRBS), which is conducted by the Centers for Disease Control and Prevention (CDC). The national YRBS, a school-based survey conducted every other year, gathers information about six types of health-related behaviors among youth and young adults: those relating to injuries and violence; tobacco use; alcohol and drug use; sexual behavior; diet; and physical inactivity. Further information about the YRBS is available from http://www.cdc.gov/healthyyouth/data/yrbs/index.htm.

Trends in the Prevalence of Marijuana, Cocaine, and Other Illegal Drug Use National YRBS: 1991–2013

The National Youth Risk Behavior Survey (YRBS) monitors priority health risk behaviors that contribute to the leading causes of death, disability, and social problems among youth and adults in the United States. The National YRBS is conducted every two years during the spring semester and provides data representative of 9th through 12th grade students in public and private schools throughout the United States.

	Percentages												Long-Term Change[1]	Change From 2011 to 2013[2]
	1991	1993	1995	1997	1999	2001	2003	2005	2007	2009	2011	2013		
Ever used marijuana (one or more times during their life)	31.3	32.8	42.4	47.1	47.2	42.4	40.2	38.4	38.1	36.8	39.9	40.7	Increased 1991–1997 Decreased 1997–2013	No change
Tried marijuana before age 13 years (for the first time)	7.4	6.9	7.6	9.7	11.3	10.2	9.9	8.7	8.3	7.5	8.1	8.6	Increased 1991–1999 Decreased 1999–2013	No change
Currently used marijuana (one or more times during the 30 days before the survey)	14.7	17.7	25.3	26.2	26.7	23.9	22.4	20.2	19.7	20.8	23.1	23.4	Increased 1991–2013 Increased 1991–1995 Decreased 1995–2013	No change
Ever used cocaine (any form of cocaine, such as powder, crack, or freebase, one or more times during their life)	5.9	4.9	7.0	8.2	9.5	9.4	8.7	7.6	7.2	6.4	6.8	5.5	Increased 1991–1999 Decreased 1999–2013	Decreased
Ever used hallucinogenic drugs (such as LSD, acid, PCP, angel dust, mescaline, or mushrooms, one or more times during their life)	—[3]	—	—	—	—	13.3	10.6	8.5	7.8	8.0	8.7	7.1	Decreased 2001–2013 Decreased 2001–2005 No change 2005–2013	Decreased

YRBSS

	1991	1993	1995	1997	1999	2001	2003	2005	2007	2009	2011	2013	Long-Term Change[1]	Change From 2011 to 2013[2]
Ever used inhalants (sniffed glue, breathed the contents of aerosol spray cans, or inhaled any paints or sprays to get high, one or more times during their life)														
	–	–	20.3	16.0	14.6	14.7	12.1	12.4	13.3	11.7	11.4	8.9	Decreased 1995–2013 Decreased 1995–1999 Decreased 1999–2013	Decreased
Ever used ecstasy (also called "MDMA", one or more times during their life)														
	–	–	–	–	–	11.1	11.1	6.3	5.8	6.7	8.2	6.6	Decreased 2001–2013 Decreased 2001–2005 No change 2005–2013	Decreased
Ever used heroin (also called "smack", "junk", or "China white", one or more times during their life)														
	–	–	–	–	2.4	3.1	3.3	2.4	2.3	2.5	2.9	2.2	No change 1999–2013	No change
Ever used methamphetamines (also called "speed", "crystal", "crank", or "ice", one or more times during their life)														
	–	–	–	–	9.1	9.8	7.6	6.2	4.4	4.1	3.8	3.2	Decreased 1999–2013	No change
Ever took steroids without a doctor's prescription (pills or shots, one or more times during their life)														
	2.7	2.2	3.7	3.1	3.7	5.0	6.1	4.0	3.9	3.3	3.6	3.2	Increased 1991–2013 Increased 1991–2001 Decreased 2001–2013	No change
Ever injected any illegal drug (used a needle to inject any illegal drug into their body one or more times during their life)														
	–	–	2.1	2.1	1.8	2.3	3.2	2.1	2.0	2.1	2.3	1.7	No change 1995–2013	No change
Were offered, sold, or given an illegal drug on school property (during the 12 months before the survey)														
	–	24.0	32.1	31.7	30.2	28.5	28.7	25.4	22.3	22.7	25.6	22.1	Decreased 1993–2013 Increased 1993–1997 Decreased 1997–2013	Decreased

[1] Based on linear and quadratic trend analyses using logistic regression models controlling for sex, race/ethnicity, and grade, $p < 0.05$. Significant linear trends (if present) across all available years are described first followed by linear changes in each segment of significant quadratic trends (if present).

[2] Based on t-test analysis, $p < 0.05$.

[3] Not available.

http://www.cdc.gov/nchs/data/series/sr_10/sr10_260.pdf

Contraceptive Use

Information in these figures and tables was drawn from the 2011–2013 National Survey of Family Growth (NSFG), conducted by the National Center for Health Statistics (NCHS) of the Centers for Disease Control and Prevention (CDC). The NSFG gathers information about family life, marriage and divorce, pregnancy, infertility, contraceptive use, and men's and women's health. More information about the NSFG is available from http://www.cdc.gov/nchs/nsfg.htm.

Figure 1. Percentage currently using any contraceptive method among all women aged 15–44, by selected characteristics: United States, 2011–2013

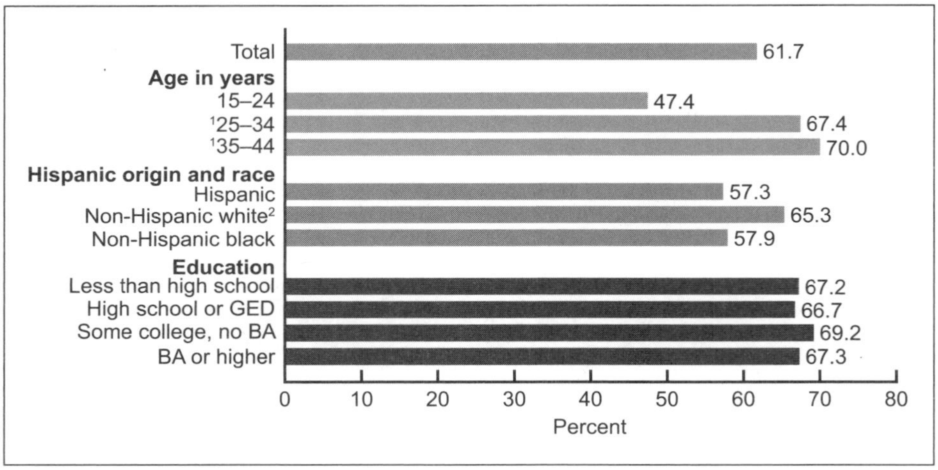

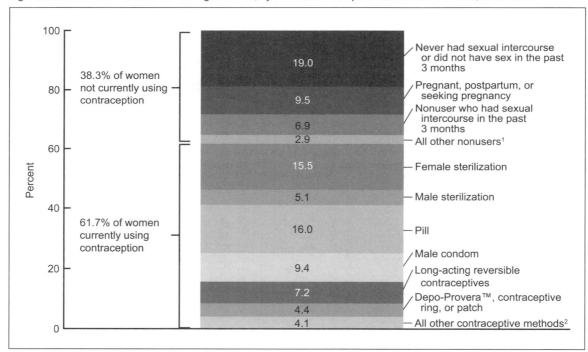

[1]Significantly different from age group 15–24.
[2]Significantly different from Hispanic and non-Hispanic black women.
NOTES: The population size referenced in this figure for women aged 15–44 is 60.9 million. Analyses of education are limited to women aged 22–44 at the time of interview. GED is General Educational Development high school equivalency diploma. BA is bachelor's degree. Access data table for Figure 1 at: http://www.cdc.gov/nchs/data/databriefs/db173_table.pdf#1.
SOURCE: CDC/NCHS, National Survey of Family Growth, 2011–2013.

Figure 2. Percent distribution of women aged 15–44, by current contraceptive status: United States, 2011–2013

[1]Additional reasons for nonuse, such as nonsurgical sterility, are shown in the accompanying data table.
[2]Other methods grouped in this category, such as withdrawal and natural family planning, are shown in the accompanying data table.
NOTES: Percentages may not add to 100 due to rounding. Women currently using more than one method were classified according to the most effective method they were using. Long-acting reversible contraceptives include contraceptive implants and intrauterine devices. Access data table for Figure 2 at: http://www.cdc.gov/nchs/data/databriefs/db173_table.pdf#2.
SOURCE: CDC/NCHS, National Survey of Family Growth, 2011–2013.

Figure 3. Percentage of all women aged 15–44 who were using female sterilization, the pill, the male condom, and long-acting reversible contraceptives, by age: United States, 2011–2013

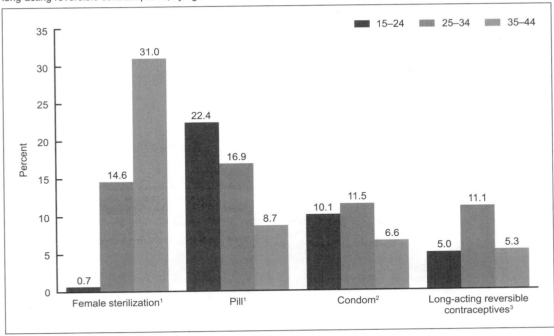

[1]All percentages are significantly different from each other across age groups.
[2]Percentages for age groups 15–24 and 25–34 are significantly different from age group 35–44.
[3]Percentages for age groups 15–24 and 35–44 are significantly different from age group 25–34.
NOTES: Women currently using more than one method were classified according to the most effective method they were using. Long-acting reversible contraceptives include contraceptive implants and intrauterine devices. Access data table for Figure 3 at: http://www.cdc.gov/nchs/data/databriefs/ db173_table.pdf#1.
SOURCE: CDC/NCHS, National Survey of Family Growth, 2011–2013.

Figure 4. Percentage of all women aged 15–44 who were currently using female sterilization, the pill, the male condom, and long-acting reversible contraceptives, by Hispanic origin and race: United States, 2011–2013

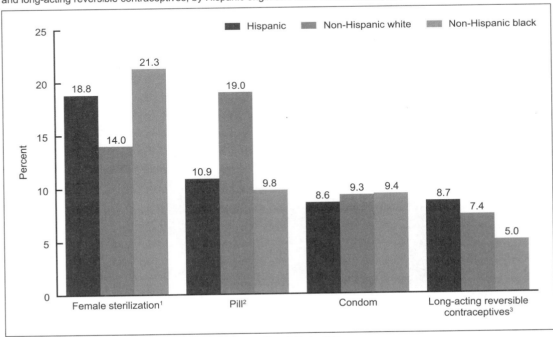

[1]Percentage for non-Hispanic white women is significantly different from non-Hispanic black women.
[2]Percentage for Hispanic and non-Hispanic black women is significantly different from non-Hispanic white women.
[3]Percentage for Hispanic and non-Hispanic white women is significantly different from non-Hispanic black women.
NOTES: Women currently using more than one method were classified according to the most effective method they were using. Long-acting reversible contraceptives include contraceptive implants and intrauterine devices. Access data table for Figure 4 at: http://www.cdc.gov/nchs/data/databriefs/ db173_table.pdf#1.
SOURCE: CDC/NCHS, National Survey of Family Growth, 2011–2013.

Figure 5. Percentage of all women aged 22–44 who were currently using female sterilization, the pill, the male condom, and long-acting reversible contraceptives, by educational attainment: United States, 2011–2013

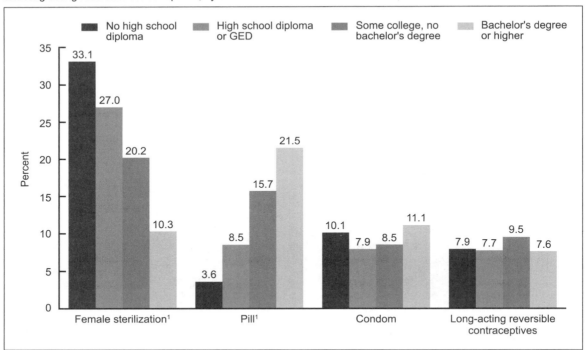

[1]Significant linear trend.
NOTES: Women currently using more than one method were classified according to the most effective method they were using. Long-acting reversible contraceptives include contraceptive implants and intrauterine devices. GED is General Educational Development high school equivalency diploma. Access data table for Figure 5 at: http://www.cdc.gov/nchs/data/databriefs/db173_table.pdf#1.
SOURCE: CDC/NCHS, National Survey of Family Growth, 2011–2013.

Data Brief 173. Current Contraceptive Status Among Women Aged 15–44: United States, 2011–2013

Data table for Figures 1, 3, 4, and 5. Current use of any method of contraception, female sterilization, the contraceptive pill, the male condom, and long-acting reversible contraceptives among all women aged 15–44: United States, 2011–2013

Characteristic	Number in thousands	Currently using any method		Female sterilization		Pill		Condom		Long-acting reversible contraceptives	
		Percent and standard error									
Total	60,887	61.7	1.10	15.5	1.01	16.0	0.89	9.4	0.57	7.2	0.53
Age in years											
15–24	19,885	47.4	1.91	0.7	0.19	22.4	1.55	10.1	1.05	5.0	0.58
25–34	20,790	67.4	1.57	14.6	1.69	16.9	1.09	11.5	1.13	11.1	1.11
35–44	20,212	70.0	1.61	31.0	1.86	8.7	1.36	6.6	0.90	5.3	0.92
Hispanic origin and race											
Hispanic	12,024	57.3	2.05	18.8	2.09	10.9	1.49	8.6	1.05	8.7	1.26
Non-Hispanic white	34,674	65.3	1.44	14.0	1.34	19.0	1.26	9.3	0.92	7.4	0.74
Non-Hispanic black	8,491	57.9	2.03	21.3	2.00	9.8	0.95	9.4	1.41	5.0	0.67
Other single and multiple race	5,698	54.8	4.42	9.1	2.27	17.5	3.42	12.1	1.57	5.8	1.23
Education[1]											
No high school diploma or GED	4,904	67.2	3.22	33.1	2.85	3.6	0.74	10.1	2.05	7.9	2.14
High school diploma or GED	11,891	66.7	2.19	27.0	2.18	8.5	1.10	7.9	1.61	7.7	1.43
Some college, but no bachelor's degree	14,851	69.2	1.58	20.2	1.62	15.7	1.51	8.5	1.10	9.5	1.24
Bachelor's degree or higher	15,446	67.3	2.05	10.3	1.58	21.5	1.73	11.1	1.12	7.6	0.93

[1]Limited to women aged 22–44 years at the time of interview.
NOTES: GED is General Equivalency Development high school equivalency diploma. Women currently using more than one method were classified according to the most effective method they were using.

Data Brief 173. Current Contraceptive Status Among Women Aged 15–44: United States, 2011–2013

Data table for Figure 2. Current contraceptive status and method used among women aged 15–44: United States, 2011–2013

Characteristic	Percent	Standard error
All women (total)[1]	100.0	. . .
Using contraception	61.7	1.10
Female sterilization	15.5	1.01
Male sterilization	5.1	0.50
Pill	16.0	0.89
Long-acting reversible contraceptives	7.2	0.53
Intrauterine device (IUD)	6.4	0.48
Implant	0.8	0.16
3-month injectable (Depo-Provera™)	2.8	0.26
Contraceptive ring or patch	1.6	0.28
Diaphragm	*	*
Condom	9.4	0.57
Periodic abstinence—calendar rhythm	0.7	0.11
Periodic abstinence—natural family planning	0.1	0.06
Withdrawal	3.0	0.30
Other methods[2]	0.3	0.11
Not using contraception[3]	38.3	1.10
Surgically sterile—female (noncontraceptive)	0.7	0.15
Nonsurgically sterile—female or male	2.2	0.26
Pregnant or postpartum	5.0	0.45
Seeking pregnancy	4.5	0.37
Other nonuse:		
Never had intercourse	10.8	0.78
No intercourse in 3 months before interview	8.2	0.55
Had intercourse in 3 months before interview	6.9	0.35

. . . Category not applicable.
* Figure does not meet standards of reliability or precision.
[1] Total equals 60.9 million women.
[2] Includes emergency contraception, female condom, foam, cervical cap, sponge, suppository, jelly, and other methods.
[3] Includes male sterilization for unknown reasons and male surgical sterilization for noncontraceptive reasons, not shown separately.
NOTES: Percentages may not add to 100 due to rounding. Women currently using more than one method were classified according to the most effective method they were using.

Complementary Medicine Use

Information in these tables was drawn from the National Health Interview Survey (NHIS), a survey conducted by the National Center for Health Statistics (NCHS) of the Centers for Disease Control and Prevention (CDC). The information in these tables was drawn from the 2002, 2007, and 2012 NHIS, for adults age 18 and older. More information about the NHIS is available from http://www .cdc.gov/nchs/nhis/about_nhis.htm.

Table 1. Trends in the use of selected complementary health approaches during the past 12 months, by type of approach: United States, 2002, 2007, and 2012

Complementary health approach	2002 Number (in thousands)	2002 Age-adjusted percent[1] (standard error)	2007 Number (in thousands)	2007 Age-adjusted percent[1] (standard error)	2012 Number (in thousands)	2012 Age-adjusted percent[1] (standard error)	Percentage point change 2002–2007	Percentage point change 2007–2012	Percentage point change 2002–2012	Trend
Nonvitamin, nonmineral dietary supplements	38,183	18.9 (0.28)	38,797	17.7 (0.37)	40,579	17.7 (0.37)	††	0.0	††	††
Deep-breathing exercises[2]	23,457	11.6 (0.24)	27,794	12.7 (0.30)	24,218	10.9 (0.26)	§1.1	††	††	††
Yoga, tai chi, and qi gong[2]	11,766	5.8 (0.17)	14,436	6.7 (0.22)	22,281	10.1 (0.25)	0.9	§3.4	§4.3	*Linear
Chiropractic or osteopathic manipulation[3]	15,226	7.5 (0.19)	18,740	8.6 (0.27)	19,369	8.4 (0.22)	††	-0.2	††	††
Meditation[4]	15,336	7.6 (0.20)	20,541	9.4 (0.27)	17,948	8.0 (0.21)	§1.8	††	††	††
Massage therapy	10,052	5.0 (0.16)	18,068	8.3 (0.23)	15,411	6.9 (0.15)	§3.3	§-1.6	§1.9	*Quadratic
Special diets[5]	6,765	3.3 (0.12)	6,040	2.8 (0.14)	6,853	3.0 (0.13)	-0.5	0.4	-0.5	**Quadratic
Homeopathic treatment[6]	3,433	1.7 (0.09)	3,909	1.8 (0.11)	5,046	2.2 (0.11)	0.1	0.4	0.5	***Linear
Progressive relaxation	6,185	3.0 (0.12)	6,454	2.9 (0.15)	4,766	2.1 (0.10)	-0.1	§-0.8	§-0.9	*Linear
Guided imagery	4,194	2.1 (0.10)	4,866	2.2 (0.16)	3,846	1.7 (0.10)	0.1	-0.5	-0.4	None
Acupuncture	2,136	1.1 (0.07)	3,141	1.4 (0.10)	3,484	1.5 (0.08)	0.3	0.1	0.4	***Linear
Energy healing therapy	1,080	0.5 (0.05)	1,216	0.5 (0.06)	1,077	0.5 (0.05)	0.0	0.0	0.0	None
Naturopathy	498	0.2 (0.03)	729	0.3 (0.04)	957	0.4 (0.04)	0.1	0.1	0.2	**Linear
Hypnosis	505	0.2 (0.03)	561	0.2 (0.04)	347	0.1 (0.03)	0.0	-0.1	-0.1	None
Biofeedback	278	0.1 (0.02)	362	0.2 (0.04)	281	0.1 (0.02)	0.1	-0.1	0.0	None
Ayurveda	154	†0.1 (0.02)	214	†0.1 (0.03)	241	0.1 (0.02)	0.0	0.0	0.0	None

† Estimates are considered unreliable. Data have a relative standard error greater than 30% and less than or equal to 50% and should be used with caution.

†† Direct comparisons are not available.

§ Difference between both years is statistically significant at $p < 0.05$.

0.0 Quantity more than zero but less than 0.05.

* Significance of the chi-squared statistics is < 0.05.

** Significance of the chi-squared statistics is < 0.01.

*** Significance of the chi-squared statistics is < 0.001.

1 The denominator used in the calculation of percentages was all sample adults.

2 In 2012, deep-breathing exercises included deep-breathing exercises as part of hypnosis; biofeedback; Mantra meditation (including Transcendental Meditation, Relaxation Response, and Clinically Standardized Meditation); mindfulness meditation (including Vipassana, Zen Buddhist meditation, and mindfulness-based stress reduction, and mindfulness-based cognitive therapy); spiritual meditation (including centering prayer and contemplative meditation); guided imagery; progressive relaxation; yoga; tai chi; or qi gong. In 2002 and 2007, the use of deep-breathing exercises was asked broadly and not if used as part of other complementary health approaches. No trend analyses were conducted on the use of deep-breathing exercises.

3 In 2002, the use of chiropractic care was asked broadly, and osteopathic approach was not specified on the survey. No trend analyses were conducted on the use of chiropractic or osteopathic manipulation.

4 In 2012, meditation included Mantra meditation (including Transcendental Meditation, Relaxation Response, and Clinically Standardized Meditation); mindfulness meditation (including Vipassana, Zen Buddhist meditation, mindfulness-based stress reduction, and mindfulness-based cognitive therapy); spiritual meditation (including centering prayer and contemplative meditation); and meditation used as a part of other practices (including yoga, tai chi, and qi gong). In 2002 and 2007, the use of meditation was asked broadly and not if practiced as part of other complementary health approaches.

5 Respondents used one or more named special diets for 2 weeks or more in the past 12 months. Special diets included vegetarian (including vegan), macrobiotic, Atkins, Pritikin, and Ornish diets.

6 No distinction was made between persons who sought treatment from a homeopathic practitioner and those who self-medicated.

NOTES: Estimates were age-adjusted using the projected 2000 U.S. population as the standard population and using four age groups: 18–24, 25–44, 45–64, and 65 and over. The denominators for statistics shown exclude persons with unknown complementary and alternative medicine information. Estimates are based on household interviews of a sample of the civilian noninstitutionalized population.

SOURCE: CDC/NCHS, National Health Interview Survey, 2002, 2007, and 2012.

Table 2. Trends in the use of complementary health approaches among adults aged 18 and over, by selected characteristics: United States, 2002, 2007, and 2012

Selected characteristic	2002		2007		2012		Percentage point change			Trend
	Number (in thousands)	Age-adjusted percent[1] (standard error)	Number (in thousands)	Age-adjusted percent[1] (standard error)	Number (in thousands)	Age-adjusted percent[1] (standard error)	2002–2007	2007–2012	2002–2012	
Total[2]	65,169	32.3 (0.37)	77,032	35.5 (0.48)	76,222	33.2 (0.42)	†3.2	†−2.3	0.9	*Quadratic
Sex										
Men	27,115	27.9 (0.49)	32,884	31.4 (0.61)	31,818	28.9 (0.54)	†3.5	†−2.5	1.0	**Quadratic
Women	38,053	36.4 (0.48)	44,148	39.4 (0.61)	44,404	37.4 (0.54)	†3.0	−2.0	1.0	*Quadratic
Age group (years)										
18–44	34,842	33.0 (0.48)	36,705	34.2 (0.63)	34,600	32.2 (0.57)	1.2	−2.0	−0.8	*Linear
45–64	23,041	36.5 (0.64)	29,507	40.1 (0.80)	29,048	36.8 (0.63)	†3.6	†−3.3	0.3	*Quadratic
65 and over.	7,286	22.7 (0.64)	10,820	31.1 (0.92)	11,789	29.4 (0.73)	†8.4	−1.5	†6.9	*Quadratic
Hispanic or Latino origin and race										
Hispanic.	5,626	26.4 (0.80)	6,162	21.6 (0.91)	7,525	22.0 (0.76)	†−4.8	0.4	†−4.4	*Quadratic
Non-Hispanic white	50,219	34.4 (0.44)	59,814	40.2 (0.60)	57,008	37.9 (0.53)	†5.8	†−2.3	†3.5	***Quadratic
Non-Hispanic black	5,181	22.9 (0.66)	5,688	22.9 (0.90)	4,957	19.3 (0.75)	0.0	†−3.6	†−3.6	*Linear
Non-Hispanic other[3]	4,142	41.5 (1.59)	5,368	39.6 (1.66)	5,946	37.3 (1.21)	−1.9	−2.3	−4.2	***Linear
Education										
Less than high school diploma	5,918	18.6 (0.68)	6,440	18.9 (0.85)	4,980	15.6 (0.72)	−0.3	−2.0	†−3.0	***Quadratic
High school diploma or GED[4].	15,777	26.6 (0.53)	17,457	28.1 (0.85)	14,744	24.4 (0.64)	−1.5	†−3.7	†−2.2	***Quadratic
Some college education	14,244	35.6 (0.75)	23,189	41.3 (0.80)	16,762	36.5 (0.82)	†5.7	†−4.8	0.9	*Quadratic
College degree or higher	28,953	42.1 (0.67)	29,743	46.7 (0.82)	39,586	42.6 (0.64)	†4.6	†−4.1	0.5	*Quadratic
Poverty status[5]										
Poor	4,127	25.1 (0.99)	6,107	26.6 (1.02)	6,315	20.6 (0.76)	1.5	†−6.0	†−4.5	***Quadratic
Near-poor.	6,961	27.7 (0.79)	8,380	27.9 (0.98)	9,283	25.5 (0.79)	0.2	−2.4	−2.2	***Linear
Not-poor.	41,962	36.8 (0.48)	55,953	40.3 (0.64)	55,490	38.4 (0.53)	†3.5	−1.9	1.6	***Quadratic
Health insurance[6]										
Private.	49,839	34.6 (0.42)	56,900	39.0 (0.59)	54,389	38.0 (0.50)	†4.4	−1.0	†3.4	*Quadratic
Public	6,402	25.8 (0.92)	9,401	27.0 (1.00)	11,387	24.8 (0.84)	1.2	−2.2	−1.0	**Quadratic
Uninsured.	8,730	28.4 (1.21)	10,382	27.8 (1.66)	9,505	22.9 (1.09)	−0.6	†−4.9	†−5.5	***Quadratic

† Difference between both years is statistically significant at $p < 0.05$.

0.0 Quantity more than zero but less than 0.05.

* Significance of the chi-squared statistics is < 0.001.

** Significance of the chi-squared statistics is < 0.01.

*** Significance of the chi-squared statistics is < 0.05.

[1]The denominator used in the calculation of percentages was all sample adults.

[2]Total was defined by a "yes" response to use of one or more of the following in the past 12 months: acupuncture; Ayurveda; biofeedback; chelation therapy; chiropractic care; energy healing therapy or Reiki; vegetarian and vegan, macrobiotic, Atkins, Pritikin, and Ornish diets; folk medicine; guided imagery; homeopathic treatment; hypnosis; naturopathy; nonvitamin, nonmineral, dietary supplements; massage; meditation; progressive relaxation; qi gong; tai chi; or yoga. The use of prayer for health reasons, megavitamin supplements, and special diets not listed, was not included. Respondents may have reported using more than one type of approach.

[3]Non-Hispanic other and persons of multiple races is a very broad and varied category of persons from a variety of races and ethnicities. This group may be more diverse than the other racial and ethnic groups.

[4]GED is General Educational Development high school equivalency diploma.

[5]Based on family income and family size using the U.S. Census Bureau's poverty thresholds for the previous calendar year. Poor persons had a total annual income below the poverty threshold; near-poor persons had incomes of 100% to less than 200% of the poverty threshold; not-poor persons had incomes that were 200% of the poverty threshold or greater.

[6]Based on a hierarchy of mutually exclusive categories. Persons with more than one type of health insurance were assigned to the first appropriate category in the hierarchy. "Uninsured" includes persons who had no coverage and those who had only Indian Health Service coverage or had only a private plan that paid for one type of service such as accidents or dental care.

NOTES: All estimates except age groups were age-adjusted using the projected 2000 U.S. population as the standard population and using four age groups: 18–24, 25–44, 45–64, and 65 and over. Estimates are based on household interviews of a sample of the civilian noninstitutionalized population.

SOURCE: CDC/NCHS, National Health Interview Survey, 2002, 2007, and 2012.

Table 3. Adults aged 18 and over who used selected types of nonvitamin, nonmineral dietary supplements during the past 30 days: United States, 2007 and 2012

Dietary supplements[1]	2007		2012		p value
	Number (in thousands)	Age-adjusted percent[2] (standard error)	Number (in thousands)	Age-adjusted percent[2] (standard error)	
Fish oil[3]	10,923	4.8 (0.17)	18,848	7.8 (0.22)	†
Glucosamine or chondroitin	7,236	3.2 (0.14)	6,450	2.6 (0.11)	†
Probiotics or prebiotics.	865	0.4 (0.05)	3,857	1.6 (0.09)	†
Melatonin	1,296	0.6 (0.06)	3,065	1.3 (0.08)	†
Coenzyme Q–10 (CoQ10).	2,691	1.2 (0.08)	3,265	1.3 (0.08)	††
Echinacea.	4,848	2.2 (0.12)	2,261	0.9 (0.06)	†
Cranberry (pills or capsules)	1,560	0.7 (0.06)	1,934	0.8 (0.06)	††
Garlic supplements	3,278	1.4 (0.09)	1,927	0.8 (0.06)	†
Ginseng	3,345	1.5 (0.10)	1,752	0.7 (0.06)	†
Ginkgo biloba	2,977	1.3 (0.10)	1,619	0.7 (0.06)	†
Green tea pills (not brewed tea) or EGCG (pills)[4]	1,528	0.7 (0.06)	1,503	0.6 (0.05)	††
Combination herb pill	3,446	1.5 (0.10)	1,463	0.6 (0.05)	†
MSM (methylsulfonylmethane)	1,312	0.6 (0.05)	1,051	0.4 (0.04)	†
Milk thistle (silymarin).	1,001	0.4 (0.04)	988	0.4 (0.04)	††
Saw palmetto.	1,682	0.7 (0.07)	988	0.4 (0.04)	†
Valerian	877	0.4 (0.05)	801	0.3 (0.04)	††

† $p < 0.05$.

†† Difference is not statistically significant.

[1] Respondents may have used more than one nonvitamin, nonmineral dietary supplement.

[2] The denominator used in the calculation of percentages was all sample adults.

[3] In 2007, fish oil was described as fish oil or omega 3 or DHA fatty acid. In 2012, fish oil was described as fish oil or omega 3 or DHA or EPA fatty acid.

[4] EGCG is epigallocatechin gallate.

NOTES: Estimates were age-adjusted using the projected 2000 U.S. population as the standard population and using four age groups: 18–24, 25–44, 45–64, and 65 and over. Estimates are based on household interviews of a sample of the civilian noninstitutionalized population.

SOURCE: CDC/NCHS, National Health Interview Survey, 2007 and 2012.

Information in these tables was drawn from the National Health Interview Survey (NHIS), a survey conducted by the National Center for Health Statistics (NCHS) of the Centers for Disease Control and Prevention (CDC). The data for these tables are drawn from the 2007 and 2012 NHIS, which included interviews with children age 4 through 17 years. More information about the NHIS is available from http://www.cdc.gov/nchs/nhis/about_nhis.htm.

Table 1. Frequencies and age-adjusted percentages of children aged 4–17 years who used or saw a practitioner, took a class, or received formal training for selected complementary and alternative medicine modalities during the past 12 months, by type of therapy: United States, 2007 and 2012

Therapy	2007		2012		
	Number (in thousands)	Age-adjusted percent (standard error)	Number (in thousands)	Age-adjusted percent (standard error)	p value[1]
Nonvitamin, nonmineral dietary supplements[2]	2,452	4.3 (0.38)	2,753	4.9 (0.29)	†
Chiropractic or osteopathic manipulation	1,742	3.0 (0.29)	1,854	3.3 (0.26)	†
Yoga, tai chi, or qi gong (any)	1,414	2.5 (0.23)	1,820	3.2 (0.24)	¶
Yoga (any)	1,312	2.3 (0.22)	1,741	3.1 (0.23)	¶
Tai chi (any)	‡113	‡0.2 (0.06)	139	0.2 (0.05)	†
Qi gong (any)	‡	‡	40	‡0.1 (0.03)	†
Deep-breathing exercises[3]	1,533	2.7 (0.28)	1,531	2.7 (0.21)	†
Deep breathing as part of mantra, mindful, or spiritual meditation; guided imagery; or progressive relaxation	- - -	- - -	360	0.6 (0.09)	- - -
Deep breathing as part of yoga, tai chi, or qi gong	- - -	- - -	1,387	2.5 (0.21)	- - -
Homeopathy treatment[4]	686	1.2 (0.26)	1,007	1.8 (0.19)	†
Homeopathy (practitioner based)	- - -	- - -	123	0.2 (0.06)	- - -
Meditation[5]	725	1.3 (0.16)	927	1.6 (0.16)	†
Mantra, mindful, or spiritual meditation	- - -	- - -	323	0.6 (0.09)	- - -
Meditation as part of yoga, tai chi, or qi gong	- - -	- - -	760	1.3 (0.15)	- - -
Massage	579	1.0 (0.14)	385	0.7 (0.10)	†
Special diets[6]	404	0.7 (0.12)	419	0.7 (0.12)	†
Progressive relaxation	327	0.6 (0.11)	216	0.4 (0.07)	†
Guided imagery	293	0.5 (0.11)	239	0.4 (0.08)	†
Movement therapies[7]	266	0.5 (0.08)	239	0.4 (0.09)	†
Energy healing therapy	110	0.2 (0.05)	102	0.2 (0.05)	†
Naturopathy	‡158	‡0.3 (0.10)	‡130	0.2 (0.07)	†
Craniosacral therapy	- - -	- - -	‡95	‡0.2 (0.07)	†
Acupuncture	96	0.2 (0.05)	‡79	‡0.1 (0.05)	†
Traditional healers[8]	619	1.1 (0.20)	‡69	‡0.1 (0.05)	§
Biofeedback	‡73	‡0.1 (0.04)	‡21	‡0.0 (0.02)	¶
Hypnosis	‡	‡	‡	‡	†
Ayurveda	34	‡0.1 (0.03)	‡	‡	†

† Difference is not statistically significant.

‡ Estimates are considered unreliable. Data have a relative standard error (RSE) greater than 30% and less than or equal to 50% and should be used with caution. Data not shown have an RSE greater than 50%.

- - - Data not available.

§ p value less than 0.01.

0.0 Quantity more than zero but less than 0.05.

¶ p value less than 0.05.

[1]p value for differences across years.

[2]While questions were asked about nonvitamin, nonmineral dietary supplements in 2007 and 2012, the data should be interpreted with caution due to question order and the specific nonvitamin, nonmineral dietary supplements covered.

[3]Deep-breathing exercises in 2012 included deep-breathing exercises as part of hypnosis, biofeedback, mantra meditation (including Transcendental Meditation, relaxation response, and clinically standardized meditation), mindfulness meditation (including vipassana, Zen Buddhist meditation, mindfulness-based stress reduction, and mindfulness-based cognitive therapy), spiritual meditation (including centering prayer and contemplative meditation), guided imagery, progressive relaxation, yoga, tai chi, or qi gong, while deep-breathing exercises in 2007 asked broadly about the use of deep breathing and did not distinguish between deep breathing used as part of other complementary health approach modalities.

[4]Homeopathy questions in 2007 did not distinguish between practitioner based and self-care. Therefore, estimates presented in 2012 also do not take this into account.

[5]Meditation in 2012 includes mantra meditation (including Transcendental Meditation, relaxation response, and clinically standardized meditation), mindfulness meditation (including vipassana, Zen Buddhist meditation, mindfulness-based stress reduction, and mindfulness-based cognitive therapy), spiritual meditation (including centering prayer and contemplative meditation), and meditation as part of yoga, tai chi, or qi gong. In 2007, meditation was asked broadly and did not specify subgroups of meditation.

[6]Special diets in 2007 and 2012 include vegetarian (including vegan), macrobiotic, Atkins, Pritikin, and Ornish diets.

[7]Movement therapies in 2007 and 2012 include Feldenkrais, Alexander technique, Pilates, and Trager psychophysical integration.

[8]Traditional healers in 2007 include Curandero, Espiritista, Hierbero and Yerbera, Shaman, Botanica, Native American Healer or Medicine Man, and Sobador. Traditional healers in 2012 include Curandero, Machi, or Parchero; Yerbero or Hierbista; Shaman; Native American Healer or Medicine Man; Sobador; and Huesero.

NOTES: Estimates are based on household interviews of a sample of the civilian noninstitutionalized population. Estimates were age-adjusted using the projected 2000 U.S. population as the standard population and using two age groups: 4–11 and 12–17. The denominators for statistics shown exclude persons with unknown complementary health approach use information.

SOURCE: CDC/NCHS, National Health Interview Survey, 2007, 2012.

Table 2. Age-adjusted percentages of children aged 4–17 years who used any complementary health approaches during the past 12 months, by selected characteristics: United States, 2007 and 2012

| Selected characteristic | Any complementary health approach use[1] | | p value for differences across years |
	2007	2012	
	Age-adjusted percent[2] (standard error)	Age-adjusted percent[2] (standard error)	
Total	12.0 (0.54)	11.6 (0.46)	
Sex			
Boys.	10.5 (0.77)	9.7 (0.56)	†
Girls.	13.5 (0.69)	13.5 (0.67)	†
Age (years)[3]			
4–11.	9.8 (0.67)	9.3 (0.53)	†
12–17.	15.0 (0.86)	14.7 (0.75)	†
Hispanic origin and race			
Hispanic.	8.2 (0.87)	6.1 (0.54)	‡
Non-Hispanic white, single race	14.7 (0.82)	14.9 (0.70)	†
Non-Hispanic black or African American, single race	5.5 (0.84)	5.5 (0.77)	†
Non-Hispanic all other races	13.6 (1.62)	14.2 (1.50)	†
Parent's education[4]			
Less than high school diploma.	4.1 (0.74)	2.1 (0.43)	‡
High school diploma or GED[5]	8.1 (0.89)	6.9 (0.77)	†
More than high school	15.2 (0.76)	15.0 (0.62)	†
Poverty status[6]			
Poor.	7.0 (0.96)	5.7 (0.69)	†
Near poor.	8.5 (0.95)	9.1 (0.81)	†
Not poor	14.9 (0.80)	14.8 (0.67)	†
Health insurance[7]			
Private.	14.1 (0.73)	14.6 (0.66)	†
Public.	8.1 (0.76)	7.6 (0.55)	†
Uninsured.	10.4 (1.44)	8.4 (1.20)	†

† Difference is not statistically significant.

‡ p value less than 0.01.

[1]Complementary health approach definition was a "yes" response to chelation therapy; nonvitamin, nonmineral dietary supplements; vegetarian or vegan diet; macrobiotic diet; Atkins diet; Pritikin diet; Ornish diet; acupuncture; Ayurveda; homeopathic treatment; naturopathy; Native American or Medicine Man; Shaman; Curandero, Machi, or Parchero; Yerbero or Hierbista; Sobador; Huesero; chiropractic or osteopathic manipulation; massage; Feldenkrais; Alexander technique; Pilates; Trager psychophysical integration; biofeedback; mantra meditation; Transcendental Meditation; relaxation; clinically standard meditation; spiritual meditation; guided imagery; progressive relaxation; yoga, tai chi, or qi gong (with deep breathing); hypnosis; and energy healing.

[2]The denominator used in the calculation of percentages was all sample children.

[3]Estimates for age groups are not age-adjusted.

[4]Refers to the education level of the parent with the higher level of education, regardless of that parent's age.

[5]GED is General Educational Development high school equivalency diploma.

[6]Based on family income and family size using the U.S. Census Bureau's poverty thresholds for the previous calendar year. "Poor" persons are defined as below the poverty threshold. "Near poor" persons have incomes of 100% to less than 200% of the poverty threshold. "Not poor" persons have incomes that are 200% of the poverty threshold or greater.

[7]Based on a hierarchy of mutually exclusive categories. Children with more than one type of health insurance were assigned to the first appropriate category in the hierarchy. "Uninsured" includes children who had no coverage as well as those who had only Indian Health Service coverage or had only a private plan that paid for one type of service such as accidents or dental care.

NOTES: Estimates are based on household interviews of a sample of the civilian noninstitutionalized population. Estimates are age-adjusted using the projected 2000 U.S. population as the standard population and using two age groups: 4–11 and 12–17.

SOURCE: CDC/NCHS, National Health Interview Survey, 2007, 2012.

Table 3. Frequencies and age-adjusted percentages of children aged 4–17 years who used selected types of nonvitamin, nonmineral dietary supplements for health reasons in the past 30 days, by type of product used: United States, 2007 and 2012

Nonvitamin, nonmineral dietary supplements	Used selected nonvitamin, nonmineral dietary supplements[1]				
	2007		2012		
	Number (in thousands)	Age-adjusted percent[2] (standard error)	Number (in thousands)	Age-adjusted percent[2] (standard error)	p value
Fish oil[3]	394	0.7 (0.17)	664	1.1 (0.13)	†
Melatonin	‡87	‡0.1 (0.05)	419	0.7 (0.11)	§
Probiotics or prebiotics	†	‡0.3 (0.15)	294	0.5 (0.09)	†
Echinacea	434	0.8 (0.13)	205	0.4 (0.08)	§
Garlic supplements	‡78	‡0.1 (0.04)	‡80	‡0.1 (0.04)	†
Combination herb pill	‡290	‡0.5 (0.15)	‡68	‡0.1 (0.04)	¶
Ginseng	‡	‡	‡63	‡0.1 (0.05)	†
Cranberry (pills, capsules)	‡33	‡0.1 (0.03)	‡31	‡0.1 (0.02)	†
Glucosamine or chondroitin	‡	‡	‡42	‡0.1 (0.03)	†

† Difference is not statistically significant.

‡ Estimates are considered unreliable. Data have a relative standard error (RSE) greater than 30% and less than or equal to 50% and should be used with caution. Data not shown have an RSE greater than 50%.

§ p value less than 0.01.

¶ p value less than 0.05.

[1] Respondents may have used more than one nonvitamin, nonmineral dietary supplement.

[2] The denominator used in the calculation of percentages was all sample children.

[3] In 2007, fish oil was described as fish oil or omega-3 or DHA fatty acid. In 2012, fish oil was described as fish oil or omega-3 or DHA or EPA fatty acid.

NOTES: Estimates are based on household interviews of a sample of the civilian noninstitutionalized population. Estimates were age-adjusted using the projected 2000 U.S. population as the standard population and using two age groups: 4–11 and 12–17.

SOURCE: CDC/NCHS, National Health Interview Survey, 2007, 2012.

Table 4. Frequencies and age-adjusted percentages of children aged 4–17 years who used selected types of complementary health approaches to treat a condition among those who used any complementary health approach in the past 12 months: United States, 2007 and 2012

Complementary health approach	2007 Age-adjusted percent (standard error)[1]	2012 Age-adjusted percent (standard error)[1]	p value
Any complementary health approach	44.2 (2.66)	45.6 (2.16)	†
Acupuncture	53.9 (14.71)	70.1 (17.83)	†
Naturopathy	‡50.0 (17.70)	66.0 (6.47)	†
Homeopathy treatment	88.8 (4.07)	62.9 (5.26)	§
Chiropractic or osteopathic manipulation	59.8 (5.21)	62.1 (3.86)	†
Biofeedback	‡42.1 (16.36)	‡59.7 (21.93)	†
Massage therapy	40.0 (8.77)	42.6 (8.70)	†
Nonvitamin, nonmineral dietary supplements	49.4 (5.59)	35.5 (3.47)	§
Special diets[2]	‡	25.9 (7.36)	†
Traditional healers[3]	‡14.4 (4.61)	‡23.5 (8.85)	†
Movement therapies[4]	‡	‡11.1 (3.98)	†
Energy healing therapy	57.9 (13.44)	‡	†
Hypnosis	78.3 (19.11)	‡	†

† Difference is not statistically significant.

‡ Estimates are considered unreliable. Data have a relative standard error (RSE) greater than 30% and less than or equal to 50% and should be used with caution. Data not shown have an RSE greater than 50%.

§ p value less than 0.001.

[1] The denominators used in the calculation of percentages were children who used each selected type of complementary health approach.

[2] Special diets include vegetarian (including vegan), macrobiotic, Atkins, Pritikin, and Ornish diets for both 2007 and 2012.

[3] Traditional healers in 2007 include Curandero, Espiritista, Hierbero or Yerbera, Shaman, Botanica, Native American Healer or Medicine Man, and Sobador. Traditional healers in 2012 include Curandero, Machi, or Parchero; Yerbero or Hierbista; Shaman; Native American Healer or Medicine Man; Sobador; and Huesero.

[4] Movement therapies include Feldenkrais, Alexander technique, Pilates, and Trager psychophysical integration for both 2007 and 2012.

NOTES: Estimates are based on household interviews of a sample of the civilian noninstitutionalized population. Estimates are age-adjusted using the projected 2000 U.S. population as the standard population and using two age groups: 4–11 and 12–17.

SOURCE: CDC/NCHS, National Health Interview Survey, 2007, 2012.

Table 5. Frequencies and age-adjusted percentages of children aged 4–17 years who used complementary health approaches in the past 12 months for specific conditions, among those who used complementary health approaches, by the condition for which it was used: United States, 2007 and 2012

Disease or condition[1]	2007		2012		p value
	Number (in thousands)	Age-adjusted percentage[2] (standard error)	Number (in thousands)	Age-adjusted percentage[2] (standard error)	
Back or neck pain	686	8.8 (1.12)	602	8.9 (1.14)	†
Head or chest cold	409	6.5 (1.38)	294	5.1 (0.92)	†
Other musculoskeletal conditions	345	5.0 (0.99)	416	6.0 (0.98)	†
Anxiety or stress	293	4.4 (0.94)	221	3.4 (0.72)	†
ADHD or ADD[3]	150	2.3 (0.52)	131	2.2 (0.59)	†
Insomnia or trouble sleeping	134	2.0 (0.59)	110	1.7 (0.43)	†
Constipation	‡	‡	‡70	‡1.2 (0.38)	†
Respiratory allergy	‡68	‡1.2 (0.53)	‡69	‡1.0 (0.39)	†
Sore throat other than strep or tonsillitis	‡94	‡1.4 (0.59)	‡50	‡0.9 (0.42)	†
Sinusitis	‡117	‡2.0 (0.78)	‡45	‡0.7 (0.31)	†
Abdominal pain	‡66	‡1.0 (0.39)	‡44	‡0.6 (0.26)	†
Depression	‡178	‡0.9 (0.28)	‡41	‡0.6 (0.23)	†
Asthma	112	‡1.8 (0.65)	‡34	‡0.5 (0.21)	†

† Difference is not statistically significant.

‡ Estimates are considered unreliable. Data have a relative standard error (RSE) greater than 30% and less than or equal to 50% and should be used with caution. Data not shown have an RSE greater than 50%.

[1]Respondents may have used more than one modality to treat a disease or condition, but were counted only once under each disease or condition treated. The questions about using a modality to treat a disease or condition were only asked of respondents who had used the modality within the past 12 months. The exception to this is the questions about using nonvitamin, nonmineral dietary supplements to treat a disease or condition, which were only asked of respondents who had used nonvitamin, nonmineral dietary supplements within the past 30 days.

[2]The denominator used in the calculation of percentages was the number of children who used complementary health approaches within the past 12 months, excluding persons with unknown information about whether a complementary health approach was used to treat the specified condition.

[3]ADHD is attention deficit hyperactivity disorder and ADD is attention deficit disorder.

NOTES: Estimates are based on household interviews of a sample of the civilian noninstitutionalized population. Estimates are age-adjusted using the 2000 U.S. population as the standard population and using two age groups: 4–11 and 12–17.

SOURCE: CDC/NCHS, National Health Interview Survey, 2007 and 2012.

Vaccination Coverage

Information in these tables was drawn from school vaccination data, as analyzed by the Centers for Disease Control and Prevention (CDC) in its *Morbidity and Mortality Weekly Report*. Further information about vaccination coverage for children, and school vaccination data, is available from http://www.cdc.gov/mmwr/preview/mmwrhtml/mm6341a1.htm.

TABLE 1. Estimated vaccination coverage,* by state/area and vaccination among children enrolled in kindergarten — United States, 2013–14 school year

State/Area	Kindergarten population[†]	Total surveyed	Proportion surveyed (%)	Type of survey conducted[§]	MMR[¶] (%)	DTaP** (%)	Varicella 1 dose (%)	Varicella 2 doses (%)
Alabama[††]	76,927	76,927	100.0	Census	≥92.0	≥92.0	≥92.0	NReq
Alaska[§§]	10,222	946	9.3	Stratified 2-stage cluster sample	94.4	96.0		92.5
Arizona	89,606	85,861	95.8	Census	93.9	94.3	96.4	NReq
Arkansas	42,649	41,068	96.3	Census	86.5	83.3		85.4
California[¶¶]	548,606	533,680	97.3	Census	92.3	92.2	95.3	NReq
Colorado	69,904	350	0.5	Random sample	81.7	80.9		81.7
Connecticut[††]	40,978	40,978	100.0	Census	96.9	97.0		96.7
Delaware	11,997	1458	12.2	Stratified 2-stage cluster sample	≥96.4	≥96.4		≥96.4
District of Columbia[††]	7,856	7,856	100.0	Census	89.0	88.7		88.8
Florida[††***]	233,797	233,797	100.0	Census	≥93.2	≥93.2		≥93.2
Georgia[††]	143,988	143,988	100.0	Census	≥94.0	≥94.0		≥94.0
Hawaii	20,056	1,074	5.4	Stratified 2-stage cluster sample	98.7	99.0	99.2	NReq
Idaho[††]	23,934	23,934	100.0	Census	88.2	88.0		86.5
Illinois[††]	163,316	163,316	100.0	Census	94.7	95.0	96.6	NReq
Indiana[††]	87,193	61,336	70.3	Census	92.9	81.8		90.2
Iowa	43,728	41,349	94.6	Census	≥91.0	≥91.0		≥91.0
Kansas[§§¶¶]	41,107	11,931	29.0	Stratified 1-stage sample (Public), Census (Private)	86.9	87.6		85.5
Kentucky[††]	57,857	57,857	100.0	Census	92.6	93.9		91.9
Louisiana[††]	63,976	63,976	100.0	Census	96.8	98.3		96.1
Maine	15,441	12,716	82.4	Census	89.9	94.4	93.8	NReq
Maryland[¶¶]	75,659	73,349	96.9	Census	97.6	99.0	99.0	NReq
Massachusetts	79,894	78,188	97.9	Census	95.1	93.0		93.9
Michigan[††]	120,297	120,297	100.0	Census	97.5	94.8		93.0
Minnesota[¶¶]	72,087	70,972	98.5	Census	93.4	96.6		92.6
Mississippi[††]	45,719	45,719	100.0	Census	≥99.7	≥99.7		≥99.7
Missouri[††]	78,140	78,140	100.0	Census	95.5	96.0		94.6
Montana	12,855	12,259	95.4	Census	93.7	94.8		NReq
Nebraska[¶¶]	27,000	26,282	97.3	Census	96.6	96.8		94.9
Nevada	35,782	1,114	3.1	Stratified 2-stage cluster sample	95.6	94.4		93.6
New Hampshire[††]	13,240	13,240	100.0	Census	≥94.7	≥94.7		≥94.7
New Jersey	123,085	117,477	95.4	Census	≥96.8	≥96.8	≥96.8	NReq
New Mexico[¶¶]	30,725	830	2.7	Stratified 2-stage cluster sample	95.9	97.4		93.4
New York[¶¶]	240,318	240,318	100.0	Census	96.8	98.1	98.2	NReq
North Carolina	126,084	123,192	97.7	Census	98.8	98.7	99.7	NReq
North Dakota	9,780	9,397	96.1	Census (public) Stratified 2-stage cluster sample (private)	90.0	90.2		89.4
Ohio	150,000	138,820	92.5	Census	96.2	96.1		95.7
Oklahoma	57,377	40,929	71.3	Voluntary response	96.4	96.1		98.0
Oregon[††]	47,649	47,649	100.0	Census	93.2	93.3	94.3	NReq
Pennsylvania[††¶¶]	151,253	151,253	100.0	Census	85.3	NReq[†††]		84.0
Rhode Island	11,521	11,421	99.1	Census	95.1	96.0		94.7
South Carolina	61,661	6,771	11.0	1-stage stratified sample	96.8	97.3	94.4	NReq
South Dakota[††]	12,566	12,566	100.0	Census	96.6	96.7		95.3
Tennessee	80,212	80,079	99.8	Census	≥94.9	≥94.9		≥94.9
Texas[§§] (including Houston)	409,255	397,262	97.1	Census	97.5	97.2		97.2
Houston, Texas	36,254	1,856	5.1	2-stage cluster sample, nonrandom schools selection	91.9	90.4		90.4

See table footnotes on next page.

TABLE 1. (*Continued*) Estimated vaccination coverage,* by state/area and vaccination among children enrolled in kindergarten — United States, 2013–14 school year

State/Area	Kindergarten population[†]	Total surveyed	Proportion surveyed (%)	Type of survey conducted[§]	MMR[¶] (%)	DTaP** (%)	Varicella 1 dose (%)	Varicella 2 doses (%)
Utah[††]	54,779	54,779	100.0	Census	98.5	98.1	99.6	NReq
Vermont[††]	6,771	6,771	100.0	Census	91.2	92.0		89.4
Virginia	105,692	4,287	4.1	2-stage cluster sample	93.1	98.3		91.3
Washington	89,165	78,924	88.5	Census	89.7	90.3		88.4
West Virginia	22,814	19,313	84.7	Census	96.1	96.5		95.5
Wisconsin[¶¶]	71,363	1,990	2.8	Stratified 2-stage cluster sample	92.6	96.3		91.2
Wyoming	NA	NA	NA	Not conducted				
Median[§§§]					*94.7*	*95.0*	*96.6*	*93.3*
American Samoa	NA	NA	NA	Not conducted				
Guam	2,935	1,235	42.1	Stratified 2-stage cluster sample	88.4	92.8		NReq
Marshall Islands	NA	NA	NA	Not conducted				
Micronesia	NA	NA	NA	Not conducted				
N. Mariana Islands	725	725	100.0	Census	96.0	94.3		92.3
Palau	402	NA	NA	Not conducted				NReq
Puerto Rico	39,170	6,789	17.3	Stratified 2-stage cluster sample	94.3	91.3		91.4
U.S. Virgin Islands	1,612	731	45.3	Stratified 2-stage cluster sample	90.5	91.0		87.9

Abbreviations: MMR = measles, mumps, and rubella vaccine; DTaP = diphtheria and tetanus toxoids and acellular pertussis vaccine; NA = not available; NReq = not required for school entry.

* Estimates are adjusted for nonresponse and weighted for sampling where appropriate, except where complete data were unavailable. Percentages for Delaware, Houston, Virginia, and Puerto Rico are approximations. Estimates based on a completed vaccine series (i.e., not antigen-specific) are designated by use of the ≥ symbol.

[†] The kindergarten population is an approximation provided by each state/area.

[§] Sample designs varied by state/area: census = all schools (public and private) and all children within schools were included in the assessment; simple random = a simple random sample design was used; mixed design = a census was conducted among public schools, and a random sample of children within the schools were selected; 1-stage or 2-stage cluster sample = schools were randomly selected, and all children in the selected schools were assessed (1-stage) or a random sample of children within the schools were selected (2-stage); voluntary response = a census among those schools that submitted assessment data.

[¶] Most states require 2 doses; Alaska, California, New York, and Oregon require 2 doses of measles, 1 dose of mumps, and 1 dose of rubella vaccine.

** Pertussis vaccination coverage might include some DTP (diphtheria and tetanus toxoids and pertussis vaccine) vaccinations if administered in another country or if a vaccination provider continued to use DTP after 2000. Most states require 4 doses of DTaP vaccine; 5 doses are required for school entry in Colorado, District of Columbia, Hawaii, Idaho, Indiana, Iowa, Kansas, Massachusetts, Minnesota, New Jersey, New Mexico, North Carolina, North Dakota, Oregon, Rhode Island, Tennessee, Texas, Utah, Vermont, Washington, Northern Mariana Islands, Puerto Rico, and U.S. Virgin Islands; 3 doses are required by Nebraska and New York. Pertussis vaccine is not required in Pennsylvania.

[††] The proportion surveyed is probably <100%, but is shown as 100% based on incomplete information about the actual current enrollment.

[§§] Kindergarten coverage data were collected from a sample, and exemption data were collected from a census of kindergartners.

[¶¶] Counts the vaccine doses received regardless of Advisory Committee on Immunization Practices recommended age and time interval; vaccination coverage rates shown might be higher than those for valid doses.

*** Does not include nondistrict-specific, virtual, and college laboratory schools, or private schools with fewer than 10 students.

[†††] Pertussis is not required in Pennsylvania; coverage for diphtheria and tetanus was 88.3%.

[§§§] The median is the center of the estimates in the distribution. The median does not include Houston, Guam, the Commonwealth of the Northern Mariana Islands, Puerto Rico, and the U.S. Virgin Islands.

TABLE 2. Estimated number and percentage* of children enrolled in kindergarten with exemption(s) from vaccination, by state/area and type of exemption — United States, 2013–14 school year

State/Area	Medical exemptions[†] No.	Medical exemptions[†] %	Nonmedical exemptions[†] No. of religious exemptions	Nonmedical exemptions[†] No. of philosophic exemptions	Nonmedical exemptions[†] Total no.	Nonmedical exemptions[†] %	Total exemptions[†] Total no.	Total exemptions[†] 2013–14 (%)	Total exemptions[†] 2012–13 (%)	Percentage point difference
Alabama	70	<0.1	447	§	447	0.6	517	0.7	0.7	0.0
Alaska	119	1.2	421	§	421	4.1	539	5.3	5.6	-0.3
Arizona	175	0.2	¶	4,195	4,195	4.7	4,370	4.9	4.2	0.7
Arkansas	24	<0.1	135	333	468	1.1	493	1.2	1.1	0.1
California	1017	0.2	††	17,253	17,253	3.1	18,270	3.3	3.0	0.3
Colorado	0	<0.1	195	3,097	3,292	4.6	3,291	4.6	4.3	0.3
Connecticut	128	0.3	670	§	670	1.6	725	1.9	1.7	0.2
Delaware	9	<0.1	83	§	83	0.7	92	0.8	0.7	0.1
District of Columbia	85	1.1	33	§	33	0.4	118	1.5	1.6	-0.1
Florida	772	0.3	3,991	§	3,991	1.7	4,763	2.0	1.8	0.2
Georgia	143	<0.1	2,420	§	2,420	1.7	2,563	1.8	2.3	-0.5
Hawaii	0	<0.1	634	§	634	3.2	634	3.2	2.5	0.7
Idaho	89	0.4	147	1,304	1,451	6.1	1,540	6.4	5.9	0.5
Illinois**	NA				NA		NA	NA	6.1	NA
Indiana	348	0.4	727	§	727	0.8	1,075	1.2	1.3	-0.1
Iowa	205	0.5	521	§	521	1.2	726	1.7	1.7	0.0
Kansas	213	0.8	527	§	527	1.9	739	2.6	1.1	1.5
Kentucky	148	0.3	357	§	357	0.6	505	0.9	0.7	0.2
Louisiana	83	0.1	28	394	422	0.7	505	0.8	0.7	0.1
Maine	56	0.4	30	766	796	5.2	852	5.5	4.3	1.2
Maryland	244	0.3	513	§	513	0.7	758	1.0	1.0	0.0
Massachusetts	332	0.4	860	§	860	1.1	1,192	1.5	1.5	0.0
Michigan	573	0.5	1,250	5,226	6,476	5.4	7,049	5.9	5.9	0.0
Minnesota**	NA				NA		NA	NA	1.6	NA
Mississippi	17	<0.1	¶	§	NA		17	<0.1	<0.1	0.0
Missouri**	NA				NA		NA	NA	1.8	NA
Montana	36	0.3	426	§	426	3.3	463	3.6	3.5	0.1
Nebraska	158	0.6	307	§	307	1.1	465	1.7	1.7	0.0
Nevada	7	<0.1	724	§	724	2.0	731	2.0	2.5	-0.5
New Hampshire	49	0.4	328	§	328	2.5	377	2.8	2.5	0.3
New Jersey	262	0.2	1,741	§	1,741	1.4	2,003	1.6	1.4	0.2
New Mexico	72	0.2	277	§	277	0.9	349	1.1	0.4	0.7
New York	302	0.1	1,547	§	1,547	0.6	1,849	0.8	0.7	0.1
North Carolina	161	0.1	1,105	§	1,105	0.9	1,266	1.0	0.8	0.2
North Dakota	32	0.3	45	185	230	2.3	262	2.7	1.8	0.9
Ohio	369	0.2	††	††	2,681	1.8	3,050	2.0	2.0	0.0
Oklahoma	73	0.1	221	586	808	1.4	880	1.5	1.3	0.2
Oregon	62	0.1	3,331	††	3,331	7.0	3,393	7.1	6.5	0.6
Pennsylvania	510	0.3	1,133	1,419	2,552	1.7	3,062	2.0	2.0	0.0
Rhode Island	33	0.3	81	§	81	0.7	114	1.0	1.1	-0.1
South Carolina[§§]	83	0.1	772	§	772	1.2	855	1.4	NA	NA
South Dakota[§§]	21	0.2	199	§	199	1.6	220	1.8	1.8	0.0
Tennessee	132	0.2	773	§	773	1.0	906	1.1	1.2	-0.1
Texas (including Houston)	2,266	0.6	††	††	5,536	1.4	7,803	1.9	1.7	0.2
Houston	979	0.3	NA	NA	NA		979	0.3	0.9	-0.6

See table footnotes on next page.

TABLE 2. (*Continued*) Estimated number and percentage* of children enrolled in kindergarten with exemption(s) from vaccination, by state/area and type of exemption — United States, 2013–14 school year

State/Area	Medical exemptions[†]		Nonmedical exemptions[†]				Total exemptions[†]			
	No.	%	No. of religious exemptions	No. of philosophic exemptions	Total no.	%	Total no.	2013–14 (%)	2012–13 (%)	Percentage point difference
Utah	94	0.2	16	2,296	2,312	4.2	2,406	4.4	3.8	0.6
Vermont	11	0.2	13	399	412	6.1	423	6.2	6.1	0.1
Virginia	173	0.2	446	§	446	0.4	619	0.6	0.5	-0.5
Washington[§§]	1,035	1.2	311	2,866	3,177	3.6	4,212	4.7	4.6	0.1
West Virginia	35	0.2	¶	§			35	0.2	1.2	-1.0
Wisconsin	103	0.1	373	3,042	3,415	4.8	3,519	4.9	4.5	0.4
Wyoming	NA				NA		NA	NA	2.3	NA
Median[¶¶]		*0.2*				*1.7*		*1.8*	*1.8*	*0.0*
American Samoa	NA				NA		NA	NA	NA	NA
Guam	0	<0.1	1	§	1	<0.1	1	<0.1	<0.1	0.0
Marshall Islands	NA				NA		NA	NA	NA	NA
Micronesia	NA				NA		NA	NA	NA	NA
N. Mariana Islands	0	0.0	0	0	0	0.0	0	0.0	0.1	-0.1
Palau	NA				NA		NA	NA	0.6	NA
Puerto Rico	0	<0.1	0	§	0	<0.1	0	<0.1	<0.1	0.0
U.S. Virgin Islands	0	0.0	17	§	17	1.1	17	1.1	0.6	0.5

Abbreviation: NA = not available (i.e., not collected or reported to CDC).

* Estimates are adjusted for nonresponse and sampling design where appropriate, except where complete data were unavailable. Percentages for Delaware, Houston, Virginia, and Puerto Rico are approximations.

[†] Medical and nonmedical exemptions might not be mutually exclusive. Some children might have both medical and nonmedical exemptions. Total exemptions is the number of children with an exemption. Temporary exemptions are included in the total for South Carolina, South Dakota, and Washington.

§ Exemptions because of philosophic reasons are not allowed.

¶ Exemptions because of religious reasons are not allowed.

** Lower bounds of the percentage of children with any exemptions, estimated using the individual vaccines with the highest number of exemptions are, for Illinois, 0.3% with medical exemptions, 1.0% with religious exemptions, and 1.3% for total exemptions, and for Missouri, 0.2% with medical exemptions, 1.6% with religious exemptions, and 1.8% for total exemptions. For Minnesota, the lower bounds of the percentage of children with any exemptions, estimated using the number of children exempt for all vaccines, are <0.1% with medical exemptions, 1.7% with religious exemptions, and 1.7% for total exemptions.

[††] Religious and philosophic exemptions are not reported separately.

[§§] Includes both temporary and permanent medical exemptions.

[¶¶] The median is the center of the estimates in the distribution. The median does not include Houston, Guam, the Commonwealth of the Northern Mariana Islands, Puerto Rico, and the U.S. Virgin Islands.

Information in these tables was reproduced from the Centers for Disease Control and Prevention's (CDC's) Morbidity and Mortality Weekly Report and drawn from the National Immunization Survey (NIS), a telephone and mail survey of parents and immunization providers conducted jointly by the National Center for Immunizations and Respiratory Diseases (NCIRD) and the National Center for Health Statistics (NCHS) of the CDC. Further information about the NIS is available from http://www.cdc.gov/nchs/nis.htm.

TABLE 1. Estimated vaccination coverage among children aged 19–35 months, by selected vaccines and dosages — National Immunization Survey, United States, 2009–2013*

Vaccine and dosage	2009		2010		2011		2012		2013	
	%	(95% CI)	%	(95% CI)	%	(95% CI)	%	(95% CI)	%	(95% CI)
DTaP										
≥3 doses	95.0	(±0.6)	95.0	(±0.6)	95.5	(±0.5)	94.3	(±0.7)	94.1	(±0.9)
≥4 doses	83.9	(±1.0)	84.4	(±1.0)	84.6	(±1.0)	82.5	(±1.2)	83.1	(±1.3)
Poliovirus (≥3 doses)	92.8	(±0.7)	93.3	(±0.7)	93.9	(±0.6)	92.8	(±0.7)	92.7	(±1.0)
MMR (≥1 dose)	90.0	(±0.8)	91.5	(±0.7)	91.6	(±0.8)	90.8	(±0.8)	91.9	(±0.9)
Hib†										
Primary series	92.1	(±0.8)	92.2	(±0.8)	94.2	(±0.6)	93.3	(±0.7)	93.7	(±0.9)
Full series	54.8	(±1.4)	66.8	(±1.3)	80.4	(±1.1)	80.9	(±1.2)	82.0	(±1.3)
HepB										
≥3 doses	92.4	(±0.7)	91.8	(±0.7)	91.1	(±0.7)	89.7	(±0.9)	90.8	(±1.0)
1 dose by 3 days (birth)§	60.8	(±1.3)	64.1	(±1.3)	68.6	(±1.3)	71.6	(±1.4)	74.2	(±1.4)¶
Varicella (≥1 dose)	89.6	(±0.8)	90.4	(±0.8)	90.8	(±0.7)	90.2	(±0.8)	91.2	(±0.9)
PCV										
≥3 doses	92.6	(±0.7)	92.6	(±0.8)	93.6	(±0.6)	92.3	(±0.8)	92.4	(±1.0)
≥4 doses	80.4	(±1.2)	83.3	(±1.0)	84.4	(±1.0)	81.9	(±1.1)	82.0	(±1.3)
HepA										
≥1 dose	75.0	(±1.1)	78.3	(±1.1)	81.2	(±1.0)	81.5	(±1.1)	83.1	(±1.2)¶
≥2 doses	46.6	(±1.4)	49.7	(±1.4)	52.2	(±1.4)	53.0	(±1.5)	54.7	(±1.6)
Rotavirus**	43.9	(±1.4)	59.2	(±1.4)	67.3	(±1.3)	68.6	(±1.4)	72.6	(±1.5)¶
Combined series††	44.3	(±1.4)	56.6	(±1.3)	68.5	(±1.3)	68.4	(±1.4)	70.4	(±1.5)
Children who received no vaccinations	0.6	(±0.1)	0.7	(±0.2)	0.8	(±0.2)	0.8	(±0.1)	0.7	(±0.3)

Abbreviations: CI = confidence interval; DTaP = diphtheria, tetanus toxoids, and acellular pertussis vaccine (includes children who might have been vaccinated with diphtheria and tetanus toxoids vaccine, or diphtheria, tetanus toxoids, and pertussis vaccine); MMR = measles, mumps, and rubella vaccine; Hib = *Haemophilus influenzae* type b vaccine; HepB = hepatitis B vaccine; PCV = pneumococcal conjugate vaccine; HepA = hepatitis A vaccine.

* For 2009, includes children born January 2006–July 2008; for 2010, children born January 2007–July 2009; for 2011, children born January 2008–May 2010; for 2012, children born January 2009–May 2011; and for 2013, children born January 2010–May 2012.

† Hib primary series: receipt of ≥2 or ≥3 doses, depending on product type received. Full series: receipt of ≥3 or ≥4 doses, depending on product type received (primary series and booster dose). Hib coverage for primary or full series not available until 2009.

§ HepB administered from birth through age 3 days.

¶ Statistically significant change in coverage compared with 2012 (*p*<0.05).

** Rotavirus vaccine includes ≥2 or ≥3 doses, depending on the product type received (≥2 doses for Rotarix [RV1] or ≥3 doses for RotaTeq [RV5]).

†† The combined (4:3:1:3*:3:1:4) vaccine series includes ≥4 doses of DTaP, ≥3 doses of poliovirus vaccine, ≥1 dose of measles-containing vaccine, full series of Hib vaccine (≥3 or ≥4 doses, depending on product type), ≥3 doses of HepB, ≥1 dose of varicella vaccine, and ≥4 doses of PCV.

TABLE 2. Estimated vaccination coverage among children aged 19–35 months, by selected vaccines and dosages, race/ethnicity,* and poverty level[†] — National Immunization Survey, United States, 2013[§]

Vaccine and dosage	White, non-Hispanic % (95% CI)	Black, non-Hispanic % (95% CI)	Hispanic % (95% CI)	American Indian/Alaska Native only, non-Hispanic % (95% CI)	Asian, non-Hispanic % (95% CI)	Native Hawaiian or other Pacific Islander, non-Hispanic % (95% CI)	Multiracial, non-Hispanic % (95% CI)	At or Above % (95% CI)	Below % (95% CI)
DTaP									
≥3 doses	95.1 (±0.9)	92.4 (±2.3)[¶]	93.4 (±2.4)	92.4 (±6.4)	96.0 (±4.6)	NA (±NA)	92.4 (±3.6)	95.6 (±0.8)	91.2 (±2.1)**
≥4 doses	85.3 (±1.4)	74.7 (±4.2)[¶]	82.3 (±3.2)	78.1 (±8.8)	89.0 (±5.2)	NA (±NA)	83.1 (±4.5)	86.0 (±1.3)	77.8 (±2.7)**
Poliovirus (≥3 doses)	93.7 (±1.0)	91.2 (±2.6)	91.6 (±2.7)	92.2 (±6.4)	95.5 (±4.7)	NA (±NA)	90.8 (±3.7)	94.4 (±0.8)	89.2 (±2.4)**
MMR (≥1 dose)	91.5 (±1.1)	90.9 (±2.5)	92.1 (±2.5)	96.3 (±2.8)[¶]	96.7 (±1.7)[¶]	90.4 (±9.7)	91.5 (±3.1)	92.5 (±0.9)	90.5 (±2.1)
Hib[††]									
≥3 doses	93.7 (±1.0)	90.7 (±2.5)[¶]	92.7 (±2.5)	89.5 (±6.8)	92.9 (±4.9)	90.5 (±9.6)	91.4 (±3.7)	94.6 (±0.8)	89.6 (±2.2)**
Primary series	94.6 (±0.8)	91.4 (±2.4)[¶]	93.3 (±2.4)	94.3 (±6.1)	93.8 (±4.8)	90.5 (±9.6)	92.3 (±3.6)	95.1 (±0.8)	91.0 (±2.0)**
Full series	84.2 (±1.4)	74.9 (±4.2)[¶]	80.9 (±3.3)	82.9 (±7.8)	82.0 (±6.2)	NA (±NA)	84.9 (±4.1)	85.3 (±1.4)	75.8 (±2.8)**
HepB									
≥3 doses	91.0 (±1.0)	91.1 (±2.4)	89.7 (±2.6)	96.1 (±4.3)[¶]	92.0 (±5.1)	94.9 (±5.6)	90.7 (±3.5)	92.0 (±0.9)	88.3 (±2.2)**
1 dose by 3 days (birth)[§§]	71.9 (±1.8)	76.7 (±3.7)[¶]	77.8 (±3.5)[¶]	NA (±NA)	73.7 (±6.5)	NA (±NA)	72.3 (±5.9)	72.1 (±1.7)	78.3 (±2.7)**
Varicella (≥1 dose)	90.0 (±1.2)	92.1 (±2.2)	92.0 (±2.5)	95.4 (±3.1)[¶]	96.0 (±2.0)[¶]	88.7 (±9.2)	91.0 (±3.0)	91.6 (±0.9)	90.3 (±2.1)
PCV									
≥3 doses	93.1 (±1.0)	90.8 (±2.6)	92.2 (±2.5)	92.3 (±6.1)	92.0 (±4.9)	90.9 (±8.6)	91.5 (±3.6)	94.2 (±0.8)	88.8 (±2.3)**
≥4 doses	84.1 (±1.5)	76.1 (±3.8)[¶]	80.4 (±3.4)	79.0 (±8.3)	85.6 (±5.4)	NA (±NA)	83.0 (±4.4)	86.1 (±1.4)	74.5 (±2.7)**
HepA (≥2 doses)	53.4 (±1.9)	49.1 (±4.3)	56.6 (±4.0)	NA (±NA)	67.3 (±6.8)[¶]	NA (±NA)	57.8 (±6.0)	56.1 (±1.9)	53.5 (±2.9)
Rotavirus[¶¶]	74.8 (±1.7)	62.1 (±4.3)[¶]	73.7 (±3.5)	NA (±NA)	74.9 (±6.7)	NA (±NA)	72.8 (±5.3)	76.9 (±1.6)	64.3 (±2.9)**
Combined series*	72.1 (±1.8)	65.0 (±4.4)[¶]	69.3 (±3.8)	70.1 (±9.2)	72.7 (±6.6)	NA (±NA)	71.8 (±5.2)	73.8 (±1.7)	64.4 (±3.0)**

Abbreviations: CI = confidence interval; DTaP = diphtheria, tetanus toxoids, and acellular pertussis vaccine (includes children who might have been vaccinated with diphtheria and tetanus toxoids vaccine, or diphtheria, tetanus toxoids, and pertussis vaccine); NA = not available (estimate not available if the unweighted sample size for the denominator was <30 or 95% CI half width / estimate >0.588 or 95% CI half width was ≥10); MMR = measles, mumps, and rubella vaccine; Hib = *Haemophilus influenzae* type b vaccine; HepB = hepatitis B vaccine; PCV = pneumococcal conjugate vaccine; HepA = hepatitis A vaccine.

 * Children's race/ethnicity was reported by parent or guardian. Children identified in this report as white, black, Asian, American Indian/Alaska Native, Native Hawaiian or other Pacific Islander, or multiracial were reported by the parent or guardian as non-Hispanic. Children identified as multiracial had more than one race category selected. Children identified as Hispanic might be of any race.

 [†] Children were classified as below poverty if their total family income was less than the poverty threshold specified for the applicable family size and number of children aged <18 years. Children with total family income at or above the poverty threshold specified for the applicable family size and number of children aged <18 years were classified as at or above poverty. A total of 535 children with adequate provider data and missing data on income were excluded from the analysis. Poverty thresholds reflect yearly changes in the Consumer Price Index. Additional information available at http://www.census.gov/hhes/www/poverty.html.

 [§] Children in the 2013 National Immunization Survey were born January 2010–May 2012.

 [¶] Statistically significant difference (p<0.05) in estimated vaccination coverage by race/ethnicity. Children identified as non-Hispanic white were the reference group.

 ** Statistically significant difference (p<0.05) in estimated vaccination coverage by poverty level. Children living at or above poverty were the reference group.

 [††] Hib primary series: receipt of ≥2 or ≥3 doses, depending on product type received; full series: primary series and booster dose includes receipt of ≥3 or ≥4 doses, depending on product type received.

 [§§] HepB administered from birth through age 3 days.

 [¶¶] Includes ≥2 or ≥3 doses, depending on product type received (≥2 doses for Rotarix [RV1] or ≥3 doses for RotaTeq [RV5]).

 *** The combined (4:3:1:3*:3:1:4) vaccine series includes ≥4 doses of DTaP, ≥3 doses of poliovirus vaccine, ≥1 dose of measles-containing vaccine, full series of Hib vaccine (≥3 or ≥4 doses, depending on type), ≥3 doses of HepB, ≥1 dose of varicella vaccine, and ≥4 doses of PCV.

TABLE 3. Estimated vaccination coverage with selected individual vaccines and a combined vaccine series* among children aged 19–35 months, by U.S. Department of Health and Human Services (HHS) region and state and local area — National Immunization Survey, United States, 2013[†]

HHS region, state and local area	MMR (≥1 dose)		DTaP (≥4 doses)		Hep B (birth)[§]		HepA (≥2 doses)		Rotavirus[¶]		Combined vaccine series*	
	%	(95% CI)	%	(95% CI)	%	(95% CI)	%	(95% CI)	%	(95% CI)	%	(95% CI)
United States overall	**91.9**	**(±0.9)**	**83.1**	**(±1.3)**	**74.2**	**(±1.4)****	**54.7**	**(±1.6)**	**72.6**	**(±1.5)****	**70.4**	**(±1.5)**
HHS Region I	**94.2**	**(±2.2)**	**90.9**	**(±2.5)**	**74.6**	**(±3.7)**	**63.2**	**(±4.4)**	**81.4**	**(±3.5)**	**77.1**	**(±3.7)**
Connecticut	91.4	(±5.4)	88.0	(±5.9)	75.2	(±7.5)	72.1	(±7.5)	81.1	(±6.3)	78.2	(±6.8)
Maine	91.0	(±4.5)	87.9	(±5.7)	68.9	(±7.4)	57.4	(±7.7)	72.0	(±7.1)	68.0	(±7.5)
Massachusetts	95.8	(±3.6)	93.3	(±4.0)	78.0	(±6.4)	62.7	(±8.0)	84.0	(±6.3)	78.5	(±6.6)
New Hampshire	96.3	(±2.6)	91.3	(±3.9)	74.1	(±6.5)	53.3	(±7.7)	78.2	(±6.7)	74.9	(±6.8)
Rhode Island	95.6	(±3.3)	91.6	(±4.9)	72.7	(±7.0)	60.9	(±8.2)	84.4	(±6.2)	82.1	(±6.7)**
Vermont	91.2	(±4.0)	85.8	(±5.1)	44.8	(±6.8)	48.5	(±6.8)**	73.4	(±6.1)**	66.9	(±6.6)
HHS Region II	**95.5**	**(±1.9)****	**86.5**	**(±3.1)**	**62.5**	**(±4.2)**	**49.3**	**(±4.4)**	**72.3**	**(±4.0)****	**72.4**	**(±4.1)****
New Jersey	95.6	(±3.3)	86.4	(±5.3)	59.8	(±7.2)	51.2	(±7.4)	69.0	(±6.9)	72.9	(±6.8)
New York	95.5	(±2.3)**	86.6	(±3.8)	63.7	(±5.2)	48.4	(±5.5)	73.8	(±4.8)**	72.2	(±5.0)**
City of New York	96.8	(±2.5)**	86.0	(±5.3)	61.2	(±7.1)	49.4	(±7.3)	67.0	(±7.1)**	69.8	(±6.9)
Rest of state	94.2	(±3.9)	87.2	(±5.5)	66.3	(±7.6)	47.3	(±8.2)	80.7	(±6.4)	74.6	(±7.4)**
HHS Region III	**92.1**	**(±2.6)**	**85.2**	**(±3.4)**	**77.9**	**(±3.8)**	**55.1**	**(±4.3)**	**77.8**	**(±3.7)****	**73.1**	**(±4.0)**
Delaware	94.8	(±3.4)	87.9	(±5.0)	83.6	(±5.3)**	64.2	(±7.0)	83.9	(±5.6)	71.8	(±6.6)
District of Columbia	96.2	(±3.1)	86.2	(±5.8)	78.3	(±6.9)	66.2	(±8.4)	68.4	(±8.1)**	76.9	(±7.2)
Maryland	95.3	(±4.4)	87.4	(±6.5)	75.4	(±7.7)	55.6	(±9.2)	83.7	(±6.6)**	75.8	(±8.0)
Pennsylvania	93.3	(±3.2)**	88.7	(±3.9)**	83.3	(±4.3)	58.3	(±5.8)	77.2	(±5.3)	75.5	(±5.2)
Philadelphia	95.9	(±2.7)	88.7	(±4.5)	77.9	(±5.9)	59.5	(±7.2)	73.4	(±6.4)	76.7	(±6.4)
Rest of state	92.8	(±3.8)**	88.7	(±4.5)**	84.4	(±5.0)	58.1	(±6.7)	78.0	(±6.2)	75.3	(±6.1)
Virginia	88.6	(±7.0)	78.8	(±9.3)	72.3	(±10.2)	48.0	(±10.8)	76.2	(±9.2)	69.2	(±10.0)
West Virginia	86.0	(±5.8)	83.4	(±6.2)	73.9	(±7.9)	57.5	(±8.4)	68.4	(±7.8)	65.5	(±7.9)
HHS Region IV	**93.0**	**(±1.7)**	**82.8**	**(±3.0)**	**73.5**	**(±3.3)**	**51.3**	**(±3.4)**	**68.9**	**(±3.4)**	**70.8**	**(±3.5)**
Alabama	89.7	(±5.8)	84.0	(±7.3)	81.7	(±7.1)	59.2	(±8.9)	74.8	(±7.8)	77.0	(±7.8)
Florida	93.4	(±4.0)	80.3	(±7.7)	58.0	(±8.3)	48.7	(±8.0)	66.0	(±8.1)	70.0	(±8.7)
Georgia	93.9	(±4.1)	83.5	(±7.9)	76.4	(±8.8)**	58.0	(±10.1)	64.6	(±10.2)	69.8	(±9.8)
Kentucky	89.5	(±5.1)	84.1	(±6.4)	88.0	(±5.6)	41.4	(±8.6)	66.4	(±8.5)	72.7	(±8.0)
Mississippi	95.2	(±3.0)	87.4	(±5.4)	79.2	(±7.1)	39.1	(±8.8)	63.2	(±8.6)	74.6	(±7.7)
North Carolina	96.0	(±3.3)**	87.5	(±5.3)	82.1	(±6.1)	51.6	(±7.7)	75.4	(±7.2)	72.0	(±7.5)
South Carolina	89.2	(±5.3)	77.3	(±7.5)	76.1	(±7.4)	52.5	(±8.8)	69.9	(±8.2)	66.5	(±8.3)
Tennessee	92.3	(±4.4)	81.1	(±6.0)	76.6	(±5.8)	52.6	(±7.1)	73.3	(±7.2)	68.5	(±6.8)
HHS Region V	**90.1**	**(±1.9)**	**81.6**	**(±2.5)**	**76.5**	**(±2.6)**	**53.0**	**(±3.0)**	**70.9**	**(±2.8)**	**68.0**	**(±2.9)**
Illinois	91.4	(±3.1)	82.7	(±4.5)	71.4	(±5.1)	48.4	(±5.5)	72.6	(±5.0)	66.8	(±5.3)
City of Chicago	90.0	(±5.2)	82.0	(±7.3)	78.9	(±8.2)	43.6	(±9.3)	76.1	(±7.7)	64.4	(±8.5)
Rest of state	91.9	(±3.8)	83.0	(±5.5)	68.7	(±6.2)	50.1	(±6.7)	71.4	(±6.2)	67.7	(±6.5)
Indiana	92.0	(±3.6)	82.1	(±5.3)	82.8	(±5.7)	61.0	(±6.9)**	65.7	(±7.1)	68.5	(±6.7)
Michigan	89.2	(±5.1)	79.6	(±6.6)	82.5	(±6.1)	51.2	(±7.9)	70.1	(±7.2)	70.0	(±7.4)
Minnesota	90.8	(±5.5)	90.5	(±5.0)	63.8	(±8.6)	54.3	(±9.1)	80.3	(±6.9)	74.1	(±7.8)
Ohio	86.0	(±5.2)	75.8	(±7.0)	78.1	(±6.4)	49.2	(±7.6)	66.5	(±7.5)	61.7	(±7.5)
Wisconsin	93.2	(±4.2)	84.0	(±6.1)	80.5	(±6.0)	63.2	(±7.5)	73.6	(±6.9)	72.8	(±7.1)

See table footnotes on next page.

TABLE 3. (*Continued*) Estimated vaccination coverage with selected individual vaccines and a combined vaccine series* among children aged 19–35 months, by U.S. Department of Health and Human Services (HHS) region and state and local area — National Immunization Survey, United States, 2013[†]

HHS region, state and local area	MMR (≥1 dose) %	MMR (95% CI)	DTaP (≥4 doses) %	DTaP (95% CI)	Hep B (birth)[§] %	Hep B (95% CI)	HepA (≥2 doses) %	HepA (95% CI)	Rotavirus[¶] %	Rotavirus (95% CI)	Combined vaccine series* %	Combined vaccine series* (95% CI)
HHS Region VI	**91.5**	**(±2.1)**	**80.4**	**(±3.2)**	**80.5**	**(±2.8)****	**58.9**	**(±3.8)**	**70.5**	**(±3.8)**	**69.8**	**(±3.6)**
Arkansas	88.3	(±5.9)	74.3	(±8.3)	79.7	(±7.3)	35.8	(±7.9)	56.0	(±9.0)	57.1	(±8.9)
Louisiana	88.1	(±5.1)	78.5	(±6.4)	81.6	(±5.7)	50.4	(±7.7)	69.6	(±7.3)	69.1	(±7.5)
New Mexico	89.1	(±4.6)	79.8	(±6.4)	67.5	(±7.0)	49.3	(±7.5)	68.7	(±7.0)**	65.7	(±7.2)
Oklahoma	89.8	(±3.8)	79.2	(±5.4)	76.7	(±5.4)**	51.8	(±6.5)	58.8	(±6.4)	62.7	(±6.3)
Texas	92.7	(±2.8)	81.5	(±4.5)	81.8	(±3.9)**	64.2	(±5.3)**	73.8	(±5.2)	72.5	(±5.0)**
Bexar County	93.0	(±3.7)	79.4	(±6.5)	73.0	(±6.9)	64.3	(±7.2)	67.2	(±7.5)	70.6	(±7.1)
City of Houston	92.4	(±4.5)	85.0	(±6.3)	83.2	(±7.9)	65.8	(±9.0)	80.8	(±7.6)	77.6	(±7.4)
El Paso County	93.7	(±3.3)**	76.7	(±6.1)	74.5	(±6.2)	64.8	(±6.8)	70.6	(±6.7)	69.7	(±6.6)
Rest of state	92.7	(±3.5)	81.4	(±5.7)	82.7	(±4.8)**	63.9	(±6.7)	73.5	(±6.6)**	72.0	(±6.3)**
HHS Region VII	**91.1**	**(±2.7)**	**84.5**	**(±3.3)**	**79.1**	**(±3.5)**	**54.9**	**(±4.5)**	**73.5**	**(±4.0)**	**71.9**	**(±4.0)**
Iowa	94.5	(±3.9)	89.6	(±4.4)	79.5	(±7.2)**	57.5	(±8.6)	74.7	(±8.2)	78.3	(±6.7)
Kansas	89.4	(±4.7)	81.6	(±6.1)	77.2	(±6.5)	60.2	(±7.6)	72.6	(±6.9)**	68.7	(±7.1)
Missouri	89.8	(±5.3)	82.1	(±6.6)	79.2	(±6.3)	45.9	(±8.5)	72.4	(±7.5)	67.9	(±7.7)
Nebraska	92.5	(±4.1)	88.3	(±4.7)	81.3	(±5.3)	69.5	(±6.5)	76.2	(±6.2)	79.0	(±5.9)
HHS Region VIII	**89.2**	**(±2.7)**	**84.2**	**(±3.0)**	**70.4**	**(±3.7)**	**54.5**	**(±4.0)**	**74.1**	**(±3.5)**	**71.4**	**(±3.7)**
Colorado	86.0	(±5.5)	81.2	(±6.0)	60.2	(±7.3)	47.6	(±7.4)	73.8	(±6.6)	69.2	(±6.9)
Montana	87.3	(±5.2)	79.0	(±6.4)	73.9	(±6.8)	46.4	(±8.5)	65.5	(±8.2)	65.4	(±8.1)
North Dakota	91.4	(±3.8)	78.6	(±5.9)	82.0	(±5.9)	59.5	(±6.8)	78.4	(±5.4)	72.0	(±6.2)
South Dakota	93.1	(±4.4)	86.5	(±5.8)	70.9	(±7.8)	55.4	(±8.3)	68.7	(±7.8)	73.8	(±7.7)**
Utah	92.6	(±3.6)	90.3	(±4.1)**	81.2	(±5.5)	67.6	(±6.8)**	78.3	(±5.8)	75.2	(±6.1)
Wyoming	89.0	(±5.4)	80.9	(±6.6)	67.0	(±8.0)	33.6	(±7.6)	65.7	(±8.0)	70.0	(±7.7)
HHS Region IX	**90.8**	**(±4.2)**	**82.1**	**(±5.1)**	**71.9**	**(±6.1)**	**56.8**	**(±6.7)**	**75.1**	**(±5.7)**	**68.2**	**(±6.2)**
Arizona	91.4	(±3.7)	76.6	(±6.6)	79.1	(±5.8)	55.4	(±8.1)	70.9	(±7.5)	65.1	(±7.7)
California	90.7	(±5.3)	83.1	(±6.4)	70.3	(±7.7)	56.8	(±8.4)	76.8	(±7.2)	69.3	(±7.8)
Hawaii	92.8	(±3.8)	83.7	(±6.1)	77.3	(±6.7)	54.2	(±8.0)	73.3	(±6.9)	66.5	(±8.2)**
Nevada	90.4	(±3.5)	81.1	(±5.0)	75.4	(±5.6)	61.1	(±6.4)	62.1	(±6.5)	60.6	(±6.4)
HHS Region X	**91.9**	**(±2.5)****	**81.2**	**(±4.1)**	**71.6**	**(±4.3)**	**56.2**	**(±5.0)**	**72.1**	**(±4.4)**	**69.2**	**(±4.6)**
Alaska	90.5	(±3.6)	75.5	(±6.1)	59.4	(±7.0)	52.5	(±7.2)	64.2	(±6.8)	63.9	(±6.8)
Idaho	91.1	(±4.3)	84.2	(±5.3)	72.7	(±6.5)	60.7	(±7.3)	74.6	(±6.4)	70.2	(±6.9)
Oregon	89.4	(±4.4)	83.8	(±5.2)	66.8	(±6.3)	55.9	(±6.7)	64.3	(±6.7)	66.6	(±6.5)
Washington	93.5	(±3.9)**	79.8	(±7.0)	75.0	(±7.1)	55.7	(±8.4)	76.3	(±7.3)	70.8	(±7.8)
Range	*(86.0–96.3)*		*(74.3–93.3)*		*(44.8–88.0)*		*(33.6–72.1)*		*(56.0–84.4)*		*(57.1 – 82.1)*	
Territories												
Guam	84.9	(±5.5)	71.5	(±7.2)	87.7	(±4.7)	45.8	(±7.5)	8.0	(±3.8)	50.3	(±7.8)
U.S. Virgin Islands	59.0	(±8.7)	51.1	(±8.8)	78.5	(±6.6)	18.6	(±6.5)	23.7	(±7.8)	39.8	(±8.5)

Abbreviations: MMR = measles, mumps, and rubella vaccine; DTaP = diphtheria, tetanus toxoids, and acellular pertussis vaccine (includes children who might have been vaccinated with diphtheria and tetanus toxoids vaccine, or diphtheria, tetanus toxoids, and pertussis vaccine); HepB = hepatitis B vaccine; HepA = hepatitis A vaccine; CI = confidence interval; Hib = *Haemophilus influenzae* type b vaccine; PCV = pneumococcal conjugate vaccine.

   * The combined (4:3:1:3*:3:1:4) vaccine series includes ≥4 doses of DTaP, ≥3 doses of poliovirus vaccine, ≥1 dose of measles-containing vaccine, full series of Hib vaccine (≥3 or ≥4 doses, depending on product type), ≥3 doses of HepB, ≥1 dose of varicella vaccine, and ≥4 doses of PCV.

   [†] Children in the 2013 National Immunization Survey were born January 2010–May 2012.

   [§] HepB administered from birth through age 3 days.

   [¶] Either ≥2 or ≥3 doses of rotavirus vaccine, depending on product type received (≥2 doses for Rotarix [RV1] or ≥3 doses for RotaTeq [RV5]).

** Statistically significant increase in coverage compared with 2012 estimates from the National Immunization Survey (*p*<0.05).

Information in these tables was reproduced from the Centers for Disease Control and Prevention's (CDC's) *Morbidity and Mortality Weekly Report* and drawn from the 2012 National Health Interview Survey (NHIS), a survey conducted by the National Center for Health Statistics (NCHS) of the Centers for Disease Control and Prevention (CDC). More information about the NHIS is available from http://www.cdc.gov/nchs/nhis/about_nhis.htm.

TABLE 1. Estimated proportion of adults aged ≥19 years who received selected vaccinations, by age group, high-risk status,* race/ethnicity, and other selected characteristics — National Health Interview Survey, United States, 2012

Vaccination, age group, high-risk status, and race/ethnicity[†]	Sample size	%	(95% CI)	Difference from 2011
Pneumococcal vaccination, ever[§]				
19–64 yrs, high risk				
Total	9,333	20.0	(18.9–21.1)	-0.1
White	5,736	21.4	(20.1–22.9)	1.3
Black	1,605	19.7	(17.4–22.2)	-3.1
Hispanic	1,326	13.8	(11.5–16.4)[¶]	-4.6**
Asian	350	13.2	(9.5–18.1)[¶]	1.2
Others	316	20.2	(15.2–26.2)	-1.5
≥65 yrs				
Total	7,076	59.9	(58.4–61.4)	-2.4
White	4,993	64.0	(62.3–65.7)	-2.5
Black	919	46.1	(41.7–50.6)[¶]	-1.5
Hispanic or Latino	698	43.4	(39.0–48.0)[¶]	0.3
Asian	373	41.3	(35.4–47.5)[¶]	1.0
Others	93	44.7	(32.6–57.5)[¶]	-22.7**
Tetanus vaccination, past 10 yrs[††]				
19–49 yrs				
Total	16,927	64.2	(63.2–65.1)	-0.3
White	8,969	69.7	(68.5–70.9)	0.1
Black	2,491	56.1	(53.5–58.6)[¶]	1.3
Hispanic	3,772	53.9	(51.9–56.0)[¶]	-2.4
Asian	1,195	54.3	(50.6–58.0)[¶]	1.9
Others	500	71.9	(66.5–76.8)	2.3
50–64 yrs				
Total	8,525	63.5	(62.1–64.8)	-0.4
White	5,577	67.5	(65.9–69.0)	-0.2
Black	1,373	52.3	(49.0–55.7)[¶]	-2.1
Hispanic	1,031	52.3	(47.8–56.8)[¶]	-0.3
Asian	371	48.2	(41.8–54.7)[¶]	3.1
Others	173	69.9	(60.3–78.0)	2.0
≥65 yrs				
Total	6,905	55.1	(53.6–56.7)	0.7
White	4,864	57.7	(55.9–59.5)	0.8
Black	904	44.6	(40.8–48.4)[¶]	0.2
Hispanic	678	44.8	(40.1–49.6)[¶]	-0.3
Asian	366	45.8	(39.5–52.2)[¶]	7.9
Others	93	50.2	(36.8–63.6)	-13.0
Tetanus vaccination including pertussis vaccine, past 7 yrs[§§]				
≥19 yrs				
Total	22,653	14.2	(13.6–14.9)	NA
White	13,135	16.1	(15.3–17.0)	NA
Black	3,434	9.8	(8.4–11.6)[¶]	NA
Hispanic	4,051	8.7	(7.6–10.0)[¶]	NA
Asian	1,526	14.7	(12.5–17.2)	NA
Others	507	21.4	(17.0–26.7)[¶]	NA
Living with an infant aged <1 yr	722	25.9	(22.4–29.8)	NA
Not living with an infant aged <1 yr	21,931	13.8	(13.2–14.5)	NA
19–64 yrs				
Total	17,695	15.6	(14.9–16.4)	3.2**
White	9,729	18.2	(17.2–19.2)	4.4**
Black	2,746	10.5	(8.9–12.3)[¶]	-0.5
Hispanic	3,544	9.2	(8.0–10.6)[¶]	1.5
Asian	1,237	16.2	(13.8–19.0)	4.5**
Others	439	22.7	(17.8–28.5)	3.0
Living with an infant aged <1 yr	716	25.9	(22.3–29.8)	4.4
Not living with an infant aged <1 yr	16,979	15.1	(14.4–15.9)	3.1**
≥65 yrs				
Total	4,958	8.0	(7.0–9.1)	NA
White	3,406	8.8	(7.6–10.2)	NA
Black	688	5.9	(3.7–9.4)	NA
Hispanic	507	3.3	(2.0–5.4)[¶]	NA
Asian	289	4.2	(2.4–7.3)[¶]	NA
Others	68	—[¶¶]		NA
Living with an infant aged <1 yr	6	—[¶¶]		NA
Not living with an infant aged <1 yr	4,952	8.0	(7.0–9.1)	NA

See table footnotes on next page.

TABLE 1. (*Continued*) Estimated proportion of adults aged ≥19 years who received selected vaccinations, by age group, high-risk status,* race/ethnicity, and other selected characteristics — National Health Interview Survey, United States, 2012

Vaccination, age group, high-risk status, and race/ethnicity[†]	Sample size	%	(95% CI)	Difference from 2011
Hepatitis A vaccination (≥2 doses), ever*				
19–49 yrs				
Total	14,834	12.2	(11.5–13.0)	-0.3
White	7,887	12.2	(11.2–13.2)	-0.1
Black	2,207	11.3	(9.6–13.2)	0.1
Hispanic	3,341	10.5	(9.2–11.9)[¶]	-0.8
Asian	992	18.7	(15.7–22.1)[¶]	-0.4
Others	407	16.1	(11.4–22.2)	-5.0
Had traveled outside the United States since 1995, other than to Europe, Japan, Australia, New Zealand, or Canada	5,259	18.9	(17.6–20.3)	-1.2
Had not traveled outside the United States since 1995, other than to Europe, Japan, Australia, New Zealand, or Canada	9,548	8.6	(7.8–9.5)	0.2
With chronic liver conditions, overall	121	—[¶¶]		—[¶¶]
Hepatitis B vaccination (≥3 doses), ever[†††]				
19–49 yrs				
Total	15,649	35.3	(34.3–36.2)	-0.7
White	8,296	37.5	(36.3–38.8)	-0.3
Black	2,338	34.2	(31.5–36.9)[¶]	1.2
Hispanic	3,465	27.1	(25.1–29.2)[¶]	-1.8
Asian	1,105	39.7	(35.5–44.0)	-0.9
Others	445	37.4	(31.9–43.3)	-6.7
With diabetes				
Overall	1,286	28.6	(25.4–32.1)	1.7
≥60 yrs, overall	1,907	15.1	(12.9–17.4)	2.6
Herpes Zoster (shingles) vaccination, ever[§§§]				
≥60 yrs				
Total	9,924	20.1	(19.1–21.2)	4.4**
White	6,957	22.8	(21.5–24.0)	5.2**
Black	1,354	8.8	(6.9–11.2)[¶]	0.9
Hispanic	990	8.7	(6.6–11.4)[¶]	0.7
Asian	487	16.9	(13.2–21.5)[¶]	3.0
Others	136	19.7	(11.5–31.6)	7.7
Human papillomavirus (HPV) vaccination among females (≥1 dose), ever[¶¶¶]				
19–26 yrs				
Total	2,300	34.5	(31.7–37.3)	5.0**
White	1,165	42.2	(38.5–46.0)	9.7**
Black	385	29.1	(23.4–35.7)[¶]	0.9
Hispanic	507	18.7	(14.9–23.1)[¶]	-1.5
Asian	148	15.6	(9.5–24.5)[¶]	-6.7
Others	95	41.2	(28.7–55.0)	2.2
19–21 yrs, total	760	44.3	(39.5–49.2)	1.2
22–26 yrs, total	1,540	28.2	(25.2–31.5)	6.7**
Human papillomavirus (HPV) vaccination among males (≥1 dose), ever[¶¶¶]				
19–26 yrs, total	1,783	2.3	(1.6–3.4)	0.2
19–21 yrs, total	634	2.4	(1.4–4.4)	-0.3
22–26 yrs, total	1,149	2.2	(1.3–3.8)	0.5

* Adults were considered at high risk for pneumococcal disease or its complications if they had ever been told by a doctor or other health professional that they had diabetes, emphysema, chronic obstructive pulmonary disease, coronary heart disease, angina, heart attack, or other heart condition; had a diagnosis of cancer during the previous 12 months (excluding nonmelanoma skin cancer); had ever been told by a doctor or other health professional that they had lymphoma, leukemia, or blood cancer; had been told by a doctor or other health professional that they had chronic bronchitis or weak or failing kidneys during the preceding 12 months; had an asthma episode or attack during the preceding 12 months; or were current smokers. Comprehensive information on high-risk conditions for hepatitis B or A was not collected in 2012.

[†] Race/ethnicity was categorized as Hispanic, black, white, Asian, and "other." Persons identified as Hispanic might be of any race. Persons identified as black, white, Asian, or other race are non-Hispanic. "Other" includes American Indian/Alaska Native and multiple race. The five racial/ethnic categories are mutually exclusive.

[§] Respondents were asked if they had ever had a pneumonia shot.

[¶] p<0.05 by t-test for comparisons, with non-Hispanic white as the reference.

** p<0.05 by t-test for comparisons between 2012 and 2011 within each level of each characteristic.

[††] Respondents were asked if they had received a tetanus shot in the past 10 years. Vaccinated respondents included adults who received tetanus-diphthera toxoid vaccine (Td) during the past 10 years or tetanus, diphthera, and acellular pertussis vaccine (Tdap) during 2005–2012.

[§§] Respondents who had received a tetanus shot in the past 10 years were asked if their most recent shot was given in 2005 or later. Respondents who had received a tetanus shot since 2005 were asked if they were told that their most recent tetanus shot included the pertussis or whooping cough vaccine. Among 34,218 respondents aged ≥19 years, those without a "yes" or "no" classification for tetanus vaccination status within the preceding 10 years (n = 1,861 [5.4%]), for tetanus vaccination status during 2005–2012 (n = 1,261 [3.7%]), or those who reported tetanus vaccination during 2005–2012, but were not told vaccine type by the provider (n = 6,986 [20.4%]) or did not know vaccine type (Td or Tdap) (n = 1,457 [4.3%]) were excluded, yielding a sample of 22,653 respondents aged ≥19 years for whom Tdap vaccination status could be assessed. In February 2012, the Advisory Committee on Immunization Practices recommended Tdap vaccination for all adults aged ≥19 years, including adults aged ≥65 years.

[¶¶] Estimate is not reliable because of small sample size (<30) or relative standard error (standard error/estimates) >0.3.

*** Respondents were asked if they had ever received the hepatitis A vaccine, and if yes, were asked how many shots were received.

[†††] Respondents were asked if they had ever received the hepatitis B vaccine, and if yes, if they had received ≥3 doses or <3 doses.

[§§§] Respondents were asked if they had ever received a shingles vaccine.

[¶¶¶] Respondents were asked if they had ever received the HPV shot or cervical cancer vaccine.

TABLE 2. Type of tetanus vaccine received, and proportion that were tetanus, diphtheria, acellular pertussis vaccine (Tdap), among adults aged ≥19 years who received a tetanus vaccination, by selected characteristics — National Health Interview Survey, United States, 2005–2012

Characteristic	No. in sample	Type of vaccine received									Proportion that received Tdap*		
		Received Tdap		Received other tetanus vaccine		Doctor did not inform the patient		Could not recall vaccine type			No. in sample	%	(95% CI)
		%	(95% CI)	%	(95% CI)	%	(95% CI)	%	(95% CI)				
≥19 yrs													
All adults	13,145	23.8	(22.7–24.9)	12.6	(11.8–13.4)	52.6	(51.2–54.0)	11.1	(10.2–12.0)		4,699	65.4	(63.5–67.3)
Health-care personnel[†]	1,501	44.0	(40.2–47.8)	13.7	(11.4–16.3)	33.1	(29.8–36.6)	9.3	(7.5–11.4)		857	76.3[§]	(72.0–80.1)
Non–health-care personnel	11,631	21.2	(20.2–22.3)	12.4	(11.6–13.3)	55.1	(53.6–56.5)	11.3	(10.4–12.2)		3,840	63.1	(61.0–65.1)
19–64 yrs													
All adults	10,932	24.9	(23.8–26.1)	12.5	(11.6–13.3)	51.5	(50.0–53.1)	11.1	(10.1–12.0)		4,065	66.7	(64.7–68.6)
Health-care personnel	1,394	44.8	(40.9–48.8)	13.5	(11.2–16.2)	32.7	(29.3–36.3)	8.9	(7.1–11.2)		809	76.8[§]	(72.5–80.6)
Non–health-care personnel	9,527	22.2	(21.0–23.3)	12.3	(11.4–13.3)	54.2	(52.6–55.8)	11.3	(10.3–12.4)		3,254	64.3	(62.0–66.4)
≥65 yrs													
All adults	2,213	16.8	(14.8–19.0)	13.1	(11.4–15.1)	59.0	(56.2–61.7)	11.1	(9.6–12.8)		634	56.1	(50.8–61.2)
Health-care personnel	107	30.1	(19.7–43.0)	16.2	(9.1–27.2)	39.0	(27.9–51.3)	14.7	(7.9–25.8)		48	65.0	(46.5–79.9)
Non–health-care personnel	2,104	16.2	(14.1–18.5)	13.0	(11.2–15.1)	59.9	(56.9–62.8)	10.9	(9.3–12.6)		586	55.4	(50.0–60.7)

* Calculated by dividing number of respondents who reported receiving Tdap by the sum of those who reported receiving Tdap and those who reported receiving other tetanus vaccinations. Respondents who reported that the doctor did not inform them of the vaccine type they received and those who could not recall the vaccine type were excluded.

† Adults were classified as health-care personnel if they reported they currently volunteer or work in a hospital, medical clinic, doctor's office, dentist's office, nursing home, or other health-care facility, including part-time and unpaid work in a health-care facility or professional nursing care provided in the home.

§ $p<0.05$ by t-test for comparisons between health-care personnel and non–health-care personnel.

TABLE 3. Estimated proportion of health-care personnel* who received selected vaccinations, by age group and race/ethnicity[†] — National Health Interview Survey, United States, 2012

Vaccination status	Sample size	%	(95% confidence Interval)	Difference from 2011
Tetanus vaccination including pertussis vaccine, past 7 years[§]				
≥19 yrs				
Total	2,105	31.4	(28.7–34.3)	NA
White	1,262	33.0	(29.5–36.7)	NA
Black	359	22.5	(17.4–28.5)[¶]	NA
Hispanic	262	25.1	(19.0–32.3)[¶]	NA
Asian	169	39.4	(30.2–49.5)	NA
Other	53	46.1	(27.7–65.7)	NA
19–64 yrs				
Total	1,911	32.6	(29.7–35.6)	5.8**
White	1,123	34.5	(30.7–38.5)	7.3**
Black	337	22.9	(17.7–29.1)[¶]	1.3
Hispanic	247	25.1	(18.8–32.7)[¶]	-4.9
Asian	154	41.4	(31.7–51.8)	13.7
Other	50	46.1	(27.2–66.1)	14.8
≥65 yrs				
Total	194	16.9	(11.3–24.6)	NA
White	139	17.5	(11.0–26.8)	NA
Black	22	—[††]	—	NA
Hispanic or Latino	15	—[††]	—	NA
Asian	15	—[††]	—	NA
Other	3	—[††]	—	NA
Hepatitis B vaccination (≥3 doses), ever[§§]				
≥19 yrs				
Total	2,767	65.0	(62.7–67.2)	1.1
White	1,692	65.5	(62.5–68.4)	0.4
Black	479	61.7	(56.4–66.7)	4.6
Hispanic	332	60.1	(53.1–66.7)	0.6
Asian	195	72.3	(63.4–79.7)	1.9
Other	69	75.9	(62.2–85.7)	5.9

Abbreviation: NA = not available.

 * Adults were classified as health-care personnel if they reported that they currently volunteer or work in a hospital, medical clinic, doctor's office, dentist's office, nursing home, or other health-care facility, including part-time and unpaid work in a health-care facility or professional nursing care provided in the home.

 [†] Race/ethnicity was categorized as Hispanic, black, white, Asian, and "other." Persons identified as Hispanic might be of any race. Persons identified as black, white, Asian, or other race are non-Hispanic. "Other" includes American Indian/Alaska Native and multiple race. The five racial/ethnic categories are mutually exclusive.

 [§] Respondents who had received a tetanus shot in the past 10 years were asked if their most recent shot was given in 2005 or later. Respondents who had received a tetanus shot since 2005 were asked if they were told that their most recent tetanus shot included the pertussis or whooping cough vaccine. Among 2,911 health-care personnel aged ≥19 years, those without a "yes" or "no" classification for tetanus vaccination status within the preceding 10 years ($n = 63$ [2.2%]) for tetanus vaccination status during 2005–2012 ($n = 100$ [3.4%]) or those who reported tetanus vaccination during 2005–2012, but who were not told vaccine type by the provider ($n = 516$ [17.7%]) or did not know vaccine type (tetanus and diphtheria vaccine [Td] or tetanus and diphtheria with acellular pertussis vaccine [Tdap]) ($n = 127$ [4.4%]) were excluded, yielding a sample of 2,105 respondents aged ≥19 years for whom Tdap vaccination status could be assessed. In February 2012, the Advisory Committee on Immunization Practices recommended Tdap vaccination for all adults aged ≥19 years, including adults aged ≥65 years.

 [¶] $p < 0.05$ by t-test for comparisons with non-Hispanic white as the reference.

 ** $p < 0.05$ by t-test for comparisons between 2012 and 2011 within each level of each characteristic.

 [††] Estimate is not reliable because of small sample size (<30) or relative standard error (standard error/estimates) >0.3.

 [§§] Respondents were asked if they had ever received the hepatitis B vaccine, and if yes, if they had received ≥3 doses or <3 doses.

Health Insurance

Information in these tables was drawn from the Current Population Survey (CPS), a survey conducted by the U.S. Census Bureau, part of the U.S. Department of Commerce. Further information about the CPS is available from http://www.census.gov/cps, and further technical details about the information in these tables is available from http://www.census.gov/prod/2013pubs/p60-245.pdf (pp. 65–75).

Table 7.
People Without Health Insurance Coverage by Selected Characteristics: 2011 and 2012

(Numbers in thousands, confidence intervals [C.I.] in thousands or percentage points as appropriate. People as of March of the following year. For information on confidentiality protection, sampling error, nonsampling error, and definitions, see *www.census.gov/prod/techdoc/cps/cpsmar13.pdf*)

Characteristic	2011					2012					Change in uninsured[1,*]	
		Uninsured					Uninsured					
	Total	Number	90 percent C.I.[2] (±)	Percent	90 percent C.I.[2] (±)	Total	Number	90 percent C.I.[2] (±)	Percent	90 percent C.I.[2] (±)	Number	Percent
Total	308,827	48,613	626	15.7	0.2	311,116	47,951	673	15.4	0.2	−663	*−0.3
Family Status												
In families	252,316	36,749	582	14.6	0.2	252,863	35,830	631	14.2	0.2	*−919	*−0.4
Householder.	80,529	11,870	215	14.7	0.3	80,944	11,921	250	14.7	0.3	52	Z
Related children under 18	72,568	6,647	271	9.2	0.4	72,545	6,348	231	8.8	0.3	−299	−0.4
Related children under 6.	23,860	1,969	122	8.3	0.5	23,604	1,960	110	8.3	0.5	−8	0.1
In unrelated subfamilies.	1,623	462	71	28.5	3.4	1,599	371	65	23.2	3.2	*−91	*−5.3
Unrelated individuals.	54,888	11,402	321	20.8	0.5	56,654	11,749	361	20.7	0.5	347	Z
Race[3] and Hispanic Origin												
White	241,586	35,991	595	14.9	0.2	242,469	35,625	568	14.7	0.2	−366	−0.2
White, not Hispanic.	195,148	21,681	460	11.1	0.2	195,330	21,585	478	11.1	0.2	−96	−0.1
Black	39,696	7,722	242	19.5	0.6	40,208	7,629	296	19.0	0.7	−93	−0.5
Asian	16,094	2,696	194	16.8	1.2	16,433	2,477	177	15.1	1.0	−219	*−1.7
Hispanic (any race)	52,358	15,776	369	30.1	0.7	53,230	15,500	360	29.1	0.7	−276	*−1.0
Age												
Under age 65.	267,320	47,923	620	17.9	0.2	267,829	47,312	663	17.7	0.2	−612	−0.3
Under age 18.	74,108	6,964	278	9.4	0.4	74,187	6,586	236	8.9	0.3	*−379	*−0.5
Under age 19[4]	78,384	7,634	284	9.7	0.4	78,177	7,193	245	9.2	0.3	*−441	*−0.5
Aged 19 to 25[4]	29,909	8,272	230	27.7	0.7	30,207	8,205	232	27.2	0.8	−66	−0.5
Aged 26 to 34.	37,174	10,237	249	27.5	0.7	37,631	10,228	242	27.2	0.6	−9	−0.4
Aged 35 to 44.	39,927	8,399	212	21.0	0.5	39,877	8,428	221	21.1	0.6	29	0.1
Aged 45 to 64.	81,926	13,382	304	16.3	0.4	81,937	13,257	303	16.2	0.4	−125	−0.2
Aged 65 and older	41,507	690	66	1.7	0.2	43,287	639	69	1.5	0.2	−51	−0.2
Nativity												
Native born	268,851	35,436	533	13.2	0.2	271,010	35,127	572	13.0	0.2	−309	−0.2
Foreign born.	39,976	13,177	392	33.0	0.8	40,107	12,824	394	32.0	0.8	−353	*−1.0
Naturalized citizen.	17,934	3,431	162	19.1	0.8	18,200	3,322	158	18.3	0.8	−109	−0.9
Not a citizen	22,042	9,746	354	44.2	1.2	21,906	9,502	345	43.4	1.1	−244	−0.8
Region												
Northeast.	55,035	6,061	251	11.0	0.5	55,135	5,939	271	10.8	0.5	−123	−0.2
Midwest	66,115	8,425	305	12.7	0.5	66,422	7,937	315	11.9	0.5	*−489	*−0.8
South	115,068	21,059	450	18.3	0.4	116,130	21,587	513	18.6	0.4	527	0.3
West	72,610	13,067	335	18.0	0.5	73,429	12,488	343	17.0	0.5	*−579	*−1.0
Residence												
Inside metropolitan statistical areas . .	261,455	41,299	730	15.8	0.2	263,328	40,694	733	15.5	0.3	−605	*−0.3
Inside principal cities	100,302	19,045	585	19.0	0.5	101,363	18,836	544	18.6	0.4	−209	−0.4
Outside principal cities.	161,153	22,255	669	13.8	0.3	161,965	21,859	680	13.5	0.4	−396	−0.3
Outside metropolitan statistical areas[5]	47,372	7,314	497	15.4	0.6	47,788	7,256	496	15.2	0.6	−58	−0.3

See footnotes at end of table.

Table 7.
People Without Health Insurance Coverage by Selected Characteristics: 2011 and 2012—Con.

(Numbers in thousands, confidence intervals [C.I.] in thousands or percentage points as appropriate. People as of March of the following year. For information on confidentiality protection, sampling error, nonsampling error, and definitions, see *www.census.gov/prod/techdoc/cps/cpsmar13.pdf*)

Characteristic	2011					2012					Change in uninsured[1],*	
		Uninsured					Uninsured					
	Total	Number	90 percent C.I.[2] (±)	Percent	90 percent C.I.[2] (±)	Total	Number	90 percent C.I.[2] (±)	Percent	90 percent C.I.[2] (±)	Number	Percent
Work Experience												
Total, aged 18 to 64	193,213	40,959	501	21.2	0.3	193,642	40,726	560	21.0	0.3	−233	−0.2
All workers	144,163	27,863	442	19.3	0.3	145,814	28,378	447	19.5	0.3	515	0.1
Worked full-time, year-round	97,443	14,926	314	15.3	0.3	98,715	15,309	333	15.5	0.3	383	0.2
Less than full-time, year-round. . .	46,720	12,937	303	27.7	0.6	47,099	13,069	292	27.7	0.5	132	0.1
Did not work at least one week	49,049	13,096	286	26.7	0.5	47,828	12,348	318	25.8	0.6	*−748	*−0.9
Disability Status[6]												
Total, aged 18 to 64	193,213	40,959	501	21.2	0.3	193,642	40,726	560	21.0	0.3	−233	−0.2
With a disability	14,968	2,484	131	16.6	0.8	14,996	2,493	129	16.6	0.8	8	Z
With no disability	177,309	38,473	480	21.7	0.3	177,727	38,233	539	21.5	0.3	−240	−0.2

*An asterisk preceding an estimate indicates change is statistically different from zero at the 90 percent confidence level.

Z Represents or rounds to zero.

[1] Details may not sum to totals because of rounding.

[2] A 90 percent confidence interval is a measure of an estimate's variability. The larger the confidence interval in relation to the size of the estimate, the less reliable the estimate. Confidence intervals shown in this table are based on standard errors calculated using replicate weights. For more information see "Standard Errors and Their Use" at <www.census.gov/hhes/www/p60_245sa.pdf>.

[3] Federal surveys give respondents the option of reporting more than one race. Therefore, two basic ways of defining a race group are possible. A group such as Asian may be defined as those who reported Asian and no other race (the race-alone or single-race concept) or as those who reported Asian regardless of whether they also reported another race (the race-alone-or-in-combination concept). This table shows data using the first approach (race alone). The use of the single-race population does not imply that it is the preferred method of presenting or analyzing data. The Census Bureau uses a variety of approaches. Information on people who reported more than one race, such as White *and* American Indian and Alaska Native or Asian *and* Black or African American, is available from Census 2010 through American FactFinder. About 2.9 percent of people reported more than one race in Census 2010. Data for American Indians and Alaska Natives, Native Hawaiians and Other Pacific Islanders, and those reporting two or more races are not shown separately.

[4] These age groups are of special interest because of the Affordable Care Act of 2010. Children under the age of 19 are eligible for Medicaid/CHIP, and individuals aged 19 to 25 may be a dependent on a parent's health plan.

[5] The "Outside metropolitan statistical areas" category includes both micropolitan statistical areas and territory outside of metropolitan and micropolitan statistical areas. For more information, see "About Metropolitan and Micropolitan Statistical Areas" at <www.census.gov/population/www/estimates/aboutmetro.html>.

[6] The sum of those with and without a disability does not equal the total because disability status is not defined for individuals in the Armed Forces.

Source: U.S. Census Bureau, Current Population Survey, 2012 and 2013 Annual Social and Economic Supplements.

Table 8.

Coverage Rates by Type of Health Insurance: 2011 and 2012

(People as of March of the following year. For information on confidentiality protection, sampling error, nonsampling error, and definitions, see *www.census.gov/prod/techdoc /cps/cpsmar13.pdf*)

Coverage type	2011	2012
Any private plan[1]	63.9	63.9
Any private plan alone[2]	52.0	52.0
Employment-based[1]	55.1	54.9
Employment-based alone[2]	45.1	44.8
Direct-purchase[1]	9.8	9.8
Direct-purchase alone[2]	3.6	3.6
Any government plan[1]	32.2	*32.6
Any government plan alone[2]	20.4	*20.7
Medicare[1]	15.2	*15.7
Medicare alone[2]	4.9	*5.4
Medicaid[1]	16.5	16.4
Medicaid alone[2]	11.5	*11.3
Military health care[1,3]	4.4	4.4
Military health care alone[2,3]	1.3	1.3
Uninsured	15.7	*15.4

   * Changes between the 2011 and 2012 estimates are statistically different from zero at the 90 percent confidence level.
   [1] The estimates by type of coverage are *not* mutually exclusive; people can be covered by more than one type of health insurance during the year.
   [2] The estimates by type of coverage are mutually exclusive; people did not have any other type of health insurance during the year.
   [3] Military health care includes Tricare and CHAMPVA (Civilian Health and Medical Program of the Department of Veterans Affairs), as well as care provided by the Department of Veterans Affairs and the military.
   Source: U.S. Census Bureau, Current Population Survey, 2012 and 2013 Annual Social and Economic Supplements.

Information in these tables was drawn from 2014 CMS Statistics, a report from the Center for Medicare and Medicaid Services within the U.S. Department of Health and Human Services. The full report is available from http://www.cms.gov/Research-Statistics-Data-and-Systems/Statistics-Trends-and-Reports/CMS-Statistics-Reference-Booklet/Downloads/CMS_Stats_2014_final.pdf, and further information about the Medicare and Medicaid programs is available from http://www.cms.gov/.

Table I.1
Medicare enrollment/trends

	Total persons	Aged persons	Disabled persons
July	In millions		
1966	19.1	19.1	—
1970	20.4	20.4	—
1975	24.9	22.7	2.2
1980	28.4	25.5	3.0
1985	31.1	28.1	2.9
1990	34.3	31.0	3.3
1995	37.6	33.2	4.4
Average monthly			
2000	39.7	34.3	5.4
2005	42.6	35.8	6.8
2010	47.7	39.6	8.1
2011	48.9	40.5	8.4
2012	50.9	42.2	8.6
2013	52.3	43.5	8.8
2014	54.0	45.0	9.0

NOTES: Represents those enrolled in HI (Part A) and/or SMI (Part B and Part D) of Medicare. Data for 1966–1995 are as of July. Data for 2000–2014 represent average actual or projected monthly enrollment. Numbers may not add to totals because of rounding. Based on 2014 Trustees Report.

SOURCE: CMS, Office of the Actuary.

Table I.2
Medicare enrollment/coverage

	HI and/or SMI	HI	SMI Part B	SMI Part D	HI and SMI	HI only	SMI only
	In millions						
All persons	53.6	53.2	49.0	40.3	48.6	4.6	0.3
Aged persons	44.6	44.3	41.0	—	40.6	3.7	0.3
Disabled persons	8.9	8.9	8.0	—	8.0	0.9	0.0

NOTES: Projected average monthly enrollment during fiscal year 2014. Aged/disabled split of Part D enrollment not available. Based on 2014 Trustees Report. Numbers may not add to totals because of rounding.

SOURCE: CMS, Office of the Actuary.

Table I.3
Medicare enrollment/demographics

	Total	Male	Female
	In thousands		
All persons	52,456	23,783	28,673
Aged	43,614	19,192	24,422
65–74 years	24,552	11,546	13,005
75–84 years	13,117	5,653	7,464
85 years and over	5,945	1,993	3,952
Disabled	8,843	4,591	4,251
Under 45 years	1,995	1,069	926
45–54 years	2,575	1,326	1,248
55–64 years	4,273	2,196	2,076
White	42,711	19,341	23,370
Black	5,490	2,372	3,118
All Other	3,811	1,794	2,017
Native American	236	106	131
Asian/Pacific	1,127	488	639
Hispanic	1,424	672	753
Other	1,023	529	494
Unknown Race	443	276	168

NOTES: Data as of July 1, 2013. Numbers may not add to totals because of rounding. Race information obtained from the Enrollment Database.

SOURCE: CMS, Office of Information Products and Data Analytics.

Table I.4
Medicare Part D enrollment/demographics

	Total	Male	Female
	In thousands		
All persons	35,740	15,041	20,699
Aged			
65–74 years	15,818	6,847	8,971
75–84 years	9,260	3,710	5,550
85 years and over	4,069	1,214	2,855
Disabled			
Under 45 years	1,764	921	842
45–54 years	1,820	919	902
55–64 years	3,010	1,430	1,580

NOTES: Data for calendar year 2013, as reported on the Part D Denominator File. Numbers may not add to totals because of rounding.

SOURCE: CMS, Office of Information Products and Data Analytics.

Table I.10
Medicare Part D enrollment by CMS region

	Total Medicare Enrollees	Total Part D Enrollees	Percent of Total Enrollees
	In thousands		
All regions[1]	52,456	35,740	68.1
Boston	2,626	1,717	65.4
New York	5,391	3,884	72.0
Philadelphia	5,239	3,382	64.6
Atlanta	11,160	7,717	69.2
Chicago	8,792	6,135	69.8
Dallas	5,710	3,797	66.5
Kansas City	2,398	1,676	69.9
Denver	1,581	998	63.1
San Francisco	7,009	5,074	72.4
Seattle	2,137	1,345	62.9

[1] Foreign residents and unknowns are not included in the regions but included in the total figure.

NOTE: Data for calendar year 2013 as reported on the Part D Denominator file.

SOURCE: CMS, Office of Information Products and Data Analytics.

Table I.11
Medicare Part D enrollment by plan type/CMS region

	Total Part D Enrollees	Total PDP Enrollees	Total MA-PD Enrollees
	In thousands		
All regions[1]	35,740	22,686	13,054
Boston	1,717	1,246	471
New York	3,884	2,140	1,744
Philadelphia	3,382	2,244	1,139
Atlanta	7,717	4,842	2,875
Chicago	6,135	4,443	1,692
Dallas	3,797	2,593	1,204
Kansas City	1,676	1,268	408
Denver	998	620	378
San Francisco	5,074	2,540	2,534
Seattle	1,345	740	605

[1] Foreign residents and unknowns are not included in the regions but included in the total figure.

NOTE: Data for calendar year 2013 as reported on the Part D Denominator file.

SOURCE: CMS, Office of Information Products and Data Analytics.

Table I.16
Medicaid and CHIP enrollment

	Fiscal year					
	1995	2000	2005	2010	2013	2014
	Average monthly enrollment in millions					
Total	34.2	34.5	46.5	53.5	57.4	64.9
Age 65 years and over	3.7	3.7	4.6	4.7	5.2	5.4
Blind/Disabled	5.8	6.7	8.1	9.5	9.6	9.8
Children	16.5	16.2	22.3	26.3	27.9	29.5
Adults	6.7	6.9	10.6	12.1	13.7	19.2
Other Title XIX[1]	0.6	NA	NA	NA	NA	NA
Territories	0.8	0.9	1.0	1.0	1.0	1.0
CHIP	NA	2.0	5.9	5.4	5.9	6.0
	Unduplicated annual enrollment in millions					
Total	43.3	44.2	58.7	67.7	72.8	80.6
Age 65 years and over	4.4	4.3	5.5	5.6	6.1	6.3
Blind/Disabled	6.5	7.5	9.0	10.6	10.7	10.9
Children	21.3	20.9	27.8	33.0	35.0	35.4
Adults	9.4	10.6	15.4	17.6	20.1	27.1
Other Title XIX[1]	0.9	NA	NA	NA	NA	NA
Territories	0.8	0.9	1.0	1.0	1.0	1.0
CHIP	NA	3.4	6.8	8.0	8.6	9.6

[1] In 1997, the Other Title XIX category was dropped and the enrollees therein were subsumed in the remaining categories.

NOTES: Aged and Blind/Disabled eligibility groups include Qualified Medicare Beneficiaries (QMB) and Specified Low-Income Medicare Beneficiaries (SLMB). Children and Adult groups include both AFDC/TANF and poverty-related recipients who are not disabled. Medicaid enrollment excludes Medicaid expansion CHIP programs. CHIP numbers include adults covered under waivers. Medicaid and CHIP figures for FY 2013-2014 are estimates from the President's FY 2015 Budget. Enrollment for Territories for FY 2000 and later is estimated. Numbers may not add to totals because of rounding.

SOURCES: CMS, Office of the Actuary, and Center for Medicaid and CHIP Services.

Table III.3
Benefit outlays by program

	1967	1980	2010	2013
	Amounts in billions			
Annually				
CMS program outlays	$5.1	$57.8	$915	$1,038
Federal outlays	NA	47.2	793	861
Medicare[1]	3.2	33.9	518	587
HI	2.5	23.8	250	273
SMI	0.7	10.1	209	249
Prescription (Part D)	NA	NA	59	65
Medicaid[2]	1.9	23.9	386	437
Federal share	NA	13.2	266	265
CHIP[3]	NA	NA	11	14
Federal share	NA	NA	8	9

[1] The Medicare benefit amounts reflect gross outlays (i.e., not net of offsetting premiums). These amounts exclude outlays for the SMI transfer to Medicaid for premium assistance and the Quality Improvement Organizations (QIOs).

[2] The Medicaid amounts include total computable outlays (Federal and State shares) for Medicaid benefits and outlays for the Vaccines for Children program.

[3] The CHIP amounts reflect both Federal and State shares of Title XXI outlays as reported by the States on line 4 of the CMS-21. Please note that CHIP-related Medicaid expansions began to be financed under CHIP (Title XXI) in FY 2001.

NOTES: Fiscal year data. Numbers may not add to totals because of rounding.

SOURCE: CMS, Office of Financial Management.

Adverse Events

Information in this table is drawn from the FDA Adverse Events Reporting Systems (FAERS) of the U.S. Food and Drug Administration (FDA), as of December 31, 2013. Further information about the FAERS program is available from http://www.fda.gov/Drugs/GuidanceCompliance-RegulatoryInformation/Surveillance/AdverseDrugEffects/ucm070434.htm.

This table represents the number of reports received by FDA and entered into FAERS by type of report since the year 2004 through 2013.

FAERS YEAR	Expedited	DIRECT	Non Expedited Entered	Total Entered	Non Expedited Received	Total Rcvd
2004	161,382	21,654	89,841	272,877	239,271	422,307
2005	212,140	25,311	84,486	321,937	225,183	462,634
2006	219,231	20,979	95,556	335,766	230,065	470,275
2007	230,000	23,035	110,407	363,442	228,206	481,241
2008	274,315	32,900	132,686	439,901	218,205	525,420
2009	330,441	34,172	126,192	490,805	216,264	580,877
2010	409,637	28,951	234,699	673,287	320,341	758,929
2011	499,576	28,064	255,362	783,002	346,745	874,385
2012	585,208	29,162	323,077	937,447	475,993	1,090,363
2013	643,293	28,501	406,235	1,078,029	506,512	1,178,306

Pharmacist Workforce

Information in this table is drawn from a report by the National Center for Health Workforce Analysis of the Health Resources and Services Administration (HRSA) of the U.S. Department of Health and Human Services. Further information about the data, including the modeling procedure used to make the estimates in it, is available from http://bhw.hrsa.gov/healthworkforce/supplydemand/simulationmodeldocumentation.pdf.

Exhibit 1.   Estimated Supply and Demand for Pharmacists in the U.S., 2012 – 2025

	Pharmacists
Supply	
Estimated supply, 2012	264,100
Total supply growth, 2012-2025:	91,200 (35%)
New entrants	160,500
Changing work patterns (e.g., part time to full time hours)	(7,960)
Attrition (e.g., retirements, mortality)	(61,340)
Projected supply, 2025	355,300
Demand	
Estimated demand, 2012	264,100
Total demand growth, 2012-2025:	42,300 (16%)
Changing demographics impact	35,800 (14%)
ACA insurance coverage impact	6,500 (2%)
Projected demand, 2025	306,400
Adequacy of supply, 2025	
Projected supply (minus) projected demand	48,900

Disease Statistics

Information for these tables was drawn from the National Health Interview Survey (NHIS), a survey conducted by the National Center for Health Statistics (NCHS) of the Centers for Disease Control and Prevention (CDC). More information about the NHIS is available from http://www.cdc.gov/nchs/nhis/about_nhis.htm, and more technical information about the data in these tables is available from http://www.cdc.gov/nchs/data/series/sr_10/sr10_260.pdf (pp. 110–117).

Table 1. Frequencies of selected circulatory diseases among adults aged 18 and over, by selected characteristics: United States, 2012

Selected characteristic	All adults aged 18 and over	Selected circulatory diseases[1]			
		Heart disease[2]		Hypertension[4]	Stroke
		All types	Coronary[3]		
		Number in thousands[5]			
Total[6]	234,921	26,561	15,281	59,830	6,370
Sex					
Male	113,071	13,820	8,752	28,940	2,898
Female	121,850	12,741	6,529	30,890	3,472
Age (years)					
18–44	111,034	4,168	980	9,187	635
45–64	82,038	9,939	5,796	27,578	2,293
65–74	23,760	5,792	3,848	12,404	1,505
75 and over	18,089	6,661	4,657	10,661	1,936
Race					
One race[7]	230,994	26,086	15,036	59,039	6,212
White	188,261	22,218	12,715	47,158	4,918
Black or African American	27,943	2,897	1,693	8,964	1,031
American Indian or Alaska Native	1,916	189	109	416	*57
Asian	12,542	743	487	2,391	198
Native Hawaiian or Other Pacific Islander	332	*39	*	110	*
Two or more races[8]	3,926	474	245	791	158
Black or African American, white	778	*39	*	66	*
American Indian or Alaska Native, white	1,611	317	175	460	136
Hispanic or Latino origin[9] and race					
Hispanic or Latino	34,946	2,020	1,280	5,588	642
Mexican or Mexican American	21,741	1,180	752	3,110	392
Not Hispanic or Latino	199,974	24,540	14,002	54,242	5,728
White, single race	156,173	20,345	11,522	41,952	4,315
Black or African American, single race	26,961	2,841	1,650	8,801	1,008
Education[10]					
Less than a high school diploma	28,311	4,607	3,295	10,324	1,553
High school diploma or GED[11]	52,795	7,154	4,483	16,969	1,802
Some college	59,577	7,761	4,412	17,851	1,803
Bachelor's degree or higher	63,036	6,080	2,892	13,525	1,067
Current employment status[12]					
Employed	142,783	8,812	3,539	25,333	1,279
Full-time	114,915	6,616	2,671	20,631	833
Part-time	25,610	1,982	779	4,249	384
Not employed but has worked previously	78,811	16,460	10,932	31,570	4,632
Not employed and has never worked	13,135	1,278	802	2,883	459
Family income[13]					
Less than $35,000	74,224	10,627	6,798	22,315	3,289
$35,000 or more	146,587	14,080	7,353	33,543	2,570
$35,000–$49,999	31,186	3,695	2,209	8,248	880
$50,000–$74,999	39,348	4,190	2,358	9,734	779
$75,000–$99,999	27,052	2,140	1,097	6,183	463
$100,000 or more	49,001	4,055	1,689	9,378	448
Poverty status[14]					
Poor	30,576	3,637	2,427	7,686	1,213
Near poor	38,167	4,910	3,018	10,378	1,472
Not poor	147,021	15,167	8,056	35,686	2,894

See footnotes at end of table.

Table 1. Frequencies of selected circulatory diseases among adults aged 18 and over, by selected characteristics: United States, 2012—Con.

Selected characteristic	All adults aged 18 and over	Selected circulatory diseases[1]			
		Heart disease[2]		Hypertension[4]	Stroke
		All types	Coronary[3]		
Health insurance coverage[15]		Number in thousands[5]			
Under 65:					
Private.	125,065	7,909	3,141	22,517	1,246
Medicaid.	19,101	2,333	1,330	4,888	799
Other.	8,734	1,524	1,155	3,339	425
Uninsured.	39,391	2,323	1,142	5,901	453
65 and over:					
Private.	21,580	6,631	4,400	11,518	1,539
Medicare and Medicaid	2,546	861	664	1,764	417
Medicare only	14,327	3,958	2,733	7,910	1,227
Other.	3,033	946	661	1,685	251
Uninsured.	286	*34	*31	*137	*
Marital status					
Married.	124,149	14,792	8,592	33,615	3,217
Widowed.	14,119	4,277	2,896	8,120	1,276
Divorced or separated.	26,499	3,736	2,317	8,968	1,067
Never married.	52,444	2,656	983	6,348	526
Living with a partner.	17,367	1,060	490	2,725	283
Place of residence[16]					
Large MSA	125,511	12,524	6,907	29,026	2,693
Small MSA.	72,095	8,545	5,110	19,111	2,182
Not in MSA	37,315	5,492	3,264	11,693	1,495
Region					
Northeast	42,760	4,549	2,463	10,126	824
Midwest	53,378	6,397	3,636	13,577	1,406
South.	85,578	10,612	6,468	24,395	2,796
West	53,205	5,003	2,714	11,732	1,344
Hispanic or Latino origin[9], race, and sex					
Hispanic or Latino, male	17,505	929	661	2,459	251
Hispanic or Latina, female	17,442	1,092	619	3,129	392
Not Hispanic or Latino:					
White, single race, male	75,739	11,007	6,935	21,267	1,923
White, single race, female	80,434	9,338	4,587	20,685	2,392
Black or African American, single race, male	12,022	1,223	750	3,529	520
Black or African American, single race, female	14,939	1,618	900	5,272	489

* Estimates are considered unreliable. Data preceded by an asterisk have a relative standard error (RSE) greater than 30% and less than or equal to 50% and should be used with caution. Data not shown have an RSE greater than 50%.

[1]In separate questions, respondents were asked if they had ever been told by a doctor or other health professional that they had: hypertension (or high blood pressure), coronary heart disease, angina (or angina pectoris), heart attack (or myocardial infarction), any other heart condition or disease not already mentioned, or a stroke. A person may be represented in more than one column.

[2]Includes coronary heart disease, angina, heart attack, or any other heart condition or disease.

[3]Includes coronary heart disease, angina, or heart attack.

[4]Persons had to have been told on two or more different visits that they had hypertension or high blood pressure to be classified as hypertensive.

[5]Unknowns for the columns are not included in the frequencies, but they are included in the "All adults aged 18 and over" column. See Appendix I.

[6]Includes other races not shown separately and persons with unknown education, employment status, family income, poverty status, health insurance, and marital status characteristics. Estimates may not add to totals due to rounding.

[7]Refers to persons who indicated only a single race group, including those of Hispanic or Latino origin. See Appendix II.

[8]Refers to persons who indicated more than one race group, including those of Hispanic or Latino origin. Only two combinations of multiple-race groups are shown due to small sample sizes for other combinations.

[9]Refers to persons who are of Hispanic or Latino origin and may be of any race or combination of races. "Not Hispanic or Latino" refers to persons who are not of Hispanic or Latino origin, regardless of race.

[10]Shown only for adults aged 25 and over. Estimates are age-adjusted to the projected 2000 U.S. population as the standard population using four age groups: 25–44, 45–64, 65–74, and 75 and over.

[11]GED is General Educational Development high school equivalency diploma.

[12]"Full-time" employment is 35 or more hours per week. "Part-time" employment is 34 or fewer hours per week. See Appendix II.

[13]Includes persons who reported a dollar amount or who would not provide a dollar amount but provided an income interval. See Appendix I.

[14]"Poor" persons are defined as having income below the poverty threshold. "Near poor" persons have incomes of 100% to less than 200% of the poverty threshold. "Not poor" persons have incomes that are 200% of the poverty threshold or greater. See Appendix I.

[15]Based on a hierarchy of mutually exclusive categories. Adults with more than one type of health insurance were assigned to the first appropriate category in the hierarchy. "Uninsured" includes adults who had no coverage, as well as those who had only Indian Health Service coverage or had only a private plan that paid for one type of service such as accidents or dental care. See Appendix II.

[16]MSA is metropolitan statistical area. Large MSAs have a population of 1 million or more; small MSAs have a population of less than 1 million. "Not in MSA" consists of persons not living in a metropolitan statistical area.

NOTE: Estimates are based on household interviews of a sample of the civilian noninstitutionalized population.

SOURCE: CDC/NCHS, National Health Interview Survey, 2012.

Table 2. Age-adjusted percentages of selected circulatory diseases among adults aged 18 and over, by selected characteristics: United States, 2012

	Selected circulatory diseases[1]			
	Heart disease[2]		Hypertension[4]	Stroke
Selected characteristic	All types	Coronary[3]	Hypertension[4]	Stroke
	Percent[5] (standard error)			
Total[6] (age-adjusted)	10.8 (0.20)	6.1 (0.15)	23.9 (0.29)	2.6 (0.10)
Total[6] (crude)	11.3 (0.22)	6.5 (0.17)	25.5 (0.33)	2.7 (0.11)
Sex				
Male	12.1 (0.32)	7.6 (0.25)	24.7 (0.42)	2.6 (0.16)
Female	9.7 (0.25)	4.8 (0.18)	23.2 (0.37)	2.6 (0.13)
Age[7] (years)				
18–44	3.8 (0.19)	0.9 (0.09)	8.3 (0.28)	0.6 (0.08)
45–64	12.1 (0.39)	7.1 (0.32)	33.7 (0.61)	2.8 (0.19)
65–74	24.4 (0.88)	16.2 (0.75)	52.3 (1.04)	6.3 (0.51)
75 and over	36.9 (1.07)	25.8 (0.92)	59.2 (1.07)	10.7 (0.64)
Race				
One race[8]	10.7 (0.21)	6.1 (0.15)	23.9 (0.29)	2.5 (0.10)
White	10.9 (0.23)	6.1 (0.17)	22.9 (0.32)	2.4 (0.11)
Black or African American	10.8 (0.54)	6.5 (0.43)	32.9 (0.69)	3.9 (0.32)
American Indian or Alaska Native	12.5 (2.35)	8.1 (2.23)	24.8 (2.65)	*4.3 (1.74)
Asian	6.8 (0.63)	4.5 (0.54)	21.2 (0.95)	1.8 (0.33)
Native Hawaiian or Other Pacific Islander	*12.5 (3.90)	*10.3 (3.33)	36.5 (6.50)	*
Two or more races[9]	16.4 (2.22)	9.6 (1.83)	26.8 (2.27)	5.7 (1.29)
Black or African American, white	16.0 (2.50)	*4.8 (2.17)	22.9 (1.97)	*
American Indian or Alaska Native, white	20.2 (3.34)	12.0 (2.58)	27.5 (3.17)	8.2 (2.08)
Hispanic or Latino origin[10] and race				
Hispanic or Latino	7.8 (0.47)	5.3 (0.39)	20.9 (0.63)	2.7 (0.30)
Mexican or Mexican American	7.8 (0.63)	5.4 (0.54)	20.1 (0.82)	2.9 (0.40)
Not Hispanic or Latino	11.2 (0.22)	6.2 (0.16)	24.5 (0.32)	2.6 (0.11)
White, single race	11.4 (0.26)	6.2 (0.18)	23.4 (0.36)	2.4 (0.12)
Black or African American, single race	11.0 (0.55)	6.5 (0.43)	33.2 (0.70)	3.9 (0.32)
Education[11]				
Less than a high school diploma	13.6 (0.61)	9.6 (0.48)	32.2 (0.80)	4.5 (0.35)
High school diploma or GED[12]	11.9 (0.41)	7.3 (0.31)	28.7 (0.58)	3.0 (0.23)
Some college	13.1 (0.42)	7.4 (0.34)	29.2 (0.57)	3.1 (0.21)
Bachelor's degree or higher	10.4 (0.39)	5.1 (0.29)	21.9 (0.53)	1.8 (0.17)
Current employment status[13]				
Employed	8.4 (0.41)	3.7 (0.31)	20.5 (0.49)	1.4 (0.24)
Full-time	8.3 (0.66)	3.6 (0.48)	21.1 (0.71)	0.9 (0.21)
Part-time	9.2 (0.67)	4.0 (0.49)	19.6 (0.86)	2.0 (0.42)
Not employed but has worked previously	14.4 (0.41)	9.0 (0.32)	29.1 (0.50)	4.0 (0.21)
Not employed and has never worked	10.6 (0.94)	6.9 (0.80)	24.7 (1.20)	3.6 (0.54)
Family income[14]				
Less than $35,000	13.2 (0.36)	8.3 (0.27)	28.3 (0.46)	4.1 (0.21)
$35,000 or more	10.0 (0.27)	5.3 (0.20)	22.4 (0.36)	1.9 (0.12)
$35,000–$49,999	10.9 (0.56)	6.4 (0.47)	24.5 (0.68)	2.6 (0.25)
$50,000–$74,999	10.7 (0.48)	6.1 (0.39)	23.9 (0.68)	2.0 (0.23)
$75,000–$99,999	9.0 (0.62)	5.0 (0.49)	22.9 (0.79)	2.2 (0.37)
$100,000 or more	9.3 (0.55)	3.9 (0.39)	19.6 (0.68)	1.0 (0.18)
Poverty status[15]				
Poor	14.0 (0.69)	9.8 (0.61)	29.5 (0.71)	4.8 (0.38)
Near poor	12.6 (0.48)	7.7 (0.38)	27.1 (0.69)	3.7 (0.27)
Not poor	9.9 (0.25)	5.2 (0.18)	22.3 (0.35)	1.9 (0.11)

See footnotes at end of table.

Table 2. Age-adjusted percentages of selected circulatory diseases among adults aged 18 and over, by selected characteristics: United States, 2012—Con.

	Selected circulatory diseases[1]			
	Heart disease[2]			
Selected characteristic	All types	Coronary[3]	Hypertension[4]	Stroke
	Percent[5] (standard error)			
Health insurance coverage[16]				
Under 65:				
Private.	5.7 (0.22)	2.1 (0.13)	15.7 (0.34)	0.9 (0.09)
Medicaid.	12.7 (0.76)	7.4 (0.56)	26.6 (0.93)	4.4 (0.42)
Other.	12.0 (1.13)	8.8 (1.08)	28.3 (1.51)	3.8 (0.77)
Uninsured.	6.2 (0.41)	3.2 (0.29)	16.0 (0.59)	1.2 (0.20)
65 and over:				
Private.	31.3 (1.01)	20.9 (0.88)	54.0 (1.06)	7.4 (0.52)
Medicare and Medicaid	34.2 (2.57)	26.3 (2.31)	69.2 (2.48)	16.5 (1.93)
Medicare only	28.4 (1.15)	19.6 (1.01)	55.6 (1.30)	8.8 (0.74)
Other.	31.6 (2.46)	22.1 (2.12)	55.8 (2.54)	8.3 (1.30)
Uninsured.	*9.8 (3.53)	*7.7 (2.87)	51.6 (8.70)	*
Marital status				
Married.	10.8 (0.29)	6.1 (0.21)	23.5 (0.41)	2.3 (0.14)
Widowed.	16.6 (2.79)	8.5 (1.21)	33.7 (3.22)	4.4 (1.22)
Divorced or separated.	12.1 (0.54)	7.0 (0.40)	28.9 (0.74)	3.6 (0.38)
Never married.	9.3 (0.61)	4.9 (0.51)	23.3 (0.83)	2.6 (0.41)
Living with a partner.	10.3 (1.13)	5.7 (0.93)	22.6 (1.34)	3.2 (0.66)
Place of residence[17]				
Large MSA	10.0 (0.28)	5.5 (0.22)	22.7 (0.37)	2.2 (0.13)
Small MSA.	11.1 (0.36)	6.5 (0.27)	24.6 (0.55)	2.8 (0.20)
Not in MSA	12.7 (0.57)	7.3 (0.38)	27.1 (0.74)	3.4 (0.28)
Region				
Northeast	10.0 (0.46)	5.3 (0.33)	21.4 (0.63)	1.8 (0.21)
Midwest	11.6 (0.48)	6.5 (0.34)	24.1 (0.64)	2.5 (0.20)
South.	11.6 (0.34)	7.0 (0.26)	26.6 (0.50)	3.0 (0.20)
West	9.3 (0.37)	5.1 (0.27)	21.5 (0.50)	2.5 (0.19)
Hispanic or Latino origin[10], race, and sex				
Hispanic or Latino, male	7.7 (0.70)	5.9 (0.64)	19.2 (0.93)	2.4 (0.41)
Hispanic or Latina, female	7.8 (0.63)	4.9 (0.49)	22.3 (0.86)	3.0 (0.45)
Not Hispanic or Latino:				
White, single race, male	13.1 (0.42)	8.0 (0.31)	25.2 (0.54)	2.3 (0.18)
White, single race, female.	9.9 (0.31)	4.5 (0.21)	21.6 (0.44)	2.4 (0.16)
Black or African American, single race, male	10.6 (0.84)	6.6 (0.67)	30.3 (1.08)	4.7 (0.57)
Black or African American, single race, female	11.1 (0.68)	6.3 (0.54)	35.4 (0.95)	3.3 (0.38)

* Estimates are considered unreliable. Data preceded by an asterisk have a relative standard error (RSE) greater than 30% and less than or equal to 50% and should be used with caution. Data not shown have an RSE greater than 50%.

[1]In separate questions, respondents were asked if they had ever been told by a doctor or other health professional that they had: hypertension (or high blood pressure), coronary heart disease, angina (or angina pectoris), heart attack (or myocardial infarction), any other heart condition or disease not already mentioned, or a stroke. A person may be represented in more than one column.

[2]Includes coronary heart disease, angina, heart attack, or any other heart condition or disease.

[3]Includes coronary heart disease, angina, or heart attack.

[4]Persons had to have been told on two or more different visits that they had hypertension or high blood pressure to be classified as hypertensive.

[5]Unknowns for the columns are not included in the denominators when calculating percentages. See Appendix I.

[6]Includes other races not shown separately and persons with unknown education, family income, poverty status, health insurance, and marital status characteristics. Estimates may not add to totals due to rounding.

[7]Estimates for age groups are not age-adjusted.

[8] Refers to persons who indicated only a single race group, including those of Hispanic or Latino origin. See Appendix II.

[9] Refers to persons who indicated more than one race group, including those of Hispanic or Latino origin. Only two combinations of multiple-race groups are shown due to small sample sizes for other combinations.

[10] Refers to persons who are of Hispanic or Latino origin and may be of any race or combination of races. "Not Hispanic or Latino" refers to persons who are not of Hispanic or Latino origin, regardless of race.

[11]Shown only for adults aged 25 and over. Estimates are age-adjusted to the projected 2000 U.S. population as the standard population using four age groups: 25–44, 45–64, 65–74, and 75 and over.

[12]GED is General Educational Development high school equivalency diploma.

[13]"Full-time" employment is 35 or more hours per week. "Part-time" employment is 34 or fewer hours per week. See Appendix II.

[14] Includes persons who reported a dollar amount or who would not provide a dollar amount but provided an income interval. See Appendix I.

[15] "Poor" persons are defined as having an income below the poverty threshold. "Near poor" persons have incomes of 100% to less than 200% of the poverty threshold. "Not poor" persons have incomes that are 200% of the poverty threshold or greater. See Appendix I.

[16]Based on a hierarchy of mutually exclusive categories. Adults with more than one type of health insurance were assigned to the first appropriate category in the hierarchy. "Uninsured" includes adults who had no coverage, as well as those who had only Indian Health Service coverage or had only a private plan that paid for one type of service such as accidents or dental care. See Appendix II.

[17]MSA is metropolitan statistical area. Large MSAs have a population of 1 million or more; small MSAs have a population of less than 1 million. "Not in MSA" consists of persons not living in a metropolitan statistical area.

NOTES: Estimates are based on household interviews of a sample of the civilian noninstitutionalized population. Unless otherwise specified, estimates are age-adjusted to the projected 2000 U.S. population as the standard population using four age groups: 18–44, 45–64, 65–74, and 75 and over. For crude percentages, refer to Table IV in Appendix III.

SOURCE: CDC/NCHS, National Health Interview Survey, 2012.

Table 3. Frequencies of selected respiratory diseases among adults aged 18 and over, by selected characteristics: United States, 2012

Selected characteristic	All adults aged 18 and over	Selected respiratory conditions[1]						
		Emphysema	Asthma		Hay fever	Sinusitis	Chronic bronchitis	Chronic obstructive pulmonary disease
			Ever had	Still has				
					Number in thousands[2]			
Total[3]	234,921	4,108	29,660	18,719	17,596	28,504	8,658	6,790
Sex								
Male	113,071	2,293	12,268	6,770	7,656	10,302	3,199	3,389
Female	121,850	1,815	17,392	11,950	9,940	18,202	5,458	3,400
Age (years)								
18–44	111,034	292	14,929	8,943	6,774	10,889	2,721	512
45–64	82,038	1,853	10,380	6,852	7,965	12,542	3,831	3,074
65–74	23,760	1,121	2,863	1,837	1,882	3,291	1,165	1,646
75 and over	18,089	843	1,489	1,088	975	1,783	940	1,558
Race								
One race[4]	230,994	4,074	28,969	18,206	17,268	28,035	8,456	6,668
White	188,261	3,662	23,594	14,562	14,559	23,351	7,151	6,066
Black or African American	27,943	339	4,098	2,855	1,636	3,393	1,038	497
American Indian or Alaska Native	1,916	*	262	147	161	221	*112	*
Asian	12,542	*36	927	591	903	1,045	156	69
Native Hawaiian or Other Pacific Islander	332	–	*88	*	*	*	–	–
Two or more races[5]	3,926	*35	691	513	328	470	201	122
Black or African American, white	778	*	138	86	*34	60	*	*
American Indian or Alaska Native, white	1,611	*18	308	273	154	268	*138	94
Hispanic or Latino origin[6] and race								
Hispanic or Latino	34,946	178	3,493	2,145	1,964	2,729	789	288
Mexican or Mexican American	21,741	*96	1,539	869	1,174	1,641	425	160
Not Hispanic or Latino	199,974	3,930	26,167	16,575	15,632	25,775	7,869	6,502
White, single race	156,173	3,494	20,459	12,621	12,763	20,859	6,426	5,804
Black or African American, single race	26,961	329	3,985	2,795	1,584	3,329	1,016	484
Education[7]								
Less than a high school diploma	28,311	1,116	3,249	2,463	1,791	2,898	1,445	1,459
High school diploma or GED[8]	52,795	1,472	5,800	3,831	3,357	6,441	2,547	2,232
Some college	59,577	1,049	8,299	5,224	5,404	9,312	2,452	2,100
Bachelor's degree or higher	63,036	423	7,465	4,354	5,871	7,976	1,406	853
Current employment status[9]								
Employed	142,783	629	16,380	9,596	10,997	16,602	3,565	1,238
Full-time	114,915	471	12,920	7,532	8,975	13,455	2,703	817
Part-time	25,610	145	3,262	1,929	1,756	2,873	775	378
Not employed but has worked previously	78,811	3,309	11,611	7,995	5,848	10,746	4,677	5,269
Not employed and has never worked	13,135	167	1,653	1,113	739	1,142	405	281
Family income[10]								
Less than $35,000	74,224	2,244	10,646	7,506	4,350	8,600	3,956	3,588
$35,000 or more	146,587	1,655	17,690	10,442	12,245	18,350	4,233	2,799
$35,000–$49,999	31,186	796	3,988	2,515	2,163	3,960	1,348	1,102
$50,000–$74,999	39,348	431	4,962	2,923	3,097	4,902	1,282	890
$75,000–$99,999	27,052	232	3,301	1,876	2,152	3,412	805	490
$100,000 or more	49,001	196	5,440	3,129	4,834	6,077	799	317
Poverty status[11]								
Poor	30,576	960	5,200	3,836	1,651	3,427	1,876	1,434
Near poor	38,167	1,097	5,001	3,271	2,233	4,600	1,791	1,601
Not poor	147,021	1,665	17,335	10,280	12,294	18,456	4,319	3,067

See footnotes at end of table.

Table 3. Frequencies of selected respiratory diseases among adults aged 18 and over, by selected characteristics: United States, 2012—Con.

Selected characteristic	All adults aged 18 and over	Selected respiratory conditions[1]						
		Emphysema	Asthma		Hay fever	Sinusitis	Chronic bronchitis	Chronic obstructive pulmonary disease
			Ever had	Still has				
		Number in thousands[2]						
Health insurance coverage[12]								
Under 65:								
Private.............................	125,065	673	15,357	9,141	10,311	16,102	3,196	1,236
Medicaid............................	19,101	607	4,017	3,050	1,599	2,424	1,422	990
Other..............................	8,734	441	1,356	927	736	1,559	725	696
Uninsured...........................	39,391	422	4,467	2,590	2,078	3,276	1,191	663
65 and over:								
Private.............................	21,580	843	2,182	1,448	1,291	2,615	1,072	1,423
Medicare and Medicaid	2,546	138	393	297	203	354	218	266
Medicare only	14,327	769	1,431	973	1,151	1,728	640	1,122
Other..............................	3,033	196	284	186	203	364	162	378
Uninsured...........................	286	–	*	–	*	*	*	–
Marital status								
Married..............................	124,149	2,060	13,804	8,525	9,922	15,823	4,026	3,517
Widowed.............................	14,119	714	1,558	1,117	957	1,918	871	1,136
Divorced or separated................	26,499	841	3,910	2,841	2,376	4,180	1,602	1,449
Never married.......................	52,444	274	7,749	4,697	3,074	4,613	1,556	444
Living with a partner.................	17,367	220	2,614	1,518	1,239	1,910	583	232
Place of residence[13]								
Large MSA	125,511	1,678	15,575	9,647	9,606	14,438	4,137	2,710
Small MSA...........................	72,095	1,345	8,862	5,783	5,687	9,164	2,754	2,237
Not in MSA	37,315	1,086	5,223	3,289	2,303	4,902	1,767	1,843
Region								
Northeast	42,760	598	5,686	3,953	3,531	4,736	1,446	1,013
Midwest	53,378	1,165	7,080	4,358	3,462	6,621	2,438	1,860
South...............................	85,578	1,778	10,071	6,280	5,929	12,585	3,449	2,781
West	53,205	567	6,822	4,129	4,674	4,563	1,325	1,135
Hispanic or Latino origin[6], race, and sex								
Hispanic or Latino, male	17,505	98	1,527	745	960	1,126	325	170
Hispanic or Latina, female	17,442	*80	1,966	1,399	1,003	1,603	464	118
Not Hispanic or Latino:								
White, single race, male................	75,739	1,954	8,388	4,571	5,548	7,537	2,423	2,905
White, single race, female..............	80,434	1,541	12,071	8,050	7,216	13,323	4,003	2,899
Black or African American, single race, male	12,022	185	1,506	942	566	1,004	285	224
Black or African American, single race, female	14,939	144	2,479	1,853	1,018	2,325	730	259

* Estimates are considered unreliable. Data preceded by an asterisk have a relative standard error (RSE) greater than 30% and less than or equal to 50% and should be used with caution. Data not shown have an RSE greater than 50%.

– Quantity zero.

[1]Respondents were asked in two separate questions if they had ever been told by a doctor or other health professional that they had emphysema or asthma. Respondents who had been told they had asthma were asked if they still had asthma. Respondents were asked in four separate questions if they had been told by a doctor or other health professional in the past 12 months that they had hay fever, sinusitis, bronchitis, or chronic obstructive pulmonary disease. A person may be represented in more than one column.

[2]Unknowns for the columns are not included in the frequencies, but they are included in the "All adults aged 18 and over" column. See Appendix I.

[3]Includes other races not shown separately and persons with unknown education, employment status, family income, poverty status, health insurance, and marital status characteristics. Estimates may not add to totals due to rounding.

[4]Refers to persons who indicated only a single race group, including those of Hispanic or Latino origin. See Appendix II.

[5]Refers to persons who indicated more than one race group, including those of Hispanic or Latino origin. Only two combinations of multiple-race groups are shown due to small sample sizes for other combinations.

[6]Refers to persons who are of Hispanic or Latino origin and may be of any race or combination of races. "Not Hispanic or Latino" refers to persons who are not of Hispanic or Latino origin, regardless of race.

[7]Shown only for adults aged 25 and over. Estimates are age-adjusted to the projected 2000 U.S. population as the standard population using four age groups: 25–44, 45–64, 65–74, and 75 and over.

[8]GED is General Educational Development high school equivalency diploma.

[9]"Full-time" employment is 35 or more hours per week. "Part-time" employment is 34 or fewer hours per week. See Appendix II.

[10]Includes persons who reported a dollar amount or who would not provide a dollar amount but provided an income interval. See Appendix I.

[11]"Poor" persons are defined as having income below the poverty threshold. "Near poor" persons have incomes of 100% to less than 200% of the poverty threshold. "Not poor" persons have incomes that are 200% of the poverty threshold or greater. See Appendix I.

[12]Based on a hierarchy of mutually exclusive categories. Adults with more than one type of health insurance were assigned to the first appropriate category in the hierarchy. "Uninsured" includes adults who had no coverage, as well as those who had only Indian Health Service coverage or had only a private plan that paid for one type of service such as accidents or dental care. See Appendix II.

[13]MSA is metropolitan statistical area. Large MSAs have a population of 1 million or more; small MSAs have a population of less than 1 million. "Not in MSA" consists of persons not living in a metropolitan statistical area.

NOTE: Estimates are based on household interviews of a sample of the civilian noninstitutionalized population.

SOURCE: CDC/NCHS, National Health Interview Survey, 2012.

Table 4. Age-adjusted percentages of selected respiratory diseases among adults aged 18 and over, by selected characteristics: United States, 2012

Selected characteristic	Emphysema	Asthma — Ever had	Asthma — Still has	Hay fever	Sinusitis	Chronic bronchitis	Chronic obstructive pulmonary disease
			Percent[2] (standard error)				
Total[3] (age-adjusted)	1.6 (0.09)	12.7 (0.25)	8.0 (0.20)	7.3 (0.19)	11.8 (0.24)	3.6 (0.13)	2.7 (0.11)
Total[3] (crude)	1.7 (0.10)	12.6 (0.25)	8.0 (0.20)	7.5 (0.19)	12.1 (0.24)	3.7 (0.13)	2.9 (0.12)
Sex							
Male	2.0 (0.15)	10.9 (0.35)	6.0 (0.26)	6.6 (0.26)	9.0 (0.30)	2.8 (0.18)	3.0 (0.18)
Female	1.3 (0.10)	14.3 (0.35)	9.8 (0.30)	7.9 (0.25)	14.5 (0.34)	4.3 (0.18)	2.5 (0.13)
Age[4] (years)							
18–44.	0.3 (0.05)	13.4 (0.37)	8.1 (0.30)	6.1 (0.26)	9.8 (0.31)	2.5 (0.17)	0.5 (0.08)
45–64.	2.3 (0.21)	12.7 (0.42)	8.4 (0.34)	9.7 (0.34)	15.3 (0.43)	4.7 (0.26)	3.8 (0.23)
65–74.	4.7 (0.40)	12.1 (0.67)	7.8 (0.52)	7.9 (0.53)	13.9 (0.65)	4.9 (0.41)	6.9 (0.49)
75 and over	4.7 (0.49)	8.2 (0.58)	6.0 (0.51)	5.4 (0.50)	9.9 (0.59)	5.2 (0.48)	8.6 (0.68)
Race							
One race[5]	1.6 (0.09)	12.6 (0.26)	7.9 (0.21)	7.3 (0.19)	11.8 (0.24)	3.5 (0.13)	2.7 (0.11)
White.	1.7 (0.10)	12.6 (0.29)	7.7 (0.23)	7.5 (0.22)	12.0 (0.27)	3.6 (0.15)	2.9 (0.13)
Black or African American	1.3 (0.17)	14.5 (0.64)	10.2 (0.53)	5.8 (0.42)	11.9 (0.55)	3.7 (0.30)	1.9 (0.24)
American Indian or Alaska Native	*	12.6 (2.12)	7.1 (1.64)	8.9 (1.93)	10.9 (2.10)	*5.8 (1.94)	*
Asian.	*	7.6 (0.73)	4.9 (0.56)	7.3 (0.71)	8.3 (0.85)	1.4 (0.29)	0.8 (0.21)
Native Hawaiian or Other Pacific Islander	–	*27.2 (8.99)	*17.0 (8.20)	*	*	–	–
Two or more races[6]	*1.2 (0.44)	17.7 (1.85)	12.9 (1.79)	9.3 (1.56)	13.4 (1.76)	5.0 (1.17)	4.2 (1.10)
Black or African American, white	*	16.9 (3.72)	11.4 (3.18)	*6.3 (2.80)	17.1 (2.87)	*2.8 (1.35)	*
American Indian or Alaska Native, white	*1.1 (0.55)	19.3 (3.06)	17.2 (3.44)	9.0 (2.25)	16.2 (2.80)	*8.3 (3.13)	5.9 (1.69)
Hispanic or Latino origin[7] and race							
Hispanic or Latino	0.7 (0.17)	10.4 (0.54)	6.5 (0.45)	5.9 (0.43)	8.3 (0.44)	2.5 (0.28)	1.1 (0.19)
Mexican or Mexican American	*0.7 (0.22)	7.2 (0.57)	4.1 (0.45)	5.9 (0.56)	8.1 (0.55)	2.2 (0.33)	1.2 (0.26)
Not Hispanic or Latino.	1.7 (0.10)	13.3 (0.29)	8.3 (0.24)	7.6 (0.21)	12.5 (0.27)	3.7 (0.15)	2.9 (0.12)
White, single race	1.9 (0.11)	13.4 (0.35)	8.2 (0.28)	8.0 (0.26)	13.0 (0.32)	3.9 (0.18)	3.1 (0.14)
Black or African American, single race	1.3 (0.17)	14.7 (0.65)	10.3 (0.54)	5.8 (0.42)	12.1 (0.57)	3.7 (0.31)	1.9 (0.24)
Education[8]							
Less than a high school diploma	3.5 (0.33)	11.6 (0.66)	8.8 (0.58)	6.3 (0.47)	9.9 (0.58)	4.8 (0.40)	4.6 (0.39)
High school diploma or GED[9]	2.4 (0.20)	10.9 (0.49)	7.2 (0.39)	6.2 (0.37)	11.6 (0.49)	4.5 (0.31)	3.6 (0.24)
Some college	1.7 (0.19)	13.9 (0.49)	8.8 (0.39)	8.8 (0.40)	15.3 (0.50)	4.0 (0.27)	3.5 (0.25)
Bachelor's degree or higher	0.8 (0.12)	11.7 (0.43)	6.8 (0.34)	9.1 (0.40)	12.4 (0.44)	2.3 (0.19)	1.5 (0.16)
Current employment status[10]							
Employed	0.6 (0.12)	11.2 (0.36)	6.5 (0.26)	7.3 (0.30)	11.2 (0.33)	2.6 (0.18)	1.3 (0.20)
Full-time.	0.5 (0.13)	10.8 (0.49)	6.1 (0.26)	7.4 (0.47)	11.0 (0.39)	2.4 (0.26)	*1.2 (0.37)
Part-time	0.7 (0.21)	12.5 (0.76)	7.5 (0.59)	6.8 (0.55)	11.4 (0.71)	3.1 (0.40)	1.8 (0.32)
Not employed but has worked previously	3.1 (0.22)	16.5 (0.56)	11.2 (0.47)	7.2 (0.34)	13.3 (0.46)	5.5 (0.32)	4.9 (0.26)
Not employed and has never worked	1.8 (0.42)	12.8 (1.10)	9.2 (0.96)	6.3 (0.75)	10.2 (0.95)	3.8 (0.60)	2.8 (0.51)
Family income[11]							
Less than $35,000	2.9 (0.20)	14.6 (0.41)	10.3 (0.37)	5.9 (0.25)	11.6 (0.35)	5.3 (0.25)	4.6 (0.23)
$35,000 or more	1.2 (0.11)	12.1 (0.33)	7.1 (0.25)	8.1 (0.27)	12.1 (0.32)	2.9 (0.16)	2.0 (0.13)
$35,000–$49,999	2.2 (0.33)	13.0 (0.72)	8.1 (0.61)	6.8 (0.47)	12.6 (0.69)	4.2 (0.44)	3.2 (0.38)
$50,000–$74,999	1.1 (0.16)	12.6 (0.61)	7.5 (0.45)	7.7 (0.45)	12.1 (0.56)	3.2 (0.30)	2.2 (0.23)
$75,000–$99,999	0.9 (0.23)	12.2 (0.77)	6.8 (0.55)	7.8 (0.60)	12.1 (0.68)	3.2 (0.41)	2.1 (0.36)
$100,000 or more	*0.7 (0.21)	11.0 (0.58)	6.2 (0.46)	9.3 (0.53)	11.8 (0.58)	1.6 (0.24)	0.9 (0.21)
Poverty status[12]							
Poor.	3.6 (0.41)	16.9 (0.70)	12.5 (0.63)	5.7 (0.39)	12.0 (0.58)	6.6 (0.51)	5.5 (0.48)
Near poor	2.9 (0.30)	13.2 (0.60)	8.7 (0.49)	5.9 (0.36)	12.2 (0.53)	4.7 (0.35)	4.2 (0.36)
Not poor	1.1 (0.09)	11.8 (0.32)	7.0 (0.24)	8.1 (0.27)	12.1 (0.32)	2.8 (0.15)	2.0 (0.12)

See footnotes at end of table.

Table 4. Age-adjusted percentages of selected respiratory diseases among adults aged 18 and over, by selected characteristics: United States, 2012—Con.

		Selected respiratory diseases[1]					
		Asthma				Chronic bronchitis	Chronic obstructive pulmonary disease
Selected characteristic	Emphysema	Ever had	Still has	Hay fever	Sinusitis		
			Percent[2] (standard error)				
Health insurance coverage[13]							
Under 65:							
Private.	0.4 (0.06)	12.4 (0.37)	7.3 (0.28)	7.9 (0.28)	12.5 (0.33)	2.4 (0.15)	0.8 (0.08)
Medicaid.	3.3 (0.42)	21.1 (0.96)	16.1 (0.85)	8.5 (0.68)	13.0 (0.79)	7.6 (0.60)	5.5 (0.48)
Other.	3.0 (0.63)	15.5 (1.68)	10.4 (1.41)	8.5 (1.19)	16.3 (1.51)	6.4 (1.11)	5.5 (0.96)
Uninsured.	1.2 (0.20)	11.4 (0.58)	6.6 (0.42)	5.4 (0.39)	8.5 (0.47)	3.1 (0.33)	1.9 (0.25)
65 and over:							
Private.	3.9 (0.39)	9.9 (0.64)	6.6 (0.50)	5.9 (0.46)	12.0 (0.65)	5.0 (0.44)	6.8 (0.53)
Medicare and Medicaid	5.3 (0.98)	15.2 (1.78)	11.5 (1.59)	7.9 (1.34)	13.9 (1.64)	8.5 (1.58)	10.3 (1.63)
Medicare only	5.3 (0.58)	9.9 (0.74)	6.7 (0.64)	7.8 (0.73)	11.8 (0.77)	4.4 (0.50)	7.8 (0.68)
Other.	6.6 (1.38)	9.3 (1.42)	6.1 (1.15)	6.7 (1.41)	11.8 (1.77)	5.4 (1.23)	12.6 (1.79)
Uninsured.	—	*	—	*	*	*	—
Marital status							
Married.	1.4 (0.12)	11.0 (0.34)	6.7 (0.27)	7.5 (0.27)	12.2 (0.35)	3.0 (0.17)	2.5 (0.16)
Widowed.	2.6 (0.44)	12.0 (2.38)	9.1 (2.29)	*8.9 (2.79)	13.6 (2.95)	6.9 (1.75)	5.6 (1.31)
Divorced or separated.	2.6 (0.27)	15.4 (0.77)	11.2 (0.67)	8.7 (0.58)	15.2 (0.76)	5.8 (0.52)	4.4 (0.39)
Never married.	1.4 (0.31)	13.9 (0.60)	8.7 (0.48)	6.5 (0.43)	10.0 (0.49)	3.9 (0.40)	2.2 (0.38)
Living with a partner.	2.2 (0.62)	15.0 (1.14)	9.6 (0.98)	8.1 (0.90)	12.2 (1.04)	3.6 (0.56)	2.5 (0.63)
Place of residence[14]							
Large MSA	1.3 (0.11)	12.4 (0.34)	7.7 (0.27)	7.5 (0.26)	11.3 (0.32)	3.2 (0.18)	2.1 (0.14)
Small MSA.	1.7 (0.17)	12.3 (0.42)	8.0 (0.36)	7.7 (0.37)	12.3 (0.46)	3.6 (0.21)	2.8 (0.20)
Not in MSA	2.4 (0.23)	14.0 (0.76)	8.8 (0.55)	6.0 (0.38)	12.6 (0.59)	4.4 (0.39)	4.1 (0.30)
Region							
Northeast	1.3 (0.16)	13.4 (0.68)	9.2 (0.56)	8.0 (0.50)	10.8 (0.57)	3.2 (0.28)	2.2 (0.24)
Midwest	2.0 (0.21)	13.3 (0.58)	8.1 (0.48)	6.3 (0.36)	12.1 (0.49)	4.4 (0.32)	3.2 (0.28)
South.	1.9 (0.15)	11.8 (0.38)	7.3 (0.30)	6.7 (0.32)	14.3 (0.43)	3.9 (0.23)	3.0 (0.18)
West	1.0 (0.17)	12.9 (0.50)	7.8 (0.38)	8.7 (0.40)	8.4 (0.39)	2.4 (0.20)	2.1 (0.20)
Hispanic or Latino origin[7], race, and sex							
Hispanic or Latino, male	0.9 (0.24)	8.6 (0.67)	4.2 (0.48)	5.6 (0.57)	6.9 (0.57)	1.7 (0.29)	1.3 (0.29)
Hispanic or Latina, female	*0.6 (0.23)	11.8 (0.77)	8.5 (0.70)	6.1 (0.58)	9.6 (0.66)	3.1 (0.43)	0.9 (0.24)
Not Hispanic or Latino:							
White, single race, male	2.2 (0.19)	11.3 (0.46)	6.1 (0.34)	7.1 (0.36)	9.8 (0.40)	3.0 (0.24)	3.4 (0.23)
White, single race, female	1.6 (0.13)	15.4 (0.49)	10.2 (0.41)	8.7 (0.35)	16.1 (0.48)	4.7 (0.25)	2.9 (0.18)
Black or African American, single race, male	1.6 (0.31)	12.6 (0.99)	8.0 (0.77)	4.7 (0.58)	8.3 (0.83)	2.5 (0.39)	2.2 (0.48)
Black or African American, single race, female	1.0 (0.20)	16.4 (0.83)	12.2 (0.75)	6.7 (0.59)	15.1 (0.76)	4.8 (0.45)	1.7 (0.22)

* Estimates are considered unreliable. Data preceded by an asterisk have a relative standard error (RSE) greater than 30% and less than or equal to 50% and should be used with caution. Data not shown have an RSE greater than 50%.

– Quantity zero.

[1] Respondents were asked in two separate questions if they had ever been told by a doctor or other health professional that they had emphysema or asthma. Respondents who had been told they had asthma were asked if they still had asthma. Respondents were asked in four separate questions if they had been told by a doctor or other health professional in the past 12 months that they had hay fever, sinusitis, bronchitis, or chronic pulmonary obstructive disease. A person may be represented in more than one column.

[2] Unknowns for the columns are not included in the denominators when calculating percentages. See Appendix I.

[3] Includes other races not shown separately and persons with unknown education, employment status, family income, poverty status, health insurance, and marital status characteristics. Estimates may not add to totals due to rounding.

[4] Estimates for age groups are not age-adjusted.

[5] Refers to persons who indicated only a single race group, including those of Hispanic or Latino origin. See Appendix II.

[6] Refers to persons who indicated more than one race group, including those of Hispanic or Latino origin. Only two combinations of multiple-race groups are shown due to small sample sizes for other combinations.

[7] Refers to persons who are of Hispanic or Latino origin and may be of any race or combination of races. "Not Hispanic or Latino" refers to persons who are not of Hispanic or Latino origin, regardless of race.

[8] Shown only for adults aged 25 and over. Estimates are age-adjusted to the projected 2000 U.S. population as the standard population using four age groups: 25–44, 45–64, 65–74, and 75 and over.

[9] GED is General Educational Development high school equivalency diploma.

[10] "Full-time" employment is 35 or more hours per week. "Part-time" employment is 34 or fewer hours per week. See Appendix II.

[11] Includes persons who reported a dollar amount or who would not provide a dollar amount but provided an income interval. See Appendix I.

[12] "Poor" persons are defined as having an income below the poverty threshold. "Near poor" persons have incomes of 100% to less than 200% of the poverty threshold. "Not poor" persons have incomes that are 200% of the poverty threshold or greater. See Appendix I.

[13] Based on a hierarchy of mutually exclusive categories. Adults with more than one type of health insurance were assigned to the first appropriate category in the hierarchy. "Uninsured" includes adults who had no coverage, as well as those who had only Indian Health Service coverage or had only a private plan that paid for one type of service such as accidents or dental care. See Appendix II.

[14] MSA is metropolitan statistical area. Large MSAs have a population of 1 million or more; small MSAs have a population of less than 1 million. "Not in MSA" consists of persons not living in a metropolitan statistical area.

NOTES: Estimates are based on household interviews of a sample of the civilian noninstitutionalized population. Unless otherwise specified, estimates are age-adjusted to the projected 2000 U.S. population as the standard population using four age groups: 18–44, 45–64, 65–74, and 75 and over. For crude percentages, refer to Table V in Appendix III.

SOURCE: CDC/NCHS, National Health Interview Survey, 2012.

Table 5. Frequencies of selected types of cancer among adults aged 18 and over, by selected characteristics: United States, 2012

Selected characteristic	All adults aged 18 and over	Males aged 18 and over	Females aged 18 and over	Any cancer	Selected type of cancer[1]		
					Breast cancer	Cervical cancer	Prostate cancer
	Number in thousands[2]						
Total[3]	234,921	113,071	121,850	20,073	3,312	1,330	2,453
Sex							
Male	113,071	113,071	. . .	8,626	*53	–	2,453
Female	121,850	. . .	121,850	11,447	3,259	1,330	–
Age (years)							
18–44	111,034	54,892	56,142	2,265	171	524	*
45–64	82,038	39,761	42,277	7,629	1,242	558	546
65–74	23,760	11,133	12,628	5,014	909	*156	907
75 and over	18,089	7,285	10,804	5,165	989	91	995
Race							
One race[4]	230,994	111,201	119,793	19,712	3,276	1,299	2,439
White	188,261	91,763	96,498	17,897	2,798	1,175	2,026
Black or African American	27,943	12,536	15,407	1,215	314	89	346
American Indian or Alaska Native	1,916	894	1,022	*88	*	*	–
Asian	12,542	5,842	6,700	495	139	*	*67
Native Hawaiian or Other Pacific Islander	332	166	166	*	*	*	–
Two or more races[5]	3,926	1,870	2,057	361	*	*	*14
Black or African American, white	778	348	430	*17	*	–	*
American Indian or Alaska Native, white	1,611	690	921	246	*	*	*
Hispanic or Latino origin[6] and race							
Hispanic or Latino	34,946	17,505	17,442	982	268	115	*67
Mexican or Mexican American	21,741	11,287	10,454	533	159	*73	*33
Not Hispanic or Latino	199,974	95,566	104,408	19,091	3,044	1,215	2,386
White, single race	156,173	75,739	80,434	16,998	2,538	1,079	1,962
Black or African American, single race	26,961	12,022	14,939	1,185	314	70	346
Education[7]							
Less than a high school diploma	28,311	13,724	14,587	2,178	398	181	296
High school diploma or GED[8]	52,795	26,002	26,794	5,430	1,016	378	681
Some college	59,577	26,974	32,603	6,079	951	505	605
Bachelor's degree or higher	63,036	30,724	32,312	6,089	916	192	823
Current employment status[9]							
Employed	142,783	75,363	67,420	7,502	989	631	766
Full-time	114,915	65,257	49,658	5,741	677	519	551
Part-time	25,610	8,952	16,658	1,625	278	101	182
Not employed but has worked previously	78,811	33,571	45,240	11,890	2,089	653	1,671
Not employed and has never worked	13,135	4,034	9,101	670	234	*	*
Family income[10]							
Less than $35,000	74,224	32,711	41,513	6,221	1,162	645	561
$35,000 or more	146,587	74,210	72,376	12,191	1,865	644	1,649
$35,000–$49,999	31,186	15,220	15,966	2,769	486	142	364
$50,000–$74,999	39,348	19,441	19,907	3,164	549	194	542
$75,000–$99,999	27,052	13,853	13,199	2,203	362	*93	225
$100,000 or more	49,001	25,697	23,304	4,055	468	215	519
Poverty status[11]							
Poor	30,576	12,999	17,576	1,767	331	342	99
Near poor	38,167	17,730	20,436	2,780	524	245	219
Not poor	147,021	74,294	72,728	13,409	2,080	646	1,870

See footnotes at end of table.

Table 5. Frequencies of selected types of cancer among adults aged 18 and over, by selected characteristics: United States, 2012—Con.

Selected characteristic	All adults aged 18 and over	Males aged 18 and over	Females aged 18 and over	Any cancer	Selected type of cancer[1]		
					Breast cancer	Cervical cancer	Prostate cancer
Health insurance coverage[12]				Number in thousands[2]			
Under 65:							
Private...............................	125,065	61,101	63,965	6,958	995	565	480
Medicaid.............................	19,101	6,813	12,287	1,067	194	219	*
Other.................................	8,734	4,759	3,975	733	93	*39	*38
Uninsured............................	39,391	21,527	17,864	1,120	131	256	*
65 and over:							
Private...............................	21,580	9,543	12,037	5,729	1,030	131	1,091
Medicare and Medicaid	2,546	805	1,740	561	138	*	*73
Medicare only	14,327	6,183	8,144	3,084	641	*56	533
Other.................................	3,033	1,729	1,304	757	*89	*	202
Uninsured............................	286	130	156	*	–	*	*
Marital status							
Married...............................	124,149	62,674	61,476	11,978	1,683	585	1,778
Widowed..............................	14,119	2,928	11,191	2,989	840	148	242
Divorced or separated...............	26,499	10,987	15,512	2,875	543	275	222
Never married........................	52,444	28,007	24,436	1,338	197	140	*112
Living with a partner.................	17,367	8,356	9,011	882	*49	182	*99
Place of residence[13]							
Large MSA	125,511	60,407	65,103	9,476	1,730	544	1,071
Small MSA...........................	72,095	34,980	37,115	6,488	980	473	863
Not in MSA	37,315	17,684	19,632	4,109	602	313	519
Region							
Northeast	42,760	20,238	22,522	3,561	705	182	486
Midwest	53,378	25,744	27,634	4,559	662	343	571
South.................................	85,578	40,968	44,610	7,336	1,214	496	954
West..................................	53,205	26,121	27,084	4,617	731	308	441
Hispanic or Latino origin[6], race, and sex							
Hispanic or Latino, male	17,505	17,505	...	306	–	–	*67
Hispanic or Latina, female	17,442	...	17,442	677	268	115	–
Not Hispanic or Latino:							
White, single race, male..............	75,739	75,739	...	7,429	*49	–	1,962
White, single race, female............	80,434	...	80,434	9,569	2,489	1,079	–
Black or African American, single race, male	12,022	12,022	...	579	*	–	346
Black or African American, single race, female	14,939	...	14,939	606	310	70	–

... Category not applicable.

* Estimates are considered unreliable. Data preceded by an asterisk have a relative standard error (RSE) greater than 30% and less than or equal to 50% and should be used with caution. Data not shown have an RSE greater than 50%.

– Quantity zero.

[1]Respondents were asked if they had ever been told by a doctor or other health professional that they had a cancer or malignancy of any kind. They were then asked to name the kind of cancer they had. A person may be represented in more than one column.

[2]Unknowns for the columns are not included in the frequencies, but they are included in the "All adults aged 18 and over" column. See Appendix I.

[3]Includes other races not shown separately and persons with unknown education, employment status, family income, poverty status, health insurance, and marital status characteristics. Estimates may not add to totals due to rounding.

[4]Refers to persons who indicated only a single race group, including those of Hispanic or Latino origin. See Appendix II.

[5]Refers to persons who indicated more than one race group, including those of Hispanic or Latino origin. Only two combinations of multiple-race groups are shown due to small sample sizes for other combinations.

[6]Refers to persons who are of Hispanic or Latino origin and may be of any race or combination of races. "Not Hispanic or Latino" refers to persons who are not of Hispanic or Latino origin, regardless of race.

[7]Shown only for adults aged 25 and over.

[8]GED is General Educational Development high school equivalency diploma.

[9]"Full-time" employment is 35 or more hours per week. "Part-time" employment is 34 or fewer hours per week. See Appendix II.

[10]Includes persons in families that reported either a dollar amount or would not provide a dollar amount but provided an income interval. See Appendix I.

[11]"Poor" persons are defined as having income below the poverty threshold. "Near poor" persons have incomes of 100% to less than 200% of the poverty threshold. "Not poor" persons have incomes that are 200% of the poverty threshold or greater. See Appendix I.

[12]Based on a hierarchy of mutually exclusive categories. Adults with more than one type of health insurance were assigned to the first appropriate category in the hierarchy. "Uninsured" includes adults who had no coverage, as well as those who had only Indian Health Service coverage or had only a private plan that paid for one type of service such as accidents or dental care. See Appendix II.

[13]MSA is metropolitan statistical area. Large MSAs have a population of 1 million or more; small MSAs have a population of less than 1 million. "Not in MSA" consists of persons not living in a metropolitan statistical area.

NOTE: Estimates are based on household interviews of a sample of the civilian noninstitutionalized population.

SOURCE: CDC/NCHS, National Health Interview Survey, 2012.

Table 6. Age-adjusted percentages of selected types of cancer among adults aged 18 and over, by selected characteristics: United States, 2012

Selected characteristic	Any cancer	Selected type of cancer[1]		
		Breast cancer	Cervical cancer	Prostate cancer
		Percent[2] (standard error)		
Total[3] (age-adjusted)	8.1 (0.17)	1.3 (0.07)	1.1 (0.09)	2.3 (0.14)
Total[3] (crude)	8.5 (0.19)	1.4 (0.07)	1.1 (0.10)	2.2 (0.14)
Sex				
Male	7.6 (0.24)	*0.1 (0.02)	–	2.3 (0.14)
Female	8.6 (0.24)	2.4 (0.12)	1.1 (0.09)	–
Age[4] (years)				
18–44	2.0 (0.15)	0.2 (0.03)	0.9 (0.13)	*
45–64	9.3 (0.33)	1.5 (0.13)	1.3 (0.17)	1.4 (0.22)
65–74	21.1 (0.85)	3.8 (0.38)	*1.2 (0.38)	8.2 (0.89)
75 and over	28.6 (1.07)	5.5 (0.51)	0.8 (0.25)	13.7 (1.17)
Race				
One race[5]	8.0 (0.17)	1.3 (0.07)	1.1 (0.10)	2.3 (0.14)
White	8.6 (0.20)	1.3 (0.08)	1.2 (0.11)	2.1 (0.15)
Black or African American	4.8 (0.32)	1.2 (0.17)	0.6 (0.15)	3.7 (0.50)
American Indian or Alaska Native	*5.2 (1.65)	*	*	–
Asian	4.7 (0.69)	1.4 (0.37)	*	*2.0 (0.65)
Native Hawaiian or Other Pacific Islander	*	*	*	–
Two or more races[6]	11.0 (1.69)	*1.1 (0.53)	*1.5 (0.74)	*
Black or African American, white	*5.7 (2.76)	*	–	*6.9 (2.16)
American Indian or Alaska Native, white	14.6 (2.83)	*	*	*
Hispanic or Latino origin[7] and race				
Hispanic or Latino	3.8 (0.38)	1.1 (0.24)	0.6 (0.16)	*0.9 (0.32)
Mexican or Mexican American	3.5 (0.46)	1.1 (0.26)	*0.7 (0.24)	*0.9 (0.43)
Not Hispanic or Latino	8.6 (0.19)	1.3 (0.07)	1.1 (0.11)	2.4 (0.15)
White, single race	9.3 (0.22)	1.4 (0.08)	1.3 (0.14)	2.3 (0.17)
Black or African American, single race	4.8 (0.32)	1.3 (0.17)	0.5 (0.12)	3.8 (0.51)
Education[8]				
Less than a high school diploma	6.2 (0.38)	1.0 (0.14)	1.8 (0.27)	1.4 (0.34)
High school diploma or GED[9]	9.0 (0.36)	1.6 (0.16)	2.8 (0.33)	1.4 (0.24)
Some college	10.3 (0.36)	1.6 (0.16)	2.6 (0.33)	1.5 (0.20)
Bachelor's degree or higher	10.2 (0.39)	1.5 (0.15)	2.7 (0.32)	0.6 (0.13)
Current employment status[10]				
Employed	7.3 (0.38)	0.8 (0.11)	1.0 (0.16)	2.5 (0.39)
Full-time	6.9 (0.57)	0.8 (0.20)	1.2 (0.29)	1.9 (0.43)
Part-time	8.0 (0.60)	1.2 (0.24)	0.6 (0.18)	2.9 (0.65)
Not employed but has worked previously	9.7 (0.35)	1.6 (0.11)	1.6 (0.21)	2.3 (0.17)
Not employed and has never worked	5.2 (0.66)	2.2 (0.54)	*	*
Family income[11]				
Less than $35,000	7.5 (0.26)	1.4 (0.11)	1.6 (0.19)	1.7 (0.18)
$35,000 or more	8.5 (0.25)	1.3 (0.10)	0.9 (0.11)	2.6 (0.21)
$35,000–$49,999	8.1 (0.45)	1.4 (0.18)	0.9 (0.23)	2.2 (0.33)
$50,000–$74,999	7.8 (0.44)	1.4 (0.18)	0.9 (0.19)	2.9 (0.42)
$75,000–$99,999	8.9 (0.62)	1.4 (0.25)	*0.7 (0.22)	2.6 (0.57)
$100,000 or more	9.8 (0.55)	1.2 (0.24)	0.9 (0.22)	2.7 (0.47)
Poverty status[12]				
Poor	7.0 (0.46)	1.4 (0.23)	1.9 (0.33)	1.6 (0.39)
Near poor	7.0 (0.35)	1.3 (0.15)	1.2 (0.21)	1.4 (0.24)
Not poor	8.6 (0.23)	1.3 (0.09)	0.9 (0.11)	2.6 (0.19)

See footnotes at end of table.

Table 6. Age-adjusted percentages of selected types of cancer among adults aged 18 and over, by selected characteristics: United States, 2012—Con.

Selected characteristic	Any cancer	Breast cancer	Cervical cancer	Prostate cancer
		Percent[2] (standard error)		
Health insurance coverage[13]				
Under 65:				
Private.	4.8 (0.20)	0.7 (0.07)	0.8 (0.11)	0.6 (0.11)
Medicaid.	5.8 (0.57)	1.1 (0.24)	1.8 (0.40)	*
Other.	6.0 (1.03)	0.9 (0.23)	*0.8 (0.29)	*0.5 (0.19)
Uninsured.	3.0 (0.27)	*0.4 (0.11)	1.4 (0.25)	*
65 and over:				
Private.	26.9 (0.98)	4.8 (0.43)	1.1 (0.29)	11.9 (1.07)
Medicare and Medicaid	22.1 (2.22)	5.5 (1.55)	*	10.9 (3.09)
Medicare only	21.9 (1.05)	4.7 (0.55)	0.7 (0.20)	8.6 (1.09)
Other.	25.1 (2.17)	*2.9 (0.94)	*	12.0 (2.39)
Uninsured.	*	–	*	*
Marital status				
Married.	8.6 (0.25)	1.1 (0.09)	0.9 (0.13)	2.4 (0.18)
Widowed.	14.2 (2.79)	2.1 (0.27)	*3.4 (1.66)	1.8 (0.32)
Divorced or separated.	10.0 (0.56)	1.8 (0.23)	1.9 (0.34)	1.7 (0.30)
Never married.	5.9 (0.53)	1.2 (0.24)	0.8 (0.25)	*1.7 (0.62)
Living with a partner.	9.3 (1.13)	*0.4 (0.18)	*2.2 (0.70)	*3.2 (1.10)
Place of residence[14]				
Large MSA	7.5 (0.24)	1.4 (0.11)	0.8 (0.12)	2.0 (0.20)
Small MSA.	8.4 (0.30)	1.3 (0.11)	1.3 (0.18)	2.5 (0.27)
Not in MSA	9.3 (0.42)	1.3 (0.14)	1.6 (0.26)	2.4 (0.27)
Region				
Northeast	7.7 (0.44)	1.5 (0.19)	0.8 (0.22)	2.5 (0.38)
Midwest	8.2 (0.36)	1.2 (0.12)	1.3 (0.22)	2.4 (0.30)
South.	8.0 (0.25)	1.3 (0.11)	1.1 (0.15)	2.3 (0.25)
West	8.5 (0.38)	1.3 (0.14)	1.1 (0.20)	1.8 (0.22)
Hispanic or Latino origin[7], race, and sex				
Hispanic or Latino, male	2.9 (0.47)	–	–	*0.9 (0.32)
Hispanic or Latina, female	4.7 (0.56)	2.0 (0.41)	0.6 (0.16)	–
Not Hispanic or Latino:				
White, single race, male	8.6 (0.29)	*0.1 (0.03)	–	2.3 (0.17)
White, single race, female.	10.1 (0.33)	2.5 (0.15)	1.3 (0.14)	–
Black or African American, single race, male	5.8 (0.62)	*	–	3.8 (0.51)
Black or African American, single race, female	4.1 (0.39)	2.1 (0.28)	0.5 (0.12)	–

* Estimates are considered unreliable. Data preceded by an asterisk have a relative standard error (RSE) greater than 30% and less than or equal to 50% and should be used with caution. Data not shown have an RSE greater than 50%.

– Quantity zero.

[1]Respondents were asked if they had ever been told by a doctor or other health professional that they had a cancer or malignancy of any kind. They were then asked to name the kind of cancer they had. A person may be represented in more than one column.

[2]Unknowns for the columns are not included in the denominators when calculating percentages; see Appendix I. Further, the denominators for calculating cervical cancer and prostate cancer percentages are sex-specific, while the denominators for calculating breast cancer percentages encompass all adults.

[3]Includes other races not shown separately and persons with unknown education, employment status, family income, poverty status, health insurance, and marital status characteristics. Estimates may not add to totals due to rounding.

[4]Estimates for age groups are not age-adjusted.

[5]Refers to persons who indicated only a single race group, including those of Hispanic or Latino origin. See Appendix II.

[6]Refers to persons who indicated more than one race group, including those of Hispanic or Latino origin. Only two combinations of multiple-race groups are shown due to small sample sizes for other combinations.

[7]Refers to persons who are of Hispanic or Latino origin and may be of any race or combination of races. "Not Hispanic or Latino" refers to persons who are not of Hispanic or Latino origin, regardless of race.

[8]Shown only for adults aged 25 and over. Estimates are age-adjusted to the projected 2000 U.S. population as the standard population using four age groups: 25–44, 45–64, 65–74, and 75 and over.

[9]GED is General Educational Development high school equivalency diploma.

[10]"Full-time" employment is 35 or more hours per week. "Part-time" employment is 34 or fewer hours per week. See Appendix II.

[11]Includes persons who reported a dollar amount or who would not provide a dollar amount but provided an income interval. See Appendix I.

[12]"Poor" persons are defined as having income below the poverty threshold. "Near poor" persons have incomes of 100% to less than 200% of the poverty threshold. "Not poor" persons have incomes that are 200% of the poverty threshold or greater. See Appendix I.

[13]Based on a hierarchy of mutually exclusive categories. Adults with more than one type of health insurance were assigned to the first appropriate category in the hierarchy. "Uninsured" includes adults who had no coverage, as well as those who had only Indian Health Service coverage or had only a private plan that paid for one type of service such as accidents or dental care. See Appendix II.

[14]MSA is metropolitan statistical area. Large MSAs have a population of 1 million or more; small MSAs have a population of less than 1 million. "Not in MSA" consists of persons not living in a metropolitan statistical area.

NOTES: Estimates are based on household interviews of a sample of the civilian noninstitutionalized population. Unless otherwise specified, estimates are age-adjusted to the projected 2000 U.S. population as the standard population using four age groups: 18–44, 45–64, 65–74, and 75 and over. For crude percentages, refer to Table V in Appendix III.

SOURCE: CDC/NCHS, National Health Interview Survey, 2012.

Table 7. Frequencies of selected diseases and conditions among adults aged 18 and over, by selected characteristics: United States, 2012

Selected characteristic	All adults aged 18 and over	Diabetes[1]	Ulcers[1]	Kidney disease[2]	Liver disease[2]	Arthritis diagnosis[3]	Chronic joint symptoms[3]
				Number in thousands[4]			
Total[5]	234,921	21,319	15,435	3,882	3,034	51,830	63,085
Sex							
Male	113,071	10,357	6,871	1,882	1,350	20,878	28,044
Female	121,850	10,961	8,564	2,000	1,684	30,951	35,041
Age (years)							
18–44	111,034	2,673	4,555	633	688	7,582	16,734
45–64	82,038	10,273	6,452	1,548	1,662	24,223	28,984
65–74	23,760	4,863	2,393	746	491	11,111	10,076
75 and over	18,089	3,509	2,035	954	193	8,914	7,291
Race							
One race[6]	230,994	20,949	14,997	3,801	2,878	51,110	61,960
White	188,261	16,188	12,809	2,960	2,472	43,586	52,649
Black or African American	27,943	3,463	1,527	629	265	5,777	6,731
American Indian or Alaska Native	1,916	272	114	*59	*	323	493
Asian	12,542	1,005	531	150	126	1,377	2,015
Native Hawaiian or Other Pacific Islander	332	*21	*	*	*	*46	*73
Two or more races[7]	3,926	369	438	81	156	720	1,125
Black or African American, white	778	*28	*61	*	*	61	132
American Indian or Alaska Native, white	1,611	225	263	*46	133	428	626
Hispanic or Latino origin[8] and race							
Hispanic or Latino	34,946	3,166	1,679	533	422	4,194	6,382
Mexican or Mexican American	21,741	1,953	975	352	220	2,292	3,879
Not Hispanic or Latino	199,974	18,153	13,756	3,349	2,612	47,635	56,703
White, single race	156,173	13,227	11,269	2,480	2,097	39,658	46,870
Black or African American, single race	26,961	3,382	1,489	617	252	5,690	6,537
Education[9]							
Less than a high school diploma	28,311	4,511	2,696	962	540	7,815	8,529
High school diploma or GED[10]	52,795	6,504	3,965	965	851	15,223	16,871
Some college	59,577	6,134	5,042	1,266	969	16,071	18,991
Bachelor's degree or higher	63,036	3,850	3,038	551	606	11,883	15,254
Current employment status[11]							
Employed	142,783	7,763	6,558	795	1,108	20,807	30,702
Full-time	114,915	6,071	5,127	628	880	16,143	24,197
Part-time	25,610	1,553	1,253	157	184	4,129	5,953
Not employed but has worked previously	78,811	12,266	8,299	2,729	1,614	28,765	29,835
Not employed and has never worked	13,135	1,273	566	354	306	2,229	2,510
Family income[12]							
Less than $35,000	74,224	8,959	6,018	2,015	1,382	18,015	22,333
$35,000 or more	146,587	10,899	8,601	1,616	1,456	30,259	36,921
$35,000–$49,999	31,186	3,148	2,273	650	352	7,657	8,991
$50,000–$74,999	39,348	3,286	2,453	468	432	8,621	10,285
$75,000–$99,999	27,052	1,833	1,621	233	253	5,303	6,652
$100,000 or more	49,001	2,632	2,254	265	419	8,678	10,993
Poverty status[13]							
Poor	30,576	3,466	2,431	877	682	6,364	8,375
Near poor	38,167	4,048	3,011	1,016	671	8,574	10,887
Not poor	147,021	11,367	8,710	1,594	1,424	32,235	38,637

See footnotes at end of table.

Table 7. Frequencies of selected diseases and conditions among adults aged 18 and over, by selected characteristics: United States, 2012—Con.

Selected characteristic	All adults aged 18 and over	Selected diseases and conditions					
		Diabetes[1]	Ulcers[1]	Kidney disease[2]	Liver disease[2]	Arthritis diagnosis[3]	Chronic joint symptoms[3]
		Number in thousands[4]					
Health insurance coverage[14]							
Under 65:							
Private.	125,065	7,117	5,900	871	1,057	19,970	28,099
Medicaid.	19,101	2,500	1,675	696	566	4,241	5,608
Other.	8,734	1,337	1,061	234	330	3,143	3,554
Uninsured.	39,391	1,974	2,360	375	395	4,372	8,354
65 and over:							
Private.	21,580	4,075	2,112	754	353	10,764	9,258
Medicare and Medicaid	2,546	798	264	207	103	1,485	1,264
Medicare only	14,327	2,801	1,647	524	167	6,183	5,367
Other.	3,033	659	378	210	*60	1,489	1,381
Uninsured.	286	*23	*	*	*	58	63
Marital status							
Married.	124,149	12,220	8,334	1,974	1,434	29,778	34,829
Widowed.	14,119	2,703	1,616	632	279	7,039	6,263
Divorced or separated.	26,499	3,266	2,536	629	695	7,946	9,050
Never married.	52,444	2,205	1,853	448	450	4,445	8,790
Living with a partner.	17,367	908	1,086	199	170	2,563	4,080
Place of residence[15]							
Large MSA	125,511	10,252	7,020	1,875	1,491	24,320	29,880
Small MSA	72,095	6,662	5,135	1,057	1,016	17,012	20,810
Not in MSA	37,315	4,406	3,280	950	527	10,497	12,395
Region							
Northeast	42,760	3,533	2,049	469	519	9,133	10,121
Midwest	53,378	4,701	3,966	1,049	666	13,003	15,442
South.	85,578	9,091	6,126	1,598	1,102	19,301	23,250
West	53,205	3,994	3,293	767	747	10,392	14,273
Hispanic or Latino origin[8], race, and sex							
Hispanic or Latino, male	17,505	1,551	612	283	153	1,497	2,866
Hispanic or Latina, female	17,442	1,615	1,066	250	269	2,697	3,516
Not Hispanic or Latino:							
White, single race, male.	75,739	6,540	5,190	1,196	962	16,260	21,311
White, single race, female.	80,434	6,686	6,080	1,284	1,134	23,398	25,559
Black or African American, single race, male	12,022	1,484	619	275	107	2,150	2,558
Black or African American, single race, female	14,939	1,898	870	342	146	3,540	3,979

* Estimates are considered unreliable. Data preceded by an asterisk have a relative standard error (RSE) greater than 30% and less than or equal to 50% and should be used with caution. Data not shown have an RSE greater than 50%.

[1]In separate questions, respondents were asked if they had ever been told by a doctor or other health professional that they had an ulcer (including a stomach, duodenal, or peptic ulcer) or diabetes (or sugar diabetes; female respondents were instructed to exclude pregnancy-related diabetes). Responses from persons who said they had "borderline" diabetes were treated as unknown with respect to diabetes. A person may be represented in more than one column.

[2]In separate questions, respondents were asked if they had been told in the last 12 months by a doctor or other health professional that they had: weak or failing kidneys (excluding kidney stones, bladder infections, or incontinence) or any kind of liver condition.

[3]Respondents were asked if they had ever been told by a doctor or other health professional that they had some form of arthritis, rheumatoid arthritis, gout, lupus, or fibromyalgia. Those who answered yes were classified as having an arthritis diagnosis. Respondents were also asked: "During the past 30 days, have you had pain, aching or stiffness in or around a joint?" (excluding back and neck) and, if yes, "Did your joint symptoms first begin more than 3 months ago?" Respondents with symptoms that began more than 3 months ago were classified in this table as having chronic joint symptoms.

[4]Unknowns for the columns are not included in the frequencies, but they are included in the "All adults aged 18 and over" column. See Appendix I.

[5]Includes other races not shown separately and persons with unknown education, employment status, family income, poverty status, health insurance, and marital status characteristics. Estimates may not add to totals due to rounding.

[6]Refers to persons who indicated only a single race group, including those of Hispanic or Latino origin. See Appendix II.

[7]Refers to persons who indicated more than one race group, including those of Hispanic or Latino origin. Only two combinations of multiple-race groups are shown due to small sample sizes for other combinations.

[8]Refers to persons who are of Hispanic or Latino origin and may be of any race or combination of races. "Not Hispanic or Latino" refers to persons who are not of Hispanic or Latino origin, regardless of race.

[9]Shown only for adults aged 25 and over.

[10]GED is General Educational Development high school equivalency diploma.

[11]"Full-time" employment is 35 or more hours per week. "Part-time" employment is 34 or fewer hours per week. See Appendix II.

[12]Includes persons who reported a dollar amount or who would not provide a dollar amount but provided an income interval. See Appendix I.

[13]"Poor" persons are defined as having income below the poverty threshold. "Near poor" persons have incomes of 100% to less than 200% of the poverty threshold. "Not poor" persons have incomes that are 200% of the poverty threshold or greater. See Appendix I.

[14]Based on a hierarchy of mutually exclusive categories. Adults with more than one type of health insurance were assigned to the first appropriate category in the hierarchy. "Uninsured" includes adults who had no coverage, as well as those who had only Indian Health Service coverage or had only a private plan that paid for one type of service such as accidents or dental care. See Appendix II.

[15]MSA is metropolitan statistical area. Large MSAs have a population of 1 million or more; small MSAs have a population of less than 1 million. "Not in MSA" consists of persons not living in a metropolitan statistical area.

NOTE: Estimates are based on household interviews of a sample of the civilian noninstitutionalized population.

SOURCE: CDC/NCHS, National Health Interview Survey, 2012.

Table 8. Age-adjusted percentages of selected diseases and conditions among adults aged 18 and over, by selected characteristics: United States, 2012

Selected characteristic	Diabetes[1]	Ulcers[1]	Kidney disease[2]	Liver disease[2]	Arthritis diagnosis[3]	Chronic joint symptoms[3]
	Percent[4] (standard error)					
Total[5] (age-adjusted)	8.6 (0.18)	6.3 (0.17)	1.6 (0.08)	1.2 (0.07)	20.6 (0.27)	25.6 (0.32)
Total[5] (crude)	9.2 (0.20)	6.6 (0.18)	1.7 (0.08)	1.3 (0.07)	22.1 (0.31)	26.9 (0.34)
Sex						
Male	8.9 (0.26)	6.0 (0.24)	1.7 (0.13)	1.1 (0.09)	17.8 (0.36)	24.1 (0.47)
Female	8.3 (0.23)	6.7 (0.23)	1.5 (0.10)	1.3 (0.10)	23.2 (0.36)	27.0 (0.40)
Age[6] (years)						
18–44.	2.4 (0.16)	4.1 (0.21)	0.6 (0.07)	0.6 (0.07)	6.8 (0.29)	15.1 (0.39)
45–64.	12.7 (0.39)	7.9 (0.33)	1.9 (0.16)	2.0 (0.15)	29.6 (0.56)	35.3 (0.58)
65–74.	21.1 (0.79)	10.1 (0.58)	3.1 (0.32)	2.1 (0.30)	46.8 (1.01)	42.5 (1.00)
75 and over	19.8 (0.90)	11.3 (0.68)	5.3 (0.50)	1.1 (0.25)	49.4 (1.11)	40.4 (1.14)
Race						
One race[7]	8.5 (0.18)	6.2 (0.17)	1.6 (0.08)	1.2 (0.07)	20.6 (0.27)	25.5 (0.32)
White.	7.9 (0.20)	6.5 (0.20)	1.5 (0.09)	1.2 (0.08)	21.1 (0.30)	26.3 (0.37)
Black or African American	13.1 (0.51)	5.6 (0.39)	2.5 (0.26)	0.9 (0.14)	21.4 (0.62)	24.3 (0.78)
American Indian or Alaska Native	17.9 (2.55)	5.9 (1.23)	*3.6 (1.27)	*	18.7 (3.17)	26.3 (2.77)
Asian.	8.9 (0.78)	4.5 (0.60)	1.4 (0.30)	1.1 (0.30)	12.3 (0.84)	16.9 (1.03)
Native Hawaiian or Other Pacific Islander	*7.3 (2.90)	*	*	*	*14.2 (4.46)	*21.7 (7.80)
Two or more races[8]	13.1 (2.06)	11.9 (1.82)	*3.2 (1.07)	4.9 (1.30)	23.1 (2.17)	32.9 (2.53)
Black or African American, white	*10.2 (4.06)	*4.7 (1.90)	*	*	16.3 (4.13)	30.2 (3.91)
American Indian or Alaska Native, white	13.5 (2.71)	15.5 (3.04)	*2.4 (0.90)	7.3 (1.92)	25.2 (3.14)	38.1 (3.69)
Hispanic or Latino origin[9] and race						
Hispanic or Latino	12.2 (0.64)	5.4 (0.42)	1.9 (0.23)	1.4 (0.19)	16.1 (0.61)	21.1 (0.68)
Mexican or Mexican American	13.1 (0.86)	5.3 (0.52)	2.1 (0.33)	1.3 (0.25)	15.6 (0.82)	21.8 (0.90)
Not Hispanic or Latino.	8.2 (0.19)	6.5 (0.19)	1.5 (0.08)	1.2 (0.07)	21.4 (0.30)	26.5 (0.36)
White, single race.	7.3 (0.21)	6.7 (0.23)	1.4 (0.10)	1.2 (0.09)	22.1 (0.35)	27.6 (0.42)
Black or African American, single race	13.2 (0.52)	5.6 (0.40)	2.5 (0.26)	0.9 (0.14)	21.6 (0.63)	24.4 (0.80)
Education[10]						
Less than a high school diploma	14.3 (0.64)	8.9 (0.54)	2.9 (0.29)	1.9 (0.23)	23.8 (0.76)	27.9 (0.81)
High school diploma or GED[11]	11.1 (0.43)	7.1 (0.36)	1.6 (0.17)	1.4 (0.16)	25.7 (0.57)	29.7 (0.67)
Some college	10.0 (0.38)	8.3 (0.39)	2.1 (0.19)	1.6 (0.17)	26.0 (0.57)	30.7 (0.64)
Bachelor's degree or higher	6.2 (0.30)	4.9 (0.28)	1.0 (0.13)	0.9 (0.12)	19.0 (0.49)	24.1 (0.57)
Current employment status[12]						
Employed	6.7 (0.37)	5.2 (0.31)	0.7 (0.11)	0.7 (0.08)	17.0 (0.47)	22.3 (0.50)
Full-time.	6.8 (0.59)	5.0 (0.47)	0.9 (0.25)	0.7 (0.10)	16.0 (0.68)	21.9 (0.70)
Part-time	7.3 (0.62)	5.5 (0.52)	0.7 (0.18)	0.7 (0.16)	18.7 (0.83)	24.6 (0.96)
Not employed but has worked previously	11.7 (0.37)	9.3 (0.38)	2.6 (0.19)	1.9 (0.15)	27.2 (0.54)	32.1 (0.62)
Not employed and has never worked	11.8 (1.03)	5.0 (0.65)	3.5 (0.71)	3.1 (0.71)	19.3 (1.14)	22.0 (1.32)
Family income[13]						
Less than $35,000.	11.8 (0.34)	7.9 (0.30)	2.6 (0.16)	1.9 (0.14)	22.8 (0.44)	29.4 (0.52)
$35,000 or more	7.3 (0.23)	5.8 (0.22)	1.2 (0.10)	1.0 (0.09)	20.1 (0.36)	24.2 (0.40)
$35,000–$49,999	9.4 (0.55)	7.0 (0.50)	2.0 (0.28)	1.1 (0.16)	22.6 (0.72)	27.6 (0.80)
$50,000–$74,999	7.9 (0.43)	6.2 (0.39)	1.2 (0.16)	1.0 (0.17)	21.0 (0.66)	25.1 (0.69)
$75,000–$99,999	7.1 (0.53)	6.1 (0.59)	1.2 (0.29)	0.8 (0.17)	19.8 (0.76)	24.2 (0.89)
$100,000 or more	5.5 (0.44)	4.8 (0.39)	0.6 (0.15)	1.0 (0.24)	17.6 (0.68)	21.7 (0.75)
Poverty status[14]						
Poor.	13.7 (0.61)	8.7 (0.49)	3.4 (0.32)	2.4 (0.26)	24.3 (0.74)	30.1 (0.85)
Near poor	11.0 (0.50)	7.9 (0.44)	2.7 (0.28)	1.8 (0.21)	22.4 (0.63)	28.7 (0.77)
Not poor	7.1 (0.21)	5.7 (0.21)	1.1 (0.09)	0.9 (0.08)	20.0 (0.34)	24.5 (0.39)

See footnotes at end of table.

Table 8. Age-adjusted percentages of selected diseases and conditions among adults aged 18 and over, by selected characteristics: United States, 2012—Con.

Selected characteristic	Diabetes[1]	Ulcers[1]	Kidney disease[2]	Liver disease[2]	Arthritis diagnosis[3]	Chronic joint symptoms[3]
			Percent[4] (standard error)			
Health insurance coverage[15]						
Under 65:						
Private	5.0 (0.20)	4.5 (0.20)	0.6 (0.08)	0.8 (0.07)	14.0 (0.33)	20.7 (0.40)
Medicaid	13.9 (0.78)	9.0 (0.64)	3.8 (0.45)	3.1 (0.40)	23.1 (0.95)	30.2 (1.03)
Other	10.4 (1.14)	8.5 (0.94)	2.0 (0.45)	2.5 (0.44)	26.6 (1.64)	33.6 (1.89)
Uninsured	5.5 (0.35)	6.1 (0.42)	1.0 (0.18)	1.1 (0.15)	11.9 (0.50)	22.1 (0.72)
65 and over:						
Private	19.3 (0.82)	9.8 (0.59)	3.6 (0.38)	1.6 (0.28)	50.0 (1.05)	42.9 (1.06)
Medicare and Medicaid	32.2 (2.39)	10.3 (1.48)	8.1 (1.28)	4.0 (0.98)	58.4 (2.49)	49.7 (2.68)
Medicare only	20.0 (1.05)	11.5 (0.84)	3.8 (0.52)	1.2 (0.31)	43.4 (1.28)	37.4 (1.26)
Other	22.6 (2.33)	12.7 (1.83)	7.0 (1.37)	*2.0 (0.81)	48.9 (2.65)	45.4 (2.82)
Uninsured	*9.1 (4.02)	*	*	*	28.1 (7.48)	29.6 (7.36)
Marital status						
Married	8.5 (0.26)	6.3 (0.23)	1.5 (0.12)	1.0 (0.09)	20.7 (0.38)	25.2 (0.46)
Widowed	11.5 (1.62)	7.8 (1.64)	2.0 (0.43)	1.1 (0.32)	34.1 (3.90)	33.0 (3.34)
Divorced or separated	10.2 (0.47)	9.0 (0.59)	2.1 (0.24)	2.0 (0.25)	24.8 (0.78)	29.6 (0.80)
Never married	8.7 (0.57)	4.5 (0.36)	1.7 (0.32)	1.3 (0.17)	16.6 (0.73)	24.1 (0.80)
Living with a partner	9.1 (1.16)	7.2 (0.85)	1.4 (0.31)	1.2 (0.32)	21.3 (1.30)	28.7 (1.43)
Place of residence[16]						
Large MSA	8.1 (0.25)	5.5 (0.23)	1.5 (0.11)	1.1 (0.10)	18.8 (0.35)	23.2 (0.42)
Small MSA	8.6 (0.34)	6.8 (0.32)	1.4 (0.12)	1.3 (0.13)	21.8 (0.49)	27.4 (0.61)
Not in MSA	10.4 (0.42)	8.2 (0.44)	2.2 (0.24)	1.3 (0.14)	24.6 (0.79)	30.6 (0.90)
Region						
Northeast	7.6 (0.40)	4.6 (0.38)	1.0 (0.14)	1.1 (0.18)	19.3 (0.57)	21.8 (0.75)
Midwest	8.4 (0.39)	7.2 (0.37)	1.9 (0.20)	1.2 (0.13)	23.1 (0.66)	27.8 (0.75)
South	10.0 (0.32)	6.9 (0.31)	1.8 (0.14)	1.2 (0.10)	20.9 (0.42)	25.8 (0.49)
West	7.3 (0.32)	6.1 (0.31)	1.4 (0.16)	1.3 (0.16)	18.9 (0.49)	26.1 (0.65)
Hispanic or Latino origin[9], race, and sex						
Hispanic or Latino, male	12.5 (0.92)	4.2 (0.57)	2.3 (0.40)	1.0 (0.22)	12.2 (0.81)	19.0 (1.03)
Hispanic or Latina, female	11.9 (0.77)	6.7 (0.62)	1.6 (0.25)	1.7 (0.31)	19.3 (0.85)	22.9 (0.92)
Not Hispanic or Latino:						
White, single race, male	7.7 (0.30)	6.5 (0.32)	1.5 (0.15)	1.2 (0.12)	19.2 (0.47)	26.4 (0.61)
White, single race, female	7.1 (0.28)	7.0 (0.30)	1.4 (0.12)	1.3 (0.13)	24.9 (0.47)	28.6 (0.54)
Black or African American, single race, male	13.1 (0.82)	5.6 (0.63)	2.6 (0.47)	0.8 (0.18)	18.9 (0.94)	21.6 (1.35)
Black or African American, single race, female	13.1 (0.68)	5.8 (0.51)	2.4 (0.33)	1.0 (0.19)	23.7 (0.81)	26.5 (0.93)

* Estimates are considered unreliable. Data preceded by an asterisk have a relative standard error (RSE) greater than 30% and less than or equal to 50% and should be used with caution. Data not shown have an RSE greater than 50%.

[1]In separate questions, respondents were asked if they had ever been told by a doctor or other health professional that they had an ulcer (including a stomach, duodenal, or peptic ulcer) or diabetes (or sugar diabetes; female respondents were instructed to exclude pregnancy-related diabetes). Responses from persons who said they had "borderline" diabetes were treated as unknown with respect to diabetes. A person may be represented in more than one column.

[2]In separate questions, respondents were asked if they had been told in the last 12 months by a doctor or other health professional that they had: weak or failing kidneys (excluding kidney stones, bladder infections, or incontinence) or any kind of liver condition.

[3]Respondents were asked if they had ever been told by a doctor or other health professional that they had some form of arthritis, rheumatoid arthritis, gout, lupus, or fibromyalgia. Those who answered yes were classified as having an arthritis diagnosis. Respondents were also asked: "During the past 30 days, have you had pain, aching or stiffness in or around a joint?" (excluding back and neck) and, if yes, "Did your joint symptoms first begin more than 3 months ago?" Respondents with symptoms that began more than 3 months ago were classified in this table as having chronic joint symptoms.

[4]Unknowns for the columns are not included in the denominators when calculating percentages. See Appendix I.

[5]Includes other races not shown separately and persons with unknown education, employment status, family income, poverty status, health insurance, and marital status characteristics. Estimates may not add to totals due to rounding.

[6]Estimates for age groups are not age-adjusted.

[7]Refers to persons who indicated only a single race group, including those of Hispanic or Latino origin. See Appendix II.

[8]Refers to persons who indicated more than one race group, including those of Hispanic or Latino origin. Only two combinations of multiple-race groups are shown due to small sample sizes for other combinations.

[9]Refers to persons who are of Hispanic or Latino origin and may be of any race or combination of races. "Not Hispanic or Latino" refers to persons who are not of Hispanic or Latino origin, regardless of race.

[10]Shown only for adults aged 25 and over. Estimates are age-adjusted to the projected 2000 U.S. population as the standard population and using four age groups: 25–44, 45–64, 65–74, and 75 and over.

[11]GED is General Educational Development high school equivalency diploma.

[12]"Full-time" employment is 35 or more hours per week. "Part-time" employment is 34 or fewer hours per week. See Appendix II.

[13]Includes persons who reported a dollar amount or who would not provide a dollar amount but provided an income interval. See Appendix I.

[14]"Poor" persons are defined as having income below the poverty threshold. "Near poor" persons have incomes of 100% to less than 200% of the poverty threshold. "Not poor" persons have incomes that are 200% of the poverty threshold or greater. See Appendix I.

[15]Based on a hierarchy of mutually exclusive categories. Adults with more than one type of health insurance were assigned to the first appropriate category in the hierarchy. "Uninsured" includes adults who had no coverage, as well as those who had only Indian Health Service coverage or had only a private plan that paid for one type of service such as accidents or dental care. See Appendix II.

[16]MSA is metropolitan statistical area. Large MSAs have a population of 1 million or more; small MSAs have a population of less than 1 million. "Not in MSA" consists of persons not living in a metropolitan statistical area.

NOTES: Estimates are based on household interviews of a sample of the civilian noninstitutionalized population. Unless otherwise specified, estimates are age-adjusted to the projected 2000 U.S. population as the standard population using four age groups: 18–44, 45–64, 65–74, and 75 and over. For crude percentages, refer to Table VII in Appendix III.

SOURCE: CDC/NCHS, National Health Interview Survey, 2012.

Table 9. Frequencies of migraines or pain in neck, lower back, face, or jaw among adults aged 18 and over, by selected characteristics: United States, 2012

Selected characteristic	All adults aged 18 and over	Migraines or severe headaches[1]	Pain in neck[2]	Pain in lower back[3]	Pain in face or jaw[4]
		Number in thousands[5]			
Total[6]	234,921	32,453	33,515	65,823	11,326
Sex					
Male	113,071	10,156	13,102	29,124	3,677
Female	121,850	22,296	20,414	36,699	7,649
Age (years)					
18–44	111,034	18,920	12,528	26,611	5,457
45–64	82,038	11,136	15,053	26,495	4,296
65–74	23,760	1,545	3,452	7,104	963
75 and over	18,089	851	2,482	5,613	611
Race					
One race[7]	230,994	31,587	32,720	64,290	11,002
White	188,261	26,040	27,925	54,218	9,483
Black or African American	27,943	3,972	3,003	6,996	985
American Indian or Alaska Native	1,916	338	352	549	154
Asian	12,542	1,162	1,384	2,412	346
Native Hawaiian or Other Pacific Islander	332	*76	*56	115	*
Two or more races[8]	3,926	865	796	1,533	325
Black or African American, white	778	117	100	264	*52
American Indian or Alaska Native, white	1,611	481	441	825	224
Hispanic or Latino origin[9] and race					
Hispanic or Latino	34,946	4,689	4,573	8,940	1,490
Mexican or Mexican American	21,741	2,689	2,569	5,143	871
Not Hispanic or Latino	199,974	27,764	28,942	56,884	9,836
White, single race	156,173	21,803	23,763	45,999	8,177
Black or African American, single race	26,961	3,813	2,888	6,786	966
Education[10]					
Less than a high school diploma	28,311	4,394	4,795	9,480	1,461
High school diploma or GED[11]	52,795	6,542	8,295	16,756	2,413
Some college	59,577	9,684	10,528	18,982	3,663
Bachelor's degree or higher	63,036	7,014	7,826	14,663	2,385
Current employment status[12]					
Employed	142,783	18,306	17,476	35,029	5,646
Full-time	114,915	14,152	14,032	27,730	4,256
Part-time	25,610	3,741	3,088	6,627	1,237
Not employed but has worked previously	78,811	12,267	14,827	28,139	5,184
Not employed and has never worked	13,135	1,875	1,201	2,630	493
Family income[13]					
Less than $35,000	74,224	12,712	12,597	24,638	4,762
$35,000 or more	146,587	18,249	19,133	37,918	6,078
$35,000–$49,999	31,186	4,365	4,661	9,228	1,496
$50,000–$74,999	39,348	5,151	5,412	11,167	1,825
$75,000–$99,999	27,052	3,403	3,235	6,583	1,021
$100,000 or more	49,001	5,330	5,824	10,940	1,735
Poverty status[14]					
Poor	30,576	6,504	5,358	10,566	2,277
Near poor	38,167	6,162	6,330	12,035	2,380
Not poor	147,021	17,402	19,318	38,168	5,884

See footnotes at end of table.

Table 9. Frequencies of migraines or pain in neck, lower back, face, or jaw among adults aged 18 and over, by selected characteristics: United States, 2012—Con.

Selected characteristic	All adults aged 18 and over	Migraines or severe headaches[1]	Pain in neck[2]	Pain in lower back[3]	Pain in face or jaw[4]
Health insurance coverage[15]	Number in thousands[5]				
Under 65:					
Private	125,065	16,630	16,042	30,735	5,254
Medicaid	19,101	4,749	3,913	7,745	1,675
Other	8,734	2,073	2,179	3,737	736
Uninsured	39,391	6,552	5,400	10,716	2,059
65 and over:					
Private	21,580	1,029	3,128	6,422	739
Medicare and Medicaid	2,546	249	571	1,011	202
Medicare only	14,327	857	1,796	4,183	520
Other	3,033	222	406	1,010	99
Uninsured	286	*40	*29	*	*
Marital status					
Married	124,149	15,509	17,789	34,811	5,138
Widowed	14,119	1,192	2,346	4,759	731
Divorced or separated	26,499	4,566	5,199	9,293	1,929
Never married	52,444	7,874	5,438	11,464	2,508
Living with a partner	17,367	3,272	2,713	5,416	1,010
Place of residence[16]					
Large MSA	125,511	16,380	16,876	33,392	5,679
Small MSA	72,095	10,453	10,806	20,742	3,611
Not in MSA	37,315	5,619	5,834	11,689	2,037
Region					
Northeast	42,760	5,100	5,390	11,332	1,665
Midwest	53,378	8,288	8,122	15,079	2,986
South	85,578	11,617	11,471	24,218	4,049
West	53,205	7,449	8,533	15,193	2,627
Hispanic or Latino origin[9], race, and sex					
Hispanic or Latino, male	17,505	1,354	1,769	4,172	601
Hispanic or Latina, female	17,442	3,336	2,805	4,767	889
Not Hispanic or Latino:					
White, single race, male	75,739	7,142	9,546	20,945	2,588
White, single race, female	80,434	14,661	14,217	25,054	5,589
Black or African American, single race, male	12,022	931	904	2,393	284
Black or African American, single race, female	14,939	2,882	1,984	4,393	682

* Estimates are considered unreliable. Data preceded by an asterisk have a relative standard error (RSE) greater than 30% and less than or equal to 50% and should be used with caution. Data not shown have an RSE greater than 50%.

[1]Respondents were asked, "During the past three months, did you have a severe headache or migraine?" Respondents were instructed to report pain that had lasted a whole day or more, and conversely, not to report fleeting or minor aches or pains. Persons may be represented in more than one column.

[2]Respondents were asked, "During the past three months, did you have neck pain?" Respondents were instructed to report pain that had lasted a whole day or more, and conversely, not to report fleeting or minor aches or pains. Persons may be represented in more than one column.

[3]Respondents were asked, "During the past three months, did you have low back pain?" Respondents were instructed to report pain that had lasted a whole day or more, and conversely, not to report fleeting or minor aches or pains. Persons may be represented in more than one column.

[4]Respondents were asked, "During the past three months, did you have facial ache or pain in the jaw muscles or the joint in front of the ear?" Respondents were instructed to report pain that had lasted a whole day or more, and conversely, not to report fleeting or minor aches or pains. Persons may be represented in more than one column.

[5]Unknowns for the columns are not included in the frequencies, but they are included in the "All adults aged 18 and over" column. See Appendix I.

[6]Includes other races not shown separately and persons with unknown education, employment status, family income, poverty status, health insurance, and marital status characteristics. Estimates may not add to totals due to rounding.

[7]Refers to persons who indicated only a single race group, including those of Hispanic or Latino origin. See Appendix II.

[8]Refers to persons who indicated more than one race group, including those of Hispanic or Latino origin. Only two combinations of multiple-race groups are shown due to small sample sizes for other combinations.

[9]Refers to persons who are of Hispanic or Latino origin and may be of any race or combination of races. "Not Hispanic or Latino" refers to persons who are not of Hispanic or Latino origin, regardless of race.

[10]Shown only for adults aged 25 and over.

[11]GED is General Educational Development high school equivalency diploma.

[12]"Full-time" employment is 35 or more hours per week. "Part-time" employment is 34 or fewer hours per week. See Appendix II.

[13]Includes persons who reported a dollar amount or who would not provide a dollar amount but provided an income interval. See Appendix I.

[14]"Poor" persons are defined as having income below the poverty threshold. "Near poor" persons have incomes of 100% to less than 200% of the poverty threshold. "Not poor" persons have incomes that are 200% of the poverty threshold or greater. See Appendix I.

[15]Based on a hierarchy of mutually exclusive categories. Adults with more than one type of health insurance were assigned to the first appropriate category in the hierarchy. "Uninsured" includes adults who had no coverage, as well as those who had only Indian Health Service coverage or had only a private plan that paid for one type of service such as accidents or dental care. See Appendix II.

[16]MSA is metropolitan statistical area. Large MSAs have a population of 1 million or more; small MSAs have a population of less than 1 million. "Not in MSA" consists of persons not living in a metropolitan statistical area.

NOTE: Estimates are based on household interviews of a sample of the civilian noninstitutionalized population.

SOURCE: CDC/NCHS, National Health Interview Survey, 2012.

Table 10. Age-adjusted percentages of migraines or pain in neck, lower back, face, or jaw among adults aged 18 and over, by selected characteristics: United States, 2012

Selected characteristic	Migraines or severe headaches[1]	Pain in neck[2]	Pain in lower back[3]	Pain in face or jaw[4]
	Percent[5] (standard error)			
Total[6] (age-adjusted)	14.1 (0.26)	13.9 (0.25)	27.6 (0.34)	4.8 (0.15)
Total[6] (crude)	13.8 (0.26)	14.3 (0.26)	28.0 (0.34)	4.8 (0.15)
Sex				
Male	9.0 (0.32)	11.3 (0.33)	25.4 (0.47)	3.2 (0.20)
Female	18.9 (0.40)	16.3 (0.36)	29.6 (0.46)	6.3 (0.23)
Age[7] (years)				
18–44	17.1 (0.40)	11.3 (0.32)	24.0 (0.48)	4.9 (0.22)
45–64	13.6 (0.43)	18.4 (0.46)	32.3 (0.56)	5.2 (0.25)
65–74	6.5 (0.48)	14.5 (0.66)	29.9 (0.90)	4.1 (0.36)
75 and over	4.7 (0.47)	13.7 (0.74)	31.1 (1.06)	3.4 (0.40)
Race				
One race[8]	14.0 (0.26)	13.8 (0.25)	27.4 (0.34)	4.8 (0.15)
White	14.3 (0.30)	14.4 (0.30)	28.3 (0.39)	5.1 (0.18)
Black or African American	14.0 (0.62)	10.7 (0.52)	24.8 (0.73)	3.5 (0.28)
American Indian or Alaska Native	17.7 (2.96)	18.0 (2.70)	29.3 (2.96)	7.8 (1.74)
Asian	9.2 (0.78)	11.4 (0.88)	19.7 (1.09)	2.8 (0.41)
Native Hawaiian or Other Pacific Islander	21.2 (6.12)	17.0 (5.09)	34.0 (8.19)	*
Two or more races[9]	21.2 (2.18)	20.9 (2.20)	41.2 (2.74)	8.4 (1.33)
Black or African American, white	15.9 (3.77)	21.1 (3.57)	28.9 (4.47)	*5.8 (2.53)
American Indian or Alaska Native, white	30.2 (3.92)	27.1 (3.67)	50.8 (4.15)	13.3 (2.66)
Hispanic or Latino origin[10] and race				
Hispanic or Latino	12.9 (0.56)	13.9 (0.59)	26.5 (0.75)	4.4 (0.34)
Mexican or Mexican American	11.9 (0.65)	13.1 (0.77)	24.6 (0.91)	4.2 (0.44)
Not Hispanic or Latino	14.5 (0.29)	14.0 (0.28)	27.8 (0.37)	5.0 (0.17)
White, single race	14.9 (0.34)	14.7 (0.33)	28.8 (0.45)	5.4 (0.21)
Black or African American, single race	14.0 (0.63)	10.7 (0.53)	24.9 (0.74)	3.6 (0.29)
Education[11]				
Less than a high school diploma	16.6 (0.77)	16.7 (0.68)	33.3 (0.90)	5.1 (0.41)
High school diploma or GED[12]	12.9 (0.48)	15.2 (0.54)	31.1 (0.72)	4.7 (0.31)
Some college	16.5 (0.53)	17.4 (0.51)	31.6 (0.66)	6.1 (0.33)
Bachelor's degree or higher	11.0 (0.41)	12.2 (0.42)	23.2 (0.56)	3.8 (0.23)
Current employment status[13]				
Employed	11.8 (0.30)	11.5 (0.32)	24.2 (0.47)	3.7 (0.17)
Full-time	11.4 (0.38)	11.1 (0.35)	23.6 (0.65)	3.4 (0.19)
Part-time	13.6 (0.78)	12.1 (0.67)	25.9 (0.95)	4.6 (0.44)
Not employed but has worked previously	20.1 (0.61)	18.9 (0.54)	35.5 (0.67)	7.6 (0.39)
Not employed and has never worked	15.7 (1.22)	10.4 (0.91)	21.9 (1.25)	4.3 (0.64)
Family income[14]				
Less than $35,000	17.8 (0.44)	17.0 (0.42)	33.2 (0.54)	6.5 (0.29)
$35,000 or more	12.5 (0.33)	12.6 (0.31)	25.6 (0.44)	4.1 (0.19)
$35,000–$49,999	14.5 (0.74)	14.8 (0.74)	29.3 (0.87)	4.9 (0.42)
$50,000–$74,999	13.3 (0.67)	13.4 (0.57)	27.9 (0.77)	4.6 (0.34)
$75,000–$99,999	12.3 (0.72)	11.6 (0.65)	24.5 (0.97)	3.8 (0.40)
$100,000 or more	10.7 (0.56)	11.2 (0.53)	21.9 (0.77)	3.6 (0.37)
Poverty status[15]				
Poor	20.5 (0.72)	18.3 (0.70)	35.7 (0.85)	7.6 (0.49)
Near poor	16.4 (0.67)	16.8 (0.62)	31.9 (0.77)	6.3 (0.40)
Not poor	12.2 (0.32)	12.6 (0.31)	25.5 (0.43)	4.0 (0.18)

See footnotes at end of table.

Table 10. Age-adjusted percentages of migraines or pain in neck, lower back, face, or jaw among adults aged 18 and over, by selected characteristics: United States, 2012—Con.

Selected characteristic	Migraines or severe headaches[1]	Pain in neck[2]	Pain in lower back[3]	Pain in face or jaw[4]
Health insurance coverage[16]	Percent[5] (standard error)			
Under 65:				
Private	13.8 (0.36)	12.3 (0.33)	24.0 (0.46)	4.2 (0.20)
Medicaid	25.0 (1.05)	21.0 (0.92)	41.2 (1.16)	8.9 (0.66)
Other	25.8 (2.20)	21.4 (1.66)	37.6 (2.02)	8.3 (1.09)
Uninsured	16.6 (0.63)	14.0 (0.59)	27.6 (0.75)	5.2 (0.38)
65 and over:				
Private	4.7 (0.45)	14.5 (0.77)	30.0 (1.04)	3.4 (0.38)
Medicare and Medicaid	9.7 (1.56)	22.3 (2.00)	39.5 (2.42)	7.9 (1.31)
Medicare only	5.8 (0.60)	12.4 (0.78)	29.1 (1.18)	3.6 (0.43)
Other	7.3 (1.44)	13.4 (1.73)	33.3 (2.29)	3.2 (0.82)
Uninsured	*21.3 (7.39)	*19.6 (7.13)	*19.2 (7.20)	*
Marital status				
Married	13.1 (0.38)	13.5 (0.35)	27.3 (0.49)	4.1 (0.21)
Widowed	21.6 (3.75)	18.7 (3.13)	30.9 (3.69)	9.8 (2.70)
Divorced or separated	19.3 (0.92)	19.0 (0.79)	33.2 (0.92)	7.2 (0.55)
Never married	13.5 (0.51)	11.8 (0.53)	24.0 (0.75)	4.4 (0.29)
Living with a partner	16.9 (0.97)	17.2 (1.21)	32.4 (1.45)	6.3 (1.05)
Place of residence[17]				
Large MSA	13.1 (0.35)	13.1 (0.34)	26.3 (0.46)	4.5 (0.20)
Small MSA	15.0 (0.51)	14.6 (0.48)	28.3 (0.59)	5.0 (0.27)
Not in MSA	15.8 (0.77)	15.0 (0.63)	30.7 (0.90)	5.6 (0.42)
Region				
Northeast	12.3 (0.63)	11.9 (0.64)	25.7 (0.82)	3.8 (0.30)
Midwest	15.8 (0.57)	14.9 (0.53)	28.0 (0.79)	5.6 (0.36)
South	13.9 (0.43)	13.0 (0.41)	27.8 (0.54)	4.8 (0.25)
West	14.0 (0.52)	15.7 (0.52)	28.2 (0.64)	4.9 (0.30)
Hispanic or Latino origin[10], race, and sex				
Hispanic or Latino, male	7.4 (0.59)	11.0 (0.77)	24.8 (1.08)	3.3 (0.39)
Hispanic or Latina, female	18.4 (0.91)	16.8 (0.85)	28.1 (1.01)	5.4 (0.52)
Not Hispanic or Latino:				
White, single race, male	9.8 (0.43)	12.1 (0.43)	27.1 (0.61)	3.5 (0.27)
White, single race, female	19.8 (0.54)	17.2 (0.49)	30.4 (0.60)	7.2 (0.33)
Black or African American, single race, male	7.5 (0.72)	7.5 (0.65)	19.7 (1.06)	2.3 (0.36)
Black or African American, single race, female	19.3 (0.94)	13.2 (0.78)	29.1 (1.03)	4.6 (0.44)

* Estimates are considered unreliable. Data preceded by an asterisk have a relative standard error (RSE) greater than 30% and less than or equal to 50% and should be used with caution. Data not shown have an RSE greater than 50%.

[1]Respondents were asked, "During the past three months, did you have a severe headache or migraine?" Respondents were instructed to report pain that had lasted a whole day or more, and conversely, not to report fleeting or minor aches or pains. Persons may be represented in more than one column.

[2]Respondents were asked, "During the past three months, did you have neck pain?" Respondents were instructed to report pain that had lasted a whole day or more, and conversely, not to report fleeting or minor aches or pains. Persons may be represented in more than one column.

[3]Respondents were asked, "During the past three months, did you have low back pain?" Respondents were instructed to report pain that had lasted a whole day or more, and conversely, not to report fleeting or minor aches or pains. Persons may be represented in more than one column.

[4]Respondents were asked, "During the past three months, did you have facial ache or pain in the jaw muscles or the joint in front of the ear?" Respondents were instructed to report pain that had lasted a whole day or more, and conversely, not to report fleeting or minor aches or pains. Persons may be represented in more than one column.

[5]Unknowns for the columns are not included in the denominators when calculating percentages. See Appendix I.

[6]Includes other races not shown separately and persons with unknown education, employment status, family income, poverty status, health insurance, and marital status characteristics. Estimates may not add to totals due to rounding.

[7]Estimates for age groups are not age-adjusted.

[8]Refers to persons who indicated only a single race group, including those of Hispanic or Latino origin. See Appendix II.

[9]Refers to persons who indicated more than one race group, including those of Hispanic or Latino origin. Only two combinations of multiple-race groups are shown due to small sample sizes for other combinations.

[10]Refers to persons who are of Hispanic or Latino origin and may be of any race or combination of races. "Not Hispanic or Latino" refers to persons who are not of Hispanic or Latino origin, regardless of race.

[11]Shown only for adults aged 25 and over. Estimates are age-adjusted to the projected 2000 U.S. standard population using four age groups: 25–44, 45–64, 65–74, and 75 and over.

[12]GED is General Educational Development high school equivalency diploma.

[13]"Full-time" employment is 35 or more hours per week. "Part-time" employment is 34 or fewer hours per week. See Appendix II.

[14]Includes persons who reported a dollar amount or who would not provide a dollar amount but provided an income interval. See Appendix I.

[15]"Poor" persons are defined as having income below the poverty threshold. "Near poor" persons have incomes of 100% to less than 200% of the poverty threshold. "Not poor" persons have incomes that are 200% of the poverty threshold or greater. See Appendix I.

[16]Based on a hierarchy of mutually exclusive categories. Adults with more than one type of health insurance were assigned to the first appropriate category in the hierarchy. "Uninsured" includes adults who had no coverage, as well as those who had only Indian Health Service coverage or had only a private plan that paid for one type of service such as accidents or dental care. See Appendix II.

[17]MSA is metropolitan statistical area. Large MSAs have a population of 1 million or more; small MSAs have a population of less than 1 million. "Not in MSA" consists of persons not living in a metropolitan statistical area.

NOTES: Estimates are based on household interviews of a sample of the civilian noninstitutionalized population. Unless otherwise specified, estimates are age-adjusted to the projected 2000 U.S. population as the standard population using four age groups: 18–44, 45–64, 65–74, and 75 and over. For crude percentages, refer to Table VIII in Appendix III.

SOURCE: CDC/NCHS, National Health Interview Survey, 2012.

Table 11. Frequencies of hearing trouble, vision trouble, and absence of teeth among adults aged 18 and over, by selected characteristics: United States, 2012

| Selected characteristic | All adults aged 18 and over | Selected sensory problems | | Absence of all natural teeth[3] |
		Hearing trouble[1]	Vision trouble[2]	
		Number in thousands[4]		
Total[5]	234,921	37,567	20,609	17,952
Sex				
Male	113,071	21,291	8,255	8,200
Female	121,850	16,276	12,354	9,753
Age (years)				
18–44	111,034	6,830	6,014	2,785
45–64	82,038	15,731	9,292	6,345
65–74	23,760	6,992	2,607	4,164
75 and over	18,089	8,013	2,696	4,659
Race				
One race[6]	230,994	36,896	20,070	17,672
White	188,261	32,973	16,561	14,708
Black or African American	27,943	2,604	2,573	2,208
American Indian or Alaska Native	1,916	207	236	*112
Asian	12,542	1,080	668	611
Native Hawaiian or Other Pacific Islander	332	*	*33	*
Two or more races[7]	3,926	671	538	280
Black or African American, white	778	*52	*77	*
American Indian or Alaska Native, white	1,611	445	332	201
Hispanic or Latino origin[8] and race				
Hispanic or Latino	34,946	3,050	2,876	1,603
Mexican or Mexican American	21,741	1,899	1,724	829
Not Hispanic or Latino	199,974	34,517	17,733	16,350
White, single race	156,173	30,164	14,008	13,168
Black or African American, single race	26,961	2,513	2,537	2,182
Education[9]				
Less than a high school diploma	28,311	5,813	3,948	5,137
High school diploma or GED[10]	52,795	10,800	5,123	6,028
Some college	59,577	11,433	5,828	3,965
Bachelor's degree or higher	63,036	8,045	4,078	2,153
Current employment status[11]				
Employed	142,783	15,885	8,877	5,509
Full-time	114,915	12,689	6,744	4,454
Part-time	25,610	2,896	1,912	979
Not employed but has worked previously	78,811	20,090	10,358	10,827
Not employed and has never worked	13,135	1,575	1,365	1,609
Family income[12]				
Less than $35,000	74,224	13,355	9,097	9,136
$35,000 or more	146,587	21,838	10,416	7,784
$35,000–$49,999	31,186	5,660	2,883	2,608
$50,000–$74,999	39,348	6,195	3,071	2,429
$75,000–$99,999	27,052	3,562	1,615	1,318
$100,000 or more	49,001	6,421	2,846	1,429
Poverty status[13]				
Poor	30,576	4,452	3,917	3,375
Near poor	38,167	6,352	4,324	4,093
Not poor	147,021	23,338	10,821	8,429

See footnotes at end of table.

Table 11. Frequencies of hearing trouble, vision trouble, and absence of teeth among adults aged 18 and over, by selected characteristics: United States, 2012—Con.

Selected characteristic	All adults aged 18 and over	Selected sensory problems		Absence of all natural teeth[3]
		Hearing trouble[1]	Vision trouble[2]	
Health insurance coverage[14]	Number in thousands[4]			
Under 65:				
Private.	125,065	13,931	7,925	4,493
Medicaid.	19,101	2,679	2,618	1,577
Other.	8,734	2,148	1,309	1,016
Uninsured.	39,391	3,745	3,377	2,012
65 and over:				
Private.	21,580	8,088	2,519	3,525
Medicare and Medicaid	2,546	884	530	1,065
Medicare only	14,327	4,700	1,836	3,440
Other.	3,033	1,251	355	690
Uninsured.	286	*48	*52	67
Marital status				
Married.	124,149	21,646	9,692	8,837
Widowed.	14,119	4,919	2,244	3,593
Divorced or separated.	26,499	5,107	3,413	2,811
Never married.	52,444	3,664	3,750	1,733
Living with a partner.	17,367	2,191	1,467	969
Place of residence[15]				
Large MSA	125,511	17,189	9,486	7,670
Small MSA.	72,095	12,582	7,184	5,583
Not in MSA	37,315	7,796	3,939	4,699
Region				
Northeast	42,760	5,881	2,951	3,263
Midwest	53,378	9,489	4,783	4,005
South.	85,578	13,834	8,086	7,740
West.	53,205	8,363	4,789	2,945
Hispanic or Latino origin[8], race, and sex				
Hispanic or Latino, male	17,505	1,741	1,245	637
Hispanic or Latina, female	17,442	1,309	1,630	965
Not Hispanic or Latino:				
White, single race, male.	75,739	17,543	5,601	6,287
White, single race, female.	80,434	12,621	8,407	6,882
Black or African American, single race, male	12,022	1,045	880	859
Black or African American, single race, female	14,939	1,468	1,658	1,324

* Estimates are considered unreliable. Data preceded by an asterisk have a relative standard error (RSE) greater than 30% and less than or equal to 50% and should be used with caution. Data not shown have an RSE greater than 50%.

[1]Respondents were asked, "These next questions are about your hearing without the use of hearing aids or other listening devices. Is your hearing excellent, good, [do you have] a little trouble hearing, moderate trouble, a lot of trouble, or are you deaf?" For this table, "a little trouble hearing," "moderate trouble," "a lot of trouble," and "deaf" are combined into one category. Estimates of hearing trouble for 2012 may not be comparable with estimates from 2006 and earlier. A person may be represented in more than one column.

[2]Regarding their vision, respondents were asked, "Do you have any trouble seeing, even when wearing glasses or contact lenses?" Respondents were also asked, "Are you blind or unable to see at all?" For this table, "any trouble seeing" and "blind" are combined into one category. A person may be represented in more than one column.

[3]Respondents were asked, "Have you lost all of your upper and lower natural (permanent) teeth?" A person may be represented in more than one column.

[4]Unknowns for the columns are not included in the frequencies, but they are included in the "All adults aged 18 and over" column. See Appendix I.

[5]Includes other races not shown separately and persons with unknown education, employment status, family income, poverty status, health insurance, and marital status characteristics. Estimates may not add to totals due to rounding.

[6]Refers to persons who indicated only a single race group, including those of Hispanic or Latino origin. See Appendix II.

[7]Refers to persons who indicated more than one race group, including those of Hispanic or Latino origin. Only two combinations of multiple-race groups are shown due to small sample sizes for other combinations.

[8]Refers to persons who are of Hispanic or Latino origin and may be of any race or combination of races. "Not Hispanic or Latino" refers to persons who are not of Hispanic or Latino origin, regardless of race.

[9]Shown only for adults aged 25 years and over.

[10] GED is General Educational Development high school equivalency diploma.

[11]"Full-time" employment is 35 or more hours per week. "Part-time" employment is 34 or fewer hours per week. See Appendix II.

[12]Includes persons who reported a dollar amount or who would not provide a dollar amount but provided an income interval. See Appendix I.

[13]"Poor" persons are defined as having income below the poverty threshold. "Near poor" persons have incomes of 100% to less than 200% of the poverty threshold. "Not poor" persons have incomes that are 200% of the poverty threshold or greater. See Appendix I.

(Continued)

Table 11. Frequencies of hearing trouble, vision trouble, and absence of teeth among adults aged 18 and over, by selected characteristics: United States, 2012—Con.

[14]Based on a hierarchy of mutually exclusive categories. Adults with more than one type of health insurance were assigned to the first appropriate category in the hierarchy. ``Uninsured'' includes adults who had no coverage, as well as those who had only Indian Health Service coverage or had only a private plan that paid for one type of service such as accidents or dental care. See Appendix II.

[15]MSA is metropolitan statistical area. Large MSAs have a population of 1 million or more; small MSAs have a population of less than 1 million. ``Not in MSA'' consists of persons not living in a metropolitan statistical area.

NOTE: Estimates are based on household interviews of a sample of the civilian noninstitutionalized population.
SOURCE: CDC/NCHS, National Health Interview Survey, 2012.
http://www.cdc.gov/nchs/data/series/sr_10/sr10_260.pdf

Information in these tables was drawn from the *HIV Surveillance Report*, vol. 25, produced by the Division of HIV/AIDS Prevention of the Centers for Disease Control and Prevention (CDC). The complete report may be accessed from http://www.cdc.gov/hiv/pdf/g-l/hiv_surveillance_report_vol_25.pdf. More information about HIV/AIDS is available from http://www.cdc.gov/hiv/default.html.

Table 1a. Diagnoses of HIV infection, by year of diagnosis and selected characteristics, 2009–2013—United States

| | 2009 | | | 2010 | | | 2011 | | | 2012 | | | 2013 | | |
| | | Estimated[a] | | | Estimated[a] | | | Estimated[a] | | | Estimated[a] | | | Estimated[a] | |
	No.	No.	Rate	No.	No.	Rate	No.	No.	Rate	No.	No.	Rate	No.	No.	Rate
Age at diagnosis (yr)															
<13	218	223	0.4	225	232	0.4	187	196	0.4	232	250	0.5	164	187	0.4
13–14	30	31	0.4	40	41	0.5	44	47	0.6	49	53	0.6	39	45	0.5
15–19	2,187	2,228	10.3	2,069	2,123	9.7	1,988	2,074	9.6	1,846	1,989	9.3	1,652	1,863	8.8
20–24	6,741	6,875	31.9	7,064	7,265	33.5	7,066	7,386	33.3	7,196	7,752	34.3	7,059	8,053	35.3
25–29	6,510	6,641	30.6	6,342	6,533	30.9	6,366	6,658	31.3	6,556	7,083	33.1	6,844	7,825	36.3
30–34	5,714	5,835	29.3	5,481	5,652	28.2	5,262	5,508	26.9	5,589	6,037	28.9	5,404	6,165	29.0
35–39	5,659	5,779	28.1	5,028	5,184	25.8	4,456	4,673	23.8	4,264	4,611	23.7	4,246	4,858	24.8
40–44	5,991	6,120	29.2	5,233	5,402	25.8	4,800	5,032	23.9	4,554	4,923	23.4	4,217	4,820	23.1
45–49	5,297	5,413	23.7	4,860	5,014	22.1	4,628	4,859	21.9	4,449	4,822	22.2	4,311	4,961	23.4
50–54	3,659	3,742	17.2	3,512	3,629	16.2	3,364	3,532	15.6	3,274	3,554	15.7	3,254	3,747	16.6
55–59	2,163	2,212	11.7	2,065	2,137	10.8	1,992	2,095	10.3	1,975	2,146	10.3	2,151	2,467	11.6
60–64	1,007	1,031	6.5	1,073	1,109	6.5	1,069	1,123	6.3	1,066	1,164	6.5	1,150	1,316	7.3
≥65	823	842	2.1	789	815	2.0	812	858	2.1	825	901	2.1	896	1,045	2.3
Race/ethnicity															
American Indian/Alaska Native	167	169	7.2	180	183	8.1	172	177	7.8	194	202	8.8	197	218	9.4
Asian	718	734	5.4	717	742	5.0	787	827	5.4	833	901	5.8	862	973	6.0
Black/African American	21,661	22,136	58.7	20,510	21,148	55.6	19,453	20,436	53.3	19,079	20,803	53.7	18,803	21,836	55.9
Hispanic/Latino[b]	9,411	9,620	19.9	9,009	9,317	18.4	8,852	9,299	17.9	8,980	9,710	18.3	8,878	10,117	18.7
Native Hawaiian/Other Pacific Islander	64	65	14.5	59	61	12.1	56	59	11.5	71	75	14.4	61	67	12.7
White	12,518	12,750	6.4	11,957	12,290	6.2	11,465	11,923	6.0	11,593	12,372	6.3	11,672	13,101	6.6
Multiple races	1,460	1,497	32.8	1,349	1,395	24.7	1,249	1,318	22.6	1,125	1,223	20.4	914	1,039	16.8
Transmission category															
Male adult or adolescent															
Male-to-male sexual contact	21,811	27,394	—	21,712	27,106	—	21,791	27,357	—	21,962	28,967	—	21,498	30,689	—
Injection drug use	1,507	2,501	—	1,306	2,205	—	1,076	1,879	—	922	1,799	—	887	1,942	—
Male-to-male sexual contact and injection drug use	1,251	1,611	—	1,177	1,507	—	1,024	1,346	—	978	1,316	—	851	1,270	—
Heterosexual contact[c]	3,120	4,501	—	2,871	4,176	—	2,725	3,959	—	2,452	3,776	—	2,199	3,887	—
Other[d]	7,625	56	—	6,935	55	—	6,415	53	—	6,953	79	—	7,745	99	—
Subtotal	35,314	36,062	29.1	34,001	35,049	28.0	33,031	34,595	27.4	33,267	35,937	28.2	33,180	37,887	29.4

(Continued)

Table 1a. Diagnoses of HIV infection, by year of diagnosis and selected characteristics, 2009–2013—United States (cont)

	2009	Estimated[a]		2010	Estimated[a]		2011	Estimated[a]		2012	Estimated[a]		2013	Estimated[a]	
	No.	No.	Rate	No.	No.	Rate	No.	No.	Rate	No.	No.	Rate	No.	No.	Rate
Female adult or adolescent															
Injection drug use	931	1,687	—	777	1,426	—	661	1,288	—	599	1,227	—	510	1,154	—
Heterosexual contact[c]	5,014	8,943	—	4,669	8,382	—	4,200	7,905	—	3,800	7,811	—	3,446	8,031	—
Other[d]	4,522	56	—	4,109	46	—	3,955	57	—	3,977	61	—	4,087	93	—
Subtotal	10,467	10,686	8.3	9,555	9,855	7.5	8,816	9,250	7.0	8,376	9,099	6.8	8,043	9,278	6.9
Child (<13 yrs at diagnosis)															
Perinatal	175	179	—	175	180	—	135	142	—	154	165	—	93	107	—
Other[e]	43	44	—	50	52	—	52	54	—	78	85	—	71	80	—
Subtotal	218	223	0.4	225	232	0.4	187	196	0.4	232	250	0.5	164	187	0.4
Region of residence															
Northeast	9,006	9,209	16.7	8,421	8,711	15.7	7,865	8,307	14.9	7,829	8,629	15.5	7,499	8,908	15.9
Midwest	5,812	5,917	8.9	5,559	5,698	8.5	5,444	5,634	8.4	5,608	5,906	8.8	5,600	6,109	9.0
South	23,032	23,513	20.7	21,895	22,564	19.6	21,244	22,285	19.2	20,804	22,629	19.3	21,066	24,323	20.5
West	8,149	8,332	11.6	7,906	8,163	11.3	7,481	7,814	10.7	7,634	8,122	11.0	7,222	8,013	10.8
Total[f]	45,999	46,971	15.3	43,781	45,136	14.6	42,034	44,040	14.1	41,875	45,287	14.4	41,387	47,352	15.0

Note. Data include persons with a diagnosis of HIV infection regardless of stage of disease at diagnosis.

a Estimated numbers resulted from statistical adjustment that accounted for reporting delays and missing transmission category, but not for incomplete reporting. Rates are per 100,000 population. Rates are not calculated by transmission category because of the lack of denominator data.

b Hispanics/Latinos can be of any race.

c Heterosexual contact with a person known to have, or to be at high risk for, HIV infection.

d Includes hemophilia, blood transfusion, perinatal exposure, and risk factor not reported or not identified.

e Includes hemophilia, blood transfusion, and risk factor not reported or not identified.

f Because column totals for estimated numbers were calculated independently of the values for the subpopulations, the values in each column may not sum to the column total.

Table 2a. Stage 3 (AIDS), by year of diagnosis and selected characteristics, 2009–2013 and cumulative—United States

	2009			2010			2011			2012			2013			Cumulative[b]	
	No.	Estimated[a] No.	Rate	No.	Estimated[a] No.	Rate	No.	Estimated[a] No.	Rate	No.	Estimated[a] No.	Rate	No.	Estimated[a] No.	Rate	No.	Est. No.[a]
Age at diagnosis (yr)																	
<13	14	14	0.0	23	24	0.0	15	16	0.0	10	10	0.0	7	8	0.0	9,399	9,421
13–14	45	46	0.6	47	49	0.6	37	39	0.5	28	29	0.4	25	30	0.4	1,442	1,461
15–19	439	450	2.1	454	470	2.1	428	447	2.1	340	361	1.7	381	435	2.1	8,636	8,793
20–24	1,947	1,996	9.3	1,987	2,062	9.5	1,971	2,064	9.3	1,863	1,982	8.8	1,996	2,239	9.8	50,040	50,787
25–29	3,140	3,220	14.9	2,884	2,993	14.2	2,763	2,896	13.6	2,701	2,877	13.4	2,787	3,123	14.5	138,724	139,957
30–34	3,651	3,743	18.8	3,302	3,423	17.1	3,129	3,276	16.0	3,218	3,424	16.4	2,927	3,268	15.4	222,750	224,308
35–39	4,335	4,442	21.6	3,708	3,844	19.1	3,179	3,329	17.0	2,891	3,074	15.8	2,869	3,200	16.3	241,443	243,169
40–44	4,989	5,116	24.4	4,304	4,463	21.3	3,753	3,930	18.7	3,424	3,640	17.3	3,121	3,496	16.8	202,176	204,006
45–49	4,813	4,935	21.6	4,273	4,431	19.6	3,953	4,138	18.7	3,614	3,843	17.7	3,386	3,781	17.8	137,405	139,062
50–54	3,492	3,578	16.4	3,180	3,298	14.8	2,900	3,043	13.5	2,863	3,045	13.5	2,803	3,135	13.9	81,518	82,718
55–59	1,939	1,987	10.5	1,759	1,826	9.2	1,793	1,874	9.2	1,756	1,872	9.0	1,789	1,998	9.4	44,927	45,628
60–64	917	939	5.9	933	967	5.7	910	950	5.3	984	1,049	5.9	1,019	1,144	6.3	23,899	24,274
≥65	777	796	2.0	741	767	1.9	724	754	1.8	721	766	1.8	740	831	1.9	20,169	20,455
Race/ethnicity																	
American Indian/Alaska Native	104	106	4.5	119	122	5.4	114	117	5.1	101	105	4.5	96	104	4.5	3,486	3,514
Asian[c]	374	384	2.8	365	380	2.6	367	384	2.5	358	382	2.4	374	415	2.6	9,560	9,712
Black/African American	14,326	14,687	39.0	13,440	13,951	36.7	12,353	12,946	33.7	11,949	12,735	32.9	11,678	13,172	33.7	491,715	497,267
Hispanic/Latino[d]	6,454	6,629	13.7	5,599	5,817	11.5	5,215	5,469	10.5	4,981	5,307	10.0	4,814	5,336	9.9	213,246	215,685
Native Hawaiian/Other Pacific Islander	37	38	8.4	39	40	8.1	32	33	6.5	30	32	6.1	34	37	6.9	845	855
White	7,917	8,097	4.1	6,979	7,208	3.7	6,505	6,786	3.4	6,079	6,429	3.3	6,090	6,759	3.4	433,681	436,557
Multiple races	1,286	1,322	29.0	1,054	1,097	19.4	969	1,020	17.5	915	984	16.4	764	867	14.0	29,995	30,448
Transmission category																	
Male adult or adolescent																	
Male-to-male sexual contact	12,574	15,530	—	11,635	14,575	—	11,157	13,958	—	10,700	13,821	—	10,542	14,611	—	520,784	577,403
Injection drug use	1,741	2,432	—	1,482	2,152	—	1,242	1,825	—	1,105	1,705	—	932	1,610	—	164,750	187,218
Male-to-male sexual contact and injection drug use	1,322	1,595	—	1,130	1,389	—	977	1,232	—	860	1,115	—	716	1,026	—	77,304	83,828
Heterosexual contact[e]	2,626	3,549	—	2,239	3,155	—	2,093	2,918	—	1,891	2,790	—	1,774	2,865	—	64,842	82,447
Other[f]	4,398	125	—	4,138	116	—	3,696	122	—	3,821	115	—	4,164	144	—	106,136	11,545
Subtotal	22,661	23,232	18.7	20,624	21,387	17.1	19,165	20,055	15.9	18,377	19,546	15.3	18,128	20,256	15.7	933,816	942,440

(Continued)

Table 2a. Stage 3 (AIDS), by year of diagnosis and selected characteristics, 2009–2013 and cumulative—United States (cont)

| | 2009 | | | 2010 | | | 2011 | | | 2012 | | | 2013 | | | Cumulative[b] | |
| | | Estimated[a] | | | Estimated[a] | | | Estimated[a] | | | Estimated[a] | | | Estimated[a] | | | | |
	No.	No.	Rate	No.	No.	Rate	No.	No.	Rate	No.	No.	Rate	No.	No.	Rate	No.	Est. No.[a]
Female adult or adolescent																	
Injection drug use	1,160	1,734	—	959	1,472	—	839	1,313	—	755	1,225	—	645	1,143	—	74,970	89,790
Heterosexual contact[e]	4,108	6,156	—	3,584	5,599	—	3,265	5,240	—	3,003	5,077	—	2,696	5,109	—	111,561	146,521
Other[f]	2,555	125	—	2,405	136	—	2,271	132	—	2,268	114	—	2,374	172	—	52,782	5,868
Subtotal	7,823	8,016	6.2	6,948	7,206	5.5	6,375	6,684	5.0	6,026	6,417	4.8	5,715	6,424	4.8	239,313	242,178
Child (<13 yrs at diagnosis)																	
Perinatal	13	13	—	17	18	—	12	13	—	9	9	—	6	7	—	8,532	8,553
Other[g]	1	1	—	6	6	—	3	3	—	1	1	—	1	1	—	867	869
Subtotal	14	14	0.0	23	24	0.0	15	16	0.0	10	10	0.0	7	8	0.0	9,399	9,421
Region of residence																	
Northeast	6,516	6,750	12.2	5,639	5,923	10.7	5,119	5,449	9.8	4,771	5,173	9.3	4,301	4,872	8.7	348,674	352,167
Midwest	3,652	3,714	5.6	3,369	3,456	5.2	3,249	3,356	5.0	3,130	3,283	4.9	2,944	3,221	4.8	125,360	126,372
South	14,718	15,036	13.3	13,715	14,183	12.3	12,908	13,466	11.6	12,382	13,109	11.2	12,769	14,345	12.1	473,007	477,964
West	5,612	5,761	8.0	4,872	5,054	7.0	4,279	4,484	6.2	4,130	4,408	6.0	3,836	4,251	5.7	235,487	237,536
Total[h]	30,498	31,262	10.2	27,595	28,616	9.3	25,555	26,755	8.6	24,413	25,973	8.3	23,850	26,688	8.4	1,182,528	1,194,039

Note. Reported numbers less than 12, as well as estimated numbers (and accompanying rates and trends) based on these numbers, should be interpreted with caution because the numbers have underlying relative standard errors greater than 30% and are considered unreliable.

a Estimated numbers resulted from statistical adjustment that accounted for reporting delays and missing transmission category, but not for incomplete reporting. Rates are per 100,000 population. Rates are not calculated by transmission category because of the lack of denominator data.

b From the beginning of the epidemic through 2013.

c Includes Asian/Pacific Islander legacy cases (see Technical Notes).

d Hispanics/Latinos can be of any race.

e Heterosexual contact with a person known to have, or to be at high risk for, HIV infection.

f Includes hemophilia, blood transfusion, perinatal exposure, and risk factor not reported or not identified.

g Includes hemophilia, blood transfusion, and risk factor not reported or not identified.

h Because column totals for estimated numbers were calculated independently of the values for the subpopulations, the values in each column may not sum to the column total.

Table 3a. Diagnoses of HIV infection, by race/ethnicity and selected characteristics, 2013—United States

	American Indian/Alaska Native			Asian			Black/African American			Hispanic/Latino[a]			Native Hawaiian/Other Pacific Islander			White			Multiple races			Total		
		Estimated[b]			Estimated[b]			Estimated[b]			Estimated[b]			Estimated[b]			Estimated[b]			Estimated[b]			Estimated[b]	
	No.	No.	Rate	No.	No.	Rate	No.	No.	Rate	No.	No.	Rate	No.	No.	Rate	No.	No.	Rate	No.	No.	Rate	No.	No.[c]	Rate
Age at diagnosis (yr)																								
<13	0	0	0.0	14	15	0.6	108	122	1.7	11	13	0.1	0	0	0.0	23	26	0.1	8	10	0.5	164	187	0.4
13–14	1	1	1.4	1	1	0.3	26	30	2.6	4	4	0.2	0	0	0.0	6	7	0.2	1	1	0.4	39	45	0.5
15–19	3	4	2.2	9	10	1.1	1,107	1,257	41.1	305	340	7.4	1	1	2.6	184	202	1.7	43	49	7.6	1,652	1,863	8.8
20–24	34	37	18.4	126	145	12.2	4,004	4,611	135.3	1,384	1,575	33.7	7	8	16.2	1,327	1,481	11.6	177	196	36.1	7,059	8,053	35.3
25–29	33	36	20.8	152	174	13.0	3,220	3,741	131.4	1,659	1,887	42.9	12	13	26.7	1,606	1,793	14.5	162	181	44.1	6,844	7,825	36.3
30–34	35	39	24.5	144	161	11.7	2,151	2,489	91.4	1,435	1,635	37.4	14	15	32.9	1,502	1,682	13.8	123	144	39.7	5,404	6,165	29
35–39	17	18	12.6	124	140	10.6	1,681	1,955	79.0	1,112	1,268	31.3	5	5	13.6	1,208	1,360	12.1	99	112	37.7	4,246	4,858	24.8
40–44	21	22	15.2	125	137	10.3	1,598	1,868	71.6	958	1,090	29.1	5	7	18.4	1,435	1,609	12.7	75	86	31.6	4,217	4,820	23.1
45–49	20	22	14.2	81	90	7.8	1,723	2,027	76.5	826	946	28.8	8	9	26.5	1,564	1,765	12.9	89	102	42.7	4,311	4,961	23.4
50–54	19	23	14.3	34	39	3.7	1,370	1,609	59.3	569	652	23.3	7	7	22.4	1,198	1,351	8.7	57	66	27.7	3,254	3,747	16.6
55–59	5	6	3.9	29	35	3.6	936	1,088	44.8	340	388	17.7	1	1	4.2	799	903	5.9	41	46	22.4	2,151	2,467	11.6
60–64	4	4	3.6	12	13	1.6	494	580	30.2	147	168	10.4	1	1	4.9	470	523	3.9	22	26	16.6	1,150	1,316	7.3
≥65	5	6	2.6	11	12	0.7	385	458	11.9	128	150	4.5	0	0	0.0	350	398	1.1	17	21	6.8	896	1,045	2.3
Transmission category																								
Male adult or adolescent																								
Male-to-male sexual contact	91	120	—	487	703	—	7,902	12,069	—	5,273	7,199	—	33	47	—	7,212	9,853	—	500	699	—	21,498	30,689	—
Injection drug use	19	22	—	17	26	—	265	903	—	230	480	—	0	0	—	337	473	—	19	37	—	887	1,942	—
Male-to-male sexual contact and injection drug use	6	10	—	8	12	—	139	331	—	188	271	—	2	3	—	488	611	—	20	32	—	851	1,270	—
Heterosexual contact[d]	14	17	—	38	56	—	1,254	2,493	—	483	718	—	1	2	—	360	530	—	49	71	—	2,199	3,887	—
Other[e]	24	0	—	157	2	—	4,092	52	—	1,461	16	—	11	0	—	1,851	28	—	149	0	—	7,745	99	—
Subtotal	154	169	18.4	707	799	12.5	13,652	15,847	105.7	7,635	8,686	41.8	47	52	24.1	10,248	11,495	13.8	737	839	44.1	33,180	37,887	29.4

(Continued)

1693

Table 3a. Diagnoses of HIV infection, by race/ethnicity and selected characteristics, 2013—United States (cont)

	American Indian/Alaska Native			Asian			Black/African American			Hispanic/Latino[a]			Native Hawaiian/Other Pacific Islander			White			Multiple races			Total		
		Estimated[b]			Estimated[b]			Estimated[b]			Estimated[b]			Estimated[b]			Estimated[b]			Estimated[b]			Estimated[c]	
	No.	No.	Rate	No.	No.	Rate	No.	No.	Rate	No.	No.	Rate	No.	No.	Rate	No.	No.	Rate	No.	No.	Rate	No.	No.	Rate
Female adult or adolescent																								
Injection drug use	7	14	—	1	7	—	151	532	—	75	175	—	2	3	—	259	393	—	15	31	—	510	1,154	—
Heterosexual contact[d]	12	34	—	67	150	—	2,182	5,268	—	559	1,232	—	5	13	—	551	1,174	—	70	159	—	3,446	8,031	—
Other[e]	24	0	—	73	2	—	2,710	67	—	598	11	—	7	.	—	591	13	—	84	0	—	4,087	93	—
Subtotal	43	49	5.1	141	159	2.2	5,043	5,867	34.8	1,232	1,419	7.0	14	15	7.3	1,401	1,579	1.8	169	190	9.3	8,043	9,278	6.9
Child (<13 yrs at diagnosis)																								
Perinatal	0	0	—	7	8	—	60	68	—	8	10	—	0	0	—	14	16	—	4	5	—	93	107	—
Other[f]	0	0	—	7	7	—	48	54	—	3	4	—	0	0	—	9	10	—	4	5	—	71	80	—
Subtotal	0	0	0.0	14	15	0.6	108	122	1.7	11	13	0.1	0	0	0.0	23	26	0.1	8	10	0.5	164	187	0.4
Region of residence																								
Northeast	11	11	9.1	165	192	5.7	3,127	3,704	59.2	2,012	2,402	31.8	2	2	10.3	1,897	2,267	6.0	285	329	38.4	7,499	8,908	15.9
Midwest	25	27	6.8	84	92	4.7	2,764	3,016	43.3	614	698	14.0	2	2	7.2	1,968	2,121	4.1	143	153	12.9	5,600	6,109	9
South	56	69	8.9	231	263	7.2	11,616	13,669	60.8	3,634	4,080	20.6	12	15	18.2	5,162	5,814	8.4	355	412	20.5	21,066	24,323	20.5
West	105	111	10.7	382	426	6.0	1,296	1,447	43.0	2,618	2,937	13.5	45	49	12.1	2,645	2,898	7.5	131	145	6.8	7,222	8,013	10.8
Total[g]	197	218	9.4	862	973	6.0	18,803	21,836	55.9	8,878	10,117	18.7	61	67	12.7	11,672	13,101	6.6	914	1,039	16.8	41,387	47,352	15

Note. Data include persons with a diagnosis of HIV infection regardless of stage of disease at diagnosis.

Reported numbers less than 12, as well as estimated numbers (and accompanying rates and trends) based on these numbers, should be interpreted with caution because the numbers have underlying relative standard errors greater than 30% and are considered unreliable.

[a] Hispanics/Latinos can be of any race.

[b] Estimated numbers resulted from statistical adjustment that accounted for reporting delays and missing transmission category, but not for incomplete reporting. Rates are per 100,000 population. Rates are not calculated by transmission category because of the lack of denominator data.

[c] Because the estimated totals were calculated independently of the corresponding values for each subpopulation, the subpopulation values may not sum to the totals shown here.

[d] Heterosexual contact with a person known to have, or to be at high risk for, HIV infection.

[e] Includes hemophilia, blood transfusion, perinatal exposure, and risk factor not reported or not identified.

[f] Includes hemophilia, blood transfusion, and risk factor not reported or not identified.

[g] Because column totals for estimated numbers were calculated independently of the values for the subpopulations, the values in each column may not sum to the column total.

Table 4a. Stage 3 (AIDS), by race/ethnicity and selected characteristics, 2013—United States

	American Indian/Alaska Native [a]			Asian [a]			Black/African American			Hispanic/Latino [b]			Native Hawaiian/Other Pacific Islander			White			Multiple races			Total		
	No.	Estimated[c] No.	Rate	No.	Estimated[c] No.	Rate	No.	Estimated[c] No.	Rate	No.	Estimated[c] No.	Rate	No.	Estimated[c] No.	Rate	No.	Estimated[c] No.	Rate	No.	Estimated[c] No.	Rate	No.	Estimated[d] No.	Rate
Age at diagnosis (yr)																								
<13	0	0	0.0	0	0	0.0	3	3	0.0	2	2	0.0	0	0	0.0	0	0	0.0	2	2	0.1	7	8	0.0
13–14	0	0	0.0	0	0	0.0	21	26	2.2	1	1	0.1	0	0	0.0	3	4	0.1	0	0	0.0	25	30	0.4
15–19	0	0	0.0	3	4	0.4	288	332	10.9	62	69	1.5	0	0	0.0	20	22	0.2	8	9	1.4	381	435	2.1
20–24	5	5	2.7	24	27	2.3	1,307	1,476	43.3	349	386	8.3	2	2	4.4	244	270	2.1	65	72	13.3	1,996	2,239	9.8
25–29	10	11	6.3	42	46	3.4	1,541	1,740	61.1	632	699	15.9	6	6	13.2	466	518	4.2	90	103	24.9	2,787	3,123	14.5
30–34	19	20	12.9	57	63	4.5	1,385	1,557	57.2	740	817	18.7	2	2	4.7	633	705	5.8	91	104	28.6	2,927	3,268	15.4
35–39	8	8	5.9	62	68	5.1	1,280	1,437	58.1	730	808	20.0	4	4	11.1	687	763	6.8	98	110	37.0	2,869	3,200	16.3
40–44	13	14	9.6	73	82	6.1	1,367	1,541	59.1	673	748	20.0	4	5	12.7	887	988	7.8	104	118	43.3	3,121	3,496	16.8
45–49	14	15	9.9	53	59	5.2	1,540	1,735	65.5	659	730	22.2	9	10	28.2	1,021	1,129	8.2	90	103	43.1	3,386	3,781	17.8
50–54	15	17	10.2	28	31	2.9	1,260	1,422	52.4	461	510	18.2	6	6	19.3	940	1,044	6.7	93	106	44.5	2,803	3,135	13.9
55–59	4	4	2.9	16	18	1.9	861	969	39.8	246	273	12.4	0	0	0.0	601	665	4.4	61	69	33.8	1,789	1,998	9.4
60–64	3	3	2.7	9	10	1.2	490	555	28.9	137	155	9.5	0	0	0.0	349	386	2.9	31	36	23.1	1,019	1,144	6.3
≥65	5	5	2.4	7	8	0.4	335	379	9.9	122	138	4.1	1	1	2.7	239	265	0.8	31	35	11.5	740	831	1.9
Transmission category																								
Male adult or adolescent																								
Male-to-male sexual contact	40	53	—	200	300	—	3,990	5,804	—	2,439	3,310	—	15	25	—	3,526	4,664	—	332	455	—	10,542	14,611	—
Injection drug use	6	7	—	5	11	—	401	816	—	224	386	—	0	0	—	265	340	—	31	49	—	932	1,610	—
Male-to-male sexual contact and injection drug use	5	8	—	4	6	—	189	338	—	138	194	—	1	2	—	338	420	—	41	58	—	716	1,026	—
Heterosexual contact[e]	9	11	—	24	36	—	1,085	1,892	—	372	529	—	1	2	—	235	330	—	48	66	—	1,774	2,865	—
Other[f]	13	0	—	87	1	—	2,255	81	—	839	24	—	10	0	—	854	34	—	106	4	—	4,164	144	—
Subtotal	73	79	8.6	320	354	5.5	7,920	8,930	59.6	4,012	4,443	21.4	27	29	13.6	5,218	5,788	6.9	558	633	33.3	18,128	20,256	15.7

(Continued)

Table 4a. Stage 3 (AIDS), by race/ethnicity and selected characteristics, 2013—United States (cont)

| | American Indian/ Alaska Native | | | Asian[a] | | | Black/African American | | | Hispanic/Latino[b] | | | Native Hawaiian/ Other Pacific Islander | | | White | | | Multiple races | | | Total | | |
| | | Estimated[c] | | | Estimated[c] | | | Estimated[c] | | | Estimated[c] | | | Estimated[c] | | | Estimated[c] | | | Estimated[c] | | | Estimated[c] | |
	No.	No.	Rate	No.	No.	Rate	No.	No.	Rate	No.	No.	Rate	No.	No.	Rate	No.	No.	Rate	No.	No.	Rate	No.	No.[d]	Rate
Female adult or adolescent																								
Injection drug use	5	8	—	1	4	—	281	597	—	95	165	—	0	0	—	230	314	—	33	55	—	645	1,143	—
Heterosexual contact[e]	9	17	—	28	54	—	1,800	3,514	—	388	707	—	4	7	—	372	641	—	95	169	—	2,696	5,109	—
Other[f]	9	0	—	25	2	—	1,674	128	—	317	19	—	3	0	—	270	16	—	76	7	—	2,374	172	—
Subtotal	23	25	2.6	54	60	0.8	3,755	4,238	25.1	800	891	4.4	7	7	3.5	872	971	1.1	204	231	11.3	5,715	6,424	4.8
Child (<13 yrs at diagnosis)																								
Perinatal	0	0	—	0	0	—	3	3	—	2	2	—	0	0	—	—	0	—	1	1	—	6	7	—
Other[g]	0	0	—	0	0	—	—	0	—	—	0	—	0	0	—	—	0	—	1	1	—	1	1	—
Subtotal	0	0	0.0	0	0	0.0	3	3	0.0	2	2	0.0	0	0	0.0	—	0	0.0	2	2	0.1	7	8	0.0
Region of residence																								
Northeast	4	4	3.4	73	82	2.4	1,980	2,251	36.0	1,151	1,304	17.3	0	0	0	895	1,008	2.7	198	223	26.1	4,301	4,872	8.7
Midwest	14	15	3.8	40	43	2.2	1,463	1,606	23.1	320	351	7.0	0	0	0	1,009	1,098	2.1	98	108	9.1	2,944	3,221	4.8
South	20	22	2.9	83	93	2.5	7,555	8,557	38.0	1,980	2,178	11.0	8	9	10.9	2,757	3,068	4.4	366	418	20.8	12,769	14,345	12.1
West	58	62	6.0	178	197	2.8	680	758	22.5	1,363	1,503	6.9	26	28	6.9	1,429	1,585	4.1	102	117	5.5	3,836	4,251	5.7
Total[h]	96	104	4.5	374	415	2.6	11,678	13,172	33.7	4,814	5,336	9.9	34	37	6.9	6,090	6,759	3.4	764	867	14.0	23,850	26,688	8.4

Note. Reported numbers less than 12, as well as estimated numbers (and accompanying rates and trends) based on these numbers, should be interpreted with caution because the numbers have underlying relative standard errors greater than 30% and are considered unreliable.

[a] Includes Asian/Pacific Islander legacy cases (see Technical Notes).

[b] Hispanics/Latinos can be of any race.

[c] Estimated numbers resulted from statistical adjustment that accounted for reporting delays and missing transmission category, but not for incomplete reporting. Rates are per 100,000 population. Rates are not calculated by transmission category because of the lack of denominator data.

[d] Because the estimated totals were calculated independently of the corresponding values for each subpopulation, the subpopulation values may not sum to the totals shown here.

[e] Heterosexual contact with a person known to have, or to be at high risk for, HIV infection.

[f] Includes hemophilia, blood transfusion, perinatal exposure, and risk factor not reported or not identified.

[g] Includes hemophilia, blood transfusion, and risk factor not reported or not identified.

[h] Because column totals for estimated numbers were calculated independently of the values for the subpopulations, the values in each column may not sum to the column total.

Table 10a. Deaths of persons with diagnosed HIV infection, by year of death and selected characteristics, 2009–2012—United States

	2009	Estimated[a]		2010	Estimated[a]		2011	Estimated[a]		2012	Estimated[a]	
	No.	No.	Rate	No.	No.	Rate	No.	No.	Rate	No.	No.	Rate
Age at death (yr)												
<13	6	6	0.0	6	6	0.0	0	0	0.0	5	6	0.0
13–14	3	3	0.0	3	3	0.0	1	1	0.0	2	2	0.0
15–19	34	35	0.2	38	40	0.2	25	27	0.1	21	25	0.1
20–24	189	197	0.9	190	202	0.9	194	211	1.0	156	188	0.8
25–29	502	523	2.4	414	440	2.1	409	446	2.1	386	460	2.2
30–34	850	885	4.5	746	789	3.9	674	728	3.5	640	767	3.7
35–39	1,503	1,561	7.6	1,184	1,250	6.2	1,029	1,105	5.6	854	1,005	5.2
40–44	2,572	2,676	12.7	2,087	2,205	10.6	1,800	1,940	9.2	1,438	1,691	8.0
45–49	3,439	3,576	15.7	3,186	3,375	14.9	2,899	3,122	14.1	2,384	2,799	12.9
50–54	3,326	3,462	15.9	3,161	3,342	15.0	3,098	3,340	14.8	2,832	3,325	14.7
55–59	2,588	2,695	14.2	2,551	2,700	13.6	2,610	2,811	13.9	2,401	2,814	13.5
60–64	1,566	1,625	10.3	1,679	1,776	10.5	1,693	1,826	10.2	1,689	1,998	11.2
≥65	1,741	1,814	4.6	1,671	1,767	4.4	1,798	1,939	4.7	1,781	2,092	4.8
Race/ethnicity												
American Indian/Alaska Native	66	68	2.9	75	79	3.5	56	59	2.6	53	63	2.7
Asian[b]	78	81	0.6	72	75	0.5	87	93	0.6	64	73	0.5
Black/African American	9,203	9,599	25.5	8,182	8,686	22.9	7,798	8,444	22.0	6,880	8,171	21.1
Hispanic/Latino[c]	2,832	2,916	6.0	2,695	2,812	5.5	2,634	2,799	5.4	2,259	2,586	4.9
Native Hawaiian/Other Pacific Islander	7	7	1.6	7	7	1.4	10	11	2.1	3	4	0.7
White	5,326	5,545	2.8	5,090	5,395	2.7	4,920	5,307	2.7	4,604	5,426	2.7
Multiple races	807	842	18.5	794	842	14.9	725	783	13.4	726	849	14.1
Transmission category												
Male adult or adolescent												
Male-to-male sexual contact	5,597	7,110	—	5,360	6,854	—	5,235	6,857	—	4,788	6,777	—
Injection drug use	2,816	3,417	—	2,546	3,133	—	2,265	2,864	—	1,991	2,723	—
Male-to-male sexual contact and injection drug use	1,335	1,514	—	1,176	1,355	—	1,147	1,343	—	1,030	1,303	—
Heterosexual contact[d]	1,310	1,871	—	1,272	1,787	—	1,235	1,781	—	1,114	1,719	—
Perinatal	19	20	—	28	30	—	34	37	—	38	44	—
Other[e]	2,407	100	—	2,148	92	—	2,119	94	—	1,802	79	—
Subtotal	13,484	14,032	11.3	12,530	13,250	10.6	12,035	12,977	10.3	10,763	12,645	9.9

(Continued)

Table 10a. Deaths of persons with diagnosed HIV infection, by year of death and selected characteristics, 2009–2012—United States (cont)

	2009			2010			2011			2012		
		Estimated[a]			Estimated[a]			Estimated[a]			Estimated[a]	
	No.	No.	Rate	No.	No.	Rate	No.	No.	Rate	No.	No.	Rate
Female adult or adolescent												
Injection drug use	1,523	1,914	—	1,315	1,684	—	1,304	1,669	—	1,133	1,611	—
Heterosexual contact[d]	2,092	3,030	—	1,956	2,895	—	1,823	2,767	—	1,705	2,832	—
Perinatal	44	45	—	30	32	—	44	47	—	39	45	—
Other[e]	1,170	31	—	1,079	29	—	1,024	36	—	944	34	—
Subtotal	4,829	5,020	3.9	4,380	4,640	3.5	4,195	4,519	3.4	3,821	4,521	3.4
Child (<13 yrs at death)												
Perinatal	5	5	—	4	4	—	—	—	—	4	5	—
Other[e]	1	1	—	1	1	—	—	—	—	1	1	—
Subtotal	6	6	0.0	5	6	0.0	0	0	0.0	5	6	0.0
Region of residence												
Northeast	4,800	4,994	9.0	4,603	4,874	8.8	4,291	4,616	8.3	3,752	4,362	7.8
Midwest	1,972	2,042	3.1	1,917	2,016	3.0	1,845	1,979	2.9	1,620	1,907	2.8
South	8,908	9,307	8.2	7,901	8,401	7.3	7,616	8,263	7.1	6,886	8,218	7.0
West	2,639	2,715	3.8	2,494	2,605	3.6	2,478	2,638	3.6	2,331	2,686	3.7
Total[f]	**18,319**	**19,058**	**6.2**	**16,915**	**17,896**	**5.8**	**16,230**	**17,496**	**5.6**	**14,589**	**17,173**	**5.5**

Note. Data include persons with a diagnosis of HIV infection regardless of stage of disease at diagnosis. Deaths of persons with diagnosed HIV infection may be due to any cause.

Reported numbers less than 12, as well as estimated numbers (and accompanying rates and trends) based on these numbers, should be interpreted with caution because the numbers have underlying relative standard errors greater than 30% and are considered unreliable.

[a] Estimated numbers resulted from statistical adjustment that accounted for reporting delays and missing transmission category, but not for incomplete reporting. Rates are per 100,000 population. Rates are not calculated by transmission category because of the lack of denominator data.

[b] Includes Asian/Pacific Islander legacy cases (see Technical Notes).

[c] Hispanics/Latinos can be of any race.

[d] Heterosexual contact with a person known to have, or to be at high risk for, HIV infection.

[e] Includes hemophilia, blood transfusion, and risk factor not reported or not identified.

[f] Because column totals for estimated numbers were calculated independently of the values for the subpopulations, the values in each column may not sum to the column total.

Table 11a. Deaths of persons with diagnosed HIV infection ever classified as stage 3 (AIDS), by year of death and selected characteristics, 2009–2012 and cumulative—United States

| | 2009 | | | 2010 | | | 2011 | | | 2012 | | | Cumulative[b] | |
| | | Estimated[a] | | | Estimated[a] | | | Estimated[a] | | | Estimated[a] | | | |
	No.	No.	Rate	No.	No.	Rate	No.	No.	Rate	No.	No.	Rate	No.	Est. No.[a]
Age at death (yr)														
<13	3	3	0.0	0	0	0.0	0	0	0.0	1	1	0.0	4,943	4,951
13–14	2	2	0.0	2	2	0.0	1	1	0.0	1	1	0.0	293	295
15–19	28	28	0.1	27	28	0.1	20	21	0.1	14	16	0.1	1,293	1,302
20–24	142	145	0.7	145	151	0.7	145	154	0.7	121	139	0.6	9,732	9,796
25–29	404	416	1.9	311	325	1.5	307	329	1.5	298	340	1.6	46,742	46,950
30–34	707	730	3.7	607	634	3.2	547	581	2.8	514	594	2.8	101,463	101,897
35–39	1,298	1,339	6.5	991	1,034	5.1	873	925	4.7	706	804	4.1	127,398	128,057
40–44	2,168	2,238	10.7	1,770	1,851	8.9	1,506	1,600	7.6	1,212	1,382	6.6	120,682	121,596
45–49	2,925	3,019	13.2	2,671	2,799	12.4	2,448	2,602	11.7	2,048	2,342	10.8	92,972	94,089
50–54	2,748	2,835	13.0	2,599	2,713	12.1	2,589	2,753	12.2	2,362	2,688	11.9	62,731	63,752
55–59	2,113	2,180	11.5	2,057	2,148	10.8	2,132	2,260	11.2	2,003	2,272	10.9	38,733	39,477
60–64	1,246	1,278	8.1	1,367	1,427	8.4	1,372	1,454	8.2	1,358	1,548	8.7	22,554	23,020
≥65	1,314	1,351	3.4	1,304	1,356	3.4	1,385	1,463	3.5	1,404	1,585	3.7	22,873	23,323
Race/ethnicity														
American Indian/Alaska Native	51	52	2.2	59	61	2.7	49	51	2.2	39	43	1.9	1,852	1,867
Asian[c]	62	64	0.5	57	59	0.4	71	75	0.5	55	60	0.4	3,420	3,441
Black/African American	7,536	7,791	20.7	6,702	7,030	18.5	6,362	6,787	17.7	5,676	6,540	16.9	267,545	270,726
Hispanic/Latino[d]	2,453	2,505	5.2	2,301	2,370	4.7	2,232	2,333	4.5	1,942	2,155	4.1	100,169	100,888
Native Hawaiian/Other Pacific Islander	6	6	1.3	7	7	1.4	9	9	1.9	2	2	0.4	354	356
White	4,281	4,412	2.2	4,044	4,225	2.1	3,964	4,205	2.1	3,702	4,199	2.1	267,750	269,653
Multiple races	709	735	16.1	681	715	12.7	638	683	11.7	626	713	11.9	11,319	11,577
Transmission category														
Male adult or adolescent														
Male-to-male sexual contact	4,743	5,804	—	4,450	5,503	—	4,414	5,509	—	4,021	5,380	—	287,753	311,087
Injection drug use	2,362	2,802	—	2,106	2,531	—	1,877	2,306	—	1,698	2,215	—	117,934	130,406
Male-to-male sexual contact and injection drug use	1,181	1,317	—	1,030	1,164	—	988	1,131	—	891	1,088	—	46,795	50,001
Heterosexual contact[e]	1,080	1,493	—	1,070	1,453	—	1,019	1,410	—	929	1,359	—	27,498	35,230
Perinatal	19	20	—	25	26	—	31	33	—	36	42	—	363	376
Other[f]	1,777	78	—	1,618	78	—	1,533	80	—	1,350	66	—	50,816	8,658
Subtotal	11,162	11,514	9.3	10,299	10,754	8.6	9,862	10,469	8.3	8,925	10,150	8.0	531,159	535,758

(Continued)

Table 11a. Deaths of persons with diagnosed HIV infection ever classified as stage 3 (AIDS), by year of death and selected characteristics, 2009–2012 and cumulative—United States (cont)

	2009			2010			2011			2012			Cumulative[b]	
		Estimated[a]			Estimated[a]			Estimated[a]			Estimated[a]			
	No.	No.	Rate	No.	No.	Rate	No.	No.	Rate	No.	No.	Rate	No.	Est. No.[a]
Female adult or adolescent														
Injection drug use	1,286	1,578	—	1,100	1,371	—	1,106	1,375	—	954	1,299	—	49,370	56,322
Heterosexual contact[e]	1,751	2,402	—	1,630	2,288	—	1,544	2,225	—	1,416	2,191	—	45,702	57,383
Perinatal	40	41	—	28	30	—	42	45	—	39	45	—	474	490
Other[f]	856	27	—	794	25	—	771	28	—	707	25	—	20,761	3,603
Subtotal	3,933	4,048	3.1	3,552	3,713	2.8	3,463	3,674	2.8	3,116	3,561	2.7	116,307	117,797
Child (<13 yrs at death)														
Perinatal	3	3	—	0	0	—	0	0	—	1	1	—	4,483	4,491
Other[f]	0	0	—	0	0	—	0	0	—	0	0	—	460	461
Subtotal	3	3	0.0	0	0	0.0	0	0	0.0	1	1	0.0	4,943	4,951
Region of residence														
Northeast	4,013	4,141	7.5	3,755	3,927	7.1	3,526	3,737	6.7	3,106	3,482	6.2	206,850	208,570
Midwest	1,594	1,631	2.4	1,533	1,585	2.4	1,460	1,535	2.3	1,300	1,474	2.2	66,318	66,856
South	7,235	7,494	6.6	6,480	6,810	5.9	6,252	6,688	5.8	5,656	6,550	5.6	249,947	253,080
West	2,256	2,299	3.2	2,083	2,145	3.0	2,087	2,184	3.0	1,980	2,206	3.0	129,294	130,001
Total[g]	15,098	15,565	5.1	13,851	14,467	4.7	13,325	14,143	4.5	12,042	13,712	4.4	652,409	658,507

Note. Deaths of persons with diagnosed HIV infection may be due to any cause.

Reported numbers less than 12, as well as estimated numbers (and accompanying rates and trends) based on these numbers, should be interpreted with caution because the numbers have underlying relative standard errors greater than 30% and are considered unreliable.

[a] Estimated numbers resulted from statistical adjustment that accounted for reporting delays and missing transmission category, but not for incomplete reporting. Rates are per 100,000 population. Rates are not calculated by transmission category because of the lack of denominator data.

[b] From the beginning of the epidemic through 2012.

[c] Includes Asian/Pacific Islander legacy cases (see Technical Notes).

[d] Hispanics/Latinos can be of any race.

[e] Heterosexual contact with a person known to have, or to be at high risk for, HIV infection.

[f] Includes hemophilia, blood transfusion, and risk factor not reported or not identified.

[g] Because column totals for estimated numbers were calculated independently of the values for the subpopulations, the values in each column may not sum to the column total.

Table 12a. Survival for more than 12, 24, and 36 months after a diagnosis of HIV infection during 2004–2009, by selected characteristics—United States

	No. of persons	Proportion survived (in months)		
		>12	>24	>36
Age at diagnosis (yr)				
<13	1,577	0.98	0.98	0.98
13—14	271	0.98	0.98	0.98
15—19	11,013	0.99	0.99	0.98
20—24	33,984	0.99	0.98	0.98
25—29	38,137	0.98	0.97	0.96
30—34	37,674	0.97	0.96	0.95
35—39	42,776	0.96	0.94	0.93
40—44	43,990	0.94	0.93	0.91
45—49	34,490	0.92	0.89	0.88
50—54	22,290	0.89	0.86	0.84
55—59	12,724	0.86	0.83	0.80
60—64	6,039	0.82	0.78	0.75
≥65	5,157	0.73	0.67	0.62
Race/ethnicity				
American Indian/Alaska Native	1,010	0.91	0.90	0.88
Asian	3,878	0.95	0.95	0.94
Black/African American	135,131	0.94	0.92	0.90
Hispanic/Latino[a]	57,987	0.95	0.94	0.93
Native Hawaiian/Other Pacific Islander	365	0.96	0.94	0.93
White	82,192	0.95	0.93	0.92
Multiple races	9,559	0.95	0.93	0.92
Transmission category				
Male adult or adolescent				
Male-to-male sexual contact	127,941	0.97	0.96	0.95
Injection drug use	14,360	0.90	0.87	0.84
Male-to-male sexual contact and injection drug use	9,927	0.96	0.95	0.93
Heterosexual contact[b]	21,013	0.94	0.91	0.90
Other[c]	43,715	0.88	0.86	0.84
Subtotal	216,956	0.94	0.93	0.91
Female adult or adolescent				
Injection drug use	8,465	0.93	0.90	0.88
Heterosexual contact[b]	36,159	0.96	0.95	0.94
Other[c]	26,965	0.92	0.90	0.89
Subtotal	71,589	0.94	0.93	0.91
Child (<13 yrs at diagnosis)				
Perinatal	1,288	0.98	0.98	0.98
Other[d]	289	0.99	0.99	0.99
Subtotal	1,577	0.98	0.98	0.98
Region of residence				
Northeast	59,549	0.94	0.93	0.92
Midwest	35,380	0.95	0.94	0.93
South	144,548	0.94	0.92	0.90
West	50,645	0.95	0.94	0.93
Year of diagnosis				
2004	49,135	0.93	0.91	0.90
2005	48,455	0.94	0.92	0.90
2006	48,752	0.94	0.92	0.91
2007	49,749	0.95	0.93	0.92
2008	48,323	0.95	0.94	0.92
2009	45,708	0.95	0.94	0.93
Total	**290,122**	**0.94**	**0.93**	**0.91**

Note. Data include persons with a diagnosis of HIV infection regardless of stage of disease at diagnosis. Data exclude persons whose month of diagnosis or month of death is unknown.

See Technical Notes for method for calculating proportion of persons surviving.

[a] Hispanics/Latinos can be of any race.

[b] Heterosexual contact with a person known to have, or to be at high risk for, HIV infection.

[c] Includes hemophilia, blood transfusion, perinatal exposure, and risk factor not reported or not identified.

[d] Includes hemophilia, blood transfusion, and risk factor not reported or not identified.

Table 12b. Survival for more than 12, 24, and 36 months after a diagnosis of HIV infection during 2004–2009, by selected characteristics—United States and 6 dependent areas

	No. of persons	Proportion survived (in months)		
		>12	>24	>36
Age at diagnosis (yr)				
<13	1,609	0.98	0.98	0.98
13–14	281	0.98	0.98	0.98
15–19	11,156	0.99	0.99	0.98
20–24	34,482	0.99	0.98	0.98
25–29	38,896	0.98	0.97	0.96
30–34	38,519	0.97	0.96	0.95
35–39	43,717	0.95	0.94	0.93
40–44	44,962	0.94	0.92	0.91
45–49	35,272	0.92	0.89	0.87
50–54	22,870	0.89	0.86	0.83
55–59	13,074	0.86	0.82	0.80
60–64	6,232	0.82	0.78	0.74
≥65	5,398	0.73	0.67	0.62
Race/ethnicity				
American Indian/Alaska Native	1,010	0.91	0.90	0.88
Asian	3,879	0.95	0.95	0.94
Black/African American	135,251	0.94	0.92	0.90
Hispanic/Latino[a]	64,179	0.94	0.93	0.92
Native Hawaiian/Other Pacific Islander	374	0.95	0.94	0.93
White	82,208	0.95	0.93	0.92
Multiple races	9,567	0.95	0.93	0.92
Transmission category				
Male adult or adolescent				
Male-to-male sexual contact	129,286	0.97	0.96	0.95
Injection drug use	15,845	0.89	0.86	0.83
Male-to-male sexual contact and injection drug use	10,146	0.96	0.95	0.93
Heterosexual contact[b]	22,065	0.93	0.91	0.89
Other[c]	44,021	0.88	0.86	0.84
Subtotal	221,363	0.94	0.92	0.91
Female adult or adolescent				
Injection drug use	8,820	0.93	0.90	0.87
Heterosexual contact[b]	37,542	0.96	0.95	0.93
Other[c]	27,134	0.92	0.90	0.89
Subtotal	73,496	0.94	0.93	0.91
Child (<13 yrs at diagnosis)				
Perinatal	1,315	0.98	0.98	0.98
Other[d]	294	0.99	0.99	0.99
Subtotal	1,609	0.98	0.98	0.98
Region of residence				
Northeast	59,549	0.94	0.93	0.92
Midwest	35,380	0.95	0.94	0.93
South	144,548	0.94	0.92	0.90
West	50,645	0.95	0.94	0.93
U.S. dependent areas	6,346	0.86	0.84	0.82
Year of diagnosis				
2004	50,302	0.93	0.91	0.89
2005	49,711	0.94	0.92	0.90
2006	49,841	0.94	0.92	0.91
2007	50,738	0.95	0.93	0.92
2008	49,301	0.95	0.93	0.92
2009	46,575	0.95	0.94	0.93
Total	**296,468**	**0.94**	**0.93**	**0.91**

Note. Data include persons with a diagnosis of HIV infection regardless of stage of disease at diagnosis. Data exclude persons whose month of diagnosis or month of death is unknown.

See Technical Notes for method for calculating proportion of persons surviving.

[a] Hispanics/Latinos can be of any race.

[b] Heterosexual contact with a person known to have, or to be at high risk for, HIV infection.

[c] Includes hemophilia, blood transfusion, perinatal exposure, and risk factor not reported or not identified.

[d] Includes hemophilia, blood transfusion, and risk factor not reported or not identified.

Information in this table was reproduced from the Centers for Disease Control and Prevention's (CDC's) *Morbidity and Mortality Weekly Report* and drawn from the 2010–2012 National Health Interview Survey (NHIS), a survey conducted by the National Center for Health Statistics (NCHS) of the Centers for Disease Control and Prevention (CDC). More information about the NHIS is available from http://www.cdc.gov/nchs/nhis/about_nhis.htm.

TABLE. Unadjusted and age-adjusted* annualized prevalence of doctor-diagnosed arthritis and arthritis-attributable activity limitation (AAAL)[†] among adults aged ≥18 years, and prevalence of AAAL among those with doctor-diagnosed arthritis, by selected characteristics — National Health Interview Survey, United States, 2010–2012

		Prevalence in the adult population								Prevalence of AAAL among adults with doctor-diagnosed arthritis			
		Doctor-diagnosed arthritis				AAAL							
		Unadjusted		Adjusted		Unadjusted		Adjusted		Unadjusted		Adjusted	
Characteristic	%	%	(95% CI)	%	(95% CI)	%	(95% CI)	%	(95% CI)	%	(95% CI)	%	(95% CI)
Overall	—	22.7	(22.3–23.0)	21.4	(21.1–21.7)	9.8	(9.5–10.1)	9.2	(9.0–9.4)	43.2	(42.4–44.1)	40.7	(39.5–41.9)
Age group (yrs)													
18–44	47.8	7.3	(7.0–7.6)	—	—	2.7	(2.6–2.9)	—	—	37.5	(35.4–39.7)	—	—
45–64	34.9	30.3	(29.8–30.9)	—	—	13.4	(12.9–13.9)	—	—	44.2	(42.9–45.5)	—	—
≥65	17.3	49.7	(48.7–50.6)	—	—	22.0	(21.3–22.8)	—	—	44.4	(43.2–45.6)	—	—
Sex													
Men	48.3	19.1	(18.6–19.7)	18.6	(18.2–19.0)	8.0	(7.7–8.4)	7.8	(7.5–8.1)	41.9	(40.5–43.3)	39.2	(37.2–41.3)
Women	51.7	26.0	(25.5–26.5)	23.9	(23.5–24.3)	11.5	(11.1–11.8)	10.5	(10.2–10.8)	44.2	(43.2–45.2)	41.7	(40.2–43.2)
Race/Ethnicity[§]													
White	68.0	25.9	(25.5–26.4)	22.9	(22.5–23.3)	10.8	(10.5–11.1)	9.5	(9.2–9.7)	41.7	(40.7–42.6)	39.3	(37.8–40.8)
Black	11.9	21.3	(20.3–22.2)	22.4	(21.6–23.2)	10.5	(9.8–11.2)	11.0	(10.4–11.7)	49.3	(47.2–51.4)	47.0	(44.4–49.7)
Hispanic	14.3	12.1	(11.5–12.7)	15.9	(15.2–16.6)	5.9	(5.5–6.3)	8.0	(7.5–8.6)	48.8	(46.3–51.4)	44.8	(41.5–48.2)
Asian	4.9	11.0	(10.0–12.0)	12.1	(11.2–13.1)	4.5	(3.9–5.2)	5.1	(4.5–5.8)	41.1	(36.6–45.7)	30.4	(25.2–36.2)
Other races	0.8	27.0	(23.2–31.2)	27.9	(24.3–31.9)	16.3	(13.3–19.8)	17.0	(14.1–20.4)	60.1	(52.4–67.4)	55.8	(45.7.65.4)
Education level													
<High school diploma	14.2	25.7	(24.8–26.6)	21.9	(21.2–22.7)	14.2	(13.5–15.0)	12.2	(11.5–12.8)	55.4	(53.6–57.3)	53.9	(50.4–57.3)
High school diploma	26.6	25.6	(25.0–26.3)	23.0	(22.4–23.5)	11.4	(11.0–11.9)	10.2	(9.8–10.6)	44.6	(43.1–46.0)	42.2	(40.0–44.4)
At least some college	31.0	22.7	(22.1–23.4)	23.3	(22.8–23.8)	9.6	(9.2–10.1)	9.9	(9.5–10.3)	42.4	(40.9–43.8)	40.6	(38.6–42.6)
Completed college or greater	28.1	18.3	(17.7–18.9)	17.8	(17.2–18.3)	6.2	(5.8–6.5)	6.0	(5.7–6.3)	33.7	(32.1–35.3)	30.4	(28.4–32.4)
Body mass index (BMI)[¶]													
Under/Normal weight	37.1	15.9	(15.4–16.4)	16.3	(15.9–16.7)	6.3	(6.0–6.6)	6.5	(6.2–6.8)	39.8	(38.4–41.3)	38.2	(35.8–40.7)
Overweight	34.7	22.6	(22.0–23.2)	20.3	(19.8–20.8)	8.8	(8.4–9.2)	7.9	(7.5–8.2)	38.9	(37.6–40.2)	37.2	(35.3–39.2)
Obese	28.2	31.2	(30.5–32.0)	28.9	(28.3–29.5)	15.2	(14.7–15.7)	14.0	(13.5–14.5)	48.6	(47.3–49.9)	44.8	(42.9–46.6)
Physical activity[**]													
Meeting recommendations	48.3	17.4	(17.0–17.8)	18.6	(18.2–19.0)	5.3	(5.0–5.5)	5.6	(5.4–5.9)	30.2	(29.0–31.5)	29.3	(27.7–31.0)
Insufficient activity	20.0	25.3	(24.6–26.1)	23.3	(22.6–24.0)	10.3	(9.8–10.8)	9.4	(8.9–9.9)	40.6	(38.8–42.4)	38.9	(36.6–41.3)
Inactive	31.6	28.9	(28.2–29.7)	24.0	(23.4–24.6)	16.3	(15.8–16.9)	13.5	(13.0–13.9)	56.5	(55.2–57.7)	54.8	(52.7–56.8)
Employment status													
Employed/Self-employed	64.9	18.8	(18.4–19.2)	20.9	(20.5–21.4)	7.9	(7.7–8.2)	9.0	(8.7–9.4)	42.3	(41.1–43.6)	40.0	(38.5–41.5)
Unemployed	7.2	14.0	(12.8–15.2)	19.0	(17.3–20.8)	6.1	(5.5–6.9)	8.4	(7.2–9.8)	43.9	(40.0–47.9)	43.2	(38.8–47.8)
Unable to work/Disabled	1.5	29.5	(26.7–32.5)	29.0	(26.3–31.8)	18.1	(15.8–20.7)	17.5	(15.1–20.2)	61.4	(55.7–66.9)	61.7	(54.2–68.7)
Other[††]	26.5	34.2	(33.4–35.1)	21.4	(20.8–22.1)	14.9	(14.4–15.4)	9.2	(8.8–9.6)	43.4	(42.2–44.6)	41.0	(37.7–44.5)
Self-rated health													
Very good/Excellent	60.3	14.4	(14.0–14.8)	15.8	(15.4–16.1)	3.4	(3.2–3.6)	3.7	(3.5–5.9)	23.5	(22.4–24.6)	22.3	(20.8–23.9)
Good	26.7	28.0	(27.3–28.7)	24.4	(23.8–25.0)	11.6	(11.1–12.0)	10.0	(9.6–10.4)	41.3	(40.0–42.7)	39.9	(37.7–42.1)
Fair/Poor	13.0	50.1	(49.1–51.2)	40.7	(39.5–41.9)	35.9	(34.9–36.9)	28.8	(27.8–29.9)	71.8	(70.5–73.0)	69.8	(67.8–71.8)
Heart disease[§§]													
Yes	11.5	49.0	(47.9–50.2)	35.4	(34.0–36.8)	26.8	(25.8–27.7)	19.4	(18.4–20.4)	54.6	(53.0–56.1)	54.0	(50.6–57.3)
No	88.5	19.2	(18.9–19.6)	19.6	(19.3–19.9)	7.6	(7.3–7.8)	7.7	(7.5–7.9)	39.4	(38.5–40.3)	37.8	(36.6–39.1)
Diabetes[¶¶]													
Yes	9.0	47.3	(46.0–48.6)	34.0	(32.5–35.7)	25.7	(24.6–26.9)	18.8	(17.6–20.1)	54.4	(52.4–56.3)	55.9	(52.0–59.7)
No	91.0	20.2	(19.9–20.6)	20.2	(19.9–20.5)	8.2	(8.0–8.5)	8.2	(8.0–8.4)	40.6	(39.7–41.5)	38.7	(37.4–39.9)

Abbreviation: CI = confidence interval.
* Age adjusted to the 2000 U.S. projected adult population, using three age groups: 18–44, 45–64, and ≥65 years.
[†] Doctor-diagnosed arthritis was defined as an affirmative response to the question, "Have you ever been told by a doctor or other health professional that you have some form of arthritis, rheumatoid arthritis, gout, lupus, or fibromyalgia?" Those who answered "yes" were asked, "Are you now limited in any way in any of your usual activities because of arthritis or joint symptoms?" Persons responding "yes" to both questions were defined as having AAAL.
[§] Race/ethnicity categories are mutually exclusive. Persons identified as Hispanic might be of any race. Persons identified as white, black, Asian, or other race all were non-Hispanic.
[¶] BMI = self-reported weight (kg) / (height [m]) ^{2} Categorized as follows: underweight/normal weight (<25.0), overweight (25.0 to <30.0), obese (≥30.0).
[**] Determined from responses to six questions regarding frequency and duration of participation in leisure-time activities of moderate or vigorous intensity and categorized according to the U.S. Department of Health and Human Services *2008 Physical Activity Guidelines for Americans*. Total minutes (moderate to vigorous) of physical activity per week were categorized as follows: meeting recommendations (≥150 min per week), insufficient activity (1–149 min), and inactive (0 min).
[††] Students, volunteers, homemakers, and retirees.
[§§] Adults were considered to have doctor-diagnosed heart disease if they answered "yes" to any of the following four questions: "Have you ever been told by a doctor or other health professional that you had coronary heart disease? Angina, also called angina pectoris? A heart attack (also called myocardial infarction)? Any kind of heart condition or heart disease (other than the ones I just asked about)?"
[¶¶] Adults were considered to have doctor-diagnosed diabetes disease if they answered "yes" to "Have you ever been told by a doctor or health professional that you have diabetes or sugar diabetes?"

Index

Entry titles and their page numbers are in **bold**, and a volume number precedes the page number. Figures and tables are indicated with (fig.) and (table).

Abbott Laboratories, 1:1–4
Abbott Diabetes Care, **1:3**
acquisitions, **1:3**
current status of, **1:3–4**
defining, **1:2**
history of, **1:1–2**
Mylan and, **2:932–933**
products and devices by, **1:2–3**
Takeda and, **4:1347**
AbbVie, **1:1, 1:3**
Abel, John Jacob, **1:xxxi, 1:xxxvii, 2:723–725**
Abuse of prescription drugs, 1:4–10.
 See also **Addiction to prescription drugs;** *individual names of legislation*
addiction to prescription drugs, **1:30–38**
adherence to prescription directions, **1:44–49**
in adolescents, **1:55–56**
amphetamines and, **1:102–106**
behavioral pharmacology and substance abuse, **1:260–265**
impact on society, **1:6, 1:8–9**
overview, **1:xxxiii–xxxiv, 1:4–5**
perception of prescription drug abuse, **1:6–7**
psychotropic prescription drugs (PPDs), **1:43–44** (*See also* **ADHD drugs**)
remedies for, **1:9–10**
types of abuse, **1:5–6**
types of drugs abused, **1:7–8**
youth drug use data, **4:1616** (table), **4:1617** (table), **4:1618** (table)
Acamprosate, **1:81, 1:82**

Access to essential medicines as a human right: history, 1:11–14
competing interests of consumers and producers, **1:12–13**
Heinz Dilemma, **1:11–12**
history of global processes and movements, **1:13–14**
Access to medicines (developing world), 1:14–21
access to medicines, defined, **1:15–16**
challenge for developing countries, **1:16**
disparities between population groups, **1:20**
mandated in health policies and frameworks, **1:15**
outcomes of global interventions, **1:19–20**
overview, **1:xxxiii, 1:14–15**
promoting access to medicines in developing countries, **1:16–19**
role of medicines in health care and quality of life, **1:15**
Access to medicines (industrialized world), 1:21–26
overview, **1:xxxii–xxxiii, 1:21**
patent protection and costs, **1:21–24**
ACEIs, **1:317**
Acetaminophen overdose risk, 1:26–28
mechanisms of action (MOA), **1:26–27**
overview, **1:26**
risks, **1:27–28**
Achiote, **4:1408**
Acid reducers, **2:637**
Acinteobacter, **2:547**
ACT UP, **3:1036–1037**

Actavis, **1**:28–30
  global office and facilities, **1**:30
  history of, **1**:29–30
  overview, **1**:28–29
  products, **1**:29
  specialty research and development, **1**:30
Actiq, **4**:1355
Actos, **4**:1345, **4**:1347–1348
Actrapid, **3**:986
Adderall
  addiction to prescription drugs, **1**:32, **1**:36–37
  black-box warnings about, **1**:40–41
    (*See also* **ADHD drugs**)
Addiction to prescription drugs, 1:30–38
  addictive prescription drugs, **1**:34–37
  cross-addiction/cross-dependence, **1**:37
  escalation to addiction, **1**:32–33
  history of, **1**:31–32
  legal prescriptions, **1**:37–38
  overview, **1**:30–31
  scope of problem, **1**:31
  societal attitude toward, **1**:33–34
  treatment for, **1**:38
ADHD drugs, 1:38–44
  addiction to prescription drugs, **1**:32, **1**:36–37
  ADHD pharmacotherapy and schools, **1**:39, **1**:43
  African Americans and, **1**:71
  CDC on children with ADHD, **1**:xliv
  central nervous system depressants and stimulants, **1**:330–331
  drugs as study aids and, **2**:551–552
  Johnson & Johnson, **2**:806
  neuro-enhancement through pharmacy, **3**:962–963
  nonmedicinal abuse of stimulants, **1**:43–44
  nonstimulants for ADHD pharmacological therapy, **1**:42–43
  overview, **1**:38–39
  prescription drug use and abuse in adolescents, **1**:54, **1**:55–56
  psychotropic intervention for children's behavioral issues, **1**:40
  stimulants for ADHD pharmacological therapy, **1**:40–42
  varying views of, **1**:39–40

Adherence to prescription directions, 1:44–49
  AIDS/HIV drugs, **1**:77–79
  determinants of, **1**:46
  individual variability and, **1**:46–48
  measures to increase adherence, **1**:48–49
  measuring problem of, **1**:45–46
  overview, **1**:44–45, **1**:44–49
Adjudicated claims data, 1:49–52
  insurance benefits manager (IBM), **1**:50
  National Council for Prescription Drug Programs (NCPDP), **1**:49, **1**:51–52
  off-label audits, **1**:51
  overview, **1**:49–50
  pharmacy benefit management (PBM), **1**:50–51
Adolescents, 1:52–56. *See also* Youth drug use data
  AIDS/HIV drugs for, **1**:78
  antipsychotic drugs used by, **1**:xliv–xlv
  contraception use data among, **4**:1620 (table), **4**:1621 (table), **4**:1622 (table), **4**:1623 (table), **4**:1624 (table), **4**:1625 (table), **4**:1626 (table), **4**:1627 (table), **4**:1628 (table), **4**:1629 (table)
  drug testing of high school and college athletes in U.S., **2**:532–537
  football (American) and performance-enhancing drugs, school policies, **2**:627–628
  mental health of, **1**:54–55
  overview, **1**:52
  physical health of, **1**:52–54
  prescription drug use and abuse in, **1**:55–56
Ado-trastuzumab emtansine, **2**:639
Advair, **2**:932
Adverse drug effects reporting systems, 1:56–59. *See also* **Adverse drug reactions (ADR) and adverse events (AE)**
  FDA and, **1**:56, **1**:57–59, **4**:1664 (table)
  medication errors and, **2**:892–895
  MedWatch program, **1**:57
  overview, **1**:56–57
  pharmacogenomics and, **3**:1096
  polypharmacy and, **3**:1137

Sentinel's Initiative and data collection,
	1:59–60
in U.K., 4:1464
women's health issues and, 4:1544–1545
Adverse drug reactions (ADR) and adverse
	events (AE), 1:59–61
cause, 1:59–60
common medication association, 1:60–61
monitoring and reporting, 1:61
overview, 1:59
prevalence, 1:60
Advertising to doctors, 1:61–66
controversy of, 1:62–63
forms of, 1:63
history of, 1:63–65
overview, 1:61–62
Advertising to patients, 1:66–70
direct-to-consumer pharmaceutical
	advertising (DTCPA), defined, 1:66–67
FDA on, 1:66–68
impact of, 1:69–70
types of, 1:68–69
Afrezza, 3:1265
Africa. *See also individual country names*
access to medicines (developing world),
	1:15–20
history of pharmacology in, 2:765–767
history of pharmacy as a profession in,
	2:733–736
Muti (traditional South African medicine),
	2:736, 2:929–931, 4:1417–1418
nganga (traditional African healers),
	3:968–970, 4:1416
Nigeria and polio vaccination programs,
	1:xliv
Pharmacology for Africa initiative,
	3:1102–1105
South Africa, 3:1315–1319
traditional and herbal medicines,
	regulation, 4:1370–1373
traditional medicine, 4:1415–1419
African Americans, 1:70–75
African-American Heart Failure Trial
	(A-HeFT), 3:1200–1201
AIDS/HIV drugs for, 1:79
cardiovascular drug response, 1:72–73

discrimination in prescribing practice,
	2:476–477
health issues of low-income people,
	2:833–834
inclusion of ethnopharmacology in health
	care approach, 1:70, 1:74–75
mental health/psychotropic drug response,
	1:71–72
other drug responses, 1:73–74
overview, 1:70–71
race-based pharmaceuticals, 3:1199–1202
Tuskegee syphilis study and, 2:759,
	4:1447–1454, 4:1517–1518
Agency for Healthcare Research and Quality,
	2:870
Agensys, 1:226
Agent Orange, 1:xli
Aggrenox, 1:284–285
AIDS, and patient activism, 3:1035–1037
AIDS/HIV drugs, 1:75–80
access to medicines (developing world),
	1:15–16, 1:18
adherence and retention in care, 1:77–79
antiretroviral therapy (ART), initiation
	and development of regiments,
	1:76–77
antiretroviral therapy (ART), overview,
	1:75–76
first HIV vaccine, 1:xlii
generic medicines and, 2:647–648
Gilead Sciences and, 2:656–658
Johnson & Johnson, 2:806
overview, 1:75–76
patient awareness of status, 1:xliv
WHO on equitable access to antiretroviral
	treatment for HIV-positive girls and
	women, 1:xliii
Aircept, 2:561
AIs, 1:340
AkaRx, 2:560
Alaska Natives. *See* **Native Americans/**
	Alaska Natives
Albucasis, 4:1460
Alcohol
drug interactions with, 2:519
as relaxant, 3:1334

Alcohol cessation drugs, 1:80–84
  alcoholism statistics, 1:81
  medications, 1:81–83
  overview, 1:80–81
Alios BioPharma, 2:805
Alival, 3:974–977
Alkeman, 1:322–323
Alkylating agents, 1:309
Allegra, 3:1164
Allergan, 1:84–85
Allergic reactions, to drugs, 1:369–370
Alles, Gordon, 1:101–102
Aloe vera (herbal medicine), 1:85–88
  aloe vera plant, 1:86
  cultural importance, 1:86–87
  overview, 1:85–86
  precautions, 1:88
  traditional modern uses, 1:87–88
Alpha-glucosidase inhibitors, 1:172
Alprolix, 1:276
Alupent, 1:284
Amaryl, 3:1164
Ambien, 3:1164
AmBisome, 2:658
American Board of Clinical Pharmacology, 1:88–91
  goals of, 1:89–90
  organization of, 1:89
  overview, 1:88–89
American College of Clinical Pharmacy, 1:91–94
  awards, 1:92
  founding and organization of, 1:91–92
  initiatives, 1:92–93
  overview, 1:91
  resources, 1:93–94
  specialties, 1:92
American College of Physicians, 1:69–70
American Council on Education, 1:xxxix
American Druggists' Circular and Chemical Gazette, 4:1475
American Indian Religious Freedom Act (AIRFA), 4:1414
American Journal of Health-System Pharmacy, 1:98

American Medical Association (AMA), 1:64, 1:70, 2:747
American Pharmacists Association, 1:94–96
  as American Pharmaceutical Association, 1:xxxvii, 1:95, 4:1474–1475
  American Pharmacists Association Foundation, 1:95
  Code of Ethics, 1:xl, 1:95, 2:742–743
  conscience clauses and, 1:415
  governance, 1:96
  history of, 1:94–95, 2:742–743
  medication therapy management (MTM) and, 2:895–897
  MedWatch and, 1:57
  mission of, 1:95–96
American Society of Health-System Pharmacists, 1:96–99
  activities of, 1:97–99
  history, 1:97
  organizational structure, 1:97
  overview, 1:96–97
Amerisource Bergen, 3:1312
Amersham, 3:990
Amgen, 1:99–101
  ethics, 1:100–101
  history, 1:99–100
  overview, 1:99
  research, 1:100
Amodiaquine, 1:191
Amphetamines, 1:101–106
  addiction to prescription drugs, 1:32
  ADHD drugs, 1:44
  appetite stimulants, 1:209–210
  athletes and, 1:235
  children and, 1:105–106
  Comprehensive Methamphetamine Control Act (1996), 1:410–412
  dexamphetamine, 1:40
  history of, 1:101–104
  overview, 1:101
  regulation and, 1:105–106
  stimulants and sports, 3:1323
  3,4-methylenedioxy-methamphetamine (MDMA), 1:394–396
  uses of, 1:104–105
Amylin, 1:173

Anabolic steroids (sport), 1:106–110.
    See also **BALCO scandal**
    baseball and performance-enhancing
        drugs, 1:250
    consumption, 1:108–109
    distribution and sale, 1:107–108
    overview, 1:106–107
    production, 1:107
    regulation, 1:109–110
    as Schedule III drug, 3:1266
    state-sponsored doping programs and,
        3:1321
    swimming and, 3:1333
Anatomical Therapeutic Chemical
    Classification System (WHO), 1:110–113
    history, 1:110–111
    regulation, 1:112
    system, 1:111–112
    uses, 1:111
Anderson, Greg, 4:1368
Andreasen, Nancy, 4:1366
Androgens, 1:310
Anesthetics, abuse of prescription drugs
    and, 1:8
Animal Medicinal Drug Use Clarification Act
    (AMDUCA), 4:1527
Animal testing, 1:113–117
    Amgen and "3Rs," 1:100–101
    benefits derived from, 1:113–115
    criticism of use of animals in research,
        1:115
    major discoveries in basic research
        and medical treatments from,
        1:114 (table)
    overview, 1:113
    regulation, 1:116–117
    responsibilities of researchers involved in,
        1:115–116
    U.S. pharmacology history and, 2:728–729
Antiaging medicines, 1:117–120
    conditions associated with use of,
        1:118–119
    criticism of antiaging movement, 1:119
    history and formation of, 1:118
    overview, 1:117–118
Antiandrogens, 1:310

Antianxiety drugs, 1:120–126
    alternatives to drugs, 1:122
    obstacles, 1:123–124
    overview, 1:120–121
    pharmaceutical companies' roles,
        1:124–126
    prescription patterns, 1:122–123
    purpose of, 1:123
    types of, 1:121–122
Antiasthma drugs, 1:126–131
    anti-Immunoglobulin E (IgE) monoclonal
        antibodies, 1:130
    for emergency management of asthma,
        1:130
    fast-acting drugs, 1:127–128
    long-term control drugs, 1:128–129
    overview, 1:126–127
    use of methylxanthines in, 1:129–130
Antibiotic revolution, the, 1:131–136.
    See also **MRSA (methicillin-resistant**
        ***Staphylococcus* aureus)**
    antibiotic resistance, 1:132
    end of, 1:134–135
    history of antibiotics in Europe,
        2:715
    impact of, 1:133–134
    MRSA and, 1:133
    overuse of antibiotics, 1:132
    overview, 1:131–132
    penicillin, 1:xxxix, 1:131, 2:727–728,
        2:738
    prescription medication use data,
        4:1591 (table)
    U.S. pharmacology history and,
        2:727–728
    veterinary pharmacology and,
        4:1528–1529
    water pollution and, 4:1533
Antibiotic/antimicrobial resistance,
    1:136–139
    antibiotic resistance, 1:136–137, 4:1601,
        4:1602–1603 (table)
    antibiotic resistance as global problem,
        1:137–138
    diagnostic methods, 1:138–139
    overview, 1:136

Antibiotics, 1:139–145
 antibiotic resistance, super bugs,
  superinfection, **1**:142–143
 antimicrobial pesticides, **1**:142
 antimicrobial treatments for bacteria,
  viruses, fungi, parasites, **1**:141–142
 geographic variations in prescribing
  practices, **2**:651
 history of, **1**:139–141
 malaria, **1**:144–145
 S. aureus and MRSA, **1**:143
 tuberculosis, **1**:143–144
Anticaries drugs, 1:145–148
 calcium- and phosphate-based products,
  1:147–148
 chlorhexidine, **1**:146–147
 fluoride, **1**:146
 iodine, **1**:147
 overview, **1**:145–146
 probiotics, **1**:148
 sodium bicarbonate, **1**:147
 triclosan, **1**:147
 xylitol, **1**:147
Anticholesterol drugs, 1:148–153
 bile acid sequestrants, **1**:151–152
 cholesterol absorption inhibitors,
  1:151
 fibric acid derivatives, **1**:150–151
 niacin, **1**:152
 omega-3 fatty acids, **1**:152
 overview, **1**:148–149
 statins, **1**:149–150
Anticoagulants, 1:153–157
 bleeding and, **1**:156–157
 fondaparinux (Arixtra), **1**:155
 oral agents, **1**:154, **1**:156
 overview, **1**:153–154
 parenteral, **1**:154–155
 warfarin (Coumadin), **1**:155–156
Anticonvulsant drugs, 1:157–160
 description of, **1**:158–159
 interactions, **1**:159
 overview, **1**:157–158
 recommended dosage, **1**:159
 side effects, **1**:159
 special conditions, **1**:159–160

Antidepressants, 1:160–168
 adolescents and, **1**:54–55
 anxiety and, **1**:166–167
 atypicals, **1**:163–164
 depression and, **1**:166
 discontinuance of, **1**:168
 MAOIs, **1**:161–162
 overview, **1**:160–161
 Prozac and early U.S. availability, **1**:xli
 sexual dysfunction and, **1**:167–168
 SNRIs, **1**:165–166
 specific serotonin reuptake inhibitors (SSRIs),
  1:xli, **1**:54, **3**:1034–1035, **3**:1276
 SSRIs, **1**:xli, **1**:54, **1**:164–165, **3**:1034–1035,
  3:1276
 substances used through the evolvement
  of psychopharmacology, **2**:702–703
  (*See also* **History of pharmacological
  treatments for mental health;** Mental
  health)
 suicide risk and, **1**:167
 TCAs, **1**:162–163
 water pollution and, **4**:1533
Antidiabetic medications, 1:168–175
 injectable noninsulin medications,
  1:172–174
 insulin therapy, **1**:174 (table)
 monitoring diabetes, **1**:174
 oral antidiabetic medications, **1**:169
 oral antidiabetic medications versus
  insulin by injection, **1**:169
 oral medications, characteristics by class,
  1:169–172, **1**:170 (table)
 overview, **1**:168–169
Antidiarrheals, **2**:636
**Anti-Doping Convention, Council of Europe,
 1:175–177**
 issues of, **1**:175–177
 overview, **1**:175–176
 World Anti-Doping Agency (WADA), **1**:175
Antiflatulence drugs, **2**:637
Antihistamines, 1:177–183
 classification, **1**:180–182
 overview, **1**:177–180
 trade names, by type and generation,
  1:178–179 (table)

Antihypertensive drugs, 1:183–186
alpha-2 receptors, 1:185–186
angiotensin-converting enzyme (ACE) inhibitors, 1:185
beta-blockers, 1:184–185
calcium channel blockers, 1:185
carbonic anydrase inhibitors, 1:184
direct renin inhibitors, 1:186
diuretics, 1:183–184 (*See also* **Diuretics**)
loop diuretics, 1:184
overview, 1:183
potassium-sparing diuretics, 1:184
vasodilators, 1:186
Anti-inflammatory drugs, 1:186–190
corticosteroid medications, 1:187–188
NSAIDs, 1:188–190
prostaglandin synthesis, 1:186–187
Anti-Kickback Statute, 2:675–676
Antimalarials, 1:190–192
diagnosis, 1:190
drug resistance, 1:192
treatment, 1:192
types of, 1:190–192
Antimetabolites, 1:309
Antimicrobials, 2:546–550
Antiobesity medications, 3:1244–1245
Antiparasitic drugs, 1:193–195
drug resistance, 1:194–195
extent of parasitic disease, 1:193
overview, 1:193–194
types of, 1:193
Antipsychiatry movement, 1:195–198
antipsychiatry lobby emergence, 1:196
impact of, 1:198
leaders of movement, 1:196–198
overview, 1:195–196
Antipsychotics, 1:198–206
alternative treatments, 1:202–203
atypical antipsychotics, 1:201–202
butyrophenones, 1:200
children and, 1:203–205
dopamine hypothesis, 1:200–201
overview, 1:198–199
phenothiazines, 1:199–200
side effects, 1:203

typical antipsychotics, 1:201
use in children and adolescents, 1:xliv–xlv
Antipyretic drugs, 1:206–208
fever reducers, defined, 1:206
fever treatment, 1:206–208
Antiretroviral therapy (ART)
Development of AntiRetroviral Therapy (DART), 2:760
highly active antiretroviral therapy (HAART), 1:76
for HIV, 1:75–79 (*See also* **AIDS/HIV drugs**)
initiation and development of regiments, 1:76–77
overview, 1:18–20, 1:75–76
WHO on equitable access to antiretroviral treatment for HIV-positive girls and women, 1:xliii
Antitumor antibiotics, 1:309
Antivert, 3:1064
Anxiolytics, 1:250–251
Aotearoa New Zealand, 2:774–777
Apidra, 3:1164
Apothecary, terminology for, 1:xxxv, 2:738
Appetite depressants and stimulants, 1:208–212
amphetamine-based, 1:209–210
appetite stimulants, 1:210–211
overview, 1:208–209
research, 1:211–212
Arab influence, on pharmacy history, 2:717–718, 2:740–742
ARBs, 1:317
Aricept, 2:560, 3:1064
Arnold, Patrick, 4:1368
Aromatase inhibitors, 1:310
Arrhythmias, 1:315–316
Arrow Therapeutics, 1:230
Arsemin (drug), 2:441
Arsemin Shokai (company), 2:441
Artemisinin, 1:192
Arthritis data, 4:1703 (table)
Arts: prescription drugs and creativity, 1:212–219
altered states, 1:214–217
arts as alternative to medication, 1:218

aspects of creativity, **1**:214
drugs as aid to arts, **1**:217–218
importance of creativity, **1**:213
overview, **1**:212–213
variables of, **1**:218–219
Asasantin, **1**:284
Asian Americans, 1:219–222
health issues, **1**:220–221
health issues of low-income people,
    2:833–834
overview, **1**:219–220
traditional medical practices, **1**:221–222
Aspirin, 1:222–225
acetaminophen as alternative to, **1**:26
Bayer and, **1**:258–259
as cardiovascular drug, **1**:318
history of, **1**:223
overview, **1**:222–223
uses of, **1**:223–224
ASR, **2**:807
Association of Southeast Asia Nations
    (ASEAN), **3**:1143
Astellas Pharma, 1:225–227
corporate philosophy and recent strategy,
    1:225
history of, **1**:225–226
overview, **1**:225
Zepharma, **2**:442
Astemizole (Hismanal) controversy,
    1:227–229
allergies and, **1**:227
overview, **1**:227
research, **1**:227–229
Asthma
adolescents and, **1**:53–54
African Americans and drug responses,
    1:72–73
Astra AB, **1**:229–230
AstraZeneca, 1:229–231
overview, **1**:229–230
Pfizer and, **3**:1065
products of, **1**:230–231
Asylums: Essays on the Social Situation of
    Mental Patients and Other Inmates
    (Goffman), **1**:197, **2**:453–454
Atarax, **3**:1064

Athletes
men's health and, **2**:905–906
Athletes, 1:231–237
amphetamines, **1**:235
anabolic steroids, **1**:106–110, **1**:133,
    1:234–235, **1**:250, **3**:1266, **3**:1321
Anti-Doping Convention, Council of
    Europe, **1**:175–177
athletic trainers and NSAIDs, **1**:235–236
BALCO scandal, **1**:247–250, **2**:628,
    2:633–635
baseball and performance-enhancing
    drugs, **1**:250–252
beta-blockers, **1**:270–276, **2**:906
biological passport, **1**:278–280
blood doping, **1**:280–283
boxing and performance-enhancing drugs,
    1:285–288
cycling and performance-enhancing drugs,
    1:435–439
diuretics, **1**:232–233
doping, origin of term, **3**:1057
drug testing, high school and college
    athletes (U.S.), **2**:532–536
drug testing, Olympic athletes (overview),
    2:537–541
drug testing, professional athletes
    (overview), **2**:541–545
ephedrine, **1**:235
ethics of performance-enhancing drugs in
    sport, **2**:583–587
football (American) and performance-
    enhancing drugs, **2**:626–630
Game of Shadows (Mark Fainaru-Wada
    and Lance Williams), **2**:633–635
glucocorticosteroids, **2**:661–663
hormones and related substances,
    1:233–234
legal issues in testing for performance-
    enhancing drugs, **2**:821–823
Olympics and, **2**:537–541, **3**:995–1004,
    3:1056–1059, **3**:1319, **3**:1320,
    3:1325–1326
overview, **1**:231–232
performance-enhancing drugs and sports:
    history, **3**:1056–1059

shooting sports and performance-enhancing drugs, 3:1287–1289

state-sponsored sports doping programs, 3:1319–1321

stimulants, 3:1321–1326

swimming and performance-enhancing drugs, 3:1332–1335

tennis and performance-enhancing drugs, 4:1351–1353

track and field and performance-enhancing drugs, 4:1367–1370

U.S. Anti-Doping Agency, 2:539–541, 4:1359–1362, 4:1495–1503

World Anti-Doping Agency (WADA), 1:106, 2:537–538, 2:585, 3:1003–1004, 4:1359–1362, 4:1546–1549

Ativan, 4:1433–1434

Atripla, 2:658

Australia, 1:237–239

Aboriginal people and bush medicine, 1:237

Chinese traditional medicine in, 1:237–238

harm reduction policies, 2:673–674

health care system of, 1:238–239

prescription drug approval process, 3:1145–1147

traditional and herbal medicines, regulation in Australia and New Zealand, 4:1373–1377

traditional medicine (bush medicine), 4:1401–1405

Australian Prescriber, 4:1375

Austria, 1:239–242

health system, 1:240–241

overview, 1:239–240

Autism and vaccines, 1:242–244

thimerosal, 1:243–244

vaccination principles, 1:242–243

Wakefield's paper and, 1:243

Autism spectrum disorder, 1:xliv

Automated dispensing, 4:1349

Auvi-Q, 3:1164

Avastin, 2:639

Aventis, 3:1264

Avicenna (ibn Sina), 1:xxxv, 2:741

Avonex, 1:277

Awareness-based methods, for contraception, 2:605

Ayurvedic medicine, 1:244–246

clinical trials, 1:245

overview, 1:244–245

preparations, 1:245–246

Bachmann, Christian, 1:xliv–xlv

BALCO scandal, 1:247–250

BALCO company, 1:247–248

football (American) and PEDs, 2:628

Game of Shadows (Mark Fainaru-Wada and Lance Williams), 2:633–635

implications, 1:249

overview, 1:247

scandal, overview, 1:248–249

Band-Aid, 2:805

Bangladesh, traditional and herbal medicines in, 4:1394

Banting, Frederick Grant, 1:xxxviii, 2:570

Barrier methods, for contraception, 2:604–605

Barron, Doug, 1:273

Baseball and performance-enhancing drugs, 1:250–252

congressional hearing (2005) and drug scandal, 1:251

overview, 1:250

types of, 1:250–251

BASF, 1:3

Bath salts (synthetic cathinones), 1:252–255

administration and abuse of, 1:253–254

overview, 1:252–253

Baxter International, 1:255–258

controversies, 1:257

major breakthroughs, 1:257

overview, 1:255–256

product quality, 1:256–257

society support initiatives, 1:256

Baycol, 1:332–334

Bayer, 1:258–260

early heroin production, 1:xxxvii

history, 1:258–259

overview, 1:258

products of, 1:259–260

during World War II, 1:259

Beal, James Hartley, 1:95

Beckman Research Institute, 2:638

Beesley, Eugene N., 2:570–571

Behavioral neuroscience, 3:966–967

Behavioral pharmacology and substance abuse, 1:260–265

methodological considerations, 1:261–262

overview, 1:260–261

psychoneuroendocrinology and, 1:264–265

substance abuse, 1:262–263

theories about, 1:263–264

Behring and Roux, 1:xxxvii

Belgium, 1:265–268

health system of, 1:266

overview, 1:265–266

pharmaceutical industry of, 1:266–267

Belladonna (traditional medicine/poison), 1:268–270

alternative uses, 1:269–270

plant description and toxicity, 1:268

research, 1:270

uses in traditional medicine, 1:268–269

Belmont Principles, 2:757, 2:759, 4:1452

Belviq, 2:560

Benadryl, 2:806

Bencao Tujing, 4:1380

Benzodiazepines, 1:32

Benzphetamine hydrochloride, 1:209–210

Berotec, 1:284

Best, Charles, 2:570

Best Pharmaceuticals for Children Act, 1:xlii

Beta-2 agonists, 3:1333

Beta2-agonists, 1:53

Beta-blockers, 3:1334

water pollution and, 4:1533

Beta-blockers (sport), 1:270–276

effectiveness, 1:274–275

ethics, 1:275

medical concerns, 1:274

men's health and, 2:906

overview, 1:270–271

prescription drugs, 1:271–272

use in sports, 1:272–274

Better Pharmaceuticals for Children Act (BPCA), 3:1054–1055

Bextra, 3:1064

BiDil, 1:119

Biguanides, 1:169–170

Bill and Melinda Gates Foundation, 1:18–19

Binder, George, 1:99

Biogen Idec, 1:276–277

history of, 1:276

manufacturing, 1:277

overview, 1:276

therapies and products, 1:276–277

Biological passport (sport), 1:278–280

guidelines, 1:278

use of, 1:278–279

Biologics Control Act of 1902, 1:xxxviii

Biologics Pharmacology Research Laboratories, 2:442

Biopress, 4:1347

Bioprospecting, 2:589

Bioterrorism

BioThrax, 4:1509

Project Bioshield Act, 1:xliii, 3:1171–1173

smallpox fears, 1:xlii, 3:1301, 4:1511

Birth control pills, 2:603, 2:608–610

Bisolvon, 1:284

Black, James, 1:270

Black, James W., 1:xli–xlii

Black Death, 2:719

Black Drink, 4:1407

Blood boosters

baseball and performance-enhancing drugs, 1:251

Blood doping, 1:280–283

overview, 1:280

risks, benefits, and outcomes, 1:281–282

types of, 1:280–281

Blood pressure

African Americans and, 1:72

Blopress, 4:1345

Bly, Stanley, 1:85

BMJ, 1:xlv

BMP Sunstone Corp., 3:1264

Boehringer Ingelheim, 1:283–285

Development of AntiRetroviral Therapy (DART), 2:760

history of, 1:283

lawsuit (2014), 1:285

products, 1:284

research and development by, 1:283–284

Boggs Act, 2:880–881

Bolivia, traditional and herbal medicines in, 4:1389

Bolt, Usain, 4:1369

Bonds, Barry, 1:247–250, 2:633–635

Boots Pure Drug Company, 1:xl

Borax, 3:1062

Bordetella pertussis, 1:xxxviii

Borrelia, 2:842

Boxing and performance-enhancing drugs, 1:285–288

　overview, 1:285–286

　regulation, 1:287–288

　rise of PEDs in professional boxing, 1:286–287

Boyer, Herbert, 2:638

Bradley Pharmaceuticals, 3:990

Brilinta, 1:230–231

Bristol-Meyers Squibb, 1:230

British East India Company, 1:xxxvi

British Journal of Clinical Pharmacology, 1:290

British Journal of Pharmacology and Chemotherapy, 1:290

British Pharmacological Society, The, 1:288–290

　history of, 1:288–289

　journals of, 1:290

　membership in, 1:289

　relationship to other organizations, 1:289–290

Bubonic plague, 1:xxxviii

Buchhein, Rufolf, 1:xxxi

Buddhism, traditional medicine and. *See* **Traditional medicine: Tibet**

Bulwer-Lytton, Edward, 1:xxxvi

Bureau of Chemistry, 1:xxxvii

Bureau of Narcotics and Dangerous Drugs (BNDD), 2:881, 3:1311

Cachexia, 1:210–211

Caffeine

　neuro-enhancement through pharmacy, 3:962

　stimulants and, 3:1322

　as study aid, 2:551, 3:1322, 3:1332

　swimming and PEDs, 3:1322

Calcium D3, 3:991

Calcium-based products, in anticaries drugs, 1:147–148

Calesnick, Benjamin, 1:89

California

　California HealthCare Foundation, 1:xliii–xliv

　Proposition 215, 2:882–883, 4:1398

　sex offenders and pharmacological interventions, 3:1274–1275

Cambridge Antibody Technology GroupZeneca, 1:229, 1:230

Camphor, 3:1062

Campylobacter, 2:547–548

Canada, 1:291–296

　clinical trials, 3:1149

　elderly people and drug coverage, 1:299

　evolution of pharmacology in, 1:291–292

　fertility control history, 2:607

　harm reduction policies, 2:673–674

　health insurance, 1:294–295

　Marketed Health Products Directorate (Canada), 2:849–851

　Medical Insurance Act, 1:xl

　medical marijuana legislation, 2:872–874

　Opium and Drug Act, 1:xxxviii

　pharmacology and economics, 1:293–294

　pharmacology as industry in, 1:292–293

　prescription drug approval process: Canada, 3:1147–1150

　racial minorities: Canada, 3:1210–1215

　sex offenders and pharmacological interventions, 3:1275

　smuggling of prescription drugs and, 3:1313

　traditional and herbal medicines, regulation: Canada, 4:1377–1379

　variation in prescription drug benefits by province/territory, 1:296–304

　world role of, 1:295–296

Canada: variation in prescription drug benefits by province/territory, 1:296–304

　barriers and solutions to improve patient's access to prescription drugs, 1:298 (table)

chronic physical condition and
 prescription drug benefits, **1**:302
controlling costs, **1**:303
coverage for nonseniors, **1**:300
demand for prescription drug benefits,
 1:301
drug prices across Canada, **1**:299
drug pricing in Ontario, **1**:300–301
drug pricing in Quebec, **1**:300
erosion of benefits, **1**:299–300
impact of being uninsured, **1**:301
mental health and out-of-pocket costs,
 1:302
mental health and prescription drug
 benefits, **1**:302–303
mental illness, impact, **1**:301–302
national system and provinces, **1**:302
overview, **1**:296–297
public drug coverage for seniors, **1**:299
public policies to control prices, **1**:300
public prescription drug benefit plans,
 1:301
role of employers, **1**:303
role of governments in regulation of drug
 prices, **1**:297–298
role of physician, **1**:298–299
Canadian Journal of Clinical Pharmacology,
 1:307
*Canadian Journal of Physiology and Phar-
 macology,* **1**:307, **1**:308
*Canadian Journal of Population Therapeutics
 and Clinical Pharmacology,* **1**:308
Canadian Medical Association Journal, **1**:xlv
Canadian provincial databases, 1:304–306
 cancer registry, **1**:305–306
 hospital services data, **1**:305
 medical service data, **1**:305
 overview, **1**:304
 population registry, **1**:305
 prescription drug data, **1**:305
 vital statistics, **1**:306
**Canadian Society of Pharmacology and
 Therapeutics, 1:306–308**
 overview, **1**:306–307
 professional pharmacology and, **1**:308
 purpose and goals of, **1**:307–308

Cancer
 access to medicines (developing world),
  1:15
 Cancer Drugs fund (U.K.), **1**:xlv
 Dartmouth-Hitchcock Norris Cotton
  Cancer Center (NCCC), **2**:443–445
 data, **4**:1674 (table), **4**:1675 (table),
  4:1676 (table), **4**:1677 (table)
 Delaney Cause, **1**:xl
 disease statistics, **4**:1674 (table),
  4:1675 (table), **4**:1676 (table),
  4:1677 (table)
 gonadotropins and, **1**:310
 hormonal therapies for, **1**:310, **1**:311–312
 hormone replacement therapy and,
  2:749–750
 Memorial Sloan Kettering Cancer Center,
  1:87
 MPDL380A, **1**:xlv
 orphan diseases and, **3**:1021
 orphan diseases and drugs for, **3**:1021
 skin cancer and sun exposure,
  3:1329–1332
 Yale Cancer Center, **1**:xlv
Cancer, drug treatments for, 1:308–312. *See
 also* Cancer; *individual pharmaceutical
 company names*
 chemoprevention, **1**:339–341
 overview, **1**:308–309
 types of, **1**:309–312
Candida, **2**:548
Cannabis. *See also* Marijuana
 cannabidiol, **1**:xlvi
 as hallucinogen, **2**:671–672
Canon of Medicine, The (Avicenna),
 1:312–315
 description of books, **1**:313–314
 legacy of, **1**:314–315
 overview, **1**:312–313
Capsaicin, **1**:349–352
Cardinal Health, **3**:1312
Cardiovascular drugs, 1:315–320
 African Americans and race-based
  pharmaceuticals, **3**:1201
 antiarrhythmic drugs, **1**:315–316
 anticoagulant drugs, **1**:319

antihypertensive drugs, 1:316–317
Digitalis, 1:319, 2:471–473
elderly people and, 2:564–565
heart failure drugs, 1:318–319
ischemic heart disease drugs, 1:318
overview, 1:315
Cardiovascular pharmacology, 1:320–322
African Americans, 1:72–73
aldosterone inhibitors, 1:321
angiotensin II receptor blockers, 1:322
angiotensin-converting enzyme inhibitors, 1:321
beta-blockers, 1:321–322
calcium channel blockers, 1:322
cardiovascular diseases, overview, 1:320–321
cholesterol-lowering drugs, 1:321
digoxin, 1:321
CareerPharm (ASHP), 1:98
Carotenoids, 3:1130–1131
Cathinones. *See* **Bath salts (synthetic cathinones)**
Cat's claw, 4:1420–1421
Caventou, Joseph Biename, 1:xxxvi
Cayenne pepper, 4:1407
CCBs, 1:316, 1:317
CD4 cell count, HIV and, 1:76
Ceclor, 2:571
Celebrex, 3:1064
Celgene, 1:322–324
overview, 1:322–323
products, 1:323–324
Center for Medicare and Medicaid Services, 4:1662
Center for the Evaluation of Value and Risk in Health (CEVR), 1:426
Centers for Disease Control and Prevention, 1:324–329. *See also* Vaccination coverage data; Vaccines
addiction to prescription drugs, 1:33–34
Advisory Committee on Immunization Practices, 4:1508 (*See also* **Vaccines**)
on autism spectrum disorder, 1:xliv
on children with ADHD, 1:xliv
diseases paramount to, 1:325–326
Division of HIV/AIDS Prevention, 4:1689 (*See also* HIV/AIDS data)

Global Disease Detection (GDD) (CDC), 1:327–328
global health campaigns, 1:326–328
Global Immunization Division, 4:1509
HIV patient awareness of status, 1:xliv
on measles, 1:xl
morbidity and mortality, from antibiotic resistant infection, 4:1601, 4:1602–1603 (table)
Morbidity and Mortality Weekly Report, 4:1605, 4:1646, 4:1651, 4:1655, 4:1703
National Center for Health Statistics, 4:1587–1984 (*See also* Prescription medication use)
National Health Interview Survey (NHIS), 4:1639, 4:1642
National Survey of Family Growth (NSFG), 4:1633 (*See also* Contraception use data)
overview, 1:324–325
President's Malaria Initiative (PMI), 1:324, 1:327
youth drug use data of (*See* Youth drug use data)
Central nervous system depressants and stimulants, 1:329–332
caffeine, 1:331
depressants, 1:329–330
nicotine, 1:331
stimulants, 1:330–331
Cerdelga, 3:1265
Cerivastatin (Baycol, Lipobay) controversy, 1:332–334
future directions, 1:333
legal action, 1:332–333
recall, 1:332
Cervical caps, 2:604
Chagas disease, 1:xlv
Chain, Ernst Boris, 1:xxxix
Chamomile (herbal medicine), 1:334–336
clinical studies, 1:335–336
cultural history, 1:334
modern cultural significance, 1:336
modern medicinal uses, 1:334–335
modern miscellaneous uses, 1:336

Chantix, 3:1065, 3:1303–1304

Chao, Allen, 1:29

Chattem Inc., 3:1164

Chemical fertilizers: human health effects,
    1:337–339
  human health effects, 1:337–338
  organic fertilizers, 1:338

Chemoprevention, 1:339–341
  agents, 1:340–341
  overview, 1:339–340

Children, 1:341–349. *See also* Vaccination
    coverage data; Youth drug use data
  AIDS/HIV drugs for, 1:78
  amphetamines and, 1:105–106
  antipsychotic drugs used by, 1:xliv–xlv
  Best Pharmaceuticals for Children Act,
    1:xlii
  CDC on children with ADHD, 1:xliv
  clinical pharmacology (industrialized
    nations), in special populations, 1:381
  complementary medicine use data,
    4:1642 (table), 4:1643 (table),
    4:1644 (table), 4:1645 (table)
  developmental pharmacology, 1:343–344
  drugs as study aids and, 2:552–553
  Essential Medicines List for Children,
    4th ed., 1:xxxiii
  fluoridation in drinking water and,
    2:616–618
  geographic variations in prescribing
    practices, 2:652
  historical perspective, 1:342–343
  Kids Inpatient Database (KID), 2:684
  neonatal abstinence syndrome, 3:957–959
  off-label use, 1:343
  orphan diseases and drugs for, 3:1021
  overview, 1:341–342
  Pediatric Pharmacology Research Units
    (PPRU), 1:346–348
  Pediatric Rule (U.S., 1998), 3:1053–1056
  pharmacokinetics, 1:342
  psychotropic intervention for children's
    behavioral issues, 1:40 (*See also*
    ADHD drugs)
  psychotropic use study in *Pediatrics,*
    1:345–346

SCHIP (State Children's Health Insurance
    Program): prescription drug benefits,
    3:1270–1274
  thalidomide controversy and, 1:211,
    2:623–625, 4:1357–1359
  WHO Model List of Essential Medicines
    for Children, 4th edition of, 1:xliv
  young children and psychotropics,
    1:344–345

Children's Vaccine Plan (WHO), 1:xlii

Child-resistant packaging, 1:9

Chili (capsaicin), 1:349–352
  overview, 1:349
  uses of, 1:349–351

China, 1:352–355
  antibiotics, 1:354–355
  drug labeling and supervision, 2:528–529
  health, 1:352–353
  health care system, 1:353
  history of pharmacology in ancient China,
    2:704–708
  opium trade, 18th century, 1:xxxvi
  Opium Wars, 1:xxxvi, 1:xxxvii
  Pen T'sao (Shen Nun), 1:xxxv
  pharmaceutical industry, 1:354
  prescription drug approval process: Asia,
    3:1143–1144
  racial minorities of Asia and, 3:1202,
    3:1206
  Sinopharm Group Company Limited and
    Chinese government, 3:1297 (*See also*
    Sinopharm Group Company Limited)
  state-sponsored sports doping programs,
    3:1319–1320
  Tibet and, 4:1425–1426
  traditional and herbal medicines, regulation
    and East Asia, 4:1379–1383
  traditional medicine and, 1:354,
    4:1408–1411 (*See also* Traditional
    medicines)
  Vietnam and, 4:1427

China National Group Corporation of
    Traditional & Herbal Medicine,
    3:1295

China National Medical Equipment Industry
    Corporation, 3:1295

China National Pharmaceutical Foreign Trade Corporation, 3:1295
China National Pharmaceutical Group Corporation, 3:1294–1295
China Pharmaceutical Advertising Limited Company, 3:1296
Chinese yew tree, 2:899
Chlorazene, 1:1
Chlorhexidine, 1:146–147
Chloroquine, 1:191
Chocola, 2:560
Cholesterol. *See* **Anticholesterol drugs**
Choline, 2:729–730
Chronic lower respiratory diseases, elderly people and, 2:565
Chronology, 1:xxxvi–xlvi
Cialis, 2:571
CiclosporinPro, 4:1355
Cigarette smoking, cessation drugs for, 3:1301–1306
Ciqorin, 4:1355
Circulatory diseases (data), 4:1666–1667 (table), 4:1668–1669 (table)
Citric acid, 3:1062
Claforan, 3:1164
Clark, Ian, 2:638
Classical conditioning, substance abuse and, 1:264–265
Classical pharmacology, 1:355–362
    clinical trials, 1:356–357
    clinical trials, history of, 1:357–358
    clinical trials, types, 1:358–359
    ethical conduct, 1:359–360
    safety, 1:360
    screening and designing new drugs, 1:360–361
    types of phenotypic screening, 1:355–356
Claxton, Karl, 1:xlv
Clinical field studies, 1:362–365
    clinical trials versus, 1:364–365
    conducting, 1:362–363
    participating in, 1:363–364
Clinical pharmacology, 1:365–370
    adverse drug reactions, 1:369
    allergic adverse drug reactions, 1:369–370

mechanism of drug action (pharmacodynamics), 1:366
    overview, 1:365–366
    pharmacokinetics, 1:367
    therapeutic drug monitoring, 1:367–369
    use of drugs, 1:366
Clinical pharmacology: developing countries, 1:370–377
    diseases, 1:374
    foreign aid, 1:373–374
    future directions, 1:376–377
    human resources, 1:372–373
    medicine use, 1:375–376
    overview, 1:370–371
    pharmacovigilance, 1:374–375
    rational use of medicine, 1:371–372
Clinical pharmacology: industrialized countries, 1:377–384
    areas of specialization in clinical pharmacology, 1:382–383
    outlook for future, 1:383–384
    overview, 1:377–378
    services to patients, 1:379–381
    special populations, 1:381
    state of profession, 1:378–379
Clinical trials, 1:384–389
    cost and time involved, 1:385–386
    critique, 1:388–389
    defined, 1:385
    EudraCT (European Union Drug Regulating Authorities Clinical Trials), 2:590–592
    gender differences in drug trials, 2:906–907
    overview, 1:384–385
    of pharmaceutical drugs in Mexico, 2:921–922
    phases of, 1:386–387
    prescription drug approval process: Australia, 3:1146–1147
    prescription drug approval process: Canada, 3:1149
    Rofecoxib (Vioxx) controversy, 3:1246–1249
Clinical trials, history of, 1:389–394
    biometrics and, 1:392–393
    blind assessment, 1:391

criticism of, 1:393
examples, 1:391
first prospective controlled trial, 1:390
importance of case studies, 1:390–391
Louis and *Méthode Numérique,* 1:390–391
making comparisons, 1:389–390
new remedies, 1:390
placebo effect, 1:391
placebos and ethics, 1:392
problems of design (19th and 20th
    centuries), 1:391–392
smallpox and "arithmetic tradition," 1:390
therapeutic perspectives (20th century), 1:392
Clinton Foundation, 1:18
Clostridia, 2:548
Club drugs, 1:394–396. *See also* **MDMA
    (Ecstasy)**
health concerns about, 1:395–396
medical use of, 1:396
pharmacology and behavioral effects,
    1:394–395
Rohypnol, 1:394–396, 2:762–763
CMC Biotech, 2:571
Coalition Against Insurance Fraud (CAIF),
    3:1312
Coca leaves, 1:xxxvii, 4:1421
Coca-Cola, 1:xxxvii
Cocaine, 1:396–399
emerging approaches, 1:398–399
historical perspective, 1:xlii
mechanisms of action and effects,
    1:397–398
overview, 1:396–397
as Schedule II drug, 3:1266
swimming and PEDs, 3:1333
youth drug use data, 4:1610 (table),
    4:1611 (table), 4:1612 (table)
Code of Ethics (American Pharmacists
    Association), 1:xl, 1:95, 2:742–743
*Code on Interactions With Healthcare
    Professionals* (Pharmaceutical Research
    and Manufacturers of America), 1:65
Cognitive enhancers, 1:399–403
drug approaches and, 1:400–402
overview, 1:399–400
stimulant drugs of abuse, 1:402

Colombia, 1:403–404
illegal drug trade and, 1:403–404
overview, 1:403
Committee on Herbal Medicinal Products
    (HMPC), 4:1385–1387
Common Rule, The, 1:404–407
criticism of, 1:406
overview, 1:404–405
scope of, 1:405–406
**Comparative effectiveness research,
    1:407–410**
current perspectives and health care
    applications, 1:409
example and value assessment, 1:409
patient-centered outcomes research
    institute, 1:408–409
Patient-Centered Outcomes Research
    Institute (PCORI), 1:408–409
purpose, 1:407
types and key components, 1:408
Complementary or alternative medicine
    (CAM). *See also* Traditional medicines;
    individual country names
children, 4:1642 (table), 4:1643 (table),
    4:1644 (table), 4:1645 (table)
Hispanic Americans and, 2:698
National Center for Complementary and
    Alternative Medicine (NIH), 3:943–946
National Center for Complementary and
    Alternative Medicine, inception, 1:xxxi
National Center for Complementary and
    Integrative Health, 1:88
National Health Interview Survey (NHIS),
    4:1639, 4:1642
selected types of nonvitamin, nonmineral
    dietary supplements, 4:1641 (table)
trends, by age, 4:1640 (table)
trends, by type of approach, 4:1639 (table)
Compound 606, 1:xxxviii
**Comprehensive Methamphetamine Control
    Act (1996), 1:410–412.** *See also*
    Methamphetamine
cold and sinus medication restrictions, 1:410
consequences of, 1:411–412
increased penalties, 1:410–411
passage of, 2:916

Compulsory licensing, 2:582
Computer-aided drug design, 1:412–414
  CADD, overview, 1:412
  ligand-based drug design (LBDD),
    1:412–413
  structure-based drug design (SBDD),
    1:412–413
  Tekturna (aliskiren), renin inhibitor (RI)
    and, 1:413–414
Comstock Act, 2:607
Concerta, 2:806
Condoms, 2:604, 2:608
"Confessions of an English Opium-eater"
  (De Quincey), 1:xxxvi
Conscience clause, 1:414–416
  criticism, 1:415–416
  overview, 1:414–415
Conte, Aubry, 4:1368
Conte, Victor, 4:1368
Contraception. *See* **Fertility control; Fertility
  control: history**
Contraception use data
  among youths, 4:1620 (table),
    4:1621 (table), 4:1622 (table),
    4:1623 (table), 4:1624 (table),
    4:1625 (table), 4:1626 (table),
    4:1627 (table), 4:1628 (table),
    4:1629 (table)
  National Survey of Family Growth
    (NSFG), 4:1633
  women and, 4:1634 (tables),
    4:1635 (tables), 4:1636 (table),
    4:1637 (table), 4:1638 (table)
Controlled Substances Act, 1:416–419
  background, 1:417
  domains impacted, 1:417–418
  medical marijuana legislation (U.S.),
    2:883, 2:884
  overview, 1:416–417
  scheduled drugs in U.S., 1:418–419,
    3:1265–1270
  smuggling of prescription drugs and,
    3:1312
Cosmetic pharmacology, 1:420–423
  debates and controversies, 1:421–422
  origin of concept, 1:420–421

Costa Rica, 1:423–424
  medicine and treatment, 1:423–424
  medicine distribution and pharmacies,
    1:424
Cost-effectiveness research, 1:425–428
  analysis, 1:425–426
  overview, 1:426–427
Counterfeit drugs/medicines, 1:428–430
  drugs most often counterfeited, 1:429–430
  earnings and growth of, 1:429
  EvaPharmacy and, 1:430
  growth of, country of origin, accreditation,
    and enforcement, 1:428–429
Crawford, A. C., 1:xxxvii
Cross-addiction/cross-dependence, 1:37
Cross-cultural pharmacology.
  See Ethnopharmacology
Cuban Society for Pharmacology, 1:431–433
  origin and contemporary developments,
    1:431–432
  overview, 1:431
Cuppari, Girolamo G., 1:89
Curandero, 1:433–435
  classification, 1:433–434
  defined, 1:433
  practice of, 1:434–435
Current Good Manufacturing Practice
  (CGMP) fraud, 3:1070–1071
Current Population Survey (CPS), 4:1659
Current state of technology-supported
  pharmacy, 4:1349–1350
Currie, James, 3:1062
CV Therapeutics Inc., 1:226
**Cycling and performance-enhancing drugs,
  1:435–439**
  in classical cycling culture, 1:436–437
  future of, 1:438
  in modern cycling culture, 1:437–438
  origins of PED in professional cycling,
    1:435–436
Cyclooxygenase (COX-2), 1:27
Cymbalta, 1:67
Cytochrome P450 enzymes, 1:72
Cytokines, 1:311
Czech Republic, medical marijuana
  legislation and, 2:876

Daiichi Sankyo, 2:441–443
  Astellas Pharma and, 1:226
  corporate philosophy and recent strategy,
      2:442–443
  history of, 2:441–442
Dairy, drug interactions with, 2:519
Dale and Betty Bumpers Vaccine Research
      Center (NIH), 1:xlii
Daliresp, 3:991
Dartmouth College, 2:443–445
  Dartmouth-Hitchcock Norris Cotton
      Cancer Center (NCCC), 2:443–445
  overview, 2:443
Darvon, 2:571
Databases/data sources. *See also* **World**
      Health Organization
  adjudicated claims data, 1:49–52
  adverse drug effects reporting systems,
      1:56–60, 2:893–894, 3:1096, 3:1137,
      4:1464, 4:1544–1545, 4:1664 (table)
  Canadian provincial databases, 1:304–306
  Centers for Disease Control and
      Prevention, 1:324–329
  computerized systems for prescription
      drugs, 4:1592 (table)
  electronic medical records, overview,
      2:489–490
  ENCePP Database (European Network of
      Centres for Pharmacoepidemiology
      and Pharmacovigilance), 2:571–573
  General Practice Research Database (UK),
      2:640–643
  Health Canada, 4:1378–1379
  Healthcare Cost and Utilization Project
      (HCUP), 2:683–685, 2:683–686
  Healthcare Effectiveness Data and
      Information Set (HEDIS), 2:686–688
  HMO Research Network (19 Regional
      Health Care Delivery Organizations),
      2:745–746
  hospital administrative data and, 2:753–756
  Medicaid and Medicare systems, 2:866–869
  medical expenditure panel survey (MEPS),
      2:869–872
  Organisation for Economic Co-operation and
      Development, 1:21–24, 3:1017–1020

  pharmacoinformatics, 3:1100–1102
  PHARMO Record Linkage System
      (The Netherlands), 3:1120–1122
  Prescription-Event Monitoring (PEM)
      Database (University of Portsmouth,
      UK), 3:1159–1162
  RxNorm (National Library of Medicine),
      3:1252–1254
  Substance Abuse and Mental Health
      Services Administration (SAMHSA),
      2:914, 3:1326–1329
  technology and pharmacy practice,
      4:1348–1351
  translational pharmacology and global
      data sharing, 4:1437–1438
Date rape drugs
  inhalants, 2:778
  Rohypnol, 1:394–396, 2:762–763
DaunoXome, 2:658
Daxas, 3:991, 4:1347
De Quincey, Thomas, 1:xxxvi
Declaration of Helsinki (1975), 2:445–447
  meetings and revisions, 2:445–447
  overview, 2:445
  Tuskegee experiment and, 4:1452
DeCODE Genetics, 1:100
Decongestants, 2:448–450
  health concerns, 2:448–450
  types of, 2:448
Deep tank fermentation (DTF),
      3:1062–1063
Defense Health Agency (DHA), 2:926
Deinstitutionalization movement, 2:450–457
  context, 2:456
  deinstitutionalization, defined, 2:450–451
  history of, 2:451–456
Delaney Cause, 1:xl
Dementia, elderly people and, 2:565
Denmark, 2:457–459
  consumption of prescription drugs in,
      2:457–458
  international conventions and prescription
      drugs, 2:459
  pharmaceutical industry, 2:459
  public debate about drugs in, 2:458
  regulation and legislation, 2:458

Dental health
   anticaries drugs, 1:145–148
   fluoridation (drinking water) and,
      2:614–617
Depakine, 3:1164
Depamine receptor agonists, 1:172
Department of Ayurveda, Yoga, Naturopathy,
      Unani, Siddha and Homeopathy
      (AYUSH) (India), 3:1291
Depression
   *The Noonday Demon: An Atlas of
      Depression* (Andrew Solomon),
      3:977–978
Dervan, Peter, 2:657
**DES (Diethylstilbestrol) controversy,
   2:459–462**
   health concerns about, 2:460–462
   overview, 2:459–460
**Developing countries, residents of,
   2:462–467.** *See also individual
   country names*
   access to essential medicines in developing
      countries, 2:464–465
   health and environment in developing
      countries, 2:463–464
   market access and, 2:466
   migration and, 2:465–466
   overview, 2:462
   poverty and, 2:462–463
Development of AntiRetroviral Therapy
      (DART), 2:760
Devinsky, Orrin, 1:xlvi
Dexamphetamine, 1:40
Diabetes
   African Americans and, 1:72–73
   aloe vera and, 1:87
   early synthetic insulin, 2:638
   elderly people and, 2:565
   endocrine pharmacology, 2:575
   in Hispanic American population, 2:698
   Merck and, 2:912
   Novo Nordisk and, 3:985–987
   percentage using diabetes medication by
      type of medication, 4:1600 (table)
   Phenformin (Azucaps) controversy,
      3:1125–1127

Diabinese, 3:1064
Diagnostic and Statistical Manual
   DSM-3 on antianxiety drugs, 1:121
   DSM-5 on cosmetic pharmacology, 1:421
   DSM-5 on prescription direction
      adherence, 1:48
   DSM-5 on substance abuse, 1:263
   on psychopharmacology, 3:1183
   Rush and, 4:1469
   on substance abuse, 1:262
Diaphragms, 2:604
Dibble, Eugene H., 4:1451
Dietary Supplement Act of 1992, 3:1157–1158
Dietary Supplement Health and Education
      Act (DSHEA), 4:1397
Dietary Supplements Compendium (USP),
      4:1504
Diethylpropion HC1, 1:210
Differential pricing, 2:521
**Diffusion of new pharmaceutical drugs,
   2:467–471**
   advertising to consumers, 2:469–470
   promotion, 2:467–468
   public relations to physicians, 2:468–469
   targeted communication in health field,
      2:469
Diflucan, 3:1064
Digitalis, 2:471–473
   digoxin, 1:319
   overview, 2:471
   precautions for, 2:472–473
   uses of, 2:471–472
DiNicolantonio, James, 1:230–231
Dipeptidyl peptidase-4 inhibitors
      (DPP4-inhibitors), 1:171–172
Diphtheria, tetanus, pertussis (DPT) vaccine,
      introduction of, 1:xxxix
Diphtheria antitoxin, 1:xxxvii
Directly observed therapy (DOT), 1:xlii
**Directly observed therapy, short-course,
   2:473–475**
   components of, 2:474–475
   inclusion of, as part of broader TB
      strategy, 2:475
   overview, 2:473–474
   uses and outcomes, 2:475

Direct-to-consumer pharmaceutical
    advertising (DTCPA), 1:66–70
Discrimination in prescribing practice,
    2:475–483
    age, 2:481–482
    ethnicity, 2:477–479
    gender, 2:479
    history of drug use, 2:480–481
    mental health history, 2:480
    overview, 2:475–476
    race, 2:476–477
    religious beliefs, 2:479–480
Disease concept of addiction: history,
    2:483–487
    historical genealogy of disease concept, 2:483
    multiple definitions of disease, 2:483–484
    strategic uses of disease concept to
        destigmatize addiction, 2:484–487
Disease management, 2:487–491
    challenges, 2:490
    new technology, 2:489–490
    patient perspective, 2:488–489
    provider perspective, 2:487–488
Disease statistics
    cancer, 4:1674 (table), 4:1675 (table),
        4:1676 (table), 4:1677 (table)
    circulatory diseases, 4:1666–1667 (table),
        4:1668–1669 (table)
    hearing trouble, vision trouble, absence of
        teeth, 4:1686–1688 (table)
    migraines, pain in neck/lower back/face/
        jaw, 4:1682–1683 (table),
        4:1684–1685 (table)
    National Health Interview Survey (NHIS),
        4:1666
    respiratory diseases, 4:1670–1671 (table),
        4:1672–1673 (table)
    selected diseases and conditions,
        4:1678–1679 (table),
        4:1680–1681 (table)
Dissociative anesthetics, 2:670–671
Disulfiram, 1:81–82
Diuretics, 2:491–494
    abuse of, 2:493
    baseball and performance-enhancing
        drugs, 1:251

as cardiovascular drug, 1:317, 1:318
    development of, 2:491–492
    hypertension in today's society, 2:494
    major classes of, 2:492–493
    overview, 1:183–184, 2:491 (*See also*
        Antihypertensive drugs)
    swimming and PEDs, 3:1334
Diuretics and masking agents (sport),
    2:494–497
    masking agents, explained, 2:485–496
    overview, 2:484–485
Division of Chemistry, U.S.D.A., 1:xxxvii
Division of HIV/AIDS Prevention,
    4:1689
Dix, Dorothea, 4:1467
Dobutrex, 2:571
"Doctor shopping," abuse of prescription
    drugs and, 1:5
Doctors
    advertising to, 1:61–66
Doering, William von Eggers, 1:xxxix
Doha Declaration (WTO), 1:18,
    4:1441–1442. *See also* **TRIPS**
    Agreement (Agreement on Trade-
    Related Aspects of Intellectual Property
    Rights), Doha Declarations, and TRIPS
    Plus
Dohme, Carl Friedrich Louise, 2:912
Dominican Republic, traditional and herbal
    medicines in, 4:1389
Dong Y, 4:1427–1428
Dopamine, 1:8, 1:36, 2:550–551
Doping, origin of term, 3:1057
Dosage safety measures, 2:497–500
    dose, defined, 2:497
    effective dose, defined, 2:498
    overview and definitions, 2:497–500
Dow Chemicals, 2:571
Doxycycline, 1:191–192, 3:1065
Dragon's blood, 4:1421
Dreser, Heinrich, 1:xxxvii
Drucker, Peter, 3:1064
Drug abuse
    abuse of prescription drugs, 1:4–10
    acetaminophen, 1:26–28
    addiction to prescription drugs, 1:30–38

Drug Abuse Control Amendments of 1965, 2:500–503, 3:1311
content of, 2:502–503
overview, 2:500–502
Drug allergies, 2:503–505
epidemiologic research, 2:504–505
overview, 2:503–504
research issues, 2:504
Drug discovery and development, 2:505–511
identifying molecules, 2:505–507
investment in R&D, 2:508–509
market development, 2:509–510
preclinical and clinical evaluation, 2:507–508
role of pharmaceutical companies and, 2:508
Drug Enforcement Administration (U.S.), 2:511–515
ADHD drugs, 1:43
Controlled Substances Act of 1970, 2:513–514
creation of, 1:xl
drug enforcement before 1973, 2:511–512
early drug enforcement history, 2:512
employment with, 2:514–515
mission and goals of, 2:512–513
modern-day, 2:514
state and local task force program, 2:514
Drug Information, 1:98
Drug interactions, 2:515–520
drug–drug interactions (pharmacodynamic), 2:516–517
drug–drug interactions (pharmacokinetic), 2:517–518
drug–food interactions, 2:518–520
overview, 2:515–516
Drug labeling: developing world, 2:520–525
access to medicines, 2:520–521
counterfeit drugs and new technologies, 2:521–522, 2:523–524
drug labels exported from U.S., 2:522–523
equity and differential pricing, 2:521
parallel imports, 2:521
World Health Organization and, 2:520, 2:523

Drug labeling: industrialized world, 2:525–530
adverse reactions labeling, 2:526
dosage and administration, 2:526
drug labeling and supervision in China, 2:528–529
European Medicines Agency, 2:527–528
FDA and, 2:525–526
package inserts, 2:526–527
package inserts, in Europe, 2:527
postmarket safety surveillance, 2:526
"Drug lag," 2:803–804
Drug poisoning deaths, involving opioid analgesics, 4:1593 (table)
Drug Price Competition and Patent Term Restoration Act (1984), 2:530–532
mechanics of, 2:531–532
overview, 2:530–531
Drug testing, high school and college athletes (U.S.), 2:532–536
college and university drug testing, 2:533–536
drug testing in high school, 2:532–533
(See also Athletes)
Drug testing, Olympic athletes (overview), 2:537–541
antidoping activities at 2014 Winter Olympics, 2:537–538
IOC medical policies, 2:538–539
overview, 2:537
U.S. Anti-Doping Agency (USADA), 2:539–540
USADA drug-testing program, 2:540–541
Drug testing, professional athletes (overview), 2:541–545
antidoping arguments, 2:543
banned substances, 2:542–543
Major League Baseball and, 2:543–544
National Basketball Association and, 2:544
National Football League and, 2:545
National Hockey League and, 2:545
overview, 2:541–542
swimming, 3:1334–1335
Drug trafficking, 3:1306–1310

Drug-resistant diseases, 2:546–550
antimicrobial resistance, 2:546
antimicrobial resistance, factors
promoting, 2:546–547
antimicrobial-resistant microorganisms,
2:547–550
diseases, 2:547
infection, 2:547
next generation of antimicrobials,
2:550
Drugs, overview, 1:xxxi–xxxiv
Drugs as study aids, 2:550–553
Drummond, M., 3:1094
Dubose Montgomery, 2:657
Duragesic, 2:806
Durata Therapeutics, 1:29
Durham-Humphrey Amendment,
3:1311

East Germany, state-sponsored sports doping
programs, 3:1320–1321
Ebers, George, 2:708
Ebers Papyrus, 1:xxxv, 2:733
Ebert Prize, 1:95
Ecstasy (MDMA), 1:394–396
Ecuador, traditional and herbal medicines in,
4:1389–1390
Edeleanu, Lazar, 1:101
Education
abuse of prescription drugs and, 1:10
ADHD pharmacotherapy and schools,
1:39, 1:43
early pharmacist degrees, U.S.,
1:xxxvi, 1:xl
pharmacology as field of study,
1:xxxi–xxxii, 1:xxxix
pharmacy technicians: training and
certification, 3:1116–1120,
3:1116–11120
Philadelphia College of Pharmacy
and Science as first U.S. school of
pharmacy, 1:xxxvi
University of Michigan, 1:xxxi, 1:xxxvii
of U.S. pharmacists, 2:743–744
WHO Model Lists of Essential Medicines
and, 1:xxxii–xxxiii, 4:1534–1537

Efalizumab (Raptiva) controversy, 2:555–557
psoriasis and, 2:555
research, 2:556
withdrawal of product, 2:557
Egbogi **(traditional Yoruba medicine),**
2:557–560
traditional training, 2:559
types medicine, 2:558
Yoruba, defined, 2:557–558
Yoruba Orishas, 2:559
Egypt (ancient)
Ebers Papyrus, 1:xxxv
history of pharmacology in, 2:708–711
Ehrlich, Paul, 1:xxxviii, 4:1448,
4:1516–1517
Eisai, 2:560–561
Biogen Idec and, 1:277
corporate philosophy and recent strategy,
2:561
history of, 2:560
Eklira Genuair, 1:231
Elanco, 2:571
Elderly people, 2:561–569
addiction to prescription drugs, 1:33–34
adherence to prescription directions,
1:45–46
age-related changes in pharmacokinetics
and pharmacodynamics, 2:564
Canada's public drug coverage for seniors,
1:299
chronic health conditions of, 2:564–566
clinical pharmacology (industrialized
nations), in special populations, 1:381
discrimination in prescribing practice,
2:481–482
economics and health care costs,
2:567–568
functional dynamics and care providing,
2:566–567
geographic variations in prescribing
practices, 2:651
geriatric medicine, 2:563–564
overview, 2:562–563
polypharmacy, 2:566
role of pharmacist in geriatric medicine,
2:568–569

Eldisine, 2:571

Electronic cigarettes, 3:1304

Electronic prescribing, 4:1348

Eli Lilly, 2:569–571
    Genentech and, 2:639
    history of, 2:569–570
    post–World War II, 2:570–571

Elion, Gertrude B., 1:xli–xlii

Elixir Sulfanilamide, 1:xxxix, 2:600–601, 2:621–623, 3:1154

Eloctate, 1:276

Emergency contraception, 2:605–606

Emetics, 2:636

Emsam, 2:932

Emtriva, 2:658

Emu bush leaves, 4:1404

ENCePP Database (European Network of Centres for Pharmacoepidemiology and Pharmacovigilance), 2:571–573
    database for research resources, 2:572
    guiding principles of, 2:572
    past and future projects, 2:572–573
    structural basis of, 2:571–572

Enders, John Franklin, 1:xl

Endocannabinoid system, appetite and, 3:1244

Endocrine pharmacology, 2:573–576
    controversies in, 2:577
    defined, 2:573–574
    for gland system and organs, 2:574–575
    history of, 2:574

Enjuvia, 4:1355

Ephedra (herbal medicine), 2:576–578
    ban in U.S., 2:578
    discovery of, 2:577
    history of, 2:576–577
    use of, in U.S., 2:577–578

Epilepsy, 1:xliv
    cannabidiol, 1:xlvi

Epinephrine, 1:xxxvii

EPO (erythropoietin), 2:578–580
    blood doping, 1:280, 1:281, 2:578–580, 3:1000–1001, 3:1334
    erythropoiesis, defined, 2:578
    Olympics and, 3:1000–1001
    swimming and PEDs, 3:1334
    uses of, 2:579–580

Epogen, 1:99

Eporatio, 4:1354

Equity pricing of essential medicines, 2:580–583
    compulsory licensing, 2:582
    drug labeling and, 2:521
    equity pricing, defined, 2:580–581
    essential medicines, defined, 2:581–582
    methods to facilitate equity pricing, 2:582–583

Equoral, 4:1355

Erectile dysfunction
    men's health and, 2:904–905
    Viagra developed, 1:xlii

Ergamisol. *See* **Levamisole (Ergamisol) controversy**

Erivedge, 2:639

Essential medicines concept
    access to essential medicines as a human right, 1:12–13
    access to medicines (developing world), 1:17

Essential Medicines List for Adults, 18th ed., 1:xxxiii

Essential Medicines List for Children, 4th ed., 1:xxxiii

Essential Medicines Lists (EMLs), 1:17

Ether, 2:722

Ethical Criteria for Medicinal Drug Promotion (WHO), 1:65

Ethics. *See also* **Athletes**
    access to essential medicines as a human right, 1:11–14
    advertising to doctors, 1:62–63
    American Pharmaceutical Association, 1:xl, 1:95, 2:742–743
    Amgen and, 1:100–101
    animal testing, 1:100–101, 1:113–117, 2:728–729
    astemizole (Hismanal) controversy, 1:227–229
    Baxter International and, 1:257
    Bayer and, 1:259–260
    beta-blocker use in sports and, 1:275
    Boehringer Ingelheim and, 1:284–285
    cerivastatin (Baycol, Lipobay) controversy, 1:332–334

Declaration of Helsinki (1975), 2:445–447

DES (Diethylstilbestrol) controversy,
2:459–462

efalizumab (Raptiva) controversy,
2:555–557

Fen-Phen (Fenfluramine/Phentermine)
controversy, 2:601–603

Genentech and, 2:639–640

human rights and pharmacology,
3:1105–1110

human subjects research, in developing
countries, 2:758–761

human subjects research, standards and
protections, 2:756–758

Johnson & Johnson and, 2:804–805,
2:806–807

levamisole (Ergamisol) controversy,
2:826–828

Merck and, 2:913

methaqualone (Quaalude) controversy,
2:917–920

nomifensine (Merital, Alival) controversy,
3:974–977

performance-enhancing drugs in sport,
2:583–587 (*See also* **Athletes**)

Pfizer and, 3:1064–1065

Phenacetin controversy, 3:1122–1125

Phenformin (Azucaps) controversy,
3:1125–1127

of placebos, 1:392

propoxyphene (Darvon, Darvocet)
controversy, 3:1173–1175

rimonabant (Acomplia) controversy,
3:1244–1246

Rofecoxib (Vioxx) controversy, 3:1246–1249

sex offenders and pharmacological
interventions, 3:1275

Takeda Pharmaceutical Co. and,
4:1347–1348

thalidomide (Contergan) controversy,
1:211, 2:623–625, 4:1357–1359

trovafloxacin (Trovan) controversy,
4:1443–1447, 4:1444–1446

Tuskegee experiment and, 2:759,
4:1447–1454, 4:1517–1518

zimelidine (Zelmid) controversy, 4:1562–1564

Ethics of performance-enhancing drugs in
sport, 2:583–587

contemporary sports culture and, 2:586

medical and professional ethics of PED,
2:586–587

therapeutic and illicit forms of PED use,
2:583–585

World Anti-Doping Agency (WADA),
2:585

Ethnicity. *See also individual names of
countries; individual names of ethnic
groups*

defined, 3:1228

ethnic discrimination in prescribing
practice, 2:477–479

low-income people and, 2:833–834

Ethnobotany, 2:587–590

current issues, 2:588–589

history of, 2:587–588

Ethnopharmacology. *See also individual
populations*

African Americans, 1:70–71, 1:74–75

International Society for
Ethnopharmacology, 2:788–791

Eucalyptus oil, 4:1403

EudraCT (European Union Drug Regulating
Authorities Clinical Trials), 2:590–592

posting trial results, 2:591–592

public area of, 2:590–591

requirements for access to, 2:591

scope of data, 2:591

secure area of, 2:591

EudraPharm (European Union Drug
Regulating Authorities Pharmaceutical
Database), 2:592–593

data sources of, 2:592–593

use of, 2:593

Europe

Denmark, 2:457–459

East Germany and state-sponsored sports
doping programs, 3:1320–1321

E.U. pharmacovigilance system, 3:1111

France, 2:630–632

harm reduction policies, 2:673–674

history of pharmacology in Middle Ages,
2:716–719

history of pharmacology in 17th–20th
    centuries, 2:711–715
history of pharmacy as profession in,
    2:737–740
medical marijuana legislation, 2:875–876
prescription drug approval process:
    Europe, 3:1150–1153
sex offenders and pharmacological
    interventions, 3:1275, 3:1276
European Medicines Agency, 2:593–596
    drug labeling and, 2:527–528
    functions, 2:594–595
    history, 2:594
    remit and structure, 2:594
    traditional and herbal medicines,
        regulation, 4:1385–1386
Exegetical Tantra, 4:1424
Expanded Programme on Immunization
    (WHO), 1:xli
Expert Committee on the Selection of
    Essential Medicines, 1:13
Extended care facility patients, polypharmacy
    and, 3:1138–1139

F. Hoffmann-La Roche AG, 2:638
False Claims Act ("Lincoln Law"), 2:597–600
    civil component to, 2:597–598
    criminal component to, 2:598
    health care fraud in U.S. and, 2:675–681
    pharmaceutical fraud and, 2:598–599,
        3:1072–1073
    state statutes, 2:598
Fampyra, 1:277
Federal Bureau of Narcotics (FBN), 2:880
Federal Food, Drug, and Cosmetic Act (1938),
        2:600–601, 2:621–623, 3:1312–1313
    Elixir Sulfanilamide deaths and, 1:xxxix,
        2:600–601, 2:621–623, 3:1154
    history of, 2:600
Feldene, 3:1064
Fen-Phen (Fenfluramine/Phentermine)
        controversy, 2:601–603
    in 1990s, 2:603
    overview, 2:601–602
    weight loss and drugs in American society,
        2:602–603

Fentora, 4:1355
Fertility control, 2:603–606
    access to contraception in developing
        countries, 1:xliv
    contraception, 2:603–605
    drugs in pregnancy, contraception,
        menopause, 4:1540–1542
    morning-after pill or emergency
        contraception, 2:605–606
    youth data on contraception use,
        4:1620 (table), 4:1621 (table),
        4:1622 (table), 4:1623 (table),
        4:1624 (table), 4:1625 (table),
        4:1626 (table), 4:1627 (table),
        4:1628 (table), 4:1629 (table)
Fertility control: history, 2:606–610
    early U.S. history, 2:606–607
    medicalization of U.S. fertility control
        (1920–1960), 2:608
    the pill and separation of contraception
        from sexual activity (1960 to present),
        2:608–610
    Title X Family Planning Program (1970),
        4:1362–1365
    U.S. legislation (1873–1920), 2:607–608
Fertility drugs, 2:610–614
    for men, 2:613
    overview, 2:610–611
    for women, 2:611–613
Ficus insipida, 4:1408
Finasteride, 1:340
First Opium War, 1:xxxvi
Five elements, 4:1428
Flavonoids, 3:1131
Fleming, Alexander, 1:xxxix, 1:131
Flex Pen, 3:986
FlexTouch, 3:986
Flibanserin, 1:xlvi
Florey, Howard Walter, 1:xxxix
Flu, Peramivir and, 1:xlv
Fluconazole, 3:1065
FluMist, 1:xlii
Fluoridation (drinking water), 2:614–617
    children's health and, 2:616–618
    health issues of, 2:615–616
    history of, 1:146, 2:614–615

Folk medicine. *See* Herbal medicine; Traditional medicine

Food, Drug, and Cosmetic Act (1938). *See* **Federal Food, Drug, and Cosmetic Act (1938)**

Food, Drug, and Insecticide Administration, **1:**xxxvii

Food additives, 2:617–620
categories and functions, **2:**617–619
food additives and human health, **2:**619–620
overview, **2:**617

Food and Drug Administration (U.S.), 2:620–626. *See also* **Adverse drug effects reporting systems; Kefauver-Harris Amendments (1962);** *individual names of drugs*
abuse of prescription drugs and, **1:**9
acetaminophen and, **1:**26
ADHD drugs, **1:**40–41
adjudicated claims data, **1:**51, **1:**52
adverse drug effects reporting systems, **1:**56, **1:**57–59
on advertising, **1:**xlii
advertising to doctors, **1:**61–66
advertising to patients, **1:**67–70
alcohol cessation drugs, **1:**81
controversies about, **2:**625–626
data on gray market drugs by, **2:**663–664
drug labeling in industrialized world, **2:**525–526
Drug Price Competition and Patent Term Restoration Act and, **2:**530–532
early forms of agency, **1:**xxxvii
Elixir Sulfanilamide deaths and 1938 Federal Food, Drug, and Cosmetic Act, **1:**xxxix, **2:**600–601, **2:**621–623, **3:**1154
Flibanserin approved by, **1:**xlvi
generic drugs and, **2:**643–649
laws affecting (1954–1960), **1:**xl
prescription drug approval process in U.S., **3:**1153–1157
Prescription Drug User Fee Act (1992), **3:**1158

Pure Food and Drug Act (1906) and, **1:**xxxviii, **1:**63–64, **2:**500–501, **2:**620–621, **3:**1190–1192, **3:**1310
reimportation of prescription drugs, **3:**1242
smuggling of prescription drugs and, **3:**1312–1313
thalidomide tragedy and Kefauver-Harris Amendment, **1:**211, **2:**623–625, **4:**1357–1359

Food and Drugs Act (U.K.), **1:**xxxix

Food Chemicals Codex (USP), **4:**1504

Football (American) and performance-enhancing drugs, 2:626–630
drugs other than steroids, THG, growth hormone, **2:**628–629
effects of, **2:**629
interviews with professional level athletes, **2:**628
legal issues, **2:**629 (*See also* **Drug testing, high school and college athletes (U.S.); Drug testing, Olympic athletes (overview); Drug testing, professional athletes (overview)**)
overview, **2:**626–627
school policies, **2:**627–628

Forest Laboratories, **1:**29

Fosamax, **2:**913

Four Tantras, **4:**1424–1425

Framework for Promoting Equitable Access to Essential Medicines (WHO), **1:**16–17

France, 2:630–632
history of pharmacology in, **2:**630–631
modern-day pharmaceutical industry in, **2:**631–632

Francke, Don, **1:**xl

Frederick II (Emperor of Germany, King of Sicily), **1:**xxxv

Fruit flavoring for drugs, advent of, **2:**570

FSH (Follistim, Bravelle, Gonal-F), **2:**611–612

Fujisawa Camphor, **1:**225

Fujisawa Pharmaceutical Co., **1:**225

Fycompa, **2:**560

Galen, **1:**xxxv, **4:**1459–1460

Gamble, James, **3:**1170

Game of Shadows (Mark Fainaru-Wada and Lance Williams), 2:633–635
  on Bonds, 2:634–635
  on MLB, 2:633–634
Gammahydroxybutyric acid (GHB), 1:394–396, 2:778
Gardasil, 2:913
Gastric drugs, 2:635–637. *See also individual names of pharmaceutical companies*
  acid reducers, 2:637
  antidiarrheals, 2:636
  antiflatulence drugs, 2:637
  categories of, 2:635
  emetics, 2:636
  history of, 2:636
  laxatives, 2:636–637
  purpose of, 2:635
GAZYVA, 2:639
GE Healthcare, 3:990
Gelatin capsule coating, advent of, 2:570
Genentech, 2:638–640
  controversies, 2:639–640
  history of, 2:638
  insulin and recombinant DNA, 1:xli
  products and production timeline, 2:638–639
General Practice Research Database (UK), 2:640–643
  description of, 2:640–641
  opportunities for improvement, 2:642
  pharmacoepidemiology and, 2:642
  strengths of, 2:641
Generic medicines, 2:643–650
  access to medicines (industrialized world) and, 1:23
  approval process, 2:645–646
  awards of generic exclusivity, 2:646
  composition, 2:645
  costs and goals of, 2:643
  future of, 2:648–649
  Generic Drug User Fee Amendments, 2:646
  issues of, 2:647–648
  men's health and bioequivalence, 2:907–908
  OTC drugs versus, 3:1025–1026
  patent protection, 2:643–645
  public perception of, 2:646–647

Genetics
  Genentech and, 2:638–640
  Gilead Sciences and, 2:657
  insulin and recombinant DNA, 1:xli
  National Center for Advancing Translational Sciences (NIH), 3:940–943
  pharmacogenomics and, 3:1096–1099
  translational pharmacology, 4:1435–1440
Genzyme Corp., 1:100, 3:1264
Geodon, 1:1–64
Geographic variation in prescribing practices, 2:650–654
  antibiotics, 2:651
  in older adults, 2:651
  painkillers, 2:650–651
  in pediatric populations, 2:652
  reason behind variation, 2:652–653
Geriatric medicine, 2:563–564, 2:568–569
Germ theory of disease, early, 2:713
Germany, 2:654–656
  health care system in, 2:654–655
  health in, 2:654
  herbal medicines used in, 2:655–656
  pharmaceutical industry of, 2:655
Gesellschaft für Geschichte der Pharmazie, 1:xxxviii
Ghana, traditional medicines in, 4:1370–1372
Gilbert, Walter, 1:276
Gilead Sciences, 2:656–658
  Development of AntiRetroviral Therapy (DART), 2:760
  drugs and products of, 2:656–657
  history of, 2:657–658
Ginseng (herbal medicine), 2:658–661
  chemistry of active compounds in, 2:660–661, 2:661 (fig.)
  medical uses and relevant chemistry, 2:659–660
  overview, 2:658–659, 2:707
Glaxo, 2:657
GlaxoSmithKline, 1:229
  Daiichi Sankyo and, 2:442
  Development of AntiRetroviral Therapy (DART), 2:760
  pharmaceutical fraud case, 3:1073

Glitinides, 1:171

Global AIDS Program (GAP), 1:326–327

Global Disease Detection (GDD) (CDC), 1:327–328

Global Fund for AIDS, Tuberculosis and Malaria (GFATM), 1:xlii, 1:18–19

Global issues
  access to essential medicines as a human right, 1:11–14
  access to medicines (developing world), 1:15–20

Globoid, 3:990

GlucaGen, 3:986

Glucerna, 1:1, 1:2

Glucocorticosteroids (sport), 2:661–663
  defined, 2:661
  history of, 2:661–662
  risks of, 2:662

Glucosinolates, 3:1131

Goeddel, David, 2:638

Goffman, Erving, 1:197, 2:453–454

Goldenseal, 2:899

Gonadotropins
  cancer and, 1:310
  gonadotropin-releasing hormone (GnRH), 2:611

Gonax, 1:225

Gonorrhea, 2:548

Good Manufacturing Practice (GMP) fraud, 3:1070–1071

Grapefruit juice, drug interactions with, 2:518

Gray market drugs, 2:663–665
  in U.S., 2:663–664
  worldwide, 2:664–665

Greece (ancient), Hippocrates and, 1:xxxv

Guangdon Techpool Bio-Pharma, 3:991

Guangdong BeiKang, 1:230

Guild of Apothecaries (Italy), 1:xxxv

$H_{1,2,3,4}$-antagonists, 1:180–182

Hagedorn, Christian, 3:985

Hahnemann, Samuel, 2:746

Halaven, 2:560

Hallucinogens, 2:667–672
  cannabis, 2:671–672 (*See also* Marijuana)
  dissociative anesthetics, 2:670–671

indolealkylamines, 2:667–668
  phenylethylamines, 2:668–670
  psilocybin, 3:1178–1180

Halofantrine, 1:191

Harm reduction policies, 2:672–674
  current approaches in Europe, Australia, Canada, 2:673–674
  current approaches in U.S., 2:674
  history, 2:673
  overview, 2:672

Harrison, L. W., 4:1450

Harrison Narcotics Tax Act of 1914
  Drug Abuse Control Amendments and, 2:501, 4:1479
  history of, 1:xxxviii
  scheduled drugs and, 3:1266, 3:1267–1268 (*See also* **Controlled Substances Act**)

Harvard Pilgrim Health Care Institute, 1:58

Harvard University, 1:xxxix

Hasegawa, Yasuchika, 4:1347

Hata, Sahachiro, 1:xxxviii

Hatch-Waxman Act, 2:530–532

Health, United States, 2013 (National Center for Health Statistics), 4:1587

Health Belief Model (HBM), 1:47

Health Canada, 1:xlv

Health care costs
  elderly people, economics and, 2:567–568

Health care fraud: United States, 2:675–683
  current and future trends, 2:678–681
  since 1996, 2:676–678, 2:677 (tables)
  statutes addressing, 2:675–676
  types of problems, 2:675

Health insurance. *See also* Health insurance data; *individual names of countries*
  adjudicated claims data, 1:49–52
  Hispanic Americans and, 2:698
  insurance benefits managers (IBM), 1:50
  nonreceipt of needed prescription drugs, 4:1590 (table)
  U.S. history of pharmacology and, 2:732

Health insurance data
  Center for Medicare and Medicaid Services, 4:1662
  coverage rates by type of insurance, 4:1661 (table)

Current Population Survey (CPS), 4:1659
Medicare enrollment (tables), 4:1662
Medicare Part D enrollment (tables), 4:1663
people without insurance, 4:1659–1660 (table)
Health Insurance Portability and Accountability Act (HIPAA)
    Common Rule and, 1:405–406
    health care fraud and, 2:675
    Healthcare Cost and Utilization Project and, 2:684 (*See also* Databases/data sources)
    HMO Research Network and, 2:745
    hospital administrative data, 2:755
    human subjects research and, 2:757
Health literacy, 2:836–838
Health Resources and Services Administration (HRSA), 4:1665
Healthcare Cost and Utilization Project (HCUP), 2:683–686
    databases, 2:684–685
    resources, 2:683–684
Healthcare Effectiveness Data and Information Set (HEDIS), 2:686–688
    overview, 2:686–687
    reporting, 2:687–688
Health-Related Quality of Life (HRQOL), 3:1193–1197
Healy, David, 4:1467
Hebert, Louis, 1:xxxv–xxxvi
Heiden, Robert, 1:284–285
Heinz Dilemma, 1:11–12
Help-seeking advertisements, 1:68
Hepatitis C infections, Baxter International and, 1:257
Herbal medicine. *See also* Traditional medicine
    in Africa, 4:1370–1373
    aloe vera, 1:85–88
    in Australia, 4:1373–1377
    in Bangladesh, 4:1394
    in Bolivia, 4:1389
    in Canada, 4:1377–1379
    chamomile, 1:334–336
    in China, 4:1379–1383

Committee on Herbal Medicinal Products (HMPC), 4:1385–1387
    in Dominican Republic, 4:1389
    in Ecuador, 4:1389–1390
    ephedra, 2:576–578
    European Medicines Agency on, 4:1385–1386
    in Germany, 2:655–656
    Ginseng, 2:658–659, 2:658–661, 2:707
    history of pharmacology: Europe, Middle Ages, 2:718–719
    history of pharmacology: U.S., 1865 to 1900, 2:725
    in India, 4:1394–1395
    in Japan, 4:1379–1383
    in Mexico, 4:1391
    of Native Americans/Alaska Natives, 4:1398–1401
    in Nepal, 4:1395
    in New Zealand, 4:1373–1377
    opium as herbal medicine, 3:1015–1017 (*See also* Opiates)
    in South Africa, 3:1316–1317
    in Sri Lanka, 4:1395
    Taiwan Herbal Pharmacopoeia, 4:1382
    Traditional Herbal Medicinal Products Directive (THMPD), 4:1385
    in United Kingdom, 4:1384
    United States regulation, 4:1396–1401
    valerian (herbal medicine), 4:1512–1515
Herbert, Gavin S., 1:84
Herbs, Chinese. *See* **Traditional medicine: China**
Herbst, Roy, 1:xlv
Heroin, 2:688–693
    ancient history, 1:xxxv
    celebrity deaths and public awareness about, 1:xl, 1:xlii
    chemistry, 2:688–689, 2:689 (fig.)
    dependency on, 2:691–692
    early history of, 1:xxxviii
    early synthesis of (1874), 1:xxxvii
    legal context, 2:692
    molecular structure, 2:689 (fig.)
    origin and production, 2:689–690
    pharmacology, 2:690–691
    prevalence, 2:690

routes of administration, 2:690
sources of, 1:xli
street price, 2:690
street terms, 2:690
treatment for dependency, 2:692, 2:693–696
withdrawal symptoms, 2:691 (table)
youth drug use data, 4:1614 (table),
    4:1615 (table), 4:1616 (table)
Heroin-assisted treatment, 2:693–696
concerns about, 2:696
criticism of, 2:696
efficacy of, 2:694–695
historical context, 2:693–694
models of, 2:695–696
High Intensity Drug Trafficking Areas
    (HIDTA), 3:1307
Highly active antiretroviral therapy
    (HAART), 1:76
Hippocrates, 1:xxxv, 2:711, 4:1459
Hippocratic Corpus, 2:711
Hires, Charles E., 1:xxxvii
Hispanic Americans, 2:696–699
contraception use data, 4:1635 (table)
defined, 2:696–697
ethnopharmacology and, 1:71, 1:74
health issues of low-income people,
    2:833–834
health of, 2:697
language and cultural barriers, 2:697–698
pharmaceutical trials and, 2:698
traditional and folk medicines of, 2:698
**History of pharmacological treatments for
    mental health, 2:699–704.** *See also*
    Mental health
conception of mental illness in ancient
    times, 2:701
conception of mental illness in Middle
    Ages and Age of Enlightenment,
    2:701–702
modern-day psychopharmacology, 2:703–704
origins of psychopharmacology, 2:699–700
psychopharmacology and other
    treatments, 2:700–701
psychopharmacology terminology, 1:260–261
substances used through evolvement of
    psychopharmacology, 2:702–703

**History of pharmacology: ancient China,
    2:704–708**
myths and folk legends, 2:705
overview, 2:704–705
plants used, 2:706–707
texts, 2:705–706
**History of pharmacology: ancient Egypt,
    2:708–711**
diagnosis and dosage, 2:709–710
medical papyri, 1:xxxv, 2:708–709
nonmedical prescriptions, 2:710–711
pharmacopoeia, 2:710
**History of pharmacology: Europe,
    2:711–715**
in 17th and 18th centuries, 2:711–713
in 19th century, 2:713–714
in 20th century, 2:714–715
antibiotics, 2:715
history of pharmacology in colonial U.S.
    and, 2:722–723
**History of pharmacology: Europe, Middle
    Ages, 2:716–719**
Arab influence, 2:717–718, 2:741
Black Death and, 2:719
early Middle Ages, 2:716
guilds, 2:718
herbals, 2:718–719
monastic medicine, 2:716–717
School of Salerno, 2:717
**History of pharmacology: U.S., colonial
    period to 1865, 2:719–723**
European history of pharmacology and,
    2:722–723
medicinal plants and traditional medicines,
    2:721–722
overview, 2:719–720
"snake oil salesmen," 2:721
soda fountains and, 2:722
training of doctors during, 2:720–721
**History of pharmacology: U.S., 1865 to
    1900, 2:723–726**
Abel and, 2:723–725
achievements in adrenal glands, 2:724–725
herbal supplements, 2:725
overview, 2:723
patent medications, 2:725–726

History of pharmacology: U.S., 1900 to 1945, 2:727–730
  antibiotic discoveries, 2:728
  choline, 2:729–730
  discovery of penicillin and, 2:727–728
  sanitation and hygiene, 2:729
  serologic testing, 2:730
  use of animals in pharmacology, 2:728–729
  viral isolation and tissue culture, 2:730
History of pharmacology: U.S., 1945 to present, 2:730–733
  costs of medications, 2:732
  new pharmaceutical products, 2:731–732
  overview, 2:730
  pharmaceutical industry, 2:731
History of pharmacy as a profession: Africa, 2:733–736
  African healing tradition origins, 2:733–734
  modern pharmacy in Africa, 2:736
  muti and, 2:736
  traditional health care services, 2:734–735
History of pharmacy as a profession: Europe, 2:737–740
  development of modern pharmaceutical products, 2:738–739
  evolution of European pharmaceutical industry, 2:739–740
  overview, 2:737–738
History of pharmacy as a profession: Middle East, 2:740–742
  overview, 2:740–741
  pharmacy in different Middle Eastern countries, 2:741
History of pharmacy as a profession: United States, 2:742–744
  American Pharmacists Association (APhA), 2:742–743
  overview, 2:742
Hitchings, George H., 1:xli–xlii
HIV Surveillance Report, 4:1689
HIV/AIDS data
  deaths of persons diagnosed HIV ever classified as Stage 3 (AIDS), 4:1699–1700 (table)
  deaths of persons diagnosed with HIV, 4:1697–1698 (table)
  diagnoses of HIV, 4:1689–1690 (table)
  diagnoses of HIV, by race/ethnicity, 4:1693–1694 (table), 4:1695–1696 (table)
  Stage 3 (AIDS), 4:1691–1692 (table)
  survival after diagnosis (more than 12, 24, 36 months), 4:1701 (table), 4:1702 (table)
HMO Research Network (19 Regional Health Care Delivery Organizations), 2:744–746
  membership, 2:744–745
  virtual data warehouse, 2:745–746
Hoechst, 2:441, 3:975
Hoffman, Albert, 1:xxxix
Home delivery of prescriptions
  mail-order pharmacies, 2:845–849
  online pharmacies, 3:1004–1008
Homeopathy, 2:746–749
  history of, 2:746–748
  scientific evaluation, 2:748
Honeybees, pesticides and, 1:259–260
Hope Medical Center, 1:xli
Hormone replacement therapy (HRT), 2:749–751
  overview, 2:749
  Women's Health Initiative, 2:749–750
Hormones
  fertility control and, 2:603, 2:604, 2:608–610, 2:609
  hormonal therapies for cancer, 1:310, 1:311–312
  testosterone and swimming, 3:1333
  water pollution and, 4:1533
Hospice treatment, 2:751–753
  defined, 2:751
  goals of, 2:751–753
  levels of, 2:752
Hospira, 1:3
Hospital administrative data, 2:753–756
  clinical metrics, 2:754–756
  databases, 2:753–754
  patient information, 2:754

Hot lips, **4:**1421

Hsia, David, **1:**29

Huangdi Neijing (Inner Canon of Huangdi),
2:705–706

Human Genome Project, **3:**1097–1098

Human growth hormone (hGH),
3:1333

**Human subjects research: standards and
protections, 2:756–758**
basic principles, **2:**757–758
history of, **2:**756–757

**Human subjects research in developing
countries, 2:758–761**
ethics in human subjects research,
2:758–759
examples of abuses in human subjects
research, **2:**760–761
special issues in developing countries,
2:759–760

Humira, **1:**1–2

Humoral theory, **4:**1460

Humulin, **2:**639

Hutcheson, Duncan, **1:**89

Hygiene, history of, **2:**729

Hypertension, elderly people and,
2:564

Hypnotics and sedatives, 2:761–764
background, **2:**761–762
Librium, **2:**762
meprobamate, **2:**762

Ibn Sina (Avicenna), **1:**xxxv, **2:**741

Ibogaine, 2:765–767
chemical composition, **2:**765
uses of, **2:**765

ICOS Corporation, **2:**571

Idec Pharmaceuticals, **1:**276

Identification of medical barcode,
4:1348–1349

IG Farben, **1:**259

IgC, **1:**276

Illegal drugs
political economics and Mexican drug
trade, **2:**922–924
prescription drug abuse compared to,
1:4, **1:**7

Imipenem, **2:**913

Immigrants and refugees, 2:767–772
cultural and social factors in immigrant
treatment-seeking approaches,
2:768–769
overview, **2:**767–768
refugees and other vulnerable populations,
2:769–770
treatment adherence and pharmaceutical
consumption among immigrants,
2:770–771

Implants, contraceptive, **2:**604

Incivio, **2:**805–806

Incretin mimetics, **1:**172–173

India, 2:772–774
health care system, **2:**772–773
health issues of, **2:**772
pharmaceutical industry, **2:**773
prescription drug approval process: Asia,
3:1143–1144
racial minorities of Asia and, **1:**106–1207,
3:1202
traditional and herbal medicines in,
4:1394–1395

Indian Health Service (IHS), **4:**1413

**Indigenous and ethnic minorities: Aotearoa
New Zealand, 2:774–777**
current context, **2:**774–775
pharmacogenomic research, **2:**776
social and cultural issues, **2:**775–776

Indolealkylamines, **2:**667–668

Indoles, **3:**1131

Inhalants, 2:777–779
inhalers and methamphetamine,
2:915
types of, **2:**777–778
use of, **2:**777, **2:**778–779
youth drug use data, **4:**1612 (table),
4:1613 (table), **4:**1614 (table)

Injected drugs, youth drug use data,
4:1619 (table), **4:**1620 (table)

InnoLet, **3:**986

Inositol, **3:**1131

Institutional Review Boards (IRBs)
Common Rule and, **1:**405–406
defined, **2:**757–758, **2:**759

Instructional Tantra, **4:**1424

Insulatard, **3:**986

Insulin. *See also* **Antidiabetic medications**
early uses of, 1:xxxviii
insulin therapy, 1:174 (table)
Novo Nordisk and, 3:985, 3:986
overview, 1:173–174
recombinant DNA and, 1:xli
Insurance benefits managers (IBM), 1:50
Intellectual property rights, 2:779–783.
See also Legal issues
defined, 2:779–780
institutions, 2:781–782
pharmacology and, 2:782
regulations, 2:780–781
Intellectual property rights, ethnobotany
and, 2:589
Interactive Promotional Media (FDA), 1:69
International Boxing Federation, 1:287
International Committee of Medical Journal
Editors, 1:65
International Council for Science, Africa
(ICSU), 3:1105
International Covenant on Economic, Social,
and Cultural Rights (ICESCR) (UN),
1:14–15, 3:1043
International Olympic Committee (IOC).
See also **Athletes**
on anabolic steroids, 1:106
drug testing, Olympic athletes (overview),
2:538–539
**International Opium Convention (1912),
2:783–785**
Hague Convention (1912) and, 2:783
issues of, 2:783–785
**International Pharmaceutical Federation,
2:785–788**
developmental history of, 2:785–786
goals, 2:786–787
International Pharmecutical Congresses
(1888–1910) and, 2:786
Statutes, 2:786
**International Society for Ethnopharmacology,
2:788–791**
history of, 2:788–789
scope of, and *Journal of
Ethnopharmacology*history of,
2:789–791
study of ethnopharmacology and, 2:788

International Society for Pharmacoeconomics
and Outcomes Research (ISPOR), 1:427
**International Society for Pharmacoepidemi-
ology, 2:791–794**
about pharmacoepidemiology, 2:791–793
membership, 2:791
pharmacoepidemiology studies, 2:791
**International Society of Regulatory Toxicol-
ogy and Pharmacology, 2:794–797**
adoption and amendment of bylaws, 2:796
council and meetings, 2:794–795
governance, 2:795–796
membership, 2:796
objectives, 2:794
International Tennis Federation, 4:1351–1353
International Union of Basic and Clinical
Pharmacology (IUPHAR), 3:1104–1105
Internet. *See also* Databases/data sources
online searches about treatments and
drugs, 1:xliii–xliv
smuggling of prescription drugs and,
3:1312–1315
Intervention, medication therapy manage-
ment and, 2:896–897
Intrauterine devices (IUDs), 2:604, 2:609
Invega Sustenna, 2:806
Inyanga, 2:930
Iodine, 1:147, 3:1062
Iproniazid phosphate, 1:xl
Isangoma, 2:930
Isis Pharmaceuticals, 1:277, 2:657
Isoflavones, 3:1131
Isothiocyanates, 3:1131
Itakura, Keiichi, 2:638
IV solution, early commercial availability,
1:255–256

Jamison, Kay Redfield, 4:1365–1367
Jamu (**traditional Indonesian medicine),
2:799–801**
background, 2:799–800
criticism, 2:800–801
overview, 2:800
Januvia, 2:912
Japan, 2:801–804
"drug lag," 2:803–804
health care system in, 2:803

international relationships of, 2:804
Japanese Pharmacopoeia, 4:1381
Kampo, 2:801–803, 2:807–812, 4:1381
pharmaceutical manufacturing, 2:803
prescription drug approval process: Asia, 3:1143
prescription drug approval process in, 3:1143
racial minorities of Asia and, 3:1202, 3:1205
traditional and herbal medicines, regulation and East Asia, 4:1379–1383
traditional medicine in, 2:801–802
Jenner, Edward, 3:1299
John A. Andrew Memorial Hospital (Tuskegee Institute), 4:1451
Johns Hopkins University School of Medicine, 4:1365
Johnson, Edward Mead, 2:805
Johnson, James Wood, 2:805
Johnson, Robert Wood, 2:805
Johnson & Johnson, 2:804–807
    Daiichi Sankyo and, 2:441
    Eisai and, 2:560
    history, 2:805
    overview, 2:804–805
    products, 2:805–806
    recalls, 2:806–807
    revenues, 1:xxxii
    Tylenol tampering case, 1:9, 2:805, 2:806, 4:1455–1458
Jones, Marion, 4:1368–1369
Joplin, Janis, 1:xl
Journal of Ethnopharmacology, 2:789–791
Journal of Experimental Pathology, 1:xxxix
Journal of the Philadelphia College of Pharmacy, 4:1475

KADCYLA, 2:639
Kakadu plum, 4:1404
Kampo (traditional Japanese medicine), 2:807–812
    diagnosis, 2:810–811
    history, 2:809–810
    overview, 2:801–803
    prevalence of, 2:801–803
    traditional and herbal medicine regulation in East Asia, 4:1381, 4:1382
    treatment, 2:811

Kangaroo apple, 4:1404
Karl XIII (king of Sweden), 2:812
Karolinska Institute (Sweden), 2:812–814
    founding of, 2:812
    medical training and library, 2:812
    Nobel Prize and, 2:813
Katen, Karen, 3:1065
Kefauver-Harris Amendments (1962), 2:814–816
    adverse drug effects reporting systems, 1:56–57
    American Board of Clinical Pharmacology and, 1:89
    Drug Abuse Control Amendments, 2:501
    FDA and, 2:623–625
    history of, 2:814
    impact of, 2:814–816
    Pfizer and, 3:1064
Keflex, 2:571
Keimatsu, Katsuzaemon, 2:441
Keitekishu (Textbook of Internal Medicine) (Manase), 2:809
Kendall, Edward Calvin, 1:xxxviii
Kentz, Frederick, 2:638
Ketamine (Special K), 1:394–396
Keytruda, 2:913
Khat, 2:816–818
Kia King (Emperor of China), 1:xxxvi
Kickbacks
    Anti-Kickback Statute, 2:675–676
    pharmaceutical fraud, definitions, 3:1070
Kim Jong-su, 1:273
Kindler, Jeff, 3:1065
King's College London, 2:818–820
    current status of, 2:819–820
    overview, 2:818
    significant researchers from, 2:818–819
Kitab al-Tasrif (Albucasis), 4:1460
Klebsiella pneumoniae, 2:548
Kleid, Dennis, 2:638
Klug, Heinz, 1:13
Knoll, 1:3
Kohlberg, Lawrence, 1:11–12
Koop, C. Everett, 1:49
Korea, traditional medicine in, 4:1382
Kraepelin, Emil, 2:700
Kramer, Peter, 1:420–422

Krogh, August, 3:985
Krogh, Marie, 3:985
Ku Nye, 4:1425
Kübler-Ross, Elisabeth, 2:751

Lactic acid, 1:283
Last Days of Pompeii, The (Bulwer-Lytton), 1:xxxvi
Latinos. *See* **Hispanic Americans**
Latisse, 1:85
Laubach, Gerald, 3:1064
Laudanum, 3:1015–1017
Laxatives, 2:636–637
Lee, Samuel, Jr., 1:xxxvi
Legal issues. *See also* **Drug testing, high school and college athletes (U.S.); Drug testing, Olympic athletes (overview); Drug testing, professional athletes (overview); Ethics; Food and Drug Administration (U.S.)**
    abuse of prescription drugs and, 1:8–9
    Bayer and copyright issues, 1:258
    False Claims Act ("Lincoln Law"), 2:597–600
    FDA and laws of 1954–1960, 1:xl
    fertility control, U.S. legislation (1873–1920), 2:607–608
    first legislation on narcotics, 1:xxxvii
    Federal Food, Drug, and Cosmetic Act (1938), 2:621–623
    football (American) and performance-enhancing drugs, 2:629
    of Genentech, 2:640
    generic medicines and, 2:643–645, 2:646
    health care fraud in United States, 2:675–681
    heroin, legal context, 2:692
    history of pharmacology: U.S., 1865 to 1900, patent medications, 2:725–726
    intellectual property rights and ethnobotany, 2:589
    of mail-order pharmacies, 2:848–849
    pharmaceutical law, 3:1074–1080
    Pure Food and Drug Act (1906), 2:620–621
    Vaccine Act of 1813 as first U.S. legislation, 1:xxxvi

Legal issues in testing for performance-enhancing drugs, 2:821–823
    overview, 2:821–822
    search issues, 2:822–823
Lemtrada, 3:1265
Lenz, Widukind, 4:1358
Lethal injection, 2:823–826
    defined, 2:823
    opposition to, 2:825
    uses of, 2:824–825
Letrozole, 1:340
Leukotriene antagonists, 1:53
Levamisole (Ergamisol) controversy, 2:826–828
    cost, 2:826–827
    use in street drugs, 2:827
Levemir, 3:986
Liber Servitoris (Zahrawi), 2:740–741
Librium, 2:762, 4:1432
Lifestyle drugs, 2:828–832
    definitions and meanings, 2:828–830
    regulatory, financial, ethical aspects, 2:831–832
    types of symptoms, illnesses, drugs, 2:830–831
Lilly, Eli, 2:569
Lilly, Josiah K., Sr., 2:569, 2:570
Lin Tse-Hsu, 1:xxxvi
Lincoln, Abraham, 4:1468–1469
Lincoln, Mary, 4:1468–1469
Lincoln Law. *See* **False Claims Act ("Lincoln Law")**
Lind, James, 1:390
Lipitor, 3:1064
Lipobay, 1:332–334
Lister, Joseph, 2:805, 4:1473
Lithium, 2:702
Liver, acetaminophen overdose risk and, 1:26–28
Loop diuretics, 1:184, 2:493
Lorcaserin, 1:209
Louis, Pierre, 1:390–391
Lovenox, 3:1164
Low-income people, 2:832–836. *See also* **Pharmacoeconomics**
    nonreceipt of needed prescription drugs, 4:1590 (table)

Patient Protection and Affordable Care
Act, 2:834
pharmaceutical issues, 2:834–835
racial and ethnic minorities, 2:833–834
relationship between health issues and
poverty, 2:832–833
residents of developing countries,
2:462–463
traditional medicine of Native American
tribes and, 4:1414–1415
Low-literacy and illiterate people, 2:836–839
health literacy in U.S., 2:838
health literacy issues, 2:836–838
literacy issues, 2:836
LSD, 2:839–842
chemical composition, 2:839
drug effects, 2:841–842
history, 1:xxxix
history and social factors, 2:839–841
Luteinizing hormone (LH), 2:611
Lycetol, 1:258
Lydia E. Pinkham's Vegetable Compound,
1:xxxvii
Lyme disease, treatments for, 2:842–844
Borrelia, 2:842
disease diagnosis, 2:843
prevention, 2:844
resistance, 2:844
seasonality, 2:842
signs and symptoms, 2:842–843
transmission, 2:842
treatment, 2:843
vaccination, 2:843–844
Lyphomed Inc., 1:225–226
Lyrica, 3:1064

Macleod, John James Rickard, 1:xxxviii, 2:570
Mail-order pharmacies, 2:845–849
potential hazards of home delivery,
2:846–847
process of, 2:845–846
U.S. and international, 2:848–849
U.S. consumers and, 2:847–848
Major League Baseball, 1:247–250,
2:543–544, 2:633–635
Malaria, 2:549–550, 2:918

Mali, traditional medicines in, 4:1372
Managed care, abuse of prescription drugs
and, 1:4–5
Management Sciences for Health, 1:13–14
M&R Dietetics, 1:3
March of Dimes, 1:xxxix
Marijuana. *See also* **Medical marijuana
legislation (Canada); Medical marijuana
legislation (Europe); Medical marijuana
legislation (Israel); Medical marijuana
legislation (U.S.)**
cannabis as hallucinogen, 2:671–672
marijuana use (youth drug use data),
4:1606 (table), 4:1607 (table),
4:1608 (table), 4:1609 (table),
4:1610 (table)
medical marijuana legislation (Canada),
2:872–874
medical marijuana legislation (Europe),
2:875–876
medical marijuana legislation (Israel),
2:877–879
medical marijuana legislation (U.S.),
2:879–886
synthetic marijuana, 3:1340–1344
**Marketed Health Products Directorate
(Canada), 2:849–851**
international collaboration, 2:850–851
MedEffect Canada, 2:850
organization of, 2:849–850
responsibilities of, 2:849
Marshall, Christopher, 1:xxxvi
Masking drugs, baseball and performance-
enhancing drugs, 1:251
Mass drug administration, 2:851–855
drug resistance, 2:854–855
effectiveness of, 2:853–854
indirect MDA, 2:852–853
malaria and, 2:851–852
MDA, defined, 2:851
Massachusetts Pharmacopoeia, 2:742
Materia medica, 2:855–857
historical background, 2:855–856
modern, 2:856–857
Materia Medica, 4:1409
Matteucci, Mark, 2:657

Maximum tolerated dose (MTD), **2:**498
Maxzide, **2:**932
McKeen, John, **3:**1063
McKesson, **3:**1312
MDMA (Ecstasy), 2:857–860
chemical composition and history of,
    2:857–858
Ecstasy use among youths, **4:**1612 (table),
    4:1613 (table), **4:**1614 (table)
health concerns, **2:**858
medical use, **2:**858–859
pharmacology and behavioral effects, **2:**858
as Schedule I drug, **3:**1266
Me too drugs, 2:860–863
advantages and disadvantages, **2:**861
cost, **2:**861–862
criticism, **2:**861
defined, **2:**860–861
impact of, **2:**862–863
Measles, **1:**xl
Measles, mumps, rubella (MMR) vaccine,
    1:xl, **1:**242–244
Mechanisms of action (MOA), of
    acetaminophen, **1:**26
Medco Containment Services Incorporated,
    2:912
Medicaid: prescription drug benefits, 2:863–866
cost containment for prescription drugs,
    2:865
Early and Periodic Screening, Diagnostic,
    and Treatment (EPSDT), **2:**863–864
prescription drug policies in Medicare, **2:**864
prescription drug utilization in Medicare,
    2:864–865
Medicaid and Medicare systems, 2:866–869
benefits provided by Medicaid, **2:**869–870
benefits provided by Medicare, **2:**867–868
differences between Medicaid and
    Medicare, **2:**866–867
history of Medicaid, **2:**868–869
history of Medicare, **2:**867
Medicaid Drug Rebate Program, **2:**865
Medicaid Expansion by States and ACA,
    3:1040–1041
Medicaid prescription drug benefits,
    2:863–866

**Medical expenditure panel survey (MEPS),
    2:869–872**
history, **2:**870
MEPS, defined, **2:**869–870
process of, **2:**870–871
publications, **2:**871–872
*Medical Inquiries and Observations Upon
    the Diseases of the Mind* (Rush),
    4:1469–1470
Medical Insurance Act (Canada), **1:**xl
**Medical marijuana legislation (Canada),
    2:872–874**
Canadian Marihuana Medical Access
    Regulations (MMAR) and Marihuana
    for Medical Purposes Regulations
    (MMPR), **2:**872–873
historical perspective, **2:**872–873
recreational use and, **2:**873–874
**Medical marijuana legislation (Europe),
    2:875–876**
Czech Republic and, **2:**876
medicinal use, **2:**875–876
Sativex, **2:**876
**Medical marijuana legislation (Israel),
    2:877–879**
marijuana's dangers and illegality,
    2:877–878
medical marijuana in Israel, **2:**878–879
positive medical effects of marijuana,
    2:877
**Medical marijuana legislation (U.S.),
    2:879–886**
historical perspective, **2:**879–882,
    4:1398
legislation in individual states, **2:**882–885
U.S. Supreme Court rulings, **2:**883–884
Medical Society (Italy), **1:**xxxv
Medicare. *See also* **Medicaid and Medicare
    systems; Medicare Prescription Drug,
    Improvement, and Modernization
    Act (2003)**
access to medicines (industrialized
    world), **1:**24
creation of, **2:**732
hospice benefit, **2:**751
Medicare (Australia), **1:**238

Medicare: prescription drug benefits,
    2:886–890
    administration of, 2:886
    Medicare Prescription Drug, Improvement,
        and Modernization Act (MMA),
        2:886, 2:890–892
    Part D program, explained, 2:886–889,
        2:891
Medicare Prescription Drug, Improvement,
    and Modernization Act (2003),
    2:890–892
    medication therapy management (MTM)
        and, 2:895–896
    overview, 2:886, 2:890–891
    Part D and, 2:886–889, 2:891
Medication compounding fraud,
    3:1071–1072
Medication errors, 2:892–895
    adverse drug effects reporting systems,
        1:56–59
    characteristics of successful programs,
        2:895
    defining, 2:892
    studying and preventing, 2:893–894
    types of, 2:893
Medication related action plan (MAP), 2:896
Medication therapy management (MTM),
    2:895–897
    components of, 2:896
    history of, 2:895–896
    medication therapy review (MTR),
        2:896–897
Medicinal plant species threatened with
    extinction, 2:897–899
    overview, 2:897–898
    some at-risk plant species, 2:898–899
    threats to medicinal plants, 2:898
Medicinal plants. See Ethnobotany
Medicines, overview, 1:xxxi–xxxiv
Medicines and Healthcare Products
    Regulatory Agency (UK), 2:899–902
    functions, 2:900–901
    history, 2:900
    operational structure, 2:900
    overview, 2:899–900
    relationship with European bodies, 2:901

Medicines Compendium (USP), 4:1504–1505
MedImmune, 1:229, 1:230
MediSense, 1:3
Medium lethal dose (LD$_{50}$), 2:498
Medley Farma, 3:1164
Medroxyprogesterone acetate (MPA),
    3:1274–1277
MedWatch, 1:57
MedWatch program, 1:57, 1:61
Melfi, constitutions of, 2:737
Melton, Doug, 2:657
Memary, 2:441
Memorial Sloan Kettering Cancer
    Center, 1:87
Men, 2:902–909
    access to medicines (developing world), 1:20
    discrimination in prescribing practice,
        2:479
    fertility drugs for, 2:613
    gender differences in bioequivalence,
        2:907–908
    gender differences in drug trials,
        2:906–907
    gender differences in prescription rates,
        2:903–904
    health issues of, 2:902–903
    male sexuality, 2:904–905
    prostate cancer, 2:905
    sports and, 2:905–906
Menlo Ventures, 2:657
Mental health. See also Diagnostic and
    Statistical Manual; Mental health parity;
    Psychopharmacology; individual names
    of countries
    of adolescents, 1:52–54
    African Americans and psychotropic drug
        response, 1:71–72
    Canadian prescription drug benefits and,
        1:301–302, 1:302–303
    discrimination in prescribing practice,
        2:480
    history of pharmacological treatments for
        mental health, 1:260–261, 2:699–704
    mental health parity, 2:909–911
    normal: definitions and controversy,
        3:979–985

psychopharmacology and history of
pharmacological treatments for
mental health, 2:699–704
Substance Abuse and Mental Health
Services Administration (SAMHSA),
3:1326–1329
*Touched With Fire: Manic-Depressive
Illness and the Artistic Temperament*
(Jamison), 4:1365–1367
in U.S., 1800–1850, 4:1466–1467
Mental health parity, 2:909–911
defined, 2:909
key provisions and history, 2:910–911
Mental Health Parity Act of 1996, 2:909
Mental Health Parity and Addiction
Equity Act (MHPAEA), 2:909
pros and cons, 2:909–910
Meprobamate, 2:762
Merck, 2:911–914
company history, 2:912
environmental record of, 2:913
Merck Chemicals, 3:1296
The Merck Manuals, 2:912
MMR, 1:xli
overview, 2:911–912
Pfizer and, 3:1063
products, 2:912–913
Rofecoxib (Vioxx) controversy,
3:1246–1249
Sinopharm and, 3:1296
size of, 1:229
Merck, George, 2:912
Merck, Jacob Friedrich, 2:912
Meridians, 4:1409
Merital, 3:974–977
Mesoptamia, early medicines in, 1:xxxv
Metabolism, 1:73
Metformin, African Americans and, 1:72
Methadone programs, 2:674, 2:692,
2:694–696
opiate replacement programs,
3:1010–1011
Methamphetamine, 2:914–917
history of, 2:914–917
overview, 2:914
as Schedule II drug, 3:1266

**Methaqualone (Quaalude) controversy,
2:917–920**
overview, 2:917–918
as Schedule I drug, 3:1266
"scrip mills," 2:919–920
in U.S., 2:918–919
Methicillin-resistant *Staphylococcus aureus*
(MRSA), 1:133, 1:143
Méthode Numérique, 1:390–391
Methylphenidate, 1:40, 1:44
Mexico, 2:920–924
Agent Orange use in poppy fields, 1:xli
clinical trials of pharmaceutical drugs in,
2:921–922
crackdown on drug trafficking
organizations, 2:923–924
cross-border sales of pharmaceuticals,
2:922–923
political economics and Mexican drug
trade, 2:922–923
regulation of new pharmaceutical drugs in,
2:921
regulation of pharmaceutical drugs in,
2:920–921
smuggling of prescription drugs and,
3:1314
traditional and herbal medicines in,
4:1391
Mexitil, 1:284
MGI Pharma, 2:560
Middle Ages, history of pharmacology in.
See **History of pharmacology: Europe,
Middle Ages**
Middle East, history of pharmacy as
profession in, 2:740–742
Migraines, pain in neck/lower back/face/jaw
(data), 4:1682–1683 (table),
4:1684–1685 (table)
Military pharmaceutical issues, 2:924–926
amphetamine history and,
1:102–103
health care provider system and,
2:925–926
humanitarian assistance and, 2:925
overview, 2:924
pharmaceutical personnel, 2:924–925

Millbrae Holistic, 4:1368

Millennium Development Goals (MDGs)
    access to medicines (developing world),
        1:15

Millennium Pharmaceuticals, 4:1346,
    4:1347

Mini-Sentinel, 1:58–59

*Minority Rights: International Standards
    and Guidance for Implementation* (UN),
    3:1230

Minot, George, 2:570

Mirabegron, 1:225

Mirror to Hospital Pharmacy (Francke),
    1:xl

Mitchill, Samuel Latham, 4:1471

Mitotic inhibitors, 1:309

Mitsubishi Tanabe Pharma Corporation,
    1:231

Mixtard 30, 3:986

Mobile technology, 4:1349

Model List of Essential Medicines (WHO),
    2:581

Molecular neuroscience, 3:967–968

Monastic medicine, 2:716–717

Monitoring adherence, 4:1349

Monitoring Medicines, 2:894

Monowitz concentration camp, 1:259

Moore, Gordon, 2:657

Morbidity and mortality, from antibiotic
    resistant infection, 4:1601,
    4:1602–1603 (table)

Morbidity and Mortality Weekly Report
    (CDC), 4:1605, 4:1646, 4:1651, 4:1655,
    4:1703

Morning-after pill, 2:605–606

Morphine
    discovery of, 1:xxxvi
    ethnobotany and, 2:588
    first injectable morphine pioneered,
        1:xxxvi
    first legislation on narcotics, 1:xxxvii

Morphotek, 2:560

Mors, Harmon Northrop, 1:26

Moton, Robert, 4:1451

Motrin, 2:806

MPDL380A, 1:xlv

MRSA (methicillin-resistant *Staphylococcus
    aureus*), 2:926–929
    categories of, 2:927–928
    diagnosis, treatment, and prevention,
        2:928
    historical perspective, 2:926–927
    resistance to bactericidal bacteriostatic
        antibiotics, 2:927

MT203, 3:991

Multidrug-resistant organisms (MDROs),
    2:546

Multilab, 4:1347

Multiple sclerosis (MS), Biogen Idec and,
    1:276–277

Murphy, William, 2:570

Murray, Kenneth, 1:276

Mushrooms, psychedelic, 3:1178–1180

Muti (traditional Southern African medicine),
    2:929–931
    background, 2:929
    delivery, 2:929–931
    historical perspective, 2:736
    overview, 2:929
    sangoma, 2:929–931

Myfenax, 4:1355

Mylan, 2:931–933
    leadership of, 2:932
    work of, 2:931–933

Myocet, 4:1354

Nabenhauer, Fred, 1:102

Naito, Toyoji, 2:560

Naloxone, 3:936–937

Narcotic antagonists, 3:935–937
    defined, 3:935
    examples, 3:936–937
    narcotic agonist-antagonists and, 3:935

Narcotics, early legislation, 1:xxxvii

Narcotics (prescription), 3:937–940
    common prescription narcotics, 3:938–940
    future of, 3:940
    history, 3:938
    overview, 3:937–938

Narcotics Division, U.S. Treasury, 1:xxxviii

National Association of Boards of Pharmacy
    (NABP), 1:428–429, 2:847

National Basketball Association, 2:544
National Center for Advancing Translational Sciences (NIH), 3:940–943
   accomplishments of, 3:941–943
   creation of, 3:940–941
National Center for Complementary and Alternative Medicine (NIH), 3:943–946
   CAM definitions, 3:943
   CAM use in U.S., 3:944–945
   creation of, 1:xxxi
   history and current priorities, 3:944
   structure and activities, 3:945
National Center for Complementary and Integrative Health, 1:88
National Center for Health Statistics (NCHS), 4:1587–1594, 4:1633, 4:1639
National Center for Health Workforce Analysis, 4:1665
National Childhood Vaccine Injury Act, 1:xli, 3:945–948. *See also* Vaccination coverage data
   history of, 1:xli, 3:945–946
   literature review by, 3:946
   National Vaccine Injury Act (NVIA), 3:947
   physician responsibility and, 3:946–947
   Vaccine Adverse Event Reporting System (VAERS), 3:946 (*See also* Adverse drug effects reporting systems)
National Commission for the Protection of Human Subjects of Biomedical and Behavioral Research, 2:757
National Committee for Quality Assurance (NCQA), 2:686
National Council for Prescription Drug Programs (NCPDP), 1:49, 1:51–52
National Football League, 2:545
National Formulary, 1:94–95
National Health and Nutrition Examination Survey (NHANES), 4:1595–1600
   different strength opioid analgesics, 4:1596 (table)
   prescription opioid analgesic use, 4:1595 (table), 4:1597 (table), 4:1598 (table), 4:1599 (table)
National Health Interview Survey (NHIS), 4:1600, 4:1639, 4:1642, 4:1666, 4:1703

National Hockey League, 2:545
National Institute for Biological Standards and Control, 3:948–950
   global role, 3:949
   history of, 3:948
   operations, 3:948–949
   statutory duties, 3:948
   UK Stem Cell Bank and Influenza Resource Center, 3:949–950
National Institute of Health and Clinical Excellence of the United Kingdom, 1:41
National Institutes of Health (NIH)
   Dale and Betty Bumpers Vaccine Research Center (NIH), 1:xlii
   National Center for Advancing Translational Sciences (NIH), 3:940–943
   National Center for Complementary and Alternative Medicine (NIH), 3:943–946
National Library of Medicine, 3:1252–1254
National Network of Excellence in Neuroscience (NNE), 4:1355
National Organization for the Reform of Marijuana Laws (NORML), 2:881
National Research Act, 2:759
National Survey of Family Growth (NSFG), 4:1633
National Vaccine Injury Act (NVIA), 3:947
National Vaccine Program Office, 4:1507
Nationwide Emergency Department Sample (NEDS), 2:684–685
Native Americans/Alaska Natives, 3:950–952
   health issues and legislation, 3:951–952
   historic background, 3:950–951
   Native American Graves Protection and Repatriation Act (NAGPRA), 4:1412
   traditional and herbal medicines, regulation, 4:1398–1401
   traditional medicine: Native American tribes, 4:1411–1415
Native Hawai'ians/Pacific Islanders, 3:952–954
   health issues of, 3:953–954
   overview, 3:952–953
   traditional medical practices of, 3:954

Natrelle Gel, 1:85
Natron, 2:710
Natural Health Products Regulations, 4:1377
Naturopathy, 3:954–957
  controversy of, 3:956
  defined, 3:954–955
  modalities of, 3:955–956
Navane, 3:1064
Needle exchange programs, 2:673–674
Neonatal abstinence syndrome, 3:957–959
  drug exposure and, 3:957–959
  treatment for, 3:959
Neonicotinoids, 1:260
Nepal, traditional and herbal medicines in, 4:1395
Nepentes Pharma, 3:1264
Netherlands, 3:959–961
  history of pharmacology in, 3:959–961
  PHARMO Record Linkage System (the Netherlands), 3:1120–1122
Neupogen, 1:99
Neuro-enhancement through pharmacy, 3:961–963
  defined, 3:961
  drugs for, 3:961–963
Neuropharmacology, 3:963–968
  basics of, 3:964–965
  behavioral neuroscience, 3:966–967
  history of, 3:964
  molecular neuroscience, 3:967–968
  neuropharmacologists' approach to their field, 3:965–966
  overview, 3:963
New chemical entity (NCE), 3:1255
New York University, 1:xlvi
New Zealand
  Aotearoa of, 2:774–777
  direct-to-consumer pharmaceutical advertising (DTCPA), 1:66–67
  traditional and herbal medicines, regulation in Australia and New Zealand, 4:1373–1377
Nexium, 2:441
NeXstar Pharmaceuticals, 2:657–658
Nganga (traditional African healers), 3:968–970

Nicotine, 3:970–974
  in brain, 3:971–972
  chemistry of, 3:971
  delivery devices, 3:972–973
  effect on human body, 3:971
  in nature, 3:970–971
  nicotine patch, 2:932
  pharmacokinetics, 3:972
  regulation, 3:973–974
Nicotine replacement products, 3:1302–1303
Nigeria
  polio vaccination programs in, 1:xliv
  trovafloxacin (Trovan) controversy, 4:1443–1446
Nihon Eisai Co. Ltd., 2:560
Nitrates, 1:318, 1:319
Nitrogen, fertilizers and, 1:337
No Free Lunch, 1:65
Nobel Prize, 2:813
Nomifensine (Merital, Alival) controversy, 3:974–977
Nonsteroidal anti-inflammatory drugs (NSAIDS)
  acetaminophen as alternative to, 1:26, 1:27
  history, 1:xl
Nonstimulants
  for ADHD pharmacological therapy, 1:42–43
  adolescents and, 1:54
Noonday Demon, The: An Atlas of Depression (Andrew Solomon), 3:977–978
Normal: definitions and controversy, 3:979–985
  capitalization, 3:983
  diversity as new normality, 3:983–984
  overview, 3:979
  personality versus personality disorder, 3:982–983
  social roles and normality, 3:979–981
  vital versus social norms, 3:981–982
Norvasc, 3:1064
Nova Terapeutisk Laboratorium, 3:986
Novartis, 1:229
Novasc, 4:1347

Novo Nordisk, 3:985–987
    modern-day work of, 3:985–987
    origin and brief history of, 3:985
Novo Syringe, 3:985
Novo Terapeutisk Laboratorium, 3:985
NovoFine, 3:986
NovoMix, 3:986
NovoPen Flex Pen, 3:986
NovoRapid, 3:986
Novoseven, 3:987
NovoTwist, 3:986
NTI (narrow therapeutic index), 2:647
Nucleoside reverse transcriptase inhibitors
    (NRTI), 1:77
Nuovo Receptario, 1:xxxv
Nuremberg Code (1947), 2:756, 2:758
Nurses, African Americans' health care and,
    1:74–75
Nutritional Labeling and Education Act
    (NLEA), 4:1397
Nutritional supplements: history, 3:987–990.
    See also Traditional medicines
    overview, 3:987–990
    use data, by selected types of nonvitamin,
        nonmineral dietary supplements,
        4:1641 (table)
Nutropin, 2:639
Nycomed, 3:990–992
    history of, 3:990
    Takeda's acquisition and, 3:990–992,
        4:1346
Nyegaard, Morten, 3:990

Obesity, adolescents and, 1:53–54
Obinutuzumab, 2:639
Office of Drug Abuse Law Enforcement
    (ODALE), 2:881
Office of National Drug Control Policy
    (ONDCP), 3:1307, 3:1311
Off-label use of pharmaceuticals,
    3:993–995
    children and, 1:343
    off-label audits, 1:51
    overview, 3:993–995
    pharmaceutical fraud and, 3:1072
Oleoresin capsicum, 1:350

Olympics. *See also* **Athletes;** *individual types*
    of sports
    athletes caught using stimulants in
        Olympics, 3:1325–1326
    drug testing, Olympic athletes (overview),
        2:537–541
    performance-enhancing drugs and sports,
        early twentieth century to modern-
        day Olympics, 3:1056–1057
    performance-enhancing drugs and sports:
        history, 3:1056–1059
    state-sponsored sports doping programs
        and, 3:1319, 3:1320
    Summer: performance-enhancing drugs,
        3:995–1000
    Winter: performance-enhancing drugs,
        3:1000–1004
    World Anti-Doping Agency (WADA),
        2:537–538, 3:1003–1004
Olympics, Summer: performance-enhancing
    drugs, 3:995–1000
    industry notes, 3:998
    PED cases at games, 3:996–998
    regulation, testing, and legislation, 3:998
    testing challenges and current testing
        policies, 3:998–999
    types of PEDs, 3:995–996
Olympics, Winter: performance-enhancing
    drugs, 3:1000–1004
    EPO and, 1:280, 1:281, 2:578–580,
        3:1000–1001, 3:1334
    industry notes, 3:1004
    notable cases, 3:1001–1002
    regulation and legislation, 3:1002
    testing, 3:1002–1003
    types of PEDs, 3:1000
    WADA and IOC efforts to improve
        monitoring, 3:1003–1004
On Death and Dying (Kübler-Ross),
    2:751
Online pharmacies, 3:1004–1008
    benefits of, 3:1008
    legal and illegal online pharmacies,
        3:1006–1007
    major differences between online and local
        pharmacies, 3:1005

pharmacy benefit managers and online pharmacies' relationship with government, 3:1005–1006
potential problems with, 3:1007–1008
process of, 3:1004–1005
Opiate replacement programs, 3:1008–1012
alternatives to methadone maintenance therapy, 3:1011
history of search for nonaddicting analgesic, 3:1008–1010
methadone maintenance therapy, 3:1010–1011
Opiates. *See also* **Salvia (drug of abuse)**
abuse of prescription drugs and, 1:8
addiction to prescription drugs, 1:31–32, 1:34–35, 1:37
ancient history of opium poppy, 1:xxxv
chronology, 1:xxxv–xlvi
different strength opioid analgesics, 4:1596 (table)
drug poisoning deaths involving opioid analgesics, 4:1593 (table)
early history of opium, 1:xxxviii
first legislation on narcotics, 1:xxxvii
harm reduction policies, 2:673–674
heroin, 2:668–693, 2:689 (fig.), 2:691 (table), 2:694–696
history of, in U.S., 2:722
for pain disorders, 3:1032–1033
prescription opioid analgesic use, 4:1595 (table), 4:1597 (table), 4:1598 (table), 4:1599 (table)
propoxyphene (Darvon, Darvocet) controversy, 3:1173–1175
as Schedule III drugs, 3:1266
Sertürner and, 2:738
Opioid prescription abuse, misuse, and overuse, 3:1012–1015
consequences of abuse, misuse, overuse, 3:1012–1013
prevention strategies, 3:1013–1014
Opium (herbal medicine), 3:1015–1017
herbal medicine use and effects of opium, 3:1016–1017
historical perspective, 3:1015–1016
Opium and Drug Act, 1:xxxviii

Organisation for Economic Co-operation and Development, 3:1017–1020
access to medicines (industrialized world), 1:21–24
global health issues and, 3:1019
history, 1:xxxii, 1:xliv
overview, 3:1017–1018
working projects of, 3:1018–1019
Orishas, 2:559
Orphan diseases, drugs for, 3:1020–1022
cancer patients and, 3:1021
development and approval process of drugs for rare or orphan diseases, 3:1020–1021
future of, 3:1021–1022
Orphan Drug Act, 1:xli
patient activism and, 3:1035
pediatric patients and, 3:1021
Prescription Drug User Fee Act (1992), 3:1158
Osbourne, Jack, 1:69
OSI Pharmaceuticals, 1:226
Over-the-counter (OTC) drugs, 3:1022–1026
country-specific regulations, 3:1023
generic drugs versus OTC drugs, 3:1025–1026
overview, 3:1022–1023
regulation of OTC drugs in U.K., 3:1024–1025
restricted OTC drugs, 3:1023–1024

P (prevention) method, 2:894
Pacific Islanders. *See* **Native Hawai'ians/ Pacific Islanders**
Pacific yew tree, 2:899
Packaging
child-resistant packaging, 1:9
inserts and drug labeling, 2:526–527
Pain control, 3:1027–1029
function of pain, 3:1027–1028
pharmacological options for, 3:1028–1029
Phenacetin controversy, 3:1122–1125
Pain disorders, 3:1030–1033
acute pain, 3:1030
chronic pain, 3:1032

combined physical and psychological pain, 3:1031

opioid medications, 3:1032–1033

physical pain, 3:1030–1031

psychological pain, 3:1031

side effects, 3:1033

treatment, 3:1032

undiagnosed or unexplained pain conditions, 3:1032

Painkillers

abuse of prescription drugs and, 1:8

addiction to prescription drugs, 1:34–35

baseball and performance-enhancing drugs, 1:250

geographic variations in prescribing practices, 2:650–651

Pan American Health Organization, 3:1300

Panoz, Don, 2:932

Papaya, 4:1407

Papyrus Ebers, 1:86

Paracelsus, 1:xxxv

Paracetamol, 1:258

Park, Davis and Company, 1:xxxvii

Pasteur, Louis, 1:xxxvii, 2:711, 2:738–739

Pasteur Institute, 1:xxxviii

Patent law. *See also* Legal issues; **Legal issues in testing for performance-enhancing drugs**

Drug Price Competition and Patent Term Restoration Act (1984), 2:530–532

early U.S. patents, 1:xxxvi

generic medicines and, 2:643–645, 2:646

Lydia E. Pinkham's Vegetable Compound, 1:xxxvii

Patient activism, 3:1033–1037

ACT UP and other AIDS activist groups, 3:1036–1037

AIDS and, 3:1035–1036

cholesterol medications and adverse effects, 3:1035

opposition to, 3:1034

patients with rare diseases, 3:1035

side effects of SSRIs, 3:1034–1035

Patient adherence. *See* **Adherence to prescription directions**

Patient Protection and Affordable Care Act (Obamacare), 3:1037–1044

access to medicines (industrialized world), 1:24

low-income people, 2:834

Medicaid and Medicare systems, 2:866

Medicaid Expansion by States and, 3:1040–1041

medication therapy management (MTM) and, 2:896

mental health parity, 2:909

overview, 1:xxxiii, 3:1037–1038

Patient's Bill of Rights, 3:1040

SCHIP and, 3:1272

strategies of, 3:1038–1040

timeline for, 3:1041–1043

traditional medicine of Native American tribes and, 4:1414–1415

Patient rights, 3:1044–1050

advertising to patients, 1:66–70

extended care facility patients and polypharmacy, 3:1138–1139

historical perspective, 3:1044–1045

Patient's Bill of Rights and ACA, 3:1040

right to autonomy, 3:1046–1049

right to privacy, 3:1046

right to receive treatment, 3:1045–1046

Paul F. Parker Medal Award, 1:92

PCP (drug of abuse), 3:1050–1053

development of, 3:1051

effects of, 3:1051–1052

phencyclidine, defined, 3:1050–1051

as Schedule II drug, 3:1266

PCS Health Systems, 2:571

Pedanios Diosocorides, 1:xxxv

Pedersen, Harald, 3:985

Pedersen, Thorvald, 3:985

Pediatric Injectable Drugs, 1:98

Pediatric Research Equity Act (PREA), 3:1055

Pediatric Rule (U.S., 1998), 3:1053–1056

Pediatric Rule, BPCA, and PREA, 3:1054–1055

timeline and evolution of pediatric drug legislation, 3:1053–1054

Pelletier, Pierre Joseph, **1**:xxxvi

Pemberton, John, **1**:xxxvii

Pen T'sao (Shen Nun), **1**:xxxv

Pen Ts'ao Kang Mu, **2**:706

Penicillin

discovery of, **1**:xxxix, **1**:131, **2**:727–728, **2**:739

early mass production, **1**:xxxix

Pennsylvania Hospital, **4**:1473–1474

Pepper spray, **1**:349–350

Peramivir, **1**:xlv

Performance-enhancing drugs and sports: history, 3:1056–1059. *See also* **Athletes**

ancient history, **3**:1056

early twentieth century to modern-day Olympics, **3**:1056–1057

PERJETA, **2**:639

Personal medication records (PMR), **2**:896

Pertussis, **1**:xxxviii

Pertuzumab, **2**:639

Pesticides: human health effects, 3:1059–1062

Bayer and, **1**:259–260

history of pesticides, **3**:1059–1060

honeybees and, **1**:259–260

regulation of pesticides, **3**:1060

risks of pesticides, **3**:1060–1062

Pew Institute, **1**:xliii

Pew Internet Project, **1**:xliii–xliv

Pew Research Center, **1**:xliii, **1**:xlv

Pfizer, 3:1062–1066

AstraZeneca and, **1**:231

Boehringer Ingelheim and, **1**:284

deep tank fermentation (DTF), **3**:1062–1063

Eisai and, **2**:560

founding of, **3**:1062

growth of and products of, **3**:1063–1065

size of, **1**:229

Takeda and, **4**:1347

trovafloxacin (Trovan) controversy, **4**:1444–1446

Pfizer, Charles, **3**:1063

Pfizer, Emile, **3**:1063

Phaedrus (Socrates), **4**:1365

Pharmaceutical benefits within health insurance plans: U.S., 3:1066–1069

basic components of drug approvals, **3**:1066–1067

delivering pharmacy benefit, **3**:1066

outcomes of pharmacy benefit management, **3**:1068–1069

plan design features aimed at decision making, **3**:1067–1068

Pharmaceutical companies. *See also individual names of countries*

Abbott Laboratories, **1**:1–4

Actavis, **1**:28–30

advertising to doctors by, **1**:61–66

advertising to patients by, **1**:66–70

Allergan, **1**:84–85

Amgen, **1**:99–101

Astellas Pharma, **1**:225–227

AstraZeneca, **1**:229–231

Baxter International, **1**:255–258

Bayer, **1**:258–260

Biogen Idec, **1**:276–277

Boehringer Ingelheim, **1**:283–285

Celgene Pharmaceutical, **1**:322–324

Daiichi Sankyo, **2**:441–443

Eisai, **2**:560–561

Eli Lilly, **2**:569–571

Genentech, **2**:638–640

Gilead Sciences, **2**:656–658

industry's critical role, **1**:xxxii

Johnson & Johnson, **2**:804–807

Merck, **2**:911–914

Mylan, **2**:931–933

Novo Nordisk, **3**:985–987

Nycomed, **3**:990–992

off-label use of pharmaceuticals, **3**:993–995

Pfizer, **3**:1062–1066

Procter & Gamble, **3**:1169–1171

role of, in drug discovery and development, **2**:508

Sanofi-Aventis, **3**:1264–1265

Sinopharm Group Company Limited, **3**:1294–1298

Takeda Pharmaceutical Co., **4**:1345–1348

Teva Pharmaceutical Industries, **4**:1353–1357

Pharmaceutical fraud, 3:1069–1074
  defined, 3:1069–1070
  harm to society from, 3:1072–1073
  importance cases of, 3:1071–1072
  types of, 3:1070–1071
Pharmaceutical law, 3:1074–1080. *See also*
  Legal issues; *individual names of laws*
  overview of contemporary issues,
    3:1074–1075
  patenting laws, 3:1075–1078
  pharmaceutical marketing laws,
    3:1078–1079
Pharmaceutical Lexicon, The (Hahnemann),
  2:746
Pharmaceutical policy: international
  cooperation, 3:1080–1084
  international cooperation projects,
    3:1081–1083
  international pharmaceutical and health
    policy organizations, 3:1083
  overview, 3:1080–1081
  WHO, 3:1081
Pharmaceutical Pricing Policy Project,
  1:22–23
Pharmaceutical products, overview,
  1:xxxi–xxxiv
Pharmaceutical Research and Manufacturers
  of America, 3:1084–1086
  access to medication, 3:1085
  adherence to prescription directions, 1:45
  biopharmaceutical innovation, value, and
    safety, 3:1085
  Code on Interactions With Healthcare
    Professionals, 1:65
  membership and organization,
    3:1084–1085, 3:1086
  PhRMApedia, 3:1085–1086
Pharmaceutical Society of Great Britain,
  1:xxxvi
Pharmaceutical Survey (American Council
  on Education), 1:xxxix
Pharmacia, 2:657, 3:1064
Pharmacists, history of profession
  abuse of prescription drugs and access
    to, 1:7
  in Africa, 2:733–734

early degrees, U.S., 1:xl
in Europe, 2:737–740
first known use of term, 1:xxxvi
in Middle East, 2:740–742
military pharmaceutical issues and
  pharmaceutical personnel,
  2:924–925
Pharmaceutical Survey (American Council
  on Education), 1:xxxix
role of pharmacist in geriatric medicine,
  2:568–569
University of Michigan, 1:xxxi, 1:xxxvii
in U.S., 2:742–744
workforce, 4:1665 (table)
Pharmacists: training and certification,
  3:1086–1089
  degrees available, 3:1087
  in different countries, 2:743–744,
    3:1087–1088
  historical perspective, 3:1086
  specialties, 3:1088–1089
Pharmacodynamics, elderly people and,
  2:564
Pharmacoeconomics, 3:1089–1096
  access to essential medicines as a human
    right, 1:12–13
  applications of, 3:1094–1095
  cost-benefit analysis, 3:1093
  cost-effectiveness analysis, 3:1092
  cost-minimization analysis, 3:1091
  cost-utility analysis, 3:1092–1093
  in developing countries, 1:xxxii
  Drummond's criteria for evaluation
    pharmoeconomic studies, 3:1094
  money spent on expensive but marginally
    expensive drugs, 1:xlv
  overview, 3:1089–1091
  pharmaceutical spending in industrialized
    countries, 1:xxxiii
  retail prescription drug expenditures,
    4:1594 (table)
  spending on pharmaceuticals, in
    transitional economies, 1:xliii
Pharmacoepidemiology
  defined, 1:382
  studies, 2:791

Pharmacogenomics, 3:1096–1099
current state and future of, 3:1098–1099
history of, 3:1097–1098
overview, 3:1096–1097
potential applications and major goals of, 3:1099
Pharmacoinformatics, 3:1100–1102
medication use process, 3:1101
overview, 3:1100–1101
Pharmacokinetics, elderly people and, 2:564
Pharmacology for Africa initiative, 3:1102–1105
goals of PharfA, 3:1102–1103
International Council for Science, Africa (ICSU), 3:1105
International Union of Basic and Clinical Pharmacology (IUPHAR), 3:1104–1105
PharfA 2010 report, 3:1103–1104
PharfA goals and successes, 3:1103
PharfA Strategic Meeting, Copenhagen (2010), 3:1104
PharfA timeline, 3:1103
sponsors, 3:1104
World Congress of Basic and Clinical Pharmacology (2014), 3:1104
Pharmacology to control and punish, 3:1105–1110
Pharmacopoeia of the United States, 1:94–95, 2:742, 2:880, 4:1471
Pharmacotherapy, 1:91, 1:93
Pharmacovigilance, 3:1110–1113
E.U. pharmacovigilance system, 3:1111
in industrialized countries, 1:382
pharmacovigilance and drug safety regulation in U.S., 3:1111–1113
WHO and, 3:1110–1111
Pharmacy and Medicines Act (U.K.), 1:xxxix
Pharmacy benefit managers, 3:1113–1116
exceptions to formulary or pharmaceutical tier system, 3:1115
formulary, 3:1114–1115
PBM activities, 3:1113–1114
PBM industry, 3:1115–1116
PBMs, defined, 3:1113
pharmacy benefit management (PBM) and adjudicated claims data, 1:50–51

Pharmacy Management Agency (PHARMAC), 2:775
Pharmacy technicians: training and certification, 3:1116–1120
education of, 3:1116–1120
medical field expansion and, 3:1116–1117
Pharmacy Technician Educators Council (PTEC), 3:1117
work environments and, 3:1119
PHARMO Record Linkage System (The Netherlands), 3:1120–1122
Phenacetin controversy, 3:1122–1125
in late nineteenth century, 3:1123
in 1950s, 3:1123
in 1960s, 3:1123–1124
in 1970s, 3:1124
overview, 3:1122
withdrawal of phenacetin, 3:1124
Phendimetrazine tartrate, 1:210
Phenformin (Azucaps) controversy, 3:1125–1127
modern-day use of, 3:1127
overview of drug, 3:1125
safety issues, 3:1125–1127
Phenylethylamines, 2:668–670
Phenylpropanolamine (PPA), 2:602–603
Philadelphia College of Pharmacy and Science, 1:xxxvi
Philippines, 3:1128–1129
Phoenix, River, 1:xlii
Phosphate-based products, in anticaries drugs, 1:147–148
Phytochemicals, 3:1130–1132
classes of, 3:1130–1131
overview, 3:1130
Pill (contraceptive), 2:608–610
Pinkham, Lydia Estes, 1:xxxvii
Plan B One-Step, 4:1355
Plasma expanders, 2:495–496, 3:1334
Plavix, 3:1164
Plegridy, 1:276–277
Plexxikon, Inc., 2:442
Polio eradication campaign, 3:1132–1135
March of Dimes, 1:xxxix
mass immunization campaigns and oral polio vaccine, 3:1133–1135

Nigeria and, **1:**xliv
overview, **3:**1132
polio vaccine, **1:**xl, **2:**731, **4:**1508, **4:**1511
Polypharmacy, 3:1135–1141
adverse drug events, **3:**1137
assessment of, **3:**1139–1140
cognitive impairment/CNS depression,
    3:1138
considerations for extended care facility
    patient, **3:**1138–1139
defined, **3:**1135
drug interactions, **3:**1138
elderly people and, **2:**566
falls, **3:**1138
functional status, **3:**1138
increased costs, **3:**1137–1138
managing, **3:**1140
nonadherence, **3:**1136–1137
prevalence of, **3:**1136
risk factors for, **3:**1136
Polyphenols, **3:**1131
Positive reinforcement, substance abuse and,
    1:265
Potassium-sparing diuretics, **1:**183–184,
    2:493
Powell, Asafa, **4:**1369
Powers, Jack, **3:**1064
Powers, Pauline, **4:**1366
Pradaxa, **1:**284, **1:**285
Praluent, **3:**1265
Prasugrel, **2:**441
Pratt, Edmund T., Jr., **3:**1064
Pregnancy. *See also* **Fertility control; Fertility**
    control: history; Fertility drugs; Women;
    individual names of drugs
    drugs used during, **4:**1540–1542
    inhalants and, **2:**779
Prescribing practices. *See also*
    Discrimination in prescribing practice;
    Geographic variation in prescribing
    practices
    in ancient Egypt, **2:**709–710
    gender differences in prescription rates,
        2:903–904
Prescription drug abuse. *See* **Abuse of**
    prescription drugs

Prescription drug approval process: Asia,
    3:1141–1145
Japan's "drug lag" and ASEAN
    harmonization, **3:**1143
overview, **3:**1141–1142
regulating pharmaceuticals as commodities
    and cures, **3:**1142–1143
rising markets in China and India,
    3:1143–1144
Prescription drug approval process:
    Australia, 3:1145–1147
clinical trials, **3:**1146–1147
overview, **3:**1145–1146
risk management and TGA, **3:**1146
Prescription drug approval process: Canada,
    3:1147–1150
clinical trials, intent, **3:**1149
drug development, **3:**1148–1149
drugs defined by, **3:**1148
overview, **3:**1147–1148
process, **3:**1149–1150
Prescription drug approval process: Europe,
    3:1150–1153
FDA compared to EMA, **3:**1152–1153
phases of process, **3:**1150–1151
presubmission process as centralized
    procedure, **3:**1151–1152
Prescription drug approval process: U.S.,
    3:1153–1157
Prescription drug monitoring programs
    (PDMPs), **1:**9–10, **3:**1311
Prescription Drug User Fee Act (1992),
    3:1157–1159
clinical trials and, **1:**384–385
Generic Drug User Fee Amendments, **2:**646
history, **1:**xlii
overview, **3:**1157–1159
prescription drug approval process,
    3:1155
Prescription medication use
    abuse of, **1:**4–10
    addiction to prescription drugs, **1:**30–38
    adherence to prescription directions,
        1:44–49
    antibiotics, **4:**1591 (table)
    arts and creativity, **1:**212–219

Canada: variation in prescription drug benefits by province/territory, **1:296–304**

computerized systems for prescription drugs, **4:1592** (table)

drug poisoning deaths involving opioid analgesics, **4:1593** (table)

Medicaid: prescription drug benefits, **2:863–866**

Medicare Prescription Drug, Improvement, and Modernization Act (2003), **2:890–892**

Medicare: prescription drug benefits, **2:886–890**

nonreceipt of needed prescription drugs, **4:1590** (table)

number of prescription drugs taken, **4:1589** (table)

prescription antidepressants, **4:1591** (table)

prescription drug approval process: Asia, **3:1141–1145**

prescription drug approval process: Australia, **3:1145–1147**

prescription drug approval process: Canada, **3:1147–1150**

prescription drug approval process: Europe, **3:1150–1153**

prescription drug approval process: U.S., **3:1153–1157**

prescription drug monitoring programs (PDMPs), **1:9–10**

prescription drug use, **4:1588** (table)

prescription drug use in past 30 days, by number of drugs taken and age, **4:1587** (table)

Prescription Drug User Fee Act (1992), **3:1157–1159**

Prescription-Event Monitoring (PEM) Database (University of Portsmouth, UK), **3:1159–1162**

reimportation of prescription drugs, **3:1242–1244**

retail prescription drug expenditures, **4:1594** (table)

SCHIP (State Children's Health Insurance Program): prescription drug benefits, **3:1270–1274**

Prescription-Event Monitoring (PEM) Database (University of Portsmouth, UK), 3:1159–1162

change from PEM to M-PEM, **3:1160–1161**

data from PEM studies, **3:1161**

Prescriptive authority, 3:1162–1166

defined, **3:1162**

history of prescribing, **3:1162–1164**

President's Emergency Plan for AIDS Relief (PEPFAR), **1:326, 1:327**

President's Malaria Initiative (PMI) (CDC), **1:324, 1:327**

Prevacid, **4:1347**

Prezista, **2:806**

Pricing, best price fraud and, **3:1071**

Principium somniferum (morphine), **1:xxxvi**

Prison pharmaceutical issues, 3:1166–1169

cost effectiveness and privatization, **3:1168–1169**

legal foundations for care, **3:1166–1167**

unique issues, **3:1167–1168**

ProAir BNO, **4:1354**

Probenicid, **2:495**

Probiotics, **1:148**

Procardia XL, **3:1064**

Procter, William, **3:1170**

Procter & Gamble, 3:1169–1171

brands, **3:1169–1170**

history of, **3:1170**

Product claim advertisements, **1:68**

Progestins, **1:310**

Proguanil, **1:191**

Project Bioshield Act (2004), 3:1171–1173

background, **3:1171**

concerns and criticism, **3:1173**

history, **1:xliii**

provisions of, **3:1171–1173**

Promoting the Quality of Medicines (PQM) Program (USP), **4:1505**

Prontosil, **1:259**

Proposition 215 (California), **2:882–883, 4:1398**

Propoxyphene (Darvon, Darvocet) controversy, 3:1173–1175

Protection Motivation Theory, 1:47

Protropin, 2:640

Provectus Biopharmaceuticals, 3:1296

Prozac
cosmetic pharmacology on, 1:420–422
U.S. availability of, 1:xli

Pseudoephedrine, restriction of access to, 3:1175–1177

Pseudomonas aeruginosa, 2:548

Psilocybin, 3:1178–1180
counterculture, 3:1179–1180
history, 3:1178–1179
legal issues, 3:1180
names and administration of, 3:1178
as Schedule I drug, 3:1266

Psychopharmacology, 3:1180–1190
ADHD drugs, 1:38–44
antipsychiatry movement, 1:195–198
antipsychotics, 1:198–206
approved classes of psychotropic drugs, 3:1183–1184
behavioral pharmacology and substance abuse, 1:260–265
chemical theories in psychiatry and use of psychotropic drugs, 3:1183
future directions, 3:1188–1189
hallucinogens, 2:667–672
historical context, 3:1181–1182
history of pharmacological treatments for mental health, 2:699–704
issues with using psychotropic drugs, 3:1186–1188
MDMA uses in 1980s and, 2:857
medicinal use, 3:1182–1183
nonmedicinal use of psychotropic drugs, 3:1185
overview, 3:1180–1181
psychiatric drug use estimates, 3:1184
psychotropic drugs in contemporary society, 3:1182
regulatory structure of psychoactive substance use, 3:1185–1186
terminology for, 1:260–261

Psychotoxic Drug Control Act of 1964, 2:501, 2:502

Pure Food and Drug Act (1906), 3:1190–1192. *See also* Food and Drug Administration (U.S.)
advertising to doctors and, 1:63–64
Drug Abuse Control Amendments of 1965 and, 2:500–501
FDA history and, 2:620–621
history, 1:xxxviii
smuggling of prescription drugs and, 3:1310

Puskar, Milan, 2:932

Pyrimethamine, 1:191

Qi, 4:1409, 4:1427

QNASL, 4:1354

Qsymia, 1:209

Quaaludes, 2:917–920

Quality of life research, 3:1193–1197
in health-related research, 3:1193–1194
measurement, 3:1194–1196
QoL, defined, 3:1193
quality of life and pharmacology, 3:1196–1197

Quartette, 4:1355

Quinine, 1:xxxvi, 1:xxxix, 1:190–191

Qvar, 4:1354

Rabies vaccine, 1:xxxvii

Race-based pharmaceuticals, 3:1199–1202. *See also individual names of groups*
African-American Heart Failure Trial (A-HeFT), 3:1200–1201
concept, 3:1200
human race and genetics, 3:1199–1200
human race and medicine, 3:1200

Racial minorities: Asia, 3:1202–1210
Asian views of race, 3:1203–1204
globalization and racial minorities in Asia, 3:1208–1209
health issues in Asia, 3:1208
overview, 3:1202–1203, 3:1215–1217
overview of Asian race by region, 3:1205–1208
racial minorities and prescription drugs, 3:1217–1219

Racial minorities: Canada, 3:1210–1215
  contemporary minority policy,
    3:1211–1212
  health issues of indigenous people and
    minorities in Canada, 3:1214–1215
  historical background, 3:1210–1211
  official and minority languages of Canada,
    3:1213–1214
  religious minorities, 3:1213
  visible minorities, 3:1212–1213
Racial minorities: Caribbean, 3:1215–1219
Racial minorities: Europe, 3:1219–1227
  brief survey of international minority
    rights in Europe, 3:1224–1225
  health issues, 3:1223–1224
  overview, 3:1219–1220, 3:1220–1222
  post–World War II, 3:1222–1223
  racial discrimination in Europe,
    3:1225–1226
Racial minorities: Latin America,
    3:1227–1233
  health issues in Latin America,
    3:1231–1232
  minorities and social class in Latin
    America, 3:1228–1230
  other minorities in Latin America, 3:1231
  overview, 3:1227–1228
  territory and minorities in Latin America,
    3:1230–1231
Raloxifene, 1:340
Ranbaxy Laboratories, Inc., 2:442
RAND Health Insurance Experiment
    (1974–1982), 3:1233–1236
  DIE design, 3:1234–1235
  mental health parity and, 2:909
  origin of RAND elasticity, 3:1235–1236
  overview, 3:1233–1234
Randomized controlled trials (RCT), 1:383
Raptiva, 2:639
Rathamann, George, 1:99
Rational drug design, 3:1236–1239
  biological target, defined, 3:1236–1237
  "drug discovery" versus, 3:1238–1239
  process of, 3:1237
  two types of, 3:1237–1238
  use of computers in, 3:1238

Rational prescribing, 3:1239–1242
  overview, 3:1239–1241
  stepwise approach to, 3:1240–1241 (table)
Raylo Chemicals, 2:658
Read, Ian, 3:1065
Reed Sinopharm Exhibitions, Co. LTD, 3:1296
Referrals, medication therapy management
    and, 2:896–897
Reimportation of prescription drugs,
    3:1242–1244
  consumers and, 3:1243
  FDA and, 3:1242
  legal issues of, 3:1243
  media and, 3:1243
  pharmaceutical industry, 3:1242–1243
Relaxants, sports and, 3:1334
Remicade, 2:913
Reminder advertisements, 1:68
Research and development. See also individ-
    ual names of pharmaceutical companies
  access to essential medicines as a human
    right, 1:12–13
  access to medicines (industrialized
    world), 1:21
  by Actavis, 1:30
  diffusion of new pharmaceutical drugs,
    2:467–471
  drug discovery and development, 2:505–511
  human subjects research, standards and
    protections, 2:756–758
Research Institute of the American College of
    Clinical Pharmacy, 1:92–93
Respiratory diseases (data),
    4:1670–1671 (table), 4:1672–1673 (table)
Review on Antimicrobial Resistance, 1:xlv
Revlimid, 1:322–323, 1:323
Rezaltas, 2:441
Rhabdomyolysis, 1:332
Richards, Mary Lea Johnson, 2:805
Riggs, Arthur, 2:638
Right to Health, 1:14–15
Rimonabant (Acomplia) controversy,
    3:1244–1246
  antiobesity medications, 3:1244–1245
  endocannabinoid system and appetite, 3:1244
  rimonabant as medication, 3:1245–1246

Riordan, Michael L., 2:657
Ritalin
    addiction to prescription drugs, 1:32, 1:36–37
Rivers, Eunice, 4:1451
Robbins, Frederick Chapman, 1:xl
Roberts, Jonathan, 1:xxxvi
Robinson, Frank, 1:xxxvii
Roche, 1:229, 2:638, 2:762
Rodengen, Jeffrey, 3:1063
Roe v. Wade, 2:609
Rofecoxib (Vioxx) controversy, 3:1246–1249
Roflumilast, 4:1347
Rohypnol, 1:394–396, 2:762–763
Rolleston Report, 2:694
Root Tantra, 4:1424
Ross Laboratories, 1:3
Royal Gist Brocades, 1:225
RU-486, 2:605
Rubella vaccine, 2:913
Rumsfeld, Donald, 2:657
Rusby, Henry Hurd, 1:xxxvii
Rush, Banjamin, 4:1469–1470
Russia, 3:1249–1251
    country description and demographics, 3:1249
    current abusers of prescription drugs in, 3:1251
    health care issues of, 3:1249–1250
    illegal use of prescription drugs in, 3:1250
    pharmaceutical industry in, 3:1249
    Russian Anti-Doping Agency (RUSADA), 2:537–538
    unique local drugs, 3:1250–1251
    U.S. situation and, 3:1251
RxNorm (National Library of Medicine), 3:1252–1254

S. E. Massengill Co., 1:xxxix, 2:600–601, 2:621–623, 3:1154
Sabin, Albert, 1:xl, 2:731, 4:1508, 4:1511
Safety Pharmacology Society, 3:1255–1259
    diplomate in safety pharmacology (DSP), 3:1257
    ICH S7A guidance, 3:1256
    regulatory agencies and nonprofit organizations, 3:1257–1258

regulatory guidance, 3:1257
    safety pharmacology, defined, 3:1255–1256
    safety pharmacology and pharmaceutical industry, 3:1256–1257
Sakuragaoka Research Laboratory, 2:560
Salicylic acid, 1:258
Saline Breast Implants, 1:85
Salk, Jonas, 1:xl, 2:731, 4:1508, 4:1511
Salmonella, 2:548
Salophen, 1:258
Salvarsan, 1:xxxviii
Salvia (drug of abuse), 3:1259–1264
    effects and risks, 3:1260–1261
    motivation for and prevalence of use, 3:1261–1262
    pharmacology, 3:1259–1260
    potential as medication, 3:1263
    public perception and legal status, 3:1262–1263
San Pedro cactus, 4:1422
Sandpaper fig, 4:1404
Sanger, Margaret, 2:607–608
Sangoma, 2:929–931
Sanitation, history of, 2:729
Sanki, Tashiro, 2:809
Sanofi-Aventis, 3:1264–1265
    overview, 3:1264–1265
    size of, 1:229
Santonin, 3:1062
Sativex, 2:876
Saunders, Dame Cicely, 2:751
Scheduled drugs (U.S.), 3:1265–1270
    debating drug scheduling under CSA, 3:1269–1270
    overview, 1:418–419, 3:1265–1266, 3:1265–1267 (*See also* **Controlled Substances Act**)
    pre-CSA drug use and regulation, 3:1267–1269
    Schedule I, 3:1266
    Schedule II, 3:1266
    Schedule III, 3:1266
    Schedule IV, 3:1266
Scheller, Richard, 2:638
Schering-Plough, 2:912

SCHIP (State Children's Health Insurance
    Program): prescription drug benefits,
    3:1270–1274
  history of, 3:1271–1272
  overview, 3:1270–1271
Schmidt, Benno C., 2:657
School of Salerno, 2:717
Second Opium War, 1:xxxvii
Second-generation sulfonylureas,
    1:170–171
Sedatives
  abuse of prescription drugs and, 1:7–8
  addiction to prescription drugs, 1:32,
    1:35–36
  baseball and performance-enhancing
    drugs, 1:250–251
Sentinel's Initiative, 1:59–60
Serologic testing, 2:730
Sertürner, Friedrich, 1:xxxvi, 2:738
Sex offenders, pharmacological interventions
    for, 3:1274–1277
Sex reassignment therapy and prescription
    drugs, 3:1277–1280
  complications, 3:1279–1280
  hormones, 3:1277–1278
  sexual minorities and, 3:1282–1283
  surgery, 3:1278–1279
Sexual minorities, 3:1280–1287
  consequences of discrimination,
    3:1281–1282
  definitions, 3:1280–1281
  focus on dysfunction, 3:1283–1284
  HIV/AIDS, 3:1282
  mental health, 3:1283
  obstacles to treatment, 3:1284–1285
  sex reassignment, 3:1282–1283
  steps needed, 3:1285–1287
Sexuality. See also Fertility control; Fertility
    control: history; Fertility drugs; Men;
    Women
  erectile dysfunction and Viagra
    development, 1:xlii
  Flibanserin for female sex drive, 1:xlvi
  men's health and, 2:904–905
Shanghai Fosun Pharmaceutical Company,
    3:1294

Shanghan Zabing Lun (Treatise on Cold
    Damage Disorders), 2:706
Sharp, Alpheus Phineas, 2:912
Sharp, Phillip, 1:276
Sharp & Dohme Incorporated, 2:912
Shen Nun, 1:xxxv, 2:705
Shepherd, Alexander M. M., 1:89
Shooting sports and performance-enhancing
    drugs, 3:1287–1289
  biathlon, 3:1288
  modern pentathlon, 3:1288
  overview, 3:1287–1288
  shooting, overview, 3:1288–1289
Sibutramine, 1:54
Sichuan Industrial Institute of Antibiotics,
    3:1296, 3:1297
Siddha medicine (Dravidian culture),
    3:1289–1292
  concepts and pathology, 3:1289–1290
  diagnosis and treatment, 3:1290–1291
  modern-day practice and industry,
    3:1291–1292
Sildenafil citrate, 1:xlii
Simpson, Sherone, 4:1369
Singapore, 3:1292–1294
  health care programs of, 3:1292–1293
  illicit drugs and drug policy, 3:1293–1294
  pharmaceutical market, 3:1293
Sinopharm Group Company Limited,
    3:1294–1298
  awards, 3:1297
  Chinese government and, 3:1297
  educational and research institutions,
    3:1297
  international collaborations, 3:1296
  overview, 3:1294–1295
  subsidiaries, 3:1295–1296
  Web site of, 3:1297
Sleep, drugs used for, 1:xlv
Slippery elm, 2:899
Smallpox eradication, 3:1298–1301
  "arithmetic tradition" and clinical trials,
    1:390
  Biologics Control Act of 1902, 1:xxxviii
  bioterrorism and, 1:xlii, 3:1301, 4:1511
  global risks, 3:1301

history of, 3:1299–1301
post-eradication, 3:1301
vaccination, 3:1298–1299
variolation, 1:xxxvi
WHO campaign (1967), 1:xl
Smith, Daniel B., 1:xxxvii
Smith, Edwin, 2:708
Smith, Kline and French (SKF), 1:102, 2:915
Smith-Hams, Denise, 2:638
Smoking cessation drugs, 3:1301–1306
electronic cigarettes, 3:1304
history of, 3:1301–1302
interventions, 3:1302
mechanism of action, 3:1303
nicotine replacement products,
      3:1302–1303
non-nicotine replacement products,
      3:1303–1304
Smuggling of drugs of abuse, 3:1306–1310
drug trafficking, overview, 3:1306
High Intensity Drug Trafficking Areas
      (HIDTA), 3:1307
Office of National Drug Control Policy
      (ONDCP), 3:1307
trends in drug smuggling, 3:1308–1309
Smuggling of prescription drugs,
      3:1310–1315
distribution and diversion of prescription
      drugs, 3:1311–1312
history of prescription drugs and,
      3:1310–1311
Internet and cross-border smuggling,
      3:1312–1315
Society for the History of Pharmacy,
      1:xxxviii
Socrates, 4:1365
Soda
   Hires Root Beer, 1:xxxvii
   soda fountains, 2:722
Sodium bicarbonate, 1:147
Sodium glucose cotransporter 2 inhibitor,
      1:172
Solomon, Andrew, 3:977–978
Solpadol, 3:1164
Solvents, 2:777–778
Songzan Ganbu (King), 4:1423

South Africa, 3:1315–1319
access to medicines, 3:1316
current prevention efforts, 3:1318
drug-related issues, 3:1317
extent of abuse of prescription medicines
      in, 3:1317
health system, overview, 3:1315–1316
influence on substance use, 3:1317
solutions to prescription medicine abuse,
      3:1318
South African Treatment Action
      Campaign, 1:19
traditional and herbal medicine in,
      3:1316–1317
traditional medicines in, 4:1372
South America. See Traditional medicine:
      South America
Southern Network on Adverse Reactions
      (SONAR), 2:676–677, 2:681
Spalding, Lyman, 4:1471
Specific serotonin reuptake inhibitors
      (SSRIs)
adolescents and, 1:54
overview, 1:164–165
patient activism and, 3:1034–1035
Prozac and early U.S. availability,
      1:xli
sex offenders and pharmacological
      interventions, 3:1276
Spermicide, 2:604–605
Spiriva, 1:284
Spirogen, 1:230
Sports. See Athletes
Sprout Pharmaceuticals, 1:xlvi
Squibb, 3:1063
Sri Lanka, traditional and herbal medicines
      in, 4:1395
St. John's wort, 4:1407–1408, 4:1421
St. Mary's Hospital Medical School,
      1:xxxvii
Staphylococcus, 2:549
State Ambulatory Surgery and Services
      Databases (SASD), 2:685
State Emergency Department Databases
      (SEDD), 2:685
State Inpatient Database (SID), 2:685

State-sponsored sports doping programs,
3:1319–1321
China, 3:1319–1320
East Germany, 3:1320–1321
Steere, William, 3:1064, 3:1065
Steroids, 1:309–310
BALCO scandal and, 1:247–250
Game of Shadows (Mark Fainaru-Wada
and Lance Williams), 2:633–635
glucocorticosteroids (sport), 2:661–663
youth drug use data, 4:1616 (table),
4:1617 (table), 4:1618 (table)
Stimulants. *See also* **Athletes; Stimulants**
(sport)
abuse of prescription drugs and, 1:7
addiction to prescription drugs,
1:36–37
for ADHD pharmacological therapy,
1:40–42 (*See also* **ADHD drugs**)
adolescents and, 1:54
baseball and performance-enhancing
drugs, 1:250
drugs as study aids and, 2:550–553
pseudoephedrine, restriction of access to,
3:1175–1177
Stimulants (sport), 3:1321–1326
athletes caught using stimulants in
Olympics, 3:1325–1326
baseball and performance-enhancing
drugs, 1:250
consumption, 3:1323–1324
distribution and sale, 3:1323
production, 3:1322–1323
regulation and legislation, 3:1324–1325
stimulants, defined, 3:1321–1322
swimming and, 3:1332–1333
Stop TB Partnership (WHO), 1:xlii
Strategic National Stockpile (SNS) (U.S.),
2:663
Strategies for Enhancing Access to Medicines
Program (Management Sciences for
Health), 1:13–14
Streptococcus, 2:549
Streptomycin, 1:xxxix, 3:1065
Study aids, drugs as, 2:550–553
Subsequent Tantra, 4:1424

Substance Abuse and Mental Health
Services Administration (SAMHSA),
3:1326–1329
methamphetamine, 2:914
organization of, 3:1327–1328
overview, 3:1326–1327
substance abuse, defined, 3:1327
Succus Alterans, 2:570
SUIAC, 3:1062
"Suicide's Soliloquy, The" (Lincoln), 4:1468
Sulfonylureas, second-generation, 1:170–171
Sumeria (ancient), medicines in, 1:xxxv
Sun Pharmaceutical, 4:1347
Sun Simiao, 4:1380
Sunscreening agents, 3:1329–1332
awareness and use, 3:1331
culture of sun worshipping, 3:1329
damaging solar effects on skin,
3:1329–1330
sunscreen issues, 3:1330
types of, 3:1330–1331
Suntory Institute for Biomedical Research,
2:442
"Surgeon General's Advisory Committee on
Smoking and Health," 3:1301–1302
Swanson, Robert, 2:638
Swimming and performance-enhancing
drugs, 3:1332–1335
building muscle and bone, 3:1333–1334
drug testing, 3:1334–1335
increasing oxygen delivery, 3:1334
masking drug use, 3:1334
relaxants, 3:1334
stimulants, 3:1332–1333
Swine flu (H1N1) vaccine, 1:257
Swiss Society of Pharmacology and Toxicol-
ogy, 3:1335–1338
aims and structure of, 3:1336–1337
composition of council, 3:1335–1336
consulting services, 3:1337
dissolution, 3:1336
member societies, 3:1335
research work, 3:1337–1338
Swiss Society for Clinical Pharmacology
and Toxicology, 3:1336
workshops and conferences, 3:1337

Switzerland, 3:1338–1340
heroin-assisted treatment in, 2:694
overview, 3:1338–1340
Swiss Society of Pharmacology and
Toxicology, 3:1335–1338
Swnw, 2:708–711
Sydenham, Thomas, 1:xxxvi
Synribo, 4:1354–1355
Synthetic marijuana, 3:1340–1344
effects and health risks, 3:1342
epidemiology, 3:1342–1343
pharmacology, 3:1340–1342
policy, 3:1343
Synthetic oxygen carriers, injecting,
1:281
Syphilis, 1:xxxviii, 2:759, 4:1447–1454,
4:1517–1518
Syrrx, 4:1347
Szostak, Jack, 2:657

TachoSil, 3:991
Tacni, 4:1355
Taiwan Herbal Pharmacopoeia,
4:1382
Takamine, Jokichi, 2:441
Takeda Pharmaceutical Co., 4:1345–1348
Abbott Laboratories and, 1:2
acquisition history and collaboration
partners, 4:1346–1347
controversies, 4:1347–1348
corporate philosophy and strategic
initiatives, 4:1345–1346
globalization, diversity, innovation,
4:1346
Nycomed and, 3:990–992
research and development, 4:1347
Tamoxifen, 1:340
TaNeDS, 2:442–443
Tanzania, traditional medicines in,
4:1372
TAP Pharmaceuticals, 1:2, 4:1347
Tarivid, 2:441
Tartic acid, 3:1062
Taxotere, 3:1164
Tea tree oil, 4:1403–1404
Tecfidera, 1:277

Technology and pharmacy practice,
4:1348–1350
automated dispensing, 4:1349
current state of technology-supported
pharmacy, 4:1349–1350
electronic prescribing, 4:1348
identification of medical barcode,
4:1348–1349
mobile technology, 4:1349
monitoring adherence, 4:1349
telecare, 4:1349
Telecare, 4:1349
Tennis and performance-enhancing drugs,
4:1351–1353
antidoping policies, 4:1352–1353
historical perspective, 4:1351–1352
motivation for doping and negative effects
of drug use, 4:1352
Tenofovir, 2:657
Ter Meer, Fritz, 1:249
Terpenes, 1:113
Terramycin, 3:1063
Tetracycline, 3:1065
Teva Pharmaceutical Industries, 4:1353–1357
advertising to patients, 1:69
National Network of Excellence in
Neuroscience (NNE), 4:1355
New Therapeutic Entities (NTEs),
4:1355–1356
overview, 4:1353–1354
products and specialty areas, 4:1354–1355
social and environmental responsibility,
4:1356
subsidiaries, 4:1354
Tevagrastim, 4:1354
Thalidomide (Contergan) controversy,
4:1357–1359
Celgene and, 1:323
history of, 4:1357–1359
Kefauver-Harris Amendment, 2:623–625
modern-day uses of, 1:211
Theophrastus, 1:xxxv
Theory of Planned Behavior (TPB), 1:47
Theory of Psychological Reactance, 1:48
Theory of Reasoned Action (TRA), 1:47
Therapeutic drug monitoring (TDM), 1:382

Therapeutic Goods Administration (TGA)
(Australia), 3:1145–1147
Therapeutic Use Exemption (performance-
enhancing drugs), 4:1359–1362
doping in sports and, 4:1360–1361
process, 4:1361–1362
TUE, defined, 4:1359–1360
TheraSenses, 1:3
Thiazide diuretics, 1:72, 1:183, 2:492–493
Thiazolidinediones, 1:171
3,4-methylenedioxy-methamphetamine
(MDMA), 1:394–396
Thuoc Bac, 4:1427
Thuoc Nam, 4:1427
Tibet. See Traditional medicine: Tibet
Ticagrelor, 1:230–231
Tide, 3:1170
Tiotropium bromide, 1:284
Tissue culture, U.S. history of, 2:730
Title X Family Planning Program (1970),
4:1362–1365
impact, 4:1363
overview, 4:1362–1363
process, 4:1363–1365
Tomek, Ales, 1:230–231
Topoisomerases, 1:309
Touched With Fire: Manic-Depressive
Illness and the Artistic Temperament
(Jamison), 4:1365–1367
Tour de France, 1:435–437
Track and field and performance-enhancing
drugs, 4:1367–1370
BALCO case and, 4:1368–1369
effects of PEDs on track and field,
4:1369
overview, 4:1367–1368
scandals (other than BALCO), 4:1369
Trade-Related Aspects of Intellectual Property Rights (TRIPS Agreement), 1:16,
1:17, 1:18, 1:21, 2:582
Traditional and herbal medicines, regulation:
Africa, 4:1370–1373
developments in traditional and herbal
medicine, 4:1370–1372
economic and cultural heritage,
4:1372–1373

Traditional and herbal medicines, regulation:
Australia and New Zealand,
4:1373–1377. See also Australia
in Australia, 4:1374
harm and, 4:1376
in New Zealand, 4:1376
product claim warnings, 4:1374–1376
terminology and legislation, 4:1373
Traditional and herbal medicines, regulation:
Canada, 4:1377–1379
Natural Health Products Regulations,
4:1377
regulation and licensing, 4:1378–1379
Traditional and herbal medicines, regulation:
East Asia, 4:1379–1384
historical regulation of medicinal herbs,
4:1379–1380
regulating pharmaceuticals and medicinal
herbs, 4:1380–1381
regulation as way toward standardization
and internationalization,
4:1382–1383
transformation of herbal medicines
through regulation, 4:1381–1382
Traditional and herbal medicines, regulation:
Europe, 4:1384–1388
European Medicines Agency, 4:1385–1386
European Union and, 4:1384–1385
licensing process, 4:1386–1387
treaties, 4:1385
U.K. case study, 4:1384
Traditional and herbal medicines, regulation:
Latin America, 4:1388–1391
Chagas disease, 1:xlv
overview, 4:1388–1391
registration of products, 4:1390–1391
standardization and, 4:1388–1390
traditional medicines, defined, 4:1388
Traditional and herbal medicines, regulation:
South Asia, 4:1392–1396
Bangladesh, 4:1394
herbal medicine, classification,
4:1392–1393
India, 4:1394–1395
literature review, 4:1393–1394
manufacturing, 4:1394

Nepal, 4:1395
safety and identification, 4:1393
Sri Lanka, 4:1395
traditional medicine, overview, 4:1392
Traditional and herbal medicines, regulation: United States, 4:1396–1401
regulation, 4:1396–1398
terminology, 4:1396
traditional medicine regulation, 4:1398–1401
Traditional Herbal Medicinal Products Directive (THMPD), 4:1385
Traditional Knowledge Digital Library, 3:1291
Traditional medicine: Australia (bush medicine), 4:1401–1405. *See also* **Australia**
bush medicine, defined, 4:1401–1402
traditional health beliefs and practices, 4:1402–1403
types of bush medicine, 4:1403–1405
Traditional medicine: Central America, 4:1405–1408
health beliefs, 4:1405–1407
pharmacology of traditional Central American medicine, 4:1407–1408
Traditional medicine: China, 4:1408–1411. *See also* **China**
safety, 4:1410–1411
TCM, overview, 4:1408–1410
Traditional medicine: Native American tribes, 4:1411–1415
contemporary practices, 4:1414–1415
history of Native Americans and traditional medicine, 4:1412–1414
traditional medicine, WHO definition, 4:1411–1412
Traditional medicine: South Africa, 4:1415–1419
muti, 2:736, 2:929–931, 4:1417–1418
nganga, 3:968–970, 4:1416
traditional medicine, as defined in South Africa, 4:1415–1416
Traditional medicine: South America, 4:1419–1422
overview, 4:1419
pharmacology of, 4:1420–1422
traditional health beliefs, 4:1419–1420

Traditional medicine: Tibet, 4:1422–1426
history, 4:1423
medical principles and science of healing, 4:1424–1425
modern-day practices, 4:1425–1426
overview, 4:1422–1423
treatment and medicinal materials, 4:1425
Traditional medicine: Vietnam, 4:1426–1430
challenges, 4:1429–1430
historical perspective, 4:1427
national policies, 4:1429
overview, 4:1426–1427
traditional Dong Y, 4:1427–1428
traditional Vietnamese medicine, 4:1428–1429
Traditional medicines. *See also individual countries and continents*
in Africa, 4:1415–1419
of Asian Americans, 1:221–222
in Australia, 1:237–238, 4:1401–1405
belladonna, 1:268–270
in Central America, 4:1405–1408
in China, 1:354, 4:1408–1411
curandero, 1:433–435
in Ghana, 4:1370–1372
history of pharmacology in ancient China, 2:704–708
homeopathy, 2:746–748
Ibogaine, 2:765–767
in Japan, 2:801–802
khat, 2:816–818
in Korea, 4:1382
in Mali, 4:1372
medicinal plant species threated with extinction, 2:897–899
Muti, 2:929–931
of Native Americans, 4:1411–1415
of Native Hawai'ians and Pacific Islanders, 3:954
nganga (traditional African healers), 3:968–970
Siddha medicine (Dravidian culture), 3:1289–1292
in South Africa, 2:736, 2:929–931, 4:1372, 4:1415–1419
in South America, 4:1419–1422

in Tanzania, **4**:1372
in Tibet, **4**:1422–1426
in U.S., colonial period to 1865,
    2:721–722
U.S. regulation of, **4**:1398–1401
in Vietnam, **4**:1426–1430
WHO on, **1**:xxxi, **4**:1411–1412
Tranquilizers, 4:1430–1435
abuse of prescription drugs and, **1**:7–8
librium and Valium, **4**:1432
"Miltown Moment," **4**:1431–1432
overview, **4**:1430–1431
pharmacological Calvinism, feminism, and
    other reactions, **4**:1433
responsible use of, **4**:1434–1435
rogue tranquilizers and sedatives, **4**:1434
Xanax, Ativan, and other "postvalium"
    tranquilizers, **4**:1433–1434
TransdermScop, **1**:xli
Transfusions, blood, **1**:281
Translational pharmacology, 4:1435–1440
future directions, **4**:1439
global data sharing, **4**:1437–1438
National Center for Advancing
    Translational Sciences (NIH),
    3:940–943
organization accelerating and promoting,
    4:1437
overview, **4**:1435–1437
potential impact on primary care,
    4:1438–1439
social justice and, **4**:1438
Trexan, **1**:81, **1**:82
Triangle Pharmaceuticals, **2**:658
Tricare Management Activity, **2**:926
Triclosan, **1**:147
Tricyclic antidepressants
adolescents and, **1**:54
TRIPS Agreement (Agreement on Trade-
    Related Aspects of Intellectual Property
    Rights), Doha Declarations, and TRIPS
    Plus, 4:1440–1443
Doha Declaration, **4**:1441–1442
generic medicines, **2**:648
intellectual property rights, overview, **2**:781
overview, **4**:1440–1441

patenting laws, **3**:1075–1078 (*See also*
    Legal issues)
TRIPS Plus, **4**:1442–1443
Trisenox, **4**:1354
Trovafloxacin (Trovan) controversy,
    4:1443–1447
legal controversy, **4**:1444–1446
overview, **4**:1443–1444
Truvada, **2**:658
Tuberculosis
directly observed therapy, short-course,
    2:473–475
drug resistance and, **2**:549
UK All Party Parliamentary Group on
    Global Tuberculosis, **1**:xlvi
Tuskegee experiment, 4:1447–1455
Alabama public health, **4**:1448–1449
end of research and aftershocks from,
    4:1453–1454
ethical issues, **4**:1452–1453
history of syphilis, **4**:1448
overview, **2**:759, **4**:1447–1448,
    4:1517–1518
start of, **4**:1449–1452
Tylenol tampering case, 4:1455–1458
Johnson & Johnson products and, **2**:805,
    2:806
packaging and, **1**:9
Type 1/2/3 antiarrhythmics, **1**:316
Tysabri, **1**:277

Ubuntu philosophy, **2**:734
UK National Health Service, **1**:xlv
UK Stem Cell Bank and Influenza Resource
    Center, **3**:949–950
Unani **(Muslim traditional medicine),**
    4:1459–1461
diagnoses and treatment of health
    problems, **4**:1460–1461
fundamentals of humoral theory, **4**:1460
history of, **4**:1459–1460
Uniform Narcotic Drug Act, **3**:1310
United Kingdom, 4:1461–1466
access to medicines (industrialized world),
    1:23
adverse event reporting, **4**:1464

Food and Drugs Act, **1:**xxxix
General Practice Research Database (UK),
    2:640–643
licensing of medicines, **4:**1463–1464
Medicines and Healthcare Products
    Regulatory Agency (UK), **2:**899–902
National Health Service, **4:**1462
National Institute of Health and Clinical
    Excellence, **1:**41
NHS England, **4:**1462–1463
NHS medicines coverage, **4:**1464–1465
opium imports, 19th century, **1:**xxxvi
overview, **4:**1461–1462
pharmaceutical manufacturing in, **4:**1465
Pharmaceutical Society of Great Britain
    founded, **1:**xxxvi
Pharmacy and Medicines Act, **1:**xxxix
Prescription-Event Monitoring (PEM)
    Database (University of Portsmouth,
    UK), **3:**1159–1162
regulation of OTC drugs in U.K.,
    3:1024–1025
traditional and herbal medicines,
    regulation in Europe, case study,
    4:1384
UK All Party Parliamentary Group on
    Global Tuberculosis, **1:**xlvi
UK National Health Service, **1:**xlv
UK Stem Cell Bank and Influenza
    Resource Center, **3:**949–950
Venereal Disease Act, **1:**xxxviii
United Nations (UN)
    access to medicines (developing world),
        1:14–15, **1:**18
    *Minority Rights: International Standards
        and Guidance for Implementation,*
        3:1230
    WHO created by, **1:**xxxix (*See also* **World
        Health Organization**)
United States. *See also* Legal issues; *individual
    names of U.S. agencies*
    animal testing and U.S. pharmacology
        history, **2:**728–729
    CAM use in, **3:**944–945
    direct-to-consumer pharmaceutical
        advertising (DTCPA), **1:**66–67

drug labels exported from U.S., **2:**522–523
drug testing, high school and college
    athletes (U.S.), **2:**532–536
drug testing, Olympic athletes,
    2:539–540
drug testing of high school and college
    athletes in U.S., **2:**532–537
early pharmacist degrees, U.S., **1:**xl
ephedra in, **2:**577–578
fertility control history and, **2:**606–608
gray market drugs, **2:**663–664
harm reduction policies, **2:**674
health care fraud in, **2:**675–683
health insurance and U.S. history of
    pharmacology, **2:**732 (*See also* **Patient
    Protection and Affordable Care Act
    (Obamacare)**)
health literacy in U.S., **2:**838
history, 1800–1850, **4:**1466–1472
history, 1851–1900, **4:**1472–1477
history, 1901–1950, **4:**1477–1483
history, 1951 to present, **4:**1483–1486
history of pharmacology: 1865 to 1900,
    2:723–726
history of pharmacology: 1900 to 1945,
    2:727–730
history of pharmacology: 1945 to present,
    2:730–733
history of pharmacology: colonial period
    to 1865, **2:**719–723
history of pharmacy as a profession,
    2:742–744
mail-order pharmacies and, **2:**847–849
medical marijuana legislation, **2:**879–886
methaqualone (Quaalude) controversy in,
    2:918–919
Pediatric Rule (U.S., 1998), **3:**1053–1056
pharmaceutical benefits within health
    insurance plans, **3:**1066–1069
pharmacovigilance and drug safety
    regulation in U.S., **3:**1111–1113
pharmacy education in, **1:**xxxvi, **1:**xl
prescription drug approval process,
    3:1153–1157
Prozac and early U.S. availability, **1:**xli
Russia and, **3:**1251

traditional and herbal medicines, regulation, 4:1396–1401
U.S. Anti-Doping Agency, 4:1495–1503 (*See also* **Athletes**)
U.S. pharmacology history, 2:727–728
U.S. Pharmacopeial Convention, 4:1503–1505
Veterans Administration and prescription drug benefits, 4:1522–1525
United States: 1800 to 1850, 4:1466–1472
    dispensing pharmaceuticals, 4:1471
    Lincolns and, 4:1468–1469
    physical illness, 4:1470–1471
    Rush and, 4:1469–1470
    treating mental illness, 4:1467
    understanding mental illness, 4:1466–1467
United States: 1851 to 1900, 4:1472–1477
    AphA founding, 4:1474–1475
    drugstores during, 4:1472–1474
    legislation and education, 4:1475–1476
    overview, 4:1472
United States: 1901 to 1950, 4:1477–1483
    education and credentials, 4:1478–1482
    legislation, 4:1479
    overview of pharmacy practice, 4:1477–1478
United States: 1951 to present, 4:1483–1486
    health system, 4:1483–1484
    pharmaceutical industry, 4:1484–1485
    pharmaceutical market, 4:1485
United States Pharmacopeia, 1:94–95, 2:742, 2:880
United States Vaccine Agency, 4:1507
Universal Declaration of Human Rights (UN), 1:15
University of California, San Diego, 4:1486–1487
    Department of Pharmacology, 4:1486–1487
    overview, 4:1486
University of California, San Francisco, 4:1487–1488
    Genentech and, 2:640
    overview, 4:1487
    research, 4:1488
    School of Pharmacy, 4:1487–1488

University of Dorpat (University of Tartu), 1:xxxi
University of Michigan, 1:xxxi, 1:xxxvii
University of Oxford, 4:1488–1490
    Department of Pharmacology, 4:1488–1489
    overview, 4:1488
    researchers, 4:1489–1490
University of Toronto, 4:1490–1493
    overview, 2:570, 4:1490–1491
    research areas, 4:1491–1492
    selected faculty research areas, 4:1492–1493
University of Warwick, 1:xlv
University of Washington, 4:1493–1495
    faculty research areas, 4:1494–1495
    overview, 4:1493–1494
University of York, 1:xlv
Upjohn, 2:657, 3:1064
URL Pharma, 4:1347
U.S. Anti-Doping Agency, 4:1495–1503
    Chronos, 4:1500
    contract testing, 4:1500
    doping regulation, 4:1495–1497
    drug reference resources, 4:1497–1498
    drug testing and Olympic athletes, overview, 2:539–541
    education, 4:1497
    implications of a failed test, 4:1499
    innovative technologies of, 4:1499–1500
    notable doping events in modern athletic competition, 4:1496 (table)
    nutritional supplements in sports, 4:1502
    results management, 4:1499
    sample analysis, 4:1499
    sample collection, 4:1498
    Simon database, 4:1500
    testing notification, 4:1499
    Therapeutic Use Exemption (performance-enhancing drugs), 4:1359–1362
    therapeutic use exemptions, 4:1498
    TrueSport, 4:1499
    USADA programs, 4:1497
    WADA Prohibited List, 4:1500–1502, 4:1501 (table)
    World Anti-Doping Code, 4:1497

U.S. Department of Agriculture, early FDA and, 1:xxxvii
U.S. Department of Commerce, 4:1659
U.S. Department of Defense, pharmaceutical issues in military and, 2:924–926
U.S. Department of Health and Human Services, 3:1326–1327, 4:1662, 4:1665
U.S. Department of Justice, DEA creation and, 1:xli. *See also* **Drug Enforcement Administration (U.S.)**
U.S. Department of Justice, on medical marijuana, 2:884
U.S. Pharmacopeial Convention, 4:1503–1505
    compendia published by (other than *U.S. Pharmacopeia*), 4:1504
    history, 4:1503
    new medicines, 4:1505
    Promoting the Quality of Medicines (PQM) Program, 4:1505
    safety of medicines, 4:1505
    structure, 4:1503
    U.S. Pharmacopeia, 4:1503–1504
U.S. President's Emergency Plan for AIDS Relief (PEPFAR), 1:18–19
U.S. State Department, on sources of drugs, 1:xli
U.S. Treasury, 1:xxxviii
USP on Compounding (USP), 4:1504

Vaccination: national and international programs, 4:1507–1510
    international programs, 4:1509
    U.S. vaccination policies and programs, 4:1507–1509
    U.S.'s global vaccine involvement, 4:1509
Vaccination coverage data
    adults, 4:1655–1656 (table)
    children (ages 19–35 months), 4:1652 (table), 4:1653–1654 (table)
    children (ages 19–35 months), by vaccines and dosage, 4:1651 (table), 4:1652 (table)
    children (kindergarten), by state/area, 4:1647–1648 (table)
    children (kindergarten), exemptions from vaccination, 4:1649–1650 (table)

health-care personnel receiving vaccinations, 4:1658 (table)
Morbidity and Mortality Weekly Report (CDC), 4:1646
tetanus vaccine, 4:1657 (table)
Vaccine Act of 1813, 1:xxxvi, 4:1507
Vaccine Information Statement (VIS), 3:947
Vaccines, 4:1510–1512. *See also* Vaccination coverage data
    CDC on global immunization, 1:328
    Children's Vaccine Plan (WHO), 1:xlii
    Dale and Betty Bumpers Vaccine Research Center (NIH), 1:xlii
    first HIV vaccine, 1:xlii
    history of, 1:xxxvii, 4:1510–1511
    introduction of DPT, 1:xxxix
    measles, 1:xl
    National Childhood Vaccine Injury Act of 1986, 1:xli
    Nigeria and polio vaccination programs, 1:xliv
    rubella vaccine, 2:913
    swine flu (H1N1) vaccine, 1:257
    vaccination: national and international programs, 4:1507–1510
    vaccination schedules, 4:1511–1512
Valerian (herbal medicine), 4:1512–1515
    mental health, 4:1513–1514
    overview, 4:1512–1513
    physical ailments, 4:1513
Valium, 4:1432
Vancomycin, 2:549
Vane, John R., 1:27
Vanquoral, 4:1355
Variolation, 1:xxxvi
Varmus, Harold, 2:657
Velcade, 2:806
Venereal Disease Act, 1:xxxviii
Venereal disease treatment: history, 4:1515–1519
    attitudes toward, 4:1515–1516
    modern-day treatment for, 4:1518–1519
    treatments for, 4:1516–1517
    Tuskegee experiment and, 2:759, 4:1447–1454, 4:1517–1518

Venereal diseases, treatments for, 4:1519–1522
    developing studies on treatments, 4:1521–1522
    infections, diseases, treatments, 4:1520–1521
    overview, 4:1519–1520
Venture Science Laboratories, 2:442
Verapharm, 1:4
Verified Internet Pharmacy Practice Sites (VIPPS) (NABP), 1:429, 2:847
Vesicare, 1:225
Veterans Administration (U.S.): prescription drug benefits, 4:1522–1525
    history of VA prescription drug benefits, 4:1522–1524
    process, 4:1524
Veterinary pharmacology, 4:1525–1529
    delivery methods, 4:1525–1527
    drug categories, 4:1527–1529
    history of, 4:1525
    prescribing veterinary medications, 4:1527
Viagra, 1:xlii, 3:1064
Vibramycin, 3:1064
Victoza, 3:986
Vietnam. See Traditional medicine: Vietnam
VIGOR study, 3:1246–1249
Viral isolation, U.S. history of, 2:730
Viread, 2:658
Vismodegib, 2:639
Vistide, 2:657
Vitamin K–rich foods, drug interactions with, 2:518–519

Wakefield, Andrew, 1:242, 1:243
Waksman, Selman, 1:xxxix, 1:140
Warner Chilcott PLC, 1:29
Warner-Lambert, 3:1064
Water pollution (prescription drugs), 4:1531–1534
    common contaminating medications, 4:1532–1533
    environmental observations, 4:1531
    medication design, 4:1533
    solutions and current research, 4:1533–1534
    sources of contamination, 4:1531–1532

Weight loss, drugs and, 2:602–603, 2:914, 3:1244–1246, 4:1375
Weintraub, Harold, 2:657
Weller, Thomas Huckle, 1:xl
West Himalayan yew tree, 2:899
White House Council on Women and Girls, 4:1364
Whitley, Richard, 1:xlv
Whitney, A. K., 1:97
WHO Model Lists of Essential Medicines, 4:1534–1537
    barriers to access, 4:1535–1536
    creation of, 1:xxxii–xxxiii
    18th edition of, 1:xliv
    essential medicines (2013), 4:1535
    original list, 1:xli
    overview, 4:1534
    Pfizer medicines and, 3:1065
Whooping cough, 1:xxxviii
Wiley Act, 1:xxxviii
Windham Pills, 1:xxxvi
Witchetty grubs, 4:1404
Women, 4:1537–1546
    access to contraception in developing countries, 1:xliv (See also Fertility control; Fertility control: history)
    addiction to prescription drugs, 1:33
    adverse drug reactions, 4:1544–1545
    African Americans and drug responses, 1:72–73
    contraception use data, 4:1634 (tables), 4:1635 (tables), 4:1636 (table), 4:1637 (table), 4:1638 (table)
    DES and, 2:459–462
    discrimination in prescribing practice, 2:479
    drug smuggling and, 3:1309
    drugs in pregnancy, contraception, menopause, 4:1540–1542 (See also Fertility control; Fertility control: history)
    fertility drugs for, 2:611–613
    Flibanserin for female sex drive, 1:xlvi
    gender differences in physiology and pharmacology, 4:1538–1539
    hormone replacement therapy, 2:749–750

pregnancy and inhalants, 2:779

relevant health conditions, 4:1542–1544

sex difference in cytochrome P450 metabolism and hepatic clearance, 4:1539 (table)

Title X Family Planning Program (1970) and, 4:1362–1365

translational pharmacy and feminism, 4:1433

WHO on equitable access to antiretroviral treatment for HIV-positive girls and women, 1:xliii

women's health, overview, 4:1537–1538

Women's Health Initiative (WHI), 2:749–750

Wood, Andrew, 1:xxxvi

Woodward, Robert, 1:xxxix

World Anti-Doping Agency (WADA), 4:1546–1549

anabolic steroids, 1:106

drug testing and, 2:537–538

ethics of performance-enhancing drugs in sport, 2:585

Olympic athletes and, 2:537–538

Olympics and, 3:1003–1004

Therapeutic Use Exemption (performance-enhancing drugs), 4:1359–1362

World Congress of Basic and Clinical Pharmacology (2014), 3:1104

World Health Assembly, 1:17

World Health Organization, 4:1549–1553

access to essential medicines as a human right, 1:11, 1:13–14

access to medicines (developing world), 1:15, 1:16–20

access to medicines (industrialized world), 1:22

adherence to prescription directions, 1:45

adverse drug reactions and adverse events, 1:60–61

AIDS/HIV drugs and, 1:76–77

Anatomical Therapeutic Chemical Classification System (WHO), 1:110–113

CDC and global immunization, 1:328

on Chagas disease, 1:xlv

Children's Vaccine Plan, 1:xlii

creation of, 1:xxxix

on epilepsy, 1:xliv

Ethical Criteria for Medicinal Drug Promotion, 1:65

Expanded Programme on Immunization, 1:xli

Global Fund for AIDS, Tuberculosis and Malaria (GFATM), 1:xlii, 1:18–19

Model List of Essential Medicines, 2:581 (*See also* **Equity pricing of essential medicines**)

pharmaceutical policy and international cooperation, 3:1081

on pharmacology's role, 1:xxxii

pharmacovigilance and, 3:1110–1111

Programme for International Drug Monitoring, 1:59

quality of life insurance (WHOQOL), 3:1195–1196

smallpox eradication campaign (1967), 1:xl (*See also* **Smallpox eradication**)

on spending for pharmaceuticals in transitional economies, 1:xliii

Stop TB Partnership, 1:xlii

traditional medicine, WHO definition, 1:xxxi, 4:1411–1412

vaccination: national and international programs, 4:1507–1510 (*See also* **Vaccines**)

WHO on equitable access to antiretroviral treatment for HIV-positive girls and women, 1:xliii

World Medicines Situation, The (WHO), 1:14

World Trade Organization (WTO)

access to medicines (industrialized world), 1:21–22

Doha Declaration, 1:18

World War II

concentration camps and Zyklon B, 1:259

Nuremberg Code (1947) and, 2:756, 2:758

Wormseed, Levant, 3:1062
Wright, Charles Romley Alder, 1:xxxvii

Xanax, 4:1433–1434
Xolair, 2:639
XOMA, 2:639
Xtandi, 1:225
Xylitol, 1:147

Yale Cancer Center, 1:xlv
Yamanouchi Pharmaceutical Co., Ltd., 1:225
Yellow Card Scheme, 4:1555–1557
Yersin, Alexandre, 1:xxxviii
Yew tree, 2:899
Yin and yang, 4:1409, 4:1428
Yoruba. *See Egbogi* **(traditional Yoruba medicine)**
Youth drug use data, 4:1605–1632
    cocaine use, 4:1610 (table), 4:1611 (table), 4:1612 (table)
    contraception use and, 4:1620 (table), 4:1621 (table), 4:1622 (table), 4:1623 (table), 4:1624 (table), 4:1625 (table), 4:1626 (table), 4:1627 (table), 4:1628 (table), 4:1629 (table)
    Ecstasy use, 4:1612 (table), 4:1613 (table), 4:1614 (table)
    heroin use, 4:1614 (table), 4:1615 (table), 4:1616 (table)
    inhalant use, 4:1612 (table), 4:1613 (table), 4:1614 (table)
    injected drugs, 4:1619 (table), 4:1620 (table)

    marijuana use, 4:1606 (table), 4:1607 (table), 4:1608 (table), 4:1609 (table), 4:1610 (table)
    methamphetamine use, 4:1614 (table), 4:1615 (table), 4:1616 (table)
    prescription drugs use, 4:1616 (table), 4:1617 (table), 4:1618 (table)
    steroids use, 4:1616 (table), 4:1617 (table), 4:1618 (table)
Youth Risk Behavior Surveillance System (YRBSS), 4:1605
Yung Cheng (Emperor of China), 1:xxxvi

Zahrawi, Abu al-Qasim al-, 2:740–741
Zeneca, 1:229–230
Zentiva, 3:1164
Zepharma, 2:442
Zero-tolerance drug policies, 4:1559–1562
    consequences, 4:1560
    overview, 4:1559–1560
    proper procedure, 4:1560–1561
Zetia, 2:912–913
Zhang Zhongjing, 4:1380
Zi Medical, 1:230
Zimelidine (Zelmid) controversy, 4:1562–1564
Zithromax, 3:1064
Zoely, 4:1355
Zoloft, 3:1064
Zuger, Abigail, 1:44
Zyban, 3:1303, 3:1304
Zyklon B, World War II concentration camps and, 1:259
Zyrtec, 2:806